Issues in African American Music

Issues in African American Music: Power, Gender, Race, Representation is a collection of twenty-one essays by leading scholars, surveying vital themes in the history of African American music. Bringing together the viewpoints of ethnomusicologists, historians, and performers, these essays cover topics including the music industry, women and gender, and music as resistance, and explore the stories of music creators and their communities.

Revised and expanded to reflect the latest scholarship, with six all-new essays, this book both complements the previously published volume *African American Music: An Introduction* and stands on its own. Each chapter features a discography of recommended listening for further study. From the antebellum period to the present, and from classical music to hip hop, this wide-ranging volume provides a nuanced introduction for students and anyone seeking to understand the history, social context, and cultural impact of African American music.

Portia K. Maultsby is Laura Boulton Professor Emerita of Ethnomusicology in the Department of Folklore and Ethnomusicology and Research Associate in the Archives of African American Music and Culture at Indiana University.

Mellonee V. Burnim is Professor of Ethnomusicology in the Department of Folklore and Ethnomusicology, Adjunct Professor of African American and African Diaspora Studies, and Director of the Archives of African American Music and Culture at Indiana University.

Issues in African American Music

Power, Gender, Race, Representation

Edited by
*Portia K. Maultsby and
Mellonee V. Burnim*

NEW YORK AND LONDON

First published 2017
by Routledge
711 Third Avenue, New York, NY 10017

and by Routledge
2 Park Square, Milton Park, Abingdon, Oxon, OX14 4RN

Routledge is an imprint of the Taylor & Francis Group, an informa business

© 2017 Taylor & Francis

The rights of Portia K. Maultsby and Mellonee V. Burnim to be identified as the authors of the editorial material, and of the authors for their individual chapters, has been asserted in accordance with sections 77 and 78 of the Copyright, Designs and Patents Act 1988.

All rights reserved. No part of this book may be reprinted or reproduced or utilised in any form or by any electronic, mechanical, or other means, now known or hereafter invented, including photocopying and recording, or in any information storage or retrieval system, without permission in writing from the publishers.

Trademark notice: Product or corporate names may be trademarks or registered trademarks, and are used only for identification and explanation without intent to infringe.

Library of Congress Cataloging in Publication Data
Names: Maultsby, Portia K., editor. | Burnim, Mellonee V. (Mellonee Victoria), 1950– editor.
Title: Issues in African American music : power, gender, race, representation / edited by Portia K. Maultsby with Mellonee V. Burnim.
Description: New York, NY ; Abingdon, Oxon : Routledge, 2016. | Includes bibliographical references and index.
Identifiers: LCCN 2016015215 (print) | LCCN 2016023479 (ebook) | ISBN 9780415881821 (hardback) | ISBN 9780415881838 (paperback) | ISBN 9781315472096 (ebook)
Subjects: LCSH: African Americans—Music—History and criticism. | African American musicians. | Music—African American influences.
Classification: LCC ML3556 .I87 2016 (print) | LCC ML3556 (ebook) | DDC 780.89/96073—dc23
LC record available at https://lccn.loc.gov/2016015215

ISBN: 978-0-415-88182-1 (hbk)
ISBN: 978-0-415-88183-8 (pbk)
ISBN: 978-1-315-47209-6 (ebk)

Typeset in Galliard
by Apex CoVantage, LLC

Printed and bound in the United States of America by Edwards Brothers Malloy on sustainably sourced paper.

*To Our Students
From Whom We Have Learned So Much*

Contents

Preface · x
Acknowledgments · xiii

PART I
Interpreting Music · 1

1. Performing Blues and Navigating Race in Transcultural Contexts · 3
   Susan Oehler Herrick

2. New Bottle, Old Wine: Whither Jazz Studies? · 30
   Travis A. Jackson

3. The Politics of Race Erasure in Defining Black Popular Music Origins · 47
   Portia K. Maultsby

4. Negotiating Blackness in Western Art Music · 66
   Olly Wilson

PART II
Mass Mediation · 77

5. Crossing Musical Borders: Agency and Process in the Gospel Music Industry · 79
   Mellonee V. Burnim

6. Industrializing African American Popular Music · 90
   Reebee Garofalo

7. The Motown Legacy: Homegrown Sound, Mass Appeal   110
Charles E. Sykes

8. Stax Records and the Impulse toward Integration   135
Rob Bowman

9. Uptown Sound—Downtown Bound: Philadelphia International Records   151
John A. Jackson

10. "And the Beat Goes On": SOLAR—The Sound of Los Angeles Records   165
Scot Brown

11. Tyscot Records: Gospel Music Production as Ministry   180
Tyron Cooper

PART III
Gender   199

12. Voices of Women in Gospel Music: Resisting Representations   201
Mellonee V. Burnim

13. Are All the Choir Directors Gay? Black Men's Sexuality and Identity in Gospel Performance   216
Alisha Lola Jones

14. Women in Blues: Transgressing Boundaries   237
Daphne Duval Harrison

15. Jazz History Remix: Black Women from "Enter" to "Center"   256
Sherrie Tucker

16. The Reception of Blackness in "Women's Music"   270
Eileen M. Hayes

17. African American Women and the Dynamics of Gender, Race, and Genre in Rock 'n' Roll   287
Maureen Mahon

18. "Ain't Nuthin' but a She Thang": Women in Hip Hop   306
Cheryl L. Keyes

PART IV
Musical Agency—African American Music as Resistance — 329

19. The Antebellum Period: Communal Coherence
    and Individual Expression — 331
    Lawrence W. Levine

20. The Civil Rights Period: Music as an Agent of Social Change — 343
    Bernice Johnson Reagon

21. The Post-Civil Rights Period: The Politics of Musical Creativity — 368
    Mark Anthony Neal

    Bibliography — 381
    Editors and Contributors — 404
    Index — 410

Preface

With the publication of *Issues in African American Music: Power, Gender, Race, Representation*, the revision of our original *African American Music: An Introduction* (2006) is complete. This current volume should be viewed as a companion to *African American Music: An Introduction*, Second Edition, which appeared in 2015. Together, these two collections provide the reader with access to the full range of coverage provided in the original text.

The revision and expansion of our 2006 compilation reflects our continuing awareness of the ever expanding breadth and depth of research and scholarship in the field of African American music. No longer relegated to the fundamental objectives of basic data recovery and content validation within the academy, this published aggregate seeks to capture and represent as fully as possible the collective spirit of African Americans whose creative genius was sparked and nurtured in North American contexts, historical and contemporary, rural and urban, sacred and secular.

The stories which come to life in these pages are accounts of human agency and resilience, of power struggles among African Americans themselves, in some instances gendered, and between African American performers and composers and their publics who often viewed Blacks as mere objects of entertainment, pleasure, or economic gain. Too frequently writers have failed to recognize and interrogate the underlying, layered complexities which have historically characterized African American communities in the United States. In these racialized narratives, distinct African American behaviors and musical values have repeatedly been cast as inherent predispositions, rather than as reflections of shared values learned and transmitted in well-defined and well-articulated socio-cultural contexts.

The writers herein chronicle African American efforts to advance representations of their musical and cultural identities as the products of rational, thinking, and feeling human beings. This body of essays acknowledges the need for and value of a collective of scholarly viewpoints which systematically and consistently engage and explore African American music production through nuanced lenses which acknowledge multiple, coexisting and sometimes contradictory African American perspectives. The angles of view we present, therefore, are many, including ethnomusicology, music education, cultural history, cultural studies, sociology, anthropology, and composition. In many instances, those who have contributed to this volume are also reputable performers in the genres they interrogate.

We encourage both undergraduate and graduate readers of this text, as well as readers who simply wish to explore African American musical expression through narratives which, as fully as possible, embody the many and varied perspectives of the musical creators themselves. In this collection, African American voices matter, not because they reflect a singular point of view, but because they affirm the existence of conscious musical agency—the inner workings of personal and collective reflection in processes of creating and performing musics celebrated across the globe.

NEW STRUCTURE

- In order to facilitate the use of this compilation in courses which utilize music to interpret broader issues (such as gender), this volume now exclusively includes treatments of both historical and contemporary issues in African American music from the vantage point of multiple genres. Original articles which outlined chronologies of African American music now appear exclusively in *African American Music: An Introduction,* Second Edition (2015).

NEW FEATURES

- Reduction in length. *Issues in African American Music* now stands as an independent volume of twenty-one synchronic explorations of African American music divided into four broad, overarching categories retained from Segment II of the original 2006 edition: (1) Interpreting Music—covering blues, jazz, popular, and classical music; (2) Mass Mediation—including general explorations of the gospel music and popular music industries as well as case studies of five prominent record labels: Motown, Stax, Philadelphia International, Los Angeles Records, and Tyscot Records; (3) Gender—which features articles on both women and men in gospel music as well as discussions of women in blues, jazz, "women's music," rock 'n' roll, and hip hop; and (4) Musical Agency—which explores the element of resistance in African American musics during three distinct historical periods: the antebellum years; the Civil Rights Movement, and the post–Civil Rights era.
- New, more descriptive chapter titles have been assigned to articles which appeared in the original 2006 volume.

NEW CONTENT

- Six entirely new chapters have been added and are dispersed among each of the four major parts of the book.
- Chapter 2 in Part I: Interpreting Music, includes "New Bottle, Old Wine: Whither Jazz Studies?" by ethnomusicologist Travis A. Jackson—a critical historiography of the field of jazz studies.

- Chapter 3 in Part I, "The Politics of Race Erasure in Defining Black Popular Music Origins" by editor and ethnomusicologist, Portia K. Maultsby, explores the deleterious scholarly and social implications of studies of African American popular music which either ignore or discount African American lived experiences as primary factors in formulating interpretations of musical meaning.
- Chapter 10 by historian Scot Brown, " 'And the Beat Goes On': SOLAR—The Sound of Los Angeles Records," in Part II: Mass Mediation, provides an account of SOLAR, one of the most successful Black-owned popular music record labels from the late 1970s through the '80s.
- Chapter 11 in Part II, "Tyscot Records: Gospel Music Production as Ministry," contributed by ethnomusicologist Tyron Cooper, juxtaposes the competing roles of gospel music as both Christian belief and capitalistic enterprise within the gospel music industry.
- In Chapter 13 of Part III: Gender, Alisha Lola Jones, ethnomusicologist, interrogates fissures in commonplace narratives on Black masculinity in African American Protestant worship contexts in her article "Are All the Choir Directors Gay? Black Men's Sexuality and Identity in Gospel Performance."
- Chapter 16, in Part III, entitled "The Reception of Blackness in 'Women's Music' " by ethnomusicologist Eileen M. Hayes, has been revised and updated to reflect ongoing changes in lesbian and queer politics surrounding music as well as subsequent changes in nomenclature used to define musics directed toward audiences composed largely of women.
- Chapter 18, also in Part III, " 'Ain't Nuthin' but a She Thang': Women in Hip Hop," contributed by ethnomusicologist Cheryl L. Keyes, profiles the role of women in shaping and defining representations of women as performers on stage and as behind-the-scenes decision-makers in the genre of hip hop.
- All remaining articles from the 2006 edition appear in this volume with updated titles but without significant changes in content.

Acknowledgments

Producing a work of this magnitude has proved to be a challenging task. The tremendous diversity of genres that can be labeled as African American is quite considerable. Furthermore, many viable and instructive approaches to the study of African American music continue to emerge from various disciplinary perspectives. While we continue to make no claims to have produced an exhaustive survey of either African American musical genres themselves or those pervasive issues that prompt our most careful scholarly scrutiny, we readily acknowledge that indeed the degree of breath and depth which we have in fact achieved results in large part from the very strong cast of contributors who have lent their highly valuable proficiencies to this effort. We extend our first and primary word of thanks to those colleagues who have devoted their considerable expertise, energy, and overall good will to the production of this compilation. For those credited in both the first and second editions, we voice our appreciation for the stabilizing role which your seminal entry provides in this second edition. To new authors, we celebrate the richness which your cutting-edge research offers, as you continue to advance and expand the boundaries of African American music scholarship.

Our highly competent and dedicated editorial assistant Rachel Hurley, who partnered with us in producing the second edition of *African American Music: An Introduction* (2015), continued to provide a much needed editorial anchor for this current work. Together with Susan Brackney, who joined the editorial team when Rachel's search for full-time employment was realized, we are fortunate to have identified assistants who were highly qualified, committed to excellence, and cooperative. We particularly acknowledge Rachel's willingness to continue to work with us long-distance after having relocated to another state. When crises came, as they so inevitably do in work of this sort, Rachel stayed the course with fierce determination to journey to the finish.

As in our previous volumes, the Archives of African American Music and Culture and its full-time staff members Brenda Nelson Strauss, head of collections, and William Vanden Dries, digital archivist, have proved to be invaluable resources in assisting our efforts to identify, locate, and assess sources critical to executing this work. To both of them, we are grateful. Critical commentary and editorial expertise provided by Adrienne Seward, Eileen M. Hayes, and Reebee Garofalo also proved invaluable during the final stages of production.

To our mutual friends and extended family members who provided much needed vocal reinforcement and unfaltering encouragement, we also express our gratitude. While we cannot name everyone, there are those whose voices of calm and prayers of faith served as true beacons of light: Jamel Dotson, Cinnamon Bowser, M. L. Hinnant, Clara Henderson, Ruth and Verlon Stone, Valerie Grim, Tyron Cooper, Fernando Orejuela, Carl Maultsby, Paula Bryant, Raili and Maxie Maultsby, Nancy Allerhand, Richard Lewis, and Darlene Harbuck immediately come to mind. Although Mellonee's dad, Arzo Burnim, passed in November 2015 prior to the completion of this new edition, his indefatigable spirit and pride in educational accomplishment continue to serve as a source of personal motivation and encouragement.

Finally, to the editorial staff at Routledge, Constance Ditzel, senior music editor, and her assistant, Denny Tek, who worked with us in the initial phases of production, we are grateful for the faith you entrusted to us to advance this second edition. We also acknowledge the support of editor Genevieve Aoki and editorial assistant Peter Sheehy in guiding this project to completion. We are extremely pleased that our work has found a significant audience, in large part through the vision and promotional efforts that you have expressed in so many profound ways. Together we celebrate with you and our many supporters for the role that *Issues in African American Music: Power, Gender, Race, Representation* will play in the lives of those who read and thoughtfully consider its content.

Portia K. Maultsby and Mellonee V. Burnim
March 2016

PART I

Interpreting Music

CHAPTER 1

Performing Blues and Navigating Race in Transcultural Contexts

Susan Oehler Herrick

MATTERS OF RACE, CULTURE, AND RESPECT: AN INTRODUCTION

Royalty routinely visit the White House in America, but how often do kings bring a guitar named Lucille to the president's home? The King of the Blues, Riley "B.B." King, performed for President Bill Clinton and First Lady Hillary Rodham Clinton on July 28, 1999, as part of a millennial celebration of American culture. King reigned as the featured performer among four other internationally recognized American artists: John Cephas and Phil Wiggins, Marcia Ball, and Johnny Lang. Later that year, the show was broadcast nationally on public television as "The Blues: In Performance at the White House." According to PBS, the series was designed "to showcase the rich fabric of American culture in the setting of the nation's most famous home."[1]

For African American performers like King and Cephas, the significance of the White House performance cannot be minimized. B.B. King and John Cephas began performing blues for Black audiences in the era of legalized racial segregation, which limited access to audiences in White social arenas. Webs of inequitable laws and unjust customs enforced racial division in the United States constructed around a binary: Whiteness in opposition to Blackness.[2] The blues grew from longstanding African American oral traditions shaped since the 1870s by working people, itinerant musicians, and urban migrants in Black social settings. The influential music has informed the sounds and lyrics of jazz, vaudeville, Tin Pan Alley pop, gospel, rhythm and blues, rock and roll, country, musicals, art music, and hip hop within and without the United States—not to mention poetry, literature, and the visual arts. Throughout the music's history, acknowledgment of the cultural value of Black vernacular music has been relatively rare in White social arenas, which routinely have diminished Black cultural contributions to "American" arts.

The broadcast of "The Blues: In Performance at the White House" acclaims the cultural value of this African American music in the United States. It pays respect to the fact that Black artists have spread appreciation for African American traditions to audiences of varied cultural backgrounds within and without the United States (Figure 1.1). Although racial barriers restricted the music's flow beyond Black American community settings through the 1950s,[3] the participation of White American performers Marcia Ball and Johnny Lang illustrates the interracial appeal of blues that has grown in the United States. At the time of the White House performance, White fans dominated the national blues audience, while African American performers remained prominent among those widely recognized as creative leaders of the blues.

The broadcast provides a glimpse of the blues in America in the late 1990s. B. B. King delivered three songs in his characteristic style flavored by Memphis rhythm-and-blues bands, including his signature tune "The Thrill Is Gone" (1969) and his "Paying the Cost to Be the Boss" (1968). The acoustic guitar/harmonica duo of John Cephas and Phil Wiggins showcased the eastern Piedmont regional style of the early twentieth century

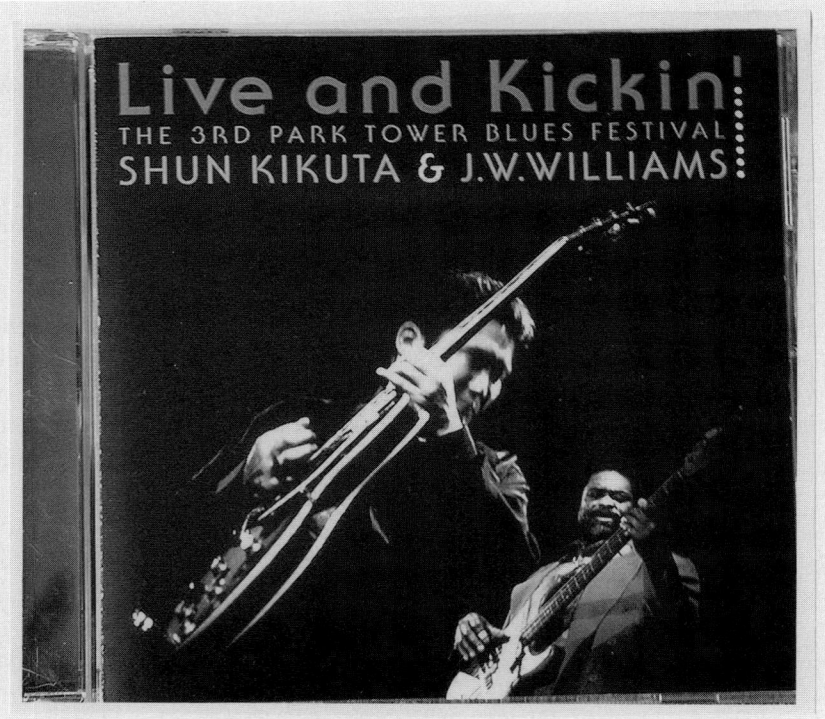

Figure 1.1
The recording project *Live and Kickin'* (BS-002) by Shunsuke "Shun" Kikuta and J.W. Williams evokes the international and transcultural dynamics of contemporary blues scenes. The 1999 release documents the collaboration of Kikuta, who hails from Japan, and Williams, a Chicagoan, with other American and Japanese artists at Tokyo's third annual Park Tower Blues Festival. Kikuta and Williams played regularly in Chicago's internationally recognized, top-level blues scene.

Courtesy Shunsuke "Shun" Kikuta

by performing two songs popularized after World War II. Pianist Marcia Ball, who honed her blend of early New Orleans rhythm and blues in the musical confluence of Austin, Texas, in the 1970s, presented her "St. Gabriel." The young crossover guitarist Johnny Lang began with a song by blues-rocker Tinsley Ellis, showing the close relationship of blues and rock, a link which continues to appeal strongly to a predominantly White blues audience. Sharing the small, well-lit stage in a closing finale, the artists collectively demonstrated the centrality of Black cultural approaches to performance.[4]

In many ways the broadcast projected an intergenerational, interracial moment of partially shared culture in a symbolic, national institution. In the political contexts of the twilight of the Clinton administration, we also could read the performance as an immediate comment on the scandals and impeachment hearings of the late 1990s. (Perhaps the lyrics of King's "Paying the Cost to Be the Boss" and "The Thrill Is Gone" spoke to Bill and Hillary Clinton.)[5]

But the varied musical repertoire and styles of the performance, as well as the long history of the blues in Black American communities, encourage a more multilayered and polyvocal interpretation. We can more fully understand blues in its contemporary interracial and transcultural settings when we analyze it in light of the music's larger cultural context. From this perspective, analysis considers the values that people have used over time to perform and interpret blues music. Experiences of performers and audiences reflect some of these legacies.

A historical perspective on blues reminds us that people have embraced, but also reinterpreted, Black traditions of blues according to values for music performed in varied cultural contexts inside and outside African American communities. From the inception of the blues in the late 1800s through the 1940s, the mass of Black America used blues music to voice, contemplate, and musically embody Black alternatives to White supremacy. Vaudevillian Maggie Jones sang, for example:

> *Goin' where they don't have no Jim Crow laws,*
> *Goin' where they don't have no Jim Crow laws,*
> *Don't have to work here like in Arkansas.*[6]

At this time and throughout much of the twentieth century, Jim Crow laws sanctioned the violently enforced denial of equitable work contracts, education, legal justice, and voting rights. Particularly in Black communities of agricultural and working-class laborers, blues performances commented on "the facts of life" outside the immediate domain of White social order. Even as the popularity of blues music has varied in Black communities, many African Americans have embraced blues as a metaphor for common political and cultural experiences of Blacks in the United States.

Race remains a structure of social stratification despite the dismantling of Jim Crow segregation. The development of scenes for blues performance outside Black community settings has required negotiations of values that navigate the tensions of racial dynamics in the United States. Black blues masters, like B.B. King and John Cephas, have used the entertainment industry to cross a historical Black–White social divide in America. Although this journey has created a route through which people of varied cultural identities have enjoyed, studied, performed, and produced blues music (Figure 1.1), the odyssey holds acute significance for African Americans who have experienced Eurocentric privilege as a disadvantage.

The subject of social race[7] has continued to ignite debates over the significance of relationships between Blacks and Whites in the blues, which is both art and business. In this respect, the blues has remained close to views of "real life" in America. At the time of the White House performance in 1999, "people of color" disproportionately faced socioeconomic struggles of poverty, discrimination, and more limited access to social services. "Colorblind" perspectives, although often issued in opposition to racism, have failed to illuminate the continued significance of racial identity as a "fundamental axis of social organization" in the United States, even as individuals continue to challenge racial barriers.[8]

From a vantage point that recognizes cultural differences, as well as their harmonies, the White House performance holds multiple meanings that bear stern insights. Like the most incisive and ironic blues lyrics that call us, in the words of Ralph Ellison, to "finger [the] jagged grain"[9] of the raw truth, this search for fuller understandings affords empowering outcomes. This essay traces the jagged grain of changes in American social conventions, cultural values, and economic practices that facilitated substantial transcultural participation in blues performances in the 1950s and 1960s. The system of segregation and its changing manifestations in law and custom pivotally shaped the routes through which this newer, largely White American audience base experienced African American blues music.

RACIAL BARRIERS AND CULTURAL INTERCHANGE: BLUES IN THE SEGREGATION ERA

The conventions of racial segregation ensured limited awareness and only qualified acceptance of blues music among White Americans until the 1960s, although blues performances were a secular centerpiece of Black communities across the nation from the late 1800s to around the mid-1950s. An examination of the movement of blues from its origins in Black laboring communities to its popularization among White middle-class audiences requires an understanding of ways that racial segregation affected the flow of Black cultural music beyond African American communities.

Under the supervision of White-led governments since the late 1800s, the laws and customs of racial segregation enforced a codified "system . . . to control interracial commerce, residency, and mobility in the interest of Whites."[10] Blues performers influenced pockets of White society while navigating barriers of legal segregation, which the Civil Rights Movement steadily dismantled during a twenty-year period after World War II. The great social magnitude of these racial barriers did not vanish systemically when individuals found ways around them. It is consequently important to notice how Blacks and Whites experienced and interpreted blues in relation to their own identities.

MONITORING MUSICAL COMMODITIES AND VALUES

White supremacist segregation channeled American experiences into separate and unequal social and economic spheres, although Blacks and Whites clearly influenced one another. Conventional views of relationships between society and the individual expected that ethnic and racial heritage would determine many social behaviors. White America existed in social terms as a legally defined and customarily distinguished sector of people, who often *claimed* a "pure" European heritage and frequently distanced themselves from the reality of African cultural influences in American life. John Edward Philips argues that "our understanding of White American society is incomplete without an understanding of the Black, and African, impact on White America."[11] The racial codification of American society into Black and White arenas obscured the reality of a culturally pluralistic America, particularly for those Americans whose experiences failed to lead them to question Eurocentric social orders. Life under segregation, however, supported worldviews that placed Black and White societies in opposition.

Racial gatekeeping reflected both aesthetic and economic aims of segregation. Although African American bandleader W.C. Handy had proved the marketability of blues commodities with the success of notated arrangements of the blues songs he first composed in 1912, the music industry discouraged recordings of blues that featured Black vocalists and Black instrumentalists until 1920. Following the vein of minstrelsy, some White popular musicians adopted formal components of blues repertoire and singing style, as in the recordings of Sophie Tucker and the compositions of popular jazzman Hoagy Carmichael, for example.[12] Actions of White managers, musicians, advertisers, and consumers converged to restrict Black musicians' access to work and compensation. From the 1920s to the 1940s blues was at the height of its popularity in Black communities, and segregation restricted Black–White social interaction in theaters, dance halls, radio stations, and record stores, as well as in professions, neighborhoods, and schools. These restrictions were most codified in the southern region of the United States, where African Americans lived in the greatest concentration of population.

The expansion of White audiences for blues recorded by Black performers occurred gradually with regard to conventions of segregation that varied according to region and dynamics of urban–rural interchange. In the northern urban centers with large African American communities, such as New York City and Chicago, African Americans made the earliest inroads to introduce Black-identified music to radio broadcasts. In cities such as New York, Chicago, Miami, and Memphis, radio shows that featured blues, gospel, and jazz music were restricted to local stations through the late 1940s.[13] As early as 1941, White-owned stations that depended on the loyalty of White audiences did feature blues in broadcasts marketed to Black audiences, such as the King Biscuit Hour on KFFA Memphis. Not until the late 1940s did powerful AM radio stations, such as WDIA Memphis, aim broadcasts at Black audiences and make the broad offerings of Black music accessible to anyone around the country who cared to transgress racial conventions and listen.

The racially coded social privilege maintained by White power holders in the music industry was about more than economic dominance alone. Attitudes toward musical performance as an embodied expression of values reveal matters at the crux of racial power in America: an intertwining of aesthetic and economic interests in society and efforts to control access to them. The highly popular stereotyped presentations of Black music in the minstrel show, which captivated White Americans before the Civil War, reflect the entanglements of racism in White engagements with Black culture, as scholar Eric Lott convincingly argues:

> . . . early blackface minstrelsy [documents] the dialectical flickering of racial insult and racial envy, moments of domination and moments of liberation, counterfeit and currency, a pattern at times amounting to no more than the two faces of racism, at others gesturing toward a specific kind of political or sexual danger, and all constituting a peculiarly American structure of racial feeling.[14]

White power holders in the segregation era closely monitored cultural expressions of Blacks, especially those involving the physical use of the body. Standards of elite White institutions viewed African American traditional performance in suspicion, with its characteristic value for a holistic and dramatic use of the body to intertwine music and dance. Ideologies supporting White supremacist segregation interpreted cultural acts according to Eurocentric cultural standards of elites, who expected complex art to evidence abstraction from the body.[15] Some Whites sought performances of Black music, but institutions monitored musical performance to support physical and ideological borders between Whiteness and Blackness.

DIFFERING CULTURAL ORIENTATIONS TO MUSIC

People of the time experienced distinctive Black and White cultural spheres, although class, region, religious affiliation, and other social factors variegated the cultural life of both Black and White communities. Americans viewed musical repertoire and performance styles as emblems of Black (or Negro or African) or White (or Caucasian or European—English, German, etc.) races. The realities of the different historical experiences of most Black and White families in the United States supported cultural practices that maintained differences among African-derived and European-derived traditions, despite points of mutual cultural interchange. Music-making in these contexts reflects that European-derived and African-derived approaches to relationships of tune/text, movement/time, and composition/performance have differed significantly. Even as White listeners encountered the music of Black communities, racial barriers restricted their access to the soundscape of Black America and the range of values that African Americans identified with it. Before the 1950s, African American traditions of blues found limited appeal among most listeners in White America.

The permeable borders marking Black and White cultural forms do not neatly conform to the strict limitations of interracial interchange evident in the ideals of segregation. Black musicians, who performed for both Black and White audiences, often supplied different songs to please the tastes of White audiences, particularly at social dances. Renowned bluesman David "Honeyboy" Edwards, and Grand Ol' Opry star DeFord Bailey, Black men who each grew up and first learned music in Black communities in the rural South, have said their performances in White social settings in the early twentieth century included repertoire for the normative tastes of Whites. Edwards and DeFord also played music familiar across Black–White social divides.[16]

Tunes, texts, and techniques of the blues were part of the interchanges through which Black culture directly influenced White culture. Bill C. Malone, a historian of country music, wrote in 1979 that the music of segregated America, particularly in southern regions, bears interracial influences:

> The folk music reservoir of the South was fashioned principally by the confluence of two mighty cultural streams, the British and the African. Yet if one looks for purity in the music of the South, the search will be in vain. . . . And the debt owed by white musicians to black sources is of course enormous. . . . In fact, one can posit the existence of a folk pool shared by both blacks and whites, a common reservoir of songs known in one form or another by the poorer rural classes, regardless of race.[17]

By the 1940s musicians' networks, recordings, and radio broadcasts had also moved blues-based music back and forth across social borders of national origin, language, and race in the southwest.[18] The idea of racially separate musical traditions in the southern United States historically proves to be a myth, even as particular cultural communities in the southern United States maintained and identified with distinctive musical traditions.

Blues performed by Black musicians, as well as blues-informed genres such as jazz and rhythm and blues, shaped the soundscape of some White American communities during segregation, but the blues did not become a cultural common denominator among people in White society at large.[19] While Black American communities offered opportunities for formal music education in art music anchored in western European traditions, no formal institution outside Black communities offered training for African American musical performance, a role that Black churches often fulfilled in Black communities. Many Black workers, including musicians, routinely crossed racial borders to work in the more diversified, capital-rich White economic zones. Far fewer people who identified as White participated on a daily basis in Black community life by following Black social norms.

Although the vernacular music of Black communities drew the attentive appreciation of pockets of White listeners, who often lived in close proximity to centers of Black population, the majority of White Americans devalued Black traditional culture as inherently inferior.[20] Even Whites' seemingly favorable views of Black culture often grew from romanticized visions of Blackness as an entertaining escape from, or freeing alternative to, White middle-class conventions. Segregationists used such narrow views of Black music as mortar for the bricks of segregation's walls.[21]

White adaptations of Black music often were viewed as White creations without Black influence, which followed the customary White denial of the impact of Black-controlled creativity upon White-identified culture. Blues historian William Barlow describes such results as an illusory "pattern of musical expropriation and racial exclusion":

> Much of the popular vocal music of the day, including the songs written by Tin Pan Alley tunesmiths, was rooted in jazz or blues, but the singers who achieved stardom on radio in the 1920s were predominantly white interpreters of black song—the best known being Al Jolson, Rudy Vallee, Eddie Cantor, and Sophie Tucker. Meanwhile, . . . African American vocalists—luminaries such as Louis Armstrong, Bessie Smith, Ma Rainey, Leroy Carr, and Florence Mills—were rarely heard on radio; nor were hundreds of black artists who recorded for race-record labels in the 1920s.[22]

Printed media and recordings provided a route for people outside Black society to learn about vernacular blues traditions without challenging conventional racial divisions of the segregation era. Particularly before the mid-1950s, it was the rare occasion when White listeners would experience blues performances outside White social settings; few entered the same contexts where African Americans organized, presented, and responded to the blues for Black audiences. Blues stars such as Bessie Smith, who sang in vaudeville tours to the accompaniment of Black musicians often skilled in jazz, attracted the attention of White urbanites beginning to explore jazz in the 1920s and 1930s. In the 1940s and 1950s, selected blues music styles gained the attention of another group of White audiences with interests in folk music, who laid the foundation for a professional blues entertainment scene in White American community settings.

FOLK MUSIC ENTHUSIASTS

The phenomenon known as the folk song movement, or folk revival,[23] gained substantial momentum in the early twentieth century in England and the United States. Drawn to the interpersonal aspects of orally transmitted musics, enthusiasts often expected folk music to carry a group's intergenerational chain of memories and values. The movement promoted selected blues artists among a broad range of folk musicians, as defined by the largely White middle class and often elitely-educated enthusiasts. Enthusiasts sought to preserve the music of "folk" communities by authenticating sources for vernacular musical texts that seemed ancient or "pre-modern," collecting traditional music in transcriptions or recordings, and publishing them. Building upon the interests of nineteenth-century antiquarians and folklorists, some intellectuals and social progressives believed folk songs revealed perspectives of working-class people or aesthetic contributions of the unlettered. With a near evangelistic ideology evident in the 1930s, revivalists broadly promoted traditional music, which they felt was in danger of extinction. A network of folk song clubs, coffee house circuits, and festivals sustained the zeal of performers, collectors, and other enthusiasts through the early 1960s. Among the pioneering Black artists in the predominantly White folk scene during the segregation era were Leadbelly (Huddie Ledbetter), Josh White, and Odetta, who featured blues numbers in their performances in the United States and western Europe.[24]

For revivalists, tracing the musical tradition of folk communities was consequently almost as important as hearing or making folk music. Collectors had published books of American folk song as early as 1911. As early as 1936, such songbooks included blues tunes and lyrics based on performances by Black musicians, who folk collectors deemed to be authentic tradition bearers.[25] Blues songs remained a featured repertoire of folk revivalists from the 1940s onward. Similar to jazz discographers, revivalists collected commercially distributed records from the 1920s to 1940s, known as "race" and "hillbilly" records, to gain the oldest available audio documents of musics in the style of vernacularly-trained regional American performers. Blues comprised a large part of the race record offerings. Revivalists contributed to the dissemination and effective canonization of folk music by selectively reissuing race and hillbilly series recordings, including blues, in the fashion of the landmark *Anthology of American Folk Music* (1952) released by Folkways. Alan Lomax, one of a number of influential collectors, particularly emphasized blues as he routed field recordings to revivalist singers in the United States and England between the early 1940s and the late 1950s.

In their focus on identifying and promoting "folk music," revivalists did elevate arts that received infrequent attention, at best, in institutions for the formal study of music. Many performers, who had learned music as a matter of course in their home communities, found increased opportunities to perform for and reap earnings from broader audiences because of the interests of folk enthusiasts. Independent and major labels recorded music that in many cases had appealed to local communities for a long time. Over the years of the folk music movement, the interest in older styles of blues outside Black community settings renewed professional opportunities for elder Black blues musicians.

Despite formidable barriers, blues repertoire performed by Black, vernacularly-trained performers did reach the ears of segments of White America before the 1950s. How White people viewed these musical exchanges, if they were aware of them, varied widely. This transfer of musical sounds across Black–White social divisions does not indicate that people using musical tunes and texts held the *same* cultural values for music. Instead, we find evidence that people maintained differing cultural values based upon *partially shared* experiences of nation, region, inter- and intra-ethnic interchange, or other aspects of

American life. Consequently, it is important to examine how people define, perform, and interpret the blues as a process that involves much more than musical form or record-buying habits alone.

BROADENING TRANSCULTURAL APPEAL: BLUES IN POSTWAR TRANSITION

Changes in the practices of the music industry in the 1950s and 1960s opened a window through which Black performers of blues, and the related genre of rhythm and blues, accessed "mainstream" markets for popular music. When reflecting on this period in a 1996 interview, "Little" Milton Campbell, who maintained a Black audience base throughout his career, explained what mainstream access meant to him as he began his recording career in the 1950s. "We got a chance," he emphasized, "to get our music exposed to audiences through the country, throughout the world."[26]

Central to the manifestation of these opportunities were Black DJs' radio broadcasts and a specialized interest in blues that began to grow among White folk revivalists and White fans of rock and roll and rhythm and blues in England and the United States. The burgeoning White audience, which collectively provided a new market outside Black communities for Black blues performers, shared interests in blues and blues-based recordings. This new market represented a route for Black blues artists to access the dominant popular music market across marketing practices and laws that segregated the marketplace of music. The fans' expectations for blues performances grew from their varied experiences of blues in the folk scene, Black-appeal radio broadcasts, blues-based pop marketed to White consumers, and, in fewer cases, live performances of rhythm and blues and blues in Black community settings. Although addressed here separately for the sake of clarity, the events in each context occurred simultaneously and with cross influences.

The National Climate

Progressive social change and countering White resistance characterized the postwar period that proved to be the final days of legalized segregation. The United States developed new technologies, used them to begin transforming the industrial economy, and waged war with arms against Korea and with diplomacy against the Soviet Union. Movements built by civil rights organizations, unions, and feminists sparked changes of great magnitude but not the social revolutions sought by the groups' most progressive advocates. Anticommunist red-baiting directly crippled media broadcasts of social commentary and the exchange of ideas, particularly in professions that attracted involvement of the political left: entertainment, broadcasting, print journalism, and publishing. During this period, the career of actor–vocalist Paul Robeson was derailed, and the folk scene was assaulted with the sentencing of Pete Seeger and the hobbling of the career of Josh White, among others. Neither political activists nor countercultural groups dismantled the stronghold of established White Anglo-Protestant society on the status quo of the American political economy.

For African Americans, gaining legal protection against racially motivated violence and discrimination was of paramount importance. Victories in civil rights legislation cracked walls of segregation in public transportation, schools, and voting booths. By 1953, African Americans held federal cabinet posts and won local and state elections in increasing numbers. Even as Black leaders' boycotts and sit-ins succeeded in changing laws and customs of segregation (as with the 1954 Supreme Court ruling in *Brown v. The Board of Education* of Topeka, Kansas, which struck down the doctrine of "separate but equal" in public schools), White supremacists denied justice in courtrooms and martyred innocents. The monumental Civil Rights Act of 1964 wrote into the US Constitution a new foundation for racial equality but did not engender it ready-made.

The Civil Rights Movement teased apart the cultural and economic resources that supported White supremacy. In the entertainment business, Black artists pursued professional avenues with their managers and recording labels beyond racially circumscribed markets for music. From 1948, advertising industry analysts recognized the untapped potential of Black consumers with a collective estimated annual income of $10 billion.[27] Recorded and live performances of artists gained airplay on radio, which previously had restricted broadcasts of the vast majority of Black popular recording artists. The changes supported Black blues performers, who circumvented racial barriers to mainstream popular music audiences and built upon a growing transcultural interest in live blues performances. Crucial to this new audience base were the tastes of a new consumer demographic: the American teenager.

Shifting Popularity of the Blues in Black America

After World War II, Black Americans literally and metaphorically distanced themselves from the legacies of slavery in southern sharecropping and Jim Crow violence. Large numbers of African Americans migrated to northern urban industrial centers to pursue the promise of higher wages and upward social mobility. African Americans' musical tastes generally reflected a declining interest in blues songs that featured instrumentation and imagery reminiscent of the rural south. Black Americans used music to dramatize new visions of their life experiences.[28] The sounds of city sophistication often promoted the sonority of the saxophone over the harmonica, the electric guitar instead of the acoustic, and lyrics that referenced urban concerns.[29] Beginning in the mid-1940s, some blues performers pulled sounds of swing jazz bands into their performances, and their characteristically upbeat innovations produced musics known as jump blues and rhythm and blues, which pleased Black dance hall patrons.

The cultural meaning of blues shifted along generational and regional lines among African Americans. Younger Black Americans embraced offshoots of blues just as younger White Americans shifted away from the Tin Pan Alley tastes of their parents' generation. When another generation of Black youth turned to soul music in the 1960s, the cutting edge of Black popular music was two generations removed from the blues. Although blues specialty labels drastically limited projects marketed to Black blues audiences after the 1960s,[30] it is historically inaccurate to say that the blues died in Black America. Many Black musicians who forged the new musical styles still drew upon the blues, having learned from older musicians in Black communities or their elders' record collections. A blues circuit in southern Black communities has continued through the early twenty-first century to support Black blues performers who drew elements of rhythm and blues and soul music into blues compositions. The blues continued to appeal to older Black Americans.

THE MUSIC INDUSTRY: BLACK-APPEAL RADIO AND WHITE AUDIENCES

In the late 1940s, pioneering DJs programmed to Black audiences, and this transformed American airwaves. Small numbers of radio stations consequently adapted formats to appeal to the mass of Black America instead of targeting sectors of White audiences. The offerings of Black-appeal radio broadened, and the initiatives of Black DJs encouraged the recognition of African Americans' consumer power by White-owned radio stations.

Record sales show that American youths of varied backgrounds found the upbeat sound of rhythm and blues particularly appealing from 1955.[31] The new White audience was captivated by the music of Black blues-based artists such as Jimmy Reed, Chuck Berry, Little Richard (Richard Penniman), and a stream of White artists' cover songs. In addition to harnessing repertoire and performance styles popularized by Black artists, the music industry recognized the financial rewards of appropriating Black DJing styles for White markets. The aim was to attract a youth demographic in the mainstream market, still defined according to the tastes of White middle-class listeners. This goal supported the marketing of White performers, such as Pat Boone, who closely rendered versions of Black performers' hits in White racial packaging. White rockabilly and rock 'n' roll kingpins Carl Perkins, Jerry Lee Lewis, and Elvis Presley were heavily influenced by Black blues and rhythm and blues artists in the 1940s and early 1950s. As formative musical influences, Presley mentioned radio, phonograph, and religious revivals, and he particularly noted the impact of "the real low-down Mississippi singers, mostly Big Bill Broonzy and Big Boy Crudup."[32]

Conversations about music aired concerns about race and class. Middle-class America, segregationists, broadcasters, and composers cautioned against the youths' focus on rhythm and blues and rock 'n' roll by claiming that it degraded moral, aesthetic, and racial conventions. Debates addressed the interracial, cross-market appeal of Black musicians and descriptions of the aesthetic and social characteristics accorded to music marketed as rhythm and blues and rock 'n' roll. Rhythm and blues star Ruth Brown has recalled that police halted concerts to separate Black majority and White minority audiences, who mixed briefly when a rope segregating the two audiences fell.[33] As sociologist Philip Ennis has documented, some White DJs around the country refused to play rhythm and blues based on racialized devaluations of Black culture. A disc jockey from Louisville, Kentucky, explained that he banned rhythm and blues:

> Not because the person is colored, but it's the rhythm and tone of the things. It's not melodic. Our audience doesn't like this sort of thing. They would be ashamed if they thought that their friends knew they were listening to it. The quality of the music is poor. . . . It brings out the—well—the savage in people.[34]

The overt movement of Black popular music into spaces associated with White mainstream society challenged past patterns for distancing Black and White culture.

The invisible airwaves of radio sent Black music into the hands of anyone who kept their radio dial tuned to Black-appeal radio shows, including White listeners. Black-appeal radio of the 1950s directly influenced White youths who became professional blues performers from the late 1950s through the 1970s. Renowned harmonica player Charlie Musselwhite remembers listening to Rufus Thomas's nightly broadcasts on WDIA, which was tagged on-air as "Your all-colored station" in Memphis. Musselwhite enjoyed turning up the volume on his car radio to listen to the show's theme song: "Hootin' Blues" by the acclaimed Black harmonica player Sonny Terry.[35] WDIA, which had employed a young Riley "B.B." King as a performing DJ, expanded to a powerful 50,000-watt broadcast capacity by the mid-1950s. The equally powerful WLAC of Nashville, Tennessee, cultivated listeners for its late-night Black-appeal formatting, who also responded to ads for race records by mail order from Randy's Records, a WLAC sponsor.[36]

Black-appeal radio, which offered White youths greater sustained access to blues-based music of Black communities, may have reinforced White musicians' interests in entering Black community settings. In regions where African Americans prominently flavored regional musical culture, White encounters with African American music in the 1950s continued to follow segregation's governance. Small numbers of White men did pursue opportunities to learn directly from blues performers in Black community settings. White professional blues performers, who effectively apprenticed with African American bands in the late 1950s and early 1960s, often augmented their interests in blues recordings by interacting with African Americans, which often began in arenas permitted by segregation. Evidence suggests this is the case whether the White men sought informal tutoring from Black blues musicians located in urban or rural communities of northern or southern regional centers for blues.

According to accounts of Mike Bloomfield and his childhood friend, Fred Glaser, Black domestic workers in Chicago's White well-to-do households expanded their exposure to Black music that began by listening to rock 'n' roll in the 1950s. Glaser explains:

> The maids always had the radio on [WVON], and they listened to black music with people like Muddy Waters and B. B. King and Ben E. King and Bo Diddley and Jimmy Reed—these were the day-to-day people that black people were listening to, when we were listening to Elvis and Buddy Holly and some of those early guys. So we heard this music . . . and we liked it. . . . I would go up to my room every night when I was supposed to go to bed, and I'd turn on [WVON].[37]

Both Glaser and Bloomfield credited domestic worker Mary Williams with introducing them to blues in the clubs of Chicago's predominantly Black Southside neighborhoods in the late 1950s, when Bloomfield had developed facility on the electric guitar.[38]

Bluesmen Charlie Musselwhite (b. 1944) and Kenny Brown (b. 1953), each White, have described the pull of Black vernacular music performed by fieldhands, drum and fife groups, and an itinerant blues singer in soundscapes they encountered in Memphis, Tennessee, and Nesbitt, Mississippi, in the late 1940s and 1950s.[39] Musselwhite and Brown overheard this music from a distance in their boyhood, while walking home from a bus stop or sitting on a riverbank, and they identify these experiences as roots for later interest in Black-oriented radio. Before Musselwhite reached the age of eighteen, he had become acquainted with elder Black musicians popularized on race recordings, such as Furry Lewis, Will Shade, and Gus Cannon. Musselwhite frequently spent time at Lewis's or Shade's home, where musicians regularly gathered and often "were very willing to show me things on the guitar" at a time when "black kids my age weren't interested in their music."[40]

Expanding the Blues Audience

Hit-makers of the late 1940s and early 1950s, such as Muddy Waters, faced declining popularity for blues in the increasingly youth-oriented markets for Black popular music. Waters, for example, had begun by the late 1950s to look outside the Black popular music market when the dance beats of rhythm and blues and the smooth ballads of young vocal groups increasingly dominated the Black music industry.[41] Spinning from the small folk revival scene and interracial marketing of rhythm and blues and its transformations, pockets of White teens and young adults gradually had become interested in old recordings of the blues in the United States and England. Following the positive reception of blues recordings among European folk and jazz fans, tours initiated between 1949 and 1958 generated favorable responses to the acoustic blues performers "Leadbelly" (Huddie Ledbetter), Josh White, Lonnie Johnson, Big Bill Broonzy (William Lee Conley), Brownie McGhee, and Sonny Terry. Studies by Bob Groom, Paul Oliver, and Jim O'Neal confirm that the growing transatlantic White audience for contemporary Black blues performers grew from musical influences of the folk revivalists and an alternative youth subculture based on rhythm and blues and rock 'n' roll.[42]

In the early 1950s, British youths influenced by folk revivalists had begun to perform a music they called "skiffle," which blended traditional American and British folk musics drawn from recordings of the race record series.[43] For most of the decade, folk song collector Alan Lomax, who had left the United States during the height of red-baiting, regularly aired radio broadcasts of folk music for the BBC that included some blues. In the mid-1950s, when Elvis Presley's blend of rhythm and blues and country-influenced pop began to chart hits for both Black and White American pop audiences, Lonnie Donnegan's skiffle cover of Leadbelly's "Rock Island Line" similarly showed the popular appeal of Black American blues songs in this style in both Europe and the United States. Among the youths fascinated by skiffle, blues, and rhythm and blues in the mid-1950s were future members of British rock groups that later included renditions of Black American recording artists' blues songs in their own hit recordings in the early 1960s.[44]

Before Black blues performers gained large followings in the new White audiences in the United States, a number of leading performers found receptive new audiences overseas in the late 1950s and early 1960s. Bereft of the offerings of Black-appeal radio, London's blues enthusiasts hunted for recordings of "country blues," amplified blues, and rhythm and blues artists. Discographies, magazines, and books published by enthusiasts in Belgium, France, and England prior to those of blues enthusiasts in the United States provided aid.[45] The Rolling Stones, the Yardbirds, and Cream began as blues purists, even questioning the validity of rhythm and blues in their repertoire, at times. Blues purists sought to authentically replicate music, indicating shared ideals promoted by folk revivalists.

After 1958, European enthusiasts of folk and jazz welcomed the amplified electric presentations of Chicago-based Muddy Waters, Otis Spann, and then Buddy Guy.[46] Responses among European audiences varied according to their readings of blues as interpreted by particular artists. After seeing Waters play in England, Brian Jones, who later led the Rolling Stones, took up electric guitar and modeled his playing after Waters's style.[47] Jeff Beck, the renowned British rock guitarist, who later pushed the use of feedback and distortion in rock, saw Guy's aggressive, explosive, lengthy, and "developed" blues solos as "total maniac abandon" that "broke all boundaries" of conventional pop form.[48]

Beginning in 1962, blues festivals, modeled on successful folk and jazz festivals, offered European and White American audiences increased access to Black blues artists' live performances. Willie Dixon, a Chicago bandleader, songwriter, and influential figure at Chess Records, recommended Black blues artists for appearances in the American Folk Blues Festival (AFBF), an annual European tour that lasted throughout the decade.[49] The AFBF artists also reached millions through appearances on European radio and television broadcasts.[50] In comparison in the United States, the large audiences for the for-profit Newport Jazz Festival (established 1954) and the Newport Folk Festival (established 1959) billed only a few Black blues performers among other featured artists, although blues songs were a staple in the repertoire of the largely White revivalist-scene performers by the early 1960s.[51] The large Ann Arbor (Michigan) blues festival did not take place until 1969.

During the apex of battles in the Civil Rights Movement in the 1960s, the presence of blues-based music in the American mainstream surely was eased across racial divides by its packaging in the hands of White British groups like the Rolling Stones, in addition to White rock 'n' roll stars like Elvis Presley. White folk revivalist queen Joan Baez launched her commercial career at the 1959 Newport Folk Festival, and by 1963 she had charted an anthem of the Civil Rights Movement, "We Shall Overcome," as a pop single. Beginning in 1963 and 1964, British rock bands fed a style of rock based on aspects of blues back into commercially mediated soundscapes of the United States, which are said to have encouraged Bob Dylan to move from folk revivalist conventions to electric instruments and a rock style.[52] The American industry continued to market music according to stylistic and racialized markets. Many White American fans of rock, who often viewed the genre as a revolutionary form, remained ignorant of the music's connection to blues or African American culture. The unacknowledged appropriation of blues repertoire and techniques by some top rock recording artists and their critics supported the illusion. For example, the 1967 "Drinking Muddy Water," credited to Dreja, McCarty, Page, and Relf and recorded by the Yardbirds (the group that later evolved into Led Zeppelin), is actually Muddy Waters' "Rollin' and Tumblin'." Willie Dixon, who held the copyright for "Rollin' and Tumblin'," later sued the band twice for copyright infringement, with some success.[53]

Blues "Revival" in America

Music promoted by folk revivalists gained attention in broader audiences in the mid-1960s, while contemporary pop markets introduced revivalist-trained folk musicians as commercial artists. Within the folk revival scenes, artists began to specialize in specific folk music styles. By the mid- to late 1960s, folk revivalists increasingly narrowed their interests in folk music at large to selectively engage in greater depth with a more limited range of folk music styles. Revivalist-trained performers of folk music turned greater attention to learning folk music directly from the "folk," or tradition bearers. In the latter half of the 1960s, revivalist promoters increasingly hired the very artists praised as masters of folk tradition. Rather than simply seeking out the music and history of all folk music, enthusiasts became interested in immersing themselves in one style or another, such as blues or bluegrass, which they hoped to hear performed by vernacularly-trained folk artists who had learned the music in their own communities. A segment of the folk revival network formed around people who were particularly interested in blues and its authentic performance, where authenticity was determined according to standards similar to those of folk purists.[54]

This impulse is known as the blues "revival," even though the blues was hardly dead, as Buddy Guy mentioned in an interview published in the inaugural volume of the blues enthusiast forum, *Living Blues Magazine*, in 1970. Guy noted that what had occurred instead was the birth of new, interested audiences and performers. He said, "Janis Joplin and Cream [featuring Eric Clapton] and all of 'em went to playin' the blues, because we never left it. If we had 'a left it, they wouldn't have found it out, you know."[55]

Blues enthusiasts in the United States, like their European counterparts, used documentation and research of recordings to build familiarity with the history of blues recording artists. Independent blues labels flourished through the 1960s. Chris Strachwitz's Arhoolie Records grew out of his International Blues Record Club, an organization to assist in the trade of old, original blues recordings.[56] A flourish of fanzines, magazines, and then books expanded printed histories of blues that continued the folk revival emphasis of artists and styles of the 1920s to 1940s race recordings.

While the late Robert Johnson and Charley Patton only were accessible on recording, revivalist promoters located a host of distinguished blues performers who had learned blues in Black cultural contexts and remained available and interested in professional opportunities. Blues societies grew in the model of folk song societies and provided new venues for Black blues artists. A short list of performers popular in these circuits includes Lightnin' Hopkins, Son House, "Mississippi" John Hurt, Sonny Terry and Brownie McGhee, and Joe Lee "Big Joe" Williams, not to mention recent blues chart-toppers from the 1950s who were making inroads among audiences of revivalist and rock scenes by the 1960s.[57]

Jeff Todd Titon, who performed, collected, and historicized blues in the revival movement of the 1960s, has noted that revivalists pursued blues according to particular values.[58] Instead of preserving the blues pristinely in its traditional contexts, revivalists selectively reconstructed it. Black blues performers likewise encountered new expectations in performances for folk scene audiences and continued the traditional African American practice of reshaping the blues to respond to new social contexts. As in the past, few White people entered Black community settings to experience blues performances, and most of the new White audience base gained transcultural understandings of blues as a result of Black performers' professional work in White social arenas.

NEW BLUES SCENES AND REVIVALIST AESTHETICS: REDEFINING THE BLUES

The development of a focused interest in blues traditions among White performers and audiences fostered specialized scenes for blues performers in White social settings beginning around 1963 in the United States. Although nourished by blues networks in Black communities and often viewed as a kind of racial integration among professional musicians, the new scenes did not unite Black and White audiences for blues. The consequent growth of specialty scenes for blues in social arenas dominated by Whites reflected the continued relevance of racial borders between Black and White social communities and the significance of aesthetic distinctions in Black- and White-identified cultural expression in the United States.

The musical interests of revivalists in documented performances, folk authenticity, and concert-style performances informed the performance practice and presentational style of the blues. Folk song collectors included recordings and notated arrangements of blues songs from Black, vernacularly-trained musicians' live performances on acoustic instruments. In contrast to African American cultural aesthetics that generally prioritize contextually responsive improvisational treatment of musical structures, the predominantly White collectors and performers usually located the essence of folk song in a relatively fixed text and tune. Through the 1950s, folk-influenced blues enthusiasts had viewed the performance of such tunes and texts as a technique for preserving authentic folk repertoire and protecting folk traditions. Concerns for preservation through replicating texts and tunes contradict African American cultural aesthetics for traditionally-performed genres that generally prioritize contextually responsive improvisational treatment of musical structures.

Revivalist aims of preservation clashed with some aesthetic values for blues performance common in Black cultural contexts, such as the importance of personalizing the delivery of traditional texts through improvisation and shaping blues music with an individually identifiable performance style.[59] Contemporary blues artist Rory Block, who learned blues at age fourteen in the heart of the 1960s New York City folk scene, emphasizes in her autobiography that she approached reissued blues recordings with an interest in achieving note-for-note accuracy in her own performances. "I spent two years of my life with my ear glued to a speaker," writes Block, "determined to figure out each and every note and play the great songs with as much accuracy as I could muster."[60] Her intensity was motivated by "a deep reverence for the music," which included acknowledging the original composers and performers. From recordings and personal interaction, performers like Block imitated pitch, rhythm, melody, harmony, and sound quality as they learned blues tunes and texts.

When established Black blues performers met such skillful novices, they often emphasized that such respectful replication, while a crucial step in learning, was an insufficient goal for meaningful blues performance. B. B. King, for instance, repeatedly passed on to younger musicians emulating his single-string melodies a lesson that he learned early in his career from Muddy Waters: "Be yourself."[61] Established White harmonica performer Charlie Musselwhite concurs: "Don't imitate anybody. Playing what you feel inside is really the key. If you want to learn harmonica, you can learn the classic tunes, but you should go on from there."[62] In 1965, with guitar riffs from Elmore James records, purposefully roughshod outfits, and a nineteen-year-old's certain confidence, Doug MacLeod, also White, quickly learned from veteran bluesman Ernest Banks of Virginia, who was Black, to shift away from self-focused imitative performance to connecting with his audiences: "[Banks] told me the idea of a bluesman is not about the bluesman, it's about the giving. By reaching other people and making them feel something, you help them get through the world easier."[63] Widely successful blues performers have continued to emphasize the value of vivifying experiential qualities of interpersonal connections through their performances.

These central understandings of blues performances in Black cultural contexts were not articulated by discs and books of the folk revival alone. Even the blues race records of performers from the Mississippi Delta region, which revivalists prized as authentic African American folk blues, were *selective* portraits of traditional performance in Black communities. Blues scholar David Evans has shown that recording company representatives for race record series downplayed repertoire, which ordinarily featured extensive repetition of core tunes and texts characteristic to live performance in the heart of the Delta.[64]

Influences characteristic of White middle-class expectations for performance were musically evident in the folk scene. Many White fans built a path of familiarity with blues through White social frameworks, although they often viewed their interracial, transcultural musical appreciation as actions that challenged conventions of established "mainstream" society, including White supremacist racism. Their experiences informed their conception of Black culture as well as their vision of blues and its relationship to contemporary Black music. While folk scenes celebrated cultural pluralism, folk scene performers like Richard Fariña (Cuban), Bruce Langhorne (African American), and Taj Mahal (African American) experienced White Anglo liberal, middle-class conventions as the dominant framework.[65]

Another aesthetic legacy of the folk scene grew from ideals of performance practice. Expository concerts were prevalent, where interlocutors typically explained folk repertoire and spoke to their audiences instead of vernacularly-trained performers. Yet blues artists schooled from within the folk scene, such as "Spider" John Koerner, spoke directly to the crowds himself.[66] Venues of concert halls distanced performers on elevated stages from their seated audiences, and middle-class standards of decorum often hushed audiences unless performers directly encouraged audience participation. Blues performers in such settings had to work around these conventions if they sought to involve all in performance through immediately responsive, active participation—a frequent characteristic of live performance in African American cultural contexts. Pauses often separated performances into a series of discrete selections bounded by the structure of single songs and their introductions, where blues performances in Black venues that promoted dancing often would avoid breaking grooves as performers moved between songs and styles. To café audiences in the early 1960s, performers like Lightnin' Hopkins brought Black cultural approaches to blues performance, which exposed the audience to varied Black oratorical styles and approaches to intertwining story with song.

In places where folk, jazz, and pop scenes collided in the 1960s, the fluid bounds of cultural forms and musical elements as artists shape the post–World War II blues soundscape cannot be denied, clearly challenging a binary racial paradigm (either Black or White).[67] Carlos Santana provides one example. Born in Mexico into a musical family, Santana took up electric guitar in high school in San Francisco and entered the city's eclectic folk, rock, and jazz scenes in the mid-to-late 1960s. Santana's biography in Santana: The Official Carlos Santana Web Site describes his early band as a "groundbreaking Afro-Latin-blues-rock fusion outfit." Santana's later reflections on the guitar players who shaped him during that time period reference B.B. King, Jimi Hendrix, Gabor Szabo, Bola Sete, and Wes Montgomery.[68] Over the course of his career, Santana's music has remained in conversation with Chicano, Puerto Rican, and other Latino artists as well.

As White blues audiences associated blues with living Black culture, the demand that performers should fulfill definitions of Blackness was an expectation issued by people who, for the most part, did not identify as Black. At times, this introduced a pungent legacy of limitations for professional artists.[69] Musician Clarence "Gatemouth" Brown, an African American, rejected the label of blues performer, even though he attracted large audiences on European and American blues circuits from the 1970s through his death in 2005. Brown strongly believed in the 1990s that the notion of blues still conjured stereotypical images of Black musicians in the minds of some. "The ignorant person," he said, "want a guy standing up there screaming the blues . . . sounding like a Baptist preacher. I just don't like that."[70] In contrast, Brown emphasized that his performances—which reflected prominent influences of swing jazz, country western, and Cajun styles in addition to conventional blues repertoire—encompassed far more than a limited shouting style he felt audiences associated with stereotypes of Black oratory.

Some White rhythm and blues or rock fans became increasingly interested in blues as they realized that artists like Eric Clapton and Janis Joplin drew heavily on blues songs. Those who developed interest in blues in folk scenes would encounter revivalist ideology that often championed folk music as an antidote to the ills of commercial consumerism. Such viewpoints may have encouraged an understanding of blues apart from, and sometimes superior to, other contemporary forms of African American music. Among an enduring base of Black blues fans, however, the most widely appealing blues artists since the 1960s have blended in conventions of rhythm and blues and soul music that resonated with the current soundscape, such as Bobby "Blue" Bland, "Little" Milton Campbell, Denise LaSalle, Z. Z. Hill, Johnnie Taylor, and Bobby Rush, among others.[71]

White Blues Scenes

By the mid-1960s, White performers of blues such as Michael Bloomfield, Paul Butterfield, Nick Gravenites, John Hammond, Geoff Muldaur, Charlie Musselwhite, Dave Van Ronk, and Eric Von Schmidt worked mainly in the folk revival or in new blues scenes of White communities. Analysis of the development of an early scene for blues in White neighborhoods of Chicago indicates that a new aesthetic trajectory emerged for blues in this transcultural scene for performance. The blues of scenes based in Black and White communities continued to differ on stylistic grounds and in terms of their appeal.

In 1963, a distinctive blues-specialty performance scene in White neighborhoods of Chicago offered new ways to access live blues based on the music of Black performers in Chicago's contemporary electric blues scene of Black Southside and Westside neighborhoods. The music-making of the Southside and Westside blues scenes had fueled the recording industry for blues based in Chicago through the early 1950s. Many hit-makers of that era continued to perform blues as the popularity of the music waned in the late 1950s. Despite the proximity of the scene to many White folk enthusiasts and rhythm and blues fans of the 1960s, a sizeable social and urban geographic distance separated White and Black neighborhoods. Whether reinforced by custom or law, segregation magnified this rift.

Examining how a blues scene grew in White Northside Chicago reveals much about the processes involved in building cultural bridges across racial divides. Values about music, race, and economic factors intersected in this new transcultural context. The view centers on performers networked among bandleaders Michael Bloomfield, Paul Butterfield, Muddy Waters, Charlie Musselwhite, and Joe Lee "Big Joe" Williams. The Northside Chicago scene that they helped to create in the early 1960s became the foundation for a local economic core of Chicago's top-level performers in a scene that has served since that time as a hub for the international blues industry.

According to a recent oral historical portrait of Bloomfield by Jan Mark Wolkin and Bill Keenom,[72] the blues of Chicago's White folk scene was divorced from the sound of electric Chicago-style blues that remained vibrant in Black Southside and Westside venues until the late 1950s. White artists, such as Bloomfield, who performed blues within folk scenes prior to 1963, reflected interests in older acoustic blues styles over contemporary Chicago electric styles. Blues venues in White neighborhoods were acoustic according to revivalist conventions. Due to prior practices of racial segregation, Northside clubs had established prohibitions against nonintegrated bands, which also inhibited Black bands from performing the electric blues styles that were so popular in Black venues.[73] When blues was introduced in White Northside clubs after 1963, it was the White performers Bloomfield, Musselwhite, and Paul Butterfield who did so.

The experiences of Paul Butterfield indicate that racial barriers did not limit skilled White players from working in venues in Black neighborhoods. Butterfield, influenced by Black innovators Little Walter and Junior Wells (Figure 1.2), became a regular feature at Southside Chicago's Blue Flame Lounge around 1962. Butterfield sat in every weekend

Figure 1.2
Junior Wells, c. early 1960s.
Photo by Raymond Flerlage. Courtesy Delmark Records.

with Little Smokey Smothers, a Black bandleader who led a band of hired Black personnel. Although Paul Butterfield musically "held his own," according to Bloomfield, Butterfield's appearance had the impact of a novelty act: "Irish white guy plays the blues."[74] Over time, White associates of Butterfield formed what Nick Gravenites described as a small "contingent" in the audience of "mostly black people" as Butterfield's White friends spread word to others of the event.[75] Sam Lay, a highly appreciated African American blues drummer, pointed out that Butterfield's draw of White audiences positively impacted the Southside club's finances; its sizeable, racially "mixed audience" supported the gigs, and the Blue Flame "became one of the most popular spots in town."[76]

Neither the electric blues scene of the Black Southside, nor the acoustic folk scene of the White Northside, was driven by purely financial or purely aesthetic goals. Venues of the folk scene in White Northside neighborhoods sponsored live music that could generate crowds. Around this time, the Northside folk club Big John's sponsored interracial billings featuring Charlie Musselwhite and Big Joe Williams, who were later joined by Michael Bloomfield on piano. When Williams left the gig, Musselwhite and Bloomfield continued with new sidemen who were White, thus ending the interracial composition of the band. Bloomfield switched to guitar, and the band played electrified blues with a smattering of jazz standards. The context made the band a novelty, although the band's level of musical achievement varied widely from "great" to "probably terrible" in the words of one member.[77] The band had no artistic competitors on the Northside, and few White fans traveled across racial barriers to the hotbed of electric blues in Black neighborhood clubs. Bloomfield's band performed as many as four nights per week at Big John's on the Northside. White patrons overflowed the relatively small establishment.

When Bloomfield's band left, Paul Butterfield continued electric blues sets at Big John's with former Howlin' Wolf sidemen Sam Lay and Jerome Arnold, two respected Black blues musicians who were drawn to the gig's promise of higher pay. According to Charlie Musselwhite, this marks the genesis of a blues scene in White social arenas of Chicago, which was styled on the contemporary performances of Black Southside blues networks:

> That started the whole flip-flop from the South Side to the North Side, because none of the clubs on the South Side could outmatch in money these North Side clubs. And [white] people loved it. They didn't want to go to the South Side. They were afraid, or they didn't know where to go. That was sort of where it really began.[78]

White audiences seeking this electric style of blues more easily could hear musicians with solid reputations. As in Butterfield's band, Black musicians skilled in the electric blues styles first popularized in Black communities in the 1950s gained avenues to perform these styles of music in integrated bands in White clubs, which offered higher wages than Southside venues where the popularity of this style of blues was declining. White Northside audiences gained access to live blues outside the Black working-class and lower-class neighborhoods of Black Southside blues clubs. In the "flip-flop," Southside venues lost a distinctive draw for the new audience base for blues, although particular venues continued to attract White audiences. As a result of a combination of cultural and socioeconomic factors, the presence of live Black music, and particularly blues bands, drastically declined in Black neighborhood clubs in the 1960s and 1970s.[79]

White blues patrons largely attended performances in White neighborhoods, and some Black blues venues cultivated White patrons in addition to their Black clientele. White Northside blues fans lacked familiarity with the offerings of Southside blues venues, the diversity of Black neighborhoods, and experiences of integration in predominantly Black areas. Southside clubs with predominantly Black patrons, such as Theresa's Lounge, successfully cultivated White patrons, however. Established in 1958 by Theresa Needham, Theresa's Lounge hosted live blues through the 1970s. Years after she closed business, Needham recalled that she had hired extra security to monitor parking lots for the vehicles that White patrons typically drove from the relatively more affluent economic zones of Northside and suburban neighborhoods. For all her patrons, Theresa Needham provided a welcoming atmosphere and tolerated no inappropriate actions.[80] Aspects of the social barriers to integration and class-mixing in such Southside clubs could be crossed by those patrons willing to challenge protocol.

White blues musicians were problematized in the discourse of the folk world and the nascent blues scene in White communities. In ways similar to jazz critics' addresses of racial identity, LeRoi Jones' *Blues People* (1963) and Paul Oliver's *The Meaning of the Blues* (1960), as well as his *Conversations with the Blues* (1965), emphasized connections between performing and living the blues.[81] The premise conjoins political and cultural expression, which aligns with definitions of blues in African American cultural contexts. Musical experience therein often comments on the "here and now" of daily life. From this standpoint, the blues should vivify a person's experiences and feelings about struggles in life as if telling the truth.

Some blues enthusiasts, like Alan Lomax, extended this maxim to question the authenticity and racial justice of White professional performers of blues. In 1965, as he introduced The Paul Butterfield Band's electric blues set at the Newport Folk Festival, Lomax drew attention to a controversy already aired in the blues revival community at a time when a number of White blues professionals were crossing over to rock audiences. More experienced Black blues artists struggled to do so. Blues researcher and record producer Samuel Charters, who also performed "old country blues" in the folk revival scene, recently captured a sense of an uneasy racial territorialism of the times:

> Even if all of us kept telling each other that young white college kids could sing the blues, at some level none of us really felt certain about it, and we were continually dismayed that there was no interest in the old country blues from the contemporary black audience. When the occasional young black singer like Taj Mahal drifted over to our camp we immediately made room for them.[82]

The continued significance of race and differences in the interests of Black and White blues audiences raised questions among some White enthusiasts regarding the meaning of blues performances as representations of Black tradition when performed by or for Whites.

Race continued to matter in financial terms as well, raising questions about the degree to which blues in White settings was an appropriation: an attempt to control Black cultural property and its financial value. White blues and blues-rock artists often achieved crossover hits in markets for rock audiences more quickly than their Black musical idols. B. B. King, Albert King, Buddy Guy, and other top Black bandleaders of the 1950s and 1960s came to the attention of pop promoters in the late 1960s when some White blues-based artists acknowledged them as musical influences.

In 1988, nearly thirty years later, White blues guitarist and crossover rock performer Stevie Ray Vaughan still commanded a greater box office draw than did veteran B. B. King. In an interview for *Guitar World* magazine that year, Vaughan pushed the spotlight onto "the pioneers and the innovators," whose recordings he used like textbooks. "Those guys are the ones who really ought to have the recognition," he said. "All the great records by Albert King and Albert Collins, Otis Rush, B.B. King's *Live at the Regal*—there's millions we could talk about. . . . There's always something new to learn in each one."[83] As discussed by researcher Paul Garon, White performers clearly are able to perform blues and succeed at it, but this interracial and transcultural move does not obliterate social structures of race in American society:

> Dismissers of white blues performance are often accused of holding the position that whites "do not have a right" to play the blues. The right to play and sing the blues is never at issue. An important factor that is at issue is that white performers have so much coverage and such high record sales (compared to blacks) that their notion of being victims of discrimination . . . is quite laughable. As if Bonnie Raitt or Stevie Ray Vaughan were drowned in obscurity![84]

Figure 1.3
Denise LaSalle.

Courtesy Ecko Records.

By the 1980s, the acclaimed vocalist and songwriter Denise LaSalle (Figure 1.3) was well aware of the irony that the blues artists most popular among African American audiences fit only with difficulty into marketing categories of the music industry:

> Z. Z. Hill and I sat down and discussed it. People like Denise LaSalle, Johnnie Taylor, Bobby Bland, Tyrone Davis, and Shirley Brown are pushed aside . . . we're too R&B to be blues, too blues to be R&B, and too blues to be pop—so then what are we? Call it soul blues—they should have a whole new category![85]
>
> Hoffman (1996), 76

The developments of Chicago's Northside scene in the early 1960s show that racial integration and transcultural interchange in musical scenes of the 1960s arose in settings informed by separate but influential Black and White social spheres. All enjoyed blues music, but Black and White audiences often held differing aesthetic expectations for its performance. Artists playing blues-specialty venues in White social arenas did not mirror musical changes in stylistic aspects of blues popularized by Black artists who appealed to predominantly Black blues audiences, particularly those of the circuit of southern Black blues shows sometimes referred to as the "chittlin' circuit."

It cannot be denied, of course, that blues artists who identify racially as Black, White, Hispanic, and other backgrounds have continued to draw audiences who include Americans of varied racial identities and international fans. Similar to nationally evident preferences of Black and White blues audiences, however, "soul blues" performers such as Bobby "Blue" Bland, Little Milton Campbell, Denise LaSalle, and Peggy Scott Adams achieved great popularity among Black blues audiences; artists marketed as "blues rock" such as Eric Clapton, Buddy Guy, Johnny Lang, and Joe Bonamassa have attracted more White blues fans and more frequently succeed in crossing over to predominantly White rock markets. "Soul blues" styles incorporate feels, instrumentation, and formal structures of post-1960 rhythm and blues, soul, and funk that have held great popularity among Black audiences. In contrast, "blues rock" styles incorporate sounds of 1950s-era blues and its interpolations in post-1960s rock.

Toward Acknowledgment: A Conclusion of Continued Negotiations

As of 1997, the Chicago scene hosted over sixty venues that regularly featured blues, located in neighborhoods where Black Chicagoans played the blues throughout the twentieth century, as well as in newer venues near predominantly White middle-class neighborhoods.[86] One venue established in the mid-1990s is a corporate franchise of The House of Blues. While Black and White performers routinely emphasize that they play music designed for people of any ethnic or national origin, since the 1980s the top-paying clubs of the Northside Chicago scene have dominated the market for patrons, the majority of whom have been White, middle-class Americans. White performers routinely cite experience working on the Black Southside blues scene as a sign of having trained at the highest level.

Through the early twenty-first century, the live and recorded performances of many Black blues artists remain prominent among those recognized as masters of the form. Venues in Southside Chicago clubs, like Lee's Unleaded Blues, attract people of varied backgrounds to cross social borders in venues connected to longstanding Black communities. Southside clubs have not maintained financial successes equivalent with blues shows of the Northside. Despite the odds, Black-managed Southside venues acknowledge the continued significance of blues in social scenes of older Black adults. Local Black blues artists continue to perform and socialize in these neighborhood clubs, although they, like other blues professionals, typically see gigs at Northside venues as a sign of having "made it" in the upper echelons of the national blues scene. Professional performers of varied backgrounds have maintained aesthetic ideals of blues performance as Black cultural music, reflecting experiences their White audiences often do not share.

A study of blues performance in transcultural contexts reveals that the aesthetic and financial interests of people involved in both Black and White social arenas are significant in the United States, and this reality has impacted blues in international scenes. Analysis of Black–White transcultural relationships reveals connections quilted in the vividly varied American cultural fabric. It complicates the narrative of how Black blues artists have navigated cultural and racial difference in performing blues. It challenges devaluations of Blackness, an element of White supremacist ideology.

People have wrestled with dynamics of racial power, however, in this transcultural process mediated by grassroots musical interest groups and the commercial music industry. Far from escaping or eradicating racial social confines, people have shaped blues music with their own expectations as they participated in blues performances with varied degrees of involvement in and identification with particular sites of Black cultural communities. Indeed, analysis focused on Black–White transcultural relationships in blues music scenes is valuable for understanding connecting points in the quilt of American culture. Examination of the cultural values of Whites also is valuable for the sake of understanding borders that separate the American fabric, specifically how seemingly benign ideals fostered in White community life sanction White privilege and "non-White" racial subordination in the United States.[87]

Historical analysis reveals how blues music lovers have navigated dynamics of social race across cultures. Rather than understanding the exchanges as a colorblind transcendence to a universal mode of harmony, it seems more historically responsive to understand the embraces as a negotiation of differences that, at the time, seemed to many to be relatively free of interpersonal racial bias. Acknowledgment of these social complexities, which not only challenged but also sustained racial and cultural barriers, does not diminish the value of the connections made across them. Acknowledgment honors these achievements and the aesthetic results of musical connections forged in moments where romanticized, market-driven, paternalistic, or other lenses have shaded the views of those involved. Recognition of the rough jagged grain of reality in the blues world calls for continued attention to the ways that individuals and institutions impact the performance of Black cultural forms in transcultural contexts.

ACKNOWLEDGMENTS

The author gratefully acknowledges the postdoctoral fellowship program of the Japan Society for the Promotion of Science (JSPS) of Japan's Ministry of Education, Science, Sports and Culture, which supported work on this article while the author was in residence at the Research Institute for the Languages and Cultures of Asia and Africa, Tokyo University of Foreign Studies. Also appreciated is assistance from the archival staff of The Chicago Blues Archive (Harold Washington Public Library, Chicago) and Indiana University's Archives of African American Music and Culture and the Archives of Traditional Music.

NOTES

1. "In Performance at the White House: Complete Series Overview," PDF document accessed via the PBS website, In Performance at the White House, http://www.pbs.org/insperformanceatthewhitehouse/pdf/IPWH/past.pdf.
2. See studies of racial consciousness discussing the significance of Whiteness and Blackness as a socially constructed racial binary in the United States and acknowledging the role of cultural values and racial identity, such as Kimberlé Crenshaw et al., 1995; Wellman 1993.
3. Barlow 1989, 325.

4. Oehler 2001.
5. As the website of the Clinton Presidential Library states, President Bill Clinton's 1998 impeachment by the House of Representatives grew from his "relationship with a young intern" (http://www.clintonlibrary.gov/william-j.-clinton-bio.html). Earlier allegations of the Clintons' involvement in questionable business deals also became media events discussed as "scandals" by the public at large.
6. "Northbound Blues," as performed by Maggie Jones (Columbia Records 14902), quoted in Barlow 1989, 146.
7. I follow Reebee Garofalo's use of the term "social race" in discussing "socially constructed race" in Black popular music in the United States (Garofalo 1993, 234–235).
8. Omi and Winant 1994, 13.
9. Ellison 1994 (1964), 78.
10. Hunter 2000, 147.
11. Philips 1990, 237.
12. Carmichael, "Washboard Blues," sheet music and lyrics [cited April 4, 2003], available from http://www.dlib.indiana.edu/collections/hoagy/; Titon 1994, 59–136.
13. Ennis 1992, 42–70, 172–173; Barlow 1999, 8–10, 20–53.
14. Lott 1995, 18.
15. Titon 1993; Gendron 1995, 31–56; Monson 1995, 397–398; Oehler 2001, 93–97.
16. Edwards 1997, 62; Bailey, quoted in Morton and Wolfe 1991, 17, 20–21, 26–27, 34.
17. Malone 1979, 4–5.
18. See Hernandez, 2010; Macías 2008, 2003.
19. Peretti 1992, 94; Barlow 1999, 109–110.
20. See Evans 1982, 38–39, 51, 90–94; Bastin 1995 (1986), 6–7; Maultsby 1990; Peretti 1992; Oehler 2001, 90–97.
21. Titon 1993; Monson 1995, 398–399; West 1999, 55–86.
22. Barlow 1999, 22.
23. Cantwell 1996, 13–47, 82–91.
24. Greenway 1960; Reuss 1971; Reagon 1975; Carawan 2002, accessed via "Guy and Candi Carawan: A Personal Story through Sight and Sound" website, http://digitalstudio.ucr.edu/studio_projects/carawan/default.html.
25. Gellert 1936; Lomax and Lomax 1936; Cohen 1995; Cantwell 1996; Filene 2000; Oehler 2001, 98–100.
26. Dolins and Campbell 1996.
27. Barlow 1999, 125.
28. Maultsby 1990; Gilroy 1991, 11–36; Maultsby 1996, 888–907.
29. Oehler 2001, 70–73.
30. Evans 1982, 85.
31. "The Early Crossovers" and "The King and His Court," in Ennis 1992, 193–255; Barlow 1999, 172–173.
32. Elvis Presley, quoted in Garofalo 1993, 57–121.
33. Oehler 2001, 118–120.
34. Unidentified individual, quoted in Ennis 1992, 233.
35. Charlie Musselwhite, quoted in Tipaldi 2002, 65.
36. Barlow 1999, 123–126, 160.
37. Fred Glaser, quoted in Wolkin and Keenom 2000, 10–11.
38. Wolkin and Keenom 2000, 19–22.
39. Charlie Musselwhite, quoted in Tipaldi 2002, 63–65; Kenny Brown, quoted in Tipaldi 2002, 45–46.
40. Musselwhite, quoted in Tipaldi 2002, 64.
41. Muddy Waters, quoted in O'Neal and Van Singel 2002, 190–191, 199–200; Gordon 2002, 155–167.
42. Groom 1971; Oliver 1991; O'Neal 1993.
43. Bird (1958) dates the beginning of the popularity of skiffle between 1949 and 1954.
44. Cantwell (1996, 308–309) indicates how songs moved from blues performers marketed to Black audiences, through folk revival scenes, to pop-marketed rock bands.
45. Charters 1959; Oliver 1960; Oliver 1991, 62.
46. Groom 1971, 7–9; Wilcock and Guy 1993, 58–78; Obrecht 2000, 11–13; Wald 2000, 170–176, 241–246, 263; Welch 2000, 8–22; Carson 2001, 18–22; Gordon 2002, 157–169.
47. Carson 2001, 18.
48. Jeff Beck, quoted in Carson 2001, 19, 41.

49. Dixon and Snowden 1989, 120–141.
50. Oliver 1991, 65–66.
51. Cantwell 1996, 296–300; Hajdu 2001, 69, 76, 83, 94–99, 107, 158.
52. See Groom 1971, 17; Palmer 1989; Bockris 1992; Ennis 1992, 322–328; Dallas 1995; Carson 2001; Hajdu 2001, 106–108, 142–148, 232, 250–251, 258–262.
53. Dixon and Snowden 1989, 222, 224; Scott Cameron, quoted in Dixon and Snowden 1989, 223.
54. Oehler 2001, 106–108.
55. Guy, O'Neal, and Zorn 1970.
56. Groom 1971, 71–74.
57. O'Neal 1993.
58. Titon 1993; Titon 1994, 261–280.
59. Evans 1982, 104–120.
60. Rory Block, "Rory Block Official Life Story" [cited April 22, 2003]; available from http://www.rory-block.com/Pages/LifeStory.htm; see also Tipaldi 2002, 165.
61. B. B. King, quoted in Gordon 2002, 114.
62. Charlie Musselwhite, quoted in Tipaldi 2002, 62.
63. Doug MacLeod, quoted in Tipaldi 2002, 269.
64. Evans 1982, 70–76, 262–264, 240–253.
65. Hajdu 2001, 94; Tipaldi 2002, 182–183.
66. Oehler 2001, 105–106; "Spider" John Koerner in University of Illinois Campus Folksong Club 1963; Zimmerman 1966.
67. Oehler, 2001; see Macías 2008, 2003.
68. Hajdu 2001, 7–9, 18–19, 21, 28–30, 33, 94; Oehler 2001, 104–105; Hammond with Townsend 1977, 154–162, 246; Groom 1971, 8–11; Titon 1993, 220–240; Wald 2000, 92–94, 116, 118–120, 139–140, 142–145, 151–153, 165–166, 177–209; Ennis 1992, 414.
69. *Carlos Santana: Influences* (DVD), Warner Brothers Productions, 2004, originally released 1995.
70. Clarence "Gatemouth" Brown, interview by the author, Bloomington, IN, September 2, 1997; Oehler 2001, 313–316.
71. Keil 1966.
72. Wolkin and Keenom 2000.
73. David Myers, personal conversation with the author, Chicago, IL, 1997.
74. Wolkin and Keenom 2000, 78.
75. Ibid., 77–78.
76. Ibid., 77.
77. Ibid., 83.
78. Charlie Musselwhite, quoted in Wolkin and Keenom 2000, 85–86.
79. Metcalf 1989; PoKempner and Schorlau 2000.
80. Metcalf 1989; PoKempner and Schorlau 2000; Tony Mangiullo, interview by the author, Chicago, IL, September 6, 1997.
81. Oliver 1960; Oliver 1965; Baraka 1999 (1963).
82. Charters 1994.
83. Stevie Ray Vaughan, quoted in Kitts et al. 1997, 48–49.
84. Garon 1995.
85. Denise LaSalle, quoted in Hoffman 1996, 76.
86. Feeney 1997.
87. Wellman 1994 (1977).

DISCOGRAPHY

Armstrong, Louis. *Louis Armstrong Plays W.C. Handy*. Originally recorded July 12, 1954–October 19, 1956. Legacy 64925, 2008. CD.

Best of Rockabilly. Various Artists. Originally released as Scena Records 271905, 2004. Play 24–7 103, 2012. CD.

Berry, Chuck. *The Great Twenty-Eight*. Originally released as Chess 92500, 1982. Geffen, 2012. CD.

Big Bill Broonzy. *Greatest Blues Licks*. Stardust Records, 2009. Digital.

Bland, Bobby "Blue." *The Best of Bobby Bland. The Millennium Collection.* Chess/MCAAA881121582, 2000. CD; Geffen/Universal Music 2000. Digital.
Block, Rory. *High Heeled Blues.* Originally released 1981. Rounder Select/Rounder ROUCD 3061, 1989. CD; Universal 2015. Digital.
Blues Is Black. Various Artists. International Music 203426, 2003. CD.
Blues Masters, Volume 7: Blues Revival. Rhino Records R2 71128, 1993. CD.
Brown, Clarence "Gatemouth." *Alright Again!* Originally released 1981. Rounder ROUCD 2028, 1991. CD; New Rounder 2028, 2011. Digital.
Brown, Kenny. *Goin' Back to Mississippi.* Originally released 1997. Big Legal Mess Records/Fat Possum BLM 0294, 2014. CD.
Butterfield, Paul. *The Paul Butterfield Band.* Elektra 7294, 1990. CD.
Crudup, Arthur "Big Boy". *Rock Me Mama.* Originally recorded September 11, 1941–April 18, 1954. Tomato TOM 2003, 2002. CD.
Donegan, Lonnie. *Talking Guitar Blues: The Very Best of . . .* Originally recorded April, 1956–December, 1965. Castle Music Ltd. CMDDD 1394, 2006. CD; Sanctuary 2011. Digital.
Guy, Buddy. *Can't Quit the Blues.* Silvertone Records/Legacy 82876 81967 1, 2006. CD.
Hopkins, Lightnin'. *Greatest Hits.* Unequal Halves, 2014. Digital.
Jolson, Al. *The Best of Al Jolson. [20th Century Masters the Millennium Collection.]* MCA Records/Decca 088 112 692-2, 2001. CD.
Kikuta, Shunsuke, and J. W. Williams. *Live and Kickin': The 3rd Park Tower Blues Festival.* Bluesox Productions BS-002, 1999. CD.
King, Albert. *The Definitive Albert King.* Stax, 2011. Two-CD set.
King, B. B. *Paying the Cost to Be the Boss.* ABC Bluesway BL 61015, 1968. Seven-inch single.
———. *B. B. King—Greatest Hits.* MCA 11746, 1998. CD.
LaSalle, Denise. *Greatest Hits.* Malaco Records 7545, 2013. CD.
Lewis, Jerry Lee. *The Best of Jerry Lee Lewis. [20th Century Masters the Millennium Collection.]* Mercury Nashville/Hip-O 314 546 736-2, 1999. CD.
Little Walter. *The Best of Little Walter.* Hallmark Recordings 713682, 2013. CD.
Muddy Waters. *Muddy Waters at Newport 1960.* MCA 088 112 515-2, 2001. CD.
Musselwhite, Charlie. *Charlie Musselwhite. Deluxe Edition.* Alligator Records, 2005. CD.
Presley, Elvis. *Elvis.* Originally released 1956. BMG/BMG Heritage 82876660592, 2005. CD.
———. *Elvis Presley.* Originally released 1956. Legacy/RCA/RSM/Legacy 90795, 2011. CD.
Rainey, Gertrude "Ma". *Ma Rainey.* Recorded October, 1924–September, 1928. Ace MCD 470212, 47021, 1995. CD.
Reed, Jimmy. *The Complete Singles As & Bs 1953–61.* Acrobat/Acrobat Licensing ADDCD 3135, 2015. CD.
Smith, Bessie. *Bessie Smith: The Complete Recordings.* Vols. 1–5. Columbia/Legacy C2K 47091, C2K 47471, C2K 47474, C2T 52838, C2K 57546, 1991–1996. Five two-CD sets.
Son House. *The Essential Son House.* Columbia/Legacy, 2014. Digital.
Spann, Otis. *Otis Spann: The Blues Collection. Vol. 1. Part 2.* Storyville Records. 2009. Digital.
Taj Mahal. *The Very Best of Taj Mahal.* Columbia/Legacy/Private Music 199580, 2012. CD.
Terry, Sonny, and Brownie McGhee. *Stranger Blues.* WNTS, 2008. Digital.
Tucker, Sophie. *The Great Sophia Tucker.* Jasmine Records JASCD 134, 2005. CD.
Wells, Junior. *Buddy Guy and Junior Wells Play the Blues (Expanded).* Originally released 1972. Reissue, Rhino/Elektra, 2013. Digital.
———. *Southside Blues Jam.* Delmark DE 628, 2012. CD.

CHAPTER 2

New Bottle, Old Wine
Whither Jazz Studies?

Travis A. Jackson

The landscape and potentials of jazz studies have changed markedly over the last forty years or so, and the projects gathered under that label have gained both depth and breadth in the process. The work done by a few generations of enthusiasts, scholars, and musicians[1] has thus borne unexpected fruit: where jazz in the mid-1970s seemed to some commentators to be dying one of several rumored deaths—with free jazz and fusion as the reputed cause[2]—today the music appears to be sharing the top of the US cultural hierarchy with, and gaining the institutional stability of much older incumbents. After its humble beginnings as a summer "classical jazz" series in 1989, for instance, New York City's Jazz at Lincoln Center is now housed in a $128 million complex overlooking Columbus Circle, thanks in part to an extensive capital campaign in the late 1990s and partly to the artistic stewardship and celebrity of Wynton Marsalis. It operates, moreover, as a full constituent of Lincoln Center—on par with the Metropolitan Opera and the New York Philharmonic Orchestra.[3] Likewise, San Francisco's SFJazz, which had nomadically relied on a range of venues from its founding by artistic director Randall Kline in 1983, used the proceeds from its own capital campaign to open a jazz-club- and Unitarian-church-inspired performing arts complex, at a cost of more than $60 million, in January of 2013.[4] These two events are signs at the very least that a range of individual and corporate donors see jazz as worthy of long-term investment, even in the midst of economic crisis.

Alongside its growing cultural sanction, jazz has perhaps never had as strong a foothold in American conservatories and academic programs as it now enjoys. Long gone are the days when students interested in jazz were prohibited from playing it in practice rooms[5] or when a conservatory wishing to receive National Association of Schools of Music (NASM) accreditation could ignore jazz or other musical styles and traditions simply by citing the need to maintain standards derived from European concert music.[6] As has been true for at least a decade, the latest edition of NASM's handbook contains mostly neutral language regarding its "threshold standards" for undergraduates seeking degrees in music—that is, the skills and repertory knowledge that they all must cultivate. Except for particular degree programs (e.g., early music, musical theater, jazz), there is no mention of any single musical tradition or geographic location that should receive priority in students' studies.[7] Even more striking, the general description of jazz studies degrees contains an acknowledgment (not, however, repeated elsewhere in the handbook) that regular study of music in the United States includes jazz.[8] One further sign of the now almost banal presence of jazz in higher education is the 2014 edition of *Down Beat* magazine's "Where to Study Jazz" special supplement. It listed 207 programs (some full-time, some summer only) for musicians beyond high school, and many of those programs employ well-known jazz performers and recording artists as tenured or tenure-track faculty.[9]

Almost certainly, the high educational profile of jazz is the product of the dedicated work of jazz educators, before and after the founding of the National Association of Jazz Educators in 1968.[10] In addition, though, the change has been underwritten by the increasingly positive presence of research-oriented jazz studies in the academy—in literature, African American studies, American studies, sociology, history, film, and anthropology departments—from the 1980s forward. The institutional locations of scholars conducting such studies outside music schools and departments is key. Although the Austrian journal *Jazzforschung* had been published continuously starting in 1969 and the *Journal of Jazz Studies* (renamed the *Annual Review of Jazz Studies* in 1982) dated back to 1973, the watershed moment in the development of academic jazz studies in the United States was arguably the publication in 1991 of "The Literature of Jazz," a special issue of *Black American Literature Forum* (BALF). The issue's topics ranged widely, encompassing photography, printed music, poetry, and fiction, and Gary Carner's introduction to the collected essays described them as embracing "the eclecticism that has always been Jazz and has always pushed it forward."[11] Such an open embrace, to Carner, stood in contrast to the narrow vision of Wynton Marsalis and like-minded "neo-conservative" musicians and critics who viewed jazz as a tradition that took a wrong turn with 1960s free jazz and 1970s fusion.[12] Carner's progressive vision, to be sure, was also critical, and the questioning it encouraged was especially evident in two essays from that issue, ones which would rank among those most widely cited over the next two decades. Rather than expressing uncritical reverence, one of them, John Gennari's "Jazz Criticism: Its Development and Ideologies," provided readers with a deep and well-documented investigation of the history of jazz criticism and the influence upon it of the backgrounds and ideological commitments of its most celebrated writers. The other, Scott DeVeaux's "Constructing the Jazz Tradition: Jazz Historiography," presented a powerful critique of the shaping force of organic metaphors and aestheticism in jazz historiography.[13]

For those writers who had produced the work that was DeVeaux's subject, jazz was first and foremost a musical style, one that they were both celebrating and attempting to legitimize in American culture. With backgrounds as critics, enthusiasts, and occasionally composers or non-music oriented academics, those writers had concentrated on identifying key figures and constructing a coherent, teleological narrative, one that functioned in DeVeaux's words as

> a pedigree, showing contemporary jazz to be not a fad or a mere popular music, subject to the whims of fashion, but an autonomous art of some substance, the culmination of a long process of maturation that has in its own way recapitulated the evolutionary progress of Western art.[14]

In the resultant histories, then, a parade of increasingly complex musical styles helped to define jazz as an instrumental music that transcended its origins in African American culture and the entertainment industry to become "America's classical music" or the nation's greatest contribution to the arts.[15] As is perhaps true of any narrative, for the story of jazz thus presented to have the power it did (and does), its crafters had to elide or omit some elements crucial to the tale's unfolding and also relegate some "characters" to minor roles (or eliminate them altogether), while simultaneously raising the status of others. Indeed, the expanded profiles that Gennari would present of jazz writers in *Blowin' Hot and Cool* (2006), ones that situated critics in broader literary and social currents, helped readers to understand what informed the aggregate shape those narratives took.

In them, the artistry of singers, when recognized, was measured in terms of their ability to emulate the virtuosity of instrumentalists, and questions of gender and sexuality were treated as ancillary to or detracting from an understanding of the progressive development of the music. Race, likewise, was more a problem that needed to be addressed (and then avoided) than it was something writers regarded as constitutive of the sweep of American history. The positioning of jazz within national and international recording industries and performance circuits threatened at every stage to undercut the developing narrative, whose creators girded their work with Romantic and Adornian ideas regarding the corrupting influence of the marketplace. For them, the admittedly modest success of recordings like Lee Morgan's "The Sidewinder" (1964) or the popularity of organ combos such as those led by Jimmy Smith were redolent of the ways that commercial concerns could lure great artists to concentrate on financial, rather than artistic, gain. In both cases, there existed good reasons to understand jazz as persisting in myriad forms both because of and in spite of the market. Relatedly, instead of understanding live performance and recording as different entities, those writers (and many fans) regarded the latter as a degraded, alienated version of the former. Had they considered the range of ideas musicians (and producers and engineers) had regarding recording, they might have understood that jazz performers—as well as those in other styles—have expectations and styles of preparation that span a continuum ranging from seeing recording as capture to understanding it as a creative medium with different affordances from those of live performance. Moreover, trusting the knowledge of the performers to a greater degree might have led writers to consider more directly the work of so-called sidemen and the ways that their agency complicated or rendered false the great-man stories the writers typically told[16] (see Figure 2.1).

Where both of the latter issues are concerned, there are perhaps few more striking examples than the title track of trumpeter Miles Davis's 1967 recording "Nefertiti," a track that many listeners find puzzling upon first audition. Having become wedded to the idea that the main interest in jazz performances and recordings is the solo work of horn players (accompanied by rhythm sections), they have difficulty understanding what is happening as Davis and saxophonist Wayne Shorter proceed to play the track's sixteen-bar theme repeatedly for almost eight minutes with only minor variations in timing and

Figure 2.1
Miles Davis. 1960.

Photograph by Franz Hubmann/Imagno/Getty Images.

dynamics. Of the thirteen iterations of the tune's structural template, in fact, only one does not feature the horns playing the theme—the twelfth chorus, in which the trumpeter and saxophonist are silent. The seeming lack of solos led at least one critic to describe the track as "soporific," decrying the monotony and apparent preciousness of the group's approach. Several years later, in an overview of the Davis Quintet's recordings from 1965 to 1968, Harvey Pekar also expressed disappointment at what the ensemble had done:

> For some reason, there are no solos on ["Nefertiti"] except for a brief Carter spot. Instead, the horns repeat the theme over and over throughout the length of the track. Frankly, I would have preferred to

hear Miles, Shorter, and Hancock solo here, but "Nefertiti" is an important selection. Its unhurried, languorous, almost hypnotic quality, caused partly by the use of rests and long tones, forecast a style of composition later employed not only by Shorter but by Joe Zawinul.[17]

Less narrowly focused listeners might have heard in "Nefertiti" the contemporary foregrounding of what was only slightly more subtle in other recordings and performances by Davis's 1960s quartet: rhythm section work that not only spurred and prodded soloists but also moved individual events in directions neither solely dictated by featured horn players nor wholly predetermined by harmonic progressions. In some ways, "Nefertiti" represents a move away from the abstraction entailed in what Ian Carr has described as the group's characteristic "time-no changes" approach to ensemble coordination, in which the only givens were a metric framework, a tempo, and a series of phrases to be played, with those givens as points of departure.[18] Here, instead, the chief interest is how pianist Herbie Hancock, bassist Ron Carter, and drummer Tony Williams distinguish each successive chorus from its predecessor—through manipulating impulse density; alternately reinforcing and obscuring the given sixteen-bar structure and its metric frames; placing conventional figures in unconventional places; exploring consonance and dissonance, harmonic stasis, and ambiguity; and much more. Again, however, these strategies are the same ones these musicians deployed on nearly every recording and in nearly every performance from their engagement at the Plugged Nickel in Chicago in December of 1965 onward.[19] Whether the participants directly intended this outcome or not, the recording registers as a powerful reminder of how varied, valuable, and indispensable the contributions of "sidemen" are in the unfolding of performance, and the source of that reminder is the musical practice itself.[20] Moreover, such a reminder might ideally encourage listeners and commentators of various kinds to listen more intently to performers on other recordings where their work is also too often interpreted as confined to the background.

Insights like these, however, have not generally been prominent features in jazz research inspired by Gennari's and DeVeaux's essays nor in addressing the issues earlier writers raised—research that has been, for better and worse, discussed under the rubric "The New Jazz Studies." Although the phrase appeared notably as the subtitle of the collection *Uptown Conversation* in 2004, differing commentators have used it to describe work with origins as far back as the late 1980s, including the BALF essays as well as those gathered in Reginald T. Buckner and Steven Weiland's *Jazz in Mind* and Krin Gabbard's edited volumes *Representing Jazz* and *Jazz among the Discourses*.[21] Nichole T. Rustin and Sherrie Tucker have described researchers in the "old" jazz studies paradigm as "being very conservative about who and what is included," as comprising "often-closed circles of discourse about jazz and its history," and as being particularly hostile toward questions of gender and sexuality. In contrast, those undertaking newer, "cultural studies of jazz" take

> a critical approach to narrative parades of individual geniuses, and . . . [are] less interested in producing grand narratives. . . . [M]any of the turns in "New Jazz Studies" indicate a moment when "gender and jazz" scholars are no longer perceived as representing a "special interest" subcategory of jazz studies, but sometimes actually received as sounding precisely the kinds of "wrong notes" that Ajay Heble argues are useful in jazz, jazz studies, and cultural theory beyond [*sic*], for their ability to "[disturb] naturalized orders of knowledge production," to analyze power, and to explore areas in a variety of jazz cultures (including academic jazz studies) in which difference produces, rather than derails, subjects; and subjects who produce difference attempt to remix power relations.[22]

In this view, the old jazz studies bore a striking resemblance to the pre-1980s great-man- and great-work-centered "old" musicology, deaf and blind as it was (so its critics maintained) to anything beyond the "music itself," while its successor ostensibly brought with it greater concern for contexts, for commerce, for agency, for conflict—in short everything that an obsession with teleology and coherence had allegedly occluded or obliterated. At the same time, however, the new jazz studies diverged from its new musicological counterpart, replacing the latter's music-analytic conservatism with what one might describe as a near-complete lack of concern with—if not a dismissive attitude regarding—music analysis or any direct engagement with the material, rather than figurative, sound of jazz.[23]

One wonders whether some researchers' avoidance of analytic approaches or engagement with the materiality of music or recordings might have flowed from their backgrounds and disciplinary training. Perhaps they did not consider themselves equipped to write convincingly in the ways they presumed music analysts might: referring, that is, with technical language to items that might feature in a performance-centered conversation among musicians or that one might notate on a score. Such fears notwithstanding, those lacking such knowledge might easily have addressed matters of form, timbre, articulation, and referentiality without recourse to potentially forbidding technical language, musicians' terms of art, or even staff notation. Given the evidence available in the writings labeled as new jazz studies, the seeming refusal of authors to embrace sound proceeds more clearly from a desire to expand the compass of jazz research beyond "adjectival accounts of important recordings" by using "research tools that are not primarily phonographic." With the latter phrase Krin Gabbard suggested that jazz studies needed to eschew the aestheticist belief in music as a "safely autonomous domain" that dominated "official" histories of jazz.[24] With few exceptions, though, adherents of the new jazz studies have never touched down long enough in the material world of sound to support any claims that they were moving beyond it or that they had ever used (or endorsed) any research tools that one might describe as phonographic.[25]

A number of reviewers of Gabbard's two 1994 volumes regarded as welcome the prospect of expanding the range of methods and approaches for the study of jazz. At the same time, though, they expressed varying levels of dismay at the balance in the essays between so-called critical theory and historically grounded investigation as well as that between theory and sonic engagement, especially when theory overshadowed or excluded its counterpart. Historian Kathy Ogren concluded that jazz studies specialists would have to "contend with many of the claims made in these volumes" but averred that people seeking more information about the history and current status of jazz in American and world cultures might want to look elsewhere.[26] Music historian Guthrie P. Ramsey Jr. lamented the "theoretical excesses" of some of the essays; and, expressing similar concerns, ethnomusicologist Ingrid Monson urged the taking of a middle way:

> Theory itself, however, is not the problem, but a lack of reciprocity between the historical and the theoretical. When critical theory is used to interrogate history and history to interrogate critical theory, then perhaps the best that poststructuralism has to offer will fully emerge.[27]

Alongside such critiques, Richard Palmer, Lee B. Brown, and Mark Tucker all highlighted an apparent disdain toward the materiality of music in the majority of the essays. Palmer put it succinctly when he wrote, "hardly any of the contributors seems interested in, able to respond to, or aware of what they are purportedly listening to. Time and again one wonders whether they are cursed with signally indifferent ears, or not simply interested in jazz as music." Regarding Michael Jarrett's "reinvestigation of allegory" inspired by the cover of the 1957 Sonny Rollins album *Way Out West*, Mark Tucker felt the essay read like a self-indulgent series of peregrinations through poststructuralist theory, record reviewing philosophy, personal anecdotes, and prized LP covers. Further, the essay lacked any discussion of the music that inspired William Claxton's photograph of Rollins as a saxophone slinger in the desert, leading Tucker to argue that such an omission was unacceptable: "Eliminating sound from the study of jazz—like avoiding reference to words and texts in literary criticism, or ignoring visual images in studies of film and painting—is a measure as extreme as it is impractical."[28]

The problems these reviewers identified in Gabbard's collections—both the overemphasis on theory and the underemphasis on history and (sound) analysis—were a product of a historical moment when 1960s and 1970s French philosophy, repackaged as (French) theory, had become "a major ideological and institutional force" in American academia.[29] As François Cusset explained, philosophy, thus appropriated and transformed, instilled in sympathetic academics a motivating suspicion of prior research paradigms that assumed two related shapes. Its "pan-textualist" form encouraged such scholars to "explain all cultural phenomena entirely from within and solely in terms of the (dys)functions of language," while its "pan-narrative" version "flatten[ed] all forms of discourse, from science to psychoanalysis, into so many narratives." In either event, "The result," he argued in the present tense,

> is an enlargement ad infinitum of the very category of literature, which remains deliberately and consciously undefined, becoming nothing other than a synonym for such a suspicion without limits. The fluctuation in its definition guarantees its porosity in relation to all adjacent fields and, more tactically, the success of its inchoate wishes to encroach upon these fields. In other words, if everything is literature, who can resist it?[30]

It isn't difficult to see how some scholars, empowered and perhaps liberated by pan-textual or pan-narrative theories, might have regarded jazz studies as a ripe target for suspicion, not merely requiring closer scrutiny but sorely needing intervention.[31] Still, however questionable the old jazz studies might have been, Gabbard's authors in effect were substituting limited, but potentially productive metaphors—music as narrative, music as literature—for the larger, messier reality that they rightly criticized previous analysts for not exploring. Rather than expanding the compass of jazz research, that is, they were simultaneously shifting emphasis away from and evacuating what arguably constituted that field's raison d'être: musical sounds and the people and practices behind them.

To be sure, in what William J. Maxwell terms "the new new jazz studies"—i.e., the body of work that followed *Representing Jazz* and *Jazz among the Discourses*—interested observers witnessed a proliferation of writing that filled many of the lacunae of the old jazz studies.[32] Arguably the most influential monographs from that period were Ingrid Monson's *Saying Something* (1996), Scott DeVeaux's *The Birth of Bebop* (1997), Sherrie Tucker's *Swing Shift* (2000) and Eric C. Porter's *What Is This Thing Called Jazz?* (2002).[33] What those books shared was their authors' interest in getting inside and taking seriously the lifeworlds of jazz musicians: their motivations, their concerns, the varied constraints—artistic, social, cultural, intellectual, economic—that they negotiated in making (or not making) careers for themselves. Along similar lines, Horace Tapscott's *Songs of the Unsung* (2001), Benjamin Looker's *Point from which Creation Begins* (2004), Steven L. Isoardi's *The Dark Tree* (2006), and George E. Lewis's *A Power Stronger Than Itself* (2008) provided detailed examinations of the aesthetic strategies, social commitments, and organizational activities of jazz-related musicians' collectives from the 1960s to the present, while Ingrid Monson's *Freedom Sounds* (2007) and Robin D. G. Kelley's *Africa Speaks, America Answers* (2012) focused more specifically on music and liberation from racial oppression.[34]

Over the same time span, several essay collections were published that shared with *Jazz in Mind*, the BALF "Literature of Jazz" special issue, and the Krin Gabbard volumes a wide-ranging set of topics; approaches that came mostly from outside music departments; and, consequently, results that made the music and musicians, perhaps, proxies for other concerns. Those collections included *The Jazz Cadence of American Culture* (1998) and *Uptown Conversation* (2004), both products of the Jazz Study Group organized by Robert G. O'Meally at Columbia University in 1994; *The Other Side of Nowhere* (2004) and *People Get Ready* (2013), both of which had origins in the regular symposia, panels, and discussions featured alongside performances at the Guelph Jazz Festival; *Big Ears: Listening for Gender in Jazz Studies* (2008); and *Jazz/Not Jazz* (2012).[35]

From my standpoint as a musician and scholar, the strongest essays in these post-Gabbard collections are those which tip the theory–music balance more toward the contingencies of musical practice, sound, and the concepts behind sound. And, not surprisingly, the authors of those works are most often musicians and other writers concerned with the affordances and materiality of musical lives, performance, and composition— people concerned, that is, with how and why musicians do what they do and with the range of ways in which performers and non-performers might respond to and understand musical activity. Alongside the contributors to more introductory works, like *The Cambridge Companion to Jazz* and *The Oxford Companion to Jazz*, the most successful writers—Lara Pellegrinelli, Michael Dessen, Jeffrey Taylor, Elijah Wald, and John Howland (among others)—have drawn largely on augmented versions of the methods that constitute the training of scholars in ethnomusicology, historical musicology, music theory, performance, and composition as well as those in history.

In the process, they have also shown that the scholars who most strongly realize the promise of the new, or new new, jazz studies are not those who reject the old jazz studies as a matter of principle, but those whose work realizes the vision Mark Tucker presented in 1998:

> scholars identified with the new jazz studies . . . need to discover they have a usable literary past that includes not just Bakhtin, Benjamin, and Cixous but also Hodeir, Schuller, and Williams. They should draw more extravagantly upon the wealth of information gathered over the years by fans, private collectors, and libraries. Above all, they might gain more followers if they lowered the rhetorical volume and showed greater tolerance toward views different from their own. Jazz writers have always been a testy bunch, quick to strike down the opinions of others and to offer up their own as superior. . . . A more productive and radical strategy would be to build a coalition of scholars, journalists, critics, and musicians united in their passion for jazz and driven to understand the worlds of meaning people have found in this music.[36]

Tucker's call remains resonant nearly two decades later, perhaps because it speaks to a perennial issue in the history and development of jazz studies, one I might describe most simply in terms of what individual researchers value and, relatedly, what they believe their audiences might value.

Getting at the worlds of meaning that people have found (and created) in jazz, in short, requires that any analyst or commentator, at minimum, needs to respect and engage with those people, surveying, cataloging, and analyzing the variety of backgrounds, motivations, skills, interpretive frames, and agendas they bring to their encounters. Too frequently, writers—whether scholars or journalists—seem more interested in playing to their chosen crowds, respectively (but not exclusively), by understanding the music and musicians in terms of dominant and emergent scholarly paradigms or by focusing on and not-so-critically reinscribing tales of genius, iconoclasm, resistance, and the like.[37] The mid-twentieth-century writers mentioned by Tucker were engaging in a long-term, distributed legitimation project, preaching as it were to a skeptical congregation rather than a supportive choir.[38] As a result, perhaps, the ideas or specific aims of musicians mattered only to the degree that they helped to verify the music's pedigree. Likewise, toward the close of the century, many of their cultural studies–influenced successors were also engaged in a legitimation project, one aimed, paradoxically perhaps, at celebrating that music and those musicians who made a virtue of subversion and one founded on mobilizing sounds and people to support a romanticized oppositional—and ultimately conformist—politics.[39] Or, more clearly, where the first set of writers seemed mostly concerned with establishing that there indeed was a jazz tradition, the second group repeatedly lavished its attention on whoever and whatever offered a challenge to the jazz tradition or any other genres. At the turn of the twenty-first century, even as a number of newer researchers clustered together under the banner of "critical improvisation studies" and cast the work of improvisers in often heroic and utopian terms,[40] what remained most clear was that the musicians and the sounds they produced were more heterogeneous than unitary and therefore did not lend themselves to single, causal arguments like those equating modernist iconoclasm or free improvisation with political liberation.

In that light, Marc Ribot's "Days of Bread and Roses," an exploration of the debates among musicians and arts presenters about how to respond to the closing of the New York club Tonic in early 2007, is a brief, but powerful, examination of the ways that creative, political, and practical agendas can diverge: people and organizations that might otherwise have had common cause failed in their efforts to build a coalition to put creative music and musicians on firmer financial and institutional footing. Building on an earlier piece published on the All about Jazz website, his essay is also a primer on the precarious positions and interdependence of music venues and the performers whom they book, both historically and currently. He observes that, three years after Tonic's closing, "Those venues booking creative musics that do advertise, that have room capacities above eighty, and that are still in Manhattan, generally pay 60 to 65 percent of the door . . . as opposed to Tonic's 75 percent. These amounts are further reduced by hidden charges," such as those for tickets purchased with credit cards. The decline in revenue for performing musicians coupled with a contraction of the recording industry dating from the early 2000s meant that jazz musicians, especially those whose work was not mainstream, found it more difficult "to develop new work and, therefore, to compete on national and global touring networks, the real economy of new, experimental, jazz, and improvisational musics."[41]

In one of the essays that followed, John Brackett provided a broader framing for Ribot's argument, responding in particular to Ribot's concerns about the effect of rising rents on the viability of venues and overlooking Ribot's almost cursory invocation of race and class issues: "The specter of gentrification has haunted the Lower East Side for a long time, so long, in fact, that the current situation should not be surprising to anyone who lives there and who has some sense of the area's history. In its most recent transformation, the image of the Lower East Side as a dark and dangerous (yet entirely thrilling) section of Manhattan was alluring for many fans of experimental, avant-garde practices. However, it was only a matter of time before real estate companies and investors began to capitalize on the subcultural capital associated with this particular region" in order to make it more appealing for (White) "bourgeois bohemians."[42] Through focusing on how the area was made hospitable for art, Brackett only alludes to the economic and legal violence that, in the 1970s and 1980s, displaced the neighborhood's poor residents, especially those who were Latino or Black.[43] Thus, where Ribot presents a view that keeps questions of contestation and negotiation in the foreground, Brackett seems to write like many other scholars, bringing those issues to the fore only when they present problems that need to be solved.

Likewise, even when the materiality of music has been central, the nuanced, contradictory, and even disturbing kinds of views that might have come from engaging frankly with, for example, musicians' ideas regarding race and agency have been less evident. The under-representation of musician-centered concerns in print and other communications media, in part, motivated drummer Arthur Taylor to conduct and record conversations with prominent jazz musicians. As he wrote in the foreword of a 1977 self-published book,

> My predominant motivation in publishing *Notes and Tones* was that it was inspired by the real voices of musicians as they saw themselves and not as critics or journalists saw them. I wanted an insider's view. These conversations, which were taped between 1968 and 1972, may not always reflect how the artists feel today, but I believe their candid statements represent important insights into a very particular period in history. . . . What all these musicians told me may shock some people and may move others, but I think their candid words, spoken in a musician-to-musician setting, are revelatory.[44]

Indeed, because of Taylor's own status as a Black musician, the interviews that appear in *Notes and Tones* read as unfiltered and revelatory in the way that few others do—even those conducted by researchers or oral historians well-acquainted with their subjects. The candor is especially evident in the way that Black musicians discuss matters of creativity, history, economics, performance, and race as they might not have with other interviewers.[45] Interestingly, despite the fact that Taylor's book preceded the emergence of the New Jazz Studies (NJS) by more than two decades and that its republication by Da Capo in 1993 occurred in the same historical moment as the newly named field's appearance, *Notes and Tones* does not figure prominently in the notes or bibliographies of much NJS research, not even as a historical footnote—with George Lewis's *A Power Stronger Than Itself* and Tony Whyton's *Jazz Icons* as notable exceptions.[46]

The series of interviews conducted by pianist Ben Sidran between 1984 and 1989 for the National Public Radio program *Sidran on Record* might also provide a resource for those concerned with the perspectives that various jazz scene participants have had on the pleasures and challenges of making lives in and with jazz. Sidran's subjects included canonized performers like Dizzy Gillespie, Betty Carter, and Miles Davis, and performers whose styles are less paradigmatically jazz like Bob James, Chuck Mangione, and Janis Siegel, as well as writers, arrangers, engineers, jazz venue proprietors, and label owners.

Among the many things listeners might have gleaned from the interviews are those concerning how musicians understand tradition and creativity, how deeply and critically they think about the worlds through which they move and how, musically and otherwise, they attempt to alter those worlds. Although many of the interviews appeared in published form in 1992 and 1995 as *Talking Jazz*, it was only in 2006 that those who missed the programs during their original run had the opportunity to hear them as part of a 24-CD boxed set, also titled *Talking Jazz*.[47]

That set includes an interview where Sidran himself responds to questions about the making of the series posed by Craig Werner of the University of Wisconsin. One of the most fascinating things about their exchange is the difference, as I hear it, between how much Werner seemed to want Sidran to discuss matters of race and how little Sidran felt compelled to oblige him. Just after the eleven-minute mark, for instance, Werner asked a question about the definition of jazz that had both stylistic and racial/cultural dimensions:

> Amiri Baraka used the phrase 'the changing same' to talk about the Black musical continuum at one point, and I think that kinda raises the question of . . . when, where . . . , when do we stop calling it jazz . . . ? You've got Donald Fagen in here. You've got Dr. John. You've got, uh, Carla Bley. You've got people like that who are not playing the same thing that Art Blakey and Sonny Rollins and Horace Silver, uh, played. You wanna talk about how they connect?

How one hears the question hinges in part on what distinguishes the first three musicians from the latter three—style? generation? race?—and in part on how we understand the latter three to be playing a different "same thing" from their counterparts. Sidran's reply focused on the unifying power of jazz as a style and approach and settled, oddly, on what musicians absorbed from their geographic locales:

> Well, I think first off we have to say that it is not a kind of music: it's an approach. And it's not just an approach to playing music, it's an approach period. You know. Jazz is . . . how you're walking down the street maybe. . . . Jazz is how you deal with the passage of time. Jazz is how you deal with improvisation. Jazz is what you do to develop a personal voice. It's how you accommodate other people to get some sort of group sensibility and swing and pulse. And all these people are clearly, are in that tradition whether they're playing a certain set of changes or they're not playing changes at all or whatever. But I think the other thing is that all these people—Donald Fagen, Steve Gadd, whoever it is—they have been informed by the same mothers and fathers that informed Johnny Griffin, that informed Miles Davis. It really is a family history with a lot of branches, and it goes back to . . . a very localized American way of life, you know. Back when there was a Chicago sound and a New Orleans sound and a Kansas City sound and, God knows, a Janesville, Wisconsin, sound [Laughs]. . . . Back then, when it was really localized and the music was, uh, flavored by the ground it stood on.

Sidran elegantly, and perhaps diplomatically, sidestepped the racial discourse the invoking of Baraka might have brought to the discussion by focusing on the raceless "Americanness" of jazz. A few minutes later, when Werner again tried to bring some aspects of race to the fore by invoking the fictional "Center for Art Detention" in Ishmael Reed's *Mumbo Jumbo* as part of a question about putting jazz in a "classical setting," Sidran made a similar move.[48] Whether or not he was aware of the specific reference, Sidran's reply again focused on Americanness:

> And I think that this idea of jazz becoming a museum music, in a way, it's inevitable. . . . This is one of the great American inventions. It's fantastic, and it's spoken all over the world. Jazz isn't going to go

away, but the core of the jazz experience may in fact be going away. And I think one of the things that is captured in these conversations is the kind of thoughts, the kind of life, the kind of emotions, the kind of questions, the kind of people that, back when nobody really cared about it, they cared everything about it. That's what they cared about.

Arguably, Sidran's references to geography and kinds of people might be read as euphemistic or veiled mentions of race, but in an interview in which the pianist is forthcoming about his dislike of recording technology and the recording industry, among other things, one wonders why he would decline to discuss race more directly.

In some ways, his interviews, as well as those that were combined with performance in the late Marian McPartland's long-running National Public Radio program *Piano Jazz*, recall the issues raised by Douglas Henry Daniels in an essay on interviews as historical data and interviewing as a research method. Daniels lamented how rarely (White) critics and other interviewers have penetrated—if they were aware of them at all—the racial veils and protocols of Black musicians, i.e., "the stratagems and ruses that Afro-Americans use when dealing with outsiders."[49] As a result, they render jazz lives—Black, White, or otherwise—as being all about the music, as though race (or gender or sexuality) had nothing to do with people's life chances, their outlooks, or their approaches.[50] What obtains in the Sidran and McPartland programs—and perhaps more pointedly in the interview collections published by Gene Lees—is not so much a failure to see behind the veil, then, as it is a will to remain ignorant of the veil or deny its existence, in the process perhaps unwittingly reproducing a racial order that renders the privileges and workings of Whiteness invisible.[51]

Whatever their merits or deficiencies, interviews, whether conducted by researchers or by others, are only part of what the synthesis imagined by Tucker would require. What jazz studies needs in greater quantities is not simply more discussions of musicians' perspectives, nor more discussions of race, not more discussions of musical practice, nor more engagement with critical theories of various kinds. Instead, the way forward for jazz studies lies in research that highlights the connections, on one hand, *between* various musicians' perspectives on different issues and, on the other, their solo and collaborative work with other musicians, other artists, or other people. Such research requires understanding musicians as beings situated in a world with other beings rather than as creators of abstracted, autonomous art. Moreover, scholars need to attend, again with musical analysis serving an essential role, to race's relational character, the way it functions as a modality through which a range of social agents *live* class, gender, and sexuality as well as their relationships to cities, regions, nations, and a host of other possibilities.[52] Likewise, and perhaps more pointedly, researchers might attend to the ways in which the ensemble of practices that lead to jazz at any particular juncture function as one modality through which musicians (and audiences) navigate their lives.

That is, in place of overworn and forced assertions that equate jazz or improvised music almost exclusively with resistance and opposition, scholars might take greater account of the ways in which musicians from differing backgrounds approach music- and world-making in strikingly different ways—even when performing in the same ensembles. In place of zero-sum debates about whether jazz is African American, American, or, increasingly, transnational, scholars might attend more explicitly to the range of views and commitments held by jazz musicians and jazz supporters (and detractors) more generally.

Exemplary in this regard is George E. Lewis's discussion of the workings and dissolution of Jazz Composers Guild in mid-1960s New York. His account juxtaposes the divergent views and recollections of Paul Bley and Bill Dixon in a way that offers an interpretation that leans toward Dixon without painting him as a hero or Bley as a villain.[53] Likewise, in my own work, I have endeavored to understand jazz musicians as people who have broad musical interests as well as deeply considered ideas regarding history, culture, society, and their places in and contributions to all of them. The simple act of turning the tables methodologically in interviews—so that the musicians were asking the questions—resulted in information about musical tastes, stylistic boundaries, tradition, and a host of other issues that I might not have gained through my pre-set interview protocol. To learn, for example, that Steve Wilson was conversant with the work of Donald Fagen or contemporary rhythm and blues performers, that Joshua Redman was fond of watching MTV and reading the novels of Thomas Pynchon, or that Sam Newsome drew musical inspiration from Toni Morrison's use of language, is to understand jazz performers as complex social agents, ones whose activities do much more than simply reflect the worlds through which they move.[54] Until such a vision can be realized, whether in the work of a single writer or in Tucker's imagined coalition, jazz research will continue to recycle the same themes regardless of their situational appropriateness. And thus, it will continue to seem like old wine being poured into new bottles, deceptively fresh but lacking the body that consideration of the complexities of individual lives might bring and carrying a taste that grows sourer with each decanting.

NOTES

1. Gennari 2006, 117–205.
2. Eric Porter 2010, 1–2; see also Radano 1993, 238–240; Nicholson 2005, 223–241. A characterization of a slightly earlier "death," with different causes, can be found in Chambers 1989, 78–81.
3. Pareles 2000.
4. Chinen 2013.
5. Hays 1999, 139–140.
6. Hays 1999, 145–148. For an essay that questions claims of concert music's superiority, see Becker 1986. For a contrary view, see Tenzer 2011.
7. See National Association of Schools of Music, *Handbook 2013–14* (Reston, VA: National Association of Schools of Music, 2013). Where musical content and repertories are concerned, the handbook reads: "NASM standards address bodies of knowledge, skills, and professional capacities. At times, the standards require breadth, at other times, depth or specialization. However, the standards do not mandate specific choices of content, repertory, or methods. . . . With regard to specifics, music has a long history, many repertories, multiple connections with cultures, and numerous successful methodologies. Content in and study of these areas is vast and growing. Each music unit is responsible for choosing among these materials and approaches when establishing basic requirements consistent with NASM standards and the expectations of the institution" ("Content, Repertories, and Methods," section III.L.1–2, of "Music Program Components," 83).
8. "Jazz and jazz studies are part of the larger musical heritage, and thus are normally included in undergraduate music studies in one or more areas such as general musicianship, repertory, music history, and theoretical studies." See National Association of Schools of Music, *Handbook 2013–14*: "Common Body of Knowledge and Skills," section VIII.B of "All Professional Baccalaureate Degrees in Music and All Undergraduate Degrees Leading to Teacher Certification," 99–100; and "Bachelor of Music in Jazz Studies," section IX.F of "Specific Professional Baccalaureate Degrees in Music," 105. In acknowledgment of the fact musicians practice improvisation in a variety of ways in a number of traditions, the improvisation requirement does not refer specifically to jazz. Further support for the integration for improvisation—and jazz in particular—appears in the report prepared by the College Music Society Task

Force on the Undergraduate Music Major, which was made publicly available in November 2014 (see Sarath et al. 2014).

9. "Student Music Guide: Where to Study Jazz 2015," *DownBeat*, October 2014. Interestingly, sixty-five of the institutions listed in the guide placed advertisements that, according to an editorial note, provide "another source of information about . . . particular jazz program[s]" (74).

10. The Music Educators National Conference, through a symposium held at the Tanglewood Festival in 1967, helped to lend legitimacy not only to the study of jazz but also the musics of various cultures throughout the world in schools of music and, eventually, music departments. For more information, see Volk 1993; Hays 1999, 150–152; Prouty 2005, 79–82, 97–99; Prouty 2008; and the article that, despite its selective reading of evidence, provides a charter historical narrative for jazz education: Murphy 1994. The role of historically Black colleges and universities in such a narrative is, according to Prouty 2008, "a subject of some dispute" (83–89), but a little-cited essay published a few years before Prouty's offers useful perspective on the matter. See Goodrich 2001. Note also that *DownBeat* began publishing education-themed special issues in the early 1950s.

11. Carner 1991, 448.

12. Ibid.

13. DeVeaux 1991; Gennari 1991.

14. DeVeaux 1991, 526.

15. Designating jazz as "America's classical music," however problematic doing so might be, is often a strategic choice. See Anderson 2002; Brown 2002; Travis Jackson 2012, 133.

16. Travis Jackson 2006, 168–177. Lara Pellegrinelli has published a related meditation on singing in jazz historiography; see Pellegrinelli 2008. On Romanticism and Theodor Adorno, see DeNora 2003, 2–3, 9–14, 16–18. On the sometimes antagonistic leadership roles rhythm section members can play in ensembles, see Bakkum 2014, 75–86. For discussion of the creative aspects of recording, see Forlenza 1993; Blair Jackson 1995a; Blair Jackson 1995b; Resner 1996; Rudolph 1996; Tolleson 1996; Tolleson 2001; and an interview with producer Steven Epstein in Massey 2009, 101–113.

17. Pekar 1997, 173.

18. Carr 1982, 145–146. See also Chambers 1989 (1985), 85. See also Bakkum 2014, 75–76.

19. Chambers 1989 (1985), 91–93; Coolman 1997, 18–21, 44, 56–58, 66–85. Coolman's dissertation, a piece some might describe as yet another genius-focused work, remains a valuable though under-recognized resource, not only for the attention to detail the author/bassist brings to the recordings he analyzes and the collaborative methods he used, but also for his willingness to raise questions about recording and process that supposedly are absent in individual artist–focused writing: see pages 35–36, 38–41.

20. John F. Szwed's biography of Davis includes the following anecdote about the recording of "Nefertiti": "When they ran through it together for the first time, Miles told Shorter, 'Wayne, we ain't gonna put no solo on this—we're just gonna play the melody over and over again.' There was nothing a soloist could add to this composition, he said. Just play it over and over again, like Coltrane's 'A Love Supreme.' But every time they played it again, it was different. . . . The complexity that always characterized bebop melodic lines was now being transferred to the rhythm section, leaving the melody instruments free to float on top of the tumult" (Szwed 2002, 263). A different transcription of the conversation between the musicians and producer Teo Macero appears on the Miles Ahead website: "Session Details: Columbia 30th Street Studio (June 7, 1967)," Miles Ahead website, accessed June 7, 2015, http://www.plosin.com/milesahead/Sessions.aspx?s=670607. Other discussions of the track and its place in jazz history include Feld 1988, 100–102, and Waters 2011, 209–210, 216–219.

21. O'Meally, Edwards, and Griffin 2004; Buckner and Weiland 1991; Gabbard 1995a; Gabbard 1995b.

22. Rustin and Tucker 2008b, 3, 8–9. The quoted segments in the cited passage are taken from the editors' "Introductory Notes" in O'Meally, Edwards, and Griffin 2004, 2, and Heble 2000, 9, respectively.

23. On "New Musicology" and analysis, see Tomlinson 1984; Agawu 1993; Agawu 1997; Currie 2009, 148–152. On the lack of attention to sound in emergent culturally oriented work on music, see Monson 1996, 3, and, more generally, Maxwell 2011, 874–876.

24. Gabbard 1995b, 3, 7. For more historicized treatments of the importance of autonomous "works" in music scholarship, see Goehr 1992; Talbot 2000. For the specific relevance of such thinking to jazz research and criticism, see Travis Jackson 2012, 7–13.

25. Two of the notable early exceptions are Jed Rasula's (1995) "The Media of Memory: The Seductive Menace of Records in Jazz History" and Robert Walser's (1995) " 'Out of Notes': Signification, Interpretation and the Problem of Miles Davis" in *Jazz among the Discourses*. To those, I might add the growing body of work by ethnomusicologists and like-minded music historians on jazz.

26. Ogren 1996, 263.
27. Ramsey 1997, 350; Monson 1997, 113. On page 112, Monson, quoting Gabbard, also asks rhetorically, "At what point does the 'fresh, if chilling, air' of poststructuralism become a new Eurocentric orthodoxy mapped onto jazz?" Lee B. Brown raises a similar issue: "For decades, black jazz musicians—with the exception of a very few—have struggled against staggering odds to serve their music. The few who had a glimpse of pop music stardom were rarely masters of their economic fates. Now, just when a new generation of black players have the possibility to lay claim not only to their music but to its financial rewards, critical theory of jazz rises to strike it down. One wonders how many of Lincoln Center's African-American players would grant Gabbard's authors the right to speak for them" (Brown 1997, 328).
28. Richard Palmer 1996, 289; Mark Tucker 1998, 139–140, see also 134–135.
29. Cusset 2008 (2003), 76.
30. Ibid., 83. See also Guillory 1993, 176–177.
31. Indeed, such is the lingering power of this brand of theory that scholars in literature and American studies departments insist on calling everything a text when it might be simpler, and more accurate, for them to think of a recording first as a recording, a film first as a film, taking into account the ontologies and material affordances of their respective media rather than disregarding them. For a general discussion of the potential of thinking about what music affords performers and listeners, see Windsor and de Bézenac 2012. For a critical look at the way that the language of affordances has perhaps been abused, see Parchoma 2014.
32. Maxwell 2011, 876–879. Before Gabbard's edited volumes were published, two of the most influential monographs that might have deserved the "new jazz studies" label—particularly since the first author published an essay in Gabbard's *Jazz among the Discourses*—used the lives of musicians as springboards. See Radano 1993; Berliner 1994. On the rise of publishing on jazz in the 1990s, see Peter Monaghan 1998.
33. Monson 1996; DeVeaux 1997; Sherrie Tucker 2000; Eric Porter 2002. Necessary complements to Tucker's work include essays and books focused on women's importance in jazz scenes as non-performers and the complex ways in which gender and race inflect relationships between performers and non-performing scene participants. See Wilmer 1980, especially chapters 11 and 12, "It Takes Two to Confirm the Truth" and "'You Sound Good—For a Woman!',", respectively; Monson 2008, 275–283; Sunderland 1992; De Jong 2007; Williams 2007.
34. Tapscott 2001; Looker 2004; Isoardi 2006; Monson 2007; Lewis 2008; Kelley 2012. Other important monographs include the following: Ake 2002; Ramsey 2003; Austerlitz 2005; Heffley 2005; Pond 2005; Solis 2008.
35. O'Meally 1998; O'Meally, Edwards, and Griffin 2004; Fischlin and Heble 2004; Heble and Wallace 2013; Rustin and Tucker 2008a; Ake, Garrett, and Goldmark 2012.
36. Mark Tucker 1998, 148. Even in 2012, Sherrie Tucker, speculating about what such a coalition still might do, observed that it remained only at the level of possibility (Sherrie Tucker 2012, 279–280).
37. Lewis Porter 1987, 3, 5.
38. Gennari 2006, 67.
39. Two of the clearest examples of knee-jerk oppositional politics appear in the introductions of Fischlin and Heble's *The Other Side of Nowhere* (2004) and Heble and Wallace's *People Get Ready* (2013). In an early piece on 1980s and 1990s cultural studies, Francis Mulhern argued its politics were limited in scope and application: "Insofar as cultural studies neglects to integrate 'high' cultural forms and practices into its field of analysis, it compromises its own theoretical ambition, which is to analyze 'whole ways of life,' or, in other, more pointed terms, the existing social relations of culture in their totality. And insofar as it insists, one-sidedly, on the active and critical element in popular cultural usages, it tends to overlook the overwhelming historical realities of inequality and subordination that condition them. . . . There is no doubt that cultural studies has attempted to further emancipatory social aims—socialist, feminist, antiracist, anti-imperialist. Its intervention has been in those substantial, specified senses political. But it is romantic to go on thinking of cultural studies as an 'intervention.' It is now an instituted academic activity, and academic activity, whatever its intrinsic merits, is inevitably not the same thing as a political project" (Mulhern 1995, 34–35).
40. MacDonald, Wilson, and Miell 2012, 244–247; see also Attali 1985 (1977), 133–136. Indeed, many of the contributions to the online journal *Critical Studies in Improvisation/Études critiques en Improvisation* read as continuations of the theory-driven early new jazz studies work rather than critical engagement with the materials and methods of improvisation. Although there are strong arguments to be made in favor of looking at improvisation across musical styles and musical cultures, one wonders how much of a role

personal ideology plays in researchers' choice of subject matter. That is, it is likely not a coincidence that the most utopian theorizing about the potentials of improvisation occurs alongside supposedly less rule-governed "free" improvisation, just as the some of the most rigidly conservative theorizing about musical democracy attends those jazz styles most prominent before the 1960s. For cross-cultural ethnomusicological considerations of improvisation, see Nettl and Russell 1998; Solis and Nettl 2009.

41. Ribot 2013, 145–146; see also "Marc Ribot: The Care and Feeding of a Musical Margin," All about Jazz website, June 5, 2007, accessed July 15, 2015, http://www.allaboutjazz.com/marc-ribot-the-care-and-feeding-of-a-musical-margin-marc-ribot-by-aaj-staff.php?page=1.
42. Brackett 2013, 172–173. See also Barzel 2013.
43. Deutsche and Ryan 1984, 94–98.
44. Taylor 1993, 5–6. Without acknowledging any debt to or knowledge of Taylor's work, saxophonist and composer John Zorn expressed the belief that he too was addressing a pressing and perennial need in 2000 in introducing the collection *Arcana*. Although he shares the same kind of Romantic/Adornian perspective as the producers of the old jazz studies, he saw himself as not surrendering to the generic/stylistic labeling that deprives an audience of "its right to the pleasure of creating its own interpretations" and keeps a critic from having "to think about what is really happening or go any deeper than the monochromatic surface" of labels. He was, instead, clearing space for the exploration of jazz and improvising musicians' own thinking about their practices: "Musical thought has vast scope, enormous depth, and approaches to it are various and dynamic, and my hope was to elicit material that would be much more direct than an interview after it's been sanitized or manipulated by someone with an agenda or an article after it's been cut, recontextualized, or sensationalized by a hungry editor trying to sell an issue of a magazine or newspaper. . . . This book exists to correct an unfortunate injustice, the incredible lack of insightful critical writing about a significant generation of the best and most important work of the past two decades" (Zorn 2000, vi).
45. Reviewing the book in his weekly *New York Times* column, critic Robert Palmer observed, "The talk ranges widely, but since all the talkers are black musicians, it tends to focus on questions of music and race. Anyone who thinks that the interviews published in jazz magazines represent how musicians talk among themselves and what they really think will be in for a shock. 'I've found through my experiences,' says Mr. Gillespie, 'that critics know what you're thinking or what you're trying to portray as much as a baby in Afghanistan would understand when you speak English.' . . . There is sure to be something in this book to offend almost anyone who is interested in jazz. Some of the most delightful passages would not bear reprinting in a family newspaper. A few of the musicians emerge as self-serving or self-indulgently bitter, and there is also a great deal of backbiting, especially among mainstream musicians who feel threatened by the avant-garde. . . . But the book is also full of historical and musical data and insights that might never have come out in more formal interview situations" (Robert Palmer 1978). See also Taylor 1993, 128.
46. See Lewis 2008, xxviii; Whyton 2010, 113–114. For a more cursory mention, see Walser 1999, 305, n1.
47. Sidran 1995 (1992). Although the boxed set is available from online retailers, audio for eighty-four of Sidran's interviews is streamable from his website. See "The Talking Jazz Project," accessed June 1, 2015, http://bensidran.com/project/talking-jazz-project. One can stream the interview discussed below from "Ben Sidran Talking Jazz," http://bensidran.com/conversation/talking-jazz-ben-sidran.
48. In the novel, the Center, located at Eighty-Second Street and Fifth Avenue in Manhattan (the site of the actual Metropolitan Museum of Art), houses a range of artworks and artifacts taken from other parts of the world that some of the novel's characters plan to steal and repatriate. Reed 1996 (1972), 84–88.
49. Daniels 1987, 162. See also Perchard 2007, 132–133.
50. Lewis Porter 1987, 8–9.
51. Debates about race in jazz are perhaps as old as the style itself and too extensive to be explored in detail here. Gene Lees was among those presenting more polemicized, anti-"politically correct" writing on Blackness and jazz, and both he and Randall Sandke have seemed at times to revel in their status as underdogs barking out uncomfortable truths that others were too ideologically deaf to hear. See Lees 1994; Lees 2001; Sandke 2010; Sandke 2011. Nonetheless, their call for colorblind discourse about jazz masked its own ideological underpinnings. For a discussion of these issues where jazz historiography is concerned, see Travis Jackson 2012, 24–36; for a broader consideration of the invisibility and hegemonic power of Whiteness, see Bonilla-Silva 2010; Bonilla-Silva 2012, 174. For perspectives from the United Kingdom, see Toynbee and Wilks 2013; Toynbee, Tackley, and Doffman 2014.
52. Hall 1980, 341; Omi and Winant 1994.
53. Lewis 2008, 92–95.
54. Travis Jackson 2012, 224–229, 236n33, and 252n32.

DISCOGRAPHY

Davis, Miles. *Nefertiti*. Originally recorded June 7, 1967–July 19, 1967. Originally released as Columbia CS 9594, 1967. Sony BMG Music Entertainment A736670, 2008. CD.
Morgan, Lee. *The Sidewinder*. Originally recorded December 21, 1963. Originally released as Blue Note BLP 4157, 1964. Blue Note 7243 4 95332 2 6, 1999. CD.
Sidran, Ben. *Talking Jazz*. Nardis Music, 2006. 24 CD boxed set of interviews.
Smith, Jimmy. *The First Decade 1953–62*. Acrobat ACQCD 7079, 2014. CD.
Sonny Rollins. *Way Out West*. Originally released as Contemporary Records C3530, 1957. Contemporary Records/Polydor #UCCO-9015, 2009. CD.

CHAPTER 3

The Politics of Race Erasure in Defining Black Popular Music Origins

Portia K. Maultsby

When we sang for black people, they called it rhythm and blues. When we sang the same song for white people, they called it rock and roll.

—Bo Diddley[1]

In the late-1970s, and as a scholar of post–World War II African American[2] popular music, I quickly became aware of the limited number of treatises and commentaries published on this topic and its disproportionate representation in studies on the broader American popular music tradition. Moreover, I became intrigued and concerned that many critics of African American and American popular music ignored or omitted the voices of the music's creators.[3] After all, in the mid-1950s, a new style of rhythm and blues evolved and traveled from the racial margins into the mainstream of society where it was marketed as rock and roll. In this new context, White artists recorded imitative and adaptive versions of rhythm and blues labeled "covers"[4] and they appropriated the vocal and instrumental stylings of Black artists in their recordings of pop songs.[5] With few exceptions, the segregated structure of the music industry prevented mainstream exposure of African American artists, whose recordings were promoted exclusively in Black communities under the "rhythm and blues" label.[6]

This racialized marketing of Black popular music, in part, accounts for the imbalance in the representation of rhythm and blues as well as the varying conceptions, meaning, and significance of rock and roll in the literature on American popular music. Written primarily by journalists,[7] accounts of Black popular music reveal the writers' personal experiences with the music based primarily on recordings and performances in mainstream venues, music festivals, White universities/colleges before predominantly White or mixed-race audiences (depending on region), and include only occasional interviews.[8] This is in contrast to the coverage of rhythm and blues artists by Black publications such as *Ebony*, *Sepia*, *Soul Illustrated*, and *Soul*.[9] Feature stories derive from the personal and musical histories recounted by artists and critiques of recordings and live performances before African American audiences. The photographs that accompany the narratives demonstrate how these audiences engage with performances, revealing the meaning and significance of rhythm and blues in Black community life.[10] As noted by popular music historian Peter Guralnick, Black musicians tailor their performances to meet the expectation of audiences. In an all-Black setting, he described bluesman Buddy Guy as "relaxed and singing for his own people in a way that was altogether different from any of the countless times I have seen him perform for white audiences."[11]

Centering my discussion on James Brown, Alan Freed, and Elvis Presley as case studies, this chapter revisits the histories and accounts of the contributions of central figures in the development of African American and American popular music. It examines Black popular music as an expression of Black life and as a mediated commodity for mass consumption. This discussion seeks to affirm how scholarly study that engages perspectives of the musical creators can generate counter narratives that reveal the complex intersections of race, culture, and power that have shaped and continue to shape the presentation and representation of African American popular music. This chapter draws from library and archival resources and interviews I conducted with artists and record company executives from 1983 to 2000.[12]

PERFORMANCE AS SOCIAL PRACTICE . . . THE LIVED EXPERIENCE

In the early 1960s James Brown, later known as the "Godfather of Soul," approached Sid Nathan, the founder-owner of King Records, with a proposal to record a live album of previously recorded material. Nathan immediately responded with an emphatic "*no!*" He simply didn't believe that Brown's fans would buy a live version of an existing studio recording. When Brown explained that the live recording he envisioned would differ from the studio version of songs, given that the audience would become active participants in the final product, Nathan quickly responded: "I am not going to spend money on something where a lot of people are going to be screaming. Who wants a lot of noise over the songs?"[13] Nathan's vehement rejection of Brown's proposal indicates that he had absolutely no comprehension of the value placed on the interactive dimension of performance in Black communities, where audience feedback is regarded as a vital contribution and an enhancement to the cultural and aesthetic experience. Audience participation is an important gauge used by Black artists to determine whether they are meeting the aesthetic expectation of the audience. As songwriter–vocalist Smokey Robinson later stated, he judges his live performance to be unsuccessful if the audience is "not involved in what's happening on stage."[14]

Despite Nathan's objection to the proposed live recording at the Apollo Theater[15] in Harlem, Brown took control of the project by making all of the arrangements and financing the production himself. *Live at the Apollo* (recorded in 1962 and released in 1963 by King Records) became one of Brown's best-selling LPs, precisely because it successfully captures the energy and the character of Black music as lived experience. As such, the recording represents much more than a mere musical performance reproduced on vinyl in time and space; it was a well-executed musical production that held both cultural and social relevance among its primary targeted audience.

Brown's live performances embody a myriad of cultural codes and musical values defined and affirmed within the context of his African American fan base. Music critic Cliff White characterizes a classic Brown performance in vivid detail, noting how the band drives the funk

> with immaculate precision so that Brown and his musicians become as one as they shift up from the underlying rhythm to intersperse his repeated and gradually fragmenting phrases with sharp horn riffs. As Brown reaches the point where he becomes like another instrument, he'll then swing back into dance with a warning scream or command that brings forth a blistering sax solo or an unexpected key change introducing a contrasting riff and perhaps a unison chant from the band.[16]

The archival footage of Brown's live performance in the biographical feature film *Get on Up* (2014)[17] and my personal observations of multiple James Brown shows over a period of thirty years allow for further elaboration: As the rhythmic drive and intensity of the show increases, Brown dances around the microphone, pushing it forward and backwards, spinning it around, and catching it before it falls to the ground. He then glides across the stage shuffling his feet in quadruple time, falls on his knees, rises up again. He claps his hands behind his head, lifts one leg, slides to the microphone on the other foot and begins singing again. As participants in the performance, audience members scream and holler, talk-back, wave hands, jump out their seats, and run down the aisles and onto the stage to dance with Brown.[18] This intense level of interaction illustrates that Brown and the "audience" are united by shared experience—one that reflects their social, cultural, and aesthetic expectations and values.[19]

The distinctive character of Brown's performance derives, in part, from the influence of the exuberant style of Black preaching he observed during his youth in the American South. He explained:

> I had been to a revival service and had seen a preacher who really had a lot of fire. He was screaming and yelling and stomping his foot and then he dropped to his knees. The people got into it with him, answering him and shouting and clapping time. After that . . . I'd watched the preachers real close. Then I'd go home and imitate them. . . . I am sure a lot of my stage show came out of the church.[20]

These musical practices and aesthetic values associated with Black worship services became signatures of Brown's live performance style. In contrast, the conventions for studio recordings were guided by a different set of principles—those representative of Euro-American musical practices and aesthetic values and applied to recordings of mainstream popular music. Although Brown had to make some aesthetic concessions on his studio recordings, he preserved those features that he considered as ethnic or cultural markers of his racial identity, which he had long embraced on the performance stage. "What most people don't realize," he states, "is that I had been doing the multiple rhythm patterns for years on stage, but . . . I had agreed to make the rhythms *on the records* [emphasis mine] a lot simpler."[21] Brown has acknowledged making other concessions for studio recordings, including shortening the length of songs and decreasing the level of intensity of his screams, shouts, and call–response interplay between the band and audience. At the same time, he retains a communal sensibility by adding live-sounding background vocals, creating dance songs that include directives which encourage participation (e.g., "Do the popcorn" and "Do the horse," "Do the mashed potato popcorn," "Do your thing, jump back, get into the swing").[22]

Despite the aesthetic adjustments Brown made in his studio recordings to fulfill the directives of those who provided access to the studios and held the purse strings, he consciously maintained features that he considered signatures of his performance style. The necessity Brown felt to fine tune his commercial studio recordings reveals the type of aesthetic negotiation that can occur when commonplace vernacular expressions of musical and cultural creativity are decontextualized as commodities, and divorced from the lived experience of its creators.

Polydor's musical director, Sid Nathan, as well as many White music critics, constantly labeled Brown's overall signature sound as "noise," while characterizing his vocal style as "stuttering" and "hollering."[23] These cultural outsiders simply could not relate to Brown's aesthetic practices because they were the polar opposite of the codes and musical values of those established in the American mainstream and embraced by Nathan and many other Whites. Writing in 1968, at the height of Brown's career, Albert Goldman, music critic for the *New York Times*, describes the cultural polarities which informed assessments of Brown's music, contending, "To whites, James is still an off-beat grunt, a scream at the end of the dial. To blacks, he's boss."[24] These radically different perspectives underscore Nathan's resistance to Brown's interest in producing a live recording and the oppositional aesthetic ideals which framed Black and White cultural boundaries. For most Whites, and for some members of the Black social and educational elite as well, those features and practices which most readily identified Brown's music as unique simply were not valued. Brown was not credited with informed, creative musical agency; instead, his culturally-derived markers of musical difference were viewed as substandard, and therefore undesirable and dispensable at the time. These markers of difference are best understood within the context of an African cultural heritage. Cameroonian composer Francis Bebey articulates underlying cultural values in African music production consonant with Brown's sound ideals.

> The objective of African music is not necessarily to produce sounds agreeable to the ear, but to translate *everyday experiences* [emphasis mine] into living sound. In a musical environment whose constant purpose is to depict life, nature, or the supernatural, the musician wisely avoids using beauty as his criterion because no criterion could be more arbitrary.[25]

Brown produces these "living sounds" by juxtaposing varying timbral qualities. Composer Olly Wilson describes the varying timbres as the heterogeneous sound ideal—an ideal that ethnomusicologist Mellonee Burnim observes "violates virtually every ideal associated with Euro-American vocal production."[26] In additional to Brown's unique timbral qualities, he creatively adapts call–response, polyrhythmic, and melodic structures in ways that reflect African musical practices. Distinguished Ghanaian ethnomusicologist J.H. Kwabena Nketia, who held dual appointments at UCLA and at the University of Ghana during his career, explains:

> What distinguishes music in the African tradition [and African-derived musics] from the music of other cultures is not merely its inventory of structural constituents but also by *the way* [emphasis mine] in which it selects, organizes, and uses particular materials in the modes of expressions it emphasizes.[27]

For those who did not share or identify with the aesthetic values and cultural practices established within the boundaries of African American communities, Brown's cultural production was of questionable musical value.

James Brown's culturally-informed signature sound resulted in seventy-seven Federal/King recordings making the *Billboard* "Top Singles R&B" charts, fourteen of which reached the #1 position, while thirty-eight placed in the top ten. This level of success over thirteen years supports the claim that Brown's recordings held significance among his fan base, which was overwhelmingly African American. Specifically, his stage performances and the live character of his studio recordings preserve stylistic features that historically have resonated with African American audiences, and have also distinguished various musics within the historical and contemporary African diaspora.

In rather graphic contrast to Brown's success on the R&B charts, only thirteen of Brown's recordings qualified for Top 20 position on *Billboard* "Pop" charts, and all of these landed at the bottom of this category.[28] These industry measures suggest that the pop music industry and its primary consumers, who were White, found Brown's music to be far less appealing than the largely Black audiences who identified with rhythm and blues music. To make it plain and simple, James Brown was never considered to be a crossover artist.

Recording for the small, independent King Records from 1958 to 1971, Brown enjoyed considerable creative freedom. This arrangement eventually changed after he signed with the German label Polydor in 1971, three years after Linn Broadcasting bought King Records as a subsidiary label. Brown explains:

> In the early years [beginning in 1971] with them I was hitting the singles in spite of the company. The songs were hits because I *forced them* [emphasis mine] through the company and made them hits myself. I was supposed to have creative control, but they started remixing my records. I mixed them, but when they came out they didn't sound like what I'd mixed. The company didn't want the funk in there too heavy. They'd take the feeling out of the record. They didn't want James Brown to be raw. Eventually [around 1979] they destroyed my sound. . . . In destroying my sound, Polydor cost me my audience.
>
> They tried to take me over into disco by bringing in a producer, Brad Shapiro. I was against it from the first. Disco had no groove, it had no sophistication, it had nothing. I fought against doing it but finally gave in. They called the album *The Original Disco Man* (1979). It wasn't disco all the way, but I was unhappy with the result.[29]

At Polydor James Brown conceded to modifying his soul and funk aesthetic to generate crossover sales; in other words, he was forced to relinquish artistic control over his creative productions. This strategy proved unsuccessful, as evidenced by Brown's failure after 1975 to make the pop charts, and his low placements on even the rhythm and blues charts beginning in 1978. Brown experienced a decline in popularity among African Americans because his new musical direction failed to meet their aesthetic expectation. Following the disappointing sales of *The Original Disco Man*, Brown and Polydor parted ways in 1980.

The crossover production formula of disco, a producer-driven music calibrated for the mainstream market, routinely minimized Black aesthetic values in producing Black artists. As crossover hits by Black performers became more common in the 1970s, the music lacked "that intangible 'something,'" a transformation music critic Nelson George describes as the "Death of Rhythm and Blues."[30] At the same time, a new music called rap began to surface on the racial margins of society. In inner cities, rap artists restored the aesthetic markers and codes of Blackness in a music that reflected their lived experience (Figure 3.1). In parks, streets, and community centers, the soul and funk samples from the music of James Brown and George Clinton, among others, provided inspiration for contemporary expressions of sonic Blackness.

Race Erasure in Black Popular Music

Figure 3.1
"Park Jam" held in the playground of Patterson Houses Project, 3rd Avenue and 143rd Street, Mott Haven district, Bronx, New York City, 1984.

Photo by Henry Chalfant. Courtesy Henry Chalfant.

CONTESTING BLACKNESS IN NARRATIVES ON BLACK MUSIC

The issue of race in Black music scholarship has been a topic of discussion since the turn of the twentieth century when scholars debated the theories of origin.[31] Nearing the end of that century, British musicologist Philip Tagg questioned the identity politics associated with the music. In an open letter titled "'Black Music,' 'Afro-American Music' and 'European Music,'" published in the October 1989 issue of the journal *Popular Music*, he contested the validity of these terms, contending that the concept of "Black" and "White" is predicated on definitions of race rather than culture. Tagg also called attention to what he called "some musicological misconceptions." He objects to the claim that blue notes, call–response technique, polyrhythms/syncopation, and improvisation are African musical traits used to distinguish African American/Black music from European/White music, establishing that these presumed markers of a Black musical identity also are found in the latter tradition.[32]

Musicologist Guthrie Ramsey, nevertheless, argues for an understanding of "*blackness as practice*" [italics Ramsey], explaining that "ethnicity and nearly every other aspect of identity should be considered performance. Blackness doesn't really exist until it is done or 'practiced,' in the world."[33] Composer Olly Wilson elaborates, describing Blackness as practice as conceptual approaches to the creative process—"the *way* [italics mine] of doing something, not simply something that is done."[34] The performance of Blackness includes both visual and sonic dimensions,[35] for in African American music they are systemically interwoven to reflect their intrinsic role in defining musical identity. James Brown's highly charged performances, as well as live performances of other African American artists of

52 Portia K. Maultsby

popular, jazz, and gospel music traditions, provide numerous concrete examples of the significance of the visual as well as the sonic in resonating with listeners.

A comparative analysis of the recording "Bridge Over Troubled Water," by popular music icons Simon and Garfunkel and Aretha Franklin, serves to illustrate the power of the sonic dimensions of performance in conveying identity. The Simon and Garfunkel version[36] is melodically straightforward, largely void of embellishment, and reserved in emotional content. In contrast, Franklin's version[37] weaves a range of improvisatory devices—melismas, varying timbres, "slides," "shouts," and moans into the melody to gradually build the emotional intensity of the song. Franklin also incorporates call–response to facilitate musical exchanges between her lead voice, the background singers, and instrumentalists. Franklin's transformation of the folk/pop song into soul, grounded in the aesthetic values which she honed from childhood in her father's Detroit Black Baptist church,[38] is a compelling example of *Blackness as practice*.

Such claims of Blackness conjures up notions of African musical continuities, which some American and European musicologists, such as Ronald Radano and Anne Danielsen, disavow, arguing against locating music in race and culture.[39] Instead, they promote a post-racial paradigm that de-contextualizes Black music and renders it either colorless or minimally interracial and devoid of cultural connections to an African past. Both put forth a narrative that argues for musical commonalities, which Radano associates with cross-racial sounds from "unlocatable origins."[40] Although cross-cultural exchanges and borrowings are common occurrences, cultural values and aesthetic priorities influence musical structures and the articulation of musical elements common in world musical traditions. Accordingly, Nketia describes the relationship between African and African American music "as dynamic and unbroken at the conceptual level," acknowledging differences in the way these concepts are applied contextually.[41]

The use of post-modern theoretical abstractions advances an approach that cultural sociologist Jon Cruz identifies as "*disengaged engagement* [italics Cruz]." Cruz contends that disengaged engagement occurs when the "cultural aesthetics becomes separated from the larger social, political, and economic conditions in which the culture being observed has taken shape." As such, "aesthetic appreciation divorced from the artist's life functions as a denial of that life."[42] The disengaged engagement study of African American music allows investigators to construct an *imagined experience* with the music in a non-contested environment where the realities of race, culture, and power can be ignored. Such narratives often dehumanize and deracialize a music that has evolved within racialized conditions. As Black popular music styles become "American," White musicians often move to the center of the narrative. This position of domination overshadows the music's creators and results in incomplete and inaccurate histories on African American and American popular musics.

African American music first became widely accessible in the mainstream as published collections (Negro spirituals) in 1867[43] and sheet music (minstrel songs, ragtime, and blues) beginning in the 1890s. This music reached even broader audiences through live radio broadcast (Negro spirituals and jazz) in the 1920s and phonograph recordings (Negro spirituals, jazz, and blues) in the 1910s and 1920s. With few exceptions, the segregated structures of society and the music industry restricted the exposure of Black musicians to Black communities. For many decades, they were denied access to mainstream publishers, booking agencies, performing venues, print and electronic media outlets, and major record companies. White publishers, songwriters, and record company executives, however, quickly recognized the potential of African American music as an economic commodity for appropriation and exploitation for mainstream consumption. White artists covered the songs performed and recorded by Black artists, imitated their styles, and financially cashed in on the mainstream popularity of their music. Critiquing this imbalance of power and the hegemonic control over the commodification process, popular music historian Reebee Garofalo writes: "Their [African Americans'] cultural contributions have been historically undervalued and/or assigned to others less deserving, and they have had to overcome systematic discrimination within the music industry itself."[44] The most popular and accepted history on the early years of rock and roll is one such example.

ALAN FREED AND ELVIS PRESLEY: THE EARLY ICONS OF ROCK AND ROLL

Both popular and scholarly works credit Cleveland disc jockey Alan Freed as having coined the phrase "rock 'n' roll." This phrase, as most scholars of popular music concur, first was used in blues songs decades before the first commercial recordings of this music. In 1947, Wild Bill Moore used the phrase as the title of his hit rhythm and blues recording, "We're Gonna Rock, We're Gonna Roll." Freed appropriated this phrase from Black culture, using it to describe the music played on his radio program "Moondog Rock 'n' Roll Party." Air-check tapes of his broadcast on WJW in Cleveland from 1952 through March 1954 reveal that the name "Moondog Rock 'n' Roll Party" referred only to the name of the program rather than the songs he played:[45]

> All right, the old Moondog is leaping out, folks. The old Moondog Rock 'n' Roll Party on Tuesday night is just getting under the way. Gotta long way to go. Two and a half hours of your favorite *blues* and *rhythm* [italics mine] records show for all the gang in the Moondog kingdom from the Midwest to the East Coast . . . this is WJW, WJW-FM in Cleveland . . .
>
> (1952)

> Hello everybody! How are you all tonight? This is Alan Freed, the old king of the Moondoggers, and it's time again for another of your favorite rock 'n' roll *session* [italics mine], blues and rhythm *records* [italics mine] for all the gang in the Moondog kingdom from the Midwest to the East Coast . . .
>
> (1954)

These air-checks provide evidence that Freed played songs labeled "rhythm and blues" by the music industry, which he inverted as blues and rhythm. Freed distinguished his use of and meaning assigned to the terms rhythm and blues and rock 'n' roll. Rhythm and blues identified the genre of music he played; "rock 'n' roll sessions" referred to the act of playing rhythm and blues records during a specific time period of two and a half hours.[46]

In the summer of 1954, Freed moved his "Moondog Rock 'n' Roll Party" from Cleveland to the 50,000-watt radio station WINS in New York City, retaining the rhythm and blues format. A year later his popularity soared as did the ratings of the station. John Jackson notes: "*Billboard* and *Variety* suddenly began referring to Freed as a 'rock and roll' disc jockey, and several record companies—majors and independents alike—began describing the rhythm and blues songs he played as 'rock & roll' in their trade advertising, eager to capitalize on the music's growing popularity," especially among White youth.[47] Concurrently, White adults protested the broadcast of this "obscene" music. To counter the negative responses from White parent groups, church leaders, and the press, who described the music as "an inciter of juvenile delinquency," industry executives repackaged and relabeled R&B as "rock 'n' roll," effectively obfuscating the racial identity of its creators.[48]

In 1955 Freed relented to public pressure to rename rhythm and blues, referencing it instead as rock 'n' roll. He eventually became famous as the first rock 'n' roll disc jockey. His repeated use of the phrase "rock 'n' roll" as a substitute for "*blues* and *rhythm*" records on his radio, and later television shows and Hollywood films, corroborated the industry's relabeling and repackaging of Black music for the consumption of White teenagers. The following excerpt from Freed's air-check tape in 1955 at WINS illustrates the erasure of the rhythm and blues label from mainstream media.

> Yours truly Alan Freed the old King of the Rock and Roller. Still to come but all ready for another big night of rockin' and rollin'. *Rock and roll* [italics mine] [is] like good to the big beat in popular music in America today. Let it go and we'll be here 'til nine o'clock reviewing the top twenty-five *rock and roll favorites* [italics mine] of the week. Welcome to Rock and Roll Party #1.[49]

Even though the mainstream media marketed Black musicians as rock 'n' roll artists, many Black artists continued to identify their repertoire and musical style as rhythm and blues, as did African American audiences. In an on-camera interview for the film *Rock and Roll: The Early Days* (1984), for example, Fats Domino is asked how rock 'n' roll got started. He responds: "Well, what they call rock and roll now is really rhythm and blues. I've been playing it for fifteen years in New Orleans." Chuck Berry's lyrics in "Roll Over, Beethoven" (1955), "Roll Over, Beethoven, an' dig these rhythm and blues!" provides evidence that he identifies the song as rhythm and blues. Similarly, Little Richard, during a 1986 television interview by Bill Boggs, makes clear that the term "rock and roll" refers to a new style of rhythm and blues, asserting: "rock and roll is rhythm and blues [played] up-tempo."[50]

Rhythm and blues pioneer Louis Jordan reveals the racial import of the term: "Rock and roll was just white imitation, a white adaptation of Negro rhythm and blues,"[51] citing country/rockabilly musician Bill Haley as an example: "I was with Decca Records from 1938 to 1953. When Bill Haley came along in '53, he was doing the same shuffle boogie I was [playing]. Only he was going faster than I was."[52] Milt Gabler, producer of Jordan's rhythm and blues recordings in the 1940s, deliberately incorporated Jordan's rhythmic style into Haley's production. Gabler explains:

> We'd begin with Jordan's shuffle rhythm. You know, dotted eighth notes and we'd build on it. I'd sing Jordan riffs to the group that would be picked up by the electric guitars and tenor sax. . . . They got the sound of The Tympany Five [Jordan's band] and the color of country and western.[53]

The appropriations of the innovations of Black artists and cover versions of rhythm and blues recordings by White artists historically has served to minimized or render invisible the contributions of Black artists in American musical development. Jordan explains: "What the white artist has done . . . they started the publicity and eliminating talk of the Black artists. They eliminated talking about who did what and how good it was, and they started talking about white artists."[54]

The first major publications on rock and roll were authored by music journalists.[55] They reported on musicians and critiqued performances and recordings for magazines and newspapers, ranging from the well-established, such as the *Washington Post* and *New York Times*, to burgeoning publications that included *Esquire* (founded in 1933), *Village Voice* (1955), *Crawdaddy* (1966), and *Rolling Stone* (1967). Their coverage of Black rock and roll artists included biographical and anecdotal information, critiques of live and/or recorded performances, song lyrics, musical skills, and influences on White artists. As expected, the reviews were subjective and some peppered with stereotypical characterizations. For example, British music journalist Nik Cohn describes Little Richard's songs as "tuneless, lyricless, pre-neanderthal." He characterizes the performance: "There was a tenor sax solo in the middle somewhere and a constant smashed-up piano and Little Richard himself was screaming his head off."[56] Similarly, Guralnick describes Little Richard's musical features as "outlandish screams and 'jungle rhythms.'" In contrast, he characterizes the style of Jerry Lee Lewis, Little Richard's imitator as: "vocal gymnastics and theatrical virtuosity."[57] Narratives such as these were widely circulated and eventually became the primary and master "text" for ensuing histories on rock and roll or popular music in the United States. With few exceptions,[58] these histories have been repeated without scholarly critique.

Songwriter and music publishing executive Arnold Shaw brought attention to this issue in the late 1970s. In the introduction to his book *Honkers and Shouters: The Golden Years of Rhythm and Blues* (1978), he wrote:

> The fact is that in its beginnings rock 'n' roll was derivative rhythm and blues—and today's mainstream . . . is preponderantly black. Yet the relation of R&B to the past and its contribution to the future has been slighted, and until now there has been no comprehensive history of its rise and development.[59]

Shaw's book stands out for the time it was written. His narrative unfolds around the voices of those who created and developed rhythm and blues as well as those who recorded, produced, marketed, and promoted the music. This firsthand account establishes a counter narrative that offers insight into the music's meaning and significance in Black community life and the process for its transformation and reception as a crossover commodity labeled rock and roll in the mainstream.[60]

The constructed stories on the immortal White superstars of rock and roll often negate the realities of life in a segregated society. That is, White privilege and notions of White superiority marginalized the people whose culture and creativity defined the genre. The early and contemporary accounts of rock and roll, as an example, often describe Presley as "King" of a musical style whose most potent articulations come from African American blues and rhythm and blues artists.[61] Minimizing the pioneering contributions of Little Richard, Chuck Berry, and other African American artists in the development of this genre, music critic John Rockwell writes:

> Bill Haley may have made the first massive rock hit ["Rock around the Clock" (recorded 1954)],[62] and people such as Chuck Berry and Little Richard *may have had* [italics mine] an equally creative impact on this raucous new American art form. But it was Elvis who defined the style and gave it an indelible image.[63]

Similar to Rockwell, country music scholar Bill Malone points to Presley's personality and showmanship as the basis for his popularity and influence as a rock and roll star: "Presley's appeal did not derive solely derive from his musical abilities; it came primarily from his personality and showmanship, and it was in this respect that Presley exerted his strongest influence."[64] Presley's showmanship was a key factor for Steve Sholes, A&R

(artists and repertoire) for RCA Victor, to sign him to the label. He told pop music historian Charlie Gillett that he "was impressed by the novelty of Presley's vocal style, his uninhibited movements on stage, and the electrifying effect he had on his audience."[65] As Ray Charles observed, Presley's uninhibited movements were imitations of African Americans: "He used to be down on *Beale* Street in *Memphis*. That's where he saw *black* [original italics] people doin' that. Ain't no way they'd let anybody like us get on TV and do that, but he could 'cause he's white."[66] He also was a frequent visitor at Black churches in Memphis, especially the East Trigg Avenue Baptist Church pastored by Rev. Herbert W. Brewster. As documented in the British Broadcast Company (BBC) documentary *Too Close to Heaven: The Story of Gospel* (1997), it was from Black churches that Presley absorbed the culture.[67]

Presley's ascent to stardom as a *rock and roll* star resulted from the strategic cross-cultural marketing of a new music, his charismatic persona, and his Black-derived vocal and stage performance style. Despised by White adults, Presley's "rock and roll" music and stage image appealed to White youth, who, in search of their own cultural identity, had rejected the musical preferences and cultural values of their parents.[68] After signing with RCA in 1955, Presley received unprecedented exposure on television variety shows[69] and Hollywood films performing country and pop ballads,[70] rhythm and blues songs, his first rock and roll hit "Don't Be Cruel," and covers of Little Richard's "Tutti Frutti," "Ready Teddy," and "Rip It Up."[71] Although country radio stations played Presley's country ballads and rockabilly songs,[72] music critics detested his rhythm and blues/rock and roll songs.

Despite negative reviews as well as the initial ban of his "rock and roll" songs on radio, Presley's shrewd and well-connected manager Colonel Parker negotiated a series of appearances on television's most popular variety shows, as well as speaking and singing roles in Hollywood films.[73] Moreover, during Presley's service in the Army from 1958 through 1960, Colonel Parker released previously recorded material, which allowed Presley to remain in the consciousness of the American public.[74] Presley benefitted from White privilege and power exercised by Parker to access mainstream media—television, Hollywood film, and radio—as well as performance venues denied to Little Richard and other Black artists in launching their careers in "rock and roll."[75]

Although several official rock/rock and roll histories identify Little Richard as a seminal figure, the focus primarily is on his flamboyant stage persona and unconventional performance style.[76] Ironically, his stage persona was deliberately constructed to counter White racial fear of a Black male star. After recording "Long Tall Sally," "Rip It Up," and "Teddy Ready," Little Richard notes:

> [W]e were breaking through the racial barrier. The white kids had to hide my records cos they daren't let their parents know they had them in the house. We decided that my image should be crazy and way out so that the adults would think I was harmless. I'd appear in one show dressed as the Queen of England and in the next as the Pope.[77]

As a consequence of the focus on his presentational persona and style, less credit was given to his musical innovations as the "architect of rock and roll."

In addition to his acknowledged percussive piano that emphasizes triplet rhythmic figures, his forceful gospel-derived vocal style, and his trademark falsetto vocal interjections, Little Richard, unlike Presley, wrote and co-wrote many of his songs. He also pioneered a distinctive rhythm and blues that ushered in the "Rock 'n' Roll" era through use of a signature rhythmic pattern called the "choo-choo beat." Charles Connor, Little Richard's original drummer explains:

> In rhythm and blues, you had a shuffle with a back-beat, but Little Richard wanted something different. He wanted something with more energy, but he didn't know how to describe the notes. So Richard brought me down to the train station in Macon, Georgia, in 1954 and he said: "Charles, listen to the choo-choo, choo-choo, choo-choo." I said, "You probably want eighth notes or sixteenth notes." We went back to his house couple of days later . . . and we came up with that beat. Now, nobody had ever played that beat before.[78]

The *choo-choo* rhythm, which became known as the rock and roll beat, distinguishes Little Richard's "Tutti Frutti" (1955), "Long Tall Sally" (1956), and "Lucille" (1957) from his earlier rhythm and blues recordings. This innovation reveals his creative genius—the ability to generate a rhythmic motive from a source that few would consider musically significant.[79] Recognizing his originality as both a musician and performer, Little Richard's producer and co-songwriter, Bumps Blackwell, describes him as "a supreme star. A once-in-a-millennium talent."[80]

In contrast to Little Richard's history of musical innovation, Elvis Presley's musical identity is riddled with accounts of imitation and appropriation. Presley covered Little Richard's "Tutti Frutti" on his first album *Elvis Presley* (1956) and "Long Tall Sally," "Rip It Up," and "Ready Teddy" on his second title, *Elvis* (1956). In addition, both albums include covers of rhythm and blues songs as well as country ballads and rockabilly songs.[81] Presley's third album *Elvis Presley/Loving You* (1957) is stylistically diverse, made up of country and pop songs, a cover of Fats Domino's "Blueberry Hill," and songs performed in the New Orleans rhythm and blues style, characterized by shuffle rhythms, a strong back beat, boogie-woogie bass line, and triplet piano. Moreover, the Black songwriter–guitarist Otis Blackwell composed and recorded the demos for Presley's first rock 'n' roll hits "Don't Be Cruel" (1956) and "All Shook Up" (1957). According to Blackwell, "When Presley recorded these songs he was copying the vocal style on the demos. I used to sing all my own demos . . ."[82] David "Panama" Francis, drummer on the demos, adds that Presley's recordings virtually copied, as well, the musical arrangements of songs note for note.[83] Presley also borrowed from the vocal styling of other Black artists, such as R&B songwriter–singer Roy Brown, whose "Good Rockin' Tonight" (1947) he covered.[84] Yet, according to author Marc Eliot, "Whenever he [Elvis] was asked about how he developed his singing style, he was always careful to avoid any mention of black music . . ."[85] The deliberate omission of Presley's appropriation of Black cultural and musical practices results in an inaccurate and incomplete account of Presley's ascension as a rock and roll superstar as well as an ongoing unacknowledgment of the innovations of African American musicians.

Cultural studies and hip hop scholar Tricia Rose critiques this trend of White artists appropriating the innovations of Black artists and covering their rhythm and blues recordings:

> [O]nce a black cultural practice takes a prominent place inside the commodity system, it is no longer considered as black practice—it is instead a 'popular' practice whose black cultural priorities and distinctively black approaches are either taken for granted as a 'point of origin,' an isolated 'technique,' or rendered invisible.[86]

White authority that dominates the discussion of African American popular music also has prevailed in jazz since its early years, as critic and record producer John Hammond asserts in his account of the early 1930s jazz scene:

> Already American jazz was attracting far more critical and public acclaim in England than in the United States, and anyone who could write jazz news, particularly of Negro players, was in demand. The English public drew no color line in music. Because Americans often did, few American jazz writers had even been to Harlem or knew enough about black players to be effective correspondents. I had and did, and for this reason I had been hired by *Gramophone* [in 1931].[87]

The British publication *Melody Maker* also hired Hammond for the same reason. Hammond recalls: "The magazine . . . was dissatisfied with its former American reporter because he wrote only about white musicians."[88] The failure to acknowledge those artists and recordings that impelled White involvement in the jazz scene created a profile of jazz that minimized the significance of Black innovation, inspiration, and influence. As a consequence the narrative of White dominance and supremacy in the media and music industry became institutionalized.

Furthermore, because White critics tended to engage African American jazz bands either through recordings or in contexts where the audiences were predominantly White, they had little, if any, awareness or knowledge of the aesthetic and cultural values that informed the music in its original African American settings. When critic George T. Simon, author of widely-read books on big bands, first heard Count Basie in live performance, he referenced the group as "the most out-of-tune bunch" he had ever heard. Simon's critical view on jazz was influenced by the aesthetic associated with the White Glenn Miller's orchestra, for whom he played drums in the early years. Later, after developing a more nuanced understanding of jazz as commonly defined among African American artists and audiences, Simon became one of Basie's biggest fans, and apologized for his rather egregious earlier misjudgment.[89]

Simon eventually acknowledged the merit of the performance aesthetic favored by Count Basie and other African American jazz musicians, which influenced his subsequent writings about African American jazz bands. This was a rare admission among music critics, whose authority over the discussion of African American popular music has resulted in the establishment of an American popular music canon where White artists and musical values most closely identified with White cultural traditions are often privileged to the detriment of opposing perspectives. This level of power has contributed to revisionist histories on popular music in which Whites emerge as the musical dominants and designated Kings and Queens of Black music. Paul Whitman was the self-appointed "King of Jazz" (1920), and the press christened Benny Goodman "King of Swing" (1930s) and Elvis Presley "King of Rock 'n' Roll" (1950s). Constructive narratives on these Kings circulated through the popular press, such as *Record World*, *Variety*, *Billboard*, *Rolling Stone*, *DownBeat*, *Metronome*, and *The New York Times*, as well as the local press in conjunction with concert promotion. These myths soon became realities in the popular imagination and they continue to circulate to this day, despite evidence that suggest a scholarly reevaluation of these titles.[90]

This trend continues today as notions of a post-racial, "color blind" society took root in the music industry in the 1990s when *Billboard*, the music industry's leading trade magazine, changed the name for its charts from "Black Music" to R&B. Accompanying this change was the following editorial:

> [I]t is becoming less acceptable to identify music in racial terms. [Furthermore] R&B as a label is less likely to create expectations about the race or ethnic origin of the music's creators. It should be made clear that *Billboard* never meant the term 'black' to refer to the color of the artists making Black music.[91]

Seventeen years following this label change, the press appointed White singers, who imitate the styles of Black artists, as the stars of Black music. The June 1, 2007, issue of *Giant*, for example, featured Robin Thicke on the cover with the headline "The New Soul Brother #1." A month later, in July 2007, British singer Amy Winehouse appeared on the cover of *Spin* magazine, with the headline "The Dangerous New Queen of Soul." Such designations ignore the contributions of Black innovators such as Eyrkah Badu, D'Angelo, Anthony Hamilton, Jennifer Hudson, Kelly Price, Tank, Tyrese, and Kim to the ongoing development of soul. Moreover, as the "African" of the African American is removed as a qualifier, as with the jazz tradition, these and other African American artists will become relegated to secondary positions or as potential footnotes in future histories on "American" music. Non-racialized approaches to narratives on African American popular music ignore the centrality of race and its institutionalization at all levels in the music industry that underscore double standards in the treatment of Black and White artists as well as in the production and marketing of their music. As sociologists Michael Omi and Howard Winant argue, "Race is not only a matter of politics, economics or culture, but all of these 'levels' of lived experience simultaneously."[92] In his analysis of post-racialism as an ideology, law professor Sumi Cho concludes that it "serves to reinstate an unchallenged white normativity."[93] Unchallenged White normativity reduces the power and influence of people of color and it may also reduce the agency of people of color in a way that simply seeks erasure and displacement. Few White Americans, for example, recognize the genius of a Buddy Guy, even though they celebrate his likeness in the appropriations of an Eric Clapton. Moreover, even fewer know the name Big Mama Thornton, an African American rhythm and blues singer who was ahead of her time and recorded the original version of "Hound Dog" that Elvis Presley popularized in the mainstream as rock and roll. Such iconic representations will continue to dominate popular music histories until the privilege and power disparity that has historically shaped accounts of American musical development is acknowledged, confronted, and systematically recalibrated to include African American voices.[94]

CONCLUSIONS

African American music emerges from the social conditions of a uniquely American experience, with a distinctiveness shaped by the cultural values translated from an African past. As lived experience, African American music is an expression of undeniable human agency through which the variables of race, culture, and power intersect with its production and reception. As a cross-cultural commodity for the American mainstream and global consumption, the music is "reused, redeployed, reinscribed, and re-encoded."[95] Within each context, African American music is experienced and interpreted differently, giving rise to multiple interpretations of the performance aesthetic, its meaning and significance. Moreover, critique of the performance aesthetic often is predicated on the writer's cultural perspective and familiarity (or lack of) with the cultural codes and musical values defined and affirmed among African Americans.

The complex history of African American popular music is best understood against the backdrop of the social and cultural contexts for origin and its appropriation by the music industry and dominant mainstream. Rather than simply repeating the master narrative of the past, an approach that engages those voices and other resources from within the culture, such as African American publications and the music industry entities involved in Black music production and marketing, will provide a more inclusive and balanced account of events that have continued to shape the presentation and representation of African American popular music. Moreover, such an approach will bring to the forefront the innovations of African Americans as songwriters, producers, artists, record company executives, and entrepreneurs who have contributed to the growth of a multi-billion dollar music and entertainment business.

ACKNOWLEDGMENTS

Segments of this essay were presented as the Seeger Lecture during the 2012 annual conference of the Society of Ethnomusicology in New Orleans, Louisiana, and the 2015 Centennial conference of the Association for the Study of African American Life and History in Atlanta, Georgia.

A special thanks to Mellonee Burnim, Miles White, and Adrienne Seward for their critical insights on earlier versions of this essay, and those from Eileen M. Hayes that contributed to the final version.

NOTES

1. Quoted in Eliot 1989, vii.
2. Throughout this study, I use the terms African American and Black interchangeably to identify the enslaved Africans brought to the United States of America and their descendants. My generalized use of these terms refers to the "critical mass," or majority, of African Americans, who, within a specific time, place, and context, established and articulated various overt signs and symbols as well as value orientations, which they self-identified and laid claim to as unique markers of their shared identity.
3. The early and most noteworthy studies on this tradition that included these voices were: Garland 1969; Shaw 1978; Joe 1980; Gillett 1984 (1970), 1974; Haralambos 1994 (1974); Broven 1995 (1974). See Meadows 2010 for additional literature on Black popular music.
4. White artists who performed such covers included the Crew Cuts, McGuire Sisters, Pat Boone, Georgia Gibbs, Elvis Presley, and Jerry Lee Lewis.
5. Those who imitated Black vocal stylings included Johnnie Ray, Elvis Presley, and Jerry Lee Lewis.
6. Pop singer Neil Sedaka confessed during an interview on *Hitmakers: The Teens Who Stole Pop Music* (2001), part of A&E's *Biography* series, that after hearing R&B on the radio as a teenager, he and his friends searched "for these [rhythm and blues] records in the Black neighborhoods because you couldn't get them in White neighborhoods except Pat Boone covers."
7. They include Eisen 1969; Cohn 1969; Williams 1969; Christgau 1973; Marcus 2015 (1975).
8. I distinguish featured interviews from narratives that incorporate interview material.
9. *Ebony*, *Sepia*, and *Soul Illustrated* are Black-owned magazines launched by John H. Johnson in 1945 (Chicago), by Horace J. Blackwell in 1947 (Ft. Worth, Texas), and by Ken and Regina Jones in 1968 (Los Angeles), respectively. *Soul* was a newsletter founded by Ken and Regina Jones in 1966. Whereas *Ebony* and *Sepia* covered all aspects of Black life and culture, *Soul Illustrated* and *Soul* were the first publications to specialize in Black popular music and entertainment.

10. For example, see the feature articles: [n.a.], "The Soul of Ray Charles," 1960; Sanders, "Aretha," 1971; Reed, "James Brown," 1968; George, "Cameo's Secret Omen," 1980.
11. Guralnick 1999 (1971), 243. In an interview with the author, Johnny Otis also said that the Southwestern swing bands played the blues and boogie-woogie type swing for Black audiences, but "for white audiences we had to play things like Glen Miller's 'String of Pearls,' 'Woodchopper's Ball' and 'South.' Of course, we'd do them in a Black style but, that's what they wanted. And we knew that what they wanted us to do was sweat and be more animated and be 'hot.' And be caricatures of ourselves" (Johnny Otis, interview by Portia K. Maultsby, Los Angeles, CA, September 13, 1984).
12. These interviews are housed in the Archives of African American Music and Culture, Indiana University, under the Portia K. Maultsby collection.
13. Brown and Tucker 1986, 130.
14. Smokey Robinson, radio interview, WBLS, January 16, 1983.
15. The Apollo theater was known as The Black Mecca in New York City at the time.
16. White 2008 (1977), 130.
17. *Get on Up*, directed by Tate Taylor and written by Jez and John-Henry Butterworth ([Universal City, CA]: Universal Pictures, 2014).
18. For other accounts of Brown's live performances, see Rose 1990, 46; Wesley 2002; Arbus 2008, 27.
19. Music critic Charles Sanders (1971, 126) observed similar performer–audience interactions during live performances of Aretha Franklin in Los Angeles; Atlanta; Greensboro, NC; Philadelphia; and New York.
20. Brown and Tucker 1986, 18.
21. Ibid., 149.
22. This "live" aura is captured on Brown's album *It's a Mother* (1969) and his singles "Say It Loud—I'm Black and I'm Proud (Parts 1 & 2)" (1968); "(Get Up I Feel Like Being) A Sex Machine (Parts 1 & 2)" (1970); and "The Payback (Parts 1 & 2)" (1973). Funk and hip hop artists adapted similar strategies in their studio recordings to produce the party ambience as illustrated in Kool & the Gang, "Funky Stuff" (1973) and Grandmaster Flash & the Furious Five, "The Birthday Party" (1981).
23. Brown and Tucker 1986, 78–79, 121.
24. Goldman 2008 (1968), 41.
25. Bebey 1975 (1969), 115.
26. Wilson 1992; Burnim 1985, 154.
27. Nketia 1981, 206.
28. Whitburn 2004, 83–85.
29. Brown and Tucker 1986, 239–240, 253.
30. George 1988, xi–xvi, and 147–159. Funk, the musical genre that developed parallel to the 1970s crossover phenomena, preserved the aesthetic values defined and shared by the Black critical mass.
31. For a critique of these works, see Maultsby and Burnim 2006, 11–13, 24.
32. Tagg 1989, 286, 288–292.
33. Ramsey 2003, 36, 38. Also see Ramsey 2004.
34. Wilson 1974, 20.
35. For detailed discussion of this concept, see Burnim 1985; Wilson 1992.
36. Originally recorded on *Bridge Over Troubled Water* (Columbia KCS 9914, 1970).
37. Originally recorded on Aretha Franklin, *Live at Fillmore West* (Atlantic, SD 7205, 1971).
38. Franklin discusses the church, especially gospel music, as the roots for her musical and performance style in the film *Aretha Franklin the Queen of Soul* (Beverly Hills, CA: Pacific Arts Video, 1988). Also see Werner 1999; Bego 2001, 11–32.
39. Radano 2003; Danielsen 2006. Also see Gilbert and Pearson 1999; Albiez 2005.
40. Radano 2003, 9–11, 49–104.
41. Nketia 1973, 9. For additional commentary on the relationship between African and African American music, see Nketia 1981, 9–10, 83, 88; Wilson 1992; Floyd 1995; Kubik 1999; Ernest Brown 2015; Maultsby 2015. Kubik's research documents intra-African musical exchanges and influences from antiquity through the twentieth century.
42. Cruz 1999, 22, 31.
43. This collection is Allen, Ware, and Garrison 1951 (1867).
44. Garofalo 2016, 90. Also see Sanjek 1988; Eliot 1989.
45. The air-check of "The Moondog Show" with host Alan Freed was originally broadcast in March 1952 on WJW (Cleveland, OH). It is available as part of "Black Radio: Telling It Like It Was," SC 39, Archives

of African American Music and Culture, Indiana University, Bloomington, and AlanFreed.com, accessed January 9, 2016, http://www.alanfreed.com/wp/archives/archives-rocknroll-1951–1959/brooklyn-paramount/moondog.

46. In conjunction with Freed's two-and-a-half-hour evening radio show, he staged live shows billed as the "Moondog Coronation Ball" and the "Biggest Rhythm and Blues Show." Photographs of this ball from May 3, 1952 (reportedly attended by 20,000 people) reveal that the audience was predominately African American, suggesting that this group made up the core of his listeners at the time. See photographs on Freed's "official" website, AlanFreed.com, accessed January 9, 2016, http://www.alanfreed.com/wp/photo-galleries/moondog-1950–1954/.
47. Jackson 1991, 88. See Eliot 1989 between pages 146 and 147 for a photograph taken on February 23, 1957, of a huge racially mixed crowd going to a Freed show at Times Square in New York. This image suggests that Freed attracted a much larger White listening audience in New York compared to the predominately Black audience in Cleveland.
48. Coincidentally, in 1954 the US Supreme Court issued the landmark *Brown v. Board of Education* ruling that struck down segregation in public schools, a decision that undoubtedly contributed to the backlash against music that many Whites viewed as encouraging race-mixing.
49. This is transcribed from Freed's broadcast on WINS in New York of a program labeled "Part I." Audio: WINS—1955, AlanFreed.com, accessed January 9, 2016, http://www.alanfreed.com/wp/on-the-air-audio-2/audio-wins-1955/.
50. "Little Richard with Bill Boggs," *YouTube*, accessed January 9, 2016, https://www.youtube.com/watch?v=B2CqEzy3iv4. In an interview with the author, Charles Connor, Little Richard's original drummer, describes rock and roll as "rhythm and blues played with a fast beat" (Charles Connor, interview by Portia K. Maultsby, Los Angeles, CA, November 10, 1990).
51. Louis Jordan quoted in Shaw 1978, 73.
52. Ibid., 43.
53. Quoted in Shaw 1978, 64.
54. Ibid., 73.
55. They include Eisen 1969; Cohn 1969; Williams 1969; Christgau 1973; Marcus 2015 (1975).
56. Cohn 1969, 22.
57. Guralnick 1971, 18.
58. For example, see Garofalo and Waksman 2014.
59. Shaw 1978, xv.
60. Authors who took a similar ethnographic or contextual approach to their studies on rhythm and blues, soul, and beyond, include: Garland 1969; Joe 1980; Gillett 1984 (1970), 1974; Hirshey 1984; George 1988; Haralambos 1994 (1974); Guralnick 1999 (1986).
61. For example, see Cohn 1970; Gillett 1970; Belz 1972; George-Warren and Romanowski 2001; Ponce de Leon 2006; Schloss, Starr, and Waterman 2012. Also see "Elvis Presley Biography," The Rock and Roll Hall of Fame, accessed August 2, 2015, http://rockhall.com/inductees/elvis-presley/bio.
62. Although Bill Haley's "Rock Around the Clock" is regarded by some rock critics as the first rock and roll song, I contend that Wild Bill Moore's "We're Gonna Rock" (1947) takes the honor. As Charlie Gillett (1970, 290) notes: "As with Bill Haley, the music and particularly the rhythms of them [rockabilly or country and western artists] had the emphatic dance beat of rhythm and blues." That dance beat was the twelve-bar boogie-woogie blues with a heavy back beat.
63. Rockwell 1977.
64. Malone 1968, 243.
65. Quoted in Gillett 1970, 54.
66. Ibid.
67. Although the documentary's official subtitle is *The Story of Gospel*, the title printed on the box is *The History of Gospel*. It was released in 1996 and aired in 1997.
68. *Variety* (1955) ran a story called "Music of Madness: Rock and Roll Music Has Stirred Up a Wind of Adult Protest." Also see Altschuler 2003; Bertrand 2005.
69. On the *Dorsey Brothers Stage Show*, Presley performed a medley of hits by R&B artists: Joe Turner's "Shake, Rattle, & Roll/Flip Flop & Fly," Ray Charles's "I Got A Woman," and Little Richard's "Tutti Frutti"; on *The Ed Sullivan Show* he performed "Don't Be Cruel," Little Richard's "Ready Teddy," and the title song to his first movie *Love Me Tender*; on the *Steve Allen Show* and *The Milton Berle Show*, he performed Big Mama Thorton's "Hound Dog." For more details, see the websites Elvis.com, ElvisPresleyMusic.com, ElvisPresleyExpert.wordpress.com, and Elvis-History-Blog.com (accessed September 15, 2015).

70. Popular culture author Marc Eliot (1989, 61) reports that the music publishers Hill and Range instructed their songwriters "to create music [for Presley] that would appeal to a wider pop audience, rather than strictly country or rockability." He continues, noting that Presley's pop idols Frank Sinatra and Dean Martin influenced his ballad vocal style as well as "Johnny [sic] Ray, a pop sensation in the early 1950s, whose one knee crooning soon became a part of the standard Presley presentation" (63). Ironically Johnnie Ray, who performed in a Black club in Detroit, was influenced by the vocal and presentation style of Black singers. See Shaw (1978, 447–449) for details.
71. These and other songs first recorded by Little Richard also were covered by Gene Vincent, Carl Perkins, Jerry Lee Lewis, The Everly Brothers, and Eddie Cochran.
72. Popular music historian Charlie Gillett (1984 [1970], 26) notes that performers of this music called themselves country rock but the music industry called it rockabilly. He describes country rock as "basically a southern white version of twelve-bar boogie-woogie blues, shouted with a minimum of subtlety by ex-hillbilly singers over an accompaniment featuring electric guitars, stand-up bass, and drums."
73. Gillett 1970, 54; Guralnick 1994; Bertrand 2005; Nash 2004; George-Warren and Romanowski 2001, 775–777. For other publications on Presley's life, music, and career, see the website *Elvis Information Network*, accessed September 12, 2015, http://www.elvisinfonet.com/index.html.
74. *Rolling Stone Encyclopedia of Rock and Roll* (George-Warren and Romanowski 2001, 776) reports that these releases generated ten hit songs while Presley was in the army.
75. A year later Little Richard, Chuck Berry, and other Black artists made brief appearances in Hollywood Rock and Roll films, such as *Don't Knock the Rock* (1956), *The Girl Can't Help It* (1956), and *Mister Rock 'n' Roll* (1957), which exposed original "rock and roll" artists in the mainstream where they were discovered by many White teenagers.
76. See Cohn 1970, 33; Gillett 1984 (1970), 33–34; George-Warren and Romanowski 2001, 570–571. See also "Little Richard Biography," The Rock and Roll Hall of Fame, accessed September 3, 2015, https://rockhall.com/inductees/little-richard/bio.
77. Quoted in White 1984, 65–66.
78. Connor, interview. Music critic Shady Grady credits Earl Palmer, session drummer on Little Richard recordings, as the creator of the rock and roll beat ("Music Reviews: Little Richard, King Floyd," *The Urban Politico*, April 12, 2014, accessed September 11, 2015, http://www.theurbanpolitico.com/2014/04/music-reviews-little-richard-king-floyd.html). Little Richard had performed "Tutti Frutti" prior to recording the song, which provides credence to Conner's account of events.
79. Charles Connor explained that Little Richard often used the "choo-choo" beat in conjunction with the shuffle rhythms (Connor, interview). Chuck Berry and Fats Domino also contributed to the development of rock and roll. Berry frequently is acknowledged for his catchy melodies, fresh, witty, and relatable teen-oriented lyrics, and innovative guitar style. Fats Domino's defining sound is signature rolling piano fifths and octave figures, and triplets over rumba rhythms, and his unique vocal style are mentioned in some histories. Domino and Berry wrote or co-wrote many of their songs, and several were recorded by White artists. For details, see George-Warren and Romanowski 2001, 69–70, 274–275; and Lydon 1971, 16–19.
80. Quoted in White 1984, 79.
81. Presley's first album (released March 1956) includes covers of R&B songs by Ray Charles ("I Got a Woman"), Little Richard ("Tutti Frutti"), and the Drifters ("Money Honey"). The 1999 reissue with bonus tracks included R&B/blues songs "Lawdy Miss Clawdy" by Lloyd Price, "Shake, Rattle, & Roll" by Joe Turner, and "My Baby Left Me" by Arthur Crudup. Presley's second album (released October 1956) also included covers of Little Richard's "Rip It Up," "Long Tall Sally," and "Ready Teddy," as well as a cover of Big Mama Thornton's "Hound Dog."
82. Blackwell quoted in "Otis Blackwell & Elvis Presley," *Elvis Australia*, accessed January 9, 2016, http://www.elvis.com.au/presley/otis_blackwell.shtml. See Otis Blackwell's performance of "Don't Be Cruel" as he recorded on the demo for Presley, available online, "Otis Blackwell—Don't Be Cruel (Live on Letterman 1987)," *YouTube*, accessed January 9, 2016, https://www.youtube.com/watch?v=ed5yIiYf8oE.
83. David "Panama" Francis, interview by author, Orlando, FL, December 3, 1983. During this interview, Francis played Blackwell's demo tape for "Don't Be Cruel." Also see "Otis Blackwell Biography," Rock and Roll Hall of Fame, accessed September 12, 2015, https://rockhall.com/inductees/otis-blackwell/bio; and "Tribute to Otis Blackwell," *YouTube*, accessed October 27, 2015, https://www.youtube.com/watch?v=ed5yIiYf8oE.
84. This is evident in "All Shook Up" and "Don't Be Cruel," where Presley's vocal style, especially his inflections and timbre, combine those of both Otis Blackwell and Roy Brown ("Good Rockin' Tonight").
85. Eliot 1989, 62.

86. Rose 1994, 83.
87. Hammond 1981 (1977), 60.
88. Ibid., 63.
89. Quoted in Hammond 1981 (1977), 173–174.
90. For example, Presley's biography on the Rock and Roll Hall of Fame website opens with the following two lines: "Elvis Presley is the undisputed King of Rock and Roll. He rose from humble circumstances to launch the rock and roll revolution with his commanding voice and charismatic stage presence" ("Elvis Presley Biography, https://rockhall.com/inductees/elvis-presley/bio). Also see Starr and Waterman 2010, 61–67, 126–129, 221–225.
91. "*Billboard* Adopts 'R&B' as New Name for 2 Charts," 1990, 6, 35.
92. Omi and Winant 2015, 162
93. Cho 2009, 1593.
94. Contemporary sources that offer counter narratives include: Mahon 2000, 2004; Altschuler 2003; Tate 2003a, 2003b; Lydon 2004; Phinney 2005; Coleman 2006; Pecknold 2013.
95. Cruz 1999, 36–37.

DISCOGRAPHY

Berry, Chuck. *The Great Twenty-Eight*. Originally released 1982. MCA 92500, 1993. CD.
Bill Haley & His Comets. *Rock around the Clock*, 1956. Geffen 000170502, 2004. CD.
Blackwell, Otis. *All Shook Up*. Originally released 1976. Shanachie Records 9204, 1995. CD.
Brown, James. *Live at the Apollo*. Originally recorded in 1962. Polydor B171502, 2004. CD.
———. *It's a Mother*. 1969. Universal/Polydor 93288, 2007. CD; Universal Music Group/Universal Republic 799295, 2014. Digital.
———. *The Original Disco Man*. 1979. Polydor/Universal Distribution E760142 2003. CD; Universal, 2014. Digital.
———. *Out of Sight: Greatest Hits*. Universal, 2002. Digital; Polydor 9849000, 2007. CD.
Fats Domino. *Fats Domino Live: His Greatest Hits*. Elap Records 50171102, 2002. CD.
Franklin, Aretha. *Live At Fillmore West*. Originally recorded February 5, 1971 and February 7, 1971. Rhino 127956, 2007. CD.
Grandmaster Flash & the Furious Five (featuring Melle Mel & Duke Bootee). *The Message (Expanded Edition.)* Originally released 1982. Reissued by Castle Music/Sanctuary 2741869, 2010. CD.
Kool & The Gang. *The Best of Kool & The Gang 1969–1976*. Mercury, 1993. Digital; Mercury 9848999, 2007. CD.
Little Richard. *Here is Little Richard*. Concord, 2012. Digital; Concord 7233840, 2012. CD.
Louis Jordan & The Tympany Five. *The Best of Louis Jordan & The Tympany Five*. Gralin Music GRM216, 2012. Digital.
Pioneers of Rock and Roll. Various artists. Phantom Import Distribution/Mbop Global 38150, 2006. CD.
Presley, Elvis. *Elvis*. Originally released 1956. BMG/BMG Heritage 82876660592, 2005. CD.
———. *Loving You*. [Bonus Tracks] BMG/RCA 82876660602, 2005. CD.
———. *Elvis Presley*. [1956.] Legacy/RCA/Sony Legacy 90795, 2011. CD.
Simon and Garfunkel. *Bridge over Troubled Water*. Originally released 1970. Columbia, 88697828292, 2011. CD.
———. *Concert in Central Park*. *Columbia/Legacy Sony Music Entertainment*, 507878, 2015. CD/DVD.
Still Stompin' at the Savoy. [1947.] Various artists. Includes "We're Gonna Rock We're Gonna Roll" by Wild Bill Moore. Giant Step/V Disc GIST 003, 2003. CD.

CHAPTER 4

Negotiating Blackness in Western Art Music

Olly Wilson

In 1969, Ralph Ellison published an essay in the *Washington Sunday Star* entitled "Homage to Duke Ellington on His Birthday" in which he made this astute observation:

> Even though few recognized it, such artists as Ellington and Louis Armstrong were the stewards of our vaunted American optimism and guardians against the creeping irrationality which ever plagues our form of society. They created great entertainment, but for them (ironically) and for us (unconsciously) their music was a rejection of that chaos and license which characterized the so-called jazz age associated with F. Scott Fitzgerald, and which has returned once more to haunt the nation. Place Ellington with Hemingway, they are both larger than life, both masters of that which is most enduring in the human enterprise: the power of man to define himself against the ravages of time through artistic style.[1]

Ellison's assessment of Ellington is a glowing tribute to Ellington as an icon of exceptional social significance in American culture. It also brings into sharp relief the unique role that African American music, in general, and African American composers, in particular, have played in defining and reflecting fundamental values of African American and American expressive culture. Ralph Ellison praises Louis Armstrong and Ellington as "the stewards of our vaunted American optimism"—a quality widely considered characteristic of the American ethos, but also of great significance in the collective consciousness of the African American community.

While acknowledging that Armstrong and Ellington created "great entertainment" designed for the popular masses, Ellison also asserts that Ellington was a master of "that which is most enduring in the human enterprise": the power of man to define himself through art. He thus highlights the irony of Ellington as a performer. Ostensibly, Ellington was an entertainer in Black show business, a tradition whose roots were in the nineteenth-century minstrel show; but in reality, he was a superb artist with an excellent grasp of the cultural ideals, assumptions, and values of his time and who possessed the ability to communicate this understanding in a profoundly compelling musical manner.

I find Ellison's statement an insightful exposition of the multiple functions African American music plays in American culture. It serves simultaneously to express the perspective of an outsider who, although present, is not recognized—*the invisible man*—and, hence, has a unique critical viewpoint of the society of which he is a part but, historically, is not considered by the majority population to be an equal participant. The "invisible man," however, does have a separate African American world in which his own basic values, ideals, and aspirations are formed. This world provides not only a context in which to critique the larger world, but also a crucible in which to develop an expressive culture that privileges values within the African American world. This insider experience is the source of a viable African American culture that both mediates and is mediated by the larger American culture.

The concept of "double consciousness" as a construct to understand African American culture was initially proposed by W.E.B. DuBois in his classic book, *The Souls of Black Folk*, written in 1903. This famous quote contains the principal statement of his concept:

> After the Egyptian and Indian, the Greek and Roman, the Teuton and Mongolian, the Negro is a sort of seventh son, born with a veil, and gifted with second-sight in this American world—a world which yields him no true self-consciousness, but only lets him see himself . . . through the eyes of others, of measuring one's soul by the tape of a world that looks on in amused contempt and pity. One ever feels this twoness—an American, a Negro; two souls, two thoughts, two unreconciled strivings: two warring ideals in one dark body, whose dogged strength alone keeps it from being torn asunder.
>
> The history of the American Negro is the history of this strife—this longing to attain self-conscious manhood, to merge his double self into a better and truer self. In this merging he wishes neither of his other selves to be lost. He would not Africanize America, for America has too much to teach the world and Africa. He would not bleach his Negro soul in a flood of White Americanism, for he knows that Negro blood has a message for the world. He simply wishes to make it possible for a man to be both a Negro and an American, without being cursed and spit upon by his fellows, without having the doors of Opportunity closed roughly in his face.[2]

Whether or not one accepts completely DuBois' view of African American culture as somewhat schizophrenic—"two warring ideals," "two unreconciled strivings"—his basic notion of the double consciousness of African American experience is compelling and reflects a recurrent theme in African American intellectual history. A contemporary reading of DuBois' analysis, however, might conclude that although one of the salient characteristics of African American culture is the duality of existence both within and outside "the veil," these existences are not necessarily warring or unreconciled, but perfectly accommodated to one another.

A consideration of music composition from the perspective of the African American tradition must therefore recognize the duality of African American culture. If the work is being produced within the veil by and for the "blues people" as an "autonomous black music,"[3] it will tend to focus on those musical qualities that reinforce the basic conceptual approaches to music-making that most vividly characterize the culture. Elsewhere, I and others have discussed these conceptual approaches, cognitive orientations, and basic assumptions about the music-making process. Among these are:

> The notion of music as a ritualistic, interactive, communal activity in which everyone is expected to participate;
>
> The concept of music as a multidimensional, sound/verbal experience in which a continuum from speech to song is expected, and the rhetorical strategies of speech as music and music as speech are shared (signifying, troping);

A conception of music based on the principle of rhythmic contrast;
The predilection for antiphonal and cyclical musical structures;
The propensity to produce percussive, stratified musical textures;
A heterogeneous timbral sound ideal; and
The notion of physical body motion as an integral part of the music-making process.[4]

An analysis of successive genres of African American music that compose the tradition within the veil consistently reveals a strong presence of these approaches, though often in new manifestations. The development of rap music beginning in the 1970s is a case in point. Emerging from inner-city African American communities, this music focuses on those basic elements that defined the music tradition: rhythmic contrast, antiphony, percussiveness, and the musical sound/verbal continuum, among others.

The concept of double consciousness is also at the core of understanding the aesthetic approaches of many African American composers who work partially or completely outside the veil. These composers often demonstrate a compositional vision that indicates an understanding of the musical values and creative strategies of the oral African American musical traditions—the music within the veil—as well as an understanding of musical values and compositional techniques associated with the literate European American musical tradition, practices clearly extrinsic to the veil. The African American composer who works within a literate tradition thus is often engaged in accommodating different musical impulses and, consciously or unconsciously, must determine the means of creating an artistically viable musical reconciliation. In general, the history of African American music indicates that, from its inception, it has had a tremendous impact on American culture. This suggests that there have been many highly successful and significant artistic reconciliations of these dual musical impulses.

Historically, most traditional African American music originated in the context of vernacular traditions and religious practices. Research on traditional African cultures before the slave trade, throughout the "Middle Passage," and during the colonial period in the Western hemisphere indicates consistently that music was an extremely prominent feature of the culture.[5] Ethnomusicological, anthropological, and musicological studies of these musical practices reveal that—although there were significant changes in musical practices over time in specific areas, and significant differences in music-making within various regions of Africa and the African Diaspora—there were important similarities in musical practices that reflect a cultural continuity of African concepts of music-making throughout most of the Diaspora.

Given this history, it is not surprising to find that seventeenth- and eighteenth-century people of African descent in the Caribbean and colonial North and South America engaged in such profound, dynamic, urgent, and ubiquitous musical practices that they became the subject of much contemporaneous commentary on the life of peoples of African descent, both slave and freedmen. The general conclusion of these chroniclers was that Africans were highly gifted musically. The most famous of these observers was Thomas Jefferson, who devoted space in his *Notes on Virginia* to his observations on the "banjar," an instrument he describes as of African origin. Regarding the musicality of Blacks, Jefferson famously stated: "In music they are more generally gifted than the Whites, with accurate ears for tune, and time."[6] This opinion appears to have been widely shared by many White colonialists. The general fascination many of the colonial settlers and European visitors seemed to have had for (what may have appeared to them to be) the African exiles' exotic musical practices and exceptional musical abilities would explain why Blacks were encouraged to perform traditional African music in selected contexts,[7] as well as learn European instruments and perform European music for the entertainment of Whites. The iconographical evidence of this practice is very strong, and the practice of seventeenth- and eighteenth-century Blacks, both slave and freedmen, performing European music for Whites is well documented.[8] Moreover, the presence of African Americans as drummers and fifers in the American Revolutionary Army also attests to the importance of African American music and musicians. Finally, scholars of the Colonial era have also documented the presence of African Americans as music tutors and music masters, particularly in the New England colonies.[9]

Given this situation, it is clear that some African American musicians had already gained a working knowledge of European musical practices before the establishment of the United States as a nation and were poised to explore the realm of composition from a European perspective with its focus on the written music manuscript. However, these composers brought their own indigenous cultural proclivities with them as they began to create new music in the written tradition with a decidedly African American character in the second and third decades of the nineteenth century.

As Eileen Southern notes in her seminal study, *The Music of Black Americans*, the dance-band music of Francis Johnson was highly successful in Philadelphia and London in the 1820s. His novel manner of bringing new vitality and musical verve to the salon music of its time was a high point in the eighteenth- and early nineteenth-century practice of African American musicians. These artists provided music, not only as entertainment in the Black and White vernacular traditions of the day, but also within the elite circles of Philadelphia White literate society. Johnson (1792–1844), "the leader of the band," was so successful that, at his death, he was memorialized in an editorial of the *Philadelphia Public Ledger* of April 6, 1844:

> Frank was one of the most celebrated personages of Philadelphia. His talents as a musician rendered him famous all over the Union, and in that portion of Europe which he had visited, while his kindness of heart and gentleness of demeanor endeared him to his own people, and caused him to be universally respected in this community.[10]

Southern writes:

> Johnson was indeed a celebrity for all times! During his short career he accumulated an amazing number of "firsts" as a black musician: first to win wide critical acclaim in the nation and in England; first to publish sheet music (as early as 1818); first to develop a "school" of black musicians; first to give formal band concerts; first to tour widely in the nation; and first to appear in integrated concerts with white musicians. His list of achievements also included "firsts" as an American, black or white: he was the first to take a musical ensemble abroad to perform in Europe and the first to introduce the promenade concert to the United States.[11]

Like Francis Johnson's published cotillions and quadrilles of the first decades of the nineteenth century, the arrangements of spirituals by Harry Burleigh and, particularly, the published ragtime music of Scott Joplin, Tom Turpin, and their associates at the end of the century, all are vivid examples of African American music that was successful within both a written and oral tradition. The most significant thing about these musicians, particularly Burleigh and Joplin, is that they each created a new musical genre based on a synthesis of different musical impulses.

It is important to understand this process as an adaptation of African American traditional concepts redesigned to accommodate new conditions. The performance traditions of ragtime existed before Scott Joplin and his contemporaries wrote this music down. Western notation obviously had an impact on Joplin's compositional thought and influenced his concept of musical form. Nevertheless, his compositions retained the most important qualities of the improvised ragtime tradition that preceded them.

Joplin was influenced by the model of late nineteenth-century salon sheet music, the thriving band music tradition, and the economic demands of a rapidly developing popular music publishing industry. In comparison, Burleigh was influenced generally by the ethos of nationalist music ideology of his time and directly by the imposing presence of Antonín Dvořák, his teacher. Similarly, Francis Johnson was influenced by popular dance music written by his European and White American contemporaries. The new musical paradigms established by these composers did not occur within a cultural vacuum. While working within a written music tradition, they reveled in musical concepts that were intrinsic to Black oral music practice. These composers were significant because they possessed those elusive sensibilities that characterize the extraordinary creative musical mind. They also thoroughly internalized musical concepts both within and outside the veil that allowed them to make that leap of creativity that resulted in a new ordering of traditional concepts.

My use of the term "duality" is not to suggest that this view of African American music is based on binary opposites, but rather a continuum of values and ideas from one set of aesthetic ideals to another. This is why a specific composer may be actively involved in what appears to be both traditions, simultaneously or successively. Joplin, Burleigh, and Johnson were familiar with the literate European as well as the African American music traditions of their time. Moreover, certainly since the high point of William Grant Still's and Duke Ellington's careers in the 1920s and 1930s, most African American composers have been involved in both traditions. Indeed, the ability to traverse successfully the perceived divide between the high-brow and low-brow, cultivated and vernacular, religious and secular has been an important contribution of African American music that helped to define a new paradigm for American music.[12]

Harry T. Burleigh's creation of the arranged solo spiritual genre commonly known as the "solo art song spiritual" is instructive. Burleigh was an exceptional baritone singer who had written several successful art songs and romantic ballads. His profound respect for and understanding of the spiritual tradition, coupled with his understanding and knowledge of European art song compositional technique, made him particularly well prepared to accomplish this task. In 1901, he published a collection entitled *Plantation Melodies, Old and New* and later contributed arrangements for Henry E. Krehbiel's *Afro-American Folksongs* (1914). Music from both of these publications was performed by Black and White singers as solo songs. In 1913 he made his first choral arrangements of spirituals, but the publication of his solo arrangement of "Deep River" in 1916 catapulted him and his new genre into prominence on the American music landscape. Jean Snyder tells us:

> The success of Burleigh's solo arrangement of "Deep River" caught the attention of concert reviewers. Several critics observed that it appeared on more recital programs in New York City and Boston than any other song. G. Ricordi, Burleigh's publishers, capitalized on its popularity, publishing advertisements in music journals listing the names of singers who were singing it. The cover of the 1917 edition listed twenty-one singers who were using it. President Wilson's daughter Margaret Wilson sang it; composer Dudley Buck's voice students sang it; African-American tenors Roland Hayes and Sidney Woodward

sang it; and Boston critic Hiram Motherwell commented that "Deep River" had "justly brought [Burleigh] into prominence which he has long deserved." Burleigh issued twelve spirituals for solo voice in 1917 and twenty more in the following five years, in addition to a number of critically acclaimed secular art songs.[13]

What made this and Burleigh's other arrangements of spirituals such as "My Lord What a Morning," "Were You There," and "By an' By" special was his ability as a composer–arranger to retain the powerful expressive essence of the spiritual and simultaneously create a piano accompaniment that complemented the song and singer without detracting from the spiritual's internal musical logic or poetic content. Burleigh's musical settings assumed the aesthetic values within the spiritual tradition, but reinterpreted the musical event using conventions associated with the concert stage. This can be demonstrated specifically in several ways.

First, Burleigh always gives hegemony to the original spiritual's vocal line in its relationship to the piano accompaniment. Accordingly, the piano line is often sparse, simple, and essentially supportive of the vocal line. This approach permits and even encourages the vocalist to take opportunities to add subtle timbral nuances and rhythmic variations in the performance of the song, a practice idiomatic within traditional performances. Second, the accompaniment often serves as a second voice that establishes an antiphonal or call-and-response relationship with the soloist, often filling in the gaps at the ends of phrases with appropriate countermelodies, as is often the case in communal vernacular spirituals. These accompaniment countermelodies and occasional interjections often contain idiomatic extended syncopated rhythmic patterns characteristic of the religious style, while usually eschewing the rhythmic ostinato techniques commonly associated with secular genres.

Third, the choice of harmonies is guided by the use of chords that appropriately support the modal implications of the original spirituals. Chromaticism is used primarily in the service of the overreaching diatonic harmonic implications, or as a color device or melodic overlay (usually a descending chromatic scale fragment), rather than as a structural element; harmonic rhythm, in general, tends to be slow. Functional harmony tends to be clearly directed toward dominant-tonic and subdominant-tonic polarities. Burleigh's most refreshing harmonic choices work, even the chromatic ones, because they adhere to the modal implications of the melodic line while implying new relationships to the tonic center, often a third above or below the original tonic. Burleigh also carefully explores timbral nuances and registral variety to clearly distinguish the piano as an accompanying voice. Yet the text is brought into sharp relief, and the multiple concepts behind its surface are evoked by its musical setting.

The result of the use of these techniques is the creation of a new model of the spiritual, a model that consists of a clearly stylized spiritual endowed with new, carefully composed elements that shape the musical content of the spiritual to reflect its composer–arranger's unique artistic reinterpretation of the original. The musical result is different from the original vernacular spiritual, but, contrary to some thought of the period, it is not an "elevation" of that tradition. The art song spiritual seeks to communicate to an audience the artistic statement of its composer–arranger as interpreted by its performer. It is an object of intrinsic perceptual interest. Marian Anderson's recorded performance of Harry Burleigh's arrangement of "Deep River" and Paul Robeson and Lawrence Brown's recording of Burleigh's "By an' By" are excellent examples of this tradition.

The orchestral compositions of African American composers reveal two general tendencies as well. On one hand, there are compositions that, on the face of it, are indistinguishable in general musical style from works written by their non–African American contemporaries. These works exhibit the general musical characteristics of their time. Their composers were conversant with the various schools of compositional thought of their generation, and their work reflects this knowledge to the degree that it was relevant to the composers' creative conception.

On the other hand, there are compositions that contain musical qualities that are clearly derived from traditional African American musical practices. The nature of those qualities varies significantly. They reflect a continuum from the foreground-level usage of musical events that range from direct quotes from, or newly composed material in the style of traditional folk forms, to more subtle referents that are abstractions and/or reinterpretations of traditional conceptual approaches to music-making. The main point here is that they reflect a consciousness of the traditional African American musical experience modified by the degree this experience has influenced the musical personality of a particular composer.

The orchestral literature of African American composers contains both types of music, and it is common for a single composer to write music that falls into both categories. The orchestral output of Clarence Cameron White (1880–1960) includes a *Violin Concerto in D minor* as well as a *Katamba Rhapsody*. William Grant Still's work includes his *Symphony No. 1: Afro-American Symphony*, as well as his *Festival Overture*, which conductor Eugene Goosens described as "Elgarian." Florence Price, Julia Perry, Howard Swanson, Ulysses Kay, George Walker, Undine Moore, Hale Smith, T. J. Anderson, David Baker, Fredrick Tillis, Wendell Logan, Noel DaCosta, Carman Moore, Alvin Singleton, Adolphus Hailstork, Dorothy Rudd Moore, Talib Hakim, and other Black composers have all written compositions whose external features are devoid of qualities commonly associated with traditional African American music, but have also written works whose conception and/or surface qualities are demonstrably and profoundly influenced by a wide array of African American musical practices. This fact is simply another indicator of the dual nature of the African American experience.

This does not mean that a composer is, in any sense, more or less "African American" when he or she writes music that appears to belong to one category or the other. The composer consciously transforms his experience by ordering sound, and that experience includes an extraordinary range of human activities, emotions, ideas, and sensibilities, each of which is reinterpreted by the act of creation. The fact that the composer's experience is an African American one will deeply influence the creative act, but that does not mean that this influence will necessarily become evident in every work of art—partially because that experience includes dimensions that transcend ethnic considerations and partially because, given the complexity of what constitutes ethnicity, it is frequently unclear which features of a creative work are derived from a particular cultural experience.

In my own compositional approach, I, too, have been influenced profoundly by traditional African American music while simultaneously exploring the full range of compositional techniques that interested me, independent of their sources. As a result, like other African American composers of the last sixty years, I have written works that, on the surface, appear to be indistinguishable in general musical style from works written by my contemporary composer colleagues who are not African American.

Two examples from my music reflect the impact of traditional music on my work. The first example is from a piece entitled *SpiritSong* for mezzosoprano, double chorus, and orchestra, written in 1974. In this work, I attempted to explore in one composition the historical development of the African American spiritual. Specifically, the composition explored the transition from the religious wordless moans, chants, and hollers that preceded the spiritual proper to the historical moment when the English text was associated with these vocal utterances and this music became the genre known as the spiritual.

The first movement of *SpiritSong* is a procession of the choir to the stage in which the main chorus sings modal, chant-like music exclusively. It explores sound locomotion and uses amplification of selected instruments, an offstage women's chorus, and the procession to achieve movement of sound in a specific space. The second movement represents the emergence of the spiritual proper and features a soprano soloist who begins the movement with a wordless chant (Figure 4.1) before gradually beginning to use the English text, ultimately singing the refrain, "Oh Lord, keep me from sinking down." In the opening of this movement, I wanted to capture the expressive quality of the traditional religious moan or chant. The use of a wide range of vocal nuances common to this tradition was an integral part of my initial conception of the piece. I attempted to achieve this quality by having the soprano change tone colors (timbres) while maintaining the same pitch, while simultaneously having the entire orchestra gradually change timbres and function as both accompaniment to, and commentary on, the soprano solo line. Because the orchestra begins on the same pitch at an extremely soft dynamic level, it creates the illusion that the orchestra emerges from the soprano solo. In addition, I use women's voices as part of this timbral mix. The orchestration is my own adaptation of late twentieth-century orchestration techniques. The movement thus reflects, both conceptually and in the usage of specific compositional procedures, the cultural plurality of my personal experience.

The second example is taken from the last movement of my composition *Sinfonia* for orchestra (1984). This movement is a stylized dance and consists of two distinct ideas: one, an angular melody stated in the high strings; and two, a propulsive rhythmic idea based on an insistent syncopated rhythmic pattern (Figure 4.2).

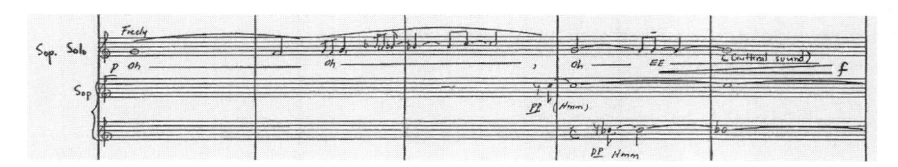

Figure 4.1
Manuscript excerpt from the second movement of *SpiritSong* (1974), showing soprano voices.

Courtesy Olly Wilson.

Figure 4.2
Syncopated rhythmic pattern from *Sinfonia* (1984).

Courtesy Olly Wilson.

The texture of the orchestral statement of this idea is clearly influenced by concepts characteristic of the African American tradition. The low strings and horns state the persistent, but constantly shifting, principal rhythmic pattern, while the percussion, trombones, and high trumpets carry on an antiphonal dialogue with this line as well as with each other. Timbrally, each is distinctly delineated, and the resultant composite texture is one in which the accents are extremely irregular, percussive, and timbrally kaleidoscopic—a textural ideal evident in many genres of African and African American music. After a development of these ideas, at the end of the movement the propulsive rhythm pattern returns but in a configuration that is more characteristic of a jazz or blues riff. In a broad sense in this work, I am using the technique of "troping" or "signifying" on previously existing rhythmic concepts as a means of creating a new, coherent musical statement.

As an individual living at the beginning of the twenty-first century, I have inherited a rich legacy of musical practices from throughout the world, and I have reveled in all of it. The music of Charlie Parker, Ludwig van Beethoven, Miles Davis, Igor Stravinsky, Bessie Smith, and Witold Lutoslawski, as well as much music of selected indigenous people of the world, all has meaning to me. I believe the composition process involves an attempt by a composer to reveal something about his or her experience by consciously ordering sound into meaningful events. That process inevitably takes place within a cultural context, and that specific cultural context shapes the nature of the produced work. This is why the work produced has meaning on so many interrelated levels: as sound-object, symbolic expression, and cultural emblem. I believe the music of Verdi or Berio would be very different if these two composers had not been Italian. The music of Benjamin Britten reflects important things about British reality in the middle of the twentieth century, just as the music of Duke Ellington tells us important things about African and African American reality in much of the twentieth century. In the broadest sense, a composer, like any artist, contemplates her or his unique reality and produces a new composition, and in so doing, makes us all a bit more aware of what it means to be human in the full richness of its various cultural manifestations. As Ralph Ellison so eloquently stated, at their best, artists are "masters of that which is most enduring in the human enterprise: the power of man to define himself against the ravages of time . . ."

ACKNOWLEDGMENTS

This chapter incorporates and revises a significant portion of an earlier article by the author, "Composition from the Perspective of the African American Tradition," *Black Music Research Journal* 16, no. 1 (Spring 1996): 43–51.

NOTES

1. Ellison 1986, 219.
2. DuBois 1961 (1903), 16–17.
3. Baraka 1963, 176, 53.
4. See, for example, Wilson 1974, 1983, 1985, 1992; Burnim 1985; Gates 1988; Maultsby 1990; Floyd 1991, 1995.
5. There are several extant descriptions of African cultural practices dating from the eighteenth century. Among the most famous are Bosman 1721; Equiano 1791; Bowdich 1819.
6. Jefferson 1954 (1781), 150.

7. Southern 1997, 52–58.
8. Epstein 1977.
9. Southern 1997, 3–52, 63–71. For an excellent annotated bibliography on African American music from the Colonial–Federalist Era (1600–1800) and the Antebellum Era (1800–1862), see Southern and Wright 1990.
10. Quoted in Southern 1997, 107.
11. Ibid.
12. Scholars who have studied the music of African American composers have shown how traditional African American music shaped the composer's works. Attention is given to this issue in Eileen Southern's (1997) work on Francis Johnson, A.J.R. Connor, and others; Linda Rae Brown 1990; Oja 1992; Floyd 1995; and Banfield 2003.
13. Snyder 1993, 137.

DISCOGRAPHY

Burleigh, Harry T. *Deep River: Songs and Spirituals of Harry T. Burleigh*. With Oral Moses, baritone, and Ann Sears, piano. Albany Music Distribution 332, 1999.

Kaleidoscope: Music by African-American Women. Includes works for piano by various artists such as Margaret Bonds, Valerie Capers, Rachel Eubanks, Nora Douglas Holt, Lena Johnson McLin, Undine Smith Moore, Julia Perry, and Florence Price. Helen Walker-Hill, piano, and Gregory Walker, violin. Leonarda 339, 2002. CD.

Kay, Ulysses. *Ulysses Kay: Works for Chamber Orchestra*. Ulysses Kay, composer, and Kevin Scott, conductor. Performed by the Metropolitan Philharmonic Orchestra. Albany Music Distribution 961, 2007. CD.

Lost Sounds—Blacks and the Birth of the Recording Industry 1891–1922. Various artists such as Harry T. Burleigh, R. Nathaniel Dett, Roland Hayes, and Clarence Cameron White. Includes "Go Down, Moses" performed by Harry T. Burleigh. Archeophone Records–ARCH 1005, 2005, 2 compact discs.

The Music of Francis Johnson and His Contemporaries: Early 19th-Century Black Composers. Music of Francis Johnson with A.J.R. Conner, Isaac Hazzard, Edward Roland, and James Hemmenway. The Chestnut Brass Company and Friends. Musicmasters 7029, 1994, CD. Recorded September 1988.

Price, Florence. *Florence Price: The Oak/Mississippi River Suite/Symphony No. 3*. Apo Hsu, artistic director and conductor. Performed by the Women's Philharmonic. Koch International Classics 375182, 2001. CD.

Ragtime Piano Roll, Vol. 1. Various artists. Includes Tom Turpin performing "St. Louis Rag." Riverside Records RLP-1006, 1953. 10-inch LP.

Robeson, Paul. *Songs of Free Men: Recital*. Includes performance of "By an' By" by Paul Robeson. Nonesuch, 63223, 1998, CD.

Scott Joplin, Classic Ragtime from Rare Piano Rolls. Remastered from original piano rolls. Micro Werks MIW 101069, 2010. CD.

Still/Dawson/Ellington: Symphony No. 2/Negro Folk Symphony/Harlem. Music by William Grant Still, William Levi Dawson, and Edward "Duke" Ellington. Chandos CHAN9226, 1993. CD.

Still, William Grant. *William Grant Still: Symphony No. 1 (Afro-American), Duke Ellington: Suite from The River*. Detroit Symphony Orchestra. Chandos 9154, 1993. CD.

Symphonic Brotherhood: The Music of African-American Composers. Music of Adolphus Hailstork, Harry T. Burleigh, Julius P. Williams, Gary Powell Nash, and David Baker. Bohuslav Martinu Philharmonic. Albany Music Distribution TROY104-2, 1994. CD.

Walker, George. *Lilacs for Voice and Orchestra: The Music of George Walker*. Faye Robinson, soprano, Arizona State University Symphony Orchestra. Summit Records DCD 274, 2000. CD.

When I Have Sung My Songs (The American Art Song 1900–1940). Various artists. Includes works by Harry Burleigh performed by Marian Anderson, Roland Hayes, and Paul Robeson. New World Records–NW 247, 1977, LP.

Wilson, Olly. *Sinfonia*. Boston Symphony Orchestra, Seiji Ozawa, cond.: New World Records, 80331-2, 1985. CD.

Works by T. J. Anderson, David Baker, Donal Fox, Olly Wilson. Various artists. New World Records 80423-2, 1992. CD.

PART II

Mass Mediation

CHAPTER 5

Crossing Musical Borders
Agency and Process in the Gospel Music Industry

Mellonee V. Burnim

The literature and film on African American gospel music frequently explore the motivation of performers in the field who sever their overt gospel ties and succumb to the lure of secular music. Major figures like Aretha Franklin and Sam Cooke—the former who grew up singing in her father's Baptist church in Detroit, the latter who rose to prominence in the male quartet tradition—are often cited as archetypes of the ubiquitous sacred–secular dichotomy in African American music. Less frequently, artists are noted who reject often lucrative careers in secular music, electing instead to pursue gospel music exclusively. Striking examples include bluesman Arnold Dwight "Gatemouth" Moore, celebrated in the film *Saturday Night, Sunday Morning: The Travels of Gatemouth Moore*, who, after an onstage conversion experience in Chicago's Club DeLisa in the 1940s, abruptly ended his blues career and entered the ministry.[1] Al Green, also documented in *Saturday Night, Sunday Morning*, as well as in the 1984 film *Al Green: The Gospel According to Al Green*, recounts a dramatic spiritual encounter that virtually compelled him to pursue gospel music in lieu of his star-studded career in soul.

Undoubtedly, the most well-known historical example of the secular-to-sacred musical switch is that of the man credited as father of gospel music, Thomas Dorsey. Previously known in the blues world as "Georgia Tom" and "Barrelhouse Tom," Dorsey's collaboration with guitarist Tampa Red (Hudson Whitaker) in 1928 resulted in his most famous double entendre hokum hit, "It's Tight Like That." Dorsey's decision to pursue a career in gospel music was prompted, in part, by a series of personal tragedies, among them the deaths of his wife and newborn son.[2] Paradoxically, although none of these men continued to publicly embrace secular music as they had done prior to their dramatic musical turnaround, it is profoundly instructive that none of them ever renounced the music of his past as a religious pariah.

Although many African Americans are both passionate and unwavering in their support or condemnation of such musical border crossings, the depth and complexity of the factors that inform these choices are rarely examined. Furthermore, these contested views of crossover in the domain of gospel music consistently fail to assess the role of the music industry in creating personalities, images, labels, and marketing strategies that transform cultural products into economic commodities, thereby fueling the flames of intercultural conflict. This investigation will explore these issues, arguing that constructs of race, culture, and, by implication, religion, are critical variables in defining how gospel music is perceived, produced, and marketed not only among African Americans but within the broader national music industry as a whole.

BORDER CROSSINGS

In 1968, the gospel music industry was unexpectedly taken by storm with the release of the single "Oh Happy Day" by the forty-six-member Church of God in Christ (COGIC) Northern California State Youth Choir (Figure 5.1). Under the direction of Betty Watson and Edwin Hawkins, the choir had been formed in 1967, and in 1968 produced its first album, *Let Us Go into the House of the Lord*. Produced by the Oakland Century Custom Recording Service, this album was a collection of eight traditional gospel songs rearranged by Hawkins, all of which were recorded in a single two-and-a-half-hour session at Ephesians Church of God in Christ in Berkeley. Conceived as a fundraising project, the album, which included "Oh Happy Day," initially sold 600 copies to a largely COGIC audience through self-promotion efforts.[3]

In March 1969, approximately ten months after its original release, "Oh Happy Day" was "discovered" (more accurately, stumbled onto) by John Lingel, a rock promotion

Figure 5.1
Edwin Hawkins Singers, circa 1970.

Photo by Michael Ochs Archives/Getty Images.

director for an Oakland music distributor, who was also a fan of gospel music. Lingel's enthusiasm for the recording led to the eventual airing of "Oh Happy Day" on underground radio station SKAN-FM in San Francisco. Lingel sensed that "Oh Happy Day" was hit material, which proved to be true; the morning following its initial airplay on SKAN, the record distributor had orders for 1,300 copies of the single.[4]

By May 1969, "Oh Happy Day" had been cited during one week by *Rolling Stone* magazine as "the most requested tune on every rock station in L.A."[5] It was among the Top 10 in San Francisco, and radio stations coast to coast gave it airplay as well. The unprecedented appeal of "Oh Happy Day" was difficult to pinpoint. Various critiques suggested that its rhythmic drive was its most compelling feature, as Thomas Dorsey, father of gospel music, suggests:

> Take "O Happy Day" [*sic*]. I've sung that song since I was a boy and nobody paid very much attention to it, but then Hawkins comes along. I guess he was inspired from on high, and he put beat into it. Not only beat, but the curves, the rhythmic curves, and the harmony. It creates a new style in gospel music, and I think he did a wonderful job.[6]

Whether or not Dorsey's assessment is correct, it is most certain that the success of "Oh Happy Day" was not the result of its production quality; only two microphones were used to cover the piano, organ, percussion (trap set), amplified bass guitar, soloist, and choir. The popularity of "Oh Happy Day" came as a complete surprise to both the industry and to the performers themselves. Edwin Hawkins acknowledged that he "had no idea that his singers were headed for fame and fortune in the top of the pops," especially given the fundraising objective of the project.[7] The tremendous interest in the recording generated an ensuing scramble from major record companies, which resulted in the group's eventual signing with Buddah Records. After having apparently purchased the master recordings, Buddah made initial orders for 250,000 albums and 350,000 singles of "Oh Happy Day."[8]

The Buddah release of "Oh Happy Day" generated industry-wide interest. Astounded by the popularity of this unlikely hit, *Rolling Stone* magazine commented:

> Like no other song in recent memory, "Oh Happy Day" has transcended all radio "formats." In San Francisco, where the song was first aired, it is being played not only on the Top 30, "progressive rock," and soul stations, but on the Bay Area's middle-of-the-road and jazz outlets as well.[9]

Having received airplay in five different markets and defying limitations generally imposed by genre and race, sales of "Oh Happy Day" eventually reached 1.5 million, ushering in the contemporary era in gospel music performance.[10] The Hawkins family continues to be a major force in the gospel music industry, noted in *Billboard* as having produced four of the Top 40 gospel albums from 1973 to 1994.[11]

It was 1993, almost twenty-five years later, before a gospel release of comparable magnitude would hit the charts. Although Aretha Franklin's 1972 LP *Amazing Grace* went gold, this record was released in the midst of Aretha's stellar career as the Queen of Soul, fully supported by the powerful industry giant Atlantic Records.[12] Neither Edwin Hawkins nor the emergent gospel phenom of the 1990s, Kirk Franklin, could boast of a professional network and name recognition that compared to that of Aretha, who already had over a dozen albums to her credit and had graced the cover of *Time* magazine when *Amazing Grace* was released.[13]

For the hit of the 1990s, the geographical locale shifted from the West Coast to the Southwest. Like Edwin Hawkins, the composer–arranger devoted exclusively to gospel music who produced the second major crossover in the genre was quite young—in his twenties. But this 1993 release by Kirk Franklin of Fort Worth, TX, called *Kirk Franklin and the Family*, was no amateur recording that accidentally received secular radio airplay. Unlike Hawkins, who had no record contract, promoter, or manager, the album *Kirk Franklin and the Family* was one of the first products of the Black, female-owned GospoCentric label, formed in 1993, the same year as Franklin's debut.[14]

Vicki Mack Lataillade, founder of GospoCentric, had worked five years at Sparrow Records as director of Gospel Marketing before launching out on her own. She had been in the gospel industry for over a decade and was known as one of the best promotional people in the field. Lataillade had worked with some of the biggest acts in the industry, including The Winans, a group of brothers from Detroit; Tremaine Hawkins, who started her career with the Edwin Hawkins Singers; and Take 6, an a cappella male sextet with a vocal texture grounded in jazz.[15] Borrowing $6,000 from her dad to start GospoCentric, reminiscent of Berry Gordy's Motown launch, Lataillade capitalized on her experience as an industry veteran to quickly establish one of the five top-selling gospel labels.[16]

After a rather lackluster debut, *Kirk Franklin and the Family* was carefully and strategically marketed to maximize airplay and availability of the album in the mainstream. Debuting in July 1993 at #32 on the gospel charts, within six months the album skyrocketed to the #1 position, with an accompanying crossover to the Contemporary Christian chart (a listing that first appeared in *Billboard* in 1980, eleven years after Hawkins's "Oh Happy Day"). A review of the Top 40 Contemporary Christian albums from the advent of the chart to June 1994 yields a list without a single African American entry.

Franklin's ascendancy up the Contemporary Christian chart reflected a breakthrough into the White Christian market. By September 1995, his position was #6, after a total of sixty-eight weeks on the chart.[17]

Following his appearance at a December holiday concert sponsored by R&B station WGCI-FM in Chicago, Franklin's album sales shot up dramatically, as did his airplay on R&B stations. In February 1994, Franklin and his group were featured on *The Arsenio Hall Show*; one year later, his recording was listed among the Top 10 R&B records.[18]

Kirk Franklin and the Family, called "the biggest phenomenon since 'Oh Happy Day,'"[19] generated sales far beyond the expectations even of the visionary president and CEO of GospoCentric. From an original GospoCentric projection of 100,000 units, a figure well above the 40,000 to 50,000 units major gospel albums typically sold at the time,[20] *Kirk Franklin and the Family* eventually went platinum, signifying sales of over one million copies. As of September 1995, the album had appeared on the biweekly Top Gospel Chart for more than 113 weeks, a total of more than two years. By October 7, 1995, the album had been listed on *Billboard*'s R&B chart for forty-two weeks. "Why We Sing," the major hit on the album, was winner of two Dove Awards from the predominantly White Gospel Music Association; two Stellar Awards, conferred by the Black gospel music industry; and the James Cleveland Gospel Music Workshop of America 1994 Excellence Award.[21]

THE CROSSOVER APPEAL

A striking similarity between these two gospel crossover hits is the fact that neither "Oh Happy Day" nor "Why We Sing" was initially conceived as having audience appeal beyond the traditional African American gospel music market. Both songs overtly referenced Jesus, avoiding the camouflage of the Christian message often associated with deliberate attempts to generate crossover appeal.[22] *Rolling Stone* magazine referred to "Oh Happy Day" as a "most unlikely hit," while Dorothy Morrison, lead singer, called its acceptance a "miracle." Alan Stone, the second disc jockey to air "Oh Happy Day" over secular radio, commented simply that people were "digging it" due to the obviousness of the singer's belief and sincerity.[23]

Hawkins expressed a desire to "leave the sincerity of the group behind us wherever we go on concerts,"[24] implying a rather subtle concern that perhaps the intended religious message of his music was being lost via translation to secular contexts and transcultural audiences. Ethnomusicologist Portia K. Maultsby recalls the commentary of one radio announcer on a Chicago soul music station who expressed ambivalence about what genre label to assign "Oh Happy Day": "I don't know what to call it; it sounds like gospel and it sounds like soul."[25] The mix of musical features that straddles sacred and secular realms invited an eclectic listening audience destined to respond to the music in ways that might sometimes conflict with those of the traditional gospel music supporter. Without question, the *Rolling Stone* journalist's choice of the phrase "digging it" to describe listening audiences' responses to "Oh Happy Day" provides just a glimpse of the oppositional forces that so often come into play when African American religious music is transformed from religious expression to cultural novelty or economic commodity. The mere use of the term "digging it" is antithetical to the way Black Christians characteristically describe their experience of gospel music.

As was true of Hawkins, Kirk Franklin, under the tutelage of his youth-directed GospoCentric label, did not set crossover record sales as his inspiration for performance:

> With the first album I didn't try to do anything special. I just had some songs that God gave me and I wanted to share them. . . . I feel like if I'm going to make music to *please people* [emphasis mine], then I'm in the wrong business. "You need to dance with the one that brung you," my mama used to tell me.[26]

Quite obviously, Franklin's dance partner was none other than the Lord. Both Hawkins and Franklin, the latter a seminary-trained Baptist minister,[27] were motivated by their desire to convey a spiritual message through song. Even Vicki Mack Lataillade saw her work as a Christian calling, indicating that she started GospoCentric because "there was a whole area of ministry that was missing [in the industry], especially with black youth," and because "there were not a lot of options for black women like me in the Christian industry, and I wanted to grow."[28] The goals and aspirations of these artists were consistent with those of pioneering gospel musicians who laid the foundation for this industry. Such gospel performers as the Roberta Martin Singers and Willie Mae Ford Smith, who was the first head of the Soloist's Bureau of the National Convention of Gospel Choirs and Choruses founded in 1932, were known to lead week-long revivals without the aid of a preacher.[29] From Shirley Caesar to Mahalia Jackson, gospel artists have historically viewed themselves as evangelists. Says Shirley Caesar: "My primary purpose as a Christian and as a gospel singer has always been to reach as many people as possible with the message of Jesus, regardless of race, gender, demographic or socioeconomic status."[30]

Lataillade notes that Franklin's music was "straight up gospel. If there's an R&B flavor, it's him."[31] Lataillade's assessment references the fact that industry efforts to generate crossover success have often pressured artists to minimize their overt references to God while maximizing their identification with current secular soundscapes. In a 1972 interview, Hawkins comments:

> Some of the things we did were gospel in the traditional sense. Of course, the name of Jesus was mentioned a lot. Our company asked us not to mention the name so much . . . because they thought it would hinder things. . . . I knew where I stood and I didn't want to jeopardize my beliefs—or sacrifice my beliefs to make the commercial world happy. I think that gospel music . . . must be appreciated as it is—just like any other music, rock 'n' roll, jazz, etc.[32]

For both "Oh Happy Day" and "Why We Sing," Hawkins and Franklin used existing hymns as source material for their compositions. In both cases, however, it is most accurate to refer to these new creations as original compositions *inspired by* hymns rather than mere arrangements, as they have been previously labeled.[33] In "Why We Sing," Franklin uses only the text of the refrain of Civilla Martin and Charles Gabriel's "His Eye Is on the Sparrow" (1905):

> *I sing because I'm happy, I sing because I'm free.*
> *His eye is on the sparrow, and I know he watches me.*

Franklin completely transformed the original composition by creating a new melody; establishing a different meter, rhythmic treatment, and form; and, of course, changing the harmony.

Combining these modifications with the aesthetic framework of gospel music performance produced a work that was fresh and imaginative, yet strongly rooted and clearly identifiable with the existing Christian (hymn and gospel) song tradition. "His Eye Is on the Sparrow" is a standard part of the repertoire of African American churches of virtually all denominations, and Franklin's "Why We Sing" skillfully contextualizes and affirms African American musical and cultural values in his text inspired by this work. "Why We Sing" has also become a standard in the African American church, crossing demographic boundaries of denomination, geography, and class. It is among those classics included in the 2001 *African American Heritage Hymnal*.[34]

Hawkins's transformation of the eighteenth-century hymn "Oh Happy Day" by P. Doddridge (words) and E. F. Rimbault followed a similar development with one major difference. A Kenneth Morris arrangement of "Oh Happy Day" that mirrors the Hawkins version appears in *The New Angelic Gospelodium, Songbook Number 1*,[35] published by Martin and Morris Music, Inc., with an original copyright of 1957. The Morris score also includes a second copyright date of 1969, the same year as the Buddah release of "Oh Happy Day." On the Buddah recording, Hawkins is given sole credit for having penned the work, even though contemporary accounts of Hawkins's success label all of the selections on the original album as "new arrangements."

The preexisting version of "Oh Happy Day," arranged by Kenneth Morris, raises question regarding the interplay between the oral and written transmission processes in gospel music. Unlike Franklin, who had a strong background in musical literacy, Hawkins did not read and write music in Western notation. It is therefore unlikely that Hawkins had been introduced to Morris's arrangement by reviewing his musical score. It is conceivable, however, that Hawkins heard the Morris arrangement performed live and absorbed it as his own. This practice is still commonplace in gospel music circles. Given the fact that the album that included "Oh Happy Day" was originally directed toward a limited COGIC audience with relatively few projected sales, it is questionable whether the issue of copyright had even been factored into the production process. Finally, Kenneth Morris (1917–1988) was still alive at the advent of Hawkins's upward career spiral. Yet even with the nationwide airplay "Oh Happy Day" received, there is no evidence that Morris ever posed a public challenge to Hawkins's receiving sole credit for the arrangement.[36]

The two-part verse–chorus structure of the hymn "Oh Happy Day" is transformed in Hawkins's recording into a three-part—verse, chorus, and vamp—external structure embedded with internal call–response throughout. But characteristic of gospel music as a genre, the work comes alive through its realization as performance. "Oh Happy Day" was characterized by a compelling drive and energy that was also evident in "Why We Sing." Neither piece is up-tempo, even though "the beat" of "Oh Happy Day" was often cited as its primary source of appeal. Thomas Dorsey calls this assessment into question, however, with his analysis that "beat" alone is not enough to guarantee the success of a song:

> There are others singing gospel who have lost the melody. All they have is the beat. When there's no melody in gospel songs, you can't get much of a story, you don't get much message. They can put all the beat in it they want, but the melody is the foundation.[37]

Comparing the relative success of "Oh Happy Day" and "Why We Sing," it becomes evident that, in both instances, young African American composer–arranger–performers were able to deftly harness the salient components of the Euro-American hymn tradition, and skillfully recast the message in such a way to capture the interest not only of the African American gospel music advocate, but of musical consumers from all walks of life, of all ages, and all denominations.

IMPLICATIONS OF CROSSOVER

According to Don Cusic, who has written extensively for *Billboard* and other trade magazines:

> The term "crossover" generally means a music that can appeal to several different audiences and can appear on several different charts—country and pop, R&B and pop, jazz and R&B, rock and easy listening—and therefore can sell in much greater numbers.

He adds further that, "Within black gospel, the term 'crossover' has a two-fold meaning."[38] Cusic unravels the two major dimensions of gospel crossover: first, from the Black consumer market into the White gospel market or onto the Contemporary Christian charts; and second, from the sacred (gospel) chart onto various secular music charts.

Writing on the popular music industry, Reebie Garofalo contends that the concept of crossover is even more complex than Cusic suggests:

> While the term can be used to indicate simply the simultaneous appearance on more than one chart, its most common usage in popular music history connotes movement from margin to mainstream. . . .

> [B]y and large African American artists must first demonstrate success in the black market before gaining access to the mainstream. It is a process which holds black artists to a higher standard of performance than white . . .[39]

Unless the complex underpinnings of gospel music crossover are fully explored, the omnipresent and powerful variables of race and culture could easily be overlooked. Cusic, whose writings appear in a wide range of religious periodicals, including *Contemporary Christian Music*, *Christian Review*, and *Christian Retailer*,[40] acknowledges that the label "Contemporary Christian" is primarily a designation for White artists, whose sales have historically depended in large part on Christian bookstores.[41] He indicates that, in 1985, stores in the Christian Bookseller's Association generated $1.269 billion in sales, with music accounting for twenty-three percent or roughly one quarter of that total.[42] By 1993, the year of Franklin's debut, Contemporary Christian music sales had passed the $500 million mark.[43]

Prior to 1990, Cusic contends that "black gospel artists [did] not really benefit from the Christian bookstore network to any degree."[44] Pioneering Black composer Kenneth Morris gives a similar account of the lack of Black access to a broad consumer market for the distribution of published song material in the 1940s:

> [D]uring that particular time, even all down through the South, nowhere was Black music sold in stores. The stores would not order from us. All the stores were white stores and they would only order from white publishers. . . . So our music could not be bought in any store in the South. That's why we set up what we called agents. Everywhere we went we would [hire] agents and you bought the music from the agents who handled the music, and they sent [the money] back [to us]. All of this was in the beginning of the business. It was not until after, after 1946, that the white stores would start to even handle the music. There was such a demand for it that they could no longer ignore it.[45]

Morris recalls that at one time Martin and Morris, his publishing company, co-owned with Sallie Martin, "had 326 agents all over the country and in the West Indies and England."[46]

Cusic advances his discussion of marketing strategies in the music industry with the conclusion that, historically, unless the Black gospel music artist (and here "Black" refers both to race as well as musical style) was able to cross over onto the Contemporary Christian music charts, record sales were likely to be restricted to the faithful but limited consumers who frequented the network of "Mom and Pop" record shops in Black neighborhoods.[47]

Although the genre of contemporary Christian music did not exist when Hawkins released "Oh Happy Day," it was clearly the exposure in the nontraditional, White FM radio consumer market that sparked its stellar rise in popularity. Comparatively, Vicki Mack Lataillade did not leave one aspect of Kirk Franklin's promotion to chance. Following the early success of his debut album, she hired an independent promotional team to help handle all the inquiries about Franklin. The new team immediately recommended that an "MTV-type video" be produced; this was uncharted territory in gospel music. As Franklin's popularity and sales began to unexpectedly soar with intense media exposure, including radio and network television, Lataillade astutely postponed the release of Franklin's second major release, *Whatcha Lookin' For*, to allow the first recording to peak.[48] Although the extent of success of Franklin's initial release was indeed surprising, Lataillade's impressive combination of experience, business acumen, and Christian commitment to the project were critical variables in implementing a promotional effort that maximized on the music's broad appeal.

The implications of restrictive, race-based marketing of religious music reaches well beyond the potential earning power and exposure of Edwin Hawkins and Kirk Franklin. Commenting on how her female group, The Caravans, formed in Chicago in 1952, benefited from Edwin Hawkins's crossover success, gospel pioneer Albertina Walker recalls:

> Really *big* money in gospel music didn't really come until Edwin Hawkins came out with "Oh Happy Day." And I have to give him his credit, you know. 'Cause when Edwin came out in the '60s with "Oh Happy Day," that's when singers were able to get *big* money. I mean *big money!!*"[49]

A second critical dimension of gospel music crossover is its movement into secular markets. In 1975, gospel music announcer and promoter Joe Bostic commented at the Gospel Announcer's Guild, a subsidiary of the James Cleveland Gospel Music Workshop of America, on the lure of crossover that gospel artists often face. According to Bostic: "Involvement by those outside the gospel field almost always produces pressures on groups to crossover, become more pop or R&B oriented, and move away from gospel roots."[50] In other words, producing a hit record that traverses sacred and secular charts is viewed as merely the first enticing step in prompting artists to switch wholesale from the sacred to the secular music industry. Such were the promptings experienced by The Edwin Hawkins Singers following the rise of "Oh Happy Day" and such was the earlier experience of gospel pioneer Mahalia Jackson, whose appeal beyond the confines of the African American audience was legion. When Mahalia moved from Apollo Records to Columbia, the label expressed a desire to "spread her artistry over everything." They queried, "Why limit yourself to gospel?"[51] At one time, Mahalia was offered $25,000 a week to sing in Las Vegas nightclubs; she refused.[52]

Whereas gospel artists who historically made the switch to secular music anticipated the benefits of improved production and marketing and increased sales, less frequently, gospel artists like Kirk Franklin, whose music did reach the secular marketplace, sometimes confronted unanticipated and unsettling responses to their work. Despite the fact that Kirk Franklin describes his gospel music expression as "chillin' with the Lord," media representations have occasionally characterized him as a "gospel-pop sex symbol," not unlike Sam Cooke as his popularity swelled as a member of The Soul Stirrers gospel quartet.[53] Occasionally, Franklin has been "pulled off stage, kissed and had his clothes ripped by adoring fans, anxious to meet the man behind the sacred music."[54] As a consequence, Franklin began to employ bodyguards, a practice atypical for major gospel music artists who, for example, are known to move freely among the membership of the 20,000-strong Gospel Music Workshop of America at its annual convention.

CONCLUSION

This discussion presents a cursory view of the complex phenomenon of crossover in the domain of the gospel music industry. Unquestionably, the issues I have addressed are not new, because gospel pioneers faced the critical and controlling gaze of the African American church-going public, as well as the larger American populace and the recording industry, in defining both the character and the content of their compositions and performances. What is inherently clear, in this highly textured maze of competing interests and multiple identities, is that the concept of music as ministry—one which lies at the very heart and core of gospel music performance ("We didn't come for form or fashion, or any outside show"[55])—faces its maximum challenge within the confines of a multimillion dollar music industry.

This study suggests that constructs of race, religion, and culture are critical variables in defining how gospel music is perceived and manipulated, not only among African Americans, but within the broader spectrum of the American music industry at large. The business of producing and marketing African American religious music is an intricate web of the variables—musical, cultural, social, political, economic, racial, and religious—that ultimately impact the resultant product at virtually every level of its development.

NOTES

1. *Saturday Night, Sunday Morning* 1992.
2. Harris 1992, 148–150; *Say Amen, Somebody* 1984 (1982).
3. Fong-Torres 1969.
4. "The Edwin Hawkins Singers: 'Oh Happy Day'" 1969, 67.
5. Fong-Torres 1969.
6. Dorsey 1973, 194.
7. Fong-Torres 1969.
8. Ibid.
9. Ibid.
10. "The Edwin Hawkins Singers: 'Oh Happy Day'" 1969, 67.
11. "Top Gospel Albums" 1994, 246.
12. Franklin and Ritz 1999, 152.
13. Ibid., 123.
14. Borzillo 1995, 23.
15. Collins 1994, 27; Franklin with Black 1998, 154.
16. Collins 1994, 27.
17. "Top Contemporary Christian Chart" 1995, 40.
18. Borzillo 1995, 23.
19. Ibid.
20. Interview by the author with Roger Holmes, manager of Richard Smallwood, 1993.
21. Jones 1995, 65.
22. "The Gospel According to . . ." 1972, 9.
23. Fong-Torres 1969, 12.
24. Ibid.
25. Maultsby 1992, 21.
26. Jones 1995, 144.
27. Ibid., 66.
28. Collins 1994, 27.
29. Boyer 1992c; *Say Amen, Somebody* 1984 (1982).
30. Caesar 1998, 118.
31. Borzillo 1995, 22–23.
32. "The Gospel According to . . ." 1972, 9.
33. Jones 1995, 144.
34. *African American Heritage Hymnal* 2001.
35. Martin and Morris 1970.
36. See Boyer 1992a; Reagon 1992a.
37. Dorsey 1973, 194.
38. Cusic 1990, 217.
39. Garofalo 1995, 281.

40. Cusic 1990, 229.
41. Ibid., 220.
42. Ibid., 215.
43. Darden 1994, 35.
44. Cusic 1990, 216.
45. Reagon 1992b, 333.
46. Ibid.
47. Cusic 1990, 218.
48. Franklin, with Black 1998, 153–155.
49. Interview by the author with Albertina Walker, 1994.
50. "Bostic Urges Gospel Folk to Be Militant" 1975, 1.
51. Goreau 1975, 178.
52. Ibid., 229.
53. Wolff et al. 1995.
54. Jones 1995, 66.
55. This is a common saying in African American religious contexts.

DISCOGRAPHY

The Edwin Hawkins Singers. *Let Us Go into the House of the Lord*. BMG Direct 75517-4951-2, 1996. CD.
Franklin, Aretha. *Amazing Grace* (with James Cleveland and the Southern California Community Choir). Atlantic 2-906-2, 1972.
Franklin, Kirk. *Kirk Franklin and the Family*. BMG/Sony Music Entertainment, 371626, 2001. CD.
Kirk Franklin and the Family. *Whatcha Lookin' 4*. Sony Music, 87194, 2011. CD.

CHAPTER 6

Industrializing African American Popular Music

Reebee Garofalo

It is, by now, common knowledge that African Americans have provided the most significant cultural inputs in the development of American music. African Americans have created, innovated, performed, and otherwise participated in the process of music-making since the United States was a colony. Their cultural contributions have been historically undervalued and/or assigned to others less deserving, and they have had to overcome systematic discrimination within the music industry itself. Still the music remains as vital and pathbreaking as ever.

RACISM AND THE MAKING OF THE MUSIC BUSINESS

The modern music industry resulted from the gradual convergence of two quite separate nineteenth-century enterprises: the fledgling recording industry, initially devoted to spoken word applications such as stenography and books for the blind, and the music publishing business, dedicated to the sale of sheet music, initially the major source of music-related revenue. African Americans were short-shrifted by both.

In the 1880s, music publishers began to centralize in an area of New York City dubbed Tin Pan Alley, initially without any African American firms among them. Tin Pan Alley dominated music publishing until the end of World War II. While these publishers had a keen ear for music and were never above borrowing from the music of African Americans when it suited their purposes, it was something of a breakthrough when White music publisher John Stillwell Stark entered into a publishing deal with composer Scott Joplin, the "King of Ragtime," at the turn of the century. Joplin's popular rags went on to sell hundreds of thousands of copies. The success of the Joplin–Stark partnership draws attention not only to the quality of Joplin's music, but also to a bias inherent in the copyright laws that militated against certain forms of African American music.

Ragtime developed alongside other forms of African American music such as jazz and the blues, which were improvisational in nature: derived more from the oral tradition of African music than the notated (written) tradition of European music. Because US copyright laws were framed in terms of melody, chord patterns, and lyrics—clearly elements of a written tradition—it was more difficult for certain forms of African American music to be defined and defended as intellectual property.

Accordingly, African Americans were poorly represented in the music publishing business. The American Society of Composers, Authors, and Publishers (ASCAP), founded in 1914 to reap the fruits of copyright, generally skewed its membership toward composers of pop tunes and semi-serious works. Of the society's 170 charter members, six were Black: Harry Burleigh, Will Marion Cook, J. Rosamond and James Weldon Johnson, Cecil Mack, and Will Tyers.[1] While other "literate" Black writers and composers (e.g., W. C. Handy, Duke Ellington) were able to gain entrance to ASCAP, the vast majority of "untutored" Black artists were excluded from the society and thereby denied the full benefits of copyright protection.

Were it not for segregation, the recording industry might have followed a different trajectory. While sound recording was developed primarily by Americans of European descent, the humor, folklore, and cultural values of many ethnic groups were introduced to each other and to the mainstream through the medium of recording. Indeed, nearly forty African American artists ranging from New Orleans minstrel Louis "Bebe" Vasnier and touring vaudevillians Cousins and DeMoss to James Reese Europe's Syncopated Society orchestra and a number of notable quartets, representing genres from blues, jazz, and ragtime to cabaret and classical, have been recently identified as having recorded during the formative years (1890–1919) of sound recording.[2] Yet relatively few of these recordings have found their way into the histories of African American music. Even after it became clear that the future of recording would be tied to music, talent scouts seldom sought out African Americans to record, and those who did record were seldom promoted, until the 1920s. While sheet music sales of Scott Joplin's "Maple Leaf Rag" dwarfed the sales of most early recordings, Joplin never made a live recording. Even "coon" songs derived from minstrelsy, a staple of early commercial recording, were almost invariably sung by Whites until World War I. Notable exceptions included George Washington Johnson, who had major hits with "The Whistling Coon" and "The Laughing Song," and Bert Williams, the extraordinary Black vaudevillian.

When a "blues" craze swept the country in the 1910s, African American composers such as the "Father of the Blues" W. C. Handy ("Memphis Blues") and Arthur Seals ("Baby Seals' Blues") joined the ranks of professional songwriters. Still, most of the blues compositions of the era were recorded by Whites singing in "Negro dialect." With the advent of recorded jazz in the late teens, patterns of segregation continued to shape public perceptions of African American music history. In 1917, when Victor decided to take a chance on "jass," the first band they recorded was the all-White Original Dixieland Jazz Band. Although ODJB was heavily influenced by the King Oliver Band (which included Louis Armstrong), the Oliver ensemble itself didn't record until 1923 (in part because some African American artists felt it enabled competitors to steal their licks more easily).[3]

The first major popular music ensemble of color to land a recording contract was James Reese Europe's Syncopated Society Orchestra, signed by Victor in 1914 to record a series of dance tunes for the unconventional White dance team of Vernon and Irene

Castle. Europe was a talented and highly trained composer who could hold his own with any writers and arrangers of the era. He also had a talent for organization; his Clef Club and later Tempo Club organizations, which assembled bands for hire, as well as the Black and Puerto Rican 369th Infantry Regiment Hell Fighters Band that he organized for the US Army with his partner Noble Sissle, proved to be quite successful. Particularly through the dances popularized by the Castles, such as the Fox Trot and the Turkey Trot, Europe introduced syncopated dance music to the mainstream audience.

It wasn't until 1920, and quite by accident, that the recording industry began to take recording African Americans seriously. When an OKeh session featuring Sophie Tucker was canceled, the enterprising Black producer/songwriter Perry Bradford convinced the record company to allow him to record a Black contralto named Mamie Smith. Her

Figure 6.1
"Race" record advertisement for Bessie Smith's "Hateful Blues," July 19, 1924.

recording of Bradford's "Crazy Blues" went on to sell 7,500 copies a week and opened up a new market for African American music. Ralph Peer, the OKeh recording director who assisted at the sessions, dubbed these records "race records," and it remained the designation for Black music, by Black artists, intended for a Black audience, until 1949. Smith's overwhelming success ushered in a decade of classic blues recordings by African American women: Ida Cox, Chippie Hill, Sarah Martin, Clara Smith, Trixie Smith, Victoria Spivey, Sippie Wallace, and, the most famous of all, Bessie Smith, "Empress of the Blues" (see Figures 6.1 and 6.2).

The initial success of the "race market" encouraged the formation of a handful of Black-owned independent labels, including Sunshine in Los Angeles and Meritt in Kansas

Figure 6.2
Advertisement for Black Swan Records.

City. Harry Pace, W. C. Handy's publishing partner, started Black Swan in 1921. Mayo "Ink" Williams, head of Paramount's race series, founded Black Patti in 1927. These companies were beset with financial problems right from the start. Not a single Black-owned label survived the 1920s intact. With the onset of the depression, they were either bought up by the major companies or forced into bankruptcy, as the race market was slowly taken over by Victor, Paramount, and Columbia; the latter absorbed OKeh in 1926.[4]

As the demand for classic blues grew, record companies discovered that there was also a considerable demand for country blues, particularly among southern Blacks. In 1924, the year Paramount acquired the Black Swan catalog, the label released recordings by Papa Charlie Jackson, Arthur "Blind" Blake, and Blind Lemon Jefferson, perhaps the most popular country blues singer of that decade. Big Bill Broonzy dominated the thirties. Throughout the twenties and early thirties, a number of companies, including OKeh, Columbia, and Victor, engaged in extensive "field" recordings. Together with John and Alan Lomax and the efforts of the Library of Congress, they became the folklorists of grassroots American culture. As a result, dozens of country blues artists—among them, Furry Lewis, Blind Willie McTell, "Mississippi" John Hurt, Son House, Charlie Patton, Huddie "Leadbelly" Ledbetter, and Robert Johnson, later immortalized as the King of the Delta Blues Singers—received wider public attention.[5]

Record companies expanded into the African American market at precisely the moment when another technological development—the birth of commercial broadcasting—threatened the very survival of the recording industry. Commercial radio, which offered free live music with better fidelity than records, decimated record sales. As a result record sales plummeted from an all-time high of $106 million in 1921 to an all-time low of $6 million in 1933, at the height of the Great Depression. While African American artists made some inroads into the recording industry as record companies went into decline, radio excluded them almost completely.

The broadcasters generally subscribed to prevailing social divisions in their programming, and, during the Depression, they could defend their choices on the basis of economic self-interest. In 1934, only 14.4 percent of Black families owned a radio.[6] If a public dissemination channel existed for so-called race music, it was the jukebox. During the Depression, new and improved jukeboxes became ubiquitous in all manner of eating and drinking establishments. In the 1930s, stocking jukeboxes accounted for as much as half of all record sales. The estimates of the number of these coin-operated machines in operation at the time range in the hundreds of thousands. It is likely that race records first came to the attention of most listeners in the "juke joints" frequented primarily by Black patrons. For those who owned a record player, repeated jukebox plays might encourage them to purchase a new record.

Jukebox operators took seriously the task of policing the moral content of their machines. This being the swing era, distinctions were made between songs with "fast" tempos and those with "fast" lyrics. No less a figure than David Rockola, owner of Rock-Ola jukebox brand, distinguished between "hot" records and "rot" records. While it was admitted that stocking the latest "hot-stuff records" might increase short-term profits, it was clear that this was not an appropriate strategy for the mainstream public. Operators were advised to "[k]eep records of this type in the places where they belong."[7] While race was seldom mentioned explicitly, it is not difficult to imagine this presupposition lurking just beneath the surface of such statements.

These patterns of racial segregation tended to obscure the origins of musical developments such as jazz, and Tin Pan Alley did little to correct the errors. To the average listener in the 1920s and 1930s, then, jazz was the product of White society dance bands, George Gershwin and Irving Berlin were early pioneers, and Paul Whiteman was its King. While such assumptions are generally acknowledged as erroneous now, at the time only a few African American bands managed to break through to the mainstream market via radio. Among the best known, Edward Kennedy "Duke" Ellington's band became famous through their live broadcasts from the Cotton Club in Harlem. William Allen "Count" Basie injected jazz with a heavy dose of the blues from the Reno Club in Kansas City. The Ellington and Basie bands not only recorded for major labels, they were among the few African American ensembles, along with those of Louis Armstrong and Fats Waller, that could be heard on radio in the 1920s and 1930s.

There were also tensions between radio and the Tin Pan Alley publishers, primarily over royalty rates. When ASCAP insisted on raising fees, in 1939 the National Association of Broadcasters (NAB), representing some six hundred radio stations, boycotted ASCAP and formed their own performing rights organization, Broadcast Music Incorporated (BMI). Because ASCAP represented the Broadway–Hollywood axis of popular music, the boycott drove BMI to the grassroots for its membership. This move signaled a new era in Black popular music in the sense that ASCAP, and its considerable influence in shaping public taste, was challenged publicly for the first time, creating a cultural space for rhythm and blues artists like Arthur "Big Boy" Crudup, Roy Brown, Ivory Joe Hunter, Fats Domino, and Wynonie Harris.[8]

The success of these artists in the late 1940s speaks to what critic Nelson George has referred to as "an aesthetic schism between high-brow, more assimilated black styles and working-class, grassroots sounds."[9] During this period, the most notable African American acts had been the more pop-sounding artists like Nat "King" Cole, Ella Fitzgerald, the Mills Brothers, and the Ink Spots, all of whom recorded for major labels. These companies failed to appreciate the appeal of rhythm and blues in working-class Black communities.

With more pronounced rhythm and a much smaller horn section, rhythm and blues followed from the demise of the big bands after World War II. Louis Jordan and the Tympani Five anticipated this transition and helped to define the instrumentation for the R&B combos which followed. Jordan's material was composed and arranged, but selections like "Saturday Night Fish Fry" (1949), "Honey Chile" (1944), and "Ain't Nobody Here But Us Chickens" (1946) evoked blues images not found in most Black pop of the day. The percussive quality and up-tempo styles of such artists as Wynonie Harris, John Lee Hooker, saxophonist Big Jay McNeely, and pianist Amos Milburn deviated significantly from the smooth and melodic sound of mainstream Black pop.

Since R&B did not readily lend itself to the production styles of the major labels (with the exception of Decca Records), the majors ignored the relatively smaller R&B market. This situation, as well as the availability of independent pressing plants, made it possible for a large number of independent labels to enter the business. By 1949 hundreds of new labels came into existence. Most important among these were Atlantic in New York; Savoy in Newark; King in Cincinnati; Chess in Chicago; Peacock in Houston; and Modern, Imperial, and Specialty in Los Angeles. While most of these labels specialized in rhythm and blues, only Don Robey's Peacock company was Black-owned. The White label heads, as well as Robey, were a combination of genuine enthusiasts, unethical opportunists, and hard-nosed businessmen who were savvy enough to see a hole in the market. Often distributing records out of the trunks of their cars (or via the national independent distribution network set up by Jack Gutshall in 1945), these entrepreneurs stocked the still-segregated jukeboxes that made hits and serviced the independent radio stations that would carry the music farther and wider.[10]

R&B RIDES THE RADIO WAVES

Independent radio brought rhythm and blues to a national audience. Prior to 1948, radio had been dominated by four national networks that tended to favor White middle-class, family-oriented programming that was largely the same from network to network. But the growth of television devastated network radio, and national programming gave way to hundreds of locally programmed stations, each appealing to its own audience. The flawless, even-toned, accent-free "radio voice" of the typical announcer was soon challenged by eccentric, fast-talking DJs—"personality jocks," as they were called—who had no trouble incorporating their own personality quirks, regional accents, and cultural preferences into their shows. These DJs forged a personal relationship with their listeners. "We were the stars in our hometown," said DJ Diggie Doo. "We went to the churches, we went to the clubs, to the schools, the little kids knew us."[11] In most cases, the key to their success was R&B.

At first, the South was the major center for R&B radio. There were pioneer Black R&B DJs as well as popular White R&B DJs who modeled themselves after these "preacher-emcees."[12] By the early 1950s, a number of so-called Negro stations in the South had proven to be quite successful. In St. Louis, Spider Burks broadcast to the city's large African American population over station KXLW. WOKJ in Jackson, Mississippi, reached over one hundred thousand Black listeners. WDIA in Memphis, "America's only 50,000 watt Negro radio station," could broadcast to nearly 10 percent of the country's twelve million African Americans. WSOK in Nashville claimed to have several Black stockholders. And, in 1951, WERD in Atlanta became the first totally Black-owned radio station in the country.[13]

R&B radio—with both Black and White DJs—soon flourished nationwide and proved to be popular with White as well as Black audiences.[14] The new cross-racial appetite for R&B was soon reflected in record sales. As early as 1952, Dolphin's Hollywood Record Shop, a Black retail outlet in Los Angeles, reported that its business was suddenly 40 percent White. The outlet's owners attributed it to independent DJs spinning R&B records. A similar pattern was developing at Mallory's Music in New Orleans and elsewhere. It signaled a change in popular music tastes that made artists such as Fats Domino, Jackie Brenston, Lloyd Price, and Joe Turner—all of whom recorded for independent labels and were promoted on independent radio—popular among both Black and White audiences.

ROCK 'N' ROLL TRANSFORMS THE MUSIC INDUSTRY

Rock 'n' roll turned the structure of the music business upside down. It brought writers and performing artists from rural grassroots and urban street corner cultures into the mainstream; it enabled small independent record labels to compete successfully with major companies; and it paved the way for eccentric DJs to become important taste makers. Because most of its formative influences as well as virtually all of its early innovators were African American, rock 'n' roll encouraged a tilt toward African American sensibilities and working-class styles. As such, it challenged the existing canons of cultural value and public taste. It upended, however momentarily, the separation of races (and classes) that had guided not just the operations of the music industry but the dynamics of all social interaction.

The powers that be responded with a number of strategies. Major labels engaged in a certain amount of talent buying, and began issuing "cover" records (pop versions of original R&B and rock 'n' roll recordings), which, owing to the superior distribution channels of the majors, often outsold the originals. Because DJs were considered largely responsible for the crossover of Black music into the pop market, ASCAP orchestrated a series of government investigations targeting questionable DJ practices, which culminated in the "payola" hearings at the end of the decade. Payola—the practice of offering financial, sexual, or other personal inducements for record play—was hardly a newcomer to the music business. Song plugging, as the practice was called earlier in the century, had been the lynchpin of industry marketing since the heyday of Tin Pan Alley. In the 1950s, however, the focus on payments to DJs became the operative strategy for neutralizing rock 'n' roll. DJs such as Alan Freed became the main casualties of these hearings, which ended up with little to show in the way of wrong-doing, but which regulated radio by inserting music and program directors and playlists to limit the autonomy of DJs.

Alan Freed had been a controversial figure in the music business since he started spinning R&B in Cleveland in 1951. He had played a major role in popularizing the music among White teenagers, and he had continued to push original Black recordings during the cover-record period. Throughout his career he promoted his interracial "Caravan of Stars" tours to the delight of his young interracial audience. For such "infractions" Freed paid dearly. By the time the payola hearings had taken off, he had been fired successively from his DJ slots at WINS and WABC in New York, where he continued to push R&B, as well as from WNEW-TV, where he had begun hosting his own TV show. After his 1960 arrest for accepting $30,000 in payola and his 1964 indictment for income tax evasion, he died of uremia, drunk and penniless.

THE MUSIC INDUSTRY AND THE CIVIL RIGHTS MOVEMENT

While the payola hearings threatened to slow the advances that African American artists had made, the burgeoning Civil Rights Movement provided a countervailing force. During this period, Black artists dominated a series of dance crazes; R&B producers emerged as artists in their own right; Black female vocal harmony groups, known collectively with their White counterparts as the "girl groups," emerged as a trend in mainstream popular music for the first time; and the most successful Black-owned record label ever was founded—Motown. There can be no doubt that in the early 1960s the Civil Rights Movement provided a climate that encouraged these and other developments.

Chubby Checker ushered in the decade with "The Twist," which hit #1 on the pop charts twice, once in 1960 and then again in 1962. The Twist craze was powerful enough to force other African American artists like Sam Cooke, Gary "US" Bonds, Ray Charles, and the Isley Brothers to get on the bandwagon. Checker himself followed up with "The Hucklebuck" (1960), "Pony Time" (1961), "The Fly" (1961), and "Limbo Rock" (1962). Relative unknowns Little Eva and Dee Dee Sharp had hits with two Twist spin-offs, "The Loco-Motion" (1962) and "Mashed Potato Time" (1962), respectively. The place where most fans learned to perform these dances was *American Bandstand*, a Philadelphia-based televised dance party hosted by Dick Clark that was picked up for national distribution by ABC in 1957. While *Bandstand* has been criticized for catering to White teenagers from Philadelphia, it was also a major showcase for Black talent. As Clark has pointed out, "over two-thirds of the people who've been initiated into the Rock and Roll Hall of Fame had their television debuts on *American Bandstand*."[15]

Producers like Luther Dixon, Phil Spector, and Berry Gordy drew on the pioneering work of Lieber and Stoller with the Drifters to create what Charlie Gillett called "uptown rhythm & blues," a precursor of soul.[16] Although Spector and Lieber and Stoller were White, they were immersed in African American (and Latino) culture and helped pioneer the R&B-based rock 'n' roll sound of the early 1960s. As a result Black female vocal groups like the Shirelles and the Crystals conquered the pop charts as never before. In 1959, Berry Gordy applied his business acumen to launch Motown, which soon became the largest Black-owned corporation in the United States. As CEO, Gordy addressed all aspects of career development for Motown's artists. As a producer, he had an uncanny ability to incorporate White audience tastes without abandoning a Black sound. In some ways this process mirrored principles then at the heart of the evolving Civil Rights Movement.

From the end of 1963 until the beginning of 1965, in the name of integration, *Billboard* discontinued its R&B charts, which had included mainly African American artists. The net effect, however, was that the number of African American artists on the pop charts actually declined. Only three of the top fifty albums for the years 1964 and 1965 were by Black artists. Accordingly, the R&B charts were reinstated by the magazine, and in 1969, R&B was replaced with the term "soul." In addition to a reduction in the number of African American artists appearing in the mainstream market, there were also a number of White artists performing Black-sounding music that was written by Whites, produced by Whites, performed by Whites, and accepted by Blacks. From 1964 to 1968, artists such as the Righteous Brothers, the Young Rascals, and Mitch Ryder and the Detroit Wheels all performed a brand of rhythm and blues that earned its own marketing category—"blue-eyed soul."

During this period, civil rights themes were evident in the music of Sam Cooke and Curtis Mayfield. James Brown and Aretha Franklin intensified the sound, capturing an emerging new spirit and, later, the call for Black pride. As the early Civil Rights Movement gave way to the more radical demand for Black Power, it was accompanied by a resurgence of grassroots rhythm and blues from the Deep South, most notably from Stax in Memphis and Fame in Muscle Shoals.[17] The new militancy was also reflected in changes in the structure of the music industry itself. In 1965, a "new breed" of Black industry personnel, led by DJ Del Shields and manager/deal-maker Clarence Avant (the man who engineered the sale of Stax to Gulf and Western), took over the leadership of the National Association of Radio Announcers (NARA) and changed its acronym to NATRA to include television as well. NARA had been born in the mid-fifties as an outgrowth of a social network of Black DJs. Shields and Avant introduced a political agenda aimed at enhancing the professional stature of Black broadcast personnel that included the creation of a NATRA School of Broadcast Science. For a time it appeared as though NATRA could be built into a viable organizational and political force, but then support turned to hostility. Whether they were perceived as too ambitious or too militant or both, the NATRA leadership was soon subjected to various forms of harassment, including government surveillance, wiretaps, and physical violence. By the end of the decade, Shields and Avant had edged out of the organization, leaving its initiatives in disarray, and Black announcers were left with one less organizational platform for advocacy and professional development.

Aside from the tumultuousness of the period, a further structural limitation on Black music had to do with format. Black music was built around the hit single, at a time when rock was incorporating extended compositions, psychedelic influences, and concept albums. A whole new radio medium—FM rock radio—opened up to accommodate these new sounds. By the early 1970s, about 80 percent of the sales dollar was in albums, and album-oriented rockers with more access to the new medium were much more likely to reap the benefits. Only a few Black artists found a ready home on FM rock radio precisely because of its orientation toward album cuts and psychedelic sounds. There were two Black-led, mixed bands in the late sixties—Sly and the Family Stone and the Jimi Hendrix Experience—who incorporated "psychedelic" sounds into their music, refusing to be limited to musical styles traditionally associated with African American culture. Hendrix's following was virtually all White throughout his career, creating a soundscape that set the stage for the further evolution of rock. But to the extent that hit singles did not translate into album sales, many Black musicians were marginalized financially for reasons that had nothing to do with the quality of their music.

BUYING (INTO) SOUL MUSIC

By the early 1970s, social forces ranging from outright repression to sheer exhaustion had begun to take a toll on the militancy of the previous decade. If there was a dominant Black sound that reflected the "quieter" mood of the early 1970s, it was Philadelphia soft soul pioneered by the writer–producer team of Kenny Gamble and Leon Huff, and producer-arranger Thom Bell, who joined forces with Sigma Sound Studios and collaborated in the tripartite administration of Mighty Three Music, their publishing arm. They hit their stride in 1971, with the formation of Philadelphia International Records (PIR) and a distribution deal with CBS. This latter point is pivotal, because this was a moment when things had calmed down enough that the major labels felt it was time to make some inroads into soul music.

In 1972, Columbia Records commissioned the Harvard Business School to undertake a study of the soul music market. Among the recommendations of the obscure but influential report—known in the industry simply as "The Harvard Report"—were the expansion of "custom label activity" with soul music providers, the development of internal soul music production, and the establishment of a "semi-autonomous" in-house soul music division. It was during this period that most of the major labels set up or consolidated Black music divisions and/or made deals with successful R&B indies, and Columbia acted accordingly. With Atlantic already owned by Warner, Stax having been recently acquired by Gulf and Western, and Motown remaining fiercely independent, a distribution deal with Philadelphia International Records appeared very attractive to Columbia at the time; soft soul had set the standard in Black popular music for the first half of the seventies and it anticipated one strand of the disco craze that was about to erupt. The

Harvard Report prompted new opportunities for Black artists to jump ship and sign with major labels; it also made numerous recommendations to fund Black business and create internal staff positions in places where previously there had been none, as the majors sought to institutionalize the process of crossing over. With some notable successes—PIR certainly comes to mind—the majors ignored or mishandled these recommendations more often than not.

One of the many recommendations that Columbia did not follow was to use its clout to enhance the distribution of the syndicated television dance party *Soul Train*. The brainchild of writer, producer, and host Don Cornelius, *Soul Train* debuted in 1970 as a local, five days a week, Black variation of *American Bandstand* on Chicago's WCIU. One year later it went into national syndication out of Los Angeles on Saturday mornings. *Soul Train* followed the time-tested formula of live dancing that made *American Bandstand* a must watch telecast and quickly attracted the top names in R&B. Jerry Butler, the Chi-Lites, and the Emotions appeared on the very first show. Over the years the program featured everyone from James Brown, Aretha Franklin, and Michael Jackson to Barry White, the Sylvers, Cheryl Lynn, and LL Cool J.

Soul Train went on to spin off award shows and specials, and as of 2005, having become the longest running show in first-run syndication, it could still boast 1.25 million viewers in 105 markets and a list of marquee advertisers that included Coca-Cola, the Gap, General Motors, McDonald's, and Hershey Foods.[18] After thirty-five years, the *Soul Train* archives have become a veritable treasure trove of African American cultural history. Don Cornelius once said, "Almost all of what I learned about mounting and hosting a dance show I learned from Dick Clark." His statement may have been too modest. Comparing the two shows early on, a *New York Times* reviewer opined that *Soul Train* was to *American Bandstand* as "Champagne is to seltzer water."[19]

PROMOTING BLACK MUSIC IN THE DISCO ERA

If *Soul Train* had put contemporary African American dance styles on display for all to see, there was also an underground party culture in the early 1970s that was quite hidden from mainstream view—until it erupted full-blown as disco. Disco began in Black, Latino, and gay all-night clubs in New York and San Francisco. At first, it was simply a nightclub DJ-created sequence of existing dance musics—primarily Motown, Philadelphia soft soul, and funk—rather than a genre unto itself. As the sound began to evolve, its influences came from far and wide. As Barbara Graustark reported in *Newsweek*:

> From Latin music, it takes its percolating percussion, its sensuous, throbbing rhythms; from the '60s "funk" music of James Brown and Sly Stone, it borrows a kicky bass-guitar line; from Afro-Cuban music, it repeats simple lyric lines like voodoo chants; and like early rock 'n' roll, it exploits the honking saxophones of black rhythm and blues.[20]

Although as many disco acts were signed to major labels as to independents, the majors often contracted with the indies for distribution. It was independent labels like TK Records (home to the Black, White, and Latino powerhouse KC and the Sunshine Band), SalSoul (which attempted to marry salsa and soul), and Casablanca (home to disco queen Donna Summer) that promoted the music and provided most of its innovations. And if disco was sparsely promoted by the majors, it was systematically ignored by radio (Frankie

Crocker on New York's WBLS being a notable exception). As a result, disco established itself as its own sub-industry, receiving its primary exposure in clubs, popularized only by the creative genius of club DJs. Because they were shunned by the record companies, disco DJs organized into distribution networks called "record pools," and in so doing, developed an alternative to the airplay marketing structure of the industry, which had failed to recognize disco's economic potential. Their efforts also created a new market for 12-inch singles and remixed releases, which thrives to this day.

More than an underground party culture, disco's fanatical following turned out to be a significant record-buying public. By the mid-1970s, the pop charts were bursting with disco acts—the Sylvers, Johnny Taylor, KC and the Sunshine Band, the Emotions, Thelma Houston, Rose Royce, Taste of Honey, Yvonne Elliman, Chic, and, of course, Donna Summer—most of whom were Black or integrated acts. Still, it was a White Australian group, the Bee Gees, who made disco safe for mainstream America.

Following the overwhelming popularity of the *Saturday Night Fever* (1977) film and Bee Gees soundtrack, radio (including Black radio) could no longer ignore the disco phenomenon. WKTU, an obscure "soft rock" station in New York, pointed the way when it converted to an all-disco format in 1978 and became the most listened-to station in the country. By 1979, two hundred stations broadcasting in almost every major market had converted to disco. Syndicated television programs like "Disco Magic" and "Dance Fever" brought the dance craze to the heartland. Some thirty-six million adults thrilled to the musical mixes of eight thousand professional DJs who serviced a portion of the estimated twenty thousand disco clubs. The phenomenon spawned a sub-industry whose annual revenues ranged from $4 billion to $8 billion.

As disco's 120-beats-per-minute formula became ubiquitous, there was an inevitable backlash. Egged on by rock radio DJs, the most vocal mouthpieces for an industry whose central focus had long been rock, the slogans that accompanied disco's collapse—like "death to disco" and "disco sucks"—sounded as much like racial epithets as statements of musical preference. In the early 1980s, rock radio reasserted its primacy (and its avoidance of African American artists) with a vengeance. Black-oriented radio, which had been reluctantly pulled into the disco orbit by its club success, was now forced to move in the direction of yet another new format—Urban Contemporary—in order to compete successfully with pop and rock stations. In the perennial struggle for ratings, the Urban Contemporary stations retained those Black artists in the soul, funk, and jazz idioms who were central to their playlists—for example, Stevie Wonder, Donna Summer, Rick James, Third World, Funkadelic, Quincy Jones, and George Benson—and added White acts, such as David Bowie or Hall and Oates, that fit an R&B format. Urban Contemporary was an interesting concept in that it was designed as a multiracial format. It was also quite successful, often surpassing rock stations in the ratings. Still, while Urban Contemporary succeeded in providing greater access to White musicians on what had been Black-oriented stations, rock radio, needless to say, did not provide any comparable access for Black artists.

INTO THE 1980S

Television had long been used to promote popular music. In the 1950s, *American Bandstand* provided national exposure for rock 'n' roll stars, Black and White, who also made regular appearances on family variety shows like *The Ed Sullivan Show*. In the 1960s, while shows like *Shindig* and *Hullabaloo* provided some exposure to Black artists, these shows tended to favor White rockers. The launching of MTV in 1981 brought acts of racial exclusion to new heights. With 85 percent of its mostly White suburban viewers falling between the ages of twelve and thirty-four, MTV promised to deliver the perfect consumers for a tight economy. MTV expanded from an initial 2.5 million subscribers to 17 million in 1983. That same year *People* magazine reported that "on MTV's current roster of some 800 acts, 16 are black."[21]

MTV executives defended their practices by claiming that few Black artists recorded the kind of rock 'n' roll that the channel's format required. Asked to explain their rejection of five Rick James videos at a time when *Street Songs* had sold almost four million copies, an MTV spokesperson told *People*: "We play rock and roll. We don't play Rick James because he's funk."[22] New music video outlets formed in reaction to MTV's restrictive programming policies. Black Entertainment Television (BET) and the long standing *Soul Train* provided the primary video exposure for Black talent in the early 1980s. Following a showdown with CBS over MTV's reluctance to air the videos for Michael Jackson's overwhelmingly popular *Thriller* LP (1982), during which CBS allegedly threatened to pull all its videos if MTV refused, the video channel relented and began relaxing its restrictions on programming Black artists. As major labels began making deals with rap indies in the late 1980s, which gave the music more exposure on pop radio outlets, MTV began programming rap around 1987. Although at first buried in a late-night weekend slot, *Yo! MTV Raps* soon moved to a daily afternoon slot and became one of the channel's most popular programs.

These restrictions of access to African American artists occurred during the first recession in the music business since the late 1940s. Recovery, beginning in 1983, was signaled by the multi-platinum, worldwide success of Michael Jackson's *Thriller*, with international sales of some forty million units making it the best-selling record in history at the time. *Thriller* began a trend toward blockbuster LPs featuring a limited number of superstar artists as the solution to the industry's economic woes. Interestingly, many of these superstars—Michael Jackson, Prince, Lionel Richie, Tina Turner, etc.—were African American.

The phenomenal pop successes of these artists immediately catapulted them into an upper-level industry infrastructure fully owned and operated by Whites. These artists were further distinguished from their less successful African American colleagues in that they were now marketed directly to the mainstream audience through the labels' pop divisions, a practice that proved to be phenomenally successful with Whitney Houston and, later, Mariah Carey. In this rarified atmosphere, African American artists were confronted with considerable pressure to sever their ties with the attorneys, managers, booking agents, and promoters who may have been responsible for building their careers in the first place. "Aside from Sammy Davis, Jr., Nancy Wilson, and Stephanie Mills," said Nelson George, there were "no other black household names with black management."[23]

In the early 1980s, record companies adopted a deliberate strategy of appealing to different demographics simultaneously. This strategy became a virtual science with the release of a number of well-calculated cross-racial duets. Releases by Stevie Wonder and Paul McCartney ("Ebony and Ivory," 1982), Michael Jackson and Paul McCartney ("The Girl Is Mine," 1982; "Say Say Say," 1983), Diana Ross and Julio Iglesias ("All of You," 1984), James Ingram and Kenny Rogers ("What about Me," 1984), Dionne Warwick and Friends ("That's What Friends Are For," 1985), Patti LaBelle and Michael McDonald ("On My Own," 1986), Aretha Franklin and George Michael ("I Knew You Were Waiting for Me," 1987), and James Ingram and Linda Ronstadt ("Somewhere Out There," 1987) brought new meaning to the term "crossover." These projects can be viewed optimistically as attempts to break down the segregation of the music industry or more cynically as commercial giants cashing in on each other's superstar audiences. Suggesting a higher purpose, Michael Jackson and Lionel Richie's "We Are the World" (1985)—the ultimate crossover recording—initiated the phenomenon of "charity rock," a string of all-star performances and mega-concerts that raised funds and consciousness for social causes.

HIP HOP, DON'T STOP

It remained for rap to take African American music back to the streets. Rap, one cultural element in the larger hip hop subculture, began in the South Bronx at about the same time as disco, but given its place of origin, the movement developed in almost complete isolation for more than five years. In the late 1970s, hip hop was "discovered," in turn, by the music business, the print media, and the film industry. Through films like the low budget *Wild Style* (1982) and the blockbuster *Flashdance* (1983), followed by *Breakin'* and *Beat Street* in 1984, hip hop was brought to the attention of a mass audience. During this period, critics regularly predicted the early death of rap, even as hip hop style set about influencing everything from ballet and modern dance, to fashion design and studio art, to pop, rock, funk, soul, and jazz.

Rap was nothing if not a window onto African American urban culture. To anyone who was listening, it was clear that much of rap spoke to positive themes. Amidst a penchant for controversy, however, rap was routinely taken to task for violence, anti-Semitism, and misogyny. As a result, Black radio avoided the music like the plague, ignoring cuts that were clearly outselling other selections on their playlists. Of the twenty-eight rap songs that reached *Billboard*'s Top Forty sales chart in the first forty-six weeks of 1988, only sixteen registered on the magazine's airplay chart. More than just a generation gap, the split between rap and other forms of Black popular music was also interpreted as an indicator of class divisions within the Black community. Bill Adler, publicist for Run-D.M.C., LL Cool J, and Public Enemy, among others, put it rather starkly:

> Black radio is run by "buppies" [Black urban professionals]. They've made a cultural commitment to a lifestyle that has nothing to do with music on the street. . . . This music very rudely pulls them back on the street corner, and they don't want to go.[24]

If the turmoil surrounding rap presented a problem for Black radio, major record companies moved to capitalize on its financial potential. In contracting Curtis Blow in 1979, Mercury was one of the few major labels to sign a rap artist directly, but buy-ins and distribution deals with small, independent rap labels—some of which, like Sugar Hill and Russell Simmons's Def Jam, were Black-owned—soon became commonplace. Columbia Records concluded a custom label deal with Def Jam in 1985. Jive Records worked with both RCA and Arista. In 1987, Cold Chillin' Records signed a distribution deal with Warner, who also bought a piece of Tommy Boy. Delicious Vinyl contracted national distribution with Island. Priority went with Capitol.[25] The majors were smart enough to leave rap's creative functions in the hands of the independents, offering them increased opportunities for distribution to mainstream outlets and greater exposure in the pop market.

Rap achieved a benchmark of mainstream acceptance when the National Academy of Recording Arts and Sciences (NARAS) added a rap category to the Grammy Awards in 1988. On March 11, 1989, *Billboard*, unceremoniously and with no editorial comment, added a rap chart to its pages. Mainstream visibility propelled rap stars into other media as well. Following his receipt of the first rap Grammy in 1989, Will Smith (the Fresh Prince) was rewarded with a starring role in a prime time sitcom, *The Fresh Prince of Bel Air*. Beginning in the late 1980s, rappers also began to show up on other African American TV shows like *A Different World* (Tupac Shakur), *Cosby* (Mos Def), and *In Living Color* (Heavy D and Biz Markie). Queen Latifah landed a starring role in her own television sitcom, *Living Single*. It was in film, however, that rap made some of its most powerful statements. Following Spike Lee's *Do the Right Thing* (1989), powered by the hip hop force of Public Enemy's "Fight the Power," there appeared a rash of Black-directed films about life in the "hood": *Straight Outta Brooklyn* (1991), *Juice*, *New Jack City* (1992) and *Boyz N the Hood* (1991), the latter two of which starred Ice-T and Ice Cube respectively, and featured their music as well. Will Smith moved on to a significant film career, with starring roles in Hollywood blockbusters like *Independence Day* and *Men in Black*.

The 1990s was also a period which showcased the creative talents and business acumen of African American producers, with Quincy Jones, Nile Rogers, Narada Michael Walden, Jimmy Jam, and Terry Lewis paving the way for Teddy Riley and Antonio "L.A." Reid and Kenneth "Babyface" Edmunds, all of whom found cultural and financial success in the mainstream market. If hip hop aesthetics had made significant impact on US popular culture, African American artists and executives were also finding themselves more at home in corporate boardrooms.

R&B/HIP HOP AND CORPORATE CULTURE

By the 1990s, the music industry had become fully implicated in the global economic system, creating a formidable marketing apparatus that demanded superstardom to pay for itself. Mariah Carey was its poster child. She started the decade with five #1 hits in a row and turned out fourteen #1 singles from 1990 to 1999, toting up sales of 105 million units as the new millennium began. Carey may have been the embodiment of the industry's superstar strategy, but the strategy itself had never been a viable model for long-term sustainable growth. After shelling out record sums for contract renewals for a handful of other superstar artists, such as Michael Jackson, R.E.M., and Madonna, who failed to deliver, the majors should not have been surprised when, after a decade or so of double-digit annual growth, sales figures for 1996 ran flat. Four of the six major labels[26] underwent significant staff cuts, with Black executives fearing the worst, as Capitol Records responded to the downturn by eliminating its Black music division. Warner soon followed suit by restructuring its Black music division and redirecting the promotion of all its artists to a single marketing department.[27]

While it is tempting to read these developments as a major label attempt to treat all its artists equally, the more common interpretation is that it was a transfer of power from

Black to White personnel. This was particularly ironic in that during this period, hip hop aesthetics had come to dominate most other styles of popular music from dance and R&B to rock and teen pop, thereby contributing measurably to the industry's return to profitability. Nowhere was the appeal of hip hop more apparent than in the success of a handful of Black-owned independents in the latter half of the decade. Artist/entrepreneurs such as Sean "Puffy" Combs and Master P built Bad Boy Entertainment and No Limit Records, respectively, into diversified business empires that generated upwards of $50 million each in a single year. After co-founding Roc-A-Fella Records and building it into a similarly diversified empire, Jay Z ascended to the presidency of Def Jam.

Just as the music industry was regaining its lost momentum, posting $38.5 billion in worldwide sales for 1999, it was hit by the double-whammy of digital downloading and the devastating after-effects of 9/11. From 2000 to 2003, the music business experienced a 25 percent loss of revenue. This period was also accompanied by another round of mega-mergers, which included severe cutbacks in artist rosters and staff positions. While no one group was spared, Black executives certainly felt the pinch. In 2001 BMG dismantled its Black music division, and by 2004, with the merger of Sony and BMG, the Big Six of the mid-1990s had become the Big Four. As *Billboard* reported in a retrospective article on Black executives: "These changes left a sizable number of talented mid-level and higher promotion, marketing, A&R and distribution executives on the street."[28]

Again there was a certain irony to the fate of Black music personnel, as the music had never performed better, culturally or economically. On October 11, 2003, *Billboard* reported that, for the first time in the magazine's history, all ten of the top ten Hot 100 pop hits in the country were by Black artists, nine of them rappers, with Beyoncé at #1 with "Baby Boy." Black dominance during this period was no fluke; it was a long-term trend. In 2004, every single recording to reach #1 on the Hot 100 was by a Black artist. And in 2005, according to *Billboard*, rap and R&B/hip hop accounted for nearly 25 percent of all album sales.

Even with all the downsizing of Black personnel, this level of Black music success was sufficiently troubling to many in the industry that, in 2005, *Billboard* initiated a new singles chart—the Pop 100—along side its perennial Hot 100, which had been the publication's primary singles chart since 1958. While the Pop 100 appeared to be a needless duplication of effort to most observers, its purpose was explained clearly by journalist and music librarian Bill Lamb:

> By the beginning of the new century, many fans and members of the music industry became concerned that the Hot 100 had become biased in favor of r&b and hip hop music. It was becoming more and more difficult for rock and mainstream pop songs to do well on the Hot 100.[29]

Simply put, the Pop 100 was designed to give White artists in pop, rock, and country a better chance to claim a #1 hit song. Notably, the strategy failed.

In 2006, for example, the top ten Hot 100 songs could be found within the first fourteen positions on the Pop 100. In 2007, the first four positions on both charts were interchangeable. In 2008, numbers one and two on both charts were the same and both were by Black artists—"Low" by Flo Rida (featuring T-Pain) and "Bleeding Love" by Leona Lewis. Indeed, all of the most popular entries on the Hot 100 in 2008 could also be found within the upper reaches of the Pop 100. Accordingly, in June 2009, *Billboard* eliminated the Pop 100 chart. It was clear that the importance of African American aesthetics for artists of all persuasions had simply become a fact of cultural life.

BLACK MUSIC ONLINE

In addition to the dominance of African American aesthetics and performance styles in US popular music, the other major development in the new millennium was the shift to an online, interactive, digital environment. This was a situation that augured well, relatively speaking, for African American sectors of the music business. The comprehensive Pew Internet and American Life project had established as early as 2000 that African Americans were more likely than Whites to listen to music online and to download music from the web.[30] And this was long before they had any kind of parity in web access. By 2010, according to Pew, the Internet population had begun to resemble the racial composition of the population as a whole. While African Americans were still less likely to own a desktop computer than Whites, both groups enjoyed equal levels of laptop ownership, and African Americans were more likely to use cell phones to access social networking sites such as Facebook, as well as to watch videos and listen to music.[31]

These trends were important because if there was one thing that all observers agreed on, it was that the future of music would be tied to online digital marketing and sales. This was a situation in which independent companies, where the majority of African Americans in music were likely to be concentrated, would be better positioned, both because they were more nimble and because their audiences tended to be younger and more tech savvy. In 2007, for example, EMI was the only major label to post a larger share of digital sales than physical ones, whereas every independent distributor reported higher earnings from digital sales than physical. Indeed, Forrester Research predicted that it would not be until 2011 that digital sales would overtake physical sales overall. To the extent that the major labels remained tethered to physical sales, they would not be able to take full advantage of what has been called the "long tail economy," the growing proportion of sales that exist beyond the top-selling products in a given field.[32]

In a digital world in which there are no manufacturing costs to speak of, no distribution costs, and no requirements for shelf space, recordings that a bricks and mortar record store couldn't even afford to stock could account for a greater proportion of profit than the ones they do stock. To give some idea of just how profitable the long tail economy can be, consider that, as early as 2004, Rhapsody streamed more songs outside of its top ten thousand than it did within its top ten thousand.[33] The picture that emerges is that of a bifurcated industry in which the entities composing the back end of the long tail could, in the aggregate, rival the major companies for market share. As *Wired* magazine noted, the future of music will be as much about "niches" as about "hits."[34]

Who are the entities that will manage the long tail? To be sure there will still be a place for major labels, blockbuster hits, superstar artists, and all the rest. In that rarified atmosphere, one will find a limited number of top-tier African American artists and executives such as power couple Jay Z and Beyoncé, and Antonio "L.A." Reid, Chairman and CEO of Epic Records. At the same time, because overall sales of recorded music have declined to less than half of what they were before the new millennium (even with digital sales added in), other aspects of music dissemination such as touring, merchandizing, sponsorships, and engaging social networks have become as important as CD sales.

Because a label deal is now only one of a number of options available to artists, management companies—indeed, artists themselves—have become as central to the task of career development as record companies once were.

The Internet has facilitated increased direct contact between artist and audience, creating the conditions under which functions like marketing, promotion, even sales, are more easily self-managed. Assisted by the Internet, artists who could sell between five and fifty thousand copies of a recording—precisely the middle tier of artists, who would never be stocked in a national record chain, which major labels have been pruning from their rosters—have a chance of achieving profitability. During its heyday, MySpace.com hosted sites for more than one million bands, many of which sold to consumers via online retailers like CD Baby.

MySpace has since been superseded in importance by more recent networks like Facebook and Twitter, just as Rhapsody has been overtaken by the more advanced algorithms of newer streaming services like Spotify, Pandora, Rdio, and the new Apple Music offering, resulting from Apple's 2015 purchase of Beats Music for $3 billion. These services hold out the possibility of a more level playing field, where African American artists are at least as likely to find success as anyone else. On the business end, Beats co-founder Dr. Dre reportedly boasted that the Beats acquisition turned him into the first hip hop billionaire. Not to be outdone, Jay Z has entered this arena by heading up the $56 million purchase of the high quality and apparently more artist friendly music service Tidal. While these examples hardly represent a solution for masses of struggling industry employees, they do suggest the top end of opportunities available to African American entrepreneurs in the digital economy. In the end, perhaps all those Black artists and executives who were downsized by the major labels in the name of profitability and economies of scale will have the last laugh by finding a comfortable and lucrative home in the long tail economy.

NOTES

1. Southern 1997, 353.
2. Brooks 2004.
3. Baraka 1966 (1963), 143–144.
4. Dixon and Godrich 1970.
5. Ibid.
6. MacDonald 1979.
7. Segrave 2002, 58.
8. Sanjek 1988.
9. George 1988, 10.
10. Shaw 1978.
11. *That Rhythm . . . Those Blues*, produced by George T. Nierenberg (Alexandria, VA: The American Experience Series, PBS Video, 1988).
12. Among the popular Black DJs in the South were "Jockey Jack" Gibson (Atlanta); "Professor Bop" (Shreveport); Larry McKinley and Vernon Winslow (New Orleans); "Sugar Daddy" (Birmingham); "Spider" Burks (St. Louis); Bruce Miller (Winston-Salem); and Nat D. Williams, "Bugs" Scruggs, Larry Dean, and George White (Memphis). Southern White R&B DJs included Zenas "Daddy" Sears (Atlanta), Bob "Wolfman Jack" Smith (Shreveport), Ken Elliott and Clarence "Poppa Stoppa" Hammon (New Orleans), Bill Gordon and Dewey Phillips (Memphis), and Gene Nobles and John Richbourgh (Nashville). A number of southern R&B recording artists—Elmore James, Rufus Thomas, Sonny Boy Williamson, Howlin' Wolf, Muddy Waters, and B. B. King, among others—had careers as DJs before they became performers. B. B. King acquired his initials from his radio moniker, "the Beale Street Blues Boy." For a detailed discussion of Black-oriented radio "personality jocks" and programming, see Barlow 1999.

13. Garofalo 2011, 78.
14. Hunter Hancock was in Los Angeles, Willie Mays in San Francisco, George Oxford in Oakland, and Phil McKernan in Berkeley. Big Bill Hill and Delta bluesman Muddy Waters held forth on WOPA in Chicago, where Al Benson, "Yo' Ol' Swingmaster," was the premier R&B DJ. In the Northeast, George "Hound Dog" Lorenz was in Buffalo and Danny "Cat Man" Stiles was in Newark. New York was the center for R&B radio in the Northeast, where Willie Bryant, "the Mayor of Harlem," and Ray Carroll broadcast *After Hours Swing Session* on WHOM. Jack Walker, "the Pear-Shaped Talker," appeared on foreign-language outlet WOV. Joe Bostic held down a late-night slot for his *Harlem Music Shop* on WINS. Tommy Smalls broadcast from WWRL, and Phil "Dr. Jive" Gordon was on WLIB. "Symphony Sid" Torin moved from Boston to New York's WMCA, as Alan Freed, the self-appointed "Father of Rock 'n' Roll," moved in from Cleveland to turn WINS into the most listened-to station in the country.
15. Schipper 1990, 70.
16. Gillett 1970, 220.
17. For more information, see Guralnick 1986.
18. Chura 2005.
19. Stelter 2008.
20. Graustark 1979, 58–59.
21. Bricker 1983, 31.
22. Ibid.
23. George 1988, 177.
24. Henderson 1988, R-21.
25. Artists associated with these labels include the following: Def Jam (LL Cool J, Oran 'Juice' Jones, the Beastie Boys, Public Enemy), Jive Records (Whodini, Kool Moe Dee, Steady B., DJ Jazzy Jeff and the Fresh Prince, Boogie Down Productions), Cold Chillin' Records (Marley Marl, Roxanne Shanté, Biz Markie, MC Shan), Tommy Boy (Stetsasonic, Force MDs, De La Soul, Queen Latifah, Black By Demand, Digital Underground), Delicious Vinyl (Tone Loc, Def Jef, Young MC), Priority (N.W.A., Eazy-E, Ice Cube). See Garofalo 2011, 484.
26. In the mid-1990s, the configuration of major labels included Sony Music, BMG, Warner Music, EMI, Polygram, and MCA. The Big Six were soon reduced to the Big Four, as Sony and BMG merged and Polygram and MCA were combined to form the Universal Music Group.
27. Leeds 2001.
28. Mitchell 2005, 25.
29. Bill Lamb, "How to Read the Billboard Charts," About.com, last modified August 7, 2015, accessed September 1, 2015, http://top40.about.com/od/popmusic101/a/billboardcharts.htm.
30. Spooner and Rainie 2000, 2, 8.
31. Smith 2010.
32. Anderson 2004.
33. Ibid.
34. Ibid.

DISCOGRAPHY

Armstrong, Louis. *The Best of Louis Armstrong: The Hot Five and Seven Recordings*. Originally recorded February 26, 1926–December 12, 1928. Columbia 86539, 2002. Four-CD set.

———. *Louis Armstrong Plays W.C. Handy*. Originally recorded July 12, 1954–October 19, 1956. Legacy 64925, 2008. CD.

Berry, Chuck. *The Best of Chuck Berry*. ATF Media, 2013. Digital.

Beyoncé. *Dangerously in Love*. Originally released as Columbia 86386, 2003. BMG/Sony Music 507224, 2015. CD.

Big Bill Broonzy. *Greatest Blues Licks*. Stardust Records, 2009. Digital.

Big Jay McNeely. *Nervous!* Saxophile Records 103, 1995. CD.

Brown, James. *Star Time*. Originally released 1991. Polydor/Strategic Marketing 007063885, 2009. Digital.

Carey, Mariah. *The Emancipation of Mimi*. Island Def Jam Music Group B0005784-02, 2005. CD.

Charles, Ray. *The Best of Ray Charles: The Atlantic Years*. Originally released as Atlantic 71722, 1994. Rhino/Rhino Atlantic, 2013. Digital.

Chic. *Chic: Greatest Hits*. Unequal Halves, 2014. Digital.

Chubby Checker. *The Very Best of Chubby Checker*. ABKCO Records 88972, 2012. CD.
Count Basie Orchestra. *Mustermesse Basel 1956 Part 2*. TCB 02202, 2008. CD.
Crudup, Arthur "Big Boy". *The Best of Arthur "Big Boy" Crudup*. Roslin Records, 2010. Digital.
The Definitive Collection of R&B Hits From 1948. Various Artists. Bofm Ltd, 2009. Digital.
Duke Ellington. *Blues in Orbit*. Columbia/Sony Music 88697492062, 2009. CD.
Duke Ellington and His Famous Orchestra. *Happy-Go-Lucky Local*. Originally recorded November 25, 1946—December 18, 1946. Discovery 70052, 1993. CD.
Fats Domino. *The Fat Man: 25 Classic Performances*. EMI 7243 8 52326 2 6, 1996. CD.
Franklin, Aretha. *Live At Fillmore West*. Originally recorded February 5, 1971 and February 7, 1971. Rhino 127956, 2007. CD.
Funkadelic. *One Nation under a Groove*. Originally recorded April 15, 1978. Charly CHARLYX 671, 2014. CD.
Hendrix, Jimi. *Fire: The Jimi Hendrix Collection*. Experience Hendrix 88697738572, 2010. CD.
Isley Brothers. *Twist and Shout/Shout*. Originally released as Wand WDS 653, 1962. Not Now Music NOT 2CD575, 2015. CD.
Jackson, Michael. *Thriller. [25th Anniversary Deluxe Edition.]* Originally released as Epic EK-38112, 1982. Legacy 7345662, 2009. CD.
James, Rick. *Street Songs*. Originally released 1981. Universal Music 0572495, 2012. CD.
Johnson, Robert. *Anthology 1911–1938*. Remastered, volume 2. Juju Classics, 2013. Digital.
LaBelle, Patti. *Winner in You*. Originally released 1986. MCA 03319, 1991 CD.
Louis Jordan and the Tympani Five. *Let The Good Times Roll: The Anthology, 1938–1953*. MCA Records MCAD2–11907, 1999. Two CD set.
Mayfield, Curtis. *People Get Ready: The Curtis Mayfield Story*. Includes "Keep On Pushing" and "People Get Ready," among others. Rhino/Warner Bros. 72262, 1996. CD Box Set.
Milburn, Amos. *Amos Milburn Rocks*. Bear Family Records BCDR16926, 2009. CD.
Mills Brothers. *The Mills Brothers: The Anthology (1931–1968)*. MCA AAMCADZ211279, 1995. CD.
N.W.A. *Straight Outta Compton*. Originally released 1988. Reissued by Priority B 002309502, 2015. CD.
Price, Lloyd. *Lloyd Price Greatest Hits*. Unequal Halves, 2014. Digital.
Queen Latifah. *Black Reign*. Originally released 1993. Universal Music 5302722, 1994. CD.
Sly & The Family Stone. *The Essential Sly & the Family Stone*. Recorded 1967–1975. Originally released 2002. Epic/Legacy 5100182, 2009. CD.
Smith, Bessie. *Bessie Smith: The Complete Recordings*. Vols. 1–5. Columbia/Legacy C2K 47091, C2K 47471, C2K 47474, C2T 52838, C2K 57546, 1991–1996. Five two—CD sets.
Summer, Donna. *The Dance Collection: A Compilation of Twelve Inch Singles*. Originally released 1987. Mercury 9849171, 2007. CD.
The Sylvers. *Classic Masters*. Originally released as Capitol/EMI Records/Capitol 37416, 2002. Capitol, 2010. Digital.
White, Barry. *Barry White: The Collection*. Originally released as Polygram/UMVD 8347902, 1989. Universal Distribution BWTVCD 1, 2004. CD.
Wonder, Stevie. *The Definitive Collection*. Originally released as Motown AA4400661642, 2002. Motown 001040902, 2007. CD.

CHAPTER 7

The Motown Legacy
Homegrown Sound, Mass Appeal

Charles E. Sykes

It happened in a white two-story house located at 2648 W. Grand Boulevard in the "Motor City," Detroit, Michigan. A sign above the large picture window prominently displayed the words, "Hitsville U.S.A." Its owner, Berry Gordy Jr., a Black songwriter, intended it to be a "factory" where hit records could be "built."[1] Young Black men and women would come and go in shifts, each doing his or her part in an assembly line that operated twenty-four hours a day, much like those in local automobile factories. They were producing a new type of rhythm and blues (R&B) that would bear the "Motown" trademark. From 1959 to 1972, Detroit was home for Motown Record Corporation, and Hitsville was the company's primary recording studio. Berry's intention to make hit records was realized as the new local phenomenon called the Motown Sound gained mass appeal.

While based in Detroit, Motown affected the careers of some of the most famous artists in the history of popular music: Diana Ross & the Supremes, Smokey Robinson and the Miracles, Martha & the Vandellas, the Temptations, Four Tops, Marvelettes, Mary Wells, Stevie Wonder, Marvin Gaye, and others. Through their voices and with the talents of esteemed musicians known as the Funk Brothers, Motown's writers and producers gave the world some of the most memorable songs ever recorded. They were songs people could relate to: upbeat, with elements of gospel, pop, and jazz fused and packaged in slick musical arrangements—tailored within the well-coordinated outfits their artists wore when they performed live. Stage routines were choreographed to project an air of "class" and "sophistication," very much within the range of acceptability for mainstream audiences, but with a subtle edge that spoke "young," "cool," "Black," "urban," and "Detroit." And most of Motown's personnel *were* young Blacks born or raised in Detroit. Motown would advertise its music as "The Sound of Young America," a slogan consistent with the ages of company personnel and with the large number of young Americans buying Motown's records.[2]

Before Motown, the music industry had no history of a Black-owned company seriously competing with White-owned companies on a national level. Motown's record sales and numbers of hit records were competitive with top independent labels and major labels in both R&B and pop categories.[3] Motown produced a product that, although delivered through Black voices and faces, crossed over into the White market at an unprecedented level of success.

In June 1972, Motown closed its Detroit offices and moved its headquarters to Los Angeles, California, completing a transition that had begun in 1966 when the company opened its West Coast office at 6255 Sunset Boulevard. In LA, Motown became strategically situated to fulfill Berry's quest to produce movies, while continuing record production in the newer, Los Angeles–based Hitsville Studios. The LA move physically disconnected Motown from its hometown, but even the company's present incorporation within media conglomerate Vivendi-owned Universal Music Group has not dislodged the Motown legacy from its Detroit roots. And the old Hitsville U.S.A., reestablished in 1985 as the Motown Historical Museum, stands as a symbol of that legacy, built during the thirteen years the company was based in the Detroit, "Motor City."

"The legacy of Motown," says Berry, "is its body of music."[4] Motown's musical foundation emerged within the context of Detroit's Black community. Here, under the leadership of Berry Gordy and his staff of writers and producers, various human, physical, social, and cultural elements coalesced in Hitsville studios as the "Motown Sound," a sound concept that would become synonymous with Detroit. This chapter examines the Motown legacy as representative of Detroit generally, and of the city's Black community in particular. By exploring issues of Black entrepreneurship, local influences, musical eclecticism, and crossover, we uncover the values that underlay the structure and operation of Motown. A glance at the production process, then, reveals ways in which Berry's exposure to the auto assembly line served as metaphor for how Berry viewed the role of artist development and as model for how Motown would make records. What follows is an overview of the "Motown Sound" and its evolution during the Detroit era, focusing on various artists, writers, and producers whose collaborations garnered mass appeal. Looking at what I term the Detroit era's "classic" phase, special attention is given to recordings written and produced by Holland-Dozier-Holland (H-D-H) for the Supremes.[5] H-D-H created a new pop-gospel R&B concept that helped propel the Supremes into stardom, while it also gave definition to the "Motown Sound." The Supremes, armed with H-D-H's material as their core repertoire, led Motown's effort to break into the mass market. The final section of this essay places the Motown legacy into perspective by highlighting the ways in which the music, people, and processes that defined the company's Detroit era have since remained timeless. Unless otherwise indicated, all dates used in reference to recordings represent the years in which the records were released, as opposed to the years in which they were recorded or peaked on record charts.

BLACK ENTREPRENEURSHIP AND COMMUNITY IDEALS

The Gordy family epitomized ideals of self-help and social consciousness, values Detroit historian Richard Thomas says represented "the heart and soul of [Black] community building" in post–World War I Detroit.[6] Berry Gordy Sr. and his wife Bertha moved from Sandersville, Georgia, to Detroit in 1922, seven years before Berry Jr. was born. Hard work, family unity, and economic prudence helped the Gordys and their eight children progress from the welfare rolls to become one of the most successful families in Detroit.[7] They owned and operated businesses in realty, building contracting, insurance, printing, and groceries, naming their grocery store after Booker T. Washington. As Black entrepreneurs and members of the Booker T. Washington Trade Association, the Gordys were part of a movement to promote economic health and community pride through patronage of Black businesses, which provided convenient access to needed products and services. In 1965, Berry Jr. received the Trade Association's business achievement award. Motown had become a multi-million-dollar operation, one of America's largest Black-owned businesses, and a testament to the ideals of self-help.

Motown's growth and success was largely based on its production of a music product that appealed to the White record-buying population, in addition to Blacks, in combination with Berry Gordy's ownership of multiple businesses that handled various essential record industry functions. Suzanne Smith explains these two factors in terms of Black nationalistic ideals of economic independence and integrationist ideals.

> In Detroit the Motown Record Company was accomplishing what Malcolm X and the Freedom Now Party advocated: black economic independence that did not rely on the industrial base of the city—auto production—to survive. At the same time, as its music began to gain more and more white fans, Motown represented the ideal of racial integration via cultural exchange advocated by Martin Luther King Jr. and SCLC.[8]

Focusing here on Berry's entrepreneurial spirit, we look now at Gordy-owned businesses that paved the way for Motown, and the transition to multiple Gordy-owned businesses that were affiliated with Motown Record Corporation.

As a member of the Gordy family, Berry Jr. was nurtured in an environment in which economic independence, through business ownership, was a way of life. What his parents did in developing businesses that served the Black community, Berry did to serve music makers and consumers. His first music business venture was the 3D Record Mart, a jazz record store established in Detroit in 1953. 3D gave Berry a sense of the local record consumer market's interests, which at that time leaned mostly toward blues and R&B, and not jazz. While this discovery came too late to save his business, it affected a shift in Berry's musical taste toward R&B as the type of music that he would write, produce, and sell in years to come.

Having become an established R&B songwriter by 1967, Berry embarked upon his next three business ventures in 1958. In partnership with soon-to-be second wife Raynoma Liles, he formed the Rayber Music Writing Company. Rayber helped local artists and songwriters create demos and masters, which could be shopped among various record labels. The Rayber Voices, a vocal group formed by Raynoma and Berry in conjunction with their business, served as their house background vocal group and would later sing background on early Motown releases. Having experienced difficulty collecting songwriter royalties from dishonest publishers, Berry established Jobete Music Company. Jobete would become the primary publisher for Motown's recordings.[9]

There seems to have been one 45-rpm single written and recorded by Wade Jones and imprinted with the Rayber Records label in 1959. On the A side we find "I Can't Concentrate," written by Wade Jones, and on the B side, "Insane," written by Smokey Robinson and Berry Gordy. Detroit record historians believe that this was a promotional record, but it certainly has historical significance in that it post-dates "Come to Me," the Marv Johnson recording that launched Berry's Tamla label, the first label to become part of Motown Record Corporation.[10]

With an $800 loan through the family's credit union, Ber-Berry Co-op, Berry became owner of his new Tamla label in 1959. Always one to draw from what people can relate to, he wanted to name his label "Tammy," the title of a #1 hit recorded by Debbie Reynolds in 1957. Since Tammy Records already had registered the label name, Berry modified the name to Tamla.[11] Later that year he established a second label, Motown, a name derived from Detroit's nickname, the "Motor City." Berry writes: "The Tamla name was commercial enough but had been more of a gimmick. Now I wanted something that meant more to me, something that would capture the feeling of my roots—my home town."[12] The company was incorporated under the name Motown, and the Motown label, bearing a map of southeast Michigan with a star marking Detroit as capital, would become the flagship label.[13] In 1962 Berry established the Gordy label, a label using his name. By the end of 1971 sixteen labels created under Berry Gordy's leadership would imprint and provide means for organizing and promoting the company's extensive and eclectic catalog. Table 7.1 shows the labels established pre-1972, the most common type of material recorded on each label, and a sample list of artists.[14] The list of labels includes the

Table 7.1 Motown labels established before 1972, with most common type of material recorded and a sample list of artists on each label.

Label	Years Active	Type	Sample Artists
Tamla	1959–1986	Popular Music	Marvin Gaye, Miracles, Barrett Strong, Stevie Wonder
Motown	1959–1988	Popular Music	Four Tops, Jackson 5, Diana Ross, Supremes
Miracle	1961	Popular Music	Freddie Gorman, Jimmy Ruffin, Temptations, Valadiers
Divinity	1962–1963	Gospel	Burnadettes, Gospel Stars, Liz Lands, Wright Specials
Gordy	1962–1987	Popular Music	Contours, Martha & the Vandellas, Temptations, Kim Weston
Melody	1962–1965	Popular Music	Howard Crockett, Lamont Dozier, Dee Mullins, Vels
Workshop Jazz	1963–1964	Jazz	George Bohannon Quartet, Earl Washington All Stars, Johnny Griffith Trio, Herbie Williams
Soul	1964–1978	Popular Music	Gladys Knight & the Pips, Jimmy Ruffin, Jr. Walker & the All Stars, Shorty Long
VIP	1964–1972	Popular Music	Elgins, Chuck Jackson, Isley Brothers, Spinners
Tamla-Motown	1965–1976	Popular Music	Mostly top Motown artists active during this period
Weed*	1969	Popular Music	Chris Clark
Chisa	1969–1971	Jazz	Jazz Crusaders, Stu Gardner, Hugh Masekela, Monk Montgomery
Rare Earth	1969–1976	Popular Music	Puzzle, Rare Earth, R. Dean Taylor, Rustix
Ecology*	1971	Popular Music	Sammy Davis Jr.
Black Forum	1970–1973	Spoken Word	Amiri Baraka, Stokely Carmichael, Langston Hughes, Martin Luther King Jr.
Mowest	1971–1973	Popular Music	G. C. Cameron, Thelma Houston, Syreeta, Bobby Taylor

* Only one record released.

London-based Tamla-Motown label, which was established in 1965 to solidify Motown's presence in the UK market.[15] It also includes Mowest, a Los Angeles–based label established the year before the company moved its headquarters from Detroit to Los Angeles.

The earliest Tamla releases showed Berry's residence, 1719 Gladstone Street, Detroit 6, Michigan, as the company's address. By early 1960 Berry had purchased the house at 2648 W. Grand Boulevard, which would become Motown Record Corporation's headquarters and sight of Hitsville Studio. Seven additional houses were eventually purchased in the West Grand Boulevard neighborhood to provide facilities for Motown's growing and flourishing operation.

Berry Gordy Enterprises was established in the early 1960s. The company handled artist management, until 1964 when International Talent Management, Inc. (ITMI) was established to manage the careers of Motown's young artists. Artist Development was formed in 1964 under Berry Gordy Enterprises to shape raw talent into professionals in all aspects of onstage and offstage presentation. Several Jobete publishing subsidiaries were formed to manage Motown's expansive catalog: Stein and Van Stock (1966), Stone Diamond (1971), and Stone Agate (1971).[16]

Motown absorbed several local record companies and, as a result, inherited individuals and groups who would become important figures in the Motown legacy. Anna Records, co-owned by Berry's sister Gwen and Roquel Billy Davis, folded in 1961 and yielded Marvin Gaye. Gwen Gordy and Harvey Fuqua's Tri-Phi and Harvey labels folded in 1963. Fuqua then joined Motown as a songwriter, producer, and head of Artist Development, and brought with him the likes of Jr. Walker & the All Stars and the Spinners. In 1966 Motown purchased Ed Wingate and Joanne Bratton's Golden World and Ric-Tic labels, a purchase that yielded not only Edwin Starr, but also Golden World's recording studio. The new studio, named Studio B, making Hitsville Studio A, provided the company with another local, and larger, recording space for string and horn overdubs.

While Motown's Detroit operation was expanding in Detroit, so was its West Coast operation. In 1968 Berry Gordy established Motown Productions in Los Angeles and hired future Motown president Suzanne de Passe as his creative assistant in charge. The establishment of Motown Productions proved significant to the company's expansion into television and, eventually, movie productions.

Although Motown remained an independent record company under Berry's ownership, it had come to resemble a major record company, owning facilities and hiring staff to handle recording, sales, promotion, touring, legal affairs, artist management and development, and other key functions of the record business. Offices were moved into the high-rise Donovan Building at 2547 Woodward Avenue in 1968. Hitsville, however, remained the hub of Motown's creative activity.

As with earlier Gordy family businesses, good community relations were important to Motown's success. Stage band students from Northwestern High School, located only a few blocks from Hitsville, observed recording sessions to learn about the process.[17] Public appearances by Motown artists helped promote local business and special causes, like Detroit United Foundation's annual Torch Drive, for which Motown permitted the use of "The Happening," the Supremes' latest record, for the campaign's theme song.[18] Motown artists' appearances at DJ record hops would bring crowds, thus increasing income for the DJs, who reciprocated with airplay for Motown's recordings.[19] Detroit was devastated by riots in July 1967. To help quell tensions, Motown released "I Care about Detroit," a promo recorded by Smokey Robinson and the Miracles. A year later, the United Foundation used the record as a theme for "Detroit is Happening," a program that provided summer jobs and recreational activities for the city's youth in an effort to prevent a recurrence of riots.[20]

Motown's success as a Detroit-based, Black-owned business spawned a large local fan base and a sense of community pride. But survival in the record business meant popularity beyond Detroit. The success that Motown would achieve in the mass market was predicated on Berry Gordy's idea that the company's output should consist of an eclectic repertoire that appealed to a general audience. Detroit provided a cosmopolitan environment in which a broad-based vision like Berry's could materialize.

LOCAL MUSIC INFLUENCES AND MUSICAL ECLECTICISM

Cities offer exposure to a "great diversity of musical behavior within a broad range of events" facilitated by education systems, public and private organizations, business and entertainment, and mass media.[21] Physical and social boundaries that define racial and cultural groups constantly crisscross, fostering the likelihood of diverse musical experiences and eclectic tastes, even within segregated neighborhoods.

Berry Gordy showed an eclectic taste for music at an early age. Uncle B.A., his first music teacher, stimulated his love for classical piano. Radio exposed him to mainstream pop and "race" music aired in small segments on local programs like WJLB's "Interracial Goodwill Hour."[22] At age seven, he composed his own "Berry's Boogie" on the family's old upright piano. He loved the Mills Brothers and the Ink Spots, two jazz-pop vocal groups whose recordings would later influence his approach to songwriting.[23] As a teenager, he was listening to jazz and dancing to the big bands of Duke Ellington and Count Basie at favorite Eastside Detroit nightspots.[24] At age twenty he wrote the song "You Are You" for the famous mainstream pop artist Doris Day. "Thinking of a general audience even then," he writes, "I had written the song with Doris Day in mind. She was America's girl next door."[25]

Berry indulged his love for jazz by opening the 3D Record Mart, only to find out that the local market was much more interested in blues and R&B. 3D failed, but Berry began listening to R&B and learned to love its infectious simplicity. Three years working on the Lincoln-Mercury (a division of Ford Motor Company) assembly line gave him opportunity to hone his R&B songwriting craft in moments between assembling parts. By 1957, Berry had become a writer for the famous R&B star, Jackie Wilson. Collaborating with co-writers Roquel Billy Davis (a.k.a. Tyran Carlo) and sister Gwen Gordy, Berry contributed to four major hits for Wilson: "Reet Petite" (1957), "To Be Loved" (1958), "Lonely Teardrops" (1959), and "I'll Be Satisfied" (1959). Collectively drawing from blues-based swing jazz, mainstream pop, and then current R&B styles, these four hits with Wilson firmly established Gordy's songwriting career. During the late 1950s his diverse musical influences congealed into songwriting concepts that would later influence the Motown Sound and the processes by which it was created.

The 1950s marked the "golden age of jazz in Detroit."[26] Some of the world's renown jazz musicians and vocalists—local greats like Barry Harris, Yusef Lateef, Kenny Burrell, and the Jones brothers, Hank, Elvin, and Thad; and guest greats like Cannonball Adderley, Billie Holiday, Sarah Vaughan, Mingus, and Miles—could be heard on any night at

Klein's, the Blue Bird, the West End, the Flame, and many other clubs. Berry Gordy frequented the Flame Show Bar, one of Detroit's most popular upscale clubs that hosted acts ranging from jazz to popular. The Flame is where Berry heard and met Billie Holiday, whose life story inspired Motown's first movie production, *Lady Sing the Blues*, which opened in 1972.

The jazz and R&B businesses intersected at the Flame, and fruitful relationships resulted, especially for Berry and Motown. Club co-owner Al Green also managed a number of local R&B acts, including Jackie Wilson. Berry's sister Gwen, who owned photo concessions at the Flame, introduced him to Green, thus launching his career as one of Jackie Wilson's songwriters. Berry would eventually hire Maurice King, the Flame's house bandleader, as music director in Motown's Artist Development department, and "Beans" Bowles, who played saxophone in King's band, as a musician and road manager for Motown's first tour.

Detroit's club scene was a breeding ground for the Funk Brothers, the musicians who played on hundreds of recordings released during the Detroit era. Their backgrounds included formal training in classical music and jazz. Band, orchestra, and stage band were their training ensembles in school music programs. But even before finishing high school, a number of them played professional jazz and blues engagements in Detroit's club scene. The nightclub environment, keyboardist Johnny Griffith claimed, nurtured the "Detroit Sound," which gave shape to the Motown Sound.[27]

Future Motown artists, writers, and producers, born during World War II, were teenagers during the 1950s and consumer-participants in a new popular culture. American popular music, formerly defined by mainstream pop, had become redefined as rhythm and blues or rock 'n' roll. Teenagers were the target market of record companies and broadcast media who disseminated and propagated this new music. Like Berry Gordy, the new generation of Detroit's Black teenagers was exposed to diverse forms of music. In church, they heard and sang gospel. In Glee Club and other school music classes, they studied European-based classical and folk traditions under the tutelage of White teachers.[28] Under Ford Motown Company sponsorship, schools provided exposure to live classical music "concerts for all of the school kids," recalls songwriter/producer Brian Holland, who views this experience as inspiration for using strings in songs that he would later produce for Motown artists.[29] Broadcast media—primarily radio and, to a lesser but growing extent, television—provided access to a broad array of musical offerings and was the core source of exposure to the popular forms of music that future Motown personnel would listen to, dance to, buy on record, and emulate.

Black radio programming had gained a substantial presence as R&B became integrated into American popular culture. White and Black DJs became leading propagators of R&B through airplay, hosting record hops, and organizing concerts that featured heroes of future Motown personnel. In the 1940s WJBK's Ed "Jack the Bellboy" McKenzie began playing blues, boogie-woogie, and R&B records "on what was essentially a pop [radio] show," and continued to do so in the 1950s.[30] Robin Seymour of WKHM and Mickey Shorr of WJBK were key promoters of R&B, although under the rock 'n' roll banner. Their live concert promotions brought to Detroit top R&B acts like Frankie Lyman and the Teenagers, whom several Motown artists note as being of major influence, and the Cadillacs, a group whose look and choreography made a profound impression on future

Temptations' Otis Williams (Figure 7.1) and whose choreographer, Cholly Atkins, would eventually groom Motown acts for the stage.[31]

While Ed McKenzie, Robin Seymour, Mickey Shorr, and other White DJs included R&B as part of eclectic playlists, WJLB aired all R&B shows with Black DJs LeRoy White, Bristoe Bryant, and Ernie Durham, one of the first Detroit DJs to host record hops. DJs at WJLB would later become important figures for breaking Motown's records in the local market, as would their counterparts at WCHB, Detroit's first Black-owned, all-Black-format radio station, located in the Inkster suburb.[32] Most of the WCHB's airtime was devoted to Black popular music, spun by DJs Joe Howard, Larry Dean, and Larry Dixon. Early morning programming, however, featured gospel music, which during the 1950s included records by the Harmonizing Four, Dixie Hummingbirds, and other gospel groups who planted the gospel roots of R&B vocal groups like the Temptations.[33]

Figure 7.1
Temptations mid-1960s. From left, Melvin Franklin (1942–1995), Paul Williams (1939–1973), Eddie Kendricks (1939–1992), David Ruffin (1941–1991), and Otis Williams (1941–).
Credit Hulton Archive.

The Motown Legacy 117

There were hundreds of teenage vocal groups in Detroit: male groups, girl groups, mixed groups. Street corners and school hallways vibrated with the sounds of blow harmonies, falsetto, doo-wop vocables, teen love lyrics, and other remnants of the vocal group tradition. Competition was stiff; talent shows frequently held in high schools provided incentive to be the best, and Ed McKenzie's "Saturday Party" on WXYZ-TV offered opportunities for young Black groups like the Five Chimes (future Miracles) to appear on television and win top talent honors.[34] Members of the Five Chimes, Matadors, Primes, Primettes, Distants, Del-Phis, and other groups would eventually take their talents to the next level as Motown artists, writers, and producers.[35]

The group concept would become central to the Motown legacy. While Motown always carried solo artists on its roster, its legacy was in large part shaped by vocal group sounds, visual images of three to five people dressed in coordinated outfits with similar hairstyles (processes for men in the early days), synchronized dance movements, and group identity, which was so much a part of youth culture in post–World War II urban contexts. As company owner, Berry Gordy faced the challenges of bringing cohesion to the disparate individuals and groups of young talent that would come to Hitsville and of positioning the company for success in the mass market.

A brochure printed sometime during the mid-1960s suggests that Motown avoided promoting itself as a Black company, promoting instead its multiple services and diverse recording repertoire released on the company's multiple labels. (See Figure 7.2.)

Figure 7.2
Motown advertising brochure cover.

Courtesy Charles E. Sykes.

The brochure's cover shows a cartoon-like image of an orchestra conductor with long, straight hair, dressed in tie and tails, smiling and posed as if introducing the title, "This Is Motown Record Corporation." The text inside boasts that Motown is "one of America's leading independent recording companies" and "a versatile, highly successful producer of single and long-playing records that satisfy a variety of preferences in popular music." Motown's eclectic nature is emphasized:

> There is a Motown record to appeal to every type of audience. The Motown, Tamla, Gordy, Soul, VIP and Mel-o-dy labels feature rhythm and blues, ballads, rock and roll, country and western, and general "pop" music. The company has increased its activity in the jazz field and offers some of the world's finest jazz artists on the Workshop label, and so that no taste is slighted, the Divinity label produces religious [gospel] records.[36]

The brochure text gives only a hint of Motown's diverse body of recordings. R&B and soul, musical traditions that are themselves diverse, constitute the core of the company's repertoire. But Motown's recording activities reached beyond R&B and soul. An album titled *The Great March to Freedom* (1963) features Martin Luther King Jr. delivering an earlier version of his "I Have a Dream" speech.[37] *The Soulful Moods of Marvin Gaye* (1961) consists of standards like "My Funny Valentine." And Marvin's *A Tribute to the Great Nat King Cole* (1965) features standards, like "Mona Lisa," that have become synonymous with Cole's recording career. The *Supremes at the Copa* (1965) album includes Broadway tunes. Covers of British pop tunes are recorded on the Supremes' *A Bit of Liverpool* (1964), and the group recorded a Christmas album, *Merry Christmas* (1965), the same year that they recorded *Supremes Sing Country, Western and Pop* (1965). The spoken words of Black political figures Martin Luther King Jr. (*Why I Opposed the War In Vietnam*, 1970) and Stokely Carmichael (*Free Huey*, 1970), and literary figures Langston Hughes (*Writers Of The Revolution*, 1970) and Imanu Amiri Baraka (*It's Nation Time*, 1972), among others, were captured and preserved on the Black Forum label, launched in 1970.[38] These are just a few examples of the range and scope of records released by Motown while the company still maintained its Detroit address as headquarters.

Berry Gordy clearly was on a mission to sell to the masses, which for a company peddling R&B records during his time meant capturing a substantial share of the White consumer market while nurturing the Black consumer base from which the music came. He proved by the mid-1960s that his mission could be accomplished by focusing less on promoting Motown's racial identity and more on implementing various means by which Motown could reach a broad audience. Motown's eclectic repertoire, which echoed Berry's diverse musical experiences and tastes formulated in Detroit, tapped the musical tastes of people across racial, social, and cultural boundaries. Motown's top acts took their eclectic repertoire into mainstream venues—the Palace in Las Vegas, Copacabana in New York—and overseas to Europe and Asia, occasionally performing for royalty. The Artist Development staff, which included music director Maurice King, choreographer Cholly Atkins, and image specialist Maxine Powell, would groom the artists to "appear in #1 places," far removed from the Black Detroit neighborhoods where most of them grew up and learned their craft.[39]

In 1964, the Supremes, with Diana Ross, Mary Wilson, and Florence Ballard, made their debut on *The Ed Sullivan Show*, a top-rated TV variety show sponsored by

Figure 7.3
The Supremes perform on *The Ed Sullivan Show*, December 27, 1964. From Left: Florence Ballard (1943–1976), Diana Ross (1944–), and Mary Wilson (1944–).
Credit: CBS Photo.

Lincoln-Mercury, broadcast nationally on CBS (Figure 7.3). The show brought the Supremes into millions of American homes, introducing their well-groomed act to a diverse range of viewers who may not otherwise have seen it and proving that young Blacks from inner-city Detroit singing R&B could be, in the words of a young White female fan, "the epitome of glamour."[40] Berry Gordy strategically scheduled subsequent appearances by the Supremes and other Motown acts on Sullivan's show to promote new releases.[41]

For many Blacks, seeing the Supremes, the Temptations, the Four Tops, and others on national television, or hearing news of their success in contexts where segregation still excluded Blacks as patrons, offered a sense of racial pride. For many Whites, the music performed and images projected by Motown's artists helped dispel Black stereotypes, or at least spoke to their musical sensibilities enough to reel them in as consumers. Yet Motown's success across racial, social, and cultural boundaries has often generated criticism narrowly focused on the notion that the company's success came with a compromise of Black roots, as evidenced in both music and presentation style.[42] Compromise or not, it is unlikely that an independent, Black-owned company operating solely on a premise of racial identity within the racially segregated climate of the 1960s would have achieved mass appeal and longevity comparable to that achieved by Motown. Berry Gordy's astute sense of what it took to be successful drove the business of Motown and was very much in tune with Maxine Powell's opinion that the company's work was not about race: "Honey, that's not Black; that's show business," she says.[43]

CROSSOVER

"Saying you listened to [DJ] 'Frantic Ernie' carried a certain amount of status for white kids who wanted to be ultracool," David Carson writes.[44] Berry was able to get Tom Clay to play Motown's records on WJBK, a pop-format station that appealed to local White listeners.[45] While R&B had its roots in the Black community, White teenagers in earshot of Black radio programming were embracing R&B, although under the rock 'n' roll banner. By the time Berry Gordy launched his Tamla label in 1959, rock 'n' roll had become the subject heading of a modern popular music narrative that included diverse forms of R&B recorded by Black artists; covers of R&B recorded by White artists whose stylistic orientations ranged from mainstream pop (Pat Boone) to rockabilly (Elvis Presley, Bill Haley); and original rock 'n' roll songs of similar range and diversity, recorded primarily by White artists and based on Black R&B models. But record charts, the measuring sticks of success in the record industry, were segregated. Black artists routinely fared better on the R&B charts, representing music recorded by Blacks for Blacks, than on the pop charts, representing music recorded by Whites for the larger White market. Optimal success in record sales required selling across defined markets, or "crossing over." Crossover was firmly wedged into the record business before Motown. During the mid-1950s, some Black artists (Platters, Silhouettes, Lloyd Price) scored #1 pop hits, while some White artists (Johnnie Ray, Elvis Presley) scored #1 R&B hits. By the time Berry started Motown, it was apparent that consumers' record collections might be integrated even while record charts and neighborhoods remained segregated.

Motown's first major step into the crossover market came with the Miracle's "Shop Around" (1960), which hit #1 on the *Billboard* R&B charts and #2 on the pop charts. A year later the Marvelettes' "Please Mr. Postman" hit #1 on both charts, an accomplishment that would be repeated in 1963 with Little Stevie Wonder's "Fingertips—Part 2" and later with other top Motown acts. Mary Wells and Martha & the Vandellas also did well in both pop and R&B charts during the early years of the Detroit era.

Billboard's temporary suspension of R&B charts from November 1963 to January 1965, which meant that popular music would all compete for ranking on the pop charts, paralleled the Temptations', Four Tops', and Supremes' first weekly Top 25 pop hits. More significantly, during this period the Supremes would record their first three of ten #1 pop hits written and produced by Holland-Dozier-Holland. The Supremes clearly held honors as Motown's top crossover act, but twenty-five other acts contributed to the company's 107 Top 10 pop hits and twenty-nine #1 pop hit singles charting before 1972, as shown in Table 7.2. However—if chart rankings have any value in measuring success within racially defined markets—Motown's success on the White pop charts did not dilute its success on the Black R&B charts; in other words, Motown was able to

Table 7.2 Motown's weekly Top 10 and #1 hits on *Billboard*'s pop and R&B charts (1959–1971).

Dates	Pop Top 10	#1	R&B/Soul Top 10	#1
1959	0	0	1	0
1960	1	1	3	1
1961	1	1	2	1
1962	6	0	11	4
1963	5	1	9	2
1964	6	4	—	—
1965	11	5	27	6
1966	13	3	30	9
1967	13	2	27	5
1968	11	2	22	6
1969*	13	3	22	7
1970	16	6	26	8
1971	11	1	20	5
Total	107	29	200	54

*1969 marks the year that *Billboard* replaced the R&B chart title with the term "soul."

maintain its Black consumer base in spite of crossover success. Cornell West asserts that Berry Gordy

> perceived a vacuum in the musical culture of the nation. He was able to convince young brothers and sisters, like me, on the Black side of town that this was my music. And at the same time convince White brothers and sisters on the other side of town listening to the Beach Boys, that Motown was also their music. Nothing like that had ever occurred.[46]

Berry Gordy developed his company around a concept that, through music, style, image, and repertoire, promoted the likelihood that non-Blacks would like and buy Motown's records. But turning the possibility of crossover into reality depended as much on a company's business networking as it did on its ability to produce records having potential cross-market appeal. Suzanne Smith explains:

> In the 1960s black popular music did not crossover to White audiences on the basis of its appeal alone. The transition involved an elaborate system of marketing the artists and behind-the-scenes deal making with distributors, disc jockeys, and record store owners.[47]

In 1960, Barney Ales, one of Motown's first White executives, joined the company as head of the sales department just in time to push "Please Mr. Postman" to #1 on the pop charts. Ales, a former distributor introduced to Berry by DJ Tom Clay, built Motown's sales department primarily by hiring experienced Whites who could get distributors to push for airplay and record sales in White markets, particularly in the racially biased South. On the other hand, Motown's promotion department consisted of industry-savvy Blacks like former DJ Jack Gibson, whose reputations enabled them to wield similar success with Black radio stations and sales outlets.

As Motown's popularity grew and racial prejudice against Black products and their representatives decreased during the mid-to-late 1960s, Motown's sales and promotion staffs became integrated, while company marketing practices used to evade racial prejudice, like avoiding use of the artists' faces on record covers (a practice that Motown used early on), became less necessary.[48] But in the process of achieving crossover success, Berry had learned how to negotiate racial prejudice. He not only managed to establish positive working relationships with key industry personnel whose cooperation was crucial to selling his records across markets, but he also hired some of the most talented members of their ranks and placed them in key roles on Motown's management roster, a strategy that helped wedge the company inside the music industry's business network. Berry's astute recognition and employment of talent in key roles would similarly manifest itself in Motown's production process, whose operation created the records his company then so skillfully promoted to the masses.

ASSEMBLING THE SOUND: PRODUCTION PROCESSES AND ROLE PLAYERS

While working at Lincoln-Mercury from 1955 to 1957, Berry became infatuated with the "pleasing simplicity" and efficiency of the assembly line process: "how everyone did the same thing over and over again" and how cars would "start out as frames and end up brand new spanking cars."[49] The assembly line concept would become manifested at Motown in two ways. One was Berry's idea that a young artist could come into the company as an "unknown" and eventually become a "star."[50] The second was the process by which various people with clearly defined roles would work collectively to create hit records.

Recollections by former Motown personnel help describe the record-making assembly line as it operated during the mid-1960s, when the company had transitioned into multi-track recording: "Usually a producer was assigned to an artist, or an artist was assigned to a producer, and they had the job of coming up with material," says the Miracles' Ron White. The material may have been created by a songwriter, but "more times than not . . . the producer would write the material for the artist."[51] Thus, songwriter–producers, often working in teams, typically generated material for the artists. The producer would teach the song to the artist. Vocal groups, however, would sometimes create their own background parts, as Smokey Robinson confirms: "I would always let the Temptations make up their own backgrounds because they were masters at it."[52] Motown's resident background vocalists, the Andantes, or artist groups were often assigned to sing background vocals for other artists and would create their own parts.

Most songwriter–producers could not read music, so Johnny Allen, Paul Riser, Hank Cosby, and other arrangers would score parts for the musicians. The producer would sing or play basic ideas so that the arranger could transcribe them to paper. The arrangement, which might include the arranger's ideas as well as those of the producer, was taken into the studio for the musicians to rehearse and record. However, the Funk Brothers, in response to the producer's instructions, often spontaneously created rhythm section arrangements as on-the-spot "head" arrangements. Once the basic rhythm arrangement was established, recording began.

The rhythm tracks, the "foundation" of the recording, were cut first. After the rhythm tracks were laid down, horns, background vocals, lead vocals, and strings (usually played by musicians from the Detroit Symphony) were overdubbed. Once all tracks were cut, the master was produced. The producer would work with the engineer to edit, balance, and mix the multiple tracks down to two (stereo) tracks, taking the liberty to augment or cut material based on his perception of what was more or less important to the sound of the recording.[53] The master was then taken to quality control, a committee consisting of several artists, writers, producers, office staff, and Berry Gordy, who determined by vote whether a record should or should not be released. Quality control might also give suggestions for additional production work to be done.[54]

Motown also created songs from tracks—i.e., rhythm tracks, or generic grooves recorded onto tape by the Funk Brothers without reference to specific songs. Tracks were given to writers to use as raw material from which to write songs. Songwriter Sylvia Moy viewed this method, unconventional at the time, as a "backwards" way of writing a song. She would later recognize that the process saved the company money.[55]

Collaboration, improvisation, and role-playing, processes inherent to Black music-making inside or outside of the studio, were key elements of Motown's assembly line. Each participant contributed in unique ways. The Funk Brothers' sense of ensemble, sound quality, musicianship, and creativity, anchored by the revolutionary bass playing style of James Jamerson, provided the musical backdrop for numerous hits.[56] Martha Reeves writes that the musicians "were responsible for all of the success of the singers at Motown because it was their music that inspired us to sing our best with excitement."[57] Yet, the vocal artists were the stars. The artists—their sounds, vocal styles, names, and looks—branded the records for consumers, arguably more so than those who wrote, arranged, played on, or produced the recordings. But the songwriters generated the stories and melodies that gave context and purpose to the work of others involved in record-making at Motown. However, the producers, who often wrote the songs as well, held ultimate responsibility for leading the production process and delivering hits that would meet the company's goals.

"We're going to make music with a great beat, with some great stories.... Our stories are going to be such that anybody can listen to them. They will not be offensive," Smokey remembers Berry saying when he started Motown.[58] Berry's words provided goals that would, in obvious and subtle ways, connect the entire body of music to the Motown legacy. The assembly line provided a process by which those goals could be achieved.

EVOLUTION OF THE MOTOWN SOUND

Berry Gordy believed that songs should tell stories that people can relate to. And, like stories, "songs need a beginning, middle and end."[59] A song "should be honest and have a good concept," he writes. "Probably the first thing people relate to is the melody." The melody should be memorable and include "hooks" (phrases of repetition and recurrence) that are "infectious," not "monotonous."[60] As the Detroit era progressed, Berry's ideas about songwriting served as a master narrative for his staff writers and producers who worked to get their records released.

The Detroit era evolved in three phases, marked by musical style and related personnel: Phase I, 1959 to 1963, the formative years; Phase II, 1964 to 1967, the "classic" period, when the Motown Sound crystallized; and Phase III, 1968 to 1972, a period of diversification and transition to the post-Detroit era.[61] The following discussion focuses on the music and music makers who had the most profound impact in the company's identity, giving special attention to the style features of Holland-Dozier-Holland's songs recorded by the Supremes during Phase II.

Phase I

Phase I releases, which were produced on Motown's two- and three-track recording systems, mirror then-past and then-current R&B styles. The first Tamla release, "Come to Me" (1959), a Berry Gordy production recorded by Marv Johnson, recalls the doo-wop vocal tradition with its "ooos," "ahhs," and vocal riffs, ingredients that were so much a part of R&B through the mid-1960s.[62] Blues elements are present in Berry Gordy productions like Motown's first national hits, "Money" (1959), recorded by Barrett Strong; the Miracles' "Shop Around (1960), co-written by Smokey Robinson; "Do You Love Me" (1962), recorded by the Contours; and "Fingertips—Part 2" (1963), co-written by several Motown personnel and recorded live by the "12 Year Old Genius," Little Stevie Wonder.

Robert Bateman and Brian Holland teamed up as "Brianbert" to write and produce, with A&R head William "Mickey" Stevenson, "Please Mr. Postman" (1961) for the Marvelettes, Motown's prototypical teenage, pop-sounding girl group. Another Marvelettes recording, "Strange I Know" (1962), is perhaps the first recording of James Jamerson's innovative, jazz-influenced, bass playing style, characterized by passing tones, eighth- and sixteenth-note combinations, syncopation, and deep, full tone quality.[63] But Jamerson also demonstrates skill in playing the shuffle pattern on "old school," boogie-woogie–based R&B pieces like Marvin Gaye's "Pride and Joy" (1963), co-written by Norman Whitfield and produced by Mickey Stevenson.

Smokey Robinson's Phase-I productions for Mary Wells are distinctive models of how lyricism and narrative can be central elements of R&B. With fellow Miracles Ron White and Bobbie Rogers as co-writers, Smokey generated seven Top 10 hits for Mary, including the Grammy-nominated "You Beat Me to the Punch" (1962). Set in verse–chorus form with a contrasting bridge, Smokey's productions for Mary project a calypso feel, which he credits to his listening to Harry Belafonte while growing up.[64]

It was clear in 1963 that something different was coming out of Detroit. Lamont Dozier and brothers Brian and Eddie Holland had formed the songwriting-production team, Holland-Dozier-Holland, or H-D-H. Early that year, Martha & the Vandellas recorded their first hit under H-D-H, "Come and Get These Memories." Martha writes, "The song had a steady beat, great background harmony parts, horns, catchy lyrics, and a story line that everyone could identify with."[65] Her comments could apply to several other 1963 hits: Martha & the Vandellas' "(Love Is Like a) Heatwave," the Miracles' "Mickey's Monkey," Marvin Gaye's "Can I Get a Witness," and the Supremes' "When the Love Light Starts Shining through His Eyes." These records, all written and produced by Holland-Dozier-Holland, echoed what Berry is reported to have said when he heard "Memories": "That's the sound I've been looking for. That's the Motown Sound!"[66]

The work generated by H-D-H at the end of Phase I launched a highly successful concept that would transform several Motown acts into hit-makers, provide leadership in reaching the masses, and give definition to a new R&B sound concept that crystallized the following year as other developments marked the beginning of a new phase.

Phase II

By 1964, records were made on Motown's new eight-track system, built by Hitsville sound engineer Mike McLean.[67] A revolutionary piece of technology at a time when four-track recording was considered state-of-the-art, the eight-track system activated the assembly line process and made it possible for priority components of the sound to be isolated and, hence, better controlled. The bass part, isolated on its own channel, became a more prominent component of the Motown Sound.[68] Motown also fed its guitars directly into the mix, as opposed to placing a microphone in front of the guitar amplifier's speaker, which was and still is the norm. Audio engineer Mark Hood comments:

> Eliminated with this minimalist signal chain are all of the customary colorations and distortions due to the guitar amplifier, speaker and enclosure. As a result, the electric guitar sounds on Motown's Detroit era records are noticeably different from electric guitar sounds on records released by almost every other label. Some describe Motown's guitar sounds as bright, present, clean, crisp and undistorted. Others think them then [thin], disembodied, stringy and plinky.[69]

Whatever the public's opinion, it is clear that multi-track recording technology provided the technological foundation for the musical concepts at work in defining the character of Motown's recordings.

Even as the Beatles invaded the top rungs of America's record charts, Motown's arrival as a major force in the popular music industry was evident in 1964. Early that year, Mary Wells hit #1 on *Billboard*'s then pop-only charts with Smokey Robinson's "My Guy." Martha & the Vandellas recorded their signature piece, "Dancing in the Street," co-written by Marvin Gaye and producer Mickey Stevenson. David Ruffin joined the Temptations as co-lead singer, along with Eddie Kendricks, and the group broke into the charts with Smokey Robinson's "The Way You Do the Things You Do." The Four Tops, previously hitless, made their way into the charts with the H-D-H hit, "Baby I Need Your Loving." And the Supremes recorded three #1 pop hits by H-D-H: "Where Did Our Love Go," "Baby Love," and "Come See about Me." Motown and the Motown sound had come of age.

Two important decisions contributed to the Supremes' success during Phase II. Berry Gordy determined that Diana Ross's "whiney voice" was preferable for their lead.[70] The other was the assignment of H-D-H as the Supremes' writers and producers. H-D-H had piloted the Supremes' first appearance in the Top 25 with "When the Love Light Starts Shining through His Eyes," an up-tempo, densely textured pop-gospel–styled production with horns blaring on the chorus, driving rhythmic accompaniment, baritone saxophone assisting with the bass line, handclaps, organ, and tambourine—all the ingredients of the "hallelujah" gospel sound of H-D-H's 1963 productions. But in 1964, H-D-H made a drastic change in the Supremes' material, beginning with "Where Did Our Love Go."

"Where Did Our Love Go" is set in a simple, transparent texture that focuses the sound squarely on Diana's voice. The other Supremes, Mary Wilson and Florence Ballard, sing a sparse two-part background accompaniment, mostly in call–response, emphasizing key thematic phrases and complementing the melody with lyrics like "baby, baby, oooo baby, baby." The lyrics deal with teenage love and longing, and project innocence. There is a constant pulsation on each beat in the measure, created in the studio (by people stomping on boards placed on the floor) and assisted by piano and bass, which add a repetitive, syncopated pattern. Guitars are mixed far into the background. A vibraphone shimmers out chords throughout the tune. The formal structure consists of a series of verses and choruses, all based on the same chords. There is no bridge, but rather an eight-bar baritone sax solo.

In "Where Did Our Love Go," H-D-H seem to have stripped their gospel-pop concept down to bare bones. Mary Wilson comments: "To my ears, 'Where Did Our Love Go' was a teenybopper song. It had childish repetitive lyrics, . . . a limited melody, and no drive. It was too smooth, and I couldn't imagine anyone liking it."[71] But people did like it: the record hit #1 in the United States and #2 in the UK.

Subsequent H-D-H releases built upon ingredients used in "Where Did Our Love Go," with handclaps, strings, punctuating horns, tambourine, modulations, and other stock H-D-H features selectively added. The Supremes' Phase II music matured as they matured. Arrangements became increasingly more sophisticated, with thicker textures and a more rhythmic drive. The teenage Supremes who joined Motown in 1961 had become young women in their twenties when they recorded "Reflections" (1967), a song whose "the way life used to be" lyrics, delivered by a deeper-voiced Diana, suggest experience and maturity. But even through change, all their "classic" period releases illustrate the gospel-pop formula that became "synonymous with the 'Motown Sound.'"[72]

The Supremes/H-D-H recordings use Black gospel elements as their foundation, evidenced in their use of tambourine, call–response, rhythmic repetition, multilayering, and handclaps, and in the ways in which the singers bend tones and anticipate and delay beats (although much more subtle than in stereotypical gospel vocal delivery). Yet Diana's clear, nasal voice, as well as the simplicity and control placed on vocal and instrumental parts, all suggest a pop orientation. In the Supremes' songs, H-D-H took Black gospel elements and packaged them into a pop production concept.

H-D-H's productions for other artists are technically and structurally very similar to those of the Supremes, but qualitatively very different, adjusting to differences in their artists' vocal styles. Richly textured orchestrations in "Baby I Need Your Loving" (1964) and "Reach Out, I'll Be There" (1966), for example, complement the maleness and maturity of the Four Tops' sound, which is centered on the dramatic, pleading, sometimes preaching voice of lead singer Levi Stubbs. Martha Reeves' intense, powerful delivery is appropriately matched with the intense lyrics and driving rhythms of "Nowhere to Run" (1965). H-D-H would periodically break from their stock formula in tunes like the shuffle rhythm–based "How Sweet It Is (To Be Loved By You)" recorded by Marvin Gaye (1965) and Jr. Walker & the All Stars (1966); the slightly funky Four Tops recording "I Can't Help Myself" (1965); the uncharacteristically funky "Roadrunner" recorded by Jr. Walker & the All Stars (1966); and "Love (Makes Me Do Foolish Things)," a slow, 1950s-type R&B ballad and an anomaly among H-D-H's regular pallet of medium- and up-tempo hits, recorded in 1966 by Martha & the Vandellas.

The focus here on H-D-H and the Supremes is not intended to assert their domination over classic Motown, but rather to give definition to a musical concept that fronted Motown's mass appeal during a period in which various artistic, technical, and management phenomena crystallized to epitomize the Motown legacy. The works of other writer-producer-artist combinations made different but no less vital contributions to shaping that legacy.

Smokey Robinson, Motown's most prolific songwriter, wrote or co-wrote and produced some of the most important Phase II hits: for Mary Wells, "My Guy" (1964), her last release before leaving Motown; for the Miracles, "Ooo Baby Baby (1965)," "Going to a Go-Go" (1965), "Tracks of My Tears" (1965), and "I Second That Emotion" (1967); for Marvin Gaye, "I'll Be Doggone" and "Ain't That Peculiar" (1965); and for the Marvelettes, "Don't Mess with Bill" (1966) and "The Hunter Gets Captured by the Game" (1967). Following "The Way You Do the Things You Do" (1964), Smokey produced several hits for the Temptations, but his "My Girl" (1965) is arguably one of the most memorable songs ever released by Motown and a song that defined the classic Temptations. Norman Whitfield, with Eddie Holland as co-writer, eventually gained primary responsibility for the Temptations' material; shifting the group to a more soulful sound, Whitfield teamed up with Holland to cut "Ain't Too Proud to Beg" (1966) and other Temptations hits.

Stevie Wonder had begun writing his own songs with Sylvia Moy, his mother Lula Hardaway, and arranger Hank Cosby, who was credited with producing "Uptight" (1965) and "I Was Made to Love Her" (1967).[73] Clarence Paul, mentor for the sightless Stevie and co-writer–producer of records for Marvin, Martha, and the Marvelettes, produced several middle-of-the-road tunes for Stevie, including a cover of Bob Dylan's "Blowing in the Wind" (1966).

Berry Gordy produced "Shotgun" (1965) for Soul label artist Jr. Walker & the All Stars. Harvey Fuqua became head of Artist Development, but produced records for Jr. Walker & the All Stars and, with Johnny Bristol, duets for Marvin Gaye and Tammi Terrell, including "Ain't No Mountain High Enough" and "Your Precious Love" (1967), written by Nick Ashford and Valerie Simpson, one of the premier writer–producer teams of Phase III.

Phase III

As Motown entered the third and final phase of the Detroit era, new sound concepts emerged amidst key personnel changes. Mickey Stevenson, Harvey Fuqua, and Clarence Paul had all left the company by the end of 1967, the same year that Supremes' Florence "Flo" Ballard was replaced by Cindy Birdsong. In 1968, H-D-H left Motown and filed a lawsuit against Motown, claiming rights to greater compensation for their work. With H-D-H gone, Top 10 hits would cease for the Four Tops until 1970, when Smokey Robinson and Frank Wilson teamed up to write "Still Water (Love)." Martha & the Vandellas never returned to the Top 10.

Diana Ross & the Supremes, the group's new name after Flo (Florence Ballad) left, recorded three #1 hits by 1970, the most unique of which was "Love Child" (1968). Produced by a new team that called themselves The Clan, which included Berry Gordy, "Love Child," in stark contrast to earlier Supremes material, delivers messages advising against teen pregnancy and illegitimacy. Diana left the group in 1970 for a solo career at Motown, and she hit #1 with a dramatic remake of "Ain't No Mountain High Enough," previously recorded by Marvin Gaye and Tammi Terrell, written and produced by Ashford and Simpson. Marvin and Tammi, with Ashford and Simpson as their primary writers and producers, would become the most successful duet ever assembled by Motown, but that all ended when Tammi died in 1970 from a brain tumor.

Dennis Edwards replaced David Ruffin, who in 1968 was dismissed from the Temptations. Barrett Strong joined Norman Whitfield as the Temptations' co-writer, replacing the departed Eddie Holland. Under Whitfield and Strong, the Temptations became Motown's leading hit act at the end of the 1960s. Their "Cloud Nine" (1968), Motown's first Grammy winner, was also the first in a series of "psychedelic soul" records that represented a complete departure from anything Motown had previously released. But Norman had already tested new waters with the mystical sounding "I Heard It through the Grapevine" (1968), recorded by Marvin Gaye, which contrasts with the gospel-based version recorded by Gladys Knight & The Pips and released in 1967.[74] Norman's Phase III work delved into social themes with songs like "War" (Edwin Starr, 1970), "Ball of Confusion" (Temptations, 1970), and "Smiling Faces" (Undisputed Truth, 1971).

Marvin Gaye and Stevie Wonder were among the few Motown artists who were also writers. Both Marvin and Stevie would reach new levels of independence in 1971 as artist–writer–producers with concept albums. For Marvin, it was *What's Going On*, a social theme-based project that became Motown's largest selling album. For Stevie, it was *Where I'm Coming From*, which, although far less successful than Marvin's work, provided a prelude to several Grammy-winning albums, and songs from albums, produced by Stevie during the 1970s.

In 1969, Motown launched the Rare Earth label, named after the White psychedelic rock group signed to the label, a move that expanded its market base. But the Jackson 5's signing that year was a far more substantial market development endeavor. With members ranging from ages eleven to eighteen, and with the dynamic Michael Jackson as the younger brother and lead singer, the Jackson 5 enabled the company to reach a new generation of teenagers and a new pre-teen audience. Motown formed a songwriter–production team named The Corporation to produce youth-oriented tunes like "I Want You Back," "ABC," and "The Love You Save," all #1 hits released in 1970. The Jackson 5 would become the company's new top hit-making act of the early 1970s, as Motown moved west.

THE LEGACY LIVES ON

In February 1966 a profile on Berry Gordy titled "Triumph of a Stay-At-Home" appeared in *Ebony* magazine. In the article Berry's sister Esther Edwards is quoted as saying "People try to get us to move away . . . to take on New York or Hollywood or one of those places. But Berry is crazy about this town."[75] Berry's love for his hometown, however, did not overshadow the possibilities that he saw for Motown in the media center of the West. Motown's Los Angeles office opened in June 1966, thus geographically situating the company for future expansion into screen-based media. Berry purchased a home in LA in 1967, and the Detroit operations were closed in June 1972.

When Motown announced that its headquarters were moving to Los Angeles, local citizens felt that the company had "abandoned Detroit."[76] Some local DJs boycotted by halting airplay of Motown's records. Motown's presence in its hometown had manifested a sense of ownership and pride among Detroiters. But company vice president and general manager Amos Wilder said that moving into "the creative center of the entertainment world" was "simply a matter of sound business judgment, economics and logistics."[77]

Some members of Motown's Detroit roster chose not to move to Los Angeles others were not invited. Some hit-making acts made the transition to LA, but a gradual exodus ensued as new, post-Detroit acts were signed. Looking at the 1980 roster, for example, we find the Temptations, who had just returned to Motown after recording three years with another label, and solo artists Marvin Gaye, Smokey Robinson, Diana Ross, and Stevie Wonder listed along with the Commodores, Dazz Band, Debarge, High Energy, Rick James, Switch, and Teena Marie. Looking at the hit records released on these newer artists we find that Motown did continue to experience success in LA, particularly with the Commodores, but certainly not at the level of consistency shown during the Detroit era. Motown's hit-making fervor had diminished. Berry saw LA as a move upward and outward into screen-based media. But he would later admit that while the company achieved some, though moderate, success in the TV and movie business, "we would have been better off with the record thing if we had stayed in Detroit."[78]

In 1988, Berry sold Motown to Boston Ventures and MCA Records, thus ending nearly thirty years of independent Black ownership and beginning the label's trek among several international media conglomerates. Dutch-owned Polygram bought Motown in 1993. Seagram, which owned Universal Studios, bought Polygram in 1998, and in 2000, France-based Vivendi bought Seagram, making Motown a division of its Universal Music Group, which is headquartered in Santa Monica, California, and New York City. Motown releases, newly created as well as remasters from pre-Universal archives, now carry the Universal Motown imprint.

Throughout changes in music style, personnel, and ownership, Detroit remains the model for what Motown is believed to be about. At the dawn of the Polygram purchase, CEO Jheryl Busby brought Berry Gordy back as chairman emeritus of Motown's board of directors.[79] Andre Harrell, Motown CEO for only one year, proposed to "lead Motown Records back to glory and back to its roots" by reestablishing the assembly line–artist development model, recruiting Detroit talent, and opening a Detroit office.[80] "Can the new Motown recapture the old magic?" read a *CNN News* headline amidst the company's fortieth anniversary celebration. Longtime company employee Georgia Ward claims that "you can't recapture that full impact of the 1960s" but "there are things that can be done to remind people what Motown was all about."[81] Current company management seems to have attempted just that.

Universal Motown maintains a *Classic Motown* website. The site contains news and information about artists, record releases, a historical overview, video clips, and links to sites where music can be purchased. A casual look at the artist roster reveals that here the term "Classic Motown" is quite broadly defined. It consists, for example, of blues artist Luther Allison, who recorded for Motown during the 1970s; blues-based R&B artist Amos Milburn, who had approximately sixteen years of recording experience before his sessions with Motown between 1962 and 1964; smooth jazz saxophonist Grover Washington Jr., whose time on the Motown roster spanned from the late 1970s to the mid-1980s; new R&B/soul/new jack artists Trina Broussard, Johnny Gill, and Boyz II Men, all of whom joined Motown after Berry Gordy had sold the company; a host of stars who signed with Motown during the post-Detroit 1970s–1980s period: the Commodores, Dazz Band, DeBarge, Willie Hutch, Rick James, Mary Jane Girls, and Teena Marie; the Jackson 5 and Rare Earth, who came to Motown toward the end of the Detroit era and were part of the Detroit to LA transition; and the iconic figures who helped define Motown during the Detroit era: Diana Ross, Smokey Robinson, Supremes, Miracles, Temptations, Four Tops, Mary Wells, Marvin Gaye, Stevie Wonder, etc. The latter group holds a strong presence on the site, especially in regard to recordings that are available for sale. The bulk of the Detroit and early LA releases now available consists of digitally remastered singles compiled into theme-based collections, which carry titles such as "Definitive Collections," "Complete Singles," "Number 1's," "Classic Gold," "Millennium Collections," "Anthology," "Originals," and "Legacy." The catalog also features records that were not previously released, particularly the "Unreleased" series, for example: *Motown Unreleased 1962: Jazz*, *Motown Unreleased 1962: Guys*, *Motown Unreleased 1962: Girls*, and *Motown Unreleased 1963*. "Timelessness" seems to be Universal's underlying theme, and other post-Detroit/post-Gordy owners have done, not only to make early Motown recordings available to consumers, but also to tell deeper stories about the talent and creativity of those who gave shape to the Motown legacy.[82]

On the subject of timelessness, it seems important to recognize Stevie Wonder as the only Detroit artist remaining with Motown to date. Stevie signed with Motown on the Tamla label in 1962, when he was twelve years old, and has remained with Motown his entire career. A multitalented, multiple-Grammy-winning, ever-evolving artist, Stevie Wonder has transcended generations of change in popular music, and in Motown, and serves as a link between Motown of yesterday and today.

The Motown legacy lives on, but it is based upon the works of Berry Gordy and his employees during the Detroit era. The body of music that they recorded remains very much a part of the world's mediascape, integrated as sound and subject in numerous movies, used in radio and TV commercials to sell various products to the masses, celebrated in televised anniversary specials, written about in books, taught in popular music courses, covered in live performances and recordings by newer Motown and non-Motown artists, sampled in digitally produced music and hip hop, remixed by music producers who use digital technology to give new perspective on classic Motown song ideas, and digitally remastered for sale and downloads as singles, albums, and box sets. Music of Motown-Detroit still has mass appeal.

CONCLUSION

Berry's vision of Motown focused prominently on reaching the masses, and he had the ability and resources to make it happen. The seed flourished from his middle-class, Detroit-based family, where he learned skills and values necessary for success in business. Post–World War II Detroit provided a cosmopolitan environment in which Berry and the next generation of Black residents could become key members of a vibrant and diverse musical culture and gain access to media that would afford others access to their talents and creativity. As a high-profile, Black-owned company whose objective was to sell records to the mainstream in a White leadership–dominated industry, Motown surely faced obstacles. But through image, sound, and marketing strategies, Motown became situated as a company with music for everyone. And while some have questioned the degree to which Motown represents its Black roots, the success that the company achieved bolstered Black representation in the music industry by creating a high-quality product that could be embraced across racial and cultural lines and transcend generations.

NOTES

1. Gordy 1994, 118.
2. A sign in the window at Hitsville reads "The Sound of Young America." It is not certain when that sign was posted, but Motown publicist Al Abrams is credited with creating the slogan. The Temptations' Greatest Hits album was the first Motown release to bear the slogan, "The Sound of Young America."
3. Based on *Billboard* record data (Whitburn 1988, 1990).
4. Berry Gordy, interview by Barbara Walters, *20/20*, ABC, October 28, 1994.

5. "Classic" Motown is often defined in a broader sense to cover the entire Detroit era, and often includes the post-Detroit Gordy period (see Classic Motown, www.classic.motown.com). Here I refer to "classic" as a peak period within the Detroit era, specifically the years 1964–1968, the period in which the Supremes recorded ten #1 hits written and produced by H-D-H.
6. Thomas 1992, 175.
7. "America's Most Amazing Family: The Famous Gordys of Detroit," *Color* Magazine, June 1949, 4–8.
8. Smith 1999, 88. The Freedom Now Party was an all-Black political party formed in Detroit in 1963. The Party focused on the election of Black officials who could push forth the Black political agenda, while also helping to promote cultural and economic change within the Black community. Malcolm X endorsed the Freedom Now Party and spoke at their first conference, named the Grass Roots Conference, on November 10, 1963 (Smith 1999, 86).
9. Berry Gordy sold half interest in Jobete to EMI in 1997, nine years after he sold Motown Record Corporation to MCA. Over time Berry would continue selling portions of Jobete to EMI until, in 2004, EMI obtained full ownership of the Jobete catalog (Betts 2014, 226).
10. According to Discogs.com, "Come to Me" was released in January 1959, and "I Can't Concentrate" was released in February. Images of and information about this recording can be found on the Motown Junkies website, accessed July 29, 2011, http://motownjunkies.wordpress.com/2009/10/05/prehistory; "Rayber" on the Seabear website, accessed July 29, 2011, http://www.seabear.se/Rayber.html. Note the similarity between the Rayber and Tamla label designs.
11. Tammy Records was founded in Youngstown, Ohio, in 1958.
12. Gordy 1994, 114.
13. The first Motown label released used a stripped label design, as illustrated by examples shown on the Seabear website, accessed October 16, 2015, http://www.seabear.se/Motown01.html. Beginning with the 1961 release of Mary Well's "I Don't Want to Take a Change," the Detroit map label design became standardized. Bianco 1988, 189.
14. Table 7.1 shows that the Tamla and Motown labels were established in 1959. The first record to carry the Motown label was "Bad Girl," recorded by the Miracles. However, this was a test pressing. "Bad Girl" was released on the Chicago-based Chess Records label 1959. The Motown label had its first released in 1960, "My Beloved" by the Satintones. In 1982 the Tamla, Motown, and Gordy labels' numbering were merged into a single number system within the company's TMG Consolidated Series. See Bianco 1988, 163. See also "TMG Consolidated Series Album Discography (1982–1988)," *Both Sides Now*, last modified July 30, 2012, accessed September 25, 2015, http://www.bsnpubs.com/motown/tmg.html.
15. Prior to establishing Tamla-Motown, the company reached the UK market by leasing its records to be issued on already established UK labels, which included London, Fantana, Oriole, and Stateside.
16. Berry created Stein and Van Stock in an effort to market songs that sounded like standards to mainstream performers. "For Once in My Life," written by Ron Miller and Orlando Murden and first released with Stevie Wonder, is an example of a "standard-type" Motown song published under Stein and Van Stock (Gordy 1994, 227). Stone Diamond and Stone Agate were create as BMI affiliates when in 1971 Jobete switched its performing rights affiliation from BMI to ASCAP (Discogs website, accessed November 23, 2015, http://www.discogs.com/label/264833-Stone-Agate-Music-Division).
17. Ollie McFarland (former Director of Music Education, Detroit Public Schools), interview by author, Detroit, MI, August 2, 2003.
18. Smith 1999, 182–185.
19. Gordy 1994, 138.
20. "It's 'I Care about Detroit' Sunday." *Detroit Free Press,* August 8, 1969.
21. Reyes-Schramm 1982, 1.
22. Carson 2000, 6.
23. Gordy 1994, 32.
24. Bjorn 2001, 108–110.
25. Gordy 1994, 53.
26. Bjorn 2001, 123–169.
27. Johnny Griffith (former Motown keyboardist), interview by author, Detroit, MI, December 2, 1994.
28. McFarland, interview; Robert Klotman (former Director of Music Education, Detroit Public Schools), interview by author, Bloomington, IN, March 2, 1996.
29. Brian Holland and Eddie Holland, interview by Portia K. Maultsby, Los Angeles, CA, April 29, 1983 (Bloomington: Archives of African American Music and Culture, Indiana University).

30. Carson 2000, 2–3.
31. Mention of Frankie Lymon and the Teenagers' influence can be found in Wilson 1986; Robinson 1989; Reeves 1994; Williams 1998. Mention of the Cadillacs can be found in Williams 1998, 25; Carson 2000, 45.
32. Gordy 1994, 111–112.
33. Cintron 1982; Carson 2000, 56–59.
34. Robinson 1989, 51; Carson 2000, 36, 67.
35. The Five Chimes evolved into the Matadors, who were renamed the Miracles. Members from the Primes and Distants formed the Temptations. The Primettes became the Supremes, and the Del-Phis became Martha & the Vandellas.
36. Motown Record Corporation brochure, published some time during the mid-1960s. The date 1963 is handwritten on the cover, but the text suggests that the brochure was printed later. For example, the Soul label, mentioned in the text, was launched in 1964. The "religious music" imprinted under the Divinity label consists of seven gospel singles released during the label's short lifespan, 1962–1963. A copy of the brochure is held at the Motown Archives, Eastern Michigan University, Ypsilanti, MI.
37. While the March on Washington, which occurred on August 28, 1963, is the event most noted for Martin Luther King's "I Have a Dream" speech, King delivered an earlier version in Detroit at a freedom rally (Walk to Freedom) on June 23, 1963. Motown released recordings of both versions of King's famous speech: *The Great March to Freedom*, from the Walk to Freedom rally, and *The Great March on Washington*, from the March on Washington. Both albums were released on the Gordy label, November 1963. The Washington, DC speech was also released as a Gordy single in November 1963.
38. The Black Forum label consists of eight albums and one single. While most of the material on Black Forum is spoken word, Baraka's *It's Nation Time* album includes song, and all tracks on an album and single by Elaine Brown are accompanied song (Sykes 2015, 12).
39. Maxine Powell (former Motown image specialist), Motown class lecture, Bloomington, IN, April 25, 1996 (Videotape recording available at the Archives of African American Music and Culture, Indiana University, Bloomington, IN).
40. Anonymous Motown fan club member, interview by the author, tape recording by telephone, October 13, 1995.
41. Smith 1999, 130–135.
42. Arnold Shaw (1986, 223–236) classifies Motown as "White Synthesis"; Peter Guralnick (1986, 1–2) states that Motown appeals "far more to a pop, white, and industry-slanted kind of audience."
43. Maxine Powell, interview by Amy Huth, Bloomington, IN, December 20, 1996.
44. Carson 2000, 54.
45. Gordy 1994, 140–141.
46. Cornell West, quoted in *Motown 40*, directed by Yvonne Smith and Hart Perry (New York: Perry Films/ABC Television, 1998).
47. Smith 1999, 106.
48. Gordy 1994, 245; Posner 2002, 168.
49. Gordy, 1994, 69.
50. Gordy, *20/20* interview.
51. Ron White and Bobby Rogers (former Miracles members), interview by author, Detroit, MI, August 4, 1994.
52. Smokey Robinson, quoted in the film "The Sounds of Soul," in *The History of Rock 'n' Roll, Volume 5* (Burbank, CA: Time Warner Entertainment, 1995).
53. Johnny Griffith, interview.
54. Ron White and Bobby Rogers, interview.
55. Sylvia Moy (former Motown songwriter), interview by author, tape recording, Detroit, MI, August 5, 1994.
56. *Standing in the Shadows of Motown*, directed by Paul Justman (Santa Monica, CA: Artisan Home Entertainment, 2003).
57. Reeves 1994, 104.
58. Robinson in "The Sounds of Soul" 1995.
59. Robinson 1989, 66.
60. Gordy 1994, 85.
61. Portia Maultsby, Consultant Report for the Motown Exhibition, October 1993.

62. "Come to Me" was released nationally on the New York–based United Artist label.
63. Allen "Dr. Licks" Slutsky, interview by Ann Felter, tape recording by telephone, Cherry Hill, NJ/Bloomington, IN, April 11, 1997.
64. Robinson 1989, 104; Robinson, quoted in *Motown 40* 1998.
65. Reeves 1994, 66.
66. Ibid.
67. The Supremes' "Baby Love" (1964) is noted as the first record to be recorded on Motown's eight-track system (Slutsky 1989, 81).
68. Mike McLean, interview by the author, videotape recording, Burbank, CA, August 2, 1995; Slutsky 1989, 81–83.
69. "Momma Don't Allow No Loud Guitar Playin' 'Round Here: The Role of Electric Guitar in Motown Recordings of the Detroit Era," graduate research paper, Motown course 2010. Mark Hood is a professional audio recording engineer and Assistant Professor of Music in the Recording Arts Department of the Jacobs School of Music.
70. Gordy, *20/20* interview.
71. Wilson 1986, 171.
72. Bianco 1988, 35.
73. In her interview with the author, Sylvia Moy claimed to have produced these records, but was not given credit.
74. The Marvin Gaye version was recorded in 1967 before the version released on Gladys Knight & The Pips, but Berry Gordy decided that the Gladys Knight version would be released first. Gordy 1994, 273–275.
75. "Triumph of a Stay-At-Home," *Ebony*, February 1966, 33.
76. McFarland, interview.
77. Thurston 1972, A3.
78. Graff 1994, A13.
79. Graff 1993.
80. McCollum 1996.
81. Katz 1998, accessed July 10, 2016, http://www.cnn.com/SHOWBIZ/9803/26/motown.anniversary.lat.
82. ClassicMotown.com, accessed November 2, 2015, http://classic.motown.com.

DISCOGRAPHY

Gaye, Marvin. *The Master, 1961–1984.* Motown Master Series 3145304922, 1995. 4-CD set.
Hitsville USA: The Motown Singles Collection, 1959–1971. Motown 3746363122, 1992. 4-CD set.
Hitsville USA: The Motown Singles Collection, 1972–1992. Motown 3746363582, 1993. 4-CD set.
The Jackson 5. *Soulsation! 25th Anniversary Collection.* Motown Master Series 3145304892, 1995. 4-CD set.
Smokey Robinson and the Miracles: The 35th Anniversary Collection. Motown Master Series 374 636 334–2, 1994. 4-CD set.
The Temptations: Emperors of Soul. Motown Master Series 31453–0338–2, 1994. 5-CD set.

CHAPTER 8

Stax Records and the Impulse toward Integration

Rob Bowman

The story of Stax Records is about as improbable and unforeseeable as any tale could possibly be. Started by a White country fiddler named Jim Stewart who, by his own admission, originally knew next to nothing and cared even less about Black music, in the 1960s Stax Records developed a readily identifiable sound that defined the very possibilities of southern soul music. While undeniably involved on a day-by-day basis in the crafting and marketing of African American culture, virtually from the beginning Stax Records was racially integrated in the studio, in the front office, and, by the midway point of its history, at the level of ownership. All this took place in Memphis, Tennessee, a city that as late as 1971 elected to close its public swimming pools rather than allow Black and White kids to swim side by side in the scorching summer heat. By any logic that one can call forth, musicologically and sociologically, Stax Records simply shouldn't have been possible.

Although Jim Stewart issued a handful of rockabilly, pop, and country 45s on Satellite Records, the precursor to Stax, between 1958 and 1960, the legacy of the company, for all intents and purposes, gets started with the summer 1960 issue of Rufus and Carla Thomas's "'Cause I Love You." From that point on, the history of Stax can be understood to divide roughly into two halves: 1960 through May 1968 and June 1968 through December 1975. In the first period, Stax was distributed by the New York–based Atlantic Records, the Volt subsidiary was created, and the company developed what became known as the "Stax Sound," manifest on the recordings of a panoply of soul greats including Otis Redding, Sam and Dave, Booker T. and the MGs, Rufus Thomas, Carla Thomas, William Bell, Eddie Floyd, and Albert King.

After the severance of the Atlantic distribution agreement in May 1968, Jim Stewart and his sister Estelle Axton sold Stax to Gulf and Western. Two years later, Jim Stewart and former Stax promotion man Al Bell bought Stax back from G&W and Stax remained an independent label until its demise in December 1975. During this second period, led by the vision and energies of Al Bell, Stax tremendously expanded its operation, releasing music of various genres recorded in various parts of the country. While the company no longer had a signature sound, it was in this period, with the popularity of Isaac Hayes, the Dramatics, the Staple Singers, and Rufus Thomas, that Stax enjoyed its greatest commercial success.

THE FIRST PERIOD

The "Stax Sound," which characterized the company's releases through the late 1960s, was the result of a number of factors. Perhaps the most fortuitous of these was Stewart's decision in early 1960 to move his fledgling company to an abandoned neighborhood movie theatre in South Memphis at the corner of College and McLemore. With his then right-hand man, Chips Moman, various members of the all-White instrumental group the Mar-Keys (whose members included Stewart's nephew, Packy Axton, as well as future Stax session musicians Steve Cropper, Duck Dunn, and Wayne Jackson), and a handful of others, Stewart converted the cavernous theatre into a recording studio. Once the seats were ripped out, a wall was constructed dividing the recording room in half, acoustic material was fastened to the walls and ceiling, and a control booth was constructed on what had been the theatre's stage. A crucial element in determining what became the Stax sound was Stewart's decision to save money by not leveling the sloping theatre floor. The finished studio turned out to be totally unique in terms of design, ambiance, and, most importantly, acoustics. With a sloping floor and angled walls, there were no directly parallel surfaces. This meant that sound waves would continuously reflect off one surface after another, ping-ponging around the room until their energy was eventually totally dissipated, in the process creating an exceedingly "live" reverberant sound that characterized each and every recording made at the company's 926 E. McLemore studio. A discerning ear can consequently identify a recording made at Stax in the 1960s within less than four bars.

While the theatre's acoustics played a large part in the "Stax Sound," so did the theatre's location. At the time that Stewart and his co-owner and sister, Estelle Axton (the name came from combining the first two letters of each of their last names), took over the Capitol Theatre, the neighborhood around College and McLemore was rapidly shifting its demographic base from White to Black. When Axton decided to convert the theatre's candy concession into the Satellite Record Shop, her clientele naturally reflected the larger shifts in the neighborhood and became nearly exclusively Black. The importance of this fact in the Stax story cannot be underestimated. Besides generating much-needed cash flow, the record shop served as a means of aiding and abetting neighborhood relations, as a ready-made test market for potential Stax releases, and as a conduit for recruiting local talent.

It was in the latter capacity that the Satellite Record Shop played a crucial role in the development of the Stax sound. When Stewart and Axton moved their operation to McLemore Avenue, they had made only one recording by a Black group, the Veltones, and they still envisioned themselves as running a company that specialized in pop and country recordings. Fortunately, it didn't take long for word to get out in the neighborhood that behind the Satellite Record Shop was a recording studio and a record company. Soon after Stewart set up shop, WDIA disc jockey and former Sun Records artist Rufus

Thomas decided to pay a visit to the fledgling company with his teenage daughter Carla in tow. Stewart was impressed with the tapes Rufus brought with him and, having achieved little success with pop and country, figured he had nothing to lose in attempting to market a Black record. When "'Cause I Love You" (1960) by Carla and Rufus sold thirty thousand copies in the mid-South, Atlantic Records decided to pick up national distribution and Satellite Records (soon to become Stax) had its first hit.

"Prior to that I had no knowledge of what Black music was about," admits Jim Stewart. "Never heard Black music and never even had an inkling of what it was all about. It was like a blind man who suddenly gained his sight. You don't want to go back, you don't even look back. It just never occurred to me [to keep recording country or pop]."[1]

In fact, Stewart's company nearly instantly changed its direction; when Carla Thomas had a Top 10 pop and R&B (rhythm and blues) hit later that fall with "Gee Whiz (Look at His Eyes)" (1960), there was no question what path Stax would take.

Playing tenor sax on the Carla and Rufus record was a sixteen-year-old named Booker T. Jones. Later to achieve fame as the organist and namesake of Booker T. and the MGs, Jones had a story typical of many of the session players who came to Stax. A student at Booker T. Washington High School, Jones would rush out of school at the end of each day, quickly deliver his newspaper route, and then head down to the Satellite Record Shop. Estelle Axton was happy to play new releases for anyone who cared to ask, so Jones, ostensibly there to buy records, spent most of his time listening to records while trying to angle a way to get through the back door into the studio. Eventually he was successful. In fact, a significant number of future Stax artists, session musicians, and songwriters used the record store as an entree into the world of Stax Records. A handful of them, including Steve Cropper, Deanie Parker, William Brown, and Homer Banks, actually worked in the store.

It is important to stress how much Stax was a part of the community. Most record companies are located in downtown office towers or suburban industrial areas. Stax was on a main street in the middle of a vibrant, dynamic neighborhood. Directly across McLemore Avenue was the Big D grocery store where most of the neighborhood residents did their weekly shopping. Adjacent to the studio was a TV repair shop, King's Barbershop, and a soul food restaurant (the latter immortalized by Booker T. and the MGs with their instrumental "Slim Jenkins' Joint," 1967). Every day, residents of the neighborhood passed the studio on their way to school or work. Over time, most people in the surrounding area knew someone who worked at Stax and the company served as a source of tremendous community pride.

The majority of the artists that recorded for the company came from the south Memphis area that surrounded the studio. This is perhaps best dramatized by the fact that Rufus Thomas, Booker T. Jones, horn players Andrew Love and Gilbert Caple, William Bell, songwriters Homer Banks and Carl Hampton, and members of the Bar-Kays, the Soul Children, and the Mad Lads all went to the same high school, Booker T. Washington. In the surfeit of commentary on the regionality of American music in general and 1960s soul music in particular, Stax recordings are commonly posited as indicative of the Memphis sound. While on one level such a statement is obviously true, Memphis itself was divided into a number of distinct neighborhoods. African Americans in the city tended to live in either south or north Memphis. Due to transportation patterns and the logic of social relationships, the majority of artists and company employees at Stax came out of the south Memphis community. Therefore, it would be more accurate to view Stax as the manifestation of the *south* Memphis sound. With the exception of Isaac Hayes, very few north Memphians made it into the company as either employees or artists. It makes one wonder about what talent didn't get to record at Stax simply because they lived a few miles in the wrong direction from the studio.

By the summer of 1962, the four original members of Booker T. and the MGs—organist Booker T. Jones, guitarist Steve Cropper, bassist Lewie Steinberg, and drummer Al Jackson Jr.—had become the "house" rhythm section at Stax Records. In 1964, Duck Dunn replaced Steinberg on bass and Isaac Hayes often sat in for Booker T. while the latter was at college. When both Booker T. and Isaac were available, they would often both play on sessions, with Hayes on organ and Jones on piano. On most recordings, the rhythm section was joined by what were originally known as the Mar-Key Horns and later dubbed the Memphis Horns. While there was some fluidity as to who played horns on a given session, in the earliest days the section mostly consisted of baritone saxophonist Floyd Newman, tenor saxophonists Gilbert Caple and Packy Axton, and trumpeter Wayne Jackson. By the mid-1960s tenor saxophonists Andrew Love and Gene Parker came on board, followed a little later by Joe Arnold, as Newman, Caple, Axton, and eventually Parker drifted away. It is crucial to recognize that both the rhythm and horn sections consisted of White and Black members. While all were engaged in the creation of African American music, the racial composition of the band invariably meant that a number of pop, rock, and country influences would also play a part in the creation of the Stax sound. Most notable among these are Steve Cropper's use of open sixth dyads (typically used by country guitarists such as Chet Atkins) and Duck Dunn's tendency to craft melodic, contrapuntal bass lines (The Beatles' bassist Paul McCartney being a big influence in this regard).

Precisely summing up the sound on the several hundred recordings issued on Stax and Volt (a subsidiary label) in the 1960s is a virtually impossible task. One can, though, delimit in general terms the main features of the Stax sound in the 1960s, all of which stand in stark contrast to the musical practices of Detroit's Motown Records, Stax's main rival in this period.

The Stax sound consisted of:

1. An emphasis on the low register sounds both in terms of arrangement and mix.
2. The prominent use of horns, which often substituted for background vocals.
3. Prearranged horn ensemble sections conceived via "head" arrangements, which often took the place of either a bridge or the more typical "improvised" guitar, keyboard, or sax solos heard on many popular music recordings (this concept was originated by Otis Redding).
4. Few instrumental solos in the "improvised" sense mentioned above.
5. A "less is more" aesthetic manifested in sparse textures—the absence of ride cymbals on many vocal recordings, unison horn lines, and the absence of strings and, for the most part, background vocals until late 1968.
6. A mix that balanced the vocal and instrumental parts, as opposed to highlighting the former.
7. A prominent gospel influence as heard in the juxtaposition of organ and piano, the extensive use of IV-I cadences, and, most importantly, in the deployment by

vocalists at Stax of extensive timbral variation, pitch inflection, melismas, and syncopated phrasing all in the service of emotional catharsis.
8. A circumscribed harmonic vocabulary largely restricted to major chords.
9. A delayed backbeat on the snare drum and rhythm guitar. The latter technique was developed in 1965 by Steve Cropper and Al Jackson Jr. in response to a new dance known as the Jerk, and it became a component of virtually every Stax recording through the end of the decade.

Less tangible but just as important with regard to the Stax sound was the process by which these recordings were made. In the 1960s, time and money were initially not important considerations at Stax when producing a recording. While northern musicians were paid by the three-hour session, for many years musicians in the South were paid on a per-song basis. Some songs were completed in a half hour, while others took up to a day and a half. In the North, where time *was* money, record company owners and producers expected to cut four songs in a typical three-hour session. This left little time to collectively work out different grooves and arrangements in the studio and instead necessitated the employment of arrangers to work out and notate as many of the parts as possible in advance of the actual session. At Stax, in contrast, the four members of Booker T. and the MGs, Isaac Hayes, and the Memphis Horns would typically saunter into the studio one at a time in the late morning, slowly getting down to the task at hand—collectively working up a song via "head" arrangements until the groove was firmly established.

Once the groove had reached the requisite level of intensity, the vocalists, horns, and rhythm section all played their parts together, recording "live" in the studio with little or no overdubbing. This, of course, meant that if someone made a mistake, they either had to live with it or everyone would have to perform the song again from the beginning. At Stax, as often as not, if the recording had achieved the desired emotional catharsis, the take would be kept, mistake and all. On Sam and Dave's recordings alone, trumpeter Wayne Jackson misses his first two responses on the repeat of the chorus after the second verse on "Hold On! I'm Comin'" (1966), and on "Soul Man" (1967) the whole band dramatically shifts the tempo down at the beginning of the first verse. Such vagaries ultimately did not matter. In fact, if anything, they contributed to the magic, giving these recordings a feeling of humanity/realness/authenticity that is often absent from high-gloss, studio-produced recordings. Through the mid-1960s, recordings at Stax were also mixed live, with Jim Stewart simply adjusting the volume control faders, governing the recording level of each instrument as the parts were actually played. While such methods were antiquated by the standards of most studios, at Stax they were part and parcel of the distinctive sound. Taken as a whole, these various aspects of the recording practice at Stax tended to make the company's releases *performance- and process-oriented*, in stark contrast to Motown's more *composition- and product-oriented* aesthetic.

The overt reliance on musical elements that stemmed from and clearly referenced blues and gospel, the emphasis on an aesthetic that favored performance and process over composition and product (and, consequently, privileged oral over written culture), and an approach to mixing that did not clearly separate the constituent elements into foreground and background to the same degree that most pop recordings of the day did—all contributed to a sound that signified and celebrated what was generally understood to be the historic Black culture of the rural, agrarian, personalized, fraternal South. This stood in direct contrast to the Motown sound which, in its use of prewritten strings, prominent foregrounding of higher register sounds, busy and dense arrangements, and copious deployment of pop conventions such as narrative lyric structures and mixes that placed the lead singer way in front of the accompaniment, signified the commonplace, assembly-line sonic practices of pop music produced in the industrial, northern city. While both companies' approaches resulted in important, valuable, and meaningful recordings, the differences between the two are palpable.

While Stax was clearly a successful company, releasing numerous hit singles from 1960 onwards, the majority of its sales through the late 1960s were to African Americans living below the Mason–Dixon line. In contrast, Motown releases tended to sell equally well to both Black and White Americans and had national appeal, selling copious numbers in the Northeast, the Midwest, the South, and the West Coast.

THE SECOND PERIOD

After May 1968, everything changed at Stax, including its sound. In December 1967, Otis Redding and two-thirds of the original Bar-Kays perished in a tragic plane crash. In April 1968, Dr. Martin Luther King Jr. was assassinated in Memphis, forever changing race relations throughout the country, in Memphis, and at Stax. In January 1968, Atlantic Records, who had been distributing Stax since October 1960, was purchased by Warner Brothers. The Stax–Atlantic distribution agreement contained a clause that allowed Stax to sever their relationship if Atlantic was sold and Jerry Wexler was no longer a shareholder. When Jim Stewart was not able to negotiate a continuance of the distribution deal at a higher percentage, he elected to terminate the agreement. At the same time that Stax was preparing to part ways with Atlantic, African American promotion and marketing executive Al Bell became a minority shareholder in the company. According to Bell, part of the verbal deal he had made with Stewart when he came to Stax in August 1965 included eventual equity in the company. Isaac Hayes claims that he and a number of the other key African American employees at the company had to get together and force Stewart's hand on this issue.[2] By mid-1969, Bell bought out Estelle Axton. At that point, with Jim Stewart and Al Bell each owning 50 percent of the company, Stax had become integrated all the way up to the level of ownership (Figure 8.1). In the fall of 1972, Bell would buy Stewart's half of the company and become the sole owner.

Bell was a larger-than-life character who, upon coming on board in the fall of 1965, transformed Stax from top to bottom. "He had energy like Otis Redding," states Booker T. Jones,

> except he wasn't a singer. He had the same type of energy. He'd come in the room, pull up his shoulders and that energy would start. He would start talking about the music business or what was going on and he energized everywhere he was. He was our Otis for promotion. It was the same type of energy [and] charisma.

"I think there were some references to him as God," adds Duck Dunn. "He was that powerful."[3]

Bell took what had been a mom-and-pop cottage industry enterprise and in a few short years guided it to the level of rhythm and blues powerhouse. In the process, Stax tremendously expanded its output, for the first time devoting considerable energies to the

Figure 8.1
Al Bel and Jim Stewart, 1963.
Photographer unknown. Courtesy of the Deanie Parker Collection, Stax Museum of American Soul Music, Memphis.

release and marketing of LPs in addition to its staple diet of 45s. A former disc jockey, Bell had a sense of marketing that was informed by the knowledge and contacts he had acquired in over a decade of radio experience at KOKY Little Rock, WLOK Memphis, and WUST Washington.

Prior to Bell's arrival, Stax had been unable to sell substantial quantities of its records in New York or Los Angeles. Reasoning that Chicago and Memphis were connected by what he termed "Mississippi River Culture," Bell decided to use Chicago as his breakout point. "My approach to marketing," Bell explained,

> was . . . from a sociological standpoint. Even though I employ some of the techniques of the industrial scientist in marketing, it is more social science. If you appreciate the cultures and what the rivers represent to the cultures in this country and the kind of music that Stax was coming up with, it would just be logical to look for exposure along the Mississippi River. . . . The people from Mississippi and New Orleans traveled along the waterways from the Gulf up the Mississippi River.

Bell observed that Black southerners settled in the cities of Chicago, St. Louis, Kansas City, and even Detroit, Michigan.

> Most of the people in Detroit were people that had left Mississippi, Alabama, or Georgia and had gone to Detroit for jobs in the automotive industry. . . . Chicago may as well have been in the suburbs of Mississippi. By and large, the majority of the African American population in Chicago was from Mississippi or you could trace their roots back to Mississippi.[4]

Once a record became popular in Chicago or Detroit, Bell could then build on that success, marketing the product on both the East and West Coasts. Extending his socioscientific analysis of the relationship between Black cultures in the South and North into the realm of "product design," Bell's conclusions eventually had a far-reaching impact on the "Stax sound" and the political economy of both the company and Black music at large.

"The problem we had then," explains Bell,

> was that Stax was viewed as a company that was coming up with that 'Bama music [a pejorative term, derived from "Alabama," referring to music with clearly defined southern roots]. We had a problem in getting the product played outside of the South, across the Mason–Dixon line. When you got into the bigger urban centers, they were doing the Motown stuff. Being a jock, I knew that, and then traveling all over the place, I knew what was happening to us in the record stores and what was happening to us at the radio level and on the street level with our music. I started looking to diversify the company and, at that time, I was talking to everybody in there about broadening the music so we could go into New York, Philadelphia, Boston, Washington, and Baltimore much more formidably.
>
> The position that I had been trying to influence production to get into was maintaining the roots music that we had, but broadening and diversifying the sound. [Eddie Floyd's fall 1968 release] "I've Never Found a Girl" was one of the first shots at that. The person that was able to contribute most to that, who thought much broader than the roots music that we had been coming up with, was Booker T. Booker was the learned guy. Booker was the only guy on staff who could write music [as in notation] and he was an arranger.[5]

Bell's goals here were two-fold. He wanted Stax to appeal to the widest constituency possible and therefore hoped these changes would enable the company's recordings to sell to the previously largely indifferent Northeast and West Coast Black communities. He also wanted to make inroads in terms of sales into the mainstream White audience.

At the same time that Booker began employing small-scale string arrangements on recordings such as "I've Never Found a Girl" (1968), even greater changes were in process. Bell went to Detroit and brought former Motown and Revilot producer Don Davis to Stax. Davis, in turn, introduced Bell to northern arrangers such as Johnny Allen and Dale Warren and other northern producers such as Freddy Briggs and Tom Nixon. All of these individuals played a tremendous role in transforming the original sound that Jim Stewart, Booker T. and the MGs, and the Memphis Horns had developed. Bringing Davis in was a brilliant move on Bell's part, from a marketing angle, as his notion that a cross-fertilization of the Memphis and Detroit sounds would be potent in the marketplace was proven correct. With Davis's productions of Johnnie Taylor and the Dramatics leading the way, Stax, sporting its new hybridized sound, ascended to its commercial peak, grossing several million dollars annually through the early 1970s.

As is usually the case, when something is gained, something else is lost. With the arrival of the Detroit contingent, recording practices changed at Stax; sessions ceased to be recorded "live," overdubbing became standard fare, massed orchestral arrangements became de rigueur, and the original Stax aesthetic and sound became distant memories of days gone by.

While Don Davis was turning out hit after hit by artists such as Johnnie Taylor ("Who's Making Love," 1968; "Jody's Got Your Girl and Gone," 1970; "I Believe in You," 1973; "Cheaper to Keep Her," 1973) and the Dramatics ("Whatcha See Is Whatcha Get," 1971; "In the Rain," 1972; "Hey You! Get Off My Mountain," 1973), the company's original rhythm and horn sections were becoming alienated. Over time, most of the overdubs and some of the rhythm section tracks weren't even recorded in Memphis. By 1969, Booker T. had moved to California. Two years later he refused to have anything to do with any artist connected to Stax. That same year, Steve Cropper gave his notice and horn players Wayne Jackson and Andrew Love asked to be taken off salary, agreeing to work at Stax only on a per-session basis.[6]

As all of these transformations took Stax long beyond the 'Bama stigma that had so concerned Bell, in 1970 he began to produce the Staple Singers himself,[7] ironically conducting all of their rhythm sessions in Muscle Shoals, Alabama, while cutting the group's vocal overdubs at Ardent Studios in Memphis. Muscle Shoals had long been an important center for the recording of southern soul music with many of Atlantic Records biggest stars, such as Aretha Franklin, Percy Sledge, Clarence Carter, and Wilson Pickett, routinely recording there. Bell elected to produce the Staples' sessions there as he felt that the musicians at Stax in Memphis, who viewed him as a record executive who could neither play an instrument nor sing, would not take him seriously as a producer. The results were impressive—the Staples reinvented themselves as contemporary soul stars, and recordings such as "Respect Yourself" (1971), "I'll Take You There" (1972), and "If You're Ready (Come Go with Me)" (1973) came to define much of what was soulful and good about the first half of the 1970s.

In her landmark 1981 article in the journal *Ethnomusicology*, Margaret Kartomi concludes that the initial and sustaining impulse for musical transculturation is normally extramusical.[8] Andrew Leyshon, David Matless, and George Revill suggest in *The Place of Music* that commonly there are economic pressures brought to bear on local musical practices to adapt aspects of repertoire, performance style, and arrangement to meet wider spaces.[9] While Kartomi's article draws its evidence largely from examples of first- and third-world cultural contact and Leyshon, Matless, and Revill focus on the world music phenomenon, Al Bell's decisions at Stax suggest that the different but related conclusions of these scholars may be equally applicable to the motivations and practices operating, on a smaller scale, within the Western pop music industry.

Stax's greatest success in the second period belonged to Isaac Hayes. A songwriter, producer, and session player, by 1969 Hayes had established an enviable reputation in partnership with David Porter, writing and producing for artists like Sam and Dave and Carla Thomas such seminal hits as "Hold On! I'm Comin'" (1966), "Soul Man" (1967), "B-A-B-Y" (1966), "When Something Is Wrong with My Baby" (1967), "I Thank You" (1968), and "Wrap It Up" (1968). In the first few months of 1969, Al Bell offered Hayes the chance to record a solo album completely on his own terms. The result was *Hot Buttered Soul* (1969), an album that transformed the political economy of the entire Black music industry. With *Hot Buttered Soul*, Al Bell's desire to diversify the company's sound and thereby eliminate the 'Bama stigma that had plagued his early marketing efforts had an impact on much more than the sound of Stax and the consequent economic fortunes of the company.

"When I did *Hot Buttered Soul*," Hayes reflects,

> it was a selfish thing on my part. It was something I wanted to do. Al said, "However you want to do it." I didn't give a damn if it didn't sell because I was going for the true artistic side, rather than looking at it for monetary value. I had an opportunity to express myself no holds barred, no restrictions, and that's why I did it. I took artistic and creative liberties. I felt what I had to say couldn't be said in two minutes and thirty seconds. So I just stretched [the songs] out and milked them for everything they were worth.[10]

Hayes, Marvell Thomas (son of Rufus, brother of Carla), and Bar-Kays members Michael Toles, James Alexander, and Willie Hall recorded *Hot Buttered Soul* at Ardent

Studios with Terry Manning engineering. Allen Jones, Marvell Thomas, and Al Bell were credited as co-producers. Only four songs were cut: an eighteen-minute version of Glen Campbell's 1967 hit "By the Time I Get to Phoenix"; a twelve-minute version of Burt Bacharach and Hal David's "Walk on By," recorded by Dionne Warwick in 1964; a nine-minute track Al Bell called "Hyperbolicsyllabicsesquedalymistic"; and a relatively short five-minute take on Memphis songwriters Charlie Chalmers and Sandra Rhodes's "One Woman." The length of the songs; the arrangements that equally fused rock, soul, pop, jazz, and classical; the long rap that preceded "Phoenix"; and Hayes's vocal style were all radically different from what was going on in mainstream soul at the time.

Hot Buttered Soul sold over one million copies, an unprecedented showing for what was nominally a soul album. Equally unprecedented was the fact that the album charted in the upper reaches of four different charts simultaneously—jazz, pop, R&B, and easy listening—a feat few, if any, artists have ever achieved. Hayes virtually owned the jazz charts for the next few years as *Hot Buttered Soul* flitted back and forth between the #1 and #2 spots on *Billboard*'s jazz LP charts for over eight months. A year and a half after it was released, it was still in the jazz Top 10, joined by Hayes's next two albums, *The Isaac Hayes Movement* and *To Be Continued*. This was the kind of across-the-board success that Al Bell had envisioned for Stax. Engineer Ron Capone quickly edited both "Phoenix" and "Walk on By" down to single length, giving Stax's newest subsidiary label, Enterprise, a double-sided hit with "Walk on By" rising to #13 and #30 on the rhythm and blues and pop charts and "Phoenix" reaching #37 on both charts.

Up to this point, virtually everyone in the record industry simply assumed that the Black audience was neither economically equipped to nor aesthetically interested in purchasing LPs in large numbers.[11] Consequently, Black artists were not afforded the luxuries enjoyed by their White counterparts in crafting extended songs or album concepts. Instead, most Black LPs were hurriedly and cheaply recorded to capitalize on a string of hit singles. Little thought, effort, or expense was put into cover art design or marketing. *Hot Buttered Soul* unquestionably proved that Black artists could sell LPs and single-handedly revolutionized the notion of the length of songs and musical palette appropriate for Black artists. Stevie Wonder, Marvin Gaye, Curtis Mayfield, and Funkadelic would all follow Hayes's lead and, over the next few years, all four would record a series of highly creative albums.

Hot Buttered Soul was the perfect manifestation of a complete transformation of both sound and business practices at Stax. The different class backgrounds of Al Bell and Jim Stewart, their consequent different attitudes toward success and marketing, and Bell's understanding of how migration patterns, regionality, and musical preferences intersected led to very different approaches to the recording process, transformed the actual sound of the recordings, and consequently changed the resulting signification-of-place of Stax releases pre- and post-May 1968. Beyond Stax, too little is known about how sales patterns of most types of popular music play out on a regional basis and how company artists and repertoire (A&R) personnel, producers, engineers, session musicians, and artists try to negotiate these sales patterns sonically in attempts to constitute the local and/or to create communities of listeners over ever wider spaces.

The session musicians on *Hot Buttered Soul*—Thomas, Hall, Toles, and Alexander, alongside guitarist Bobby Manuel—would become the main session players at the McLemore studios in Stax's second period. In various permutations, they cut hit after hit for artists such as Isaac Hayes, Rufus Thomas ("Do The Funky Chicken," 1969; "(Do

The) Push and Pull," 1970; "The Breakdown," 1971; and "Do the Funky Penguin," 1971), and Albert King ("I'll Play the Blues for You," 1972; "Breaking Up Somebody's Home," 1972; and "That's What the Blues Is All About," 1973), and newcomers Little Milton ("That's What Love Will Make You Do," 1971), the Emotions ("Show Me How," 1971; and "My Honey and Me," 1972), the Soul Children ("I'll Be the Other Woman," 1973; "Hearsay," 1972; "It Ain't Always What You Do (It's Who You Let See You Do It)," 1973; and "Don't Take My Kindness for Weakness," 1972), Veda Brown ("Short Stopping," 1973), and the Temprees ("Dedicated to the One I Love," 1972). While Stax and its Volt and Enterprise subsidiaries were storming the charts with such home-grown smashes, the company was also enjoying mass success with Johnnie Taylor's and the Staple Singers' Muscle Shoals sessions, and Al Bell was making master purchase deals for bona fide hits by Mel and Tim ("Starting All Over Again," 1972), Jean Knight ("Mr. Big Stuff," 1971), and Frederick Knight ("I've Been Lonely for So Long," 1972).

Al Bell's influence extended well beyond marketing and A&R. In fact, there were seemingly no limits to his vision of the future of Stax Records. By 1972, the company had expanded into the world of film, with Isaac Hayes's soundtrack for *Shaft* jump-starting the so-called "blaxploitation" movement while also providing the groundwork for several of the key sonic components of late seventies dance-music grooves.

Anyway one looks at it, *Shaft* (1971) was one of the crowning achievements of Stax and rhythm and blues in the 1970s. Bell, desiring to develop Stax into an all-around entertainment firm, had been wanting to move the company into the world of film since at least 1968 when Stax had been sold to Gulf and Western. (Gulf and Western owned Paramount Pictures; Bell assumed that this relationship would pave the way for Stax artists to score film soundtracks and for these soundtracks to be released on one or another of the Stax family of labels.) Isaac Hayes shared Bell's keen interest and in early 1971 signed on to compose the *Shaft* soundtrack. Considering that this was his first film assignment, Isaac's score was nothing short of ingenious, containing numerous highlights. For most people, though, the film, Isaac Hayes, and the blaxploitation era are inextricably wedded to the title song, "Theme from *Shaft*" (1971). Released as a single in September 1971, two months after the album was on the market, "Theme from *Shaft*" contains an inordinate number of hooks, or catchy and defining melodic–rhythmic phrases. The two that are invariably the most indelibly etched into the listener's ear are the sixteenth-note hi-hat riff and wah-wah rhythm guitar part that are heard virtually from the beginning to the end of the track (Figure 8.2). Both licks, or patterns, were recycled endlessly during the disco era. Topping it all off were the incredibly dramatic string parts.

The *Shaft* album went to #1 on both the pop and R&B album charts, staying on the pop listings for a staggering sixty weeks. The single, "Theme from *Shaft*," which also reached the #1 spot on the pop charts while having to settle for #2 on the R&B charts, won two Grammy Awards that year. Isaac and arranger Johnny Allen won in the Best Instrumental Arrangement category; and Dave Purple, Ron Capone, and Henry Bush won in the Best Engineered Recording category. Isaac also won a Grammy in the Best Original Score Written for a Motion Picture category for the complete album. Even bigger than the Grammies was the Academy Award Hayes walked away with on April 10, 1972, for the Best Song category. For many African Americans, Isaac's capturing of an Oscar that night was an event comparable in significance to Joe Louis's knockout of Max Schmeling in 1938. It was a victory for all of Black America.

Figure 8.2
Transcriptions from Isaac Hayes's "Theme from *Shaft*."

Source: Bob Bowman.

Hayes's success in this period led writer Chester Higgins to dub him "Black Moses." The fact that disc jockeys, other writers, and Hayes's audience immediately took up the moniker speaks volumes about the symbolic importance of Hayes's achievements to Black America at large.[12] Hayes was extremely conscious of this and, alongside Al Bell and several other Stax artists and employees, felt a tremendous responsibility to both provide leadership and to give back to the community. In addition to performing at numerous benefit concerts, Hayes established the Isaac Hayes Foundation to develop housing projects for families with low incomes.

Stax as an organization was also extremely active in supporting Black-oriented community projects in Memphis and other regions of the country. For example, Stax Records staged an all-day concert in Los Angeles that featured its artists exclusively. The event, called WattsStax, was part of the Watts Summer Festival held on August 20, 1972, at the Los Angeles Coliseum. All proceeds derived from the massive Wattstax concert in August 1972, as well as the subsequent soundtrack albums and film, were donated to Black charities in the Los Angeles area; for several years, Stax contributed heavily to Jesse Jackson's Operation PUSH organization, and, of course, the company routinely supported local Memphis-based initiatives.

In addition to providing financial support, Stax was active on a number of fronts that were clearly a part of a corporate policy in support of the ideals and goals of the Civil Rights Movement. While the majority of material recorded by the company addressed matters of the heart in an effort to meet the commercial marketplace, a few Stax writers such as Homer Banks and Randy Stewart penned overt protest material such as "The Ghetto" (1968), "Long Walk to D.C." (1968), and "When Will We Be Paid" (1969). In 1970, the company established the spoken word Respect label as a vehicle to issue recordings that were politically and socially attuned to the newly emergent Black consciousness. The label's slogan was "Tell It Like It Is" and its recordings were distributed through school systems and churches in addition to regular retail record outlets. In total, seven albums were issued on Respect: two by Jesse Jackson, four by singer–songwriter John KaSandra, and one by Detroit journalist Jim Ingram. Finally, in 1970 Stax executive Larry Shaw brought together a consortium of Black-owned communications and consulting companies into an umbrella organization called Communiplex. Communiplex worked on a number of projects over the next few years, including the Stax-issued soundtrack for the first so-called blaxploitation film, *Sweet Sweetback's Baadasssss Song* (1971). As was the case with most developments at Stax in the 1970s, Communiplex may have been formed out of a desire to increase the company's bottom line, but it was also deployed in the service of the African American community at large. On several occasions over the years, on a pro bono basis, Communiplex helped successfully market the election campaigns of a number of African American politicians, large and small.

While Isaac Hayes and Stax Records were basking in the success of *Shaft*, which, of course, had been marketed by Communiplex, Bell's expansionist vision continued apace. In 1972, Stax made what just might be the very first promotional videos in soul music's history for the Staple Singers' hits "Respect Yourself" and "I'll Take You There." Bell had been to a Phillips tradeshow in Majorca, Spain, and realized that cable television and video were coming. The Staples videos were the first step in Stax's efforts to build up a catalog of ready-made programming for such oncoming changes in media. Under Bell's guidance, Stax, now staffed by some two hundred employees, also expanded into recording comedy, gospel, rock, pop, jazz, and socially conscious programs on new labels such as Partee, Gospel Truth, Respect, Hip, and Truth. Finally, in the 1970s Stax as a company made tentative steps toward embracing Bell's pan-African vision, making marketing inroads into the Caribbean, South America, and Africa in an attempt to connect the various peoples of the African Diaspora.

It is ironic that while Al Bell was hot in pursuit of crossover success and expansion in several different directions, the company's founder, Jim Stewart, who initially wasn't even interested in Black music, would have been content to keep things a lot simpler, focusing on recording soul records that replicated the original Stax sound, mass success and mega-money be damned. As is so often the case when a cottage industry becomes a large corporation, at Stax the company's owners had become embroiled in a sea of never-ending paperwork and meetings. For Stewart, life at Stax had ceased to be fun.

In 1972, Stewart told Bell that he wanted to sell the company and get out of the business. Attempts were made to find a buyer over several months and, while there were a few offers made, none came up to the price in cash that Stewart and Bell thought the company was worth. Bell eventually worked out a deal with Columbia Records in New York where, in turn for the rights to distribute Stax, Columbia would loan the company $6 million. Out of that $6 million, Bell would begin to buy Jim Stewart's share of the company. Part of the condition of the deal was that Stewart stay with the company for an additional five years. The agreement was consummated on October 24, 1972.

It is significant to note that the fact that Bell was now sole owner of the company was kept quiet from both company employees and the public. When this did come to light during Stax's bankruptcy troubles, within Memphis there was a racist backlash. While Memphis was willing to grudgingly accept that an integrated record company within its midst was doing millions of dollars worth of business, for many the idea that the company was wholly Black-owned was simply unacceptable.

The Columbia–Stax distribution deal had been negotiated between Bell and CBS president Clive Davis. In May 1973, Davis was abruptly fired and his successors were aghast at the deal he had made with Stax. They felt that the smaller Memphis company was being overpaid. When they attempted to renegotiate the deal and Bell said no, relations between the two companies soured. That, combined with the clashes that resulted due to the two companies' different corporate cultures, eventually led to a situation where Stax was experiencing slumping sales and consequent cash flow problems. Stax contended that Columbia was overordering Stax products and then not placing the records in the marketplace. By mid-1974, Columbia decreed that Stax had been overadvanced and ceased remitting any further funds.

Faced with economic strangulation and attempts at a hostile takeover, Stax pledged its publishing interests to Union Planters National Bank in return for several million dollars in loans. Without an income stream due to Columbia's refusal to pay Stax any further funds until the advance was cleared up, Stax could not meet its loan obligations to Union Planters. When the bank found itself in serious financial troubles, it elected to force Stax into bankruptcy. Stax was padlocked shut on December 19, 1975.[13]

Although the company folded in the last days of 1975, the legacy of Stax remains potent a quarter century later. In the 1960s, rock groups such as the Rolling Stones were routinely covering Stax classics such as Rufus Thomas's "Walking the Dog" (1963) and

Otis Redding's "That's How Strong My Love Is" (1964). In the 1980s, ZZ Top hit the charts with their cover of Sam and Dave's "I Thank You" (1968), as did the Fabulous Thunderbirds with a similarly refashioned cover of the dynamic duo's "Wrap It Up" (1968). In the world of rap, the Stax influence has been even more ubiquitous. From Heavy D & the Boyz's crazed cover of "Mr. Big Stuff" (the original was 1971, the cover was 1986), to Salt-N-Pepa's reworking of Linda Lyndell's "What a Man" (the original was 1968, the cover was retitled "Whatta Man" and issued in 1994), to Will Smith's use of the Bar-Kays's "Sang and Dance" (1970) on "Gettin' Jiggy Wit It" (1998), samples of Stax recordings have been omnipresent on the rap landscape. Finally, there have been dozens of urban covers of Stax material. Notable examples include Jewell's Snoop Doggy Dogg–produced cover of Shirley Brown's "Woman to Woman" (the original was 1974, the cover was 1994), BeBe and CeCe Winans's Grammy Award–winning version of the Staple Singers' "I'll Take You There" (the original was 1972, the cover was 1991), and Janet Jackson's take on Johnny Daye's "What'll I Do for Satisfaction" (the original was in 1967, the cover was in 1993). In these and the continued recording and performing activities of Stax alumni such as Booker T. & the MGs and Sam Moore of Sam and Dave, the magic of Stax lives on.

NOTES

1. Interview with the author, April 21, 1986.
2. This information is based on statements made by Isaac Hayes in interviews with the author.
3. Interviews with the author, March 17, 1994.
4. Interview with the author, November 15, 1985.
5. Interview with the author, May 2, 1993. While all the session musicians participated in the head arrangements that were an integral part of all rhythm section and horn section dates, Booker T. Jones had obtained a university degree in music from Indiana and was the only musician on staff at that time capable of writing out string arrangements.
6. This information is based on statements made by Wayne Jackson and Andrew Love in interviews with the author.
7. Bell signed the Staple Singers to Stax Records in the fall of 1968. Steve Cropper produced the group's first two albums, neither of which generated charted material.
8. Kartomi 1981.
9. Leyshon, Matless, and Revil 1998.
10. Interview with the author, August 6, 1986.
11. This information is based on statements made by Jerry Wexler, Jim Stewart, and Al Bell in interviews with the author.
12. *Black Moses* became the name of Hayes' next studio album.
13. See the last four chapters of Bowman 1997

DISCOGRAPHY

Bell, William. *The Very Best of William Bell*. Stax STXCD 30297, 2007. CD.
Booker T. & the MGs. *Best of Booker T. & The MGs*. Originally released as Atlantic SD 8202, 1968. Stax 046, 1992. CD.
———. *Best of Booker T. & The MGs*. Originally released as Stax 60004, 1986. Stax 123, 1998. CD.
The Complete Stax/Volt Singles, 1959–1968. Various artists. Originally released as Atlantic 7567822182, 1991. Atlantic/Rhino 8122795466, 2016. CD.
The Dramatics. *The Best of The Dramatics. [20th Century Masters The Millennium Collection.]* Hip-O Records B0005217–02, 2005. CD.
The Emotions. *Chronicle: Greatest Hits*. Originally released as Stax STX-4121, 1979. Stax SCD24 4121, 2002. CD.

Floyd, Eddie. *Chronicle: Greatest Hits.* Originally released as Stax STX-4122, 1978. Stax SCD-4122–2, 1990. CD.
Hayes, Isaac. *The Isaac Hayes Movement.* Originally recorded March, 1970–April, 1970, originally released 1970. Stax SCD-4129–2, 1991. CD.
———. *To Be Continued.* Originally released 1970. Stax 4016, 2007. CD.
———. *Hot Buttered Soul.* Originally released 1969. Fantasy/Stax 7231458, 2009. CD.
———. *Shaft. [Music from the Soundtrack.]* Originally released 1971. Fantasy/Concord/Stax/Universal, 2009. Digital; Stax STX-31751, 2009. CD.
King, Albert. *Albert King/Little Milton Chronicle.* Originally released 1979. Stax SCD-4123–2, 1989. CD.
Little Milton. *The Very Best of Little Milton.* Stax 30306, 2007. CD.
The Mar-Keys. *The Best of the Mar-Keys.* Sound and Vision, 2013. Digital.
Redding, Otis. *(Sittin' On) The Dock of the Bay.* Originally released 1968. ATCO Records/Rhino Flashback 780254, 2009. CD.
———. *Otis Redding: The Complete Studio Albums Collection.* Atlantic/Rhino, 2015. Digital.
Sam and Dave. *Sam and Dave: The Greatest Hits.* Unequal Halves, 2013. Digital.
The Soul Children. *Genesis.* Originally released 1972. ZYX Music 4433, 2001. CD.
———. *Friction.* Originally released as Stax STX 1005, 1974. JVC Victor 61956, 2002. CD.
The Staple Singers. *The Best of the Staple Singers.* Originally released as Fantasy FCD-60–007, 1986. Stax 0025218300728, 2006. CD.
Taylor, Johnnie. *Johnnie Taylor Chronicle: The 20 Greatest Hits.* Originally released as Stax STX-88001, 1977. Reissued as Stax FCD-60–006, 1990. CD.
Thomas, Carla. *Stax Profiles Carla Thomas.* Fantasy/Stax 1886212, 2006. CD.
Thomas, Rufus. *The Very Best of Rufus Thomas.* Fantasy/Concord/Stax 7230307, 2007. CD.
Van Peebles, Melvin. *Sweet Sweetback's Baadasssss Song.* Originally released 1971. Stax SCD24 3001, 2002. CD.
WattsStax: The Living Word. [Concert Music from the Original Movie Soundtrack.] Various artists. Concord 7230520, 2007. CD.

CHAPTER 9

Uptown Sound—Downtown Bound
Philadelphia International Records

John A. Jackson

PROLOGUE

Philadelphia International Records was formed in 1971 by Kenneth Gamble and Leon Huff, both of whom started out as penniless Black youths from the ghettos of West Philadelphia and Camden, New Jersey, respectively. Philadelphia International was the last major American independent record label to develop a regional sound. The Sound of Philadelphia was a multilayered, bottom-heavy brand of sophisticated and glossy urban rhythm and blues. Before its demise, Philadelphia International produced nine platinum-certified albums and fifteen gold-certified albums, by Patti LaBelle, McFadden & Whitehead, Harold Melvin and the Blue Notes, the O'Jays, Billy Paul, Teddy Pendergrass, and Lou Rawls. But the vocals of those artists—and of other Philadelphia International singers—were merely one component of a rigid assembly-line formula perfected by Gamble and Huff. Relying on that hit-making precept, the two parlayed Philadelphia International Records into the second-largest Black-owned recording company, right behind Motown.

Kenny Gamble was born in South Philadelphia on August 11, 1943. When he was thirteen, Gamble, his mother, and two brothers moved to West Philadelphia, which was already one of the city's most blighted areas. By the time Gamble was a teenager, he aspired to be a singer. Around 1957, he became a "gofer" for notable WDAS rhythm and blues disc jockey Georgie Woods ("The Guy with the Goods"). Gamble periodically brought Woods copies of arcade-recorded songs the naïve teenager had made, with the hope that Woods would play them on the air.

Leon Huff was born in Camden, New Jersey, on April 8, 1942. The son of a local barber, Huff was raised in one of the city's austere and foreboding post–World War II housing projects. The streetwise teenager taught himself to play the piano after observing a local performer play boogie-woogie onstage in neighboring Philadelphia, just across the

Delaware River. By the early 1960s, Huff had acquired a reputation as a notable rhythm and blues session pianist in Philadelphia and in New York.

Gamble met Huff thanks to a White record promoter turned writer and producer, Jerry Ross. In high school, Gamble befriended piano player Thom Bell. (Bell was born in Kingston, Jamaica, on January 27, 1943, and, with his family, moved to West Philadelphia when he was four years old. Two years later, he began formal piano lessons.) In 1962, Gamble and Bell cut a record (*I'll Get By*, by "Kenny and Tommy") for Ross' label; the piano player for the session was Leon Huff. Gamble started to write songs with Ross and to learn the basics of record production. He also began singing in West Philadelphia bars. In 1963, in need of a regular backing band for his gigs, he formed the Romeos, a five-man combo that included his old singing partner Thom Bell on piano.

In 1963, Gamble and Huff each wrote their first hit records. Gamble (with Jerry Ross) wrote the Sapphires' "Who Do You Love," while Huff penned Patty & the Emblems' "Mixed Up, Shook Up Girl." That fall, Gamble, who had a smooth baritone voice similar to that of crooner Brook Benton, recorded an album for Columbia Records. Due largely to Columbia's inept promotion of Black music, however, the album proved to be a commercial failure.

By that time, Gamble and Huff both worked in the Schubert Building, Philadelphia's version of New York's Brill Building and the fountainhead of early 1960s pop music. Gamble continued to write with Ross, while, two floors below, Huff wrote for John Madara and Dave White, two White men who were former singers turned songwriter–producers. After kindling a friendship through their mutual musical interests, Gamble and Huff decided to form their own partnership. In 1965, they borrowed $700 and formed their own record label, Excel, as well as their own song publishing company. For legal reasons, Excel Records became Gamble Records after one release. The differences between the new partners were striking. The lanky Gamble was insightful, reserved, and dressed functionally. The gruff and taciturn Huff was short in stature and liked to outfit himself impeccably. The only things the two had in common were their socioeconomic backgrounds, inabilities to read or write music, and robust drives to succeed.

Until then, most of the rhythm and blues records originating in Philadelphia featured Motown licks. But that situation began to change. As the Romeos recorded a series of records for a local label, Gamble and Huff (who had replaced Thom Bell in the Romeos) continued to refine their studio production and songwriting techniques. Gamble and Huff had each learned how to play a few rudimentary musical chords. Huff, who played the piano by ear, was able to convey his musical ideas in that manner; Gamble simply sang his ideas, either to Huff or to the musicians in the recording studio.

By that time, Gamble was a recording studio denizen who compulsively observed and absorbed a wide array of production techniques from numerous sources. He was present when the landmark Philadelphia soul hits "Yes, I'm Ready," by Barbara Mason and "This Can't Be True Girl," by Eddie Holman were recorded in 1965. Those sessions had a profound effect on Gamble's evolving production philosophy. Soon he and Huff, working together, began to develop their own soulful groove. By 1967, Gamble and Huff were writing and producing minor rhythm and blues hits for a local group called the Intruders, who recorded for Gamble Records. The Intruders' records, which few White listeners heard, were largely confined to the Philadelphia–Baltimore–Washington, DC, corridor.

Everything changed late that year, however, after Gamble and Huff wrote and produced the Top 10 hit "Expressway to Your Heart" for a local "blue-eyed soul" group called the Soul Survivors. Early the following year, Gamble and Huff surpassed that milestone when they wrote and produced their first million-selling record, *Cowboys to Girls*, for the Intruders. The strong crossover proclivity of those two hits caused Gamble and Huff to reassess the appeal of their music. It was now obvious that Whites, as well as Blacks, were drawn to it.

Between 1968 and 1971, Gamble and Huff, writing to a racially mixed audience, produced Top 40 hits for a diverse group of established artists, including Archie Bell & the Drells, Jerry Butler, the Intruders, Wilson Pickett, Joe Simon, and Dusty Springfield. Their defining work during that time frame was Jerry Butler's "Only the Strong Survive," released on the singer's *The Ice Man Cometh* album in 1968 (and later as a single). The song featured all of the components—rich, layered arrangements, potent bass lines, strings, and a distinct female chorus—of what was soon to become Gamble and Huff's landmark sound.

Gamble and Huff's signature sound was rooted in their rhythm section, which consisted of drummer Earl Young; guitarists Norman Harris, Roland Chambers, and Bobby Eli; bassist Ronnie Baker; vibraphonist Vince Montana Jr.; and percussionist Larry Washington—"the guys who were beginning to mean something in Philly,"[1] said Kenny Gamble. This elite group of five Blacks and two Whites (Eli and Montana Jr.) was soon joined by two additional White musicians, organist Lenny Pakula and guitarist T. J. Tindall. The integrated group went on to become "the tightest of tight," said guitarist Bobby Eli.[2] During studio jams, they would often help develop riffs (and, sometimes, entire melodies) that were later incorporated into songs. The rhythm section, together with a horn section of about ten members and about a dozen string players, became known collectively as MFSB. Those letters ostensibly stood for "Mother, Father, Sister, Brother," but to the musicians, they were code for "Mother-fuckin' son-of-a-bitch," a complimentary expression (as in, "He plays like a mother-fuckin' son-of-a-bitch") used by many of the players in the studio. MFSB would play on every Philadelphia International hit for the next several years.

Another significant component of Gamble and Huff's trademark sound was the recording studio itself and the sound engineer who ran it. During the summer of 1968, Joe Tarsia, a White, self-taught electronics whiz (and formerly the chief engineer at Philadelphia's Cameo–Parkway Records), opened his own recording studio called Sigma Sound. Sigma became the keystone in Gamble and Huff's Philadelphia soul mix. Jerry Butler, whose recordings with Gamble and Huff were made at Sigma, called Tarsia "an acoustical genius [who] was as much a part of the Philly Sound as any of the writers and producers."[3] An ardent advocate of an open, ambient sound quality, Tarsia believed that when recording, "less is sometimes more."[4] He was able to project that roomy quality using Sigma's original, state-of-the-art, eight-track mixing board.

Throughout Gamble and Huff's career, the overwhelming majority of recording acts with which they had the greatest success were veterans of the recording studio who had never experienced a hit record or whose once-flourishing careers had taken a turn for the worse. Gamble and Huff were successful with such acts because the producers did not fall into the trap of trying to replicate the artists' past recordings. Instead, the singers were thrust into Gamble and Huff's rigid, assembly-line production process.

The first step in that process was to write the lyrics for a particular song. This was done by Gamble and Huff, who occasionally wrote with a third collaborator, or by a pair of staff songwriters who wrote songs on demand for a particular artist. Often assisted by the rhythm section, Gamble and Huff then composed the song's rhythm track. The artist, or the lead singer of the group recording the song, would then come into the studio and record the lead vocals while listening to the rhythm track. Gamble and Huff next employed someone to write an arrangement for the song. Their top arranger was the multitalented vibraphonist, Bobby Martin, who first made a splash as a musician in the late 1940s. (In the early 1960s, Martin produced Patti LaBelle & the Bluebelles' first records.) Besides Martin, Gamble and Huff regularly used Thom Bell as an arranger. (Bell was then creating his own brand of sweet Philadelphia soul, writing, arranging, and producing for the Delfonics and the Stylistics.) If the recording was of a group, the background vocals were then recorded. In the case of a solo artist, backing vocals by male and female studio singers were added to the song. The voices of the anonymous studio singers were usually added to Gamble and Huff's group recordings as well. And in some cases, the studio singers were heard in lieu of the group billed as the song's performers. (This process began at least as early as 1968, when Gamble and Huff sang as "The Drells" on their productions for Archie Bell. Besides a coterie of male studio singers, Gamble and Huff, and just about everybody else who recorded in Philadelphia during the 1970s, used the female trio of Barbara Ingram, Carla Benson, and Evette Benton—dubbed "The Sweethearts of Sigma"—on their recordings.) After all of the vocals were laid down, the track was then "sweetened" by the addition of horns and strings.

Gamble and Huff were quite successful at implementing this technique when they operated as independent producers. For the most part, though, they were unable to duplicate that success with the recordings of their own artists. (Only the Intruders enjoyed significant chart success for Gamble and Huff's own record label.) Gamble and Huff's inability to write or produce hit songs for their own artists became known around Sigma Sound as "The Curse."

Gamble and Huff's main problem was that the record business had changed drastically since they first entered it. When Gamble Records was formed, independent rhythm and blues labels such as Atlantic, Motown, and Stax flourished. But by 1970, five manufacturers (Columbia, Warner–Seven Arts, RCA Victor, Capitol–EMI, and MGM) controlled over half of the pop music business. Independent labels such as Gamble's were being squeezed out of business or absorbed by one of the five giants. In addition, record album sales had eclipsed the sales of singles in all facets of the pop music business. In an attempt to better compete with the major labels, near the end of 1968 Gamble and Huff made a deal with Chess Records to distribute their Neptune label. But in early 1969, when Chess was sold to GRT, a manufacturer of pre-recorded audiotapes, Neptune was "pushed to the side," said Gamble.[5]

Significant 1968 recording sessions with Wilson Pickett and Jerry Butler showed that Gamble and Huff possessed the talent necessary to write and produce commercially successful albums, but their tiny labels remained singles-oriented enterprises in an increasingly album-dominated market. When Neptune Records folded in 1970, Gamble and Huff set out to find a major record company with deep pockets and a potent distribution system.

At the same time Gamble and Huff began their search, Columbia Records, the reigning colossus of the recording industry, began to seek inroads into the burgeoning rhythm and blues music business. The renewed interest in rhythm and blues by Columbia (the label had operated a subsidiary called OKeh during the 1950s and Date in the 1960s) was the result of two occurrences. One was the demonstration by Stax, Atlantic, and Motown that well-promoted Black artists, given the necessary distribution, could deliver albums that appealed to a multiracial audience. With its 1969 release, Isaac Hayes' Stax album *Hot Buttered Soul* was cast as a creative force in rhythm and blues and soul. Also around that time, Motown producers Norman Whitfield and Barrett Strong began offering extended tracks on their albums, thereby challenging the industry-wide notion that a Black album need be nothing but a collection of singles and filler.

The other reason for Columbia's renewed interest in rhythm and blues was America's growing fixation on popular Black mores, which, around 1970, sparked a Black Renaissance within the country's pop culture. On network television, formerly a bastion of White conservatism, Black comedians Bill Cosby (*The Bill Cosby Show*) and Flip Wilson (*The Flip Wilson Show*) starred in landmark shows on the NBC network. The Black, sharp-tongued George Jefferson character made a timely appearance on the CBS network's hit series, *All in the Family*.

In the world of cinema, the release of *Sweet Sweetback's Baadasssss Song* (1971) kicked off a spate of blaxploitation films that featured sexy, powerful, righteous, and angry Black protagonists. Musicwise, rhythm and blues, which had traditionally been absent from network television, made a forceful national appearance in the form of *Soul Train*, a Black dance show patterned after *American Bandstand*. Taking stock of Black music's growing crossover appeal, Kenny Gamble proclaimed that "Philly soul records had the ability to break big pop if only a company could recognize that situation."[6]

THE RISE TO PROMINENCE

When Gamble and Huff contacted Columbia Records about a possible record deal, the company, then under the auspices of the erudite Clive Davis, was all ears. It had been Davis who, in 1967, realized that Columbia needed to expand into rock music in order to survive. In 1970, Davis acknowledged "the explosive crossover potential of black music"[7] and formulated another plan: Columbia would create a separate soul music division, the company would sign Black artists and producers, and it would also sign manufacturing and distribution agreements with independent soul firms. Later that year, Columbia appointed a Black man, Logan Westbrooks, as director of special markets (Columbia's euphemism for its Black music division), and ordered him to "create a black marketing staff to penetrate the black market."[8]

Gamble and Huff "were ready to make a move," said Ron Alexenburg, then president of Columbia's subsidiary label, Epic, and a participant in the label negotiations with the independent writer–producers. But a roadblock in the proceedings loomed. Clive Davis wanted to sign Gamble and Huff to a straight independent production contract. Gamble and Huff insisted on their own record label, to be funded and distributed by Columbia. After protracted bargaining, "we delivered," said Alexenburg.[9]

The formation of the corporation called Philadelphia International Records was announced in February 1971. According to the deal, Columbia initially allotted the cash-starved producers $75,000 for fifteen single releases and $25,000 per album. Gamble and Huff were given complete creative control of their new label. They signed their own artists and produced and recorded their own music. After receiving the finished master recordings, Columbia manufactured, distributed, and promoted Philadelphia International's records. In addition, the Philadelphia International agreement called for Gamble and Huff to periodically produce albums for Columbia's own recording artists. The agreement was designed to benefit both parties. With its implementation, Columbia gained an inroad to the lucrative rhythm and blues market while Gamble and Huff received the money and the distribution needed to produce and deliver their music to a mass market. This access to the White consumer market did not influence the character of Gamble and Huff's creativity; they continued to write and produce exactly as they had before. As Joe Tarsia put it, Gamble and Huff "were not thinking black or white; they were thinking *green*."[10]

While Gamble and Huff had no qualms about employing Whites when it came to creating and recording their music, the business end of Philadelphia International was operated predominantly by Blacks. Earl Shelton, who previously served as the administrative head of Cameo–Parkway Records, was hired in that capacity to run Philadelphia International. Harry Coombs, who had been associated with recording artist Ramsey Lewis in the 1960s, was named head of promotion, and Gamble's longtime friend, Phil Asbury, became the company attorney.

As promising as the Philadelphia International deal appeared to both parties, there was one disadvantage that neither Gamble and Huff nor Columbia foresaw. Contrary to popular belief, Philadelphia International was not an immediate success. During its first year of production, the label issued sixteen singles and one album. But a lack of focus on Philadelphia International's part, coupled with Columbia's inability to effectively promote Black music, resulted in a meager payoff of one modest hit, "You're the Reason Why," by the Camden-based rhythm and blues group the Ebonys in the summer of 1971.

Exacerbated by Columbia's ineffective promotion, "The Curse" continued to haunt Gamble and Huff. Racial divisions ran high within the music business as Blacks exercised recently-gained powers. At many Black-oriented radio stations, Columbia's White promotion men were not welcome. Columbia's impotent promotion of Philadelphia International product was especially difficult for Kenny Gamble, who was particularly close to many of the Black DJs in Philadelphia. The problem became so acute that, near the end of 1971, Gamble and Huff threatened to leave Columbia. At that point, Columbia agreed to turn over the promotion of Philadelphia International's records to Gamble and Huff's company. The change in tactics called for Columbia to make payments earmarked for record promotion directly to Philadelphia International. This proved to be a Damoclean decision, for while it initially helped develop hit records, it eventually threatened the welfare of Columbia, Philadelphia International, and Kenny Gamble himself.

It was the hope of Columbia Records that Gamble and Huff would make records that were appealing to Blacks and Whites alike, thereby enabling the giant company to sell large, across-the-board quantities of their albums. The marketing strategy for Philadelphia International product entailed releasing an album along with a strong single from it. If things went according to plan, the single would create enough interest on Black radio to cross over to White stations and stimulate album sales. If all of that somehow came to pass, at least one additional single (and hopefully more) would be released from the album, boosting its sales even further. But, up to that point, Columbia had been unable to work its plan, because Philadelphia International had released just one album (by Billy

Paul, a local jazz-inflected singer friendly with Kenny Gamble). Having grown impatient, Columbia sent word to Philadelphia: start producing hit records.[11]

The second coming of Philadelphia International Records occurred late in 1971, with the signing of two rhythm and blues groups: Harold Melvin and the Blue Notes and the O'Jays. At the time they signed with Philadelphia International, neither of these two shopworn groups, with a combined thirty years of recording experience for at least twenty different record labels, had ever had a Top 40 hit. But because of these two un-noteworthy signings, Gamble and Huff's underachieving record company stood on the brink of a startling breakthrough. In the spring of 1972, Philadelphia International released albums by Harold Melvin and the Blue Notes (Figure 9.1), the O'Jays, and Billy Paul, all of which contained the requisite single releases to implement Columbia's marketing strategy. To the joy (and relief) of Columbia and Gamble and Huff, four of those singles—the ballads "If You Don't Know Me by Now" by the Blue Notes and "Me and Mrs. Jones" by Billy Paul, and the O'Jays' dance floor rousers "Back Stabbers" and "Love Train"—became million sellers. The albums by the O'Jays and Billy Paul were eventually certified gold.

By the end of 1972, Philadelphia International Records hummed like a well-oiled machine. "The hits started coming, rolling in," recalled Thom Bell, who arranged several of them. "Then they started rolling even more."[12] America's established soul music centers, including Detroit, Memphis, and Muscle Shoals, were put on notice that the city of Philadelphia was a player to be reckoned with, as a potent rhythm and blues hit-maker and as the source of an entirely new soul sound.

Gamble and Huff's hit parade marched on into 1973. That year, Philadelphia International released the O'Jays' concept album, *Ship Ahoy*, which dealt with the African slave

Figure 9.1
Harold Melvin and the Blue Notes, c. 1970.
Photo by Michael Ochs Archives/Getty Images.

trade. The emotionally provocative and critically acclaimed package became Philadelphia International's best-selling album up to that time. By then, Philadelphia International had added a fourth hit-recording group to its growing roster. In addition to backing other artists, the musicians known as MFSB now made albums on their own. Their *Love Is the Message*, released near the end of 1973 and bolstered by the million-selling dance anthem, "TSOP" (The Sound of Philadelphia), went gold.

As good things continued to happen at Philadelphia International, Gamble repeatedly attempted to persuade Thom Bell to formally join him and Huff at the label. But Bell, a fiercely independent individual who enjoyed a successful career as a writer, arranger, and producer (then principally for Atlantic Records' flagship rhythm and blues group, the Spinners), refused to be tied to any record company. But Gamble, Huff, and Bell did find a way to join forces. In 1973, they formed a holding company called Great Philadelphia Trading. That company subsequently purchased a building located in the heart of Philadelphia that had previously served as headquarters for the then-defunct Cameo–Parkway Records. Desperately in need of additional operating space, Philadelphia International Records leased space in the building and moved the company's operations out of its cramped Schubert Building headquarters, located diagonally across South Broad Street. Gamble, Huff, and Bell also pooled their song publishing catalogs to form Mighty Three Music Publishing ("You'll Never Forget Our Tunes"). From then on, songs published by any and all of the three would belong to Mighty Three.

As Philadelphia's soulful dance music cast a wide shadow over the developing disco scene in 1974, America's hedonistic generation reveled in a dance explosion unseen for a decade. The rise of disco was aided by several Philadelphia International hits propelled by the masterly thrusts and bracing hi-hat of drummer Earl Young, including Harold Melvin and the Blue Notes' popular up-tempo numbers, "The Love I Lost" (1973) and "Satisfaction Guaranteed" (1974), and MFSB's "TSOP" (1974). Kenny Gamble boasted that the Philly Sound "is the best kind of dance music there is."[13]

By that time, Philadelphia International had cultivated an international audience, and the company released several albums that were recorded live overseas. (The female trio The Three Degrees had a particularly strong worldwide following.) Because of this strong international market, Columbia established several overseas branches of Philadelphia International Records. When it came to soul music, "what Philly had to give, the whole world wanted," proclaimed Gamble.[14] Now making records for an international audience, Philadelphia International's stars maintained a grueling worldwide touring schedule that was orchestrated by Huga Management, a division of the parent record company. Touring was also the recording stars' main source of income, because the bulk of the writing credit for the songs they sang went to Gamble and Huff or to their staff writers, and all of the song publishing was assigned to Mighty Three Music.

Gamble and Huff's worldwide acceptance further endeared them to Philadelphia's Black community, where the two were regarded as champions of a sort, two "brothers" able to run with the big White executives. Both men continued to live modest lives and remained eminently accessible. For the most part, they eschewed the trappings of wealth and fame. Philadelphia International's new Broad Street headquarters did not even have a sign outside the building.

All the while, Kenny Gamble became increasingly involved in social causes, most of which focused on fostering Black awareness and self-worth. He adeptly used the music of the O'Jays to project many of his socioeconomic points, with songs such as "Back Stabbers" (1972), "Shiftless Shady Jealous Kind of People" (1973), and "For the Love of Money" (1974). But the advancement of Gamble's lofty ideals did not always mesh with the well-being of Philadelphia International Records and its artists. Such was the case in 1973, when Billy Paul, coming off the million-selling "Me and Mrs. Jones," seemed to have the world at his feet. Then, over Paul's (and everyone else's) objections, Gamble released the controversial and confrontational "Am I Black Enough for You?" as the singer's follow-up record, effectively killing Paul's newfound momentum. Gamble's obstinacy in promoting "The Cause" would continue to increase at the expense of Philadelphia International's fortunes.

THE DECLINE OF POWER AND POPULARITY

The high times continued for Columbia and Philadelphia International, but there were signs of trouble ahead. In the spring of 1973, Gamble and Huff's godfather at Columbia, Clive Davis, was dismissed for allegedly misappropriating corporate funds. It was also alleged that, beginning about the time that Columbia ceded promotion of Philadelphia International records to Gamble and Huff's firm, the giant recording company spent over $250,000 per year in payola, a good deal of it going to Philadelphia International. A federal strike force was formed, and an investigation of payola in the music business, dubbed "Project Sound," was initiated. Philadelphia International Records was a main target of the investigation.

Then, during the spring of 1975, Philadelphia International was brought close to a standstill. Kenny Gamble suffered a nervous breakdown and had to be hospitalized. As a result, the company released only one new album during the first nine months of that year. Ron Alexenburg recalled that Columbia had no choice but to "back off and wait until [Gamble] was healthy enough to return."[15]

When Gamble did return later that year, rhythm and blues music had changed dramatically. Led by Van McCoy's dance floor classic, "The Hustle," disco had become the dominant force in the pop music industry. The newest and hottest genre in rhythm and blues was called funk. Gamble and Huff went so far as to establish a subsidiary label called TSOP, which was designed to showcase artists with a decidedly funkier style. TSOP did score a major funk hit in 1975 with "Do It Anyway You Wanna" by the People's Choice, but the group, as well as the label itself, was unable to duplicate that success.

Near the end of 1975, as The Sound of Philadelphia was assaulted by unprecedented competition, Gamble and Huff faced the loss of many of their key personnel. Perhaps the greatest loss was that of the multitalented Bunny Sigler. A writer, producer, and dynamic performer, Sigler, out of frustration over Gamble and Huff's refusal to promote him as a singer, left for greener pastures. Equally as injurious to Gamble and Huff was the loss of the heart of their stalwart rhythm section. Ronnie Baker, Norman Harris, and Earl Young were unhappy over not receiving writing credit (and, thus, royalties) for assisting in the development of some of the rhythm tracks that grew into hit songs. Also growing more impatient each day over the lack of opportunities to produce records at Philadelphia International, the trio left to form their own production company. Vince Montana Jr. joined Salsoul Records, where he created the Salsoul Orchestra, while a disillusioned Lenny Pakula temporarily left the music business altogether. Bobby Eli, although he continued to record for Gamble and Huff, became one of Atlantic Records' coterie of rhythm and blues producers dubbed the "Young Professionals." As if that were not enough, Philadelphia International was also about to lose its second most popular recording act.

In the fall of 1975, Philadelphia International managed to release albums by the O'Jays (*Family Reunion*) and Harold Melvin and the Blue Notes (*Wake Up Everybody*) before the mass defections occurred. Both albums became huge hits, but as the year ended, the Blue Notes' lead singer Teddy Pendergrass, who endured a contentious relationship with the acerbic Harold Melvin, split from the group. Pendergrass would continue to record for Philadelphia International, but there was no guarantee that he would be as successful on his own as he had been with his former group (who moved to another label). The title of the Blue Notes' final album for Gamble and Huff shrieked the warning: *Wake Up Everybody*! Philadelphia International Records could not survive if its current state of affairs did not improve in a hurry.

In 1976, the City of Philadelphia led America's bicentennial celebration and Philadelphia International Records began the process of recasting itself. Gamble and Huff's beleaguered company had the wherewithal to rectify its spate of problems, and acted accordingly. (By this time, Philadelphia International was then the sixth-largest Black-owned corporation in the United States, with some fifty employees and an annual payroll of $3 million.) Drummer Charles Collins, guitarist Dennis Green, and bassist Michael "Sugarbear" Foreman joined the depleted rhythm section. Arranger–producers Jack Faith and Richard Rome, who had been only marginally employed by Philadelphia International, had their roles increased, and additional producers, songwriters, and musicians were hired. One of the most predominant of Philadelphia International's new employees was Dexter Wansel, a young jazz-fusion artist and virtual wizard of the fast-developing keyboard instrument known as the synthesizer. Hired as a writer, arranger, and producer, Wansel also became A&R (artists and repertoire) and musical director for MFSB. In forging a reputation as a visionary, hit-making producer, Wansel (and, to a lesser extent, Victor Carstarphen, another newcomer) replaced Philadelphia International's classic thumping groove with a lighter, more disco-oriented, keyboard-dominated sound.

Meanwhile, another of Philadelphia International's problems was resolved. After almost three years, the payola case against the record company and Kenny Gamble came to a close. In a plea bargain, Gamble pled guilty to one count of illegal payments to radio station personnel, and he and Philadelphia International were fined. Leon Huff was indicted but, in an indication of how little Huff was involved in the company's business, the charges against him were subsequently dropped. The rather paltry payoff from the government's high-profile payola investigation gave rise to speculation that the investigation had been racially motivated—a sort of payback to those Blacks who had the temerity to rise to the top of what was essentially a White man's domain. On the surface, this was a plausible argument. Payola was historically endemic to the music business, and a nominal conviction such as Gamble's could have been made against scores of White record company executives.

A closer look at the case, however, revealed that Philadelphia International apparently relied heavily on payola to promote its records. In *Hit Men: Power Brokers and Fast Money Inside the Record Business*, author Frederic Dannen wrote that when federal investigators subpoenaed the financial records of Philadelphia International, they were "astonished . . . [to discover] the most graphic paper trail of payola that one could imagine." According to

Danren, the payoff money came from the quarterly checks that CBS gave to Philadelphia International for promotional support. One investigator involved with the case said that prosecutors had lists of "the amount of money" paid out by Philadelphia International "and who it was paid to."[16] What prosecutors did not have were people willing to testify that Philadelphia International had paid them off. Without such corroboration of the evidence, no cases could be brought against those charged. Thus, Gamble was able to work out a plea bargain. Perhaps the biggest casualty of Project Sound was Black music in general. Despite the embarrassingly insubstantial results of the government probe, the aura of scandal caused major record companies to back off from the marketing of Black music and focus instead on the comparatively safer White pop field.

Kenny Gamble and Philadelphia International Records survived the payola scandal, but the quest to imitate that company's sound, along with the rise of disco, continued to undermine the freshness of Philadelphia soul. Once again, Philadelphia International managed to bounce back, as Gamble and Huff reverted to their proven practice of working with veteran recording artists in need of a career boost.

In 1975, Philadelphia International signed the deep-toned baritone Lou Rawls, who had not had a Top 40 hit in five years. Sparked by "You'll Never Find Another Love Like Mine," the singer's first-ever million-selling single, Rawls' *All Things in Time* album, which was released in the spring of 1976, became one of Philadelphia International's biggest-selling albums ever. The reconstituted set of studio musicians who played on Rawls' album was dubbed the "Resurrection Rhythm Section." Philadelphia International's roster was also infused with new life by the meteoric success of Teddy Pendergrass, who, as a solo artist, was slickly marketed as a sex symbol as well as a dynamic singer.

For the remainder of the 1970s, Philadelphia International was essentially a three-act label. The O'Jays were Gamble and Huff's most consistent act by far. As the decade ended, each of the group's eight Philadelphia International albums of new material had been certified gold or platinum. Not quite on a par with the O'Jays, but a hefty cut above everyone else, was Teddy Pendergrass, who was responsible for four gold or platinum albums during that time. Lou Rawls, who followed his blockbuster debut album with two additional gold efforts, rounded out the trio. The only other Philadelphia International act to have a gold album during those years was McFadden & Whitehead, whose 1979 self-titled effort contained their million-selling anthem, "Ain't No Stoppin' Us Now."

Philadelphia International's new slogan declared that "The Message Is in the Music." But despite the continuing hit parade, Gamble and Huff's company was no longer the musical trendsetter it had once been. The label that once projected a classic sound now catered to distinct lead vocalists and was growing marginal within the music industry.

It was no help that Kenny Gamble, the driving force behind Philadelphia International (he exercised final say on all company matters), was now wealthy beyond his expectations and no longer regarded music with the passion he once exhibited. Gamble was a deeply spiritual person whose social consciousness began to dominate his behavior. Rather than showing an interest in competing with the ongoing disco and funk onslaught, Gamble attempted to involve Philadelphia International in a community improvement campaign. In the spring of 1977, the record company released an album called *Let's Clean Up the Ghetto*. The album was comprised of songs sung by several of Philadelphia International's biggest stars, and the title song was sung by the ensemble of stars. As part of the project, Philadelphia International bore the cost of cleaning equipment that was distributed free of charge in the city's Black neighborhoods. But Gamble's noble campaign was rebuffed by Philadelphia's race-baiting mayor, Frank Rizzo, and never really caught on. This official rejection by the city to which Gamble had remained true stiffened his resolve to further promote Black causes, come what may. Many of his views of society's ills were printed on Philadelphia International's record jackets. Gamble also became a devout Muslim. He "no longer saw Philadelphia International Records as merely a musical enterprise," wrote rhythm and blues critic and historian Nelson George, "but also a platform from which to proselytize, espousing a world view that obliquely revealed his private beliefs in the tenets of Islam."[17]

By 1978, Philadelphia International had entered into a downward spiral. Its operating capital almost depleted (Columbia's original guarantee of $25,000 per album was no longer in effect), the company's album output for the year dropped to eight releases, only half as many as the year before. There was a six-month stretch toward the middle of the year when Philadelphia International issued no new product. Compounding matters were sweeping problems that bedeviled the entire pop music business. That year saw the beginning of an industry-wide sales decline that would continue into the 1980s.

Between 1977 and 1979, Philadelphia International managed only five Top 40 hits. The late 1970s crossover success of Teddy Pendergrass, the O'Jays, and Lou Rawls masked the fact that Philadelphia International (and Black music in general) was losing most of its White audience. Of those three artists, Rawls' loss of White support was the sharpest. After three best-selling albums, his sales began to fade. In addition, Jerry Butler and Archie Bell, artists who enjoyed strong White support when they recorded with Gamble and Huff in the late 1960s, joined Philadelphia International in the late 1970s. But White record buyers no longer cared about them, and the singers were unable to duplicate their earlier successes.

In 1979, disco suffered a sudden meltdown. Philadelphia International and other Black record companies were hit hardest by the ensuing disco "backlash" and by the bottom falling out of the entire pop music industry. From the summer of 1980 to the summer of 1981, Gamble and Huff's cash-strapped company issued no records. It did not help that, by 1982, Black music faced a racist climate abetted by pop music's latest and most powerful promotional vehicle, MTV, which refused to air video clips by Black artists. Meanwhile, rap music, the antithesis of the smooth and melodious sound of Philadelphia, began to emerge as Black music's savior.

During the troubling early 1980s, Philadelphia International was almost single-handedly kept afloat by Teddy Pendergrass. The O'Jays' unbelievable run of gold and platinum had finally come to an end. But in March 1982, Philadelphia International's last great star was critically injured in an automobile accident. In an instant, Pendergrass became a paraplegic whose singing career appeared to be over. For Philadelphia International, *everything* was over. Following the loss of the label's only act capable of selling significant quantities of records, Columbia Records terminated its distribution contract with Philadelphia International. Gamble was forced to fire everybody at the company except attorney Phil Asbury.

In 1985, Gamble and Huff struck a distribution deal with Capitol–EMI Records. But after the release of only five Philadelphia International albums, the arrangement ended in 1987, marking the bitter end for Gamble and Huff's once world-famous label. In 1998–1999, under the auspices of sons and nephews of Gamble and Huff, Philadelphia

International Records was briefly revived. But after the release of two contemporary albums that went virtually unnoticed, Philadelphia International Records shut its doors for good.

THE LEGACY

The doors of Philadelphia International Records remain shuttered. Periodically, rumors of the creation of a Philadelphia International museum in the historic building appear. (Gamble, Huff, and Bell—by way of Great Philadelphia Trading—still own the choice piece of real estate.) One of the greatest successes of Gamble and Huff's record company was the establishment of the sound of Philadelphia as a significant musical genre. In the process, for a few fleeting years the City of Philadelphia (as it had done a decade earlier during the early *American Bandstand* era) became pop music's epicenter. Philadelphia International Records also demonstrated that no matter how washed-up a recording artist seemed, the possibility of career rejuvenation existed.

Ironically, Philadelphia International's strengths ultimately proved counterproductive to the company. Gamble and Huff developed an operating formula so successful that they would not (or could not) change when change was warranted. This brought about Philadelphia International's greatest failures—the inability to adapt to evolving musical styles and to develop new recording artists.

The music of Philadelphia International Records lives on through the various reissue projects that appear on the market. Today, control of the company's master recordings is split between Sony and Capitol–EMI. Sony, which purchased Columbia Records in the 1980s, controls the master records made from 1971 through 1975. When Columbia's five-year distribution deal with Philadelphia International ended in 1975, Columbia was unable to come to terms with Gamble and Huff over the control of future Philadelphia International master recordings. As a result, that control reverted to Gamble and Huff, although Columbia continued to distribute the label. As part of Capitol–EMI's 1985 agreement to distribute Philadelphia International, Capitol–EMI obtained the rights to Philadelphia International's post-1975 master recordings. Gamble, Huff, and Bell subsequently sold their Mighty Three Music catalog to Warner–Chappell Music.

Philadelphia International's legacy is also perpetuated by the live performances of some of the company's top artists, including Patti LaBelle, Teddy Pendergrass, Lou Rawls, the O'Jays, and reconstituted versions of the Intruders and the Blue Notes. In addition, remakes of Philadelphia International's hit songs continue to emerge. Simply Red's version of Harold Melvin and the Blue Notes' "If You Don't Know Me by Now" reached #1 on the charts in 1989, sold a million copies, and resulted in a Grammy nomination for Gamble and Huff. Philadelphia International's music can also be heard in "samples" used in contemporary rhythm and blues songs such as Patti LaBelle's 1981 recording of "Love Need and Want You," which, in 2002, was sampled in the #1 rhythm and blues hit, "Dilemma," by rapper Nelly with vocalist Kelly Rowland.

Philadelphia International Records should ultimately be remembered for two things: the production of extraordinary music and the proof of how two poor Black ghetto youths, who possessed little more than grit, determination, and a love of music, were able to rise to the top of their chosen profession.

NOTES

1. Cummings 1975, 86.
2. Interview by the author, November 9, 2000.
3. Interview by the author, August 5, 2001.
4. Interviews by the author, September 27, 2000.
5. Cummings 1975, 103.
6. Ibid., 107.
7. Davis 1976, 164.
8. Bowman 1997, 280.
9. Interview by the author, November 8, 2000.
10. Interviews by the author, September 27, 2000.
11. Columbia's dictate to "start producing records" was revealed by the Philadelphia-based producer Billy Jackson in his interview with the author, November 9, 2000. Jackson worked for Columbia Records from the late 1960s into the early 1970s.
12. Interviews by the author, September 30, 2001.
13. Cummings 1975, 137.
14. Ibid., 127.
15. Interview by the author, November 8, 2000.
16. Dannen 1991, 103, 104.
17. George 1988, 145.

DISCOGRAPHY

Butler, Jerry. *Nothing Says I Love You Like I Love You*. Originally released as Philadelphia International/EMI 35510, 1978. Sony Music Distribution EICP1367, 2010. CD.

Harold Melvin and the Blue Notes. *The Essential Harold Melvin and the Blue Notes featuring Teddy Pendergrass*. Originally recorded 1972–1975. Epic/Legacy 90627, 2004. CD.

———. *Wake Up Everybody*. Originally released as Philadelphia International/EMI ZK-33808, 1975. Edsel EDSM 0002, 2010. CD.

LaBelle, Patti. *The Essential Patti LaBelle [Limited Edition 3.0.]* Originally released as Philadelphia International Records/Epic/Legacy, 2008. Legacy/Sony Legacy 68643, 2010. Three CD set.

MFSB. *Love Is the Message*. Originally released 1975. BBR CDBBR 0179, 2012. CD.

———. *Love Is the Message: The Best of MFSB*. Originally released as Epic/Legacy 66689, 1995. Sbme Special Mkts. 724104, 2008. CD.

The O'Jays. *Ship Ahoy*. Originally released 1973. BBR CDBBR 0207, 2013. CD.

———. *Family Reunion*. Originally released 1975. Edsel EDSM 0001, 2010. CD.

———. *The Essential O'Jays [Limited Edition 3.0.]* Originally released as Legacy/Epic 90632, 2005. Legacy/Philadelphia International/EMI 52786, 2009. Three CD set.

Paul, Billy. *Total Soul Classic: 360 Degrees of Billy Paul*. Originally released 1972. Sony Music Distribution 733922, 2008. CD.

Pendergrass, Teddy. *Live! Coast To Coast*. Originally released as Philadelphia International Records 88474, 1978. The Right Stuff 29117, 1994. CD.

———. *Life Is a Song Worth Singing*. Originally released as Philadelphia International Records JZ 35095, 1978. Legacy 88697 29485 2, 2008. CD.

———. *Greatest Hits: Love TKO*. Originally released as Master Classics 8021, 2004. Hypnotic, 2006. CD.

———. *The Essential Teddy Pendergrass [Limited Edition 3.0.]* Originally released as Legacy 717476, 2007. Legacy/Philadelphia International/EMI 52785, 2009. Three CD set.

Rawls, Lou. *All Things in Time*. Originally released as Philadelphia International Records PZ 33957, 1976. Reissued as Philadelphia International Records ZK 33957, date unknown. CD.

———. *When You Hear Lou, You've Heard It All*. Originally released as Philadelphia International Records 25AP 857, 1977. The Right Stuff/Capitol 27628, 1998. CD.

———. *Let Me Be Good to You*. Originally released as Philadelphia International Records PIR 83658, 1979. The Right Stuff T2–66708, 1993. CD.

CHAPTER 10

"And the Beat Goes On"
SOLAR—The Sound of Los Angeles Records

Scot Brown

SOLAR (Sound of Los Angeles Records) was one of the most successful Black-owned record labels from the late 1970s through the '80s, with a lengthy run of hits and a large roster of artists including The Whispers, Shalamar, Dynasty, Lakeside, Midnight Star, Klymaxx, Carrie Lucas, The Deele, Calloway, and Babyface. The label was founded in 1977 and innovatively embraced multiple trends associated with soul, disco, and funk. SOLAR flourished in the midst of a transformation in the history of American and African American music. Large entertainment conglomerates were developing strategies to gain a stronghold in Black music consumer markets—and at a time of increased globalization and corporate consolidation in the industry at large. These changes, especially the foray of conglomerates into Black music, led to the virtual eradication of significant market share of independent labels that dominated Black music consumer markets a decade earlier.[1] The drift toward consolidation and usurpation accelerated in the decades to follow, thereby generating new competitive challenges for the survival of Black-owned record companies.

The latter 1970s was not an opportune time for a start-up Black record label, as major companies had established "Black music divisions" aimed at gaining footholds in African American music consumer markets. Larkin Arnold (Capitol), LaBaron Taylor (CBS), Logan Westbrooks (CBS), Ray Harris (RCA), and Tom Draper (Warner Bros.) were among a slew of talented Black executives who redesigned artist recruitment and/or product marketing practices to fit the particularities of the African American music market. They had expertise in business strategies that, prior to the 1970s, were the domains of Black-owned and small "boutique" labels.[2] Though Motown Records continued to reign as one of the most powerful African American enterprises, its commanding position vis-à-vis popular music was steadily declining amidst increased competition from larger corporations—a glaring symbol to this effect being the steady flight of its top artists and producers to other labels; e.g. The Jackson 5 (Epic), Four Tops (ABC), Gladys Knight & the Pips (Buddha Records), The Temptations (Atlantic), and Marvin Gaye (Columbia).[3]

Black labels had difficulty weathering the late 1970s and '80s—Stax Records was sold in 1977, Philadelphia International experienced major declines in sales by the mid-1980s, and the iconic Motown Records was sold in 1988. Pop music historian David Sanjek observed, in 1997, that SOLAR had distinguished itself from other recently established Black labels:

> [O]ne can point to such recent enterprises as Sylvia and Joe Robinson's Sugar Hill Records, Dick Griffey's Solar Records, or Paisley Park Records . . . all, with the exception of Solar Records, are no longer labels in the commercial spotlight.[4]

Part of SOLAR's ability to endure was its ability to constantly maneuver and negotiate with more powerful corporate forces in the industry—especially distributors. By 1981 SOLAR expanded to the point of launching Constellation Records. Three years later—Klymaxx, Collage, and Carrie Lucas moved over to the subsidiary which had acquired a distribution arrangement with MCA, independent of SOLAR's distributor Elektra/Asylum.[5]

This essay examines the rise and decline of SOLAR records with an interest in: (1) the origins of the label, (2) sonic strategies for commercial success, and (3) the parallel political and economic activism of its founder, Dick Griffey.

DICK GRIFFEY: ROAD TO ECONOMIC NATIONALISM

When Dick Griffey launched SOLAR in 1977, he had acquired decades of experience in multiple facets of the music business. He learned to play the drums at an early age, having grown up in a musical household in Nashville, Tennessee. His mother Juanita Hines was a gospel vocalist and keyboardist for the National Baptist Convention. In the early 1950s, he attended Pearl High School, studying with the formidable music educator and band conductor, Marcus Gunter. Trumpeter Waymon Reed (who went on to play in Count Basie's band and married Sarah Vaughn) played with Griffey in a jazz band during their high school years. In 1957, after spending a year at Tennessee State on a music scholarship and playing with the university marching band, Griffey served in the Navy as a medic and relocated to San Diego.[6] After his discharge in 1961, he settled in the West Adams/West Jefferson section of Los Angeles and worked as a private duty nurse. A few years later, Griffey's Tennessee State schoolmate and basketball player, Dick Barnett, moved to California to play for the Los Angeles Lakers. The two opened the Guys & Dolls club located at 3617 S. Crenshaw Blvd. at a time when an increasing number of African American residents and businesses were moving west of the city's historic Central Avenue district—a shift that began after the US Supreme court ban of discriminatory restrictions in housing in 1948.[7]

Griffey booked top performing acts at Guys & Dolls—regularly bringing in artists such as The Impressions, The Temptations, The Four Tops, Jackie Wilson, and Johnny "Guitar" Watson. Living up to its advertising slogan, "The Haven for the Greatest Athletes and Celebrities,"[8] the nightclub was a natural path toward Griffey's career as a concert promoter. Initially booking acts in Los Angeles venues, such as Adams West Theater, he went on to become one of the leading promoters of R&B and soul music concerts through the mid 1970s—handling the performances of Al Green, The Temptations, Aretha Franklin, as well as the international tours of The Jacksons and Stevie Wonder.[9]

While among a small clique of Black promoters of national stature in 1973, Griffey raised the issue of racism in the music industry and the need for African American empowerment (recurring concerns that would shape his entrepreneurial efforts). Noting the widespread exclusion of Black promoters from large national venues, he stated in 1973, "[T]here are a lot of capable black promoters all over the country who deserve a shot at some of these major concerts."[10] Griffey subsequently answered these concerns with activism, co-founding the United Black Concert Promoters Association. By the early 1980s, the association collaborated with Reverend Jesse Jackson's People United to Serve Humanity (PUSH) and opened the door for African American promoters to gain access to large arena tours. Out of these efforts Al Haymon emerged in 1984 as the first Black promoter of the Budweiser Superfest concert series. Concert promotion, however, was just one of the many facets of the music industry in which Griffey sought to institutionalize the Black Power call for economic empowerment.

FROM *SOUL TRAIN* TO SOLAR

Don Cornelius, former Chicago newscaster for WCIU-TV and host/executive producer of the Black music variety television show *Soul Train*, also considered his show as part of the ongoing struggle for Black economic power. While the show's programming centered on Black music, Cornelius was interested in expanding African American leadership in the television industry beyond the entertainment level, stating that "there is a place in television for blacks who don't sing, dance or tell jokes." "This is," he continued, "what I set out to prove with *Soul Train*."[11] Within two years of *Soul Train*'s debut in 1970 as a Chicago weekday program, the show emerged as a syndicated weekly program spanning media markets throughout the US. The capacity for Black financial cooperation to impact and potentially transform racially exclusionary segments of the American popular culture industry was perhaps best exemplified in *Soul Train*'s co-sponsorship by Johnson Products—one the largest African American businesses and manufacturers of Black hair care and cosmetics.[12] *Soul Train* moved to Los Angeles in 1971. L.A.'s position as the nation's media and entertainment center blurred traditional distinctions between "local" and national Black cultural trends. *Soul Train* was as much a part of the L.A. Black public sphere as it was an iconic Black cultural institution. Dance was (and remains) a profound expression of Black youth cultural identity, and *Soul Train* provided an outlet for African Americans in Los Angeles to display their unique moves to the world over.

The prize of appearing on *Soul Train* invigorated dance competitions in nightclubs, public schools, and neighborhoods throughout Los Angeles. Furthermore, the dances, fashions, and hairstyles popularized by the show were a reflection of the styles and tastes of African American youth in Los Angeles, and those transported westward by the steady migration of Black artists from other cities. John Muir High school student Temille Porter and her dance partner Charlie Allen received an honorary mention at the radio station KDAY's "Ultra Sheen, Afro Sheen, 7-Up Dance Contest," held at the Whiskey a-Go-Go club on Sunset Boulevard in June of 1975. The prize for placing in the contest was an audition for *Soul Train* at the KTTV Studios. Two months later, the two of them—donning matching tropical print outfits, made by her mother, Mazree Porter—strolled gallantly down the *Soul Train* line.[13] Popular *Soul Train* dancers Jeffrey Daniel and Jody Whatley contributed to the growth of numerous dance styles seen by

Figure 10.1
Soul Train Records executives. Left to right: Don Cornelius (co-founder), Logan Westbrooks (Vice President of Marketing), and Dick Griffey (co-founder).

Courtesy Archives of African American Music and Culture, Indiana University, Logan Westbrooks Collection.

national audiences; e.g. waacking, popping, robotics, and backsliding (popularized by Michael Jackson as moon-walking).

Also in 1975 Cornelius and Griffey (Figure 10.1) formed Soul Train Records—they were natural partners for this new business venture since Griffey had served as talent coordinator for *Soul Train* television show.

Soul Train's artist roster represented musical diversity and included: The Soul Train Gang (not to be confused with the *Soul Train* dancers), The Whispers, Shalamar, Carrie Lucas, and Sun Bear. Given the trends of the time period of the label (1975–1977), *Soul Train*'s musical direction embodied the overlapping appeal and shared styles of early '70s soul along with signature up-tempo rhythms and beats associated with disco.

Cornelius and Griffey employed a number of Los Angeles producers, musicians, and studios to work on specific projects such as Carrie Lucas' debut, *Simply Carrie* (1977) for Soul Train Records. At the same time, they often looked to the East Coast when putting together music aimed at the disco market. Producers Kenny Gamble and Leon Huff of Philadelphia International Records reigned as a top force through both early '70s soul and late '70s disco, and Soul Train Records used members of the company's creative staff to guide some of its productions. A number of selections on the eponymous second *Soul Train Gang* LP (1976), for instance, were co-produced and arranged by staff members of the famed Philadelphia International label. The Gamble and Huff imprint was also present on The Whispers' LP, *One for the Money* (1976) produced by drummer Norman Harris of the MFSB (Mother Father Sister Brother)—a collective of musicians who recorded the theme for the *Soul Train* television show, "TSOP (The Sound of Philadelphia)."

Soul Train had pulled together a number of promising artists and was likely on its way to achieving the kind of success envisioned by Cornelius and Griffey. The label, though, was closely tied to the television show and driven by Cornelius' hands-on leadership. Notoriously protective of the brand, Cornelius did not extend the option for the label to continue using the "Soul Train" name. He had grown skeptical of the record business as a profitable enterprise and decided to return to focusing exclusively on the television show and leave the record business entirely.

THE LATE 1970S: THE FIRST PHASE OF THE SOLAR SOUND

In late 1977, when Dick Griffey was faced with the abrupt departure of Don Cornelius, he promptly changed the name to SOLAR (the Sound of Los Angeles Records). In keeping with the new namesake, Griffey drew more heavily from a talent pool within the local music scene: hiring numerous artists, producers, arrangers, writers, and operations staff based in Los Angeles.[14] The most significant step toward solidifying a distinctive SOLAR sound was the hiring of Leon Sylvers III (Figure 10.2) and his team of songwriters and co-producers.

Sylvers is the most important architect of SOLAR's early sound, characterized by fast-moving bass lines, percussive guitar rhythms, bright tonal colors, and stacked harmonies. He initiated a new dimension to dance music during the final years of disco and put

Figure 10.2
Leon Sylvers of the R&B group The Sylvers sits at the console at BMI studios on March 9, 1974, in Los Angeles, California.

Photo by Michael Ochs Archives/Getty Images.

The Sound of Los Angeles Records **169**

his signature on slower tempo love ballads. The vision for this sound is tied to Sylvers' personal journey. He was the second oldest in a musical family of nine children and had been involved in music for many years prior to his debut as SOLAR's producer. In the early 1970s the family group known as The Sylvers recorded with MGM and then with Capitol Records. His experience sharing singing parts with his sisters and brothers cultivated a special ear for arranging complex harmonies. Leon, a multi-instrumentalist, learned recording skills from Freddie Perren, formerly of the Motown production team known as "The Corporation." Perren produced The Sylvers during their stint with Capitol Records, which gave way to two major hit singles: "Boogie Fever" (1975) and "Hotline" (1976). Leon left the group shortly thereafter and formed an independent production company, Silverspoon Productions.

Silverspoon was the force behind the late '70s SOLAR sound, bringing together a crew of top-notch musicians, singers, and writers, including: Nidra Beard,[15] Vincent Brantley, Gene Dixon, Joey Gallo, Marcus Hare, Dana Myers, Wardell Potts, Richard Randolph, Ernest "Pepper" Reed, William Shelby, Ricky Smith, Kevin Spencer, Foster Sylvers, Ricky Sylvers, and William Zimmerman. Their consistent outpouring of hits earned them the nickname, "The Throw Down Brothers" (a reference inspired in part by Motown's Funk Brothers). This team enhanced their recordings with string and horn arrangements done by a number of veteran composers, creating tones associated with sophistication and elegance—a common feature of disco-era hit records. Shalamar, The Whispers, and Carrie Lucas moved from Soul Train Records over to SOLAR—each of which, in their own way, were considerably impacted by the sounds of Silverspoon and The Throw Down Brothers.

Shalamar became one of SOLAR's top-selling groups. The first LP on the new label, *Disco Garden* (1978), marked a clear step in a new direction. The lineup and sound was changing. While signed to Soul Train Records, Shalamar consisted of Jeffery Daniel and Jody Whatley and lead vocalist Gary Mumford. On SOLAR, Gerald Brown, formerly of The Soul Train Gang, replaced Gary Mumford as the male lead vocalist. Brown shared leads with Whatley on *Disco Garden* and her identifiable timbre endured as a signature part of the group's sound for many years. Loaded with fresh sounds, SOLAR promoted this album by seizing national networks of radio stations and record stores through dance contests: "Radio personalities in all tour cities are being invited to host the contests held in each area's prominent disco," the *Los Angeles Sentinel* reported, "with entry blanks being distributed through record stores."[16] These events furthered Shalamar's image as a dynamic trio, in sync with dance crazes erupting in clubs all over the globe.

The 1979 Shalamar follow-up *Big Fun* brought on major commercial success. The single "Second Time Around" soared up to the very top of the *Billboard* R&B and pop charts. Opening with the laser-like summons of electronic drums (also popularized the same year in Anita Ward's disco smash, "Ring My Bell"), the song has a rhythmic magic that lays a pathway for Whatley's and Daniel's trademark male/female unison and harmony-laden hooks. Also, lead vocalist Howard Hewitt replaced Gerald Brown on *Big Fun*. Hewitt's powerful voice—capable of moving seamlessly from a high natural to silky falsetto tone—added the final addition to the Shalamar panache and lineup that would consistently deliver top SOLAR classics for years to come: "Full of Fire" (1980), "Make That Move" (1981), "This Is for the Lover in You" (1981), "I Can Make You Feel

Good" (1982), and "A Night to Remember" (1982). Lyrically Shalamar's hits tended to focus on love, and/or love drama, and celebratory feelings.

The good vibes sensibility also resonated on Carrie Lucas' first SOLAR project *Street Corner Symphony* (1978). However, this album belied the simplicity and lightheartedness of *Disco Garden*, and, moreover, Lucas' previous work on Soul Train Records. Indeed, *Street Corner Symphony* had its share of danceable songs, but much of the compositions have a jazzy feel with substantial chord changes, elaborate instrumentation, and polished background vocal arrangements (sung by The Whispers). Many of the songs have the flavor of jazz standards, including a duet Lucas sings with her husband (Griffey) called "Simpler Days," which she wrote along with her brother, session keyboardist and songwriter extraordinaire, Greg Phillinganes. Despite its artistic merit, *Street Corner Symphony* was a commercial failure. Lucas' following project, *In Danceland*, returned to a disco orientation and broke through the Top 40 of the *Billboard* R&B and dance charts with songs completely devoted to the plane of bodily movement—"Are You Dancing," "Dance with You," and "Danceland."

The band Dynasty also offered listeners a soundtrack for the dance floor, including the infectious rhythms of "I Don't Wanna Be a Freak (But I Can't Help Myself)" (1979), "I've Just Begun to Love You" (1980), "Do Me Right" (1980), "Adventures in the Land of Music" (1980), and "Here I Am" (1981). Led by Leon Sylvers, nearly all of the Dynasty's members were key players in his Silverspoon Productions.[17] The band's lively sound was enriched by Silverspoon's production style using multiple singers who traded off and shared lead verses, oftentimes in a single composition. The instruments in the band's recordings were not merely accompaniments. Keyboards and bass and guitar licks move about and share the center in Dynasty's tunes. The group's inability to chart on *Billboard*'s Top 40 has overshadowed Dynasty's charisma and rich musical catalog. Present-day interests may very well serve as a corrective. The band's dance classics have re-emerged as hidden treasures for new music producers. "Adventures in the Land of Music," for instance, is one of the most frequently utilized SOLAR singles—sampled by Angie Stone, Tha' Rayne featuring Lupe Fiasco, Brooke Valentine, Rushden and Diamonds, JadaKiss, Teedra Moses, and DJ Taso.

The Whispers' "And the Beat Goes On" (1979) ranks among the most well known SOLAR hits to have been sampled, most notably in Will Smith's "Miami" (1997). When the song took off in 1979, it began a climb that crossed over to different music markets: R&B, disco, and pop.[18] Written by Will Shelby (Dynasty), Steve Shockley (Lakeside), and Leon Sylvers, "And the Beat Goes On" blended an optimistic message (looking forward when in the midst adversity) with an upbeat and funky music track. It was an anti-blues song, akin to McFadden & Whitehead's "Ain't No Stoppin' Us Now," which came out the same year. Initially "And the Beat Goes On" was intended for a group that actually never came into existence—Myers, Philpart, and Woods—a trio comprised of Dana Myers, Mark Philpart, and Vernon Woods. After the decision was made to record the song with The Whispers, Myers went on to pen many singles for SOLAR, whereas Philpart and Woods worked primarily as background vocalists on concert tours and recordings with the label. The Whispers were unlike any other vocal group founded during the Motown-era. They successfully navigated numerous changes in Black popular music (soul, disco, funk, and '80s R&B) while maintaining a vocal group approach and sound with which their fans could consistently expect and rely.

During the first half of SOLAR's run as a Black popular music wellspring (roughly from 1978 through the early 1980s), Leon Sylvers' team of songwriters and producers was the wind carrying SOLAR's rapid rise as a major player in Black popular music. Motown, Philadelphia International, and Black music divisions of larger companies had to make room. By 1981 SOLAR was a recognized force in the industry, noted for being part of the revival of "spirited 'Black pop.'" Some music critics wondered if the label's late 1970s run would continue into the new decade.[19] The concern was justified. Musical tastes were rapidly changing, especially with the ascendency of synthesizers and drum machines as leading contributors to what came to be known as the '80s sound in R&B, funk, pop, and early hip hop (then known as "rap" music). By the mid-1980s Sylvers no longer was the main contributor to the label's endurance throughout a decade wrought with changes in technologies of sound and R&B tastes that bent toward groove-based, slower tempos. Silverspoon, in this context, would have to share production leadership of SOLAR with a new group of producers and songwriters who—often due to Sylvers' own mentorship—had come from the ranks of self-contained bands.[20]

1983–1992: NEW TRENDS IN THE SOLAR SOUND

The first half of SOLAR's reign presented commercial challenges that laid the basis for the label to reassert itself during the mid-1980s. Tapping into funk leanings in Black popular music—which roughly corresponded with the peak years of disco (1976–1980)—SOLAR signed a number of large-sized, self-contained bands. Funk bands in the late 1970s did not often cross over to the pop charts but were capable of going gold and sometimes even platinum, while remaining almost exclusively in the domain of African American consumer markets. SOLAR signed Lakeside in 1978, Midnight Star in 1980, Klymaxx in 1981, and The Deele in 1983. Each of these groups had individual members whom Griffey encouraged to become producers and songwriters—both for their respective bands and other SOLAR artists.

Lakeside was a nine-member band from Dayton, Ohio—consisting of Fred Alexander, Norman Beavers, Marvin Craig, Fred Lewis, Tiemeyer McCain, Thomas Shelby, Stephen Shockley, Otis Stokes, and Mark Wood. The band, originally formed in 1969, blended the configurations of the Motown-era singing group with the self-contained funk band set-up—with four vocalists alongside a tight five-piece band. They arrived in Los Angeles in 1972 as the result of a gig gone sour in Oklahoma. Armed with the sole resource of their performance skills, the nine of them scrambled to find work in Los Angeles' nightclub scene. Lakeside was known in Los Angeles as a show-stopping live band and became a favorite in Black L.A. clubs such as Mavericks' Flat and the Total Experience. After a brief stint with ABC records, Lakeside signed to SOLAR in 1978. The band took off with its gold single "All the Way Live" (1978)—a celebration of performance power. The verses, affirmed by a chanting hook, assured listeners that Lakeside's live concert and recordings ultimately produce the same effect: a compulsion to dance. The instrumentation and arrangement captured the energy of a "live" show—a dramatic opening, catchy hook, and an infectiously fat (bass-driven) groove. This performance aesthetic was a leitmotif on LP covers and concerts associated with eight of their nine SOLAR albums. Band members were cast in the guise of archers, cowboys, pirates, jockeys, genies, G-men, raiders of the lost ark, and border patrol officers (transformed as *The Party Patrol*). The funk classic "Fantastic Voyage" (1980) was Lakeside's biggest hit, taking listeners on a musical ride to the promised "land of funk."

The members of Lakeside wrote their own material. However, *Shot of Love* and *Rough Riders* were both produced by Leon Sylvers, who mentored them through the process of recording. The band had self-produced the third and most successful album in their discography, *Fantastic Voyage*. Songwriting is oftentimes a collective and even communal process for large-sized bands that benefit from the creative input of many ideas and voices. Nevertheless, most big funk bands had certain members that particularly excelled as writers and producers. Guitarist Steve Shockley and vocalist/multi-instrumentalist Otis Stokes both worked on numerous projects for other SOLAR artists: The Whispers, Shalamar, Carrie Lucas, and Klymaxx. Each of them, in specific instances, collaborated with very prolific songwriter and "Thrown Down Brother" Will Shelby—brother of Lakeside singer Thomas Shelby. With some variation, a pattern repeated itself with Midnight Star, Klymaxx, and The Deele: (1) placing a band with a known producer for initial recording projects, (2) moving the band to self-produce, and (3) identifying individual songwriters and producers in the band to work on other SOLAR projects.

Joining SOLAR in 1980, Midnight Star was another Ohio-born band known for burning up the stage. This group was an assemblage of highly trained musicians (many of whom attended Kentucky State University)—Reginald Calloway, Vincent Calloway, Kenneth Gant, Melvin Gentry, Belinda Lipscomb, Jeffrey Cooper, Bobby Lovelace, William Simmons, and Bo Watson. Midnight Star mirrored Lakeside in their trek toward autonomy and in supplying SOLAR with songwriters who brought their fresh ideas for hit singles on other artists.[21] Leon Sylvers produced the first two albums whereas the third, entitled *Victory* (1982), was done so by the band's leader, Reggie Calloway.[22] The following effort, *No Parking on the Dance Floor* (1983), was a double-platinum game-changer, launching Midnight Star's run as R&B and pop hit-makers through most of the 1980s. The group blended electronic sound technologies with funky music and catchy lyrics arrangements. Virtually each member of Midnight Star played multiple instruments, facilitating an ability to change toward a synthesizer-driven sound as a complement to R&B-styled vocals.

Three years before *No Parking on the Dance Floor* reached the airwaves, Roger Troutman (leader of the group Zapp) transformed the range and melodic possibilities of the talk box or voice box—a device that allows an artist to fuse vocal patterns with the sound emitted by electronic instruments and mimic speech.[23] Even more robotic in tone was the device known as the vocoder which conveyed a sci-fi aesthetic frequented in '80s dance music such as Kano's "I'm Ready" (1980), Kraftwerk's "Numbers" (1981), Earth, Wind & Fire's "Let's Groove" (1981), Afrika Bambaataa's "Planet Rock" (1982), and The Jonzun's Crew's "Pack Jam" (1982). Reggie Calloway considered these sounds as gateways to a danceable futurism. He described Midnight Star's first vocoder-laden single "Freak-A-Zoid" as

> already ahead of its time . . . you're taking a word like freak which is old as dirt and then "zoid" which is now until tomorrow and people will always deal with the freaky side of things and the whole computer age will continue and never die.[24]

Vincent Calloway's vocoder voice on other releases ["No Parking on the Dance Floor" (1983), "Electricity" (1983), and "Operator" (1984)] further cemented Midnight Star's standing as pioneering artists within this trend. Building on a lane widened by Patrice

Figure 10.3
Photo of Klymaxx, ca. 1980.
Photo by Bobby Holland/Michael Ochs Archives/Getty Images.

Rushen, Marvin Gaye, Mtume, Atlantic Starr, and Luther Vandross, Midnight Star also crafted smooth, mid-tempo R&B hits: "Wet My Whistle (1983), "Curious" (1984), and "Midas Touch" (1986).

One year after Midnight Star came onboard, SOLAR made history once again, in 1981, by signing the all-women's self-contained R&B and funk band, Klymaxx (Figure 10.3): Cheryl Cooley (guitar), Bernadette Cooper (drums and vocals), Robbin Grider (keyboards and vocals), Joyce "Fenderella" Irby (bass), Lynn Malsby (keyboards), and Lorena Stewart (lead vocals). Black women instrumentalists in blues, jazz, rock, and other genres have a long history of subverting gendered notions of propriety in their mastery of instruments not deemed "feminine."[25] Like the first two Midnight Star albums, Klymaxx's debut *Never Underestimate the Power of a Woman* (1981), was a display of great musicianship but did not yield much in the way of sales. The title track, written by Cheryl Cooley and Bernadette Cooper, was a defiant challenge to misconceptions of the "band" as an exclusive male province. The song is intentionally complex, answering any questions about women's capacity to groove hard and play intricate arrangement with numerous changes, crescendos, and modulations. The only other song written by a Klymaxx member was the ballad "I Want to Love You Tonight," by Lynn Malsby. Overall, the album bore the imprint of Lakeside, produced by Steve Shockley and Otis Stokes, who also wrote most of the songs. Unlike Lakeside and Midnight Star, Klymaxx did not have an extensive history as a working concert band prior to joining SOLAR. Formed in 1979 by drummer Bernadette Cooper, the group was signed shortly after releasing a demo video in 1980. Griffey also nudged Cooper to bring in a new bassist, Joyce "Fenderella" Irby.

Though the band went through initial growing pains while in the process of being recording artists, Klymaxx, nevertheless, experienced a similar path as that of other SOLAR groups where commercial success corresponded with the discovery of a musical identity. The sophomore project *Girls Will Be Girls* presented some of the first production opportunities for Jimmy Jam and Terry Lewis who, at that time, were still honing their skills and learning from Leon Sylvers. Klymaxx worked out core elements of their own sound on this project. Joyce Irby was added as an alternative lead voice. She added a pop sensibility to Klymaxx (especially on ballads). Bernadette Cooper appeared as a funky diva character on faster songs laced with witty spoken braggadocio. The instrumentation built on Midnight Star's brand of electronic funk. The second album did not sell very well but it inaugurated the band's move toward self-production and songwriting.[26]

Meeting in the Ladies Room (1984) thrust Klymaxx into pop stardom. The group put its own funky spin on woman-centered themes. The lyrical double entendre in the first release, "The Men All Pause," invoked feminine sensual power and beauty while signaling a challenge to gendered ageism. The song also presented Bernadette Cooper as a signifying, toasting character comparable to Morris Day. Her stylized, self-aggrandizing testimonies were similarly featured on the LP's ultra-danceable title track. Contrastingly, Klymaxx's "I Miss You," crossed over as a popular ballad, showcased Irby's distinctive voice—which remarkably resembled that of Michael Jackson. Griffey's strategy of artist development had, once again, garnered long-term results. At a time when larger labels would have quickly dropped an act for very low album sales, SOLAR gave these bands multiple opportunities to establish a commercially viable musical identity.

The ten-member band, Collage, followed this model but without the ultimate big score on the charts. *Do You Like Our Music* (1981) was the first album and, true to form, produced by The Whispers. The band maintained elements of '70s big band soul and funk, including regular choral phrasing by its full horn section. Collage's vocal arrangements reflected, in part, the sensibilities of their producers: smoothly stacked backgrounds surrounding the high natural lead vocals of Lee Peters. By the third 1985 LP, the band entered the Top 100 of the R&B and dance charts with the single "Romeo Where's Juliet," but fell short of the sales apex achieved by the aforementioned bands. World-class session keyboardist Bill Wolfer was even more of an outlier during this period. His sole album with the SOLAR subsidiary, Constellation Records, entitled *Wolf* (1982), contained instrumental compositions and songs with guest singers, such as Michael Jackson, Stevie Wonder, Finis Henderson, and Jon Gibson. Spanning multiple musical styles—electro-funk, jazz, pop, and R&B—*Wolf* was a work of imaginative vision and stellar performances. Despite its modest commercial accomplishment, the LP would later resurface as a gem for crate-diggers and 1980s retro enthusiasts.

While subject to anomalies and unanticipated results, the SOLAR strategy of patiently moving bands from supervised to independent production proved viable yet again in the trajectory of the group known as The Deele: Darnell "Dee" Bristol (vocals), Stanley "Stick" Burke (guitar), Kenny "Babyface" Edmonds (vocals, guitar, and keyboards), Carlos "Satin" Greene (vocals), Antonio "L.A." Reid (drums), and Kevin "Kayo" Roberson (bass). On one level, The Deele can be seen as SOLAR's answer to The Time, a band from the Minneapolis camp of artists produced by '80s megastar, Prince. Six of the eight titles on The Deele's first LP, *Streetbeat*, have all of the necessary ingredients to be classified as '80s funky jams: chanting hooks, steady drum machine patterns, blended "natural" and synthesized bass lines, choppy guitar rhythms, and picturesque stories sung over a bed of keyboard patterns. However, The Deele's beautiful ballads, steeped in the wedding song tradition, set them apart from the pack at SOLAR. They included "I'll Send You Roses"(1985), "Sweet November" (1985), and "Two Occasions" (1987). Babyface launched his solo career simultaneously with The Deele's run of three consecutively strong LPs. By 1989, he and "L.A." Reid broke away from the band and formed LaFace Records.

SOLAR marked its Reagan-era zenith in 1984 with the official opening of a six-story office building located on 1635 N. Cahuenga Boulevard in Hollywood, housing a recording studio, executive offices, rehearsal hall, and showcase rooms. Griffey's economic empowerment agenda was evident in the effort to include as many African Americans as possible in the construction process. After securing financing for the building project located on a lot previously occupied by game show producer Chuck Barris, SOLAR employed real estate agent Vanessa Jollivette—daughter of former Deputy Real Estate Commissioner for the State of California Bettye Jollivette—as the developer and construction manager for the project. Jollivette hired Ray Dones, the founding member of the National Association of Minority Contractors, as part of the general contractor team, and Mamie Johnson as the interior contractor.[27] "We knew," Jollivette recalled, "that we were embarking upon new territory that could instill entrepreneurial 'can do' attitudes in . . . not just the local community, [but also] the African American community throughout the United States."[28]

THE 1990S: SOLAR, PAN-AFRICANISM, DECLINE, AND TRANSITIONS

Dick Griffey's focus on economic empowerment was tied to a spirited pan-Africanist perspective. Unlike the growing protest themes in hip hop, SOLAR—consistent with trends in popular '80s R&B—did not convey explicit political messages. Strategically, Griffey kept the world of selling records and liberation politics in separate but mutually supportive spheres. In 1973, prior to founding SOLAR, he had promoted a concert, co-sponsored by the Los Angeles Pan-African Law center, to assist in raising funds for FRELIMO and the liberation struggle in Mozambique. Griffey became, though, more fully engaged with Africa in 1980, when he, along with activist Ayuko Babu, Maxine Walters, and others, mobilized to bring Guinean dance troupe Les Ballet Africains to perform at the city's bicentennial celebration. Making arrangements for the event, Griffey traveled to Guinea with the delegation and met President Sekou Touré.[29]

Thereafter, Griffey formed the Coalition for a Free Africa and became heavily involved in the US anti-apartheid movement, working closely with Reverend Jesse Jackson and PUSH/Rainbow Coalition, the NAACP, Artists and Athletes Against Apartheid, and other activists. Los Angeles, as global media/entertainment center, became a major staging ground for anti-apartheid activism, where the cause achieved heightened status given the frequent publicity accorded to high-profile celebrity support.[30]

In 1986, Griffey, Jesse Jackson, and a large group of civic and business leaders embarked on a seventeen day "fact-finding" trip to eight African nations: Nigeria, Congo,

Angola, Botswana, Mozambique, Zambia, Tanzania, and Zimbabwe. The trip spurred closer bonds between the anti-apartheid movement and liberation support of neighboring "frontline" African states.[31] The campaign to divest from the apartheid regime and pressure the US government to withdraw support of South African–backed rebels in Angola and Mozambique was, from Griffey's standpoint, part and parcel of a vision for developing Black economic solidarity.[32] While continuing to lobby for US policy changes regarding a number of issues facing the African continent, Griffey worked steadfastly to create business relationships between SOLAR and African markets for Black music.[33] He concluded that opportunities for international trade with African countries could generate an alternative to the inevitable pattern of large corporate interests overtaking the independence of smaller Black-owned boutique record labels, such as SOLAR.[34]

By the 1990s, it became clear that the SOLAR CEO's pan-Africanism framed his criticism and self-criticism of the music industry and broader obstacles to Black economic empowerment. Looking at the history of his label, Griffey conceded that power ultimately rested with the conglomerates that controlled venues for market access to musical products. "Distributors have the best of everything," he asserted, "[i]t is not necessary for them to be very talented, since they have an infrastructure that says, 'If you want to get your product to the marketplace, you have to come through me.'"[35] Griffey conceded that even SOLAR had "been dependent in that way: my record company and my music company were always distributed by RCA or Warner or MCA or Capitol or Lasky or through a joint venture with SONY."[36] He eventually started the African Development Public Investment Corporation, specializing in investment and trade in the continent's vast mineral wealth. Moving in a new direction, Griffey declared, "I feel strongly that we Africans need to do something for ourselves that can stand on its own, where we do not need those [corporate] intermediaries."[37]

Griffey's investment in pan-African commerce continued to grow, while his personal interest in the music industry steadily declined, as did SOLAR Records. By the late 1980s, a dwindling number of SOLAR artists remained on the charts. Many had moved on to more lucrative pastures at larger record companies. "I Wanna Be Rich" (1989) by the duo Calloway (formed by Reginald and Vincent Calloway, formerly of Midnight Star) was a top-charting SOLAR single that stood out at the onset of this twilight phase.

Music was changing, just as it had done a decade earlier. Hip hop had grown to become a dominant force in popular music and had a transformative effect on R&B. Griffey was instrumental in helping to launch what came to be a major force in West Coast hip hop, Death Row Records. The soundtrack to the film *Deep Cover* (1992) was one of SOLAR's last major recordings and introduced Dr. Dre (then no longer with N.W.A. and Ruthless Records) and Snoop Dogg as solo artists. The classic Dr. Dre album, *The Chronic* (1992), was recorded at SOLAR's Galaxy Studios.[38] Though participating in yet another musical paradigm shift, Griffey's vision for Black economic power extended well beyond the scope of the music business and encouraged him to eventually relocate to the other side of the Atlantic. By the end of the 1990s, SOLAR Records had closed its office doors and the SOLAR Towers building was sold to one of the label's former artists, Kenny "Babyface" Edmonds. The structure stands to this day as evidence of one of the most important African American cultural and entrepreneurial institutions of the late 1970s and '80s.

Like so many preceding Black-owned record labels (Vee-Jay Records, Motown, Stax, and Philadelphia International), SOLAR not only identified African American talent but tended to stay with and develop artists in ways that would defy the patience of major companies. Summarizing this strategy, Griffey mused: "[The] majority of the majors . . . have money, they have financing, and they have the infrastructure but they really don't have the Berry Gordys, the Kenny Gambles or the Al Bells," who can see potential beyond quick profits. "When you're looking at the diamond in the rough," he concluded, "most people don't know if it's just a rock. . . . Everybody can recognize something once it's already cut and polished."[39] The stars may have lined up perfectly for the accidental birth of SOLAR Records. The survival and accomplishments of the label, though, were the result of definite strategies and steady navigation. When considering the myriad of artists and producers involved in its run, the first word in the acronym "SOLAR" could be pluralized—"Sound[s]" rather than a singular reference. The label contributed to numerous trends in popular music: mid-1970s soul music, late-1970s disco, 1980s electro-funk and dance music, and R&B love ballads—each style and phase is marked by a uniquely SOLAR imprint.

ACKNOWLEDGMENTS

Special thanks to Carolyn Griffey, Chuck Johnson, Carrie Lucas, Dana Meyers, Tony Nwosu, Ricky "Freeze" Smith, and Logan Westbrooks for assistance and feedback. This essay draws some material from a previous publication by the author, "SOLAR: The History of the Sounds of Los Angeles Records" in *Black Los Angeles: American Dreams and Realities* (pp. 266–282). Darnell Hunt and Ana-Christina Ramon, eds. New York: New York University Press, 2010.

NOTES

1. See Burnett 1996, 1–63; Kennedy and McNutt 1999, x.
2. Matthews 1977, 7, 15, 31; George 1988, 121–146; Person-Lynn 1998, 179–197.
3. Posner 2002.
4. Sanjek 1997, 555.
5. Cuff 1983, D2.
6. Interview by the author with Dick Griffey, audio recording, Los Angeles, 2008.
7. *Westwood One Collection*, SC70; "Guys & Dolls Host Jim Brown Night," 1964, B4; interview by the author with Dick Griffey, audio recording, Los Angeles, 2008; Robinson 2010, 21–59.
8. "Guys & Dolls Host Jim Brown Night," 1964, B4.
9. Interview by the author with Dick Griffey, audio recording, Los Angeles, 2008; Myers 1995, 341.
10. Hunt 1973, C24.
11. "Don Cornelius Is Guest on WBEE's 'Minority Forum'," 1974, 15.
12. "Soul Train Hit with Teens," 1970, 13; "'Soul Train' Back for 2nd Season TV Series," 1972, 12; Walker 1998, 303–309.
13. Jim Maddox (KDAY Program Director) and Jean Tillman (KDAY Community Relations Director) to Temille Porter, June 20, 1975, personal files of Temille Porter; Pam Brown (Soul Train Teen Coordinator) to Temille Porter, August 1975, personal files of Temille Porter.
14. "Dick Griffey Concerts," 1983, B8.
15. Nidra Beard was a big part of the Silverspoon production and songwriting team, co-penning numerous songs for Carrie Lucas, Shalamar, The Sylvers, and The Whispers.
16. "Solar Launches National Dance Contest," 1978, B1A.
17. Dynasty members were: Leon Sylvers (bass and vocals), Nidra Beard (vocals), Linda Carrier (vocals), Kevin Spencer (vocals and keyboards), William Shelby (vocals and keyboards), Wayne Milstein (percussion), Wardell Potts Jr. (drums), Richard Randolph (guitar), Ernest "Pepper" Reed (guitar), and Ricky Smith (keyboards).

18. "The Whispers Say: And Beat Goes On," 1980, B.
19. Sculatti 1981, K76.
20. Sylvers remained the main producer of Shalamar through 1983 when the group began to go through major personnel changes. During the early to mid-1980s he also took on more projects from non-SOLAR artists, including Gladys Knight & the Pips, Janet Jackson, Evelyn "Champagne" King, Glenn Jones, Brothers Johnson, Five Star, and many others.
21. Reggie and Vincent Calloway and Bo Watson worked with Klymaxx, The Whispers, and The Deele. Other members of Midnight Star also produced and wrote for other SOLAR artists.
22. Harvey Mason was co-producer along with Sylvers on the first Midnight Star album, *The Beginning* (1980).
23. "Interview Transcript: Zapp (Roger Troutman)," Collector's No. 1357, 1982.
24. "Interview Transcript: Midnight Star (Reggie Calloway)," Collector's No. SE 84-15 and Collector's No. 2735A, 1984.
25. Porter 2002, 79–83; Mahon 2004, 204–230; Johnson 2007, 51–68.
26. "Jimmy Jam and Terry Lewis Have Become Synonymous with Recording Excellence," Waxpoetics.com, http://waxpoetics.com/features/articles/jimmy-jam-interview/.
27. Ibid.
28. Interview by the author with Vanessa Jollivette, audio recording, Los Angeles, 2009.
29. Interview by the author with Ayuko Babu, interview transcript, 2008, 7, 27–31; interview by the author with Dick Griffey, audio recording, Los Angeles, 2008, 15–26.
30. "ANC Mothers Inaugural Banquet," 1986, A1; "Anti-Apartheid Telethon on Drawing Board," 1986, A1.
31. Stanford 1997, 149.
32. "Tutu's U.S. Visit Stirs New Anti-Apartheid Awareness," 1986, A16; "Solar Chief Keynotes Ebonics Awards," 1986, A3.
33. *Westwood One Collection*, SC70.
34. For a debate on the usurpation of Black companies such as Motown and Johnson Products by large corporations, see Reynolds 1995, 194; Rowe 1984, 18.
35. Myers 1995, 341.
36. Ibid.
37. Ibid.
38. Touré 2006, 71–85.
39. Interview by the author with Dick Griffey, audio recording, Los Angeles, 2008.

DISCOGRAPHY

Babyface. *A Closer Look*. SOLAR/Epic CDEPC 3847, 1991. CD.
Calloway. *All the Way*. SOLAR/Epic ZK 75310, 1989. CD.
Collage. *Shine the Light*. Constellation/MCA MCA-5564, 1985. LP.
The Deele. *Greatest Hits*. The Right Stuff 7243–5–8–2078–2–8, 2003. CD.
Dynasty. *The Best of Dynasty*. SOLAR/The Right Stuff 72435–81968–2–5, 2003. CD.
Lakeside. *Shot of Love*. [1978.] The Right Stuff 7243–8–54244–2–7, 1997. CD.
———. *Fantastic Voyage*. [1980.] Capitol Records 09463–61033–2–7, 2006. CD.
Lucas, Carrie. *Greatest Hits*. SOLAR/The Right Stuff 72435–82534–2–9, 2003. CD.
Midnight Star. *Anniversary Collection*. The Right Stuff 7243–5–20664–2–1, 1999. CD.
Shalamar. *Disco Garden*. [1978.] Unidisc AGEK-2071, 2002. CD.
———. *Big Fun*. [1979.] Unidisc AGEK-2072, 2002. CD.
———. *Three for Love*. [1980.] Unidisc AGEK-2073, 2006. CD.
———. *Friends*. [1982.] Sanctuary SMBCD 348, 2006. CD.
———. *Circumstantial Evidence*. [1987.] Unidisc AGEK-2078, 2002. CD.
Westwood One Collection: Special Edition. Sound recording includes more than 200 radio programs on Black popular music from the 1970s and '80s. Karen Shearer Collection, SC70, Archives of African American Music and Culture, Indiana University, Bloomington.
The Whispers. *Open Up Your Love*. [1977] Capitol/The Right Stuff 38378, 1996. CD.
———. *Headlights*. [1978] The Right Stuff 7243–8–55793–2–5, 1997. CD.
———. *And the Beat Goes On*. [1978] Unidisc AGEK-2106, 2003. CD.
———. *Greatest Hits*. The Right Stuff 7243–8–57604–2–6 1997. CD.

CHAPTER 11

Tyscot Records
Gospel Music Production as Ministry

Tyron Cooper

Indianapolis, Indiana–based Tyscot Records is the oldest Black-owned and operated gospel music label in the United States. The label is one of three brands housed under the official company, Tyscot Incorporated, which encompasses Tyscot Records, Tyscot Films, and Tyscot Publishing, with its catalog of approximately four thousand mostly Christian-based songs. As an independent recording label that has greatly impacted the careers of numerous artists, executives, and other creative personnel in the gospel music industry, from its inception Tyscot founders conceived the label as a ministry-driven business, a concept that profoundly shapes the character of its day-to-day operations as well as its approach to achieving its fiscal goals. In other words, the intersection of faith and commerce is readily evident in the story of Tyscot Records.

The total number of industry insiders impacted by Tyscot, since its founding in 1976, is literally too extensive to cite here. Even co-founder of Tyscot, Leonard Scott, when asked how many artists the company has included on its roster over almost four decades of existence, simply stated, "Oh wow, lots!"[1] While no official comprehensive artist roster from 1976 to the present exists, many would likely be surprised to know that some of the most well-known national gospel recording performers and industry executives have been impacted by the label in various ways throughout their careers. Seven-time Grammy Award winner, Kirk Franklin, and three-time Stellar Award winner, Kim Burrell, obtained some of their early recording experiences at Tyscot. During an interview with ethnomusicologists Mellonee Burnim and Raynetta Wiggins, Leonard Scott recalls, "We've got early recordings on Kirk Franklin when he was with Trinity Temple back in the day. Kim Burrell. . . . We've got recordings on all of these people because back then [in the early 1990s] nobody knew them."[2] Indeed, both Kim Burrell and Kirk Franklin recorded with Dallas, Texas's Trinity Temple Full Gospel Mass Choir for Tyscot during the early stages of their careers.[3]

The late Al "The Bishop" Hobbs, one of gospel music's premier radio announcers and founder of independent gospel music label Aleho Records, distributed several of his company's recording releases through Tyscot. Pioneering gospel artist/producer/TV personality Bobby Jones has also released music on the Tyscot label.[4] Through its involvement in both recording and distribution, Tyscot has functioned as a launching pad for performers and other industry insiders considered mega-stars in the twenty-first-century gospel music recording community. The office of Tyscot includes an archival room stacked floor to ceiling with hard copies of recordings released by the company from its inception to the present, tangibly reflecting the extent of the label's output and impact.

TYSCOT FOUNDERS

Leonard Scott and the late Craig Tyson founded Tyscot Records in 1976 at ages twenty-seven and twenty-four, respectively. Prior to the company's launch, Tyson and Scott had seminal musical and life experiences, which prepared them well for this major undertaking. Son of the late Bishop James Tyson, who was a well-known pastor in the Apostolic denomination,[5] Craig Tyson was a prodigy church organist whose musical upbringing can be traced back to Youngstown, Ohio, where he honed his music skills during worship services at Mount Calvary Pentecostal Church, pastored by his father. During the early 1970s, Bishop Tyson moved the family to Indianapolis to pastor what is considered the city's "mother" Apostolic church, Christ Temple Apostolic Faith Assembly. At Christ Temple, Tyson continued in his role as church organist, over time developing a national reputation for his virtuoso organ performances, choir directing, and music arrangements, and as a first-call musician for regional and national gospel recording sessions. In 1976, Bishop Tyson left Christ Temple to start his own church, Christ Church Apostolic in Indianapolis, and Craig Tyson again followed his father to serve as church organist and choir director, a position that would further equip him with the artistic and religious sensibilities to co-found Tyscot Records that same year.

Leonard Scott, who attended Christ Temple Apostolic Faith Assembly as a child, gained experiences as a working musician during the late 1960s while playing alto saxophone in the Soul Messengers funk band from Terre Haute, Indiana. Unlike Tyson, whose musical experience was grounded exclusively in the church, Scott's musical boundaries stretched deeply into the realm of secular music. Speaking of the Soul Messengers, Scott reflected, "We were playing soul stuff. You know, Temptations, James Brown; you know, just covering all the pop hits . . . they played on the radio."[6] Performing with the Soul Messengers required Scott to travel from Indianapolis to Terre Haute and back to Indianapolis for concerts every weekend. While performing with the band, Scott also attended the Indiana University Dental School in Indianapolis where he enrolled in 1969. Over time, Scott's pursuits with the Soul Messengers began to threaten his academic progress, prompting his father to issue the ultimatum, "If you all ain't made it in a year, you got to do it my way."[7] Scott's father was concerned that his son's choice of life as a road musician offered little promise of economic or social stability. He wished for Scott to focus on dental school exclusively. Scott accepted his dad's challenge to forgo his aspirations for a career in popular music if he had not achieved success within one year, and one year later, he entered dental school full time.

However, Scott did not altogether end his pursuit of popular music. As a member of a band composed of his dental school peers, Scott was able to eliminate travel demands by playing a standing engagement of three days per week at Indianapolis's Fort Harrison Officer's Club. Each band member was paid fifty dollars, considered great compensation for a local artist in the early 1970s. Shrewdly, Scott was able to continue his musical pursuits while pursuing his degree in dentistry.

In 1972, during Scott's junior year in dental school, he had a profound experience, which changed his life and eventually led to the co-founding of Tyscot Records. Scott recounts:

> I was really spiritually and emotionally at a very low point in my life. . . . I was living in a little apartment by myself and I was working on somebody's teeth, and I'll never forget. The Lord spoke, and it wasn't an audible voice, but he spoke to my mind and told me, "Now is your time." You know? I put the teeth down and got in my car and just went down to Christ Temple, you know, the church I was brought [up in]—And I hadn't been to church in [years] . . .
>
> And I got in my car and went down to the church that I had come up in. And when I walked in the door I expected to see somebody preaching but wasn't nobody preaching. It was like people were . . . just praying. And I didn't know, but I found out later on that they had a big tent meeting and over a hundred [people got] . . . baptized during this tent meeting. And so, they were praying . . . in the Holy Ghost. And I found a place at the altar and just got down and started praying, and I had an experience just like in the book of Acts.[8]

Scott recollects that his encounter with God resulted in a spiritual transformation mirroring the experience of early Christians who were endowed with the Holy Spirit as referenced in Acts 2:4: "And everyone present was filled with the Holy Spirit and began speaking in other languages, as the Holy Spirit gave them this ability." Like early Christians, Scott spoke in a spiritual language that Pentecostals commonly reference as "speaking in tongues,"[9] while scholars often reference the ritual practice as "glossolalia."[10]

Scott assesses the impact of this experience: "And so that changed my life. I had a great big ole Afro. And I wanted to cut my Afro off and I got rid of all my drugs and all that kinda stuff."[11] He immediately distanced himself from those things that he felt detracted from his image and consciousness as a committed Christian. No more marijuana or popular music; no more hairstyle that some might consider radical. Scott instead embraced core Christian values and ideas representative of his faith community, and he began to attend Christ Temple regularly, where he met Craig Tyson, church organist.

In 1975 a rift occurred between Bishop Tyson and the deacons of Christ Temple, which resulted in Tyson's departure and founding of Christ Church Apostolic. Scott followed Bishop Tyson to Christ Church, where he eventually became the treasurer and worship leader, working alongside organist Craig Tyson. Nonetheless, saddened by the internal church conflict, Scott was led to fast,[12] or abstain from food, as he pursued focused and sustained prayer regarding the breach. Scott secluded himself in a hotel for three days and nights as he sought divine instruction about the direction he was to take in his life.

During this fasting period Scott wrote both the text and melodies of approximately twelve songs, an amazing feat, given the fact that he had no prior history of composing. At the conclusion of the fast, Scott immediately contacted Craig Tyson about his new divinely-inspired compositions. Subsequently, the two developed the rhythms, melodies, harmonies, and overall arrangements for Scott's songs as well as for other compositions written by Tyson. Armed with this music arsenal, they decided to produce a live recording for Christ Apostolic Church Radio Choir, which they called *Feel Good* (1977).[13] This was significant, as the "radio choir" was featured during the weekly church service radio broadcast on WTLC-AM 1310—the primary radio station programming Black gospel music in Indianapolis. Without a recording, Christ Church Apostolic's radio choir, like many other church radio choirs during that time, could only be heard during Sunday morning worship services or on the church's weekly WTLC radio program. The release of *Feel Good* allowed supporters and consumers an opportunity to engage Christ Church Apostolic's live musical and worship atmosphere in the privacy of their homes any time. More significantly, *Feel Good* led to the eventual formation of Tyscot Records, as Scott explains:

> And we started working on this recording. . . . I was practicing dentistry by now and I also had purchased a nursing home, so I was doing some other things. And my attorney told me, "If you're gonna do something in music, you probably need to start another corporation just to protect your other assets." . . . And so that's what we did. And he asked me, "What do you wanna call it?" I said, "I don't know; you . . . say I need it" (laughter). And he said, well who's doing this?" I said, "Well, me and Craig." And he said, "Why don't [you] just put y'all names together. Why don't you just call it Tyscot?" I said ok, no problem.[14]

While both Tyson and Scott founded the company, Tyscot was supported largely with monies gained from Scott's dental practice during its nascence. In fact, his dentistry has sustained the label financially through multiple critical junctures. From the outset Scott viewed the creation of this record label as a directive from God. The founding of Tyscot, therefore, illustrates the synthesis of business enterprise with music ministry—a reality that continues to be reflected in Scott's life, as his dental office, Tyscot Records, and Rock Community Church, the church which he currently co-pastors,[15] are all located in the same office building on Seventy-First Street in Indianapolis, which Scott owns (see Figure 11.1).

Figure 11.1
Left to right: Tyscot Records, Rock Community Church, and Scott Dentistry.
Photo by Tyron Cooper.

TYSCOT: THE EARLY YEARS 1976–1988

Key positions at Tyscot have shifted over time since the company's founding in 1976. For the first few years Leonard Scott and Craig Tyson were the only employees at Tyscot. Leonard Scott served as president for the first twelve years, from 1976 to 1988, personally overseeing the business aspects of the label. During this time, Scott also created other businesses such as the aforementioned dental practice and a local nursing home. The dental office, which he opened in 1973, was located at 3532 Keystone Avenue in Indianapolis, where Tyscot Records was originally housed upstairs in the same building. Scott's businesses have always been closely linked via ownership and proximity.

From the outset, co-founder Craig Tyson managed the creative dimensions of the company's recording productions. Tyson held a full-time job at American Fletcher National Bank while simultaneously working for Tyscot. Most early Tyscot staff members maintained employment elsewhere while developing the label. According to Scott, Tyson was only at the company for a few years before he left the label sometime between the late 1970s and early 1980s to pursue other ventures; he eventually became the music director for Bethel Pentecostal Church in Grand Rapids, Michigan, the church attended by young siblings now known as the 1980s R&B sensation DeBarge.[16]

Ricky Clark, another early Tyscot staff member in the 1980s, was a local DJ on WTLC radio and a police officer who also owned an R&B recording label. Recognizing the significance of Clark's experiences in the music industry, Scott invited him to join Tyscot, with the objective of pooling their resources to obtain more consistent radio airplay and maximum record sales for the company. During the 1980s, Clark's mother, Mildred Clark, became Tyscot's first full-time employee; she performed multiple tasks, including answering the phone, contacting radio stations to gain airplay for the label, and preparing mailings. As needed, Tyscot also periodically hired freelance workers to assist with tasks such as marketing and promotions.

During their youth, all seven of Scott's children also assisted with Tyscot, the nursing home, and the dental practice as needed. At Tyscot, they helped with packaging records, answering phones, and even cleaning. Scott put it plainly: "They did whatever needed to be done."[17] From the outset, Scott's hands were full, as a newly found record label executive with limited music industry experience who was leading a relatively inexperienced staff. Scott's nephew, Sidney Scott, who later became Director of Artists and Repertoire (A&R) at Tyscot, recalls instances during the early years where Scott was known to complete work on the teeth of a dental client and immediately jet upstairs to the Tyscot office to answer a phone call from a radio station inquiring about an upcoming album release of one of his artists.[18] At one point during the early 1980s, Scott's energies were so strongly fractured among his businesses that he considered disbanding Tyscot altogether. To complicate matters even further, the label was barely solvent during its formative years. However, because of the coupling of Scott's overarching desire to spread the gospel and his strong affinity for music, he continued to support Tyscot despite advice from his financial advisor to close the label. Scott recollects:

> I remember meeting with my accountant. Every year I'd meet with the accountant, and he'd look at me and say, "Okay, the dental practice is doing real good. This one's doing good." He'd always get to the record company and say, "Now this record company, you probably should shut that down . . ." because

it wasn't making any money. I was doing it because I loved it, you know? And I'd tell him, "You know some people golf. They do what they want to do. I like music. I like doing this." You know? And he said, "Well, okay."[19]

Jeopardizing his own financial stability, Scott continued to pursue the viability of Tyscot, eventually compiling a roster of some of the label's earliest flagship artists. Among them were a gospel quartet from Anderson, Indiana, called Truth and Devotion, and The Pentecostal Ambassadors, a young male trio formed through Grace Apostolic Church in Indianapolis who had previously signed to Savoy Records at the behest of their premier gospel artist, Rev. James Cleveland. Local Indianapolis staple Robert Turner and the Silver Hearts, a mixed ensemble, was also on Tyscot's roster, as well as the ensemble Bill Sawyer and Christian Tabernacle of Cleveland Ohio, which earned the label its first relative success in the industry. Reflecting on the significance of Bill Sawyer, Scott states:

> I never will forget. I was at a Gospel Music Workshop of America. It was in Chicago this year, and I was a new label. I had these records [from Truth and Devotion, Robert Turner and the Silver Hearts, and The Pentecostal Ambassadors] and I was trying to [obtain radio airplay for Tyscot recordings]. The lifeline of a gospel record company is radio airplay, and so they had all these radio announcers[20] that come meet every year, and they would give the record companies an opportunity to tell them what they got. You know—why you need to play this. And I was literally begging them, "Will you play? Will you please play this? This is good, you know?" And evidently I wasn't doing too good. And there was this minister, and he was actually the chaplain for the announcers. And I never will forget, he came up to me, put his arm around me and said, "Dr. Scott, I'm going to help you." He said, "I've got this record that is doing real good. In fact, people all over the nation want it, and I'm the church." He said, "I'm not a record label. I'm a church. I've got this record. I'm going to turn it over to you and let you run with it." And he had a song on that record that everybody wanted. He had a lady that was about ninety years old that had been a bar singer when she was young, and she was singing this song, "Jesus Keep Me Near the Cross," and killing it, you know? And everybody wanted it all over. And sure enough, as soon as I took that over—see, I used to have to call stations—"Will you play my record? Please play my record, please. Please play my record." I'd call stores, "Will you take my record?" You know? "Please take my record." But as soon as I took that one, it kind of flipped. They started calling me.[21]

According to Scott, Bill Sawyer and Christian Tabernacle's "Jesus Keep Me near the Cross" from the album *Something Old, Something New* (1983) marked the turning point for Tyscot. With the song's mid-range Hammond B3 organ, lightly touched piano, sparse guitar, soaring background unison strings, and rhythmically interactive drum set supporting a soprano-driven big sound traditional gospel choir and the infectious, mature, raspy mezzo-soprano soloist, "Jesus Keep Me near the Cross" was a sure hit for consumers across the nation who desired to experience the heart of song and performance in a traditional Black church worship service. I can remember my own home church, Little Zion Church of God in Christ in Lake Worth, Florida, singing this song to the exuberant eruption of the entire congregation in the 1980s. Sawyer, together with other early Tyscot artists, helped to brand the company as a successful independent gospel record label.

Scott's recollection regarding the ascent of the Tyscot record label documents how consumer-driven radio can impact the career trajectories of recording artists and labels. Scott also establishes how artists can be rather fortuitously "discovered." While Sawyer's entrée into Tyscot Records resulted from a seemingly happenstance encounter at a major trade conference, potential recording artists can also be identified at church conferences and other artistic and religious events, as well as through demo tape recordings. It was through the transmission of a demo tape that Tyscot discovered and signed one of its prominent artists of the 1980s and 1990s, John P. Kee. Leonard Scott recalls that on a Saturday morning in 1987, he "received a phone call from Derek Dirksen" who was then assisting Tyscot with locating new talent. Dirksen also managed Commissioned, the popular 1990s contemporary male gospel group from Michigan. After Dirksen played a few songs from Kee's demo tape over the phone, Leonard Scott shouted, "Just sign him!" a decision that would later elevate the status of Tyscot Records in the music industry even further.[22]

Shortly after signing, the singer–songwriter and multi-instrumentalist Kee began to record albums with his ensemble, New Life Community Choir: *Wait on Him* (1989), *There Is Hope* (1990), and *Wash Me* (1991). On these projects, Kee mixed traditional gospel choir and gospel quartet singing elements with eclectic contemporary secular music styles from 1960s soul to 1970s funk and early 1990s new jack swing. Through Kee, Tyscot began to expand its consumer base, offering music resonating both within and beyond the boundaries of the traditional Black church. Beginning with Kee, Tyscot generated broader attention nationally with more contemporary sounding artists like Florida's Reverend Melvin Dawson and Genesis Ensemble and Trinity Temple Full Gospel Mass Choir, which featured the young Kirk Franklin.

TYSCOT IN THE NEW ERA 1988–2009

Despite the widespread appeal of John P. Kee, other Tyscot artists were not selling enough records to sustain the company financially without Scott having to continue bailing out the label with funds from his dentistry. According to Scott, this glaring imbalance in relative artist success reflects a general trend in the music business. He notes, "only one out of nine records break even. This is across the board [industry-wide]."[23] So, while there is always the expectation that records produced will sell, the fact is few artists generate the sales projected in their contracts. Typically only one or, certainly, relatively few recording artists sustain the financial viability of a label. In Tyscot's case, not even John P. Kee in the late 1980s could pull the company out of the red. Furthermore, because of Scott's ongoing responsibilities for managing his dental practice, his ability to provide artists with the types of managerial support needed for their success remained quite limited. Consequently, Scott again considered disbanding Tyscot in 1988. Upon learning of this possibility, Scott's son, Bryant, abandoned his ambitions for attending dental school and assumed the Tyscot helm, a role he held for over a decade, from 1988 until 2009.

Bryant Scott's decision to work with the company can be considered one of divine intervention, as Leonard Scott explains:

> Bryant was supposed to go to dental school. Bryant was supposed to be a dentist. Bryant had done all of the preliminary dental schoolwork. He had been accepted into dental school and the next class, he had one physics class to take. Pending him passing that in the summer, he was already accepted in the next dental school class. During this time, he comes to me and says—(Now remember I told you I'm not making a dime in the record company, all right? The dental practice is doing real good, all right?) And he comes to me and says, "Dad, I think the Lord wants me to help you with the record company." I said, "Oh? Really?" But when he said "the Lord" told him that, now he's—If he'd said, "I think I'll—," but he said *the Lord*. And so I ain't going to box with God if God told him that. And so he didn't go to dental school, and he started actually working at the record company. When he started working at the record company is when it turned around and started making money.[24]

Bryant Scott could have chosen to become a dentist following the career path that had already proven to be profitable for his father. However, based upon his faith in God and the belief that he was ordained—divinely chosen—to run his father's business, the college-aged young man opted instead to begin his stint as president of the label. His unwavering resolve is indicative of how the business decisions of both father and son are driven first and foremost by religious belief, or faith. In essence, like Leonard Scott, Bryant Scott views his work at Tyscot as a type of ministry, even though the realities of commerce necessitate that "We're constantly looking at the market and looking at how to sell new music and how to do different things [for the financial success of the company]."[25] The shared vision of Scott and his son Bryant, which approaches business through the lens of ministry, has been a key factor in sustaining the success of the Tyscot label through its forty years of existence. As a family business, having been led only by Scott and his son since inception, the legacy of integrating music and ministry has been powerfully sustained.

With Bryant Scott at the helm providing undivided attention to building the record label, Leonard Scott was able to focus exclusively on his dentistry. Over time, Bryant Scott evolved into a widely recognized savvy businessman, who was successful in securing major artists' contracts and developing performers for the label. Under his leadership, Tyscot emerged as a household name among gospel music supporters. Tyscot became a major independent label, consisting of a small record company with national product distribution and broad industry impact. With Bryant at the helm, the label received its first Recording Industry Association of America certified Gold Record with the label's then premier artist, John P. Kee, whose CD release *Not Guilty* (1999) sold more than five hundred thousand units, an enormous sales figure for gospel artists. Ethnomusicologist Mellonee Burnim points out that during the 1990s, major gospel albums typically sold forty thousand to fifty thousand units.[26]

While Bryant Scott led the company during this period of exceptional achievement, he also was at the helm when Tyscot experienced one of its most challenging moments. In 1993, Spectra, the label's distributor, filed for bankruptcy. According to Leonard Scott, distributors have always been the primary

> way for your recordings and your products to get into stores or to be sold if you don't have somebody to put them in there. That's what the distributor does. They get them in the stores and they collect your money and take care of your inventory in the warehouse and all that kind of stuff, shipping and all of that.[27]

In essence, Spectra was the lifeblood of Tyscot; it distributed albums to store shelves and collected the money from product sales. The magnitude of Spectra's bankruptcy was compounded by the fact that, at the time of their filing, John P. Kee's Tyscot album *We Walk by Faith* (1992) was ranked the #1 gospel album in the nation by *Billboard*. Furthermore, Tyscot, by this time, had accumulated a roster of artists who were becoming highly visible in the gospel music industry through concert touring, radio airplay, and album releases. Melvin Dawson and Genesis Ensemble's *Signs of the Times* (1992), Reverend Oscar Hayes and the Abundant Life Fellowship Chorale's *Got 2 Tell It* (1991), Denise Tichenor's *Lead Me* (1992), and Dan Willis and Pentecostals of Chicago's *Bridging the Gap* (1992) were gaining traction on the label. Bobby Jones and the New Life Singers also released *Bring It to Jesus* (1993) on Tyscot during this period.

With such a strong roster of artists whose projects were released by Tyscot in the early 1990s, the impact of Spectra's bankruptcy became far more daunting. The label's economic viability was at stake. Scott reflects:

> . . . the owner of the company [Spectra] that distributed our records called. And it was on a Friday evening; I never will forget. In fact I was in my basement working on some music for one of the artists, and he said, "Doctor Scott, got some bad news for you." He said, "We're going out of business." I said, "Oh, okay." He said, "No. No, you don't understand. . . . We're going *totally* out of business, you know? We're not reorganizing or something, where you might get a dime or a dollar or something. We're going *totally* out of business. As of Monday, we'll no longer be." He said, "Your company is doing good, but the other ones we're distributing, they're not doing good at all." And then he told me, "I'm sorry."[28]

Not only is the graveness of Spectra's bankruptcy evident from Scott's narrative, the organic link between distributors and record labels, which are seemingly independent of each other, also rises to the foreground. Because labels other than Tyscot were not selling enough records for Spectra to remain economically sound, Tyscot, while in good standing, nonetheless suffered. At the time Spectra owed Tyscot approximately $300,000 for units sold by the label. Without these funds, it would be impossible for Tyscot to pay artists, manufacturers, and songwriters for their work.

While for many business executives this news could have been a death knell, Bryant and Leonard Scott's reaction was the exact opposite. Upon hearing the announcement from Spectra, Leonard Scott recalls:

> I just started praising the Lord over the phone. I said, "Hallelujah! Thank you, Lord." I never will forget. He [the Spectra representative] said to me, "Uh, are you okay? Did you hear what I said?" And I tell you, God worked it out. We called all of our artists at that time. . . . And we told every one of them, "You're out of contract, and we can't pay you." And every one of them said, "We stand with you." You know? Then we called the people we owed money to and told the manufacturers and they said, "Well, we understand what's going on, you know. . . . We can't give you credit . . . but we will continue manufacturing your [records]—even though you owe us all this money—we'll continue manufacturing for you on a pay-as-you-go basis." You know it was like, "Wow!" He [the devil] tried to take us out, but he [God] sustained us in spite of the dire circumstance.[29]

Immediately after realizing the company's financial misfortune, Scott began to "praise the Lord." His initial action represents the extent of the impact that religious values and purpose have on Scott and his label staff when challenged with issues that jeopardized their business. Instead of disbanding the company, Scott faced the problem squarely, relying on his unwavering faith. Tyscot Records had been birthed in the spiritual realm, after a period of secluded fasting and praying. Where others might have seen disaster, Scott instead saw the opportunity for God to once again reveal himself. Approaching his artist roster, his staff, and his creditors with complete honesty concerning his very grave predicament, Scott realized that what he would be able to accomplish as an individual was severely limited. "By faith," as John P. Kee sang, Scott received inexplicable understanding and mercy from his business partners, who clearly held the power to dismantle his entire enterprise, had they so chosen.

Bryant Scott, who was on vacation at the time of Spectra's collapse, received a call from Leonard Scott about the crisis: "Dad calls and says, I gotta cut my vacation short cause Spectra, our distributor declared bankrupt and they owed us a whole lot of money." After the call, Bryant Scott, like his father, did not waiver in his faith or business resolve. Rather, he instantly went to work in an effort to shore up the company financially:

> Dad made it clear that he wanted to pay everybody that we owed. I did not want to declare bankruptcy or anything so I went to work cutting deals. Because we wanted to pay people they were very favorable in how they treated us. They understood for the most part, and we were able to cut deals with manufacturers and other suppliers for . . . dimes on the dollar. They were just elated that we desired to pay and not leave them hanging.[30]

While Bryant Scott held the position of president during this defining moment, both his and his dad's responses to the looming financial crisis reflected a shared approach to business through the prism of faith. Clearly, as a business, Tyscot's ultimate objective was financial stability or fiscal soundness, and indeed they were able to resolve the immediate financial crisis via payment agreements they established with "manufacturers and other suppliers" along with others to whom they were indebted. However, the unconventional approaches the Tyscot enterprise employed to achieve that desired state, particularly in the face of such daunting potential defeat, represented their personal resolve to rely on God as their guide and leader rather than on their own human frailty.

TYSCOT: 2010–

By 2010, a series of events led to a second major financial crisis at Tyscot. First, technological advancement opened the door to illegal file sharing, which consequently impacted legal purchases of song releases and other associated revenue. Furthermore, with the advent of online retail sites like iTunes, consumer habits shifted from the purchase of full albums to cherry-picking singles for ninety-nine cents. Thirdly, by the 2008 national financial crisis in the United States, record companies, regardless of their status as mainstream or independent, were all experiencing diminishing sales. In a 2009 *Music Business Journal* article entitled "The Recession Compounds the Crisis in Recorded Music Sales," marketing consultant Brian Zarlenga highlighted the fact that

> money spent on music per capita dropped from $44 to $38 among Internet users. People just don't have the disposable income to be spending $10 on a CD, when all they really want to hear is one or two songs off the entire disc. The survey also showed that 48% of teens . . . did not buy even one CD throughout all of 2007. Not ONE CD! For the record labels to think that millions of people buying one or two songs for $.99 each can counteract the huge loss suffered by the amount of people not buying the physical product is farfetched.[31]

The purchasing of music, as outlined by Zarlenga, was indeed decreasing industry-wide, and Tyscot, a viable part of the gospel music industry by 2010, was not immune to the fiscal downturn.

During this period of industry decline, Tyscot's staff members were asked to take pay cuts, and as president, Bryant Scott also agreed to decreased compensation by resigning from his full-time position to become a part-time consultant. The elder Scott once again assumed the helm of the company. Bryant Scott also secured the position of Executive Vice President for the North Carolina upstart label Imago Dei Music Group (IDMG), while continuing to work with Tyscot. Bryant Scott's stint with IDMG was short-lived due in part to the successful entrée of Tyscot into the film industry with the company's then premier artist/producer Deitrick Haddon's first feature movie, *Blessed and Cursed* (2010).[32] Haddon's initiative to produce films, which extended the company's artistic output and financial gain, allowed Bryant Scott to return to Tyscot in 2011, resuming his position as the President and Chief Operating Officer of the label.

During Bryant Scott's time with IDMG, his sister Melanie assisted their father Leonard with the daily operations of the company, serving as General Counsel and the Senior Vice President of Marketing, beginning in 2008. Melanie Scott offers the following description of her responsibilities in this role:

> I protect the company from all lawsuits and also negotiate contracts and work out the legal logistics and ramifications of deals and pretty much anything that could come as a high-risk issue to the company or any potential deal that we may be [negotiating] . . . licensing, copyright issues, anything that's related to our intellectual property.[33]

Prior to Melanie Scott's becoming General Counsel, Tyscot did not have a full-time staffer in this capacity. In the past, the company had simply contracted attorneys with the expertise needed to fulfill legal tasks, many of whom mentored Melanie Scott in the process.

While the responsibilities of the general counsel are extensive, Melanie Scott approaches her work with an overarching view of Tyscot's distinctiveness as an independent *gospel music label* rather than an independent or major secular/mainstream music label. She states:

> Entertainment as a whole has its fair share of issues and so I don't think that's exclusive to our label . . . but you try to do your best to protect the integrity of the company. Within our company, one of the biggest things is that integrity. And the name behind Tyscot is associated with a very strong sense of family and strong sense of Christian values. And so there's a lot of morality issues that would come up with our company that wouldn't come up with . . . a hip hop indie label. So there are different laws that you have to become familiar with as a Christian company. . . . There are a lot of issues that we won't deal with because we are a smaller label. . . . We wouldn't get the huge million dollar lawsuits from like a Brittany Spears or something like that because she had this mega hit and now there's some type of lawsuit because they say that it infringed on their copyright. . . . So we have our set of issues. Larger labels have their set of issues.[34]

Very strategic in gaining the type of education that would allow her to evolve into a first-rate lawyer for Tyscot, Melanie Scott explains, "one of the reasons I attended law school was to do entertainment law with the premise that I would be general counsel for Tyscot."[35] In fact, her educational background has proven to be beneficial for her as both General Counsel and Vice President of Marketing:

> My major in undergrad was advertising communications. And so I did graphic designs for the company long before I did anything legal. And so it just fit that I would do both art and law when I came out. It kinda happened that way you know.[36]

As the Vice President of Marketing, Melanie Scott is responsible for the "organization as a whole, making sure that our [Tyscot] brand is always protected, that it's defined in the market place and that it's not infringed upon." She explains further:

> I also brand artists around what our label brand is. So that can be in the individual album. That can be in them [artists] as a whole . . . overseeing the entire imaging and creative side of an artist in a musical work and the label as a whole.

The notion behind branding, according to Melanie Scott, is to make "yourself identifiable with your marks [images, creative style, marketing, etc. . . .] and with your products in the consumer market place." Regarding Tyscot specifically, she explains:

> Tyscot is unique because it is . . . the oldest Black-owned gospel recording label in the country. In that sense, it has evolved. And so, one of the goals at this point is to . . . enhance the brand of the company by really making consumers understand that it's life-changing music and entertainment. So . . . we're trying to bring a more contemporary audience and also expand the brand. . . . But as we evolve we want to open that brand up to a larger consumer base. So right [now] we're encompassing strictly gospel music and we will continue to do gospel. But we have been known more as a traditional gospel label. But Tyscot is going to evolve in more of a "positive" music label. It will have . . . the Christian base in it but it will be entertainment and music. It won't strictly be records. It will be pervasive across quite a few different things [CDs, film, etc. . . .] but it will encompass music in all of those—but Christian music. But not necessarily traditional. There is contemporary, obviously, worship style, urban, hip hop, Christian music and in addition to that jazz, soul music. . . . So, we have a very large brand. But if you wanted to in four words sum it up it would be "life-changing music entertainment." That is Tyscot.[37]

TYSCOT PERSONNEL

Amidst the major successes and challenges facing Tyscot in the late 1980s and early 1990s, a number of new staff members were added to the roster: Robin Oliver started out in the mailroom and also completed data entry, called radio stations to provide them with record releases, packaged records, answered the phones, and secured copyrights and publishing information as needed. Having moved up through the ranks since her start in 1990, as of 2015 Oliver serves as Vice President of Operations. Sidney Scott, nephew of Leonard Scott, beginning in 1992, worked his way from the mailroom and other low-level assignments to his current position as Director of A&R, where he is charged with discovering new talent, identifying appropriate producers for recordings projects, as well as developing overarching musical and marketing concepts for Tyscot initiatives. Both Sydney Scott and Oliver have also written and produced songs for Tyscot artists such as Shirley Murdock's "He Is the Rock" (2011) and The Jesus Gang's "Bow Down My Child" (2000) over the course of their tenure at the label.

Oliver and Sydney Scott represent Tyscot staff members who participate in both the business and creative sides of the company, as they are themselves performing artists in the music industry. Indianapolis-based national gospel recording artist Lamar Campbell, and widely known choir director Sheri Garrison, minister of music at the ten-thousand-member Eastern Star (Baptist) Church in Indianapolis, are also exemplary, for they both gained their first industry experiences as multifaceted Tyscot staff members. Other remote staff, such as Atlanta-based Leighton Singleton, who works in sales, and Jeff Hargrove, who serves as Director of Promotions, as well as a host of creative transplants such as acclaimed Chicago producers/songwriters Michael Houston and Walter Smith, have been a part of the Tyscot operation since the mid- to late 1990s. Tyscot, as a result, has impacted the city of Indianapolis as well as the surrounding regional community through its creation of opportunities for economic advancement and artistic development.

As of 2015, the core staff at Tyscot consists of approximately ten people: a Chief Executive Officer (CEO), Chief Operating Officer (COO), Vice President of Marketing, General Counsel, Director of Promotions, Director of Distribution, and a Promotions/A&R Director, among others. In addition, many producers, music directors, instrumentalists, background vocalists, and engineers from around the nation are hired to craft the musical

Figure 11.2
Leonard and Christine Scott perform at "Why We Sing: Indianapolis Gospel Music Conference" at Fairview United Methodist Church, Bloomington, Indiana, 2011.

Photo by Milton Hinnant.

sounds and styles of the label's featured artists. Through the collective efforts of this creative aggregate, Tyscot offers diverse styles of traditional and contemporary gospel music along with other Christian-based media such as Tyscot Films[38] and Tyscot Loud, a new hip hop component launched in 2015 that promotes music of gospel rap artists.

Tyscot's current active roster features seasoned and up-and-coming traditional and contemporary gospel artists, including Leonard Scott himself, who has recorded over eight solo albums and partners with his wife, Christine Scott, while performing gospel music around the nation (see Figure 11.2). Other artists include Anthony Brown and Group Therapy, The Rance Allen Group, Ruth La'Ontra, Casey J, Lonnie Hunter, Tiff Joy, Danetra Moore, Clareta, and their current top-tier artist, Deitrick Haddon, with his ensemble, The Voices of Unity.[39] The label, therefore, continues to serve as a launching pad for new artists while sustaining the longevity of industry staples like Leonard Scott, The Rance Allen Group, and Deitrick Haddon. Even more, the company has become an extensive brand that continues to evolve with the pace of the ever-shifting broader music industry.

TYSCOT AS MINISTRY

Unlike secular labels such as Detroit's Motown Records founded with the sole intent to produce "hit records,"[40] Tyscot, from its inception, has functioned as a business that simultaneously serves as a vehicle for ministry. Therefore, Tyscot coincides with other successful gospel labels like GospoCentric Records,[41] founded by Vicki Lataillade in 1993, and described by Kirk Franklin as having been created with a purpose and "passion to serve God, to spread the Word, and to change people's lives through the medium of gospel music."[42] In similar fashion, Tyscot's mission statement charges label associates to have "a positive, powerful impact on every human soul worldwide."[43] Most staff members chosen to work for Tyscot are selected not only for their expertise in artistry and/or business, but also for their ability to conform to the religious framework and primary aim of the company—ministry.

The role of prayer at Tyscot is one of many ways to identify the collective ministerial intent among associates of the label. In selecting artists for the roster, for instance, Leonard Scott states, "we pray over and seek divine direction before signing an artist."[44] As Scott contends, prayer is one of the most prominent ways label staff seek God's guidance. Tyscot staff members alternate in leading prayers every morning before beginning the workday; they pray as a collective for clear direction regarding daily business tasks. Prayer is also an integral part of the recording production process. During Leonard Scott's live recording event in 2009 for his album, *My Worship Experience* (2010), in which I participated as guitarist, musicians and music directors gathered before rehearsals and performances to pray together for the success of the project and for the wellbeing of each other. Prayer functions to establish spiritual unity from the outset, for the recording is perceived as much more than economic pursuit or religious entertainment. With few exceptions, both artists and label staff view the overarching goal of their music as ministry. Their perspective illustrates Burnim's assertion that at its greatest depth, gospel music performance is an act of worship. She describes prayer rituals that accompany preparation and execution of gospel music, arguing that the "inclusion of the prayer as an essential, not optional component, at both [gospel] performances and rehearsals . . . [is] a strong indicator of the view of performance as worship."[45] Burnim's sentiments apply to the collective experience of Tyscot employees, who are chosen to be a part of this musical community, in part, because they share the same religious values; whether in a staff meeting or during an actual recording production, the business of Tyscot is approached as ministry.

Tyscot Records is a sacred venture that not only impacts how business is conducted but also influences the spiritual lives of those within and beyond the company. This reality became most clear to me when I asked staff member Robin Oliver why she had remained with the company for more than twenty years and even agreed to a pay cut in 2010 when the label was in financial crisis: "I just had a belief that things were going to get better. . . . I believed it *because we prayed a lot*."[46] I initially had assumed that Oliver chose to stay with the company because of difficulties she faced in finding another job, given the precarious state of the national economy during the downturn. To the contrary, however, she expressed the exact opposite:

> I never thought it would be difficult to find a job. Working there [at Tyscot], I ended up getting saved [converted to Christianity]. Working for that company actually brought me closer to Christ. . . . That company changed my spiritual life.[47]

Oliver was one of few people who was not a Christian prior to having been hired. In fact, she joked that when she joined the company, "almost every word that came out of my mouth was a curse word," a behavior frowned upon in the religious community with which Tyscot is associated. Nevertheless, Oliver was emphatic: "Tyscot is love," describing the company as having a welcoming atmosphere that prompted her eventually to "get saved," or become a Christian, and adapt the outward lifestyle promoted at Tyscot. She began to attend church regularly and abstain from profanity and other behaviors deemed contrary to religious character. In essence, the religious convictions she developed shaped her loyalty to Tyscot and ultimately overshadowed her financial concerns. During the company's most challenging times, Oliver remained steadfast and unmovable. Clearly, she and the entire staff "lived the life they sang about,"[48] reflecting what Leonard Scott emphatically declares: "Along with a business, Tyscot is a ministry."[49]

The prevailing religious grounding evident at Tyscot is also strongly operative in other contexts industry-wide, including Black Entertainment Television's gospel music talent competition *Sunday Best*, which completed its eighth season in 2015. Exploring distinct characteristics of *Sunday Best*, one of the most popular gospel music television shows to date, ethnomusicologist Christina Harrison illuminates how the nature of critique offered by the show's judges—who include popular gospel artists such as Donnie McClurkin, Yolanda Adams, Tina Campbell, and Kirk Franklin—is equally driven by artistic merit and spiritual engagement and commitment. Harrison argues that *Sunday Best* differs in subtle, although significant, ways from its secular model, *American Idol*, stating:

> *American Idol* places strong focus on branding, imaging, and constructing consumer relationships, factors present in *Sunday Best*, but sublimated to the overall purpose of music ministry. In *Sunday Best* there is more at stake than the pursuit of a career as a recording artist. Its winner will venture into an industry purposed to present God to the masses.[50]

When contestants achieve a heightened state of musical excellence *and* spiritual anointing during performances,[51] *Sunday Best* judges are expected to recognize the transcendent power of the merger between music and ministry. Judges have been known to become overcome in such moments, which can be neither predicted nor programmed. In one such instance, according to Harrison, Tina Campbell commented following a particularly poignant spiritual encounter:

> Of course God is all over the place 'cause He's all over you. The thing about you that gets me, you are honest. You are genuine. You are true. You are a real gospel singer, because you have the heart of God.[52]

Campbell's comments cement the fact that *Sunday Best* performances transcend musical skill or even artistry. The most effective performances on the show embody a clear manifestation of the "anointing," which shapes the collective goal to minister among artists, contestants, judges, and even audience members, who respond to artistic and spiritually potent presentations with "'go 'head,' 'that's alright,' 'yes, suh.'"[53] Tyscot, like *Sunday Best*, is a part of an extensive performance community dedicated to producing compelling musical products and outstanding artists who successfully position the gospel message firmly within the marketplace. Thus, the organic link between creativity, commerce, and faith is readily evident, as Tyscot associates and other gospel music proponents industry-wide cast their collective creative and business efforts as ministry.

CONCLUSION

Tyscot Records, while not often acknowledged, is a major independent gospel music record label that has been instrumental in advancing the careers of many well-known entertainment industry insiders. As to be expected, Tyscot seeks to produce and sell consistent product to ensure the financial gain, viability, and stability of the company. This goal is advanced through a network of highly effective family leadership, committed core staff members, and a dynamic creative collective of musicians, music directors, and songwriters.

At the same time, however, the label is equally defined by its strong religious identity and sacred intent. In other words, Tyscot's success as a business is shaped by shared collective belief in the divine, which impacts *all* areas of the company. The Tyscot label manifests an inextricable bond between music business and music ministry. This intertwined reality constitutes the uniqueness of Tyscot as a gospel music recording label, as manifest in the words of Leonard Scott: "Tyscot is a label of integrity that's gonna do right by . . . our ministry as well as by the market place."[54] At Tyscot, the business of gospel music production is undeniably ministry.

NOTES

1. Leonard Scott, interview by Mellonee Burnim and Raynetta Wiggins, July 25, 2011.
2. Ibid.
3. Kirk Franklin, however, does not mention Tyscot in his autobiography, *Church Boy* (1998).
4. Hobbs not only owned Aleho International Records but also served as gospel radio announcer on Indianapolis's WTLC, vice-chairperson of the Gospel Music Workshop of America (GMWA), which boasts thirty thousand members, and chairperson of the Gospel Announcers Guild. Jones is the host of Black Entertainment Television's *Bobby Jones Gospel*, the longest running show on cable TV since 1980. These two pioneers have been instrumental in the careers of nationally known artists such as Kathy Taylor, Marvin Sapp, Yolanda Adams, and Gospel Music Workshop of America Women of Worship, to name a few.
5. The Apostolic denomination in North America has its origins in the Pentecostal event of the Azusa Street revival in Los Angeles, California, from 1906 to 1908, where an intercultural and interracial collective of Christians, facilitated by African American preacher William Joseph Seymour, held revivals, sparking a religious evangelical movement. Primary belief in the denomination centers upon the evidence of a believer's ability to exhibit glossolalia or "speaking in tongues," as well as water baptism in the name of Jesus Christ (Anderson 2006).
6. Leonard Scott, interview with the author, December 3, 2009.
7. Leonard Scott, interview by Mellonee Burnim and Raynetta Wiggins, July 25, 2011.
8. Ibid.
9. Speaking in tongues signifies congregants' metaphysical communication with God. As they utter sounds unidentifiable to the natural ear, the sounds are transmitted as prayers in the spirit realm.
10. See Hinson 2000; Synan 2001.
11. Leonard Scott, interview with the author, December 3, 2009.
12. In her article, "Consuming Christ: The Role of Jesus in Christian Food Ethics," religious studies scholar Laura Hartman references fasting as a way to "recognize human bodies as frail, as dependent upon food and upon God, but also to recognize humans as more than their bodies" (Hartman 2010, 48). As such, while Leonard Scott fasted to gain divine instruction from God, he was also, essentially expressed by Hartman, fasting as a symbol of humility and spiritual identity.
13. Leonard Scott, interview with the author, December 3, 2009.
14. Ibid.
15. Leonard Scott and his wife, Christine Scott, co-pastor Rock Community Church, an approximately seventy-member non-denominational body, which they founded in 2000.
16. Leonard Scott, interview with the author, July 8, 2015.
17. Ibid.
18. Sidney Scott, interview with the author, July 7, 2015.
19. Leonard Scott, interview by Mellonee Burnim and Raynetta Wiggins, July 25, 2011.
20. Refers to the Gospel Announcers Guild of GMWA.
21. Leonard Scott, interview by Mellonee Burnim and Raynetta Wiggins, July 25, 2011.
22. Leonard Scott, interview with the author, July 8, 2015.
23. Leonard Scott, interview by Mellonee Burnim and Raynetta Wiggins, July 25, 2011.

24. Ibid.
25. Bryant Scott, interview with the author, July 6, 2015.
26. During an interview in 1993, Roger Holmes, who was also manager for national gospel artist Richard Smallwood, informed Mellonee Burnim about typical record sales figures for gospel performers (Burnim 2006, 429).
27. Leonard Scott, interview by Mellonee Burnim and Raynetta Wiggins, July 25, 2011.
28. Ibid.
29. Ibid.
30. Bryant Scott, interview with the author, July 6, 2015.
31. Zarlenga 2009.
32. Along with being a chart-topping artist/producer and actor, Haddon also appears regularly on network/cable TV Oxygen's *Preachers of LA* and *Fix My Choir*. The former show has become highly controversial because Haddon's personal lifestyle, which includes a very public divorce, prompts public critique of his ministry. Both shows have generated considerable ratings success.
33. Melanie Scott, interview with the author, February 24, 2010.
34. Ibid.
35. Ibid.
36. Ibid.
37. Ibid.
38. The company has produced the following films: *Blessed and Cursed*, directed by Joey Kapity (Indianapolis: Tyscot Films, 2010); *A Beautiful Soul*, directed by Jeffrey Byrd (Indianapolis: Tyscot Films, 2012); and *Switching Lanes*, directed by Tommy Ford (Indianapolis: Tyscot Films, 2015).
39. Haddon has written the screenplay and appeared in the first two of three Tyscot films, the second one *A Beautiful Soul* (2012).
40. Sykes 2006, 431.
41. GospoCentric Records became popular as the label that released Kirk Franklin's song "Why We Sing" (1993), obtaining the #1 spot on gospel music charts and receiving radio airplay on secular radio as well as winning numerous top industry awards including two Stellar Awards, two Dove Awards, and four GMWA awards. The label has become synonymous with the success of Kirk Franklin, one of the top-selling artists/producers in the gospel music industry.
42. Franklin 1998, 148.
43. Sidney Scott, interview with the author, July 7, 2015.
44. Stan North, "Interview with Dr. Leonard Scott: A Tyscot Retrospective," GospelFlava.com, last modified July 23, 2002, accessed July 13, 2015, http://gospelflava.com/articles/drleonardscott.html.
45. Burnim 1989, 58.
46. Robin Oliver, interview with the author, July 9, 2015.
47. Ibid.
48. Refers to the song, "I'm Gonna Live the Life I Sing about in My Song," composed in 1941 by Thomas Andrew Dorsey, the father of gospel music.
49. "Interview with Dr. Leonard Scott: A Tyscot Retrospective."
50. Harrison 2012, 63.
51. According to scholar Glenn Hinson, churchgoers often reference the spiritual anointing as God's "touch," or influence, upon a person or performance. The anointing, Hinson suggests, is manifested in various expressive behaviors such as empowering "a preacher's faltering words with wisdom and revelation. It can summon from the throat a shout of praise and jubilation. It can lead the tongue to revel in the phrasings of an unknown, celestial language. And it can push a singer to voice lyrics never before heard by mortal ears. Many forms, many responses, but a single source"—the anointing (Hinson 2000, 2).
52. Harrison 2012, 43.
53. Ibid., 40.
54. Leonard Scott, interview with the author, July 8, 2015.

DISCOGRAPHY

Bill Sawyer and the Christian Tabernacle Concert Choir of Cleveland. *Something Old, Something New*. Tyscot Records 12783, 1983. Cassette.
Bobby Jones and New Life. *Bring It to Jesus*. Tyscot Records 984041, 1993. CD.

Dan Willis and the Pentecostals of Chicago. *Bridging the Gap*. Tyscot Records 4029, 1992. CD.
Hobbs, Al. *Through Christ*. Tyscot Records 86515, 1995. CD.
Jesus Gang. *Live My Life for You*. Tyscot Records 1232, 2000. CD.
John P. Kee and Friends. *There Is Hope*. Tyscot Records 6127, 1990. CD.
Melvin Dawson and Genesis Ensemble. *Signs of the Times*. Tyscot Records 4034, 1992. CD.
Murdock, Shirley. *Live: The Journey*. Tyscot Records TYS 9841932, 2011. CD.
The New Life Community Choir featuring John P. Kee. *Wait On Him*. Tyscot Records TCD-89415, 1989. CD.
The New Life Community Choir featuring John P. Kee. *Wash Me*. Tyscot Records 7901401729, 1991. CD.
The New Life Community Choir featuring John P. Kee. *We Walk by Faith*. Tyscot Records 4031, 1992. CD.
The New Life Community Choir featuring John P. Kee. *Not Guilty . . . The Experience*. New Life/Tyscot/Verity 43139, 2000. CD.
Reverend Oscar Hayes and the Abundant Life Fellowship Chorale. *Got 2 Tell It*. Tyscot Records 4024, 1991. CD.
Scott, Leonard. *Bishop Leonard Scott Presents: My Worship Experience*. Tyscot Records 984188, 2010. CD.
Taylor, Kathy. *Live: The Worship Experience*. Tyscot Records 984178, 2009. CD.
Tichenor, Denise. *Lead Me*. Tyscot Records 4033, 1992. CD.
Trinity Temple Full Gospel Mass Choir. *Holy One*. Tyscot Records 4037, 1993. CD.

PART III

Gender

CHAPTER 12

Voices of Women in Gospel Music
Resisting Representations

Mellonee V. Burnim

Perhaps more than any other genre in the history of African American music, gospel music is replete with women who are highly respected icons in the field. The first million-selling gospel records were by Mahalia Jackson and Clara Ward; the art and craft of gospel piano were fashioned by Texas-born Arizona Dranes; Sallie Martin and Magnolia Lewis Butts were prominent in the founding of the National Convention of Gospel Choirs and Choruses in 1932, the first organization created to promote and disseminate gospel music. Women have been and continue to be vocalists, composers, and choir directors of repute; they have been instrumentalists, owners of music publishing companies, and radio announcers. In the history of gospel music, women have been neither invisible nor silent. Furthermore, at least on the surface, they wielded formidable respect and power, comparable to if not exceeding that of their male counterparts.

The pervasiveness of women's voices in gospel music is not new in the history of Black religious music, for women figured prominently in accounts of singing and dancing in the invisible church during slavery. In his introduction to the *Books of Negro Spirituals*, poet and lyricist James Weldon Johnson celebrates the musical prowess of "Ma" White, in the aftermath of slavery, as "a great leader of singing" whose duty it was to "'sing-down' a long-winded or uninteresting speaker . . . and even to cut short a prayer of undue length by raising a song."[1] Women were present in greater numbers than men during the first tours of the original Fisk Jubilee singers in 1871. In fact, when the founding director, George White, who was both male and White, became too ill to continue his leadership role at one point, it was a young Black woman, Ella Shepherd, who took the helm and kept the history-making tour from being dismantled.[2]

However, the pervasiveness of women gospel artists tends to sublimate the challenges they faced in achieving broad recognition and status. On the surface, the medium of music appears to be an equalizer, a meta-language through which women can communicate forthrightly, without barriers. Women's high visibility, power, and authority in gospel music provide no assurance that the gospel terrain is a level playing field. What exists on the surface as victorious presence *and* power actually obscures the battles either fought and won, or averted, that allowed women to rise to positions of renown. Just as gospel music itself is "multidimensional in construct," consisting of more than text, dress, and behavior, the lives and stories of those women who have been at the forefront of the advance of gospel music historically are equally multilayered and complex.[3]

As women, they challenged the status quo in music circles, much the same as their blues counterparts. Blues women were out on the road, confronting Jim Crow, enduring the stress of performing night after night, managing entourages of family and support staff, and singing songs that the church considered objectionable, in places that the church considered even more objectionable. Similarly, pioneering women of gospel maintained an unrelenting itinerary, often confronting Jim Crow; enduring one-night performance runs; managing entourages of family, accompanists, and ensemble members; and singing songs initially considered "too bluesy" by members of the established church community.

In order for their voices to be heard, women of gospel music constantly confronted prevailing stereotypical and restrictive images of themselves and of their music. Their challenge was against representations of who they were and what they were capable of doing as women, on the one hand, and who they were and what their capabilities were as musicians, on the other. Given the number of women who made significant contributions to gospel music, I have chosen to limit this investigation to three women who rose to the forefront of gospel music during its formative years, women who dared to bring dreams to life that others could barely imagine: Lucie Campbell, Mahalia Jackson, and Willie Mae Ford Smith. These are women for whom the most extensive body of data exists, allowing for an in-depth exploration of the dynamics, timbre, and texture of their musical, cultural, and spiritual voices. I will explore the messages embedded in the music as text and as genre, in order to more fully grasp what it meant for these pioneers to confront such formidable institutions as the music industry and the church, and such dominant individuals as ministers and spouses. The women in this discussion fill the ranks of both ordinary and extraordinary; they survived by blazing their own trails. Through music, they were liberated and empowered to profoundly touch the lives of millions.

LUCIE CAMPBELL (1885–1963)

Lucie Campbell (Figure 12.1) was born in the Deep South, in Mississippi in 1885. She was the daughter of former slaves and the youngest of eleven children. Her father died when she was a newborn; her mother raised the children alone, taking in washing and ironing after having moved to Memphis to try to make a better life for her family. When the oldest daughter in the family was given piano lessons, Lucie gleaned what she could from her sister's opportunity. Ironically, it was Lucie who became the celebrated musician. In 1899, at age fourteen, Lucie Campbell graduated as valedictorian from her high school in Memphis. She became a schoolteacher, not in music, but in English and history, a job she held for fifty years.[4]

Lucie Campbell was a pioneering figure in the development of gospel music, noted particularly for her role as Director of Music for the Christian Education Department of the National Baptist Convention, USA, the largest aggregate of African American

Figure 12.1
Lucie Campbell.

Courtesy Luvenia George.

Christians in the United States. Miss Lucie, as she was fondly called by those who knew her well, holds virtually legendary status in the annals of the National Baptist Convention. For a period of over forty years, she functioned as a powerful figure to be reckoned with. In 1915, after the convention split, Campbell was one of nine organizers invited to be a part of reorganization efforts, because she had a reputation as an "outstanding Christian worker and singer."[5]

As a composer, Campbell had an output of over one hundred songs. She directed 1,000-voice choirs and sponsored extravagant musicals and pageants. She defined the character of worship at the Baptist convention by choosing what songs were to be sung and by whom. When gospel great Clara Ward was initially rejected in her early 1950s bid for an appearance at the National Baptist Convention, it was Campbell who reversed the decision and allowed her to perform. Everybody who was anybody knew that songs selected for the convention were virtually guaranteed success. After Thomas Dorsey's "If You See My Savior" was introduced at the convention in 1930, he promptly sold 4,000 copies of the song. Music was a critical component of the National Baptist Convention meetings. As ethnomusicologist Luvenia George points out, music was strategically used as one of the tools that helped to bolster the attendance necessary "for keeping the organization intact and preventing defection by the churches."[6]

As the only female member of the Publishing Board of the Convention, Lucie Campbell helped to publish songbooks that were widely used throughout the denomination and even cut across denominational lines. In 1921, the landmark collection *Gospel Pearls* was published, which included compositions by the father of gospel music Thomas Dorsey, grandfather of gospel music Charles Albert Tindley, and Lucie Campbell's first copyrighted composition, "The Lord Is My Shepherd." The *Gospel Pearls* remained a standard resource in Black Baptist and Methodist churches throughout the 1960s. Having been raised in the Methodist church and having served as pianist in Missionary and Primitive Baptist churches in Teague, Texas, the *Gospel Pearls* was a staple in my own personal music library.

Three articles in Bernice Johnson Reagon's edited volume *We'll Understand It Better By and By: Pioneering African American Gospel Composers* (1992) center on Lucie Campbell. Each writer presents a microcosm of Lucie Campbell, which ultimately yields three vastly different renderings of her. Taken together, a somewhat fractured portrait of Campbell results. In each author's portrayal of Miss Lucie's role in the National Baptist Convention, she is projected as larger than life, a woman who effectively uses her position of power to aid in launching the international music careers of such luminaries as Mahalia Jackson, Clara Ward, Roberta Martin, J. Robert Bradley, Marian Anderson, and even Thomas Dorsey. While the writings of Horace Boyer and Luvenia George celebrate Campbell's compositional prowess, concentrating on her national persona, Rev. Clarence Walker's portrayal of Campbell includes her popularity as a speaker for Women's Day programs, conferences, and high school commencements, providing a close examination of her involvement in the musical life of local churches in Memphis, where she lived.[7] As a national figure, Miss Lucie appears virtually without blemish, whereas at the local level Walker renders her in an altogether different light.

Because Lucie Campbell was neither minister nor male, she was denied access to the pulpit when she spoke. Some who heard her believed that where she stood neither hindered her authority and power, nor reduced her effectiveness in comparison to male preachers. According to one observer, "Miss Lucie could stand down on the floor and break up a church."[8] When speaking of women in her addresses, Miss Lucie characterized the depth of their beauty, power, and influence. She made no attempt to project either submissiveness or subservience. Her words were provocative and daring, and in many ways downright radical, perhaps even subversive, for a woman born in the nineteenth century:

> From whatever viewpoint you evaluate a woman, she is the most influential being in the world. She can lead a man to the highest pinnacle of beauty, of purity, nobility and usefulness; or to the lowest depths of shame and infamy. Woman was behind the fall of Adam, the first man; behind the fall of Samson, the strongest man, behind the fall of Solomon, the wisest man. Despite man's boasted

strength, courage and intellect, he will follow a woman anywhere. Someone boastfully remarked that man is the head. A quick-witted woman replied, "Then woman is the neck—the head cannot turn without the neck."[9]

In another address, Campbell advances the physical beauty of the Black woman, speaking to audiences long before the "Black Is Beautiful" slogan of the 1960s and sending a message of empowerment that she not only envisioned, but actually lived. She exhorts:

> Women, we are somebody—clothed in the sun. No need for costume jewelry or real diamonds, rubies or pearls. The sun is enough. You can barely look at the sun with the naked eye. It is too dazzling. A perfectly dressed woman will bear heavily on the eye.[10]

Loved by the National Baptist Convention for her organizational skill, her musicianship, as well as her personal sense of style, audiences of the National Baptist Convention were known to eagerly await the 5'2," 110-pound giant as she made her entrances onto the platform; the sight of her "strutting," as it was called, across the stage brought unbridled delight.[11] Perhaps it was Miss Lucie's multifaceted greatness and her extraordinary confidence, likely perceived by some as arrogance, that opened the door to her vulnerability. This same Lucie Campbell who directed casts of thousands over the years at the National Baptist Convention also served as choir director at Baptist churches in her hometown of Memphis, Tennessee. At Metropolitan Baptist Church in 1922 and twice at Central Baptist Church in the years 1929 and 1943, Lucie Campbell was embroiled in church conflicts that twice resulted in her being involuntarily expelled from church membership.

In the 1922 incident, Lucie Campbell was on the wrong side of a dispute concerning who was to become the new pastor of Metropolitan Baptist. The later controversies at Central Baptist were fueled in one instance by differences over which choir was to sing on a given Sunday and in another instance by her refusal to apologize (as instructed by the male pastor) to a male deacon with whom she had difficulty working over an extended period. In the first and last of these three episodes, the police were summoned, and Miss Lucie is depicted as seizing her umbrella, presumably to utilize it as a weapon of defense. Both conflicts ended with Miss Lucie's removal from the membership roll. In the 1922 case, not only were Miss Lucie and one hundred of her followers "churched," or excommunicated, but Miss Lucie was personally barred from other churches in Memphis as well, and there was a reported effort to exorcize her from churches across the state of Tennessee.[12]

After the 1922 conflict, during an extended period of self-imposed exile from church in general, Miss Lucie composed one of her most famous songs "He Understands; He'll Say Well Done":[13]

> If when you give the best of your service,
> Telling the world that the Savior is come;
> Be not dismayed when men don't believe you;
> He understands; He'll say, "Well done."[14]

In this text, Ms. Lucie laments her experience of conflict and controversy at Metropolitan. The lyrics express a sense of her deep personal anguish over serving, giving her best, and spreading the gospel, only to be misunderstood and rejected by her peers. Her response through the release of her creative impulse, however, can be viewed as a conscious act of resistance to charges that represented her as difficult, uncooperative, and unapologetic. Miss Lucie utilized the same tool that African Americans had used with such success during the period of slavery and the fight for civil rights. Music served simultaneously as a healing balm and as a nonthreatening weapon for resisting and confronting oppressive representations from the church politic.

MAHALIA JACKSON (1912–1972)

Although over time Lucie Campbell's music has transcended barriers of race in some ways, as evidenced by recordings of her songs by Pat Boone and Lawrence Welk,[15] during her actual career Miss Lucie was known, loved, and "challenged" almost exclusively within the confines of the African American Christian community. In contrast, Mahalia Jackson (Figure 12.2) was a public figure, a household name who rose from humble beginnings to international recognition and fame. Her credits are impressive by any standard.

Figure 12.2
Portrait of Mahalia Jackson, April 16, 1962.
Library of Congress, Prints and Photographs Division, Carl Van Vechten Collection.

Jackson's list of accomplishments is stellar. She won two Grammy awards, as well as a lifetime Grammy issued posthumously. At the presidential inauguration of John F. Kennedy, she was a featured soloist. Among her many television credits are appearances on variety shows hosted by Dinah Shore, Bing Crosby, Steve Allen, and Ed Sullivan. In 1954, she hosted her own Chicago radio show, and in 1955 she had her own television show there as well. Hers was the first million-selling gospel record, "Move on Up a Little Higher," a 1947 release. And it was Mahalia Jackson who stirred the crowd with the musical preface to Martin Luther King Jr. at the 1963 March on Washington, singing "How I Got Over" and "I've Been 'Buked and I've Been Scorned."[16]

The great Mahalia Jackson came from humble beginnings, not unlike those of Lucie Campbell. Born poor, her mother died when she was five years old. Her father, who worked as a stevedore by day, a barber by night, and a preacher on Sundays, was unable to raise her and her ten-year-old brother, so Mahalia was "adopted" by her mother's sister, whom she called Aunt Duke. A churchgoing woman, Aunt Duke did not allow Mahalia to listen to secular music, an admonition that Mahalia shrewdly circumvented by listening to her older cousin Fred's blues recordings while her aunt was at work. Bessie Smith was her favorite singer, and, although she later carefully guarded this fact from her churchgoing audience, Bessie's influence permeated Mahalia's vocal style since childhood. She recalls: "I remember when I used to listen to Bessie Smith sing 'I Hate to See that Evening Sun Go Down.' I'd just fix my mouth and try to make my tones come out just like her."[17]

As one of the pioneers of gospel music, Mahalia played a seminal role in taking this genre into uncharted territories. She recalls how "big churches" initially, during the early 1930s, did not accept gospel music, that it was the small storefront churches that welcomed this emergent form. For many, particularly members of the educated elite, the music was considered jazz; as such, it was *not* acceptable for worship. In a 1952 interview, Mahalia countered this representation of her chosen song form with the argument that she was simply singing in the style that reflected the cultural experiences she had while growing up in New Orleans.[18] For those who found gospel music objectionable, the genre was defined first and foremost, perhaps even singularly, by its *aural* dimensions—its melodic, rhythmic, and chordal structure. For Mahalia, such representations were unfair, incomplete, *and* inaccurate. Therefore, it was simply not conceivable that she could be expected, as a musician, to reject, disavow, or discard her accumulated musical and cultural knowledge to accommodate provincial notions of religious music acceptability:

> Coming up North, a lot of people have questioned me about . . . the way I sing these religious songs. But I've heard 'em being rendered this way from a child. So that's why maybe a lot of the songs that I sing, they might think it sounds [like] jazz because the jazz musicians played it. But it was something I heard from a little bitty girl on up to this day. The type of music that I'm talking about was known to [all the] New Orleans people after they had buried the deceased [as] . . . second line. . . . That type of music is really in my soul.[19]

Mahalia Jackson embraced music as culture; her musical identity encompassed and reflected the sum total of her musical experiences. Her performance style evolved as an amalgam of her musical experience. Any effort to extract that legacy from her musical character was in fact an effort to disembody Mahalia from her concept of who she was.

Whereas established churches represented one site of contention regarding the music she offered to the world, Mahalia also faced similar indictments from a music professional, a concert tenor whom she sought out for voice lessons in 1932 in Chicago's Southside.

Using the Negro spiritual "Standing in the Need of Prayer" as her audition piece, Professor DuBois (referred to by some sources as Prof. Kendricks) quickly stopped her, exclaiming:

> That's no way to sing that song. Slow down. . . . You've got to learn to stop hollering. The way you sing is not a credit to the Negro race. You've got to learn to sing songs so that white people can understand them.[20]

Clearly, Professor DuBois' views of what constituted music of value were diametrically opposed to those of Mahalia. The aesthetic values that characterized gospel music in the 1930s are the same values that have historically distinguished all forms of African American music, sacred and secular, in the United States.[21] Mahalia had absorbed these values in her Baptist church in New Orleans, in the Sanctified church next to the house where she grew up, and in the "back o' town" streets during Mardi Gras. It was not something she chose to relinquish or suppress, even if her performance was criticized by members of the educated elite. Her reaction to Professor DuBois?

> I felt all mixed up. How could I sing songs for white people to understand when I was colored myself? It didn't seem to make any sense. It was a battle within me to sing a song in a formal way. I felt it was too polished and I didn't feel good about it. I handed over my four dollars to the Professor and left. . . . It was a long time before I had another extra four dollars, but even when I did, I never went back to Professor DuBois' music salon. It turned out to be my one and only singing lesson.[22]

Over the course of her career, Mahalia suffered public rebuke from some African American churches and from a music professional who professed Western European–derived musical values. Privately, she also endured a similar critique from her own husband, Isaac Hockenhull. A graduate of Fisk University and Tuskegee Institute, Ike, as Mahalia referred to him, had studied to be a chemist, but the only job open to him in Chicago during the Depression was that of mail carrier. When they married, Mahalia was working as a hotel maid. Her insecurities regarding their relative educational backgrounds were evident as she expressed disbelief that "this educated man who was ten years older . . . could be interested in a girl who never knew any school after the eighth grade." But Ike believed that the only thing standing between Mahalia and a career as a "great concert artist" was her gospel music repertoire. She recalls:

> He was educated and he thought gospel singing *wasn't* [emphasis mine]. He still wanted me to be a concert singer. He wanted me to take voice training and he and I were always fussing about it. "Why do you want to waste your wonderful voice on that stuff?" he would shout. "It's not art! . . . You'll never get anywhere running around to those churches hollering your head off with those gospel songs. Don't you understand that God gave you a voice and you're not using it to become a great artist?"[23]

A less confident, competent, or secure woman might have been crushed by such a harsh appraisal from one so close. But even at twenty-four years old, Mahalia was able to grasp the inherent contradictions in Ike's argument. Although admittedly feeling oppressed by the weight of Ike's desire and their precarious financial state, which he felt could be alleviated by Mahalia's switching to classical or semi-classical music, she responded by asserting:

> I didn't care whether gospel singing wasn't art. It had something for *me*. It was part of me. I loved it and sang it just the way I heard folks singing it down South during those great Baptist revival meetings on the Mississippi River when I was a child.

She continued:

> Even in those days when I was arguing with Ike, I somehow knew that what I had to give was in my singing. A lot of times we don't appreciate who we are and what we are. Even education, while it's a wonderful thing, can make a person narrow that way about himself.[24]

Mahalia's resistance to negative views of her music in the case of her husband Ike and her prospective instructor Professor DuBois are representative examples of intracultural conflict. She was an African American confronting other African Americans' devaluations of an indigenous African American music genre that she loved. The indictments were not directed toward Mahalia's voice or her person; the attacks were not *personal*, at least not directly. Yet they challenged the overarching views of gospel music that Mahalia personally held. Mahalia and Ike eventually were divorced; they came apart, as she says, "over gospel singing." Her recollections are telling of the pain she experienced as a result:

> A man doesn't want his wife running all over the country, even if it's for the Lord—but I couldn't stop doing it. When you have something deep inside of you for the world, nothing can stop you—I gave up other things for the work I wanted to do.[25]

Although music was the vehicle that allowed Mahalia to escape the hardship of a life of domestic labor, music was much more than a profession for Mahalia. It was a *calling*—a ministry sufficiently compelling for her to resist compromise even for a husband she loved:

> I was born to sing gospel music. Nobody had to teach me. . . . I was so strongly drawn to gospel music [because] I had a feeling . . . deep down inside me that it was what God wanted me to do.[26]

As a recording artist, Mahalia Jackson was equally challenged by an institution that appeared to accept and promote her music on the one hand, yet at the same time constricted and restricted her performance style to make her conform to their preconceived notions of what represented the boundaries of musical excellence and acceptability. It was her religion that was sometimes totally ignored when Mahalia Jackson moved into recording and television studios. Decisions in the studios were based on variables of time and money. Cultural or religious needs or objectives were not primary determinants of programmatic choices. In 1954, Mahalia Jackson hosted her own radio show, which commanded a sizeable local audience in Chicago. She already had a million-selling recording to her credit when she was asked to host the program; yet even the positive reviews the show garnered and its audience response were still not enough to prevent the show from being terminated after only twenty weeks. The show lacked a sponsor, without which it was doomed to fail. She was told, "You're all right here in Chicago with a local sponsor, but there isn't a sponsor who sells his product down South that would take a chance on a Negro singer."[27] Nat "King" Cole faced the same fate with his television host debut; his show premiered in 1956 and was terminated for lack of a sponsor in 1957 after sixty weeks.[28]

Mahalia's experience in the television studio illustrates further how her intimate knowledge of gospel repertoire and her demonstrated excellence and stature in the field provided few assurances that she and her music would receive the respect warranted. Mahalia recalls this episode in 1955, when she appeared on Chicago station WBBM-TV:

> When I first walked into that CBS studio, I admit I was pretty much a total unknown. None of those folks had ever been inside a black church, or listened to gospel on early records. But they had their orders

to work with me. It was *my* show certain nights, and they did work with me, but some of them may not have liked what I do! Well that first day the arranger walked over to me even before I had my coat off. He sat down on the piano bench and told me he just couldn't follow the song I'd chosen to sing for an opener. Now the song he was talking about is a very old and famous spiritual, "Nobody Knows the Trouble I've Seen." Of all the music in that studio he should have known that song! Well, that man told me that the way I was going wasn't the way the song was supposed to go! Can you believe that? So I just talked right back at him. I said: "How come, mister, you think you can tell me about that old song, when it was born in my mouth?" And, you know, he answered me back with ridicule. He talked to me real bad. But I held my tongue and said nothing more. I decided to answer him through the song itself, and the way I sing it.[29]

Both the music and its message became for Mahalia a weapon of resistance, just as it had been for Lucie Campbell. Whether or not the producer knew that Mahalia was signifying through her music is immaterial; Mahalia knew. The song served its purpose for *her*. Was the producer motivated by cultural racism or simply professional arrogance? We have no way of knowing. What is important is, although his attack exacted a wound, it did not destroy. The self-assuredness, the clarity, the conviction with which Mahalia sang anchored her and propelled her to press on to higher ground. When persecuted, Mahalia turned to God, singing words and expressing feeling that, as gospel composer William Herbert Brewster said, "were almost dangerous to say, but you could sing it."[30]

Finally, in the television studio *and* in the recording studio, Mahalia experienced the clash of aesthetic values in determining *how* she was to articulate a given piece. She had no doubt about what she wanted to do, and what would be achieved as a result. But neither the recording studio nor the television studio adhered to values and norms commonplace in the Black church. She explained:

Time is important to me . . . because I want to sing long enough to leave a message. I'm used to singing in churches where nobody would dare stop me until the Lord arrives! But the first thing those television and recording folks would do was to start warning me, "Look out! Watch your time!" And then, first thing you know, they'd start cutting the song! I always got the feeling that some of those producers and studio people were trying to slick me up, turn me into a commercial entertainer. But real gospel singing is not *just* entertainment . . .

She complained further:

I hate to see how the commercial world takes over the songs that have been the strength of my people. How they turn them into jived-up nightclub acts and rock-and-roll recordings. The dignity of a colored church—religion itself—is being debased, so that a few people can make some fast money out of them.[31]

Although Mahalia Jackson was the creative artist, she was not always in control of the product she created. She speaks of how music directors sometimes cut choral groups or strings into her recordings *after* she had completed them. Sometimes, she recalls, "those studio engineers made me sound like a pig squealing under a gate."[32] European fans who heard Mahalia in concert for the first time sometimes commented on the stark contrast between her recordings and her live performances. In the live performance, she was clearly and totally in control, choosing the repertoire she valued, singing reprises as she was so moved, and using every limb in her body and every muscle in her face to convey the message in the music. No inaccurate representations of her artistry could stand in the face of her performances. The music she produced invariably reigned supreme.

When Mahalia Jackson died in 1972, she was honored with two funerals, one in the city of Chicago where she had lived since 1927 and the second in New Orleans, the city of her birth. Together, the funeral services attracted some 18,000 mourners, including such luminaries as Chicago Mayor Richard Daley and Coretta Scott King.[33] At the Chicago funeral, Queen of Soul Aretha Franklin sang Thomas Dorsey's "Precious Lord,"[34] which Mahalia herself had sung at the funeral of Martin Luther King Jr.[35] She died a multimillionaire, with a reported estate valued at $9 million.[36]

WILLIE MAE FORD SMITH (1904–1994)

As the final icon in this trilogy, Willie Mae Ford Smith is another figure whose stature was contained for the greater part of her career within the African American community exclusively. It was only after she was featured in the 1982 film *Say Amen, Somebody* that she rose to prominence among non-Blacks as well. Celebrated throughout her career with the title "mother," the term of endearment acknowledges the role she played, as did Lucie Campbell, in launching the careers of numerous gospel greats.

Willie Mae Ford Smith's own launching pad was the National Convention of Gospel Choirs and Choruses, sometimes referred to as the Dorsey Convention, an organization created for the express purpose of promoting and disseminating gospel music. The National Convention of Gospel Choirs and Choruses was the first of over a dozen such organizations now in existence, all of which are based on the Dorsey model, including the largest, the James Cleveland Gospel Music Workshop of America. Willie Mae Ford Smith conceived of the Soloist Bureau in the convention, a unit she headed, that served to provide nurture and instruction for aspiring gospel soloists.

As did Lucie Campbell, Willie Mae Ford Smith moved as a child from her birth state of Mississippi to Memphis, Tennessee. As did Mahalia Jackson, she later moved North with her family as a part of the Great Migration. She remained in St. Louis, where they settled, until her death. She was born in 1904, the seventh of fourteen children. At age twenty, she married a man nineteen years her senior, had two children of her own, and adopted a third who became her accompanist for over twenty years. She was ordained as a minister in the A.M.E. Zion Church in the late 1930s/early 1940s. In the mid-1950s, she became a member of the Apostolic church, choosing to transfer her membership to a denomination that viewed women in the ministry in less restrictive terms. She is the only one of these three women who institutionalized her role as a preacher; she is also the only one who had children.

Willie Mae Ford Smith was not a composer, as was Lucie Campbell, and neither was she a commercial recording artist, as was Mahalia Jackson. Although she was offered a recording contract in the 1940s after singing an Easter sunrise service at Hollywood Bowl in California, her husband and father advised her to reject the offer to record, which she did. But no records were necessary to ensure Willie Mae Ford Smith an audience. Her greatest contributions were at the grassroots level, as she crisscrossed the country conducting what others called "programs" and what she referred to as "evangelistic services" or "revivals in song." Over a ten-year period during the height of Mother Smith's career in the 1940s, she was home only a week or so per month. Her daughter Jackie recalls, "Preachers resented her," yet, "people would come from miles around to hear her sing."[37] Sometimes the "doors of the church" (invitation to discipleship) would be opened at her events, even though, as was the case with Lucie Campbell, she never stood in the pulpit.

That her audiences loved and respected her is an understatement. Although she ignored the dictates of the clock when she performed, her admirers nonetheless held her in high regard. Again, her daughter Jackie recalls: "If the program was supposed to start at seven or seven thirty . . . she'd leave home at 8:30. . . . [But] nobody would leave . . . they'd just sit there and wait."[38] Jackie describes her mother as a dramatic singer who utilized gestures that conveyed the rhythm and meaning of her repertoire. Although she would never have classified herself as an entertainer, there was nonetheless an element of flair in her performances that appealed to her audiences' purely aesthetic sensibilities. She always wore a flower in her hair, and as her daughter fondly recalls, she "always tried to be as pretty as she could be." Because she perspired freely when she performed, she also carried a cape, which seems to have become part of her persona. Her daughter Jackie recounts:

> When she'd leave home, she wasn't perspiring, so she'd throw the cape back and the kids in the neighborhood used to call her Superman. She'd break out the door with that cape kind of leaning in the back. And they'd say "It's a bird—."[39]

Willie Mae Ford Smith's musical career had a challenging dimension shared by neither Mahalia Jackson nor Lucie Campbell. She had children, a son and daughter who were left behind in the care of friends and family when she traveled. Mother Smith did not take the decision to leave her children in pursuit of her ministry lightly, and, as captured in the film *Say Amen, Somebody*, neither did her husband. Three encounters in this film document the complex terrain Willie Mae Ford Smith navigated in expressing her identity as a woman in ministry, a mother, and a wife. In the first, Mother Smith confronts her own grandson, who questions her authority as a woman to teach and preach. As the sequence continues, she mentors her protégé, Zella Jackson, who is anxious about her marriage as she attempts to balance the demands of her career and family. Finally, Mother Smith weaves a powerful narrative of her husband's vociferous agitation against her travels and her musical confrontation with a minister who sought to demean and diminish her Christian mission by reducing her to an object of his own personal sexual desire.[40] In each case, as Willie Mae Ford Smith confronts traditional representations of gender, male and female, she reveals her areas of vulnerability as well as her strategies of resistance.

In response to a controlling mate who questions her extensive travel, suggesting that her children are being neglected, Willie Mae Ford Smith relies on prayer as an antidote. When her husband suffers a tragic fall down an elevator shaft as he sought to impose his own corrective for her behavior, his accident clearly is viewed as the hand of God protecting her from pending discord, from disjuncture in her evangelical mission. Her husband's experience must have indeed been completely transforming, life-changing both physically and spiritually. Not only does Mother Smith note that she never again had problems with his challenging her life's work, but in fact her adult children characterize their father as Mother Smith's greatest fan, someone who always sat on the front row of her "programs" and who protected her from undue disturbances during her intervals at home. She had wielded the weapon of prayer and triumphed.

Mother Smith's encounter with the minister brazen enough to threaten to "pat her hips" was dissipated through song, another way of turning it over to the Lord. She did not argue, she did not cower in fear, nor did she retreat. Instead, she allowed the power of the musical message to fight her battles.

To deal with her grandson's challenge, she sent him to the Bible to reconnect with God's command of all living creatures to do as He so wills. Her controversial advice to Zella Jackson:

> It's hard being a gospel singer, having a career. . . . When you realize you're not doing it just for Zella. And get the children and the support of the children and the husband and the family all that out of your mind, and see the souls out there that are drifting, and you're throwing out a lifeline. And Zella, just as true as I'm talking to you today, God has a way for you to go. And you can do what God wants you to do. But you do it with the hand of him leading you.[41]

Willie Mae Ford Smith's overriding sense of God's divine purpose for her life compelled her to go against the grain and to advise Zella accordingly. Although she faced opposition at every juncture, she was unwavering in the commitment to her call.

CONCLUSION

In her book *Outlaw Culture: Resisting Representations*, bell hooks explores the internal workings of "cultural practices and cultural icons" that she defines as "on the edge, as pushing the limits, disturbing the conventional, acceptable politics of representation."[42] Clearly, the women of gospel music I have discussed fit this description. They were ordinary women who led extraordinary lives, simply because they refused to be limited by tradition, by conventional wisdom, or by images that restricted the world they envisioned under God's directive. Although the concept of representation is most often applied to media images, visual or print, this concept is expanded here to embrace the dynamics of African American oral culture. Music existed both in print and in the oral tradition. Representative images that governed gospel music and its female practitioners existed in the conscious or subconscious minds of Blacks and Whites that these women encountered. Their ability to successfully negotiate the limiting power of these constructs depended largely on each artist's ability to recognize their existence.

Women of gospel music had to be alert, resourceful, and resilient in order to achieve their musical and spiritual goals. Lucie Campbell, Mahalia Jackson, and Willie Mae Ford Smith were all that and more. Just as gospel music itself is "multidimensional in construct," consisting of more than text, more than dress, and more than behavior, those women who have been at the forefront of the advance of gospel music historically narrate equally complex lives, as musicians and as women. The stories behind the public personae magnify their achievements even more. They did not achieve greatness based on body image or public persona or by the sole virtue of their accomplished musicianship. They sacrificed much, and they fought long and hard. Sometimes they grew weary, but their personal sense of mission, their calling, never allowed them to quit.

These pioneering women of gospel music clearly reflect the womanist paradigm advanced by theologian Jacqueline Grant, who contends:

> A womanist then is a strong black woman who has sometimes been mislabeled as a domineering, castrating matriarch. A womanist is one who has developed survival strategies in spite of the oppression of her

race and sex in order to save her family and her people. . . . For some Black women that may involve being feminine as traditionally defined, and for others it involves being masculine as stereotypically defined. In either case, womanist just means being and acting out who you are.[43]

The three women I have discussed—Lucie Campbell, Mahalia Jackson, and Willie Mae Ford Smith—defied stereotypes, resisted representation; they blazed their own trails. Through music they were liberated and empowered to profoundly touch the lives of millions.

ACKNOWLEDGMENTS

The research for this article was completed during the 2001–2002 academic year, through the generous support of the Womanist Scholar's Program at the Interdenominational Theological Center in Atlanta, Georgia (Director, Jacqueline Grant).

NOTES

1. Johnson and Johnson 1989 (1925, 1926), 22.
2. *Jubilee Singers: Sacrifice and Glory* 2000.
3. Burnim 1985, 147.
4. See Luvenia George 1992; Boyer 1992b; Walker 1992, 124–125.
5. Luvenia George 1992, 113.
6. Ibid.
7. Walker 1992, 125.
8. Ibid., 127.
9. Lucie Campbell, quoted in Walker 1992, 125.
10. Campbell in Walker 1992, 126.
11. Ibid.
12. Campbell in Walker 1992, 130.
13. Ibid.
14. *The African Methodist Episcopal Church Bicentennial Hymnal* 1984, 487.
15. Luvenia George 1992, 119.
16. Jackson and Wylie 1966; Goreau 1975; Schwerin 1992.
17. Jackson and Wylie 1966, 36.
18. Recorded interview: Jules Schwerin, compiler, *Mahalia Jackson: I Sing Because I'm Happy* (Smithsonian/Folkways Special Projects, SFSP900002, 1992. Originally issued in 1979 as Folkways 31101 and 31102).
19. Schwerin 1992.
20. Jackson and Wylie 1966, 59.
21. Burnim and Maultsby 1987.
22. Jackson and Wylie 1966, 59.
23. Ibid., 70–71.
24. Ibid., 71–72.
25. Ibid., 78.
26. Ibid., 66.
27. Jackson and Wylie 1966, 95; see also Schwerin 1992, 85.
28. Haskins and Benson 1984, 144.
29. Schwerin 1992, 103.
30. Brewster 1992, 201.
31. Ibid., 106.
32. Ibid., 152–153.
33. See "Two Cities Pay Tribute to Mahalia Jackson" 1972, 62–72; Brown 1972, 17–34; Goreau 1975, 609.
34. "Two Cities Pay Tribute to Mahalia Jackson" 1972, 62.
35. Jackson and Wylie 1966, 215.

36. Schwerin 1992, 187.
37. Dargan and Bullock 1989, 255.
38. Ibid., 254.
39. Ibid.
40. *Say Amen, Somebody* 1984 (1982).
41. All of the above references to film content pertain to *Say Amen, Somebody* 1984 (1982).
42. hooks 1994, 4.
43. Grant 1989, 205.

DISCOGRAPHY

Bradley, J. Robert. *I'll Fly Away*. Nashboro 7139, 1974. LP.
Cleveland, Rev. James. *Gospel Workshop of America*. Savoy Gospel 7100, 1990. CD.
Dorsey, Rev. Thomas A. *Precious Lord: The Great Gospel Songs of Thomas A. Dorsey*. Originally released by CBS Records KG32151, 1973. Columbia/Legacy 57164, 1994. CD.
Dranes, Arizona. *Complete Recorded Works (1926–1929)*. Document Records DOCD 5186, 2000. CD.
———. *He Is My Story: The Sanctified Soul of Arizona Dranes*. Tompkins Square TSQ 2677, 2012. CD.
The Edwin Hawkins Singers. *Let Us Go Into the House of the Lord*. Buddah Collector's Classics. BMG Direct 75517–49515–2, 1996. CD.
The Fisk Jubilee Singers. *The Fisk Jubilee Singers*. Directed by John W. Work. Originally released as Folkways Records FA2372, 1955. Reissued by Smithsonian Folkways Recordings FW02372, 2004. Digital.
———. *In Bright Mansions*. Curb Records 78762, 2003. CD.
Franklin, Aretha. *Amazing Grace*. Originally released 1972. Atlantic SD2–906–2, unknown date. CD.
———. *Precious Lord*. Passport Audio 1046, 2006. CD.
Franklin, Kirk. *Kirk Franklin and the Family*. BMG/Sony Music Entertainment, 371626, 2001. CD.
Jackson, Mahalia. *How I Got Over*. Includes "I've Been 'Buked and I've Been Scorned," "Move On Up a Little Higher," and others. Columbia C34073, 1976. LP.
———. *Mahalia Jackson 21 Greatest Hits*. Kenwood Records 20510, 1979. LP.
———. *Mahalia Jackson: I Sing Because I'm Happy*. Compiled by Jules Schwerin. Folkways 31101 and 31102, 1979. Reissue, Smithsonian/Folkways Special Projects, SFSP900002, 1992.
Martin, Roberta. *Roberta Martin . . . Live*. Jewel 144, date unknown. CD.
The Roberta Martin Singers. *Best of the Roberta Martin Singers*. Originally released 1979. Reissued by Savoy Gospel 7018, 2001. CD.
Say Amen, Somebody. Various artists. Music from the Original Soundtrack. Originally released by DRG Records SB2L 12584, 1983. Reissued by Rykodisc 10892, 2007. CD.
Smith, Willie Mae Ford. *Going on with the Spirit*. Nashboro Records 7148, 1975. LP.
———. *I'm Bound for Canaan Land*. Originally released by Savoy Records SL 14739, 1983. Reissued by ZYX Music 4906, 2001. CD.
———. *Mother Smith & Her Children*. Spirit Feel SFCD 1010, 1990. CD.
Ward, Clara. *Soul and Inspiration*. Capitol Records ST-126, 1969. LP.
———. *Famous Ward Singers*. Savoy 5001, 1990. LP.
———. *When the Gates Swing Open*. Liquid 8 12134, 2003. CD.

CHAPTER 13

Are All the Choir Directors Gay?
Black Men's Sexuality and Identity in Gospel Performance

Alisha Lola Jones

When I share with African American gospel enthusiasts that I research Black men's performance of gender and sexuality in gospel music, the most frequent responses I receive are: "Why are there so many 'effeminate' men in music ministries? And why are so many choir directors gay?" I often follow up with the questions: "In what ways are they 'effeminate'? How do you know *so many* choir directors are gay?" In their replies, "choir directors" are commonly described as male soloists and leaders who exhibit femininity. Enthusiasts use coded descriptions of performance traits such as "singing high like a woman" or dancing "with grace." Explanations of "singing high like a woman" in solo gospel music performance suggest that the higher vocal register is a woman's domain and men who traverse into that vocal territory are queer. In one instance, I asked a male cleric to explain what dancing "with grace" means. He replied, "I mean graceful like a woman. You know, the smoothness and fluidity in his hand gestures and his limp wrists." When I countered with, "Are women the only ones allowed to be graceful, smooth, or fluid?" he had difficulty formulating an answer.

In seeking clarification of meaning and assumptions embedded in the descriptions of male vocalists and choir directors in African American churches, evidence suggests that common perceptions are representative of an unstated but assumed masculine ideal. In fact, respondents in my research population frequently suggest that African American churches actually serve as magnets for queer men, evident especially in the role of choir director. Rarely do such critical commentaries acknowledge the fact that homosexual men may be found in every area of church leadership—as deacons, ushers, trustees, and even as pastors.[1] Furthermore, the projection of the choir director as gay without concrete supporting evidence (such as their self-identification) signals a conflation of men's sexuality with gender expression, which in actuality are two distinct aspects of identity. While sexual orientation references sexual partner preferences, gender expression is indicative of the socio-culturally developed male- or female-coded ways that individuals present their identity to the public.

Throughout my research in local and national gospel music scenes, gospel enthusiasts often identify what they view as a cultural obsession with sexual and gender expression among African American churchgoers. Despite this fact, these topics are often culturally marked as taboo, and the distinctions between sexual orientation and gender expression are rarely acknowledged or explored beyond superficial interpretations. Within cultural conversations regarding queer gender expression and sexuality, there is also a disparity between the ways in which women's and men's identities are scrutinized in African American churches. Gender and sexuality scholar Philip Brian Harper contends that, for Black men, in particular, there is a profound anxiety that surrounds Black American masculinity in US culture.[2] In his book *Black Men Worshipping: Intersecting Anxieties of Race, Gender, and Christian Embodiment*, American scholar of religious studies Stacy C. Boyd uses Harper's Black masculine anxieties framework to analyze the ways in which this uneasiness seeps into African American churches.[3] Additionally, according to communication studies scholar C. Riley Snorton, the Black masculine anxieties about male gospel performance are fueled by discourses surrounding the rumored pervasiveness of queer sexuality in Black churches. Male choir director leadership figures into Snorton's assessment, whereby the male musical or choir director "could almost be considered a trope in narratives about queer sexuality and the black church . . . as a proverbial ur-text of queer sexual rumors."[4] The use of "ur-text" is poignant because it connotes both the longstanding social scripts and musical rhetorics that are performed in African American churches. Further, Snorton asserts that in addition to the male choir director's capacity as an "arranger" or organizer of music performance, "his location—typically placed behind and elevated above the pulpit—makes him a focal point for surveillance."[5] The ability of choir directors to attract and vie for both the male and female observers' gaze within hetero-patriarchal social constructs evokes both scrutiny and anxiety about their potential queer duplicitousness. Harper, Boyd, and Snorton find that Black masculine anxieties stem from the negative perceptions surrounding the rise of the "down low" phenomenon which characterizes queer men as living heterosexual lives in public while living homosexual or bisexual lives in private.

There are cultural and religious tensions that surround men's display of femininity in worship. A man's vocalized and embodied display of feminine attributes is a contested and ridiculed gospel performance practice. Among respondents in my research, men's gender nonconformity in attire, mannerisms, and vocal styles can readily be interpreted as signals for sexual nonconformity. In these informal exchanges, men who are gender nonconforming or have same-gender desire are often presumed to be one and the same, which is not always the case. On the one hand, a man can be hetero-presenting; that is to say, he can be a homosexual gospel musician who can successfully deflect attention from his queer sexual orientation in heteronormative contexts. He can perform the gender role, styles, and expressions associated with heterosexual men while being in a committed, same-gender, loving relationship. In other words, there are individuals who display no readily identifiable markers that suggest their homosexual identity. On the other hand, a man described as "effeminate" can display mannerisms that are often interpreted as "feminine" or "queer," even though his desire is to be sexually intimate with women. Thus, the social tensions emerge specifically around men's display of attributes perceived as feminine.

Among some African American Christians—often members of socially conservative congregations—gender identity is regularly an imagined and oppositional state of being that bifurcates a spectrum of traits into masculine and feminine poles. Ideal masculinity and heterosexuality are monitored identities designed to distance men from any display of feminine traits. To protect the spiritual integrity of gospel music, socially conservative congregations police the musicians' marital fidelity and uphold an ideal gender expression for the archetypal male figures that facilitate worship. As Snorton sets forth, there are two archetypal male figures that are heavily scrutinized for their masculinity or sexuality at Sunday service: the musical or choir director and the pastor or preacher.[6] In particular, those two archetypes are known for their specific functions. Writing in 1990, two scholars of African American religion, C. Eric Lincoln and Lawrence H. Mamiya, characterized these two archetypes by the centrality of their preaching or singing function:

> The sermon, or more accurately, the *preaching* is the focal point of the worship in the Black Church, and all other activities find their place in some subsidiary relationship. In most black churches music, or more precisely, singing is second only to preaching as the magnet of attraction and the primary vehicle of spiritual transport for the worshipping congregation.[7]

They described the archetypal male preacher by his performance of charisma, skill with words, and, in some instances, his eloquence in closing messages with powerful song as a singing preacher. Lincoln and Mamiya also observed that the majority of the most prolific African American musicians, regardless of their musical style, were either the progeny of a preacher or received their first training and public performances of their music in Black churches.[8] Given this fact, preaching may be viewed as symbolic performance of heterosexual and paternal authority by virtue of the preachers' liturgical primacy in African American worship settings.

In contrast to the male preacher, male vocalists and choir directors can draw a degree of scrutiny about their queer sexual potential and gender expression that does not apply to the preacher archetype. Ethicist Victor Anderson wrote in 2004 that male gospel singers and especially choir directors are often stereotyped as "soft," feminine, or queer, notably when they use their entire body to demonstratively and emphatically guide the musical flow of performance during worship. Indeed, there has long been a juxtaposition of the preacher's and the choir director's perceived masculinities, which results in the monitoring of preaching and singing in African American worship as a way of policing the boundaries of men's conventional masculine gender expression, heterosexuality, and status. Despite the examination of Black men's worship styles and climates by literary and religious studies scholars,[9] ethnomusicological research on Black men's worship is limited. Expanding upon Melvin L. Butler's 2014 ethnomusicological research on queerness and masculinity in Black gospel music, I analyze the extent to which male gospel musicians' performances withstand or confirm participants' long held cultural and theological perceptions about the ways in which Black masculine identity is performed and staged to reinforce hetero-patriarchy.

In this chapter, I consider Black male vocal performance of gender and sexuality in historically African American Protestant churches as a contentious tradition that points to the role that hetero-patriarchal social structures can play in deciphering men's identity, position, and function in gospel music performance. In this discussion, I will examine first the time-tested hetero-patriarchal perceptions about "masculine" identity and sexuality associated with worship in traditional African American churches. I conclude by exploring the ways in which prominent heterosexual and homosexual male vocal musicians challenge these hetero-patriarchal norms as they negotiate narratives about their transgressive sexuality, and the consequences and implications they often confront in doing so, particularly in Black Pentecostalism.

METHODOLOGY

My transcongregational, transdenominational, and multi-sited research relies primarily on ethnographic fieldwork consisting of interviews with preachers and worship leaders who are also vocal recording artists. As a participant-observer in historically African American Protestant (African Methodist Episcopal, Baptist, Pentecostal, and non-denominational) churches, I attended gospel concerts and music conferences in Chicago, IL, and the Washington, DC, metropolitan areas from 2006–2014.[10] While visiting these sites and interviewing participants, I followed the discourses surrounding peculiar or queer masculine gospel music performance. This study is also based in part on content gathered in a series of transdenominational workshops on worship and masculinity that I facilitated following the session I conducted at the national African Methodist Episcopal (A.M.E.) Church Music and Christian Arts Ministry (MCAM) Conference in Chicago, IL, in July 2013. Participants served in various worship leader roles in their respective churches, such as preachers, vocalists, instrumentalists, dancers, and concert music composers. During the workshop that was extended from the scheduled one hour to three hours, I invited mostly male participants to comment on footage of worship that displayed, according to some of my preliminary respondents, a range of men's gospel performance styles. The performances included choir director Ricky Dillard and the New Generation Chorale's live performance of "God Is Control" from his *Hallelujah* album (1995) as an example of performance that was often referred to as "flamboyant" or "queer"[11] and male gospel go-go performance as a performance that was referred to as "hyper-masculine."[12] I sought to determine how these respondents assessed the presence or absence of masculinity in these two seemingly oppositional gospel performances of masculinity. In addition to documenting the themes that these men shared, I used those themes to form the basis of my interview questions. I later interviewed other men, including instrumentalists, whom the male respondents identified as "peculiar" or queer in their gospel performance.

THE PERFORMATIVE, SACRED, AND IDEOLOGICAL INNER WORKINGS OF HETERO-PATRIARCHY

The ideological inner workings of hetero-patriarchy in the communities I studied are at once sacred—that is, grounded in religious thought—and performative. Hetero-patriarchy is the normalization of men's paternalistic dominance over and disempowerment of women, homosexual men, and men who are woman-like, while privileging heterosexual experiences. I deploy the concept of patriarchy in my analysis to indicate the various ways in which the male domination of women, homosexual men, and feminine men—or men who are perceived as woman-like—manifest in societal and cultural structures of historically African American Protestant churches. There are various male roles played by music ministry leaders and preachers within historically African American Protestant congregations. Male vocalists and preachers perform patriarchy within the churches' gendered and sexualized constructions of the meanings generated when men are heard and observed as leaders in worship. As men interweave their most prominent liturgical roles of singing and preaching, patriarchy is also socio-culturally inscribed and negotiated. However, it is important to note that men also perform on musical instruments, use their bodies to dance, and move throughout traditional African American worship space in ways that are socio-culturally gendered.

Given the centrality of music to African American religious and quotidian life, I am drawn to the stereotypes of male musicians and the assumptions often made about their identity that influence gospel music patronage, reception, and dissemination. I asked the male participants in the A.M.E. MCAM Conference to describe the ideal models of masculine worship leadership they sought when they looked for a church. They immediately described the choir director/singer and the preacher as the paradigmatic facilitators of the worship. The former was positively characterized as a worship leader, or a vessel, while the latter was frequently imagined as a man of God or "father in the faith," imagery and terminology that associates divinity with paternalism. After further discussion, respondents' depictions revealed a Cartesian split that was associated with the symbolic performance of these roles using intellectual attributes to describe the preacher and affective traits to describe the musician.[13] For example, preachers were often referred to as "academic" while singers were viewed as "emotive." When I asked if there were negative stereotypes of male choir director/singers and preachers, they raised the stereotype of the choir director/singer as "flaming," on the "down low," or "boyish," as indicated by the popular term "choir boy"—a term which ridiculed male participants in the choir by diminishing their manhood. Participants also talked about the perception of preachers as adulterers or "pulpit pimps"[14] who use charismatic speech and virility to dominate majority female congregations and draw offerings for their financial gain. There was little speculative discussion among the workshop participants about other less-performative male archetypes—ministry adjutants, ushers, audio/sound engineers, security guards, and trustees—that transcend the preacher/vocal musician binary of masculine worship discourse. Regardless of the role in which men participate in worship, they are scrutinized for the degree to which they display femininity in their identity. Drawing from the interviews with male choir directors and preachers, they are surveilled for the extent to which they exhibit feminine characteristics in three interlinking areas: (1) the sung and spoken uses of the male voice, (2) the negotiation of social and religious domains, and (3) the style of delivery within the hetero-patriarchal context of Black churches and the gospel music industry.

GENDERED AND SEXUALIZED VOCAL MUSIC MINISTRY

When I interviewed male choir directors and music ministers, I questioned whether there are any gendered and sexualized associations with male participation in music ministry. Most of the men stated that they experienced socio-cultural tensions in many historically African American Protestant churches. They hear congregants' assumptions about their identity and experience a disparity in the enforcement of morality codes regarding musicians' sexual activity. They also stated that while there may be some degree of truth to the gender and sexuality stereotypes, there is no monolithic masculinity in male music ministry vocal or instrumental performance. Openly homosexual director of worship and the arts at historical Ebenezer Baptist Church in Atlanta, Georgia, Dr. Tony McNeill attested to assumptions that are tied to his music ministry role and principle instrument.

> I think there is an automatic association of queerness and femininity with the [singing choir director] or the choir director who plays the piano. And actually, these days there are more men who are directors than there are women, but choir directing is still thought of as feminine. People rarely question if the bass player, drummer, or Hammond B3 player are gay—not unless they have characteristics that are called into question.[15]

The "automatic" socio-cultural association of femininity with choir directing and piano performance that McNeill has experienced is connected to women's eligibility and shared participation in these performance domains. McNeill was one of several African American men who referred to himself as "homosexual" to distinguish himself from the designation "gay." While some of the men did use the term "gay," it often registered for African American homosexual men as signifying dominant White social and cultural experiences.

In my 2013 and 2015 interviews with Washingtonian music minister, choir director, and self-described "butch" homosexual man Charles Anthony Bryant, he reflected on the divergent morality codes he has experienced as a self-identified hetero-presenting male choir director. Bryant described the inequitable standard to which he was held in comparison to instrumentalists:

> If you hear anything about an instrumental musician's sexuality, it is usually after a fallout—like a woman is pregnant. You hear stories about organists, bassists, and drummers running all up and through the women in the congregation or the soprano and alto section of the choir.[16]

"Running all up and through" or "going through" is a euphemistic reference to having several sexual relationships with individuals in the congregation or choir, regardless of the instrumentalist's sexual orientation. When asked, "What do you hear about the choir director's sexuality?" his response, while laughing, was:

> It is not often that you hear about the choir director having an incident with women in the congregation. It happens, but usually that man is a *known* ladies' man. Now that I think of it, the only time that I hear about the male choir director's sexuality . . . (laughs) is when he is running all up and through the tenor section.[17]

Bryant admits that he speaks from the vantage point of a choir director and that instrumentalists may experience the perception of their identity in a different manner. In Bryant's experience, instrumentalists are presumed to be heterosexual unless they express their gender in a manner that suggests otherwise. He stated that the male instrumentalists

> could do what they wanted to do but not the [male] vocalists. . . . The vocalists or worship leaders have to live above reproach. The elders, deacons, and mothers of the church will pull aside a vocal worship leader and tell him he is not living right before they pull aside the drummer or bassist.[18]

Other participants have emphasized that there are many discourses generated about men who vocally display their potentially queer identity, especially when they sing mainly in the higher register, falsetto, during gospel solos. In the historically Protestant congregations that I studied, male soloists singing in a higher register expand in significance as a vocal display of what gender studies theorist David Halperin called "queer potential" or the social meanings ascribed to male singers who comfortably sing high "like a woman." Using falsetto stylistic approaches or a countertenor voice designation may draw scrutiny of his identity.[19] By vocal designation, I refer to men's most common performance ranges and stylistic approaches. This sonic signification of woman-like sound was illustrated in my interview with Tennessee State University professor and self-described homosexual male Patrick Dailey, who is a countertenor—a vocal designation for men who perform music that matches the vocal range and quality of female contraltos, mezzo-sopranos, or sopranos in the Western European art music tradition.[20] Dailey indicated that when he is a soloist in African American churches, he "presents like a good Baptist man" by verbalizing a traditional salutation before he sings to deflect any questions about whether or not he is a homosexual man.

> Often when I get up in front of a new audience, I am very neutral. Like, if I am at church and they want me to sing an aria, I will say (in a slightly lower register), "Praise the Lord everybody. I am Patrick Dailey. We are not going to be before you long. We are gonna sing this one aria for you and we will get out of the way."
> I will say it like a good Baptist man who loves the Lord. I don't get up and say (in a higher register), "Hey y'all he's so worthy, chile."[21] Mmmhmmm. No![22]

When asked for clarification about that "good Baptist man" persona, Dailey indicated that the persona description was a composite heterosexist and patriarchal masculinity with whom he often interacted in traditional Black church denominations and organizations.

As I indicated earlier, contemporary gospel choir directors are often imagined and stereotyped as "flaming," animated, "soft," and "flamboyant" performers who use their entire bodies to guide the choir and instrumentalists in the band. The concept of flamboyance is a salient term in these settings that refers to demonstrative and ecstatic facility in cuing the choir and instrumentalists during performance. However, the Black gospel choir director, regardless of sexual orientation, is expected to have charisma. Tony McNeill described flamboyance as

> anything that draws attention to the person instead of the content of the message being conveyed. I do not associate [flamboyance] with being gay or straight. Most people when they hear that term do have an automatic association with being gay.[23]

Worship leader Patrick Dailey similarly described flamboyance as "operating in the flesh" or being vain in performance. He said, "You should not draw attention to yourself. We were taught you draw attention to God."[24] These two concepts of "flamboyant" demonstrate a concern about worship leaders displaying their ego while leading the music ministry, but they also reveal anxieties about gendered performance registering for congregants as effeminate.

The social meanings that are ascribed to men's performance of identity are highly valued and monitored. Such values are devised to protect the spiritual vitality of gospel music participants and congregants whether or not they are Christian believers. Music minister Charles Anthony Bryant articulated his anxieties about gendered flamboyant performance in the following manner: "I am extra careful about the energy I give off. I am supposed to function in a submissive way, but I am not permitted to give off any feminine energy."[25] His perception of flamboyance characterizes the stylistic choices that are interpreted as men's use of feminine attributes, mannerisms, and symbols in their performances, which may evoke conversations about identity and sexuality. To cultivate the fellowshipping community as a worship leader, he negotiated same-gender performance interactions with other men. Bryant allowed the preacher to be the dominant figure, while he maintained a submissive performance posture—a stance that is often interpreted as feminine in a hetero-patriarchal construct. His anxiety about flamboyant performance reveals that there is a limit to the degree to which men can exude "feminine energy" in their presentation.

GENDERED AND SEXUALIZED PULPIT MINISTRY

Among gendered spaces in Black churches, the pulpit is constructed in opposition to the symbolically feminine (read: "unmanly") or boyish gospel choir loft that is a platform for the art of musical and gestural rhetorics. The pulpit, arguably the most powerful space in African American Christian worship, is a symbolically phallocentric platform from which heterosexist rhetoric is delivered. W.E.B. DuBois wrote in 1903, "The preacher is the most unique personality developed by the Negro on American soil."[26] Thirty years later, theologians Benjamin Mays and Joseph Williams Nicholson added that the preacher "played a conspicuously important part in the survival struggles of the race and has held ever since a strategic place in Negro life."[27] The previously mentioned constructions of the pastor as Godlike or father figure and the choir director as a vessel or boy-like are due in large part to how the spiritual leadership is organized, gendered, and represented in many predominantly African American Protestant churches. In the leadership hierarchies, the majority of the ministerial leadership is male, while the laypeople (including lay ministers) are mainly comprised of women. As congregational studies scholar Daphne C. Wiggins attests, "Enter most African American congregations and you are likely to see male pastors standing before predominantly female audiences."[28] In fact, according to 2014 research from the Pew Research Center, women compose an average of 59% of "historically Black Protestant" congregations.[29] However, they are not represented proportionately in the majority of church leadership structures. This is due in part to some historically Black Protestant congregations' theological rejection of women in pastoral and pulpit ministry. As a result, many of the ministerial leadership networks are homosocial and patriarchal, providing several opportunities for men's fraternal bonding, where they learn with whom they can safely share their views on nonconforming gender and sexual identity in Christian power structures. Their actions belie their beliefs and teachings; the way they live does not always reflect the messages they preach and sing.

While preachers are known to divulge their testimonies about heterosexual premarital and/or extramarital relationships, they are less likely to share about a queer and/or "questioning" sexual past. To distance themselves publicly from any womanliness, queer potential, or androgyny, some male preachers perform contradictory public and private scripts about morality. As heterosexual preachers gauge where they can safely share their views on nonconforming gender and sexual identity, they often develop distinct personal narratives appropriate for the social context. One of the publicly performed scripts sometimes attributed to Black male preachers is that of hypocrites who rail against the sexual sins of others, while they succumb to their own moral failings. In hetero-patriarchal settings, male preachers benefit from asserting their heterosexuality and manliness—whether or not their assertion of orientation and identity is appropriate—which distinguishes them from women and homosexual men. Thus, they are reinscribed as dominant within the power structure.

Sociologist and Baptist preacher Michael Eric Dyson recounts a service during which a preacher delivered a sermon about the transformational power of God. The guest preacher warned about the pitfalls of sex outside of marriage and proclaimed that God can turn lust into love, thereby giving Christians a stronger relationship with God. The preacher's sermon content, which focused on traditional heterosexual discipline of monogamy or celibacy, contradicted the private script he performed with his colleagues. Among his fellow pastors, the preacher openly admitted his sexual attraction to a woman he observed in the congregation. After the service ended, the preachers present gathered in the pastor's study, where the guest preacher asked the pastor of the church about the woman he admired during the service. By the end of the exchange, the pastor had assured the visiting preacher that he would facilitate his contact with the woman. In assessing this sequence of events, Dyson determined "how dishonest we're sometimes made by the unresolved disputes between our bodies and our beliefs," instead of being forthcoming about the spectrum of sexual appetites and experiences.[30] The church pulpit had been used as a perch to survey the pews for a potential sexual conquest. Dyson describes the visiting preacher's performance of the standard public script the believers expect to facilitate their "high time" in the Lord. To add insult to injury, the woman's pastor, or "spiritual father," not only condoned but also assisted the guest preacher's pursuit of a clandestine, heterosexual rendezvous. Male–female sexual relationships are held as sacrosanct, even when they are extramarital, defying biblical literalist teachings about sex outside of marriage.

Public and private scripts are not just performed among preachers. They are also performed between preachers and musicians, as well as among musicians themselves. With regard to public and private scripts between preachers and musicians, for example, Dyson attested to the homophobic preaching moments that are met by queer men's singing, diffusing anti-gay or homophobic speech with musical communication.

> One of the most painful scenarios of black church life is repeated Sunday after Sunday with little notice or collective outrage. A black minister will preach a sermon railing against sexual ills, especially homosexuality. At the close of the sermon, a soloist, who everybody knows is gay, will rise to perform a moving number, as the preacher extends an invitation to visitors to join the church. The soloist is, in effect, being asked to sing, and to sign, his theological death sentence. His presence at the end of such a sermon symbolizes a silent endorsement of the preacher's message. Ironically, the presence of his gay Christian body at the highest moment of worship also negates the preacher's attempt to censure his presence, to erase his body, to deny his legitimacy as a child of God. Too often, the homosexual dimension of eroticism remains cloaked in taboo or blanketed in theological attack. As a result, the black church, an institution that has been at the heart of black emancipation, refuses to unlock the oppressive closet for gays and lesbians.[31]

Dyson's observation conveys the irony of that moment between homophobic proclamation and queer musical affirmation. Homosexual men's navigation of the preacher's sermonic rejection is an intentional ritual in which the queer singer represents his presence by sonically and creatively diffusing the contentious rhetoric that was preached. Some of the homosexual men with whom I have collaborated in my research have observed that scenario directly. In fact, both McNeill and Bryant expressed resentment toward the hypocritical heterosexual men who are insensitive and condemning of queer ministers' and musicians' sexual needs, while preachers assist each other with arranging clandestine rendezvous with women. They commented about the cognitive dissonance they experience participating in gatherings such as The Hampton Ministers' Conference and Choir Directors' and Organists' Guilds that tap into their gifts to mobilize ministers for social injustice, while leaving homosexual musicians to fight for dignity in their church homes.

In July 2015, Baptist minister and gospel recording artist Rev. E. Dewey Smith delivered a controversial sermon at the 8,000-member Greater Mount Calvary Holy Church. He recounts what he calls a revelation by God about perceptions of queer sexuality in African American churches:

> If you look at half of our choirs, and a great number of our artists that we call abominations, that we call demons, we demonize and dehumanize the same people that we use. And we don't say nothing about the gay choir director, because he is good for business. As long as the choir sounds good I ain't saying nothing about his sexuality. We have done what the slave master has done to us—dehumanize us, degrade us, demonize us—but then use [gay musicians] for our advantage. It is hypocritical to talk about the Supreme Court and calling them Sodom and Gomorrah (which is not what it is all about), but, if that is the case, half of our churches have been Sodom and Gomorrah for 100 years.[32]

Pastors' and congregants' queer-shaming serves to maintain the hetero-patriarchal order that the ministries of queer gospel artists bolster. "It is good for business" resembles and distills sentiments that I have encountered in my interviews. Preachers and musicians admit, "Congregations secretly want their pastors to be a womanizer and their music minister to be gay."[33] The churches profit from the music mastery and ecstatic delivery of their gay male musical leaders, the cultural products they generate—compositions and recordings—as well as television and radio airplay. Smith points out the contradictions in denominations, churches, and ministers who preach *against* queer sexuality and identity, on the one hand, while reaping artistic and monetary benefits from these same gay musicians, on the other hand. The question is evoked: Who benefits from the anti-gay sermons that preachers deliver? In male-dominant, hetero-patriarchal church leadership structures, heterosexual men do. And, as long as certain men "struggle" with or explore queer sexuality, hetero-presenting men—those men who perform a heterosexual and monogamous identity in the public sphere—will remain the most powerful decision-makers on the payroll.

GENDERED AND SEXUALIZED INSTRUMENTALISTS

Preachers are not the only figures in worship leadership that are expected to symbolically embody heterosexuality and patriarchy. Throughout African American religious narratives, musical representations of male church roles include interpretations such as deacons lining out hymns and instrumentalists offering sermonic selections. In African American worship contexts, instrumentalists function outside the domains of the conventional cultural rhetoric(s) of singing and preaching. While preachers and singers utilize their voices as embodied instruments, instrumentalists contribute to musical participation with external instruments. In addition, instrumentalists are a culturally unmarked category; that is, there is little discussion about suspicions regarding their queer gender expression and sexuality, unless they are keyboardists (musicians who play piano, synthesizer, and/or organ) or they exhibit readily identifiable queerness.

During my interviews, some musicians' remarks revealed that when congregants observed instrumentalists' queer performance or which instrumentalists exhibited gender nonconforming cues, it was met with noticeable silence—a lack of commentary. Some participants maintained that they were socialized to silently observe and decipher gender identity cues. For example, Seattle-born trumpeter and guitarist Josiah Woodson indicated that the musicians in the pit subscribe to a "don't ask, don't tell" policy, regardless of their perceived sexual orientation.

> When I was younger, we knew when cats (men) were dealing with a different deck [read: homosexual or gender nonconforming]. They weren't shunned or cast out, but it was like . . . well, that was the minister of music, and he wears pumps [women's high heels] and he takes them off to play the organ and he is "killin" [playing really well.][34]

When I asked Woodson what his reference to "pumps" signified, he responded, "The pumps were a signal for queerness." In many of Woodson's verbal responses, he used veiled language to talk about the musicians' identities, suggesting a level of discretion and anxiety around the subject matter. Woodson maintains there was no verbal communication among the musicians or church members about the instrumentalists who exhibited gender nonconforming styles. He sensed and was socialized to be silent. No one was to speak openly concerning this perceived difference in sexual identity. Woodson later clarified that when he spoke of organists, he was referring to a composite instrumental role that included pianists, organists, or keyboardists. Even though there are instrumentalists who identify as queer, instrumentalists who do not play the keyboard are assumed to be conventionally masculine and heterosexual. Male musicians' non-rhetorical use of external instruments bolsters a symbolic hetero-patriarchal construction of their worship participation due to their distance from the contested, gendered domains of vocality that traditionally situate preachers as manly and intellectual versus singers as boyish and emotive.

Bryant and other musicians uncover contradictions that reinscribe heteronormative and misogynistic constructs of manhood. When I asked musicians how they know that the men to whom they refer are gay, I frequently got a response similar to what I received from Bryant. He comments:

> Well, they have never been married and do not have children. They never talk about [children] either. These are my mentors. I *know* them. They have never claimed to be gay publicly, but their body language changes when we are around other men. My mentors are of a particular era where you guard your image, your reputation. Your image and reputation are the same. And socially, they are asexual.[35]

Bryant's observations illustrate a recurring theme in my interviews with men who self-identify on a spectrum of identities. Their silence deflects from the absence of hetero-patriarchal social markers such as getting married to a woman and having children. Divorced or single status, being in a long-distance relationship, having adopted children, or being a godfather also serve as means through which homosexual men may deflect from their queer sexual orientation. Musicians' observations about the unspeakable—often self-negating—nature of the call to ministry simultaneously depict the virility ascribed to the pulpit, even as their singing style is thought to be queer(ing).

While there are both heterosexual and non-heterosexual keyboardists, some self-identified heterosexual men have expressed anxiety about making clear their conventional masculinity and sexual preference in social networks. During June 2008 and July 2015 interviews with Washingtonian touring musician, music minister, keyboardist, and self-identified heterosexual Anthony "Tony" Walker, he confided that there is an assumption that if a man is a heterosexual instrumentalist that he "goes through the choir loft," resembling Bryant's terminology cited above. Walker said that the instrumentalists are "on the surface" expected to be male and heterosexual.

In a similar manner, McNeill described the sexualized assumptions associated with instrumentalists' spaces. He distinguished the "instrumentalists' pit" or section from the choir loft in a gendered manner as the imagined "man-cave of worship." He explained, "The pit is the man-cave for hetero-presentation, for both the DL [down low or discretely gay] and the straight. It is the place where being macho or undetectable is required for entry."[36] Men's hetero-presentation allows them to use the gendered perceptions of musical roles (non-keyboard instrumentalist) and space ("instrumentalists' pit") to their advantage and subdue assumptions about their sexual orientation without having to verbally self-identify.

In addition to Bryant, McNeill, and Walker, there were several vocal and instrumental musicians who used the phrase "run through" or "go through the choir loft" to depict the phallocentric stereotype of promiscuous musicians. Conversely, not one of my respondents said musicians "go through the 'instrumentalists' pit'," which suggests that the instrumentalists' area is a symbolically gendered location for embarking upon sexual conquests. Likewise, the choir loft is a symbolic destination for sexual conquests. While the choir loft is imagined as a destination and the music pit as a point of departure, both vocalists and instrumentalists have been involved in (non)heterosexual relationships or encounters in music ministries.

Without a doubt, choir directors negotiate positive and negative perceptions about their gender identity among other musicians. In fact, many men elect to compartmentalize their religious and social identities while leading worship or performing gospel music. When social perceptions about the meaning of male musicians' gender nonconforming expression or sexual identity are discussed, comments often include euphemisms and various forms of non-verbal communication through noticeable silence and gestures such as lingering looks, raised eyebrows, and head tilts while observing performance and social interactions. In the following section, I focus on the consequences Black Pentecostal vocalists who challenge hetero-patriarchal constructs within the gospel music industry may face.

CONSEQUENCES AND IMPLICATIONS OF HETERO-PATRIARCHY

Within various historically African American Pentecostal churches, considerable disparity exists in the consequences homosexual and heterosexual males face for sexual transgressions. Evidence suggests that while a number of well-known heterosexual male gospel music artists have violated publicly sanctioned sexual norms of their various Pentecostal congregations, in many cases they have been able to either maintain or rather quickly reclaim leadership status within their respective churches, as well as in the gospel music industry. Such scenarios shed light on the ways in which sexual indiscretion is displayed, heterosexual identity is valued, and patriarchy is protected in various African American religious contexts.

Since the late 1990s, several prominent heterosexual male musicians have publicly acknowledged and systematically confronted accusations of addiction to pornography, adultery, and even parenting out of wedlock—sexual norms which traditional African American Christianity, particularly Pentecostal churches, publicly castigate. Musicians who acknowledge these improprieties risk losing a significant portion of their fan base, a decline in performance engagements, and a demotion in church leadership, unless they verbally or ritually apologize and demonstrate that they are working toward full spiritual redemption and restoration.

Within the last two decades, Grammy-nominated gospel artists James Moss (COGIC), (aka J. Moss) and Deitrick Haddon (PAW) both confessed to conceiving children outside of their marriages, while Grammy-nominated and Stellar Award–winning Tye Tribbett (Apostolic) confessed to an extramarital affair with a member of his group G.A. (Greater Anointing).[37] In each of these cases, the artists' narratives regarding their admitted sexual offenses emphasize their journey to spiritual restoration. As a sign of contrition, heterosexual male artists are expected to ask the church body politic for forgiveness. In addition, the process of restoration sometimes requires censure from public leadership for an extended period, during which time the artist may also receive counsel from one or more spiritual advisors. In yet other instances, punitive measures are completely self-directed and self-imposed.

In exploring the case of Deitrick Haddon, it is important to acknowledge the fact that he was not only a well-known gospel recording artist, he also held the role of ordained minister in the Pentecostal Assemblies of the World (PAW), an organization to which his father was also a ministry leader. Following his sexual indiscretion, Haddon became estranged from his father, who was then serving as his pastor. Haddon later divorced, moved from his home in Detroit to Los Angeles, and subsequently fathered a child with the partner he had been involved with during his marriage.

In a widely distributed 2013 Facebook post, Haddon described his extended period of repentance. Later, using social media to wage a public defense of his indiscretion, Haddon commented: "As a sign of humility and accountability, I have not preached on any platform in any church for one year!! I have paid my penalty for sin!!" In his view, the process of repentance was complete, and he was therefore fully restored both to God as well as to the church.

It is instructive that in his media campaign, Haddon also sought to deflect from his personal culpability and imperfection by referencing his wife's foibles. Gospel music industry wives rarely speak publicly regarding the quality or character of their marital lives. Wives are often completely silent regarding marital indiscretions, thus making women vulnerable to various degrees of misogyny. Hetero-patriarchal alignment manifests when male musicians are the sole or dominant spokespeople for whether or not they are happily married. Even though Haddon's behavior uniformly and admittedly deviates from the prevailing African American Christian ethic governing sexual behavior, his self-disclosures align him with commonplace hetero-patriarchal prescriptions in this socio-cultural and religious context.

During the same year that Haddon made his controversial Facebook post, he also released the album entitled *R.E.D. (Restoring Everything Damaged)*, which peaked at #9 on the Billboard Gospel Albums Chart and became involved in the development of the Oxygen network reality television show *Preachers of L.A.* Serving as an executive producer, Haddon envisioned the show as "redefin[ing] the public perception of the pastor"[38]—a way of exploring the imperfect private lives of prominent male ministry leaders. Five of the six principle cast members were African American, suggesting the targeting of an African American audience. Each of the six featured ministers were evangelicals, including charismatics from Full Gospel as well as non-denominational churches. Haddon's checkered personal past became an integral part of the provocative story line. The show has now completed two successful seasons. In 2014 Haddon added a second Oxygen network series to his credit called *Fix My Choir*, which he co-hosted weekly with Michelle Williams, a former member of the popular music group Destiny's Child, which featured Beyoncé. Haddon's career continues to soar, as he added the role of executive producer of *Preachers of Detroit* to his credit in 2015. Any retribution or negative reprisals that may have resulted from his prior sexual transgressions have clearly had little impact on his meteoric rise to television stardom. In the television series, he has resumed his itinerant preaching ministry with his father's blessing.

Contemporary gospel music artist Tye Tribbett represents another example of a heterosexual performer whose behavior conflicted with the espoused norms of African American Pentecostalism. Following the public revelation of Tribbett's affair with one of his backup singers, he sought spiritual counseling, together with his wife, from his fellow pastor and holy hip hop recording artist Da' T.R.U.T.H (Emanuel Lambert, Jr.).[39] Instead of healing, the controversy escalated further after Lambert became romantically involved with Tribbett's wife. For Tribbett, that breach of trust combined with his own act of infidelity fueled a desire for radical change. In order to try to save his marriage and family, Tribbett disbanded his gospel group G.A. and left Philadelphia to begin work in the music ministry at the 10,000-member Ebenezer A.M.E. church in Fort Washington, MD. Tribbett publicly acknowledged his transgressions repeatedly—on social media, radio, and television—attributing his personal failings to "insecurity" and "selfishness."[40] His process of restoration to the church fold included a self-imposed, sixty-day period of consecration, during which he did not publicly grace any pulpit as either a preacher or singer.

Tribbett's recording career continues to progressively flourish. In 2010, the year his controversial encounters first became public, he released his fourth album, *Fresh*, on Sony Records, which reached #1 on the Billboard Gospel Albums Chart, where it remained for fifty weeks. By 2013, he had moved to the Motown Gospel label, where he released the album *Greater Than*, which debuted at #1 on the Billboard Gospel Albums Chart. During the same year, Tribbett was the opening act for BET's *Celebration of Gospel*; he was also featured together with Donnie McClurkin during this major television event, which attracted 2.6 million viewers in 2014. BET's *Celebration* has been "the number one gospel or religious telecast on TV for fourteen years."[41] As Tribbett's music performance career continues to advance, he is also promoted in ministerial circles as a pastor. In 2014, Tribbett moved with his family to Houston, TX, where he serves as a youth pastor at New Life Christian Center under Bishop I.V. Hilliard and his wife and co-pastor, Rev. Bridget Hilliard.

Haddon and Tribbett are but two instances in which male heterosexual gospel music artists have violated the professed norms of marital fidelity in traditional African American

Protestant denominations, yet their careers have been minimally impacted. Another example of heterosexual transgression is that of multi-platinum-selling recording artist Kirk Franklin, who in a 2005 interview on *The Oprah Winfrey Show* acknowledged his addiction to pornography. In an interview with Christian Broadcasting Network's Scott Ross, Franklin attested that some Christian men even chastised him about admitting his addiction, saying to him, "I'd rather do that [watch pornography] than cheat on my wife." Despite this fact, in 2007 Franklin continued to advance professionally, becoming co-executive producer and host of BET's popular gospel music talent competition, *Sunday Best*, which is now in its eighth season.[42]

In the case of heterosexual transgression, tolerance and forgiveness are normative in traditional African American churches. Gospel musicians who profess deliverance through the language of spiritual restoration and who realign their behaviors with monogamous, marital heterosexuality are typically forgiven and welcomed back into the church fold. Heterosexual gospel recording artists are likely to maintain their livelihood within the gospel music industry while also retaining their roles of authority in their church music ministries.

IMPLICATIONS FOR HOMOSEXUALS AND GAY ALLIES

When male musicians traverse hetero-patriarchal social and cultural norms of the "don't ask, don't tell" policy by self-identifying as homosexual, trans, or even as a gay ally, in many traditional African American congregations these artists often face more severe consequences than that of heterosexual males, including loss of livelihood, as well as both professional and public ostracism. For example, in a 2009 television interview on Word Network, gospel music artist Tonéx (born Anthony C. Williams II), both a Grammy and Stellar Award nominee, unapologetically disclosed his attraction to men without any assertion of repentance or desire for deliverance. When asked by the host, contemporary gospel music artist Lexi, "So, have you struggled with homosexuality?" he responded, "It wasn't a struggle"—indicating lack of remorse about his transgressive sexuality. Prior to this public revelation, Tonéx had released *Rainbow* (2008) and *The Naked Truth* (2008), the latter of which the public could access for free. Both of these albums were released on his personal label Nureau Ink under the Zomba Label Group. Both albums referenced same-gender intimacy and suggested his queer identity. These releases, the latter of which was unauthorized, fueled an ongoing feud between Zomba Records and Tonéx, which eventually resulted in his termination from the label.

Rainbow explored same-gender sexuality and the "risky behavior" associated with sexually transmitted diseases, topics that are marked as taboo in gospel music circles. *The Naked Truth* was particularly controversial as the first album identified with a gospel music artist to receive a parental advisory label. On the recording, Tonéx uses profanity in disclosing the fact that a male preacher had molested him when he was six years old.[43] Many PAW church leaders policed Tonéx's language, criticizing his startling revelation and labeling his commentary as unbecoming of a minister of the gospel. Representatives of the very same power structure that had violated him as a child chose to censor his justifiable anger as an adult.

On *The Naked Truth*, Tonéx interrogated his sexual identity, posing the question: "What am I?" to which he responded, "The genius, the faggot, the weirdo, the homo, the hobo, the magnet," fueling public speculation that he was a closeted gay man. The vernacular terms point to Tonéx's shared insider knowledge and history with homosexual social networks. Never before had a gospel artist explicitly confronted critics about his queerness. Following *The Naked Truth*, he released the album *Unspoken* (2009) while signed to the Sony/BMG label, for which he received his first non-gospel Grammy nomination for the song "Blend."

Outspoken pastor, gospel musician, and self-identified "delivered" homosexual Donnie McClurkin seized the opportunity to publicly chastise Tonéx in an anti-gay sermonic script during the November 2012 Church of God in Christ (COGIC) convocation. McClurkin tapped into a customary topic that heterosexual and hetero-presenting preachers deliver at the annual November COGIC convocation. Engaging the unfolding of Tonéx's story, McClurkin exhorted the youth about the perils of identifying as homosexual, referencing Tonéx's bold lack of repentance as potentially "turning their [the youths'] hearts further away from God." With this message, Pastor McClurkin, who remorsefully referenced himself as a "forefather" of homosexual gospel music networks, rejected the legitimacy of Tonéx's homosexuality and his relationship with God.

As a consequence of Tonéx's public revelation of his homosexuality, he began to lose performance engagements and pastoral authority within his ordaining organization, the Pentecostal Assemblies of the World (PAW). The predominately male church leadership distanced itself from Tonéx, calling him a heretic and a "reprobate," referencing Romans 1:28 to condemn his homosexual identity. As a PAW exile, Tonéx began worshipping with churches that affirmed LGBTQ (lesbian, gay, bisexual, transgender, and questioning/queer) believers such as The Fellowship of Affirming Ministries in San Francisco, founded by openly "same-gender-loving" (lesbian) gospel recording artist Bishop Yvette Flunder, who had been raised in the Church of God in Christ (COGIC). Unable to secure a pastoral or musical appointment in Pentecostal networks, Tonéx sought employment as an image consultant or secular music producer within the entertainment industry. While heterosexual recording artists are commonly protected and promoted following sexual indiscretions, Tonéx faced public humiliation, was exiled from his local and national body, and suffered significant loss of income.

Eventually, Tonéx changed his stage name to B. Slade (a.k.a. Brian Slade) in 2010 and pursued openly gay performance opportunities. No longer signed with the Zomba or Sony/BMG labels, he reinvented himself and began to release music on his personal Suxxess Records label as an independent artist. His story of transformation into an openly gay identity was featured in *The New Yorker*,[44] as well as in documentaries such as *The New Black* (2013). The attention Tonéx garnered from being an outcast in gospel music provided him with exposure to new secular music networks, which allowed him to generate income through digital distribution. He went on to collaborate with notable popular music artists such as percussionist Sheila E. and R&B vocalists Chaka Khan, Faith Evans, and Angie Fisher—the latter a collaboration that netted him his third Grammy nomination.

In order for Tonéx to circumvent the professional ostracism which he encountered within gospel music networks, he was forced to reinvent himself and expand his presence in the secular entertainment industry as B. Slade. Although heterosexual male vocalists Haddon and Tribbett were restored and promoted in gospel music circles following the revelation of their acts of sexual impropriety, Tonéx's unapologetic assertion of his gay identity was perceived as an affront to the prevailing hetero-patriarchal social order that protects and privileges heterosexual male behavior.

While the narrative of Tonéx demonstrates the serious reprisal homosexual gospel music artists may face in both church and industry, heterosexual pastors who ally themselves to queer believers also place their professional stature within conservative religious groups at risk. Recording artist Bishop Carlton Pearson and Rev. Dr. Delman Coates, members of the executive board of the Hampton Ministers' Conference, are notable African American heterosexual Protestant pastors who affirm rather than condemn homosexual Christians in their sermons, writings, politics, and public media engagement. Both of their narratives illustrate the consequences fundamentalist Pentecostal ministers who challenge the hypocrisy of hetero-patriarchy may potentially face.

Bishop Pearson is a COGIC-raised gospel recording artist and former pastor of the 5,000-member Higher Dimensions Evangelistic Center in Tulsa, OK—with a multiracial, evangelical, fundamentalist following. During the recording of three *Live at Azusa* albums (1995, 1996, and 1997), Pearson developed an acute awareness of the prevalence of queer musicians in Black churches and throughout the gospel music industry. In March 2004, Pearson was declared a heretic by his male colleagues in the Joint College of African American Pentecostal Bishops, following his argument posed in his treatise *The Gospel of Inclusion*.[45] According to Pearson, religion is a means through which power structures maintain control over believers. In essence, his theological position challenges the core Christian belief that Jesus is the only way to God. Pearson was subsequently released from leadership among Pentecostal bishops and restricted from access into the prominent preaching circles in which he was formerly a part. Moreover, the Azusa Conference declined because of poor attendance, and Pearson no longer continues the recording series that he had produced during the conference.[46] Simply put, Pearson became an outcast among Pentecostals, resulting in his loss of financial and social status, as well as his loss of officially sanctioned Pentecostal affiliation.[47]

A Pentecostal outcast, Pearson attracted the attention of homosexual church leaders such as former member of the COGIC church, Bishop Yvette Flunder, who invited him to preach at her church, The City of Refuge United Church of Christ in San Francisco, a congregation known as "welcoming and affirming to gays."[48] Flunder is the very same pastor who has welcomed Tonéx. Pearson recounts, "The whole room was almost all gay, lesbian, transgender, bisexual people. . . . I had never been in a room full of almost 99 percent gay people praising God and singing and dancing."[49] Pearson considered his experience at the City of Refuge as both healing and transformational. After a brief stint at pastoring in Tulsa, OK, he later launched New Dimensions in Chicago, IL, where he became a strong advocate for gay and lesbian inclusion. In his churches, Bishop Pearson provides a safe space for all musicians, particularly believers whose sexuality is heavily assessed and challenged within hetero-patriarchal contexts.

Rev. Delman Coates serves as another example of a pastor within a conservative Protestant congregation whose public support of LGBTQ issues prompted his ouster from a prominent ministerial leadership post. The 2015 annual Hampton Ministers' Conference and Choir Directors' and Organists' Guild[50] (hereafter referred to as The Hampton Ministers' Conference) came under fire by media and activists when Rev. Coates, the senior pastor of Mt. Ennon Baptist Church in Clinton, MD, was released from the executive council.[51] As a candidate for lieutenant governor of Maryland, Coates had publicly supported marriage equality and LGBTQ rights.[52] He states:

> I never saw pastors organizing around any other policy issues. I became concerned about the reduction of morality. I didn't want my silence to be interpreted as consent. . . . When I support LGBT rights, I do so, not despite the Bible, but because of it.[53]

Although Coates had privately shared his views about "legislating morality" with members of the Hampton Executive Council, it was his public stance which proved most damaging.

The discourses surrounding Coates' release fuels the perception that pastoral alliances with the LGBTQ community are widely viewed as a threat to the hetero-patriarchal order in African American churches. As long as Coates did not use his political influence to support queer musicians, he was permitted to remain in a leadership role.

I asked Coates about the reprisals that he faced for advocating for homosexual congregants. Coates confirmed that the two major backlashes he experienced were what he called "dis-fellowship" from organizations such as the Hampton Minister Conference and colleagues telling others not to invite him to preach at their churches. Before he started advocating for marriage equality, Coates had preached three times a month outside of his church. After he took his political stance, Coates' invitations declined to a mere twice a year.[54]

Coates' and Pearson's cases exemplify the ways in which heterosexual pastors who advocate for LGBTQ issues such as same-sex marriage equality are ministering to people who would not enter the church otherwise. Instead of preaching to the proverbial choir of people who subscribe to hetero-patriarchal social constructs, they choose to risk their status in order to pastor and advocate for marginalized LGBTQ believers.

CONCLUSION

In this chapter, I examine the gendered and sexualized constructions of archetypal male gospel performance roles throughout African American religious narratives. These male musical and worship leader archetypes have historically shaped and defined African American Christian worship, word, and work. Within historically African American Protestant congregations, gendered and sexualized meanings are associated with singing and preaching roles that reflect hetero-patriarchal norms in African American worship. These meanings are often transferred to and shared in gospel music performance in the public sphere in order to maintain respectable, hetero-patriarchal constructs that stem from and resemble historically African American Protestant congregational power structures. Various gospel music and pulpit ministry-centered organizations that have modeled their leadership after African American Protestant congregation power structures are negotiating diverse representation and tangible support of homosexual men.

I have explored the ways in which Black male sexuality and gender expression is learned and presented to convey myriad meanings that do not subscribe tidily to identity binaries. Male musicians' expressions of gender nonconformity and potentially queer sexuality are signaled to participants in the public square through various practices. Participants recognize identity nonconformity, but do not always verbally address it. Conversely, men's heterosexuality is presented in the public and private sphere but is conveyed through socio-cultural scripts that are adjusted and accepted throughout the leadership ranks of historically African American Protestant congregations. While those gendered and sexualized meanings are distributed, they are also challenged through performance and everyday life.

I contend that what is at stake in Black men's performance of gender and sexuality is not only the socio-cultural fissures that widen in response to homophobic sentiments and restrictions. What is also at stake are forms of misogyny in which congregants and gospel music patrons police femininity that is performed in male bodies. In examining the anxieties and assumptions conveyed with the perennial questions about whether or not all choir directors are gay, I analyze the religious and cultural inner workings of hetero-patriarchy. In sum, contemporary gospel music performances of hetero-patriarchy privilege heterosexual men's musical and rhetorical narratives about their sexuality, while simultaneously dominating women's and homosexual and gender-nonconforming men's musical and rhetorical narratives about their identities.

NOTES

1. Anderson 2004, 310. In fact, several of the African American men who disclosed their queer identity to me referred to themselves as homosexual, distinguishing themselves from gay men. While some of the men do use the term "gay," often the word registered for African American homosexual men as signifying White social and cultural discourses.
2. Harper 1996, xi.
3. Boyd 2011, 3.
4. Snorton 2014, 98–99.
5. Ibid., 98.
6. Ibid., 97.
7. Lincoln and Mamiya 1990, 346.
8. For example, the "father of gospel music" Thomas A. Dorsey was the son of a preacher. Aretha Franklin, Nina Simone, Marvin Gaye, Kierra "Kiki" Sheard, PJ Morton, Tye Tribbett, Deitrick Haddon, Toni Braxton, John Legend, Tonéx, Isaac Carree, and Fantasia Barrino are a sample of African American musicians who are preachers' kids.
9. Anderson 2004; Boyd 2011; Snorton 2014.
10. Chicago, IL, and Washington, DC, are important ethnographic sites for this research because of the positions that they share within the popular American imagination of Black men worshipping, as places Black men sojourn in order to attend men's conferences and rallies.
11. During my March 11, 2011, interview with openly homosexual musician Tonéx, he mentioned Ricky Dillard and New G's performance of "Worked It Out" at the 2008 *Stellar Awards Show* as an example of one of the many ways in which queer expressive culture is demonstrated as an open secret in gospel music. (See also Sanneh 2010.) Toward the end of the piece, Dillard proclaimed, "The spirit of David has come upon me!" Dillard then used dance moves that closely resemble the popular "duckwalk" and movements found in vogue femme performances of Black gay ballroom expressive culture. (See also Bailey 2013, 154, 159.)
12. "Gospel go-go" refers to both an event and a music style. Gospel go-go is the gospel style of an indigenous percussive funk music that was created in Washington, DC, called go-go. Chuck Brown is held as the originator of the go-go music style, which was conceived to be an expansive live music that keeps the party going.
13. "Cartesian" refers to the term for René Descartes' (1596–1650) philosophy that regarded the mind as being separate from the body.
14. There are several memoirs about the pimp preacher figure in African American churches, including Herbert Brown's *Pimps in the Pulpit* (2012), Gerald Gibb's *The Pimp and the Preacher* (2006), and Bruce Henderson's *Pimp to Preacher: Evangelism 911 with a Former L.A. Pimp* (2013) to name a few. The recent memoirs about "pulpit pimps" that are listed focus on preachers' hypocrisy from either a first- or third-person perspective.
15. Interview by the author with Dr. Tony McNeill, July 2015.
16. Interview by the author with Charles Anthony Bryant, July 12, 2015.

17. Ibid.
18. Ibid.
19. Halperin 2002, 27.
20. Jones 2015.
21. "Chile" is a vernacular form of "child," which is a term of endearment.
22. Interview by the author with Patrick Dailey, November 2012.
23. Interview by the author with Dr. Tony McNeill, July 2015.
24. Interview by the author with Patrick Dailey, November 2012.
25. Interview by the author with Charles Anthony Bryant, May 2013.
26. DuBois 1903, 190.
27. Mays and Nicholson 1933, 39.
28. Wiggins 2005, 1.
29. "Gender Composition by Religious Group (2014)," accessed September 9, 2015, http://www.pewforum.org/religious-landscape-study/gender-composition/.
30. Dyson 1996, 80.
31. Ibid., 104–105.
32. Blair 2015.
33. Griffin 2006; Dyson 2009.
34. Interview by the author with Josiah Woodson, September 6, 2015.
35. Interview by the author with Charles Anthony Bryant, July 2015.
36. Interview by the author with Dr. Tony McNeill, July 2015.
37. "Tye Tribbett Discusses the Infidelity in his Marriage," Associated Press 2010, accessed September 8, 2016, http://www.eurweb.com/2010/10/tye-tribbett-discusses-the-infidelity-in-his-marriage/.
38. Interview by the author with Dietrick Haddon, March 2015.
39. "How Da T.R.U.T.H. Overcame the Love Triangle That Rocked the Gospel Industry: Path MEGAzine Interview" 2011.
40. McGhee 2010.
41. Morrow 2014.
42. As a reinscription of hetero-patriarchy, transgressions of a similar nature have been well documented among African American ministers, in which they also continue to professionally advance but fall outside the scope of this article. For example, in Nick Salvatore's *Singing in a Strange Land: C. L. Franklin, the Black Church, and the Transformation of America* (2005), he documented that Rev. C. L. Franklin, soul music vocalist Aretha Franklin's father, conceived a child with the twelve-year-old girl Mildred Jennings. Franklin was married to Barbara Franklin and pastor at New Salem Baptist Church in Detroit, MI. Yet, Franklin remains one of the most iconic preachers of the twentieth century. Another example of a scandal following a preacher's sexual indiscretion is when nude pictures were widely distributed via the Internet of preacher and Stellar Award–nominated recording artist Rev. Charles Jenkins, senior pastor of Fellowship Missionary Baptist Church in Chicago, IL. As the pictures were distributed right after the release of his first album, Jenkins revealed that they were released as a threat to reveal that he had an eight-year-long extramarital affair with a woman on his administrative staff who was paid a six-figure salary (See "Scandal, Lies, Cover-Up: Charles Jenkins' Deceit Revealed after 8-Year Affair," *EEW Magazine Online*, last modified May 29, 2014, http://buzz.eewmagazine.com/eew-magazine-buzz-blog/2014/5/29/scandal-lies-cover-up-charles-jenkins-deceit-revealed-after.html.) Despite the visual evidence of his affair, Jenkins has gone on to attain #1 on the Billboard Gospel Albums Chart with his second album.
43. In Tonéx's 2011 interview with Lexi for *The Lexi Show* on the Word Network, he mentions two different incidences of molestation, one at age three, the other at age six, both perpetrated by adults in his family and church circle.
44. Sanneh 2010.
45. In the subsequent book *The Gospel of Inclusion* (2009) Pearson proposes that the gospel includes everybody, regardless of his or her national, religious, cultural, or sexual identity.
46. The Azuza series preserved traditional Pentecostal repertoire and celebrated the ministry legacy of William J. Seymour as a featured musician and preacher during the Azuza Street Revival in Los Angeles, CA (1906–1908).
47. Morrison 2006.
48. Ibid.
49. Pearson, quoted in Morrison 2006.
50. The Hampton Ministers' Conference and Choir Directors' and Organists' Guild of Hampton University in Hampton, VA, were founded in 1914 when the Negro Organizational Society, the Conference for

Education in the South, the Southern Education Board, and the Cooperative Education Board sought to strengthen churches' community engagement. There were forty leaders from four denominations present at the first meeting held June 29–July 3, 1914. The Choir Directors' and Organists' Guild joined the annual conference in 1934 following a visit from the Westminster Choir School to the gathering in the previous year. In many ways, The Hampton Ministers' Conference represents the pairing of the preaching and music-making functions in African American religious practices, across denominations.

51. Cheers 2015.
52. Williams 2012.
53. Delman Coates' assertion of biblical support for his position is notable because he holds a PhD in New Testament and Early Christianity from Columbia University.
54. Coates made this statement during the question following his lecture at the "Poverty, Race and Sexuality: Reclaiming the Prophetic Voices of the Movement" conference at Boston University, in Boston, MA, on August 6, 2015. Coates and I were among the researchers and practitioners that convener Rev. Keith Magee, Th.D., invited to lecture at the conference in conjunction with The Social Justice Initiative organization.

DISCOGRAPHY

B. Slade. *Diesel*. CD Baby/Suxxess Records 5637815096, 2012. CD.
Da' T.R.U.T.H. *Moment of Truth*. Cross Movement Records 000029, 2004. CD.
———. *Open Book*. Red Urban 0029, 2007. CD.
———. *Heartbeat*. Mixed Bag Music Group MGB-CD-1001, 2014. CD.
Haddon, Deitrick. *Lost and Found*. Tyscot Records 43195, 2002. CD.
———. *Revealed*. Zomba 723471, 2008. CD
———. *R.E.D. (Restoring Everything Damaged)*. RCA 370639, 2013. CD.
Moss, J. *The J Moss Project*. GospoCentric 70068, 2004. CD.
———. *Just James*. GospoCentric 747910, 2009. CD.
———. *Grown Folks Gospel*. Central South Distribution/PMG 8412, 2014. CD.
Ricky Dillard's New Generation Chorale. *Hallelujah*. Malaco 6019, 1995. CD.
Tonéx. *The Naked Truth*. Nureau Ink, 2008. Digital.
———. *Rainbow*. Nureau Ink, 2008. Digital.
———. *Unspoken*. Battery Records/Zomba/Red Ink Records 8697446692, 2009. CD.
Tribbett, Tye. *Fresh*. Columbia/Sony Music Distribution 88697597832, 2010. CD.
———. *Greater Than*. Integrity Music/Motown 5099972195727, 2013. CD.
Tribbett, Tye and Greater Anointing. *Stand Out*. Columbia 88697161142, 2008.CD.

CHAPTER 14

Women in Blues
Transgressing Boundaries

Daphne Duval Harrison

Spirituals, ragtime, blues, and jazz are the formidable creations of Black people who were brutally oppressed, yet who gave beauty in response to enslavement and enriched the musical heritage of people throughout the world. The spiritual derived from African origins and influenced the form, expressiveness, as well as the textual and musical content of the blues, and, subsequently, jazz. The same mournful expression found in "Sometimes I feel like I'm almost gone . . . a long ways from home . . ." is felt in the lines of Ma Rainey's, "If I could break these chains and let my worried heart go free/but it's too late now, the blues has made a fool of me."[1]

This ability to capture the deepest personal emotions and frame them in a simple text loaded with metaphors and other figures of speech was the hallmark of African griots, praise singers, priests, and dirge singers. The spirituals and the blues extended the tradition while incorporating past practices of double entendres, proverbs, and allegories. Historically, the field hollers, work songs, and spirituals were formulated and reformulated according to emotional, spiritual, and physical needs of the slaves. The double entendre of corn-shucking party songs, spirituals, and work songs encapsulated sophisticated meanings in seemingly primitive lyrics and simplistic melodies. Yet, a closer examination of the lyrics, rhythms, and melodies of the slaves' songs reveals an insight and spiritual substance that was usually misunderstood by outsiders. The body of poetic literature that emerged from the horrors of slavery documents the creativity and intelligence of a so-called illiterate people.

This duality of meaning and purpose continued when the blues emerged during the latter decade of the nineteenth century as a more individualized expression of feelings by African Americans who were "freed from the bonds of slavery" but still bound to the lands they worked yet could not own. The blues are a dynamic sociocultural art form that seemingly mutates depending upon the venue, occasion, artist, and audience. Therefore, the music and musician have a fluid relationship that constantly responds to these factors. Ironically, the savagery of lynching, poverty, and racism that hindered opportunities for Blacks to develop their own economic independence was the fertile ground from which this unique song form developed.

Although women are not obviously present in many of the writings about this music, their role has been significant from the earliest days of its existence. There is no absolute proof as to where, when, or by whom the blues were created, but there is evidence that women were involved as singers as well as instrumentalists from its inception. Gertrude Pridgett (Ma Rainey) recalled having heard the blues sung by a woman while she was traveling with a tent show in the South. Commentaries by scholars Lawrence Levine, John Work, and Sandra Lieb, as well as musicians such as W. C. Handy, who performed on the circuit during that time, lend credence to the story. Other studies suggest that the itinerant revival and camp meetings may have contributed to women's active involvement as singers as well as instrumentalists in the development of blues.[2] Most scholars consider Ma Rainey as the "Mother of the Blues" because she introduced blues songs on stage in the early years of her performing career.

URBAN MIGRATION 1900–1930

One of the major factors that attracted young women to the stage in shows, at house parties, and in other venues was the beginning of the "Great Migration" in the first decade of the twentieth century. The 1896 *Plessy v. Ferguson* ruling by the Supreme Court eliminated the rights of Blacks to equal protection under the Constitution. Whites, particularly in the South, used lynching to punish any Black man or woman who dared resist total domination and degradation. The tension between rural life and the additional opportunities and mores of an urban life motivated many families, single women and men, and even children as young as ten years old, to migrate in large numbers to cities;[3] as Blacks moved from rural to urban areas, they began to adapt to a wider worldview.

One might consider that the negative aspects of peonage, Klanism, lynchings, and poverty were the impetus for the mass movement that led to the creation of a "new" South in South Chicago. Chicago was at the confluence of the migratory stream bearing the artistic, social, religious, and political aspirations and expectations of Blacks from Mississippi, Tennessee, Alabama, Texas, and other states as well. Their movement was reflected in their religious and secular music. Chicago, unlike New York, became and still is the mecca for the blues. Blues scholar William Barlow notes the importance of Chicago in the evolution of blues into a major urban cultural art form, thusly:

> The central role that Chicago played . . . stemmed from three major factors. First, the city was a key refuge for black migrants, especially . . . from the densely populated Mississippi Delta, where the blues was deeply rooted in the rural culture. . . . Second, the city was also an underworld stronghold . . . and a sizable red-light district. . . . And third, was surpassed only by New York as a center for show business during the first decades of the twentieth century. Thus, Chicago was able to provide black entertainers and musicians with rare employment and recording opportunities.[4]

As a major railroad hub, Chicago was the perfect geographic location for Blacks who migrated from the farms, chain gangs, river levees, and plantations of Tennessee, Arkansas, Mississippi, and Louisiana from the turn of the nineteenth century to the present.

The picnics, where the fife and drum and washboard bass provided the blues songs, hollers, and religious and dance songs, were now held on crowded tenement stoops. Baptist, Methodist, and Sanctified-Pentecostal congregations did not leave their southern churches behind, they carried them on the trains, cars, and boats that hauled them "up north."

Churches, cafes, and rooming houses were soon joined by hotels and small theaters as Blacks developed interest in other forms of entertainment including dramatic and musical performances. Leisure time activities expanded rapidly in such major cities such as Chicago, New York, St. Louis, and Philadelphia as Blacks began to organize clubs, churches, and fraternal orders in their newly burgeoning communities.

The stream of Black men, women, and even children, traveling in groups or alone, took the blues, country songs, and religious songs and reshaped them to fit their new home.[5] Among these were girls seeking work as domestics in cities such as Baltimore, Philadelphia, Chicago, and New York, and westward. Of particular interest are the young Black women who sought employment in the entertainment field. Some—for example, Alberta Hunter—initially worked as domestics before moving into show business. Others dreamed of joining a traveling show or circus, or performing in a dance hall or club in a city like Chicago.

ENTRÉE INTO SHOW BUSINESS

Women troupers were a part of practically every event that appeared on stage between 1900 and 1930. In some instances, their beauty surpassed their talents, but they were an important facet of Black stage life in vaudeville comedy, blues, and dance. The minstrel and so-called coon shows of the nineteenth century provided opportunities for enterprising women, such as "Black Patti" (a.k.a. Sissieretta Jones) of classical music and Ada Overton Walker of musical theater fame, to display their talents. They also were the locus for the expansion of the pool of women singers, dancers, and comediennes. The combination of comedy, romance, and race pride in those shows attracted Black and White audiences prior to World War I.

Although minstrel and "coon shows" featuring women in singing, dancing, and comedy roles at the turn of the century were popular in northern cities, the negative images that characterized these shows troubled some Black musicians and performers. Notable among those who sought to counter these images were Will Marion Cook, Will Vodery, James Weldon and J. Rosamond Johnson, James Reese Europe, Paul Laurence Dunbar, and Scott Joplin.

By the time the United States entered World War I, Black stage shows and orchestras had already made their impact on audiences in Europe. For example, Will Marion Cook's *In Dahomey* debuted at London's Shaftesbury Theater in 1903 to rave reviews, setting a precedent for all-Black shows that followed.[6] The production featured Ada Overton Walker (wife of George Walker, comedian), Abbie Mitchell (Cook's wife, Figure 14.1), Lottie Williams, and Hattie McIntosh in singing and dancing roles. The impression the show made on European audiences was later enhanced by the Black musicians under James Reese Europe's command who had fought under France's flag in World War I and gained admiration and respect as soldiers and musicians. By the war's end, Black men and women were performing in musical revues for Black and White audiences in New York, Philadelphia, and other cities on the Orpheum, Theatre Owners' Booking Association,

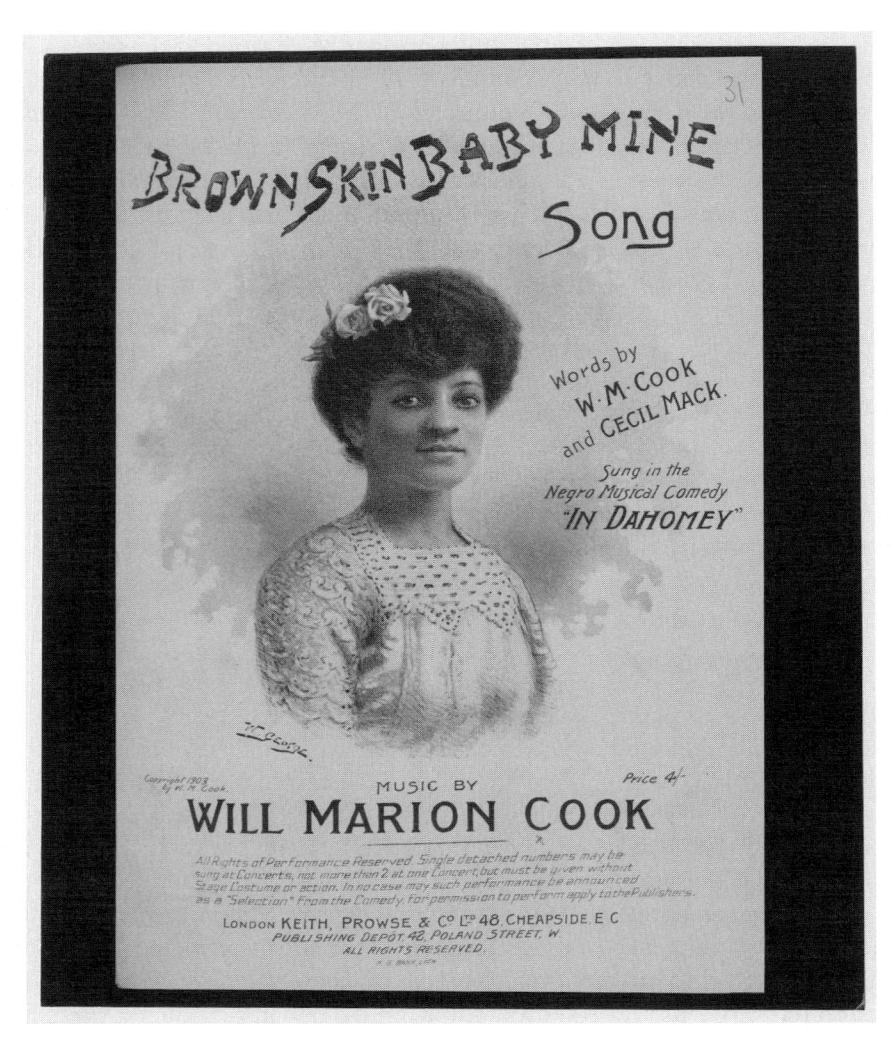

Figure 14.1
Abbie Mitchell, wife of Will Marion Cook, depicted on the sheet music cover for "Brown-Skin Baby Mine," featured in the musical *In Dahomey* (1903).

Courtesy The British Library Board, H.3983.k (31).

and other circuits. The growing working and middle classes of Blacks began to rely on the Black press for schedules and other information regarding plays, musical revues, and vaudeville shows. The *Chicago Defender*, the Baltimore *Afro-American*, the *Pittsburgh Courier*, and other papers in the South and Midwest served as key sources.

The emerging Black community transplanted its southern, rural, and urban traditions into a northern segregated city that had new opportunities linked with old prejudices and problems. Yet, the persistence of cultural practices over time suggests that the blues as a performance art was a source of sustenance in this new urban setting. One might say that the blues, coupled with its religious counterpart, gospel, demonstrates the versatility of the music and its creators in spite of a quixotic, hostile, yet nurturing environment. For example, when King Oliver, Louis Armstrong, Alberta Hunter, and other ragtime and honky-tonk musicians arrived in Chicago, the clubs, brothels, and gambling houses in the Southside's red-light district were virtual replicas of the same types of White-controlled areas of entertainment found in New Orleans and Memphis. The similarity of performance venues and opportunities in the developing northern communities provided a familiarity that was an attractive lure for young women. However, as the blues became more widespread beyond its southern origins, the pathway to fame was rough, often lurid, and exploitative for many of the women who sought careers as entertainers.

FIRST BLUES RECORDING

Piano rolls and recordings, such as those that featured "coon songs," the comedy of Bert Williams, or spirituals sung by the Fisk Jubilee Quartet, were popular in the Black community at the turn of the twentieth century. However, it was the traveling minstrel shows featuring live performances by Ma and Pa Rainey, and, later, Bessie Smith and a host of would-be stars, that carried the blues around the South and Midwest; prior to 1920, no blues recordings featuring Black women had been issued.

In partnership with lyricist Harry Pace, W. C. Handy, commonly cited as "father of the blues," founded the Memphis-based Pace & Handy Music Company Publishers around 1912, a venture that initially achieved only minimal success. In 1918, Handy left Tennessee to seek fame and fortune in New York by publishing and recording his blues songs. New York's Tin Pan Alley, where publishing flourished, kept a "closed shop" that stymied Black songwriters. Handy's initial efforts to get his vocal compositions recorded were equally unfruitful.[7]

However, enterprising young Black composer Perry Bradford persisted in hounding various companies to feature the first Black woman singer on record. In 1920, General Phonograph Company (parent company of OKeh Records) agreed, using Mamie Smith, a popular singer in various stage shows in Harlem who, like many of her counterparts, had a repertoire composed mainly of show tunes. Smith's voice could be considered typical of the show singers of the day—nothing spectacular—but, to her credit, she was viewed as very attractive, buxom, and could swing with the band. Although the popularity of singers such as Ma Rainey and Bessie Smith far exceeded that of Mamie Smith when the first blues recording was released, efforts to secure recording opportunities for these more established artists failed initially. The recording industry rejected them because their less-polished vocal styles, their southern diction, and the coarser timbres of their voices were considered unacceptable.[8]

Perry Bradford's persistence was rewarded when General Phonograph's OKeh label produced "Crazy Blues" with Mamie Smith on vocals and Willie "the Lion" Smith on piano with the Jazz Hounds (Figure 14.2). The recording reportedly sold 75,000 copies in the first month, and according to Bradford (who was known to exaggerate) "surpassed the one million mark during its first year in the stores."[9] Thus began the era of what the recording industry alternately labeled as race records or "classic" blues.[10]

After the success of Smith's "Crazy Blues," the recording industry realized the potentially lucrative market for female blues singers in major cities such as Chicago, New York, Philadelphia, Baltimore, and Atlanta. Scouts were sent to the South to seek talent, thus starting a two-way flow of southern blues artists between their home bases and Chicago

Figure 14.2
Record label from "Crazy Blues."

Courtesy Living Blues Collection, Blues Archive, J. D. Williams Library, University of Mississippi.

or New York. The astonishing demand for blues records by women spawned careers for many of them and for their accompanying musicians. In 1923, Bessie Smith and Ma Rainey were recorded for the first time, the former on the Columbia label and the latter on Paramount.

MUSICAL AND CULTURAL FORMATION

The commonality of experiences and family backgrounds of the women who chose careers as blues singers suggests that the combination of talent and a desire to perform usually outweighed the pressures for conformity to the mores and taboos of community and family regarding a performing career. The power of the images promoted by the recording industry and projected in the gorgeous photographs in Black newspapers, as well as the perceived glamor of the life on the vaudeville stage, was a heady experience for young women barely in their teens who sought to escape poverty and an uncertain future.

The style of blues sung by women reflected the type of venue where they performed, the constitution of their audiences, and their seminal musical experiences during their formative years. The minstrel, vaudeville, and medicine show circuit was the route to stardom for Rainey, Bessie Smith, Lizzie Miles, "Sippie" Wallace, Bertha "Chippie" Hill, Trixie Smith, and many others. Women typically performed with a band in traveling shows such as the Rabbit Foot Minstrels, with a guitar or jug band in tent shows or picnics in southern towns, or with a piano in saloons or at house parties.

Sarah Martin's sixty recordings on the OKeh label between 1922 and 1927 made her one of the most prolific recording artists of the "classic" blues era. Martin had the distinction of being the first classic blues singer to record with a guitar and with a jug band. She worked with Thomas Dorsey during his blues career, prior to his becoming known as "father of gospel music"; Martin later became the first "classic" blues singer to return full-time to gospel performance in the late 1930s.[11]

Ma Rainey and Bessie Smith began their careers as a part of traveling shows, whereas other artists got their starts performing in church, such as Sarah Martin, Edith Wilson, and Helen Humes, all famous blues singers from Louisville, Kentucky. Lizzie Douglas, better known in the 1930s and 1940s as Memphis Minnie, began playing guitar on the streets of Memphis in her early teens. Both Sippie Wallace (née Thomas) and Victoria Spivey were initiated into blues as pianist–singers in Houston and Dallas, Texas, respectively, before their teens. House parties and picnics, where bluesmen such as Blind Lemon Jefferson were regulars, served as the incubators for their professional careers. These settings held intriguing musical possibilities for the artists because they were freed from the time and censorship constraints they confronted in the recording process. On the other hand, these performance sites also included illegal activities such as gambling, bootleg whiskey, and prostitution.

Dance halls and "sporting clubs" in Chicago were the settings where Alberta Hunter, pianist–composer Lovie Austin, pianist Lillian Hardin, and Lucille Hegamin launched their careers in the first and second decades of the twentieth century. Hunter's style reflected the sophistication and flair of the nightclub scene in Chicago where the gamblers and big spenders preferred physically attractive women with high-style costumes and seductive airs. Ida Cox, who was also a Georgia girl, initially maintained the preaching sound that earned her the title of a Blues Queen. By the 1930s, she had gained a more polished sound as she traveled with her own troupe in a musical revue. A comparison of her recordings in the 1920s and late 1930s demonstrates her versatility and ability to adapt to the new trends in popular music. For example, in the 1939 salute to spirituals and blues at Carnegie Hall, produced by John Hammond, Cox was featured singing a jazzier rendition of her 1920s composition, "Death Letter Blues."

AESTHETICS OF BLUES PERFORMANCE

The "classic" blues singers represented a cross section of Black women in their physical appearance, their childhood performance aspirations, and their persistence in performing their music as they chose. Ma Rainey, Victoria Spivey, Sippie Wallace, Trixie Smith, Ida Cox, and Bessie Smith were known to employ a vocal style typical of "shouters" in tent and traveling shows, picnics, rowdy houses of the South, and urban red-light districts. Their voices were not considered "pretty" or "lyrical," but rather were coarse in texture. Typically, the melodic range of their songs centered around four or five notes ranging from middle C to A above middle C. However, the vocal power, slides, and vocal inflections that they employed expressed pain, anger, or joy in a manner that left no doubt about the emotional content of the song. Their voices were the familiar ones heard in the churches, picnics, and workplaces as folk expressed their spiritual joy, happiness, aches and pains, and triumphs over injustice and adversity. Bessie Smith's superior talent lay in her ability to draw the listener into the deepest realms of her feelings. She managed to defy categorization because she could take any song—blues or not—and transport the audience to her deepest level of anguish, anger, defiance, or lascivious audacity while maintaining a blues feeling.

In contrast to the classic blues "shouters," singers with light soprano or contralto voices, such as Alberta Hunter, Edith Wilson, Mamie Smith, Lucille Hegamin, and Monette Moore, were more likely to have developed their talents on dance hall stages or in clubs with a less noisy clientele. Their singing styles reflected a higher vocal range and timbre much closer to the light-hearted ballads typical of nightclubs, cabarets, and Broadway revues. Frequently backed by some of the best jazz musicians available, performances and recordings in both styles were parlayed into a lucrative business for the record companies, the singers, and the musicians.

Although the lyrics and melodies of "shouters" like Ma Rainey and Bessie Smith reflected the southern sensibilities of their youth, their performing personae demonstrated that they understood the expectations of their audiences to hear and see a fancy-dressed star singing the latest blues hit. Lavish tiaras, dangling earrings, heavily jeweled gowns, and huge feathered fans lent an air of grandeur that blues audiences admired and appreciated. Classic blues singers personified the beauty and luxury that most in their audiences could never hope to attain, for beauty was more than skin color, exquisite facial features, or comely figure. Such titles as Empress, Queen, and Mother of the Blues signified the value that classic blues women held for thousands of listeners in cities and towns in the North and South. Their measure of success made their audiences proud.

An interesting outcome of the variety of the singing styles the female blues singers employed, whether they were moaning, shouting, tearful, or teasing, was the influence they had on the young jazz musicians who performed with them. They were afforded the rare opportunity to expand their repertoire and style through the call-and-response interplay between the voice and instruments of such well-known jazz musicians as trumpeters Freddie Keppard or Louis Armstrong; pianists James P. Johnson, Jessie Crump, Sammy Price, "Little Brother" Montgomery, Thomas "Fats" Waller, Fletcher Henderson, and Earl Hines; and guitarists such as Sylvester Weaver. These artists acknowledged that performing with blues women was a major influence on their phrasing, timing, and melodic and rhythmic invention.

The numerous iterations of the "Jazz Hounds" bands that were listed in the advertisements with a plethora of classic blues singers demonstrate the close relationship between the two idioms. In fact, several women were active musicians who played with bands and recorded during the 1920s and 1930s. For example, Victoria Spivey accompanied herself on piano or organ on some of her recordings. Composer Lovie Austin had her own band in Chicago, the Blue Serenaders, that recorded with Alberta Hunter. Lillian Hardin, trained at Fisk University, joined Joe Oliver's band as pianist in Chicago. While Hardin sang and played solo blues piano on occasion, she and her then-husband, Louis Armstrong, were also featured on recordings by blues singers. Hardin played a key role in promoting Armstrong's early career and was the pianist on his classic Hot Fives and

Sevens recordings. A practical benefit for women who accompanied themselves was the ease in finding short-term engagements in the tiny clubs and bars that were the usual venues for the blues.

POST–DEPRESSION ERA

By 1930, more than one hundred Black women had recorded at least one blues song. The most noted and accomplished singers and musicians continued into the 1930s but with much-diminished opportunities. The decline of the vaudeville circuit reduced stars like Ma Rainey, who had once traveled in stylish trains or cars with her own band, to performing in seedy tent shows. In 1935, Bessie Smith, no longer the undisputed superior star of the "classic" blues era, died tragically in an automobile accident while touring in the South. Nevertheless, blues women did not disappear from the musical landscape.

The same desires and ambitions that compelled the women of the 1920s to seek their fame and fortune in the blues continued to attract girls to the scene in the South, West, and Chicago. By the mid-1930s, Memphis Minnie, who had her first recording in 1929; Lucille Bogan (a.k.a. Bertha Jackson); Mary Johnson, an exceptional honky-tonk pianist; Alice Moore; Billie Hudson Pierce; and others were in the new wave of singers and instrumentalists to take to the stage and recording studios. The Depression era may have reduced the opportunities for stage shows and recordings, but the women continued to sing as the radio, phonograph, and movies brought greater popularity and access to Black audiences.

Lizzie Douglas (Memphis Minnie), who played banjo and later guitar on the streets of Memphis in her early teens, was an early progenitor of the musical mix that grew out of these influences. She and her first husband, Joe McCoy, traveled North to make their first recording in 1929. Although this was technically still the "classic" blues era, Minnie's style was a departure from the typical recordings of women singers. She played the harmonica and sang her composition "Bumble Bee Blues," producing a fascinating mixture of blues and country styles. As she became more involved in the urban blues scene of Chicago, her performances became more hard-driving, distinctive, and sophisticated. Commuting for nearly four decades between Memphis and Chicago to record and perform, Memphis Minnie could arguably be considered the keystone of Chicago blues.

Memphis Minnie was one of the first musicians to switch to electric guitar as the technology changed the timbre and importance of the instrument. By 1942, she was playing the electric guitar in Chicago's Southside clubs, as she continually surprised her fans with her prowess as a performer and composer. Her versatility and skill were evident as she shifted from the elaborate guitar-picking style that is heard on her earliest releases to a more lyrical style prompted by the demands of the recording studio, a style she continued into the 1940s.

The guitar was no longer considered a country instrument when talented musicians such as Memphis Minnie and Bill Broonzy performed on it. Minnie gained much admiration and respect when she beat Broonzy, who was considered "the best," in a cutting session in Chicago in the late 1930s. In cutting contests, popular among both blues and jazz artists, musicians pitted their talents on a specific instrument to demonstrate their versatility, technique, and creativity in the improvisations they spontaneously performed. The competition between Memphis Minnie and Bill Broonzy established her firmly as an innovative virtuoso on the electric guitar. Her singing and playing were powerful, and she continually renewed her technique and her compositions through the years.

Other women were accomplished instrumentalists in the decades from the 1940s through the present, but few were as versatile as Minnie. Hadda Brooks could arguably be called a blues pianist, but she was an exceptional boogie-woogie pianist in the slow, loping style similar to Cow-Cow Davenport. Brooks, Camille Howard, and Julia Lee were among the few women to gain fame as blues instrumentalists, whereas Rosetta Tharpe vacillated between performing and recording first gospel, then the blues. Regardless of the setting, Tharpe was a dynamic guitarist who could sing and play with great facility and power. She, like Sippie Wallace and Victoria Spivey in the 1920s, could not completely reject her religious upbringing and eventually returned to performing mainly gospel.

BLUES REPERTOIRE

The blues repertoire expanded exponentially as new labels tried to duplicate the earning success of General Phonograph's OKeh. Alberta Hunter, Bessie Smith, Rainey, Spivey, and Wallace, as well as many of their successors from the 1930s to the present, wrote some of their own songs. Many of these compositions expressed feelings of homesickness, loneliness, abandonment, or desire to see a lover. The despair of destitution and infidelity, as well as a plethora of social commentaries on natural disasters, prostitution, death, and superstition, were subjects that frequently appeared in this vocal commentary on life among the disenfranchised. Victoria Spivey's "Arkansas Road Blues," sung in her typical moaning style, is an excellent example:

> *I got my train sack and now I'm going back*
> *Because, I got those Arkansas Blues.*
> *But I ain't gonna travel this big road by myself,*
> *If I don't take my baby, I sure won't have nobody else.*[12]

The irony in the text is that Spivey was born and raised in Texas, not Arkansas, and this blues was recorded in Chicago, though she was living and working in Missouri at the time.

Ida Cox's "Hard Times Blues" describes the same despair as Spivey's "Arkansas Blues," but it also depicts a common dilemma for Black men and women who were displaced when World War I ended and many Blacks who had migrated North lost their factory and other jobs to returning White soldiers and a new wave of immigrants. The following lines are almost pictorial:

> *I never seen such a real hard time before,*
> *The wolf keeps walking all 'round my door.*
> *I can't go outside to my grocery store.*
> *I ain't got no money and my credit don't go no more.*
> *Won't somebody please, try'n' find my man for me,*
> *Tell him I'm broke and hungry, lonely as I can be.*[13]

As a composer, Bessie Smith wrote blues that cover a wide range of topics, from despair to poverty, to desolation and cheating men. Her titles include "Poor Man's Blues," "Wasted Life Blues," "Standin' in the Rain Blues," "Hard Times Blues," and "Jailhouse Blues."[14] "Poor Man's Blues" is astounding in its direct criticism of White men's exploitation of Black men, in particular, and its subsequent degrading and deleterious effects on

Black women and children. It is powerful and poignant in its comparison of what Whites gained from Black labor during World War I and the continued poverty that Blacks suffered after the war ended.

> *Poor man fought all the battles, poor man would fight again today (2X)*
> *He would do anything you ask him in the name of the U.S.A.*
> *Now the war is over, poor man must live same as you,*
> *If it wasn't for the poor man,*
> *Mr. Rich Man what would you do?*[15]

The tragic irony is that Bessie's text dealt with a past event but forecast the same conditions that Ida Cox would sing about in her Depression-era "Pink Slip Blues," referring to the 1930s Works Project Administration:

> *'Cause a little white paper Uncle Sam has done addressed to me (2X)*
> *It meant one more week, one week of prosperity.*
> *But bad news got to spreading and my hair start to turning gray,*
> *'Cause Uncle Sam started chopping, cutting thousands off the WPA.*[16]

What is remarkable about Cox, Wallace, Rainey, Bessie Smith, and Spivey is that they could address the most pressing needs and concerns of Black women through their lyrics and melodies. The tension found in most blues, though often masked by humorous lyrics, is ever-present whether the women are singing about mistreatment, prostitution, poverty, abandonment, or natural disasters. The same themes of sexuality, mistreatment, infidelity, misery, and sexual braggadocio are found in subsequent decades.

Memphis Minnie's deft and humorous use of metaphors and double entendres was a hallmark of her lyrics. For example, her various "doctor's blues" simultaneously allude to illnesses that afflicted poor Blacks and to the status derived from being a "doctor's wife." In her rendition of "Down in New Orleans," Minnie sings:

> *Well, my man is a doctor and he lives off rice and beans,*
> *That's why he done gone and left me back down in New Orleans.*[17]

Her lyrics also echoed the same type of sexual inferences employed in the 1920s. Sexual euphemisms are sprinkled throughout the texts of many of her songs, such as "What's the Matter with the Mill?" in which she complains of her lover's impotency in the line "can't get no grinding." Minnie was an exceptional musician and composer who, in the opinion of her biographers, Paul and Beth Garon, has not been surpassed by any blues woman since her time.[18] While this may be an overstatement, there is considerable evidence to support their position.

Memphis Minnie's popularity and blues themes probably influenced singers such as Lucille Bogan (a.k.a. Bessie Jackson), a lifelong resident of Birmingham who recorded under both names with different labels. Like her predecessor Ma Rainey, Bogan addressed lesbianism directly in her songs. Rainey's "B.D. Women"[19] was one of several blues on homosexuality and lesbianism recorded in the 1920s. Bogan's 1933 release, "Women Won't Need No Men," implies lesbianism but could also be interpreted as a preemptory call for women's liberation. Bogan also boldly dealt with color prejudice and the attribution of Black or dark skin as concomitant to evil or unattractiveness. References such as "sealskin brown" or "black and evil" continued in the texts in subsequent decades. Their lyrics used color, weight ("I may be skinny," or "I'm a big fat mama"), and sometimes phrases such as "nappy hair" to challenge notions of beauty and sexual performance.

THE IMPACT OF RADIO, FILM, AND RECORDING STUDIOS

Whereas blues women's careers were controlled in the 1920s by the record companies and the club and show owners, the relative success of many women blues singers prior to, during, and after World War II was similarly influenced by recording studios. Jeff Titon notes that the practice of Black folks sharing recordings of the latest "classic" blues release was a significant factor in spreading the popularity of a given recording or artist and thereby influencing record companies.[20] Producers like Lester Melrose (active in the late 1930s and early 1940s) and the Chess brothers in Chicago (active in the 1950s) had the wherewithal to attract, promote, and also exploit Black talent. After 1951, the Chess Brothers hired blues vocalist–bass player Willie Dixon as a full-time composer–arranger–talent scout and sometimes producer.[21] Dixon brought some of the best blues artists to Chicago during that era, supervised their sessions, and wrote many of their hit blues songs.

Following the advent of the "classic" blues era of the 1920s and early 1930s, the spread of gospel music on recordings and radio in the late 1920s and in the 1930s played a critical role in the development of different styles of blues performance. The affinity of church music to blues was apparent at its inception and led to cross-fertilization of form, melody, text, and accompaniment. The church played a central role in the Black community; Baptist and Pentecostal churches, in particular, served as spawning grounds for the next generation of blues singers, especially girls. The cross-fertilization was enhanced when the broadcasts of the preaching sermons, gospel quartets, and choirs replaced the phonograph in many homes. In 1921, Thomas A. Dorsey (Baptist), pianist and bandleader for Ma Rainey during the 1920s, published his first gospel song; he later became known as father of gospel music. The recordings of gospel composer–pianist Arizona Dranes (Church of God in Christ), and vocalist Sallie Martin (Spiritualist), Dorsey's business manager, also served as seminal musical influences.

Ironically, World War II created new opportunities for Blacks in search of a better life. Wartime efforts provided more jobs and better living standards for Blacks who migrated to Chicago and New York, and in even larger numbers to Los Angeles, San Diego, and San Francisco. As in the past, radio was a major purveyor of the music that they left behind. In the South, WDIA in Memphis, WLAC in Nashville, and WERD in Birmingham were at the forefront of radio stations targeted to Black listeners and can be given some of the credit for an upsurge in blues popularity in the late 1940s. On the West Coast, literally dozens of stations in San Diego, Los Angeles, and Oakland kept the music alive for defense workers, servicemen, and others.[22]

Often the choices available to Black audiences were heavily influenced by the stations to which they had access. Although few stations broadcast directly to Black audiences during the 1920s and 1930s, many a Sunday breakfast or meal was prepared while listening to broadcasts of the Golden Gate Quartet, the Southernaires, or Wings over Jordan. Southerners also listened to country and hillbilly music regardless of whether they were Black or White. This amalgam of gospel, blues, and country music was revealed in the guitar-picking styles, yodel-type vocals, and thumping four-beat rhythms of some of the blues singers in the South.[23]

As the 1930s ended, the success of singers such as Ethel Waters, Ella Fitzgerald, and Billie Holiday, for whom blues was only a tangential part of a repertoire consisting mainly of popular songs and show tunes, overshadowed those blues singers such as Georgia White, Merline Johnson, Lillian Glinn, and Chippie Hill who had risen to prominence. Blues singers suffered because Black and White listeners now had a wider choice of music on radio, recordings, and the jukeboxes.

In the late 1930s and the 1940s, the movie industry played a pivotal role in how and by whom the blues would be performed. Movies, particularly the shorts shown before feature films at local theaters and the five- to ten-minute performances that appeared on a tiny screen connected to a few jukeboxes, rapidly influenced the shift in musical taste. Consequently, "jump blues" (rhythm and blues songs with a boogie-woogie foundation) and torch songs became the rage. Blues songs were orchestrated with strings and sometimes a full Hollywood stage backdrop for renditions of "Stormy Weather" or "Am I Blue?" For example, in the films *Cabin in the Sky* and *Stormy Weather*, Ethel Waters and Lena Horne sang the Hollywood version of blues in a sultry fashion with full orchestral arrangements. No moaning, groaning, or lascivious movements or lyrics were allowed in these films or in the jukebox "shorties."

Many Black films by major studios treated the blues characters in romanticized fashion, often as if they needed redemption through religion. Billie Holiday appeared in the film *New Orleans* (1947) as a maid, and although the original version had her singing, the portion with her songs was deleted for its distribution in the South. Comparably, radio censors removed racier versions of the blues that Black and White singers performed with dance bands. There were no more allusions to sexuality, sex, or lewd behavior.

THE NEW BLUES WOMEN

As Black neighborhoods expanded and flourished again, the opportunities for bands and singers grew, attracting a new wave of artists from the heart of the South who brought their love of the music with them. An exceptionally diverse group of blues women and men emerged during the period from the 1940s to the present. As in the past, gospel music was the lifeblood of the community, and Sallie Martin was a major influence on female performers in particular. One of her protégées, Dinah Washington (née Ruth Jones), was born in Tuscaloosa, Alabama, but moved with her parents to Chicago while still a child.

Dinah, like some of her predecessors and contemporaries (vocalist–guitarist Rosetta Tharpe and singers Della Reese, Esther Phillips, and Ruth Brown), vacillated between the sacred and the profane for a while. These singers learned to play an instrument or to sing in church choirs and quartets at an early age. Washington toured and sang in recitals featuring sacred music, performing for a short period with Sallie Martin's female gospel ensemble.[24] In 1941, Washington began to sing popular songs in the sultry style of Billie Holiday. Lionel Hampton hired her to sing with his band, and she toured with him for a short period of time. In 1943, Leonard Feather, a jazz entrepreneur and writer, was successful in getting her to record his songs, "Salty Papa Blues," "I Know How to Do It," and "Evil Gal Blues." Feather's "Blow Top Blues," on the Decca label, became one of Washington's biggest hits; it was probably her most well-known recording.

Washington's career had the ups and downs that typified the careers of many blues–pop singers. Her temperament onstage and off mirrored the legendary accounts of Bessie Smith, who had a reputation for cussing and fighting if someone crossed her. Nevertheless, Washington had sensitive timing, fluid phrasing, and deep emotional impact, whether backed by strings while singing Clyde Otis's "This Bitter Earth" or when belting out "Evil Gal Blues." Recording companies and agents realized that they could market a talent like Washington to a broader segment of the population—that is, more Whites—if they softened the sound to simulate a concert hall rather than a smoke-filled club where raunchier lyrics and a jazz band were the fare.

"I Know How to Do It," "Salty Papa Blues," "Blow Top Blues," and "Good Daddy Blues" were staples in Washington's repertoire because her fans loved the sexual innuendoes and hard-edged brashness of her vocals. When James Petrillo, head of the American Federation of Musicians, banned all recorded music on radio in 1942, Washington retorted with "Record Ban Blues," even though it could not be played on air. The musical *Dinah Was*, staged in the late 1990s, portrayed her struggles with temper, failed marriages, anguish, and the discrimination she and other Black entertainers were confronted with on and off stage.

Atlantic Records, Savoy, Vee-Jay, and several other labels were among the most influential and prolific in the country for blues and rhythm and blues. During the 1950s, the Muscle Shoals, Alabama studio, known best for its records produced by Jerry Wexler for Atlantic, also produced several of the singers in the Chess stable. Among them was Etta James, a belter in the style of Ma Rainey and Bessie Smith. Her most popular releases, "Tell Mama" and "I'd Rather Go Blind," were recorded there. James, who spent her early childhood with her maternal grandparents, began studying piano at age five with a Baptist church musician, who encouraged her to sing to raise money for the church. Through this early instruction, she learned to sing dramatically and use her powerful voice effectively.

When James's grandparents died in 1950, her mother moved to San Francisco seeking a better life. Etta learned to play upright bass in a school ensemble and formed a vocal trio, with two of her girlfriends, that later auditioned for rhythm and blues pioneer Johnny Otis. When Etta was fourteen, Otis began promoting her on stage. One of her first recorded hits was "Roll with Me, Henry," which she and Otis wrote but later renamed "The Wallflower" to avoid potential censorship.[25]

In 1959, James went to Chicago to record on the Chess label. Her distinctive style combines sensuous, melismatic phrasing that connotes pleading in "I'd Rather Go Blind" but easily switches to boisterous boasting in "Tell Mama." "At Last," a bold arrangement with strings a la Dinah Washington, reflects the tender and lyrical dimension of her performance style. Her bouts with drugs, obesity, and finances have not diminished her musicianship, and she remains in demand at blues and rock concerts in the United States and abroad. Although she performed for a period in 1998–1999 from a motorized wheelchair due to illnesses attributed to addiction and extreme obesity, she fought for control of her life and returned to the stage slimmer and healthier. At this writing, James has a new release, *Burning Down the House*, on the Private/RCA Victor label. James's autobiography, *Rage to Survive* (co-authored by David Ritz), was published in 1995 by Villard Books and later released in paperback by Da Capo Press.[26]

"Little Esther" Phillips was born in Texas but moved with her mother to the Watts section of Los Angeles as a child. She sang in the Sanctified church and was discovered by Johnny Otis when, at age thirteen, she won a talent show at the Largo Theatre.[27] Her first recording with Otis was "Double Crossing Blues," a hit with Black teenagers. Fortunately, Otis, a man of integrity, took a fatherly approach when she began touring with his band and allowed her mother to travel with them. Nonetheless, Esther's life was still a constant struggle with men, drugs, and temper tantrums.

Esther Phillips's recordings on Savoy are superb examples of urban blues in the 1960s. Her voice and style reflect her admiration for Dinah Washington, and Phillips's unique tremolo is characteristic of most of her early recordings. With her comeback in the 1980s and early 1990s, she had become a mere shadow of the audacious, hot-tempered, and openly sexy young woman she had once been; her voice was reduced to a very limited range that bordered on rhythmic talking. Her final recordings reflected an artist who relied on style as a substitute for vocal dexterity and quality.

Mabel Louise Smith, better known as Big Maybelle, was born in 1924 in Jackson, Tennessee. She played piano in the Sanctified church as a child, but like many of her counterparts, a prize in a 1932 Memphis amateur contest sparked her desire to sing the blues. By age twelve, she was singing with a band, and shortly thereafter she joined the famous all-woman International Sweethearts of Rhythm, a jazz orchestra composed of Black women who began as students at the Piney Woods School in Mississippi. Her first recording was for Decca Records; she later went to King Records where she recorded three singles with jazz trumpeter Hot Lips (Oran) Page and his band. Subsequent recordings on OKeh and Savoy led to her popularity on rhythm and blues stations in the 1950s.

Big Maybelle's most famous song is "Candy," which was totally different from her usual R&B fare. Rather than a spirited "jump blues," her sultry, rich-as-dark-chocolate voice was tender and seductive. She was backed by strings on the 1959 Savoy release *Blues, Candy and Big Maybelle*. Audiences of the *Cosby Show* will recognize "Candy" as Cliff Huxtable's background favorite when he sought to romance his wife, Clair. As with some of her contemporaries and predecessors, Maybelle continually fought addiction to drugs and overeating. She died of diabetes in 1972.[28]

Willie Mae "Big Mama" Thornton, a native of Montgomery, Alabama, was a preacher's daughter who, in her early teens, toured on the southern nightclub circuit with Sammy Green's Hot Harlem Revue. During a booking at Houston's Bronze Peacock Lounge, Don Robey, the club's Black owner, recorded her for his Peacock Label. Her third release on Peacock was "Hound Dog" (1952), a blistering attack that characterized men as dogs chasing after a female dog in heat. Elvis Presley's 1956 cover of "Hound Dog" reportedly sold seven million copies, reaching #1 on the pop charts.

Thornton dressed in men's attire all the time, although in her early days with Otis she wore her hair in the prevailing women's styles. As years passed, she added a hat or cap to her outfit, and was easily mistaken for a man by people who did not know her. Gladys Bentley, singer and pianist of the "classic" blues era, also confounded her audiences by dressing in male attire. The assumption that homosexuality was the reason for the cross-dressing has not been verified in either of these cases.

Thornton's output diminished in the 1960s until Arhoolie recorded her singing and playing "Ball and Chain" in 1968. Ironically, a young, White rock singer, Janis Joplin, who admired Thornton, recorded a cover of "Ball and Chain," which gave Thornton a boost on the blues circuit. By this time, she was an outstanding harmonica player and occasionally played drums as well, but she never had another hit record.

One of Big Mama's final performances was at the 1979 San Francisco Blues Festival. Suffering from prolonged battles with addiction, she had to be helped on stage, but her fans greeted her with a standing ovation that must have been the medicine she needed. According to Richard Cohen, "In the next 50 minutes, she gave one of her best performances in recent years." She "sang, moaned, yelled and did about everything there is to do to a song."[29] Not surprisingly, she was honored with the San Francisco Blues Festival Award. She never regained her health and died of unknown causes, alone in a rooming house in Los Angeles, the city where she began performing with Johnny Otis.

Denise LaSalle, a native of Mississippi based in Jackson, Tennessee, is a singer who writes many of her own blues songs. She came on the scene in the late 1960s, and her first big hit was "Trapped by a Thing Called Love," recorded by Westbound in 1971. LaSalle has a powerful voice and direct style that easily accommodates her brash, saucy lyrics. As did many other blues women, she began her musical career by singing at various churches in her childhood; she was further influenced by singers on the Grand Ole Opry radio broadcasts and later by music that flowed from the juke joints across the street from her home in Belzoni, Mississippi. Her early influences included Dinah Washington, Ruth Brown, and Laverne Baker, among others.

Denise LaSalle frequently traveled between her home and Chicago to see performers at the Regal Theater and other Southside venues. Unlike her 1920s predecessors, most often she was not traveling to record but to keep abreast of the latest music. Upon returning home, she composed more songs. LaSalle performed on occasion at some of the clubs in Chicago, and Chess Records expressed interest in recording her but did not issue her a contract. Consequently, she independently produced her own record with the help of Billy Anderson, a minor executive of Chess.

LaSalle's blues are direct and laced with sexual innuendo and boasting, such as "Breaking Up Somebody's Home," "Man Sized Job," and "Fast Hands and a Dirty Mind." Her topics recapitulate 1920s blues such as the Lizzie Miles recording, "I Hate a Man Like You," and "Up the Country," which Sippie Wallace composed and recorded. LaSalle continues to write and perform southern soul blues on stage and for the Malaco label.[30]

Barbara Carr, another product of the South, also writes and performs her own blues. Her lyrics border on risking censorship because of their graphic sexual references, but Carr has steadily gained popularity. Her more recent recordings include topics that are less torrid and suggestive and her styling is a combination of down-home blues and slick city sophistication.[31]

REIGNING BLUES QUEEN KOKO TAYLOR

Koko Taylor (Figure 14.3), née Cora Walton, was born in 1938 in Memphis. When the children in her neighborhood could not pronounce Cora, she became known as Koko; because the name seemed to fit her personality and style, it stuck. As did so many other blues women, Taylor began singing in church choirs, but it is unclear whether that was in Memphis or Chicago. In an interview she recalls singing, along with Buddy Guy and

Figure 14.3
Koko Taylor.

Courtesy Alligator Records.

Junior Wells, in clubs, at dances, and at schools on the Southside of Chicago beginning in 1953. Willie Dixon of Chess Records assisted Koko in recording the single "Honky Tonky" on the minor US label in 1963, but it was 1964 when she made her debut recording for Chess, singing "What Kind of Man Is This?" and "Don't Mess with My Man," which launched her highly successful career. Her signature song, "Wang Dang Doodle," followed as a million-record hit the next year.[32]

Taylor's voice is strong and easily recognized by the power that seemingly could raise a roof, but she lacks flexibility in phrasing and range. Apparently, she never thought that a woman had to sound any different than the shouters and down-home bluesmen she liked so much. Howlin' Wolf, B. B. King, Muddy Waters, Sonny Boy Williamson, and Memphis Minnie were the blues singers that she listened to and admired.

Partying White college students were particularly fond of Taylor's song "Wang Dang Doodle," and its popularity made it her theme song. She was soon on the folk and blues festival circuits in the United States and Europe. Her 1975 album *I Got What It Takes*, on the Alligator label, renewed her popularity; she and her band, the Blues Machine, have a tight act that continues to draw crowds. Hers is electric blues at its best. Perhaps the most poignant commentary regarding the "state of the blues" comes from Taylor's assessment of the contemporary blues audience, which is mainly White:

> I consider myself a blues singer. I wouldn't be nothing else! . . . I have to sing the way I feel . . . but some peoples. . . . Maybe they ain't really cut out to sing the blues, and some of 'em, they don't sing it because, you know, originally this is a Negro inheritance, the blues, wherein they've heard it so much in their life until they don't want to hear any more. They like running from it, they wants to hear something different. They ashamed of it, so they do what the next person do. They say I don't want to sing the blues, don't nobody like the blues today. . . . But me, I want the world to know I like the blues. That's the reason I sing it. So they'll know![33]

Other lesser-known contemporary blues women artists include Margie Evans with her big, beautiful tone and styling, who expatriated to Switzerland; Jessie Mae Hemphill of Mississippi, a scion of a highly acclaimed country blues family beginning with Sidney Hemphill, who plays guitar, harmonica, tambourine (with her feet), and sings in the traditional country style; and Mary Jefferson, who continued to sing at blues fests and special programs in Washington, DC, venues until she died of addiction and poor health in 2002. "Big Time Sarah" Streeter, another southerner, apprenticed as a child in Chicago's Southside gospel ensembles and began singing the blues at Morgan's lounge before her fifteenth birthday. Buddy Guy, Junior Wells, and Sunnyland Slim were influential in shaping her style. She is a shouter who is popular at Chicago's new blues clubs on the Northside. Valerie Wheeler, who was classically trained, chose to sing the blues rather than opera and was attracting new and younger crowds before she died unexpectedly in her twenties.

Shemekia Copeland, daughter of bluesman Johnny Copeland, is a rising star in the Delta blues region. By age twenty-three, she already had a hit recording and has become popular at blues and jazz clubs like Blues Alley and the 9:30 Club in Washington, DC. She was one of the few Black, female blues singers chosen to appear in the 2003 PBS series *The Blues*.[34] She follows in the footsteps of Sippie Wallace, Bessie Smith, Ma Rainey, and other blues women who wrote and performed their own material.

Although present-day blues women may not have the province and popularity of those in past decades, they nonetheless keep singing, assured of the fact that somewhere there are listeners who, like Koko Taylor, want the world to know they love the blues.

NOTES

1. Lieb 1981, 85.
2. Work 1969 (1915), 32–33.
3. *Negro Population in the United States* 1918.
4. Barlow 1989, 287.
5. Swartz 1919, 5.
6. Beerbohm 1903, 13.
7. Handy 1970 (1941), 193–210.
8. Ibid., 193–210.
9. Barlow 1989, 128.
10. Harrison 1988, 45–46.
11. O'Neal 1982, 23.
12. Harrison 1988, 152.
13. Ibid.
14. Albertson 1975, 64, 66, 80, 116, 119.

15. Harrison 1988, 71.
16. Ibid., 72.
17. Garon and Garon 1992, 155.
18. Ibid.
19. "B.D." is an abbreviation for "bull dyke."
20. Titon 1994 (1977).
21. Dixon and Snowden 1989, 81.
22. See DjeDje and Meadows 1998, discussions in several chapters.
23. Cantor 1992.
24. As a contemporary of Thomas Dorsey, Martin was a seminal figure in the development and dissemination of gospel music beginning in the 1930s. See Harris 1992, 256-ff.
25. Otis 1993, 91–98.
26. For further discussion on James, see James and Ritz 1998; Joyce 2002. See also Otis 1993.
27. Otis 1993, 91–98.
28. Erlwine et al. 1996.
29. Cohen 1971–1972, 46–47.
30. Erlwine et al. 1996, 157–158.
31. Ibid., 45.
32. Ibid., 539.
33. O'Neal 1971–1972, 46–47.
34. *Martin Scorsese Presents: The Blues: A Musical Journey*, produced by Martin Scorsese (New York: PBS and Columbia Music Video, 2003).

DISCOGRAPHY

Dranes, Arizona. *Complete Recorded Works (1926–1929)*. Document Records DOCD 5186, 2000. CD.
———. *He Is My Story: The Sanctified Soul of Arizona Dranes*. Tompkins Square TSQ 2677, 2012. CD.
Dorsey, Rev. Thomas A. *Precious Lord: The Great Gospel Songs of Thomas A. Dorsey*. Originally released by CBS Records KG32151, 1973. Columbia/Legacy 57164, 1994. CD.
The Early Minstrel Show. Various artists. New World Records 80338, 1998. CD
The Fisk Jubilee Singers. *In Bright Mansions*. Curb Records 78762, 2003. CD.
———. *The Fisk Jubilee Singers*. Directed by John W. Work. Originally released as Folkways Records FA2372, 1955. Reissued by Smithsonian Folkways Recordings FW02372, 2004. Digital.
James, Etta. *The Essential Etta James*. Legacy/Masterworks 71773, 2010. CD.
Ma Rainey. *Ma Rainey*. Recorded October, 1924–September, 1928. Ace MCD 470212, 47021, 1995. CD.
Martin, Sallie, and Martin, Cora. *Just a Little Talk With Jesus: 1940–1952*. Gospel Friend PN-1509, 2014. CD.
Martin Scorsese Presents the Blues: A Musical Journey. Hip-O B0000393–02, 2003. 5-CD set.
Sallie Martin Singers. *Throw Out the Lifeline*. Specialty Records SPCD-7043–2, 1993. CD.
Smith, Bessie. *Do Your Duty: The Essential Recordings of Bessie Smith*. Includes "St. Louis Blues," "Empty Bed Blues," parts 1 and 2, and others. Recorded February 16, 1923–May 15, 1929. Indigo 2008, 1997. CD.
———. *Sweet Mistreater*. Includes "Poor Man's Blues," "Young Woman's Blues," and "Nobody's Blues But Mine," among others. United States of Distribution 599, 2005. CD.
———. *Bessie Smith: The Complete Columbia Recordings*. Columbia/Sony Legacy 88725403102, 2012. CD.
Williams, Bert. *Bert Williams: The Remaining Titles 1915–1921*. Recorded October 1, 1915–October 28, 1921. Document DOCD 5661, 2000. CD.

CHAPTER 15

Jazz History Remix
Black Women from "Enter" to "Center"

Sherrie Tucker

Do you know, in Bessie Smith's time and all that, you don't hear too much about the men. They were piano players. But on stage it was the black woman. But now, to get an instrument? No, sir, a woman couldn't bring an instrument in no house, especially with a husband that was a musician. And not today either. . . . But if it wasn't for the women there would be no culture a-tall, a-tall.
—Trombonist Melba Liston, interviewed by Linda Dahl[1]

"Only the black woman can say, 'when and where I enter . . . then and there the whole Negro race enters with me.'"[2] This familiar quote from Black protofeminist Anna Julia Cooper (1858–1964) emphasizes the radical potential of African American women to open doors for "those hampered by multiple oppressions" as they make their own entrances into historically exclusive realms.[3] But what does one say about those many "whens and wheres" that African American women have not only "entered," but cocreated, and in which they dynamically resided and labored, only to disappear from historical memory? It is impossible to know what jazz would sound like today without Billie Holiday's phrasing, timbre, and timing; without Mary Lou Williams' shaping of the distinctive Kansas City sound through her rolling piano swing and her lasting touch on jazz arranging and composition of swing, bebop, and religious concert music; or without the participation of countless other women, both known and unknown, whose lives are woven through the entire history of this music. Yet it is possible, and common, for jazz to be thought of and historicized as a "man's world," sometimes decorated by "girl singers" (usually not taken seriously as musicians) into which, on rare occasion, an "exceptional" woman artist may enter, with the understanding, of course, that she will shut the door behind her.[4]

"Invisibilize" is the eminently useful verb coined by Brenda Dixon Gottschild to name those slippery processes where "sins of omission and commission" can be difficult to untangle.[5]

> **"Invisibilize"**
>
> To remove from or omit from official histories, thus obscuring the true role of certain groups.

From history books and textbooks to documentaries and record catalogs, jazz history has been memorialized in ways that "invisibilize" women as productive cultural citizens.[6] Despite evidence of jazzwomen's existence, the perception of jazz as a lineage of male geniuses overshadows community efforts that included both men and women and obscures the multiple entrances and long careers of trumpet players such as Dolly and Dyer Jones, Ann Cooper, Valaida Snow, Tiny Davis, and Clora Bryant; saxophonists such as Vi Burnside, Margaret Backstrom, and Bert Etta "Lady Bird" Davis; and trombonists such as Melba Liston.

This chapter proceeds from the belief articulated by Liston in the epigraph: that an understanding of jazz history without women is culturally incomplete. More research needs to be conducted on women's participation, possibilities, contributions, roles, and statuses in specific historical contexts before we can narrate jazz history in this more complete way. We do know that, at times, women have made a palpable impact on the music and have done so with a high level of status and recognition during their day, as with the blues women of the 1920s. In some settings, women's participation was acceptable as long as it remained within boundaries thought to be gender appropriate: as vocalists, playing instruments thought to be feminine or ambiguous (violin, piano), in family or "all-girl" bands, or as music educators. At other times, women's jazz participation was socially and economically discouraged, especially when they played instruments thought of as masculine (such as brass instruments and drums).[7] Yet a surprising number of women, including trombonist Melba Liston, forged ahead, making careers, building the music, and earning respect from their peers, while investing their talents and lives in a world that all too often invisibilized their efforts. We may not yet know all of the intricacies of the "whens and wheres" of these musical women and their influences, but we do know enough to seriously consider Liston's point: "If it wasn't for the women," jazz, as we know it, would not exist.[8]

"VISIBILIZING" WOMEN IN JAZZ HISTORY

In the 1980s, in response to the "invisibilization" of women from jazz historiography and fueled by new interest in recovering lost histories of people whose knowledge had been devalued and excluded, several writers produced important book-length studies that documented women's participation throughout the history of jazz. According to these treatises, women were not just on the verge of bursting into the field of jazz (as reviews of female jazz artists have typically heralded, even today), they had been there all along. What they hadn't yet entered was the historical record. Between 1981 and 1984, D. Antoinette Handy (1998), Sally Placksin (1982), and Linda Dahl (1989) produced first editions of painstaking studies drawn from overlooked primary and secondary sources, including the Black press (which often paid more attention to women musicians than did the mainstream news media and White-owned music magazines) and interviews with women musicians who remembered themselves and other women in jazz history even if nobody else did. Because previous historians weren't necessarily looking for women musicians, the women-in-jazz historians not only had to incorporate overlooked sources, but also had to carefully revisit traditional sources such as trade magazines (e.g., *DownBeat*, *Billboard*, *International Musician*, etc.) for clues. Not only did these researchers find evidence of women musicians in the history of every jazz style and on every instrument, but they found that women musicians were often marketed as novelties rather than as skilled artists. Regardless of how seriously many of the women took themselves and their music, they found themselves constructed as trivial and inconsequential by the ways that they were presented, received, booked, advertised, and reviewed. They were confounded with presenting acceptable and marketable forms of femininity while at the same time performing music associated with male musicians—and frequently found themselves costumed and choreographed in ways that called attention to their visual performance and away from their music.

These studies made it possible, if not popular, to map jazz history with women in it. They showed that African American women had participated in many of the musical forms that preceded and developed into early jazz, including work songs, spirituals, blues, gospel, and ragtime. Women had danced, and chanted, and even drummed in nineteenth-century New Orleans at Congo Square, the gathering place of slaves where public music-making associated with *vodun* (voodoo) practices was allowed to take place, and where some say that jazz improvisation was prefigured.[9] While most brass bands were made up of all men, women also played in early brass bands, usually as members of all-female units such as the 16-piece Colored Female Brass Band led by cornetist Viola Allen in East Saginaw, Michigan, in the late 1800s. In the late nineteenth and early twentieth century, it was not uncommon to find women, usually on piano but sometimes on other instruments, in tent shows; circus, family, and vaudeville bands; and minstrel shows. In the early 1900s, women pianists such as Laura Brown, Lucy Williams, and Luella Anderson broke up the usual rhythms with the best of them as pianists of the new craze known as ragtime. Women worked as pianists and directors of orchestras in Black theaters in the teens and 1920s.[10]

The place where Black women's influence on the precursors of jazz is most readily apparent is as vocalists. Many of the earliest recordings of now-canonized male jazz soloists are available to us now precisely because instrumentalists such as Coleman Hawkins, Louis Armstrong, and Sidney Bechet were hired to accompany blues "queens" such as Mamie Smith, Bessie Smith, and Ma Rainey.[11] Indeed, the one area where African American women are readily acknowledged as having indisputably entered, early on and with impact, is in vocal jazz. Yet the importance of singers, as well as women, to the development of jazz tends to be minimized and couched in more personal and less professional terms, in relation to the status accorded instrumentalists. Jazz history, for example, typically casts Bessie Smith and other "classic" blues women as irrepressible, natural powerhouses—raw material that would inspire the artistic creators of instrumental jazz, rather than as possessing the status described by Melba Liston when she said, "in Bessie Smith's time" you didn't "hear too much about the men. They were piano players. But on stage it was the Black woman."[12] Thankfully, the position historically accorded to vocal music in jazz is being rethought by current scholars, notably Farah Jasmine Griffin and Lara Pellegrinelli.[13]

Indeed, many of the musical precursors to jazz were vocal music forms, including blues, spirituals, work songs, and the *vodun* (voodoo) chants from Congo Square. In her book on Bessie Smith, Ma Rainey, and Billie Holiday, Angela Davis argues that part of the power of jazz to express what Sidney Finkelstein has called "the hope and struggle for freedom" stems from "its roots in the vocal music that stands at the beginning of the African American music tradition."[14] Slaves in the United States were largely banned from playing musical instruments, so they created vocal music that could facilitate community building and critical expression while sounding harmless to slave masters. A rethinking of the relative status of vocalists and instrumentalists in jazz historiography is certainly an important step in increasing our understanding of women as jazz musicians, because the women who *have* been acknowledged as contributors to the music have been, for the most part, singers. The simultaneity of acknowledgment and dismissal affects our knowledge about the entire history of jazz and is epitomized by the ways in which Billie Holiday is frequently treated in the jazz literature. As Davis, Robert O'Meally, and Farah Jasmine Griffin have pointed out, many writers who acknowledge Holiday's contributions to the music see her genius as naive and undisciplined.[15] This, of course, is part of a larger set of race stereotypes that have also affected African American men (including instrumentalists), yet the effects of this discourse on Black female vocalists presents a more complete erasure of their artistry and skill from the canon of jazz history.

From the eras of pre-jazz blues and religious music, African American women vocalists played definitive musical roles *as Black women*, performing with audible difference and high status at the same time and exerting an influence that one can still hear in vocal and instrumental jazz today. Where would jazz be without the women blues and gospel singers—those of local renown and beyond—who inspired instrumentalists, vocalists, and audiences? Some, like blues and gospel singer Ann Cook of New Orleans, played these key roles primarily at parties, sporting houses, juke joints, and/or churches in the communities in which they lived; others imparted their music, style, and spirit to audiences in towns and cities on the rugged itineraries of traveling shows and revivals; and yet others carried their influence to even broader audiences through emerging mass culture technologies. In addition, Black women's voices were crucial to the sounds and meanings of arranged spirituals in concert settings, such as those of the Fisk Jubilee Singers. Black women's involvement in church singing and church piano playing has been, and continues to be, an important site of training and influence for jazz musicians throughout the history of the music.[16] In Linda Dahl's words, "The black church, it could almost be said, was the first jam session—and black women were always powerhouses in it."[17]

Women's relative acceptance in dance has also made possible their active participation in the jazz community, although, even more so than vocalists, the musical contributions of dancers are not emphasized in typical versions of jazz history. Dancers, both women and men, contributed a great deal to the music; however, one can read most jazz historiography without learning how the lindy-hoppers at the Savoy Ballroom, for example, influenced the music in collaboration with the musicians in Chick Webb's band.[18] Another niche where women have been accepted in jazz culture and have had an active effect on the music of local scenes, but whose presence remains historically obscured, is as music educators. Musicians have spoken individually about Alma Hightower, for example, as a tremendous influence on a generation of African American jazz musicians in Los Angeles, but she and other teachers of jazz musicians are generally lost from our historical perspectives.[19] Many women have also actively participated in jazz culture as fans and in family and business partnerships. As Robin D. G. Kelley has pointed out, many spouses of jazz musicians (including Nellie Monk and Gladys Hampton, married to Thelonius Monk and Lionel Hampton, respectively) were involved with jazz long before meeting their husbands and remained actively immersed in the music, often as managers.[20]

Of the instrumentalists, the impact of pianists is most widely acknowledged, although it is important to note that this typically occurs when a pianist or two, usually Mary Lou Williams and/or Lil Hardin Armstrong, inherits a place in the story as an "exceptional woman." The "exceptional woman" narrative, or stories of isolated women so remarkable that they enter a "man's world," ironically functions as one more way of "invisibilizing" women as constituents of jazz culture. In fact, women's careers as pianists in early jazz were hardly "exceptional." Piano was one of the few roles and one of the best jobs available to Black women in the early days of jazz.

The pianists in early jazz bands in cities such as New Orleans and Chicago were quite frequently women, including Emma Barrett and Lil Hardin Armstrong, due to the preponderance of women skilled at playing this "feminized" instrument at the very time that piano entered the jazz band.[21] While piano remained the most common and accepted instrument for women, some female cornetists, trumpet players, and saxophonists were celebrated in the Black press in the 1920s, including the trumpet-playing mother and daughter, Dyer and Dolly Jones (also known as Dolly Armenra or Dolly Hutchinson).

Women who played instruments other than piano in jazz bands of the 1920s usually did so in the contexts of all-woman bands. All-woman bands continued to provide employment (and marginalization in the press, recording industry, and subsequent historiography) for women, on both Black and White entertainment circuits, in the 1930s and 1940s. These bands were marketed in very gender marked ways, as novelties, indicated by their titles—the Harlem Playgirls, the International Sweethearts of Rhythm (Figure 15.1), the Darlings of Rhythm—although, again, these bands were quite often treated seriously in the Black press, sometimes showing up in polls of readers' favorite bands.

When these bands traveled, they did so in racially segregated circuits, with the Black bands facing the same obstacles encountered by other African Americans who traveled, especially in the Jim Crow South. During World War II, all-woman bands (then called "all-girl" bands) were in high demand to fill in for men's bands depleted by the draft, but they were also more likely to be seen as "substitute" rather than "authentic" musical outfits, even if the women in them had been playing professionally long before the war.[22] Also due to the war, some "all-men" bands supplemented their ranks with female players: African Americans Gerald Wilson and Lionel Hampton hired Melba Liston (trombone) and Elsie Smith (saxophone), respectively. White bandleader Woody Herman hired Billie Rogers (trumpet) and Marjorie Hyams (vibes).

The postwar return of male musicians, as well as the related polarization of gender roles in hiring and social norms, resulted in many women musicians moving from band employment into musical fields traditionally considered "appropriate" for women, such as teaching or accompaniment, or switching from horns to piano or Hammond organ, from bandstands to cocktail lounges. Some women managed to keep working in combos, such as the Hell Divers led by trumpet player Tiny Davis. The new technology of television

Figure 15.1
The International Sweethearts of Rhythm saxophone section, Chicago, 1944. Top left to right: Helen Saine, Rosalind "Roz" Cron, Vi Burnside. Bottom left to right: Grace Bayron, Willie Mae Wong.

Courtesy Rosalind Cron.

brought employment for some White women musicians, while continuing the racist history of separate and unequal working conditions and opportunities for women of color. Some Black women, including violinist Ginger Smock, appeared on short-lived television shows in the early 1950s that failed to secure sponsorships. Only White women found employment in the sponsored television programs built around the big bands led by Ina Rae Hutton and Ada Leonard in the 1950s.[23]

In the 1960s, some women participated in jazz ensembles associated with the cultural responses to racism that continued during and after the Civil Rights Movement, with Black Power, Afrocentrism, Cultural Nationalism, and Third World Liberation.

Pianist-harpist-percussionist-composer Alice McLeod Coltrane joined John Coltrane's group in 1966.[24] Pianist-organist Amina Claudine Myers is among the women who participated in the Association for the Advancement of Creative Musicians (AACM), an organization devoted to supporting Black music and Black musicians in Chicago in the 1960s and 1970s.[25] The theatrical performance aspects of AACM groups such as the Art Ensemble of Chicago also opened spaces of musical involvement for women who were dancers, although these women, like so many other dancers from other jazz eras, are usually omitted from the story. Women jazz players also participated in cultural responses to continued gender discrimination, through involvement in newly formed all-woman bands, such as the Jazz Sisters and Maiden Voyage, and in women's jazz festivals. The first such event was held in Kansas City in March 1978, immediately followed by the Universal Jazz Coalition's first annual Salute to Women in Jazz in New York. In the same year, Stash Records reissued several collections of recordings featuring women in jazz historically. These recordings were accompanied by Frank Driggs' informative booklet with its explicit call for more research in the field of women's historical participation in jazz. Such is the context for the emergence of the books by Handy, Dahl, and Placksin. Unfortunately, subsequent histories of jazz made little use of this knowledge.[26]

The 1980s women-in-jazz histories presented impressive accountings of women's presence in all eras and on all instruments in jazz history, and they demonstrate the importance of including questions about gender and race in conducting jazz research. However, they also pointed to a need for in-depth historical research on specific jazz scenes, bands, genres, and other foci. Responding to this call, researchers over the ensuing years produced biographical, thematic, and more historically narrow studies, deepening our knowledge of artists such as Mary Lou Williams, Valaida Snow, and Alice Coltrane; women in local scenes, such as Central Avenue in Los Angeles; all-woman bands; and gender issues of representations, identity, labor, and education.[27] As women of color feminists persuasively argued in the 1970s and 1980s, "women" is not simply a category of sameness, but an experience differentiated by gender, race, and class.[28] If the meanings associated with gender vary radically across social groups and across time and place, then the generalizations that we may draw from the broad sweep of jazz history are likely inadequate for examining concurrent differences in women's opportunities, experiences, and contributions to jazz. Attitudes toward women's "appropriate" instruments, genres, labor, status, etc., may very well differ drastically among different social groups of the same time and place. While it is difficult to address complex differences in broad historical surveys, the insights and meticulous historical maps provided by the women-in-jazz histories render in-depth studies possible.

NEW ORLEANS: A CASE STUDY

From 2002 to 2004, I had the privilege of conducting research on women in a single city, New Orleans, for the New Orleans Jazz National Historical Park. That the National Park Service sought and contracted a research study of women in jazz is a hopeful indicator of support that will help us to tell more complete histories. Because most jazz history books begin in late nineteenth-century New Orleans, this local scene serves as an excellent example of the need for focused studies. While the report, *A Feminist Perspective on New Orleans Jazzwomen* (2004) is complete and available through the New Orleans

Jazz National Historical Park,[29] I want to emphasize that it barely scratches the record. My hope is that other researchers will be inspired by unanswered questions and underexplored areas of local research, as doorways to expand the historical record of jazz to hear women and gender as specific, nuanced, changing, constitutive parts of the story. I share some questions that arose for me as I conducted my research, in hopes that other scholars will build on the report and continue the work of remixing the historical record to better hear and understand women and gender as part of jazz history. I would like to spin for you some of my ideas, as well as some of the unanswered questions, from the New Orleans research study, in hopes that they will be useful for thinking through how detailed local and comparative studies of women and jazz may benefit from, and build on, the works of Dahl, Handy, and Placksin.

As a cosmopolitan Caribbean hub, turn-of-the-century New Orleans comprised many kinds of ethnic, racial, linguistic, religious, class, and national identifications—and with them, many kinds of music and many different definitions of proper roles for women and men (what we might call different "sex-gender systems"). It is likely not only that all of these diverse cultural contacts accounted for diverse and ever-changing gender roles in music around the city, but also that gender variety, as part of cultural variety, contributed to the development of early jazz. Some theorists have argued for what Olly Wilson has called a "heterogeneous sound ideal" in jazz and other forms of Black music.[30] So one question that addresses gender and music together in a local sense is how, in New Orleans, has gender variety, as well as other kinds of cultural variety, contributed to the development of this aesthetic of difference?[31]

While it is true that women were less likely than men to play brass instruments in New Orleans marching bands, nonetheless some did. A focused study would allow us to determine which women. New Orleans jazz historian Karl Koenig, who has made a concerted effort to include women in his studies, found that in Houma, Louisiana, a small town southwest of New Orleans, the town band included a number of women.[32] A local study of gender and music in Houma (in comparison with towns whose brass bands did not include women) would be a site to look for clues about one cultural trajectory of women's musical participation and status. While little is known about them, four women appear in a 1928 photo of the Tonic Triad Band, an African American New Orleans brass band.[33] Is it enough to say most brass bands were all-men, or to simply celebrate the presence of the four women in one band? Or are there other ways to explore how gender operated in the communities of the players, both male and female, of the Tonic Triad? For example, were women more likely to participate in brass bands in Treme, a primarily African American residential area, than in other sections of New Orleans? If so, what is the cultural context for their involvement? Jazz developed at a time when African Americans and Creoles-of-color, who identified as separate racial groups, were legally being fused as "colored" by the rise of Jim Crow, even though these communities had different cultural, linguistic, and musical histories. How did gender constructions and ethnic and class identifications factor into the musical differences and fusions that developed in New Orleans after the demise of Radical Reconstruction (1867–1877)?

Pianist Dolly Adams came from an influential Creole-of-color family of musicians, which included her mother, Olivia Douroux (née Manetta), who played trumpet duets with her husband, Louis Douroux, at private parties. While playing trumpet professionally was acceptable for Louis but unacceptable for Olivia, it is significant that it was acceptable for both to play trumpets at private parties and for their daughter (born 1904) to become a jazz pianist and bandleader who doubled on bass and drums. The gender organization of instrument and genre seems more nuanced and dynamic in the Manetta and Douroux families than an analysis that simply says it was not considered proper for women to play brass instruments or jazz in Creole-of-color communities. We must know more about specific histories of race and gender in local contexts.

A complex look at how different communities negotiated gender and music in late nineteenth- and early twentieth-century New Orleans must address the fact that African American, European American, and Creole-of-color women were, without question, more likely to play piano and organ than brass instruments. How did this common association between instrument and gender come about? African American women who played jazz piano often came from church music backgrounds and were more likely than men to have taken piano lessons, two factors that made them more likely than men to read music. As pianists, and as reading musicians, African American women contributed important elements to jazz when the bands were no longer limited to mobile street units and when bandleaders desperately needed someone in the band with knowledge of chords and the ability to teach new charts to non-reading members. While Lil Hardin Armstrong is often acknowledged as an "exceptional woman" for performing this role in early Chicago-based New Orleans bands, some scholars of New Orleans jazz and women in jazz demonstrate that there was already a precedent for this practice in New Orleans before Joe "King" Oliver hired Hardin for his jazz band.[34] Olivia "Lady Charlot" Cook recalled being in demand as a reading pianist for men's bands, but she also recalled that male bandleaders were ambivalent about her skills: "They liked that I could read it, but they hated that it was a woman."[35] Was this "like–hate" relationship between male bandleaders and the skilled female pianists they hired common? Did gender bias curtail women pianists' creative freedom, as when Joe "King" Oliver denied Lil Hardin's "urge to run up and down the piano and make a few runs and things?"[36] Were women reed and horn players similarly restricted? Did this "like–hate" relationship affect the careers of women of all cultural groups in New Orleans?

Paradoxically, while gender typically defines power hierarchically within a culture, gender constructions are also common ways by which cultural groups define themselves as different from one another. In other words, the dominant groups' ideological definitions of gender frequently function to define their culture as superior to all others. Women outside dominant culture membership are affected both by the gender construction of their cultural group and by the social "norms" defined by the dominant culture from which they may be excluded. For instance, even as the dominant culture may have exerted a strong message that it wasn't "ladylike" to work for wages, many women, of course, needed to work. It may not have been ideologically "ladylike" to play trombones or trumpets, or to enter the spaces where jazz was played, but for some women, playing jazz was not considered wholly transgressive in the local sense, but rather a viable way to earn a living. African American women who played classical music often found that careers in jazz were more open to them, as masculinist as we may think of the genre today and despite the fact that classical music may have been considered more "ladylike," even in their own cultural group. Pianist and organist Olivia "Lady Charlot" Cook is just one celebrated African American jazz musician whose dream was to have been a classical concert pianist.[37] Many women, by virtue of race or class, were already barred from the ideological definition of "lady," but would still be affected by contradictory and restrictive messages about gender.

While it is a mistake to restrict a telling of early New Orleans jazz history to the red-light district, many jazz history narratives are skewed in favor of this part of the story. And indeed, it is another place that may provide instructive glimpses into diverse gender systems and women's participation in early New Orleans jazz. The gender ideology of the day certainly did not tell women that it was "ladylike" to be prostitutes or madams, yet economic and domestic conditions presented these roles to women, some of whom had musical talents. Antonia P. Gonzales advertised her famous Storyville brothel by billing herself as a cornet-playing madam.[38] Not all women who played music in Storyville brothels doubled as prostitutes, however. In 1917, thirteen-year-old Dolly Adams began playing piano in her uncle Manuel Manetta's band.[39] Her son, Placide Adams Jr., later told filmmaker Kay D. Ray that Manetta hired his mother in part for safety reasons, because Manetta thought that no one would attack a preadolescent girl carrying money and instruments to and from gigs.[40] Pianists Camilla Todd and Edna Mitchell played in Storyville bordellos as non-resident musicians.[41] Ann Cook was remembered by musicians as a singer who often worked in Storyville (where the workers were racially mixed, but the clientele was White), but who was also a prostitute in the non-racially-restrictive Black Storyville. Black Storyville was located in a part of town known as the Battlefield, the area where Louis Armstrong grew up and where, as one musician recalled, "women and men were tough."[42] Did other women musicians emerge from the Battlefield? Did Cook's alleged "toughness" connote a sound that was Battlefield specific? How did the New Orleans sex industry, with its own rules of gender, race, sexuality, culture, and commerce, differently configure musical women?[43]

The Northern migration of jazz out of New Orleans is a staple of jazz historiography, although recent historians of New Orleans jazz have reminded us that jazz continued to be played in New Orleans even as musicians and audiences migrated,[44] and historians of jazz in California, Japan, Canada, Latin America, Europe, and other locales have helped to dispel the myth that jazz traveled only to Kansas City, Chicago, and New York.[45] It would be very helpful to know more about how women traveled in these circuits. Were some destinations more open to women jazz artists due to local understandings of gender, music, and labor? We know, for example, that when jazz pianist and singer Nellie Lutcher left Louisiana, she did not move to Chicago, Kansas City, or New York, but headed due west for a career in Los Angeles.[46] Although not an Orleanean, we know that Tennessee-born African American trumpet player Valaida Snow played in Shanghai as early as 1926.[47] Many women musicians, including Blue Lu Barker, Lovie Austin, and Lil Hardin Armstrong, were part of the ongoing cultural exchange between New Orleans and Chicago.[48]

Although it is not part of the typical story, musicians and other workers also migrated *into* New Orleans during the period that jazz was headed north and east (and south and west). The African American population of New Orleans grew, rather than diminished, during the Great Migration, as southern urban centers were also destinations for migrants. To what extent did women musicians arrive in New Orleans, not during the period of early jazz, but as migrants or traveling musicians during the years between World Wars I and II? One such migrant was African American trumpet player Ann Cooper, who in 1935 left Chicago for New Orleans, where she would work with Joe Robichaux's Rhythm

Boys. According to the Black press and oral histories of musicians who remembered working with her, she eventually went back to Chicago, continuing a long career of working in highly regarded men's and women's bands.[49] Cooper, Snow, Dyer and Dolly Jones, and many other female trumpet players are described in glowing terms by the Black press yet are excluded by general jazz history narratives. This historical oversight may be changing, given new attention to Snow,[50] and the inclusion of more entries on women instrumentalists in recently published reference books, such as the *New Grove Dictionary of Jazz*.[51] There is still, however, considerable distance between the gender and jazz expectations of reporters for the Black press in the 1920s, 1930s, and 1940s, and the authors of the most widely circulated stories about jazz in history books, textbooks, compilation CDs, and documentaries. What other articulations of jazz and gender go missing in the dominant histories, and how might local studies help us piece together a more complex view?

These are just some of the questions raised by my New Orleans research, and I share them in hopes that they will continue to be explored by scholars looking into these, and other, local, particular, and specific "whens and wheres."

CONCLUSION

I began this piece with a quote by trombonist and arranger Melba Liston, whose importance to jazz is legendary among musicians, if not with the general public. Also legendary was Liston's modesty, so one can be sure that she was not simply "tooting her own horn" in her account of jazz history, which placed women squarely in the center of the genre's development. In fact, it is largely through the memories of women musicians, and their willingness to recall and narrate their lost histories, that historians of women and jazz have come closest to accessing a jazz history narrative that includes women. Such narratives often describe their careers as complex social negotiations.

Liston's own career exemplifies the complexity of this thing called gender in various contexts, including jazz. The Kansas City–born trombonist and arranger worked for such well-known male jazz bandleaders as Dizzy Gillespie, Quincy Jones, and Randy Weston. But to get *anywhere near* that point, she had to defy her grandmother, more than one husband, and countless male musicians just to be able to play her horn and go out to the venues where jazz was played. On the other hand, she was sustained by the encouragement of her mother, grandfather, and many other musicians, both male and female. This complicated social web of acceptance and rejection, participation and invisibility, makes the struggles of women instrumentalists extremely difficult to discern. These stories certainly do not fit neatly into the usual linear narrative where bands of men innovate on instruments, while a solitary woman sexily sings her private joys and (mostly) woes. And it certainly doesn't mean that the so-called entrance of women into the realm of jazz culture has guaranteed that the door would stay open for others, or that their presence would be noted by historical documentation, prestigious roles, and access to lucrative areas of the jazz profession.

As many feminist historians have pointed out, without an analysis of gender it is difficult to see women in history. In terms of jazz history, gender analysis can help us move beyond tidy representations of musicians produced by record companies, jazz magazines, Hollywood films, critics, and historians that accept "normative" gender constructions as typical rather than ideological. Analyses of race, class, culture, ethnicity, nation, sexuality, and other social categories can help us to see that gender does not exist in a vacuum; that what is considered "feminine" or "masculine" or "musical" will vary from context to context. Jazz is not unique in this respect; many scholars study the ways that social categories such as race and gender shape, and are shaped by, cultural performances. But neither is jazz unique as a social and historical sphere that is often presented as purely aesthetic and measurable by barometers of "greatness" and "genius." Black music historians who work from perspectives of African American and African Diaspora studies have long warned of the dangers of disconnecting aesthetics from history and culture, though gender is often overlooked as an important category in this regard.

As Melba Liston's life and opening commentary suggest, if women are invisible, it becomes impossible to understand the culture—even such a supposedly male-oriented culture as jazz. Yet the solution to this problem is not a future grand entrance of jazz-women into jazz. They have entered. And entered. And entered. Perhaps the question is, when and where will women enter our common-sense pool of knowledge about jazz history and culture? The answer depends on continued research that seeks to understand the ways women have inhabited, produced, supported, and developed jazz, and that analyzes the conditions of their contributions, their status, and the cultural possibilities open to them, in specific times and places. It will be interesting to see who and what else is made visible once those doors are finally opened.

NOTES

1. Dahl 1989, 258–259.
2. Anna Julia Cooper, quoted in Giddings 1984, 82.
3. James 1997, 20.
4. See Tucker 2001–2002.
5. Gottschild 1998, 2–3.
6. See the documentary, Ken Burns' *Jazz*, for an example of this pattern. Burns did not invent this dominant narrative, but the high-profile circulation of his documentary, not only on television but in libraries and jazz history classes, make for a handy touch-stone for anyone in need of evidence of the gender bias of dominant jazz historiography. See Jacques, et al. 2001, 207–225; Kelley 2001.
7. For more on the gender-coding of styles, venues, roles, and instruments, see Tucker 2001, 249–255.
8. Dahl 1989, 258–259.
9. See Cavin 1975; Placksin 1985, 5.
10. For more information on women's participation in all of these areas, see Placksin 1985; Dahl 1989; Handy 1998.
11. Placksin 1985; Harrison 1988; Dahl 1989; Handy 1998.
12. Dahl 1989, 258–259.
13. See Griffin 2001, 2004; Pellegrinelli 2005, 2008.
14. Davis 1998, 166–167.
15. Griffin 2001, 15–16. See also Davis 1998, 184–188; O'Meally 1991.
16. For more on blues women's roles as early recording stars, see Harrison 1988. For a discussion of gospel and its influence on secular music, see Maultsby 1992.
17. Dahl 1989, 6.
18. A growing body of dance literature helps to fill out this history. See Hazzard-Gordon 1990; Malone 1996, 91–110; Miller and Jensen 1996; Gottschild 1998; Brooks 2006; Brown 2008a, 2008b; Hubbard and Monaghan 2009.
19. An exception to this omission is the remarkable study by Kennedy 2002.
20. Kelley 2002, 24. Maxine Gordon is contributing the historical record of jazz communities as project director of "Women Who Listen: An Oral History with Women Jazz Fans."
21. See Chamberlain 2001.
22. For more on the women's bands of this period, see Tucker 2000.

23. Tucker 2000, 322.
24. See Berkman 2007, 2010; Kernodle 2010.
25. See de Jong 2007; Lewis 2008, especially 459–480.
26. For more on this period of historiography, see Rustin and Tucker 2008b, 10–16.
27. Research on individual women jazz instrumentalists includes Dahl 1999 and Kernodle 2004 on Mary Lou Williams; Brown 2006 and Miller 2007 on Valaida Snow (see also Allen 2005 for a fiction based on Snow's life); and the articles in the special issue of *Black Music Research Journal* on Melba Liston guest edited by Monica Hairston O'Connell. For an example of a local study that draws into relief the centrality of African American women, see Bryant et al. 1998. On Black women and jazz outside the United States, see Brown 2006; Miller 2007; Muller and Benjamin 2011. Recent studies of themes and issues include Rustin and Tucker 2008a; McGee 2009.
28. See, for example, the essays in Hull, Scott, and Smith 1982; Moraga and Anzaldúa 1983; Anzaldúa 1990.
29. "New Orleans Jazz," National Park Service, last modified April 10, 2012, http://www.nps.gov/jazz/historyculture/people.htm.
30. Wilson 1992.
31. See also Ake 2002; Long 2004; Hersch 2009.
32. Koenig 1996, 18.
33. Handy 1998, 166. The photograph appears in Rose and Souchon 1984 (1967), 194.
34. Chamberlain 2001, 3.
35. Olivia Charlot Cook, *Oral History Interview*, August 30, 1999 (New Orleans: Hogan Jazz Archive, Tulane University).
36. Placksin 1985, 60–61.
37. Cook interview, 1999.
38. Rose 1984, 103; Placksin 1985, 46.
39. Dolly Adams, *Oral History Digest*, April 18, 1962 (New Orleans: Hogan Jazz Archive, Tulane University).
40. Placide Adams Jr., interview with filmmaker Kay D. Ray for her documentary, *Lady Be Good: Instrumental Women in Jazz* (2014). Full interview in possession of Kay D. Ray.
41. Punch Miller, interview, September 1, 1959, quoted in Chamberlain 2001, 4.
42. Manuel Manetta, *Oral History Digest*, March 28, 1957, four reels (New Orleans: Hogan Jazz Archive, Tulane University), Reel III of IV, 11. See also Willie Parker, *Oral History Transcript*, November 7, 1958 (New Orleans: Hogan Jazz Archive, Tulane University), 34.
43. For an excellent analysis of Storyville, gender, race, and sexuality, see Long 2004.
44. See Suhor 2001.
45. See Lotz 1997; Miller 1997; Yoshida 1997; Fernandez 2002.
46. Nellie Lutcher, oral history, interview by Patricia Willard, February 15, 1979, Smithsonian Jazz Oral History Project (Newark: Institute of Jazz Studies, Dana Cotton Library, Rutgers, the State University of New Jersey), transcript, 21.
47. Miller 2007.
48. Danny Barker and Lu Barker, oral history, interview by Milt Hinton, April 30, 1980 (Newark: Institute of Jazz Studies, Dana Cotton Library, Rutgers, the State University of New Jersey), transcript; Taylor 2008, 48–63.
49. For examples of coverage of women trumpet players in the Black press, see "They Blew Horns" 1938, 19; "Ann Cooper to 'Darlings of Rhythm' Band" 1944, 6; and "Ann Cooper Plays with Bibbs' Band" 1940, 10.
50. Allen 2005; Brown 2006; Miller 2007.
51. Kernfeld 2002. See also Price, Kernodle, and Maxille 2010.

DISCOGRAPHY

Armstrong, Lil Hardin. *1936–1940 Anthology*. Reissue, Stardust Records, 2011. MP3 download.
Bryant, Clora. *Gal With a Horn*. Originally released 1947. Reissue, VSOP 42, 1995. CD.
Carrington, Terri Lyne. *The Mosaic Project*. Concord Jazz CJA-33016–02, 2011. CD.
Coltrane, Alice. *Journey to Satchidananda*. Originally released 1971. Reissue, GRP/Impulse! AAIMPD228, 2009. CD.
Forty Years of Women in Jazz. Various artists. Jass CD-9/10, 1989. CD.
International Sweethearts of Rhythm. *Hot Licks*. Reissued from 1944–46, Sounds of Yesteryear, 2006. CD.

Jazz Women: Great Instrumental Gals. Various artists. Universal Saga Jazz 42, 2003. CD.
Liston, Melba. *Melba Liston and Her 'Bones.* Originally released 1958. Reissue, Fresh Sound 408, 2010. CD.
Sax in the City. Various artists. Apria Records, 2004. CD.
Snow, Valaida. *Valaida, Vol. 2: 1935–1940.* Harlequin HQCD 18, 1994. CD.
———. *Queen of the Trumpet and Song.* DRG 8455, 1999. CD.
Williams, Mary Lou. *Zoning.* Originally released 1974. Reissue, Smithsonian Folkways SFW40811, 1995. CD.
A Woman's Place Is in the Groove: Women in Jazz 1923–1947. Various artists. Acrobat ACRCD 163, 2002. CD.
The Women: Classic Female Jazz Artists 1939–1952. Various artists. RCA Bluebird 6755–2-RB, 1990. CD.

CHAPTER 16

The Reception of Blackness in "Women's Music"

Eileen M. Hayes

INTRODUCTION

Societal advances initiated by LGBT activists and cultural workers over the past fifteen years have effaced a longer and deeper history of lesbian feminists and others making music and producing concerts and festivals addressed primarily toward lesbian audiences and consumers in the 1970s and decades following. This essay writes Black women into that history as performers and as "women's music" festival attendees. In *Songs in Black and Lavender*, I suggested that "women's music" is less a type of music than it is a site of women's thinking about music, a context for the enactment about lesbian, feminist politics and notions of community.[1] While the latter is true, in that these music festivals still attract lesbian and queer women predominantly, the wider political and social context for LGBT-related popular culture is significantly different from the cultural environment spawned three or more decades ago. While the differences between then and now cannot be overestimated, the first instance of obvious change is in the name used to describe this community organized under the umbrella of music. Although part of this essay relates Black women's early efforts to distance themselves from use of the moniker of "women's music" in favor of the term "women-identified," the latter term also fell out of circulation in lesbian/feminist political circles more than fifteen years ago. Therefore, I use the term "women's music," although it is instructive that the website for the Michigan Womyn's Music Festival (michfest.com) attributes no adjective to "music" when describing the festival on its web pages, thereby eschewing any identification of the music itself as "women's music." This is an indication of a new era in terms of lesbian and queer cultural politics. This phenomenon adds validity to musician Sue Fink's observation, later paraphrased, that there is no women's music—only women's music audiences.[2]

"Women's music" emerged in the early 1970s as part of a subculture of lesbian feminism. Proponents (Holly Near, Margie Adam, Chris Williamson, and Meg Christian, among others) described the emerging genre as "music by women, for women and about women."[3] As women's music festival historian Bonnie Morris writes, "For those women—lesbian, bisexual, and heterosexual—whose hearts responded to any message of women-identified music, the next challenge was learning how to produce and market albums outside male commercial confines."[4] Feminist musician–activists sought increased opportunities for women in rock and folk music performance, sound engineering, and concert production including lighting design. In short, they sought to carve out a professional–social space in which women could give voice to lesbian sensibilities through performance. The women-identified (or women's) music recording and distribution industry, controlled financially by women (Olivia Records was the first), became a focal point for the dissemination of this music.[5]

Understandably, even those feminist and/or Black activists engaged in movement practices from the 1970s to 1990s might not be familiar with the musical scenes this essay describes. Part of the reason lies in the contradictory nature of the enterprise itself. Writes Cynthia Lont, "Rather than directly confronting patriarchy, women's music for the most part ignored it, and by its very existence, created an alternative culture."[6] The alternative culture Lont describes was referred to as "cultural feminism," distinguished by its counterpart, radical feminism, in that cultural feminism was a countercultural movement based on traits associated with traditional notions of femaleness (e.g., nurturance, softness, politeness). Cultural feminism encompassed more than the values and behaviors, which were posed "in direct opposition to the hierarchical, competitive, aggressive, and violent male world view."[7]

Cultural feminism had conflicting consequences. Eventually, the movement came to involve goods, services, artistic and intellectual work, and other cultural elements. This meant that on the one hand, women gained unparalleled opportunities to experience *esprit de corps* with other women as they engaged in mutual support for their artistic and creative endeavors. On the other hand, the fact that cultural feminism was in part based on essentialist notions of women served to circumscribe and, later, contain the genre of women's music.

Women-only venues, such as women's music festivals held annually in the states of Illinois, Indiana, Ohio, Michigan, and, later, Mississippi, became privileged sites for the performance of this music. Historically, some festivals, such as the National Women's Music Festival (NWMF), were held on college campuses over four-day weekends that afforded attendees access to residence halls and other amenities of the university. Outdoor festivals, such as the six-day Michigan Womyn's Music Festival, take place on privately owned land, as did the Gulf Coast Women's Music Festival held in Ovett, Mississippi, many years ago. In previous years, workshops (on everything from "unlearning racism" to "car maintenance for women") were held in an attempt to raise and solve lesbian–feminist problems.[8] In order to be sensitive to a host of needs, organizers also provided vegetarian meals, access for disabled women, sign interpreters for the deaf, and sliding-scale entrance fees. These efforts at inclusion have a long history in communities that were organized around women's music.

Over the years, many argued that middle-class sensibilities permeated the festivals, although awareness of class issues waxed and waned; as Morris reminds us, personal camping gear, rainproof dome tents, down sleeping bags, and collapsible folding toilets all cost money.[9] The 2003 Wiminfest, a weekend women's music festival held in Albuquerque, New Mexico, offered consumers accommodations at an upscale city center hotel. Most festivals, however, took place at rented summer camp facilities, state parks, or rural ranches.[10] Although open to *all* women (and occasionally to men) the women's music festivals are produced, organized, and attended by a White lesbian majority and serve as in-gatherings for lesbian activists and musicians from across North America.[11]

Despite their relatively low numbers, Black women have played—and occupy an important niche—at women's music festivals. The highly acclaimed Black women's a cappella ensemble, Sweet Honey in the Rock, is by far the most well known and, historically, the first Black women's a cappella ensemble whose performances intersected nodes of the women's music network. Prominent Black musicians who have performed at women's music festivals include: Edwina Tyler, Odetta, Linda Tillery and the Cultural Heritage Choir, Judith Casselberry/J.U.C.A., Rashida Oji, In Process . . . , Deidre McCalla, Rachel Bagby, Laura Love, Toshi Reagon, Melanie DeMore, Vicki Randle, Ubaka Hill, The Washington Sisters, Mary Watkins, Pam Hall, Urban Bush Women, the late Gwen Avery, and Casselberry-DuPree—to name a few.

My aim is to insert the experiences of Black performers of "women's music" into the genealogy of African American music, addressing, in particular, issues of realness that arose in this sphere during the course of my research. During interviews, musicians discussed their performance of African American culture in a predominantly White lesbian social field, their commitment to feminist ideals, homophobia in Black communities, and their comfort level as artists who perform also in gender-inclusive environments. This constellation of issues, best characterized as the politics of authenticity in the women's music community, forms the basis of this discussion.

THE POLITICS OF NAMING

As mentioned earlier, the website of the Michigan Womyn's Music Festival ostensibly bypasses any efforts to characterize the music performed at the festival. In the past, there was no real agreement among supporters as to the definition of the term "women's music," nor did participants agree on the types of musical performances that were consistent with women's music ideals. In spite of the frequently voiced declaration that women's music is "music by, for, and about women," the term was enigmatic. Questions I posed at that time included: How does one differentiate women's music with its localized meanings from the broader rubric of "women in music" or, for that matter, "women and music"? The waters became muddier when we consider that even some musicians active in the first decade of the women's music network express disappointment that the network's roots in lesbian sensibilities could not be more publicly acknowledged. Black singer–percussionist Vicki Randle shared her thinking about proponents' formulation of the genre early on:

> Instead of defining "women's music" in the most obvious, confrontational and controversial way—as music by lesbians for lesbians, which would have been the most honest at the time—the spokeswomen for this movement tried to sidestep this overt declaration by attempting instead to define what "female-oriented" and "male-oriented" music was.[12]

Ultimately, this term reinforced the notion of the universal woman, ignoring the specific ways that female-gendered experiences—including those of lesbian feminists—were inflected by race and class. Many feminists, including feminists of color, began to refer to themselves and to their politics as "woman-identified," following Adrienne Rich's suggestion that same-sex bonds among women—heterosexual, bisexual, and lesbian—be established in a mutual "woman-focused vision."[13] Although for many women of color, the use of "women-identified" was offered as a corrective, Randle, in this interview, yearned for a greater acknowledgment of the genre's association with its lesbian consumer base.

It is perhaps difficult now to understand the relevance of the focus on "naming" the genre. One contributing factor is that African American women who began to affiliate with the women's music network brought with them a unique set of cultural values. Men, for example, were a necessary part of the African American cultural equation. In interviews, Black musicians and festival attendees (festigoers) shared with me their preference for the term "women-identified" as opposed to "women's" music. Black women and other women of color suggest that the term "women's music" evoked hearings of "(White) women's music," a universalized women's experience that was undifferentiated by race, class, nationality, and musical style. In contrast, the label "women-identified music" was held to be more inclusive. Toni Armstrong Jr., White feminist and former editor and co-founder of *HOT WIRE: Journal of Women's Music and Culture*, most aptly characterizes the thinking of Black festigoers and others about the term, "women-identified":

> Being women-identified may or may not have anything to do with being lesbian, but it's always focused on the female sensibility, and on relationships between females. The specific topic could be mothers and daughters and grandmothers, friends, sisters, the women's movement, lesbian love relationships, the love between women musicians, the relationship a woman has to the world at large, "the woman in your life is you," whatever. Being women-identified means by, for, and about women.[14]

Broad references for the term "woman-identified" as described by Armstrong, combined with common-sense understandings, provide a framework for understanding the occasional "collisions" I experienced during conversations with Black festival attendees about their favorite Black *women-identified* performers. For example, when I asked a Black lesbian festigoer to name her "favorite" Black women-identified artists, she responded: "Janet Jackson—oh, I'm sorry. That's not considered women's music. Ubaka Hill, the drumming."[15]

Clearly, the festigoer adjusted her response to meet what she thought were my expectations. Indeed, when told the subject of my research was Black performers of women-identified music, most interlocutors heard "Black women performers" instead. Therefore, a response of "Janet Jackson," a well-known, Black, popular music artist, is not surprising. Initially, this encounter led me to monitor my own assumptions that the women I interviewed would speak as cultural "insiders"—aficionados, if you will, of the women-identified music scene. Later, I realized that my consultant had indeed been functioning "bi-musically." Her response reflected her appreciation for both Black women in popular music and Black performers of women-identified music. Scholars argue that "the emergence of a strong lesbian/queer studies in the 1990s with its interrogation of sexual identity and a concomitant liberation movement has supplanted a concern with issues falling under the rubric of 'women-identified.'"[16]

SWEET HONEY IN THE ROCK

The involvement of women of color altered the political landscape as well as the soundscape of women's music. In 1977, the African American women's ensemble Sweet Honey in the Rock became the first Black ensemble whose performances intersected nodes of the women's music community. Founder and artistic director Bernice Johnson Reagon, an African American cultural historian, was leader of the ensemble.

The daughter of a Black Baptist minister, Bernice Reagon attained musical experience growing up in a region in southwest Georgia that had "developed a strong sacred-music singing tradition."[17] Reagon received her early political experience during the 1960s as a member of the Freedom Singers, a male/female a cappella ensemble that participated in the campaign for desegregation and voting rights in Albany, Georgia. Noting that by the time of the Albany desegregation movement, schisms had emerged between the various Civil Rights organizations,[18] historian Paula Giddings observes:

> It would take a special effort to keep the disparate elements of the Albany Movement together and SNCC [the Student Nonviolent Coordinating Committee] discovered a key to that unity. . . . Albany became known as a "singing movement" and it was the rich, darkly timbred voice of Bernice Reagon, an Albany State College student, who joined SNCC, that evoked the resonance of centuries-old memories and strength.[19]

Almost a decade later, Reagon conducted vocal workshops for the women and men of the D.C. Black Repertory Company, where she served as vocal director beginning in 1972.

Sweet Honey in the Rock emerged from one of Reagon's vocal workshops in 1973.[20] The ensemble had its first performance at a conference held at Howard University in November of that year and produced its first concert in 1974. Reagon writes that for that concert, Sweet Honey sang

> the full range of what would mark the group's performances, such as traditional songs like "No More Auction Block for Me," gospel songs like "Traveling Shoes," a blues medley of Jimmy Reed's "You got me runnin'/you got me hidin'; you got me runnin' hidin' hidin'/anyway you want it, let it roll," and "See See Rider," and songs depicting struggle, like Len Chandler's "I'm Going to Get My Baby out of Jail."[21]

After its formation as an ensemble, Sweet Honey in the Rock performed in racially integrated venues inclusive of women and men. The singers performed for predominantly Black audiences and also for racially diverse audiences at concerts held at churches, schools, theaters, folk festivals, and political rallies.

A significant event in the history of both Sweet Honey in the Rock and the women-identified music community was the collaboration of Sweet Honey with women's music founders, peace activist–singer–songwriter Holly Near, singer–songwriter Meg Christian, and Olivia Records. In 1977, Reagon, scheduled for a residency at the University of Santa Cruz, decided to launch a West Coast tour for Sweet Honey in the Rock. After anticipated funding sources failed to materialize, Sweet Honey agreed to collaborate in a recording with Olivia Records in exchange for financial support for the ensemble's tour. Although the Olivia activists were varied in sexual orientation, they described themselves as "political lesbians." This naming practice had been adopted by radical feminists across the nation. The appellation signified women's commitment to other women as a political entity. Thus, especially during the 1970s, heterosexual feminists frequently identified as "political lesbians." Reagon recalls that she found important congruencies between the Black Nationalist sentiments with which she was familiar and sentiments of the radical women's movement, to which she was introduced through Sweet Honey's West Coast tour.

This tour facilitated the ensemble's introduction to the "radical, separatist, White-women–dominated, lesbian cultural network in California," a network that differed radically from that which had nurtured the formation and development of Sweet Honey.[22] Conflicts highlighting both race and cultural differences arose between Sweet Honey in the Rock and the West Coast women-identified music community. "Many of these conflicts," Reagon writes,

> came from our being "people-identified" (which included men), rather than "women-identified." We were working in a community [California women's network] that excluded men. The communities we moved among did a lot of checking, they wanted to be sure that they protected themselves and that they were dealing with women-identified women. I think we came up short, but they took us in anyway.[23]

Reagon relates that another source of conflict was that early sponsors of the concert tour questioned the ensemble's collective identity as a feminist group, so much so that Sweet Honey's name was called into question:

> When we insisted on our name, Sweet Honey in the Rock, an ensemble of Black women singers, we were asked what was wrong with being called feminist. I would answer, "What is wrong with being a Black radical woman and calling your organization an ensemble of Black women singers?" I explained that our radicalness was rooted in our history and models, and that the words and phrases we used were used by our mothers and our mothers' mothers, and we wanted to always name that connection.[24]

According to Reagon, the character of that connection recalls the name of the ensemble that references "the legacy of African American women in the United States." Her father, she states, related to her a non-biblical parable about "a land that was so rich that when you cracked the rocks, honey would flow from them." Reagon compares the sturdiness of Black women to rocks and mountains and the sweetness of Black women to honey.[25]

Part of the subtext surrounding the conflict Sweet Honey experienced with members of the West Coast women's music community had to do with the perception, even among women-of-color activists such as Reagon, that the women's movement was foremost a vehicle for perpetuating the interests of "white middle-class women."[26] That this perception was widespread comes as no surprise. As a Black woman who had grown up with numerous strong African American role models who worked both inside and outside the home, Reagon relates, for example, that she did not immediately share the feminist call for women to become gainfully employed. What, then, inspired Reagon's political consciousness, already sensitive to racial issues, to become inflected with gender concerns? A turning point seems to have come when Joan Little, a Black woman in North Carolina, was arrested on a burglary conspiracy charge in 1974. The highly publicized case involving rape, retaliatory murder, and escape galvanized Black feminists and allies. Reagon composed "Joan Little" in response and the song became the first of Sweet Honey in the Rock's to be played on Black-oriented radio. Sweet Honey produced its first recording, self-titled, in the autumn of 1976.

In 1977, inspired by Sweet Honey in the Rock's experience with the radical women's movement, Reagon composed "Every Woman," the text of which calls for honoring the various roles women play in relationship to one another ("mother, sister, daughter, lover"). Reagon's penning of "Every Woman" coincided with the increased influence of religious conservatives in US politics. Anita Bryant, former pop singer and spokesperson for Florida's orange growers, led a campaign to repeal Dade County's nondiscrimination ordinance that included sexual orientation in its list of protected minorities in hiring and housing. A national boycott of orange juice followed; the song, celebrating the many ways that women love and bond was, as Reagon suggests, "important to that struggle."[27]

Reagon recollects that prior to the song's debut before Sweet Honey's East Coast–based, Black community audience in the spring of that year, she was concerned about its reception. Although she does not elaborate, perhaps it was the last verse that caused her the most anxiety: "Woke up this morning feeling fine/rolled over, kissed a friend of mine." Admittedly, the song's text is not particularly radical by today's standards; however, for a Black women's ensemble to perform such a song in the late 1970s before a gender-inclusive Black audience most certainly was a transgressive act. Sweet Honey performed "Every Woman" as part of its repertoire until 1985 when Reagon penned "Mae Frances" (which appears on their album *The Other Side* on Flying Fish records), a song which spoke to similar issues.

The ensemble continues to incorporate songs in its repertoire that advocate for respect and justice for women and same-sex partnerships. With its trenchant voicing of women's concerns through a wide range of African American musical genres, Sweet Honey has been described as providing a cultural "bridge" in musical style and thematic content between the aftermath of the Civil Rights Movement and the women's movement.[28] As Reagon states:

> To sing a Sweet Honey concert, it is necessary to sing songs in the nineteenth-century congregational style, as well as the performance styles required for arranged concert spirituals, quartet singing, early and classical gospel, jazz, West African traditional, rhythm and blues, and rap—all in the same evening.[29]

CONCURRENT ACTIVISM BY BLACK RADICAL FEMINISTS

African American women's critique of the universalization of White women's experience was manifest in the emergence of independent Black feminist organizations throughout the country. In addition to their perspectives on race and gender inequity, Black women who had been active in the "New Left" incorporated class analysis into their organizational framework. According to historian Sara Evans, the term "New Left politics" refers to the fusion of "the personal and moral optimism of the southern Civil Rights Movement with the cultural alienation of educated middle-class youth." Evans writes that "the intellectual mode that dominated the early years of the new left operated to exclude women as leaders, and only those with roots in an older left tradition ever thought to raise the 'women question' before the mid-sixties."[30] The National Black Feminist Organization (NBFO), founded in 1973, articulated the need for political, social, and economic equality especially for Black women. Within a year of its founding, the NBFO had a membership of 2,000 women in ten chapters; similar groups followed in its wake.[31] In 1974, members of the Boston chapter of the NBFO decided to form an independent group, the Combahee River Collective. In 1977, this small group of African American women outlined a Black feminist politic emphasizing the simultaneity of Black women's oppression as Blacks and as women.[32] Members of Combahee described themselves as "political lesbians."[33]

Implicit in the term "political lesbian" was a call for the eradication of homophobia and a rejection of lesbian separatism, because such a philosophy, *A Black Feminist Statement* reads, "leaves out far too many people, particularly black men, women, and children."[34] This stance is similar to the one taken by Sweet Honey in the Rock. Individuals within Combahee pursued multi-issue activist involvement in lesbian politics, abortion rights, and combating sterilization abuse. Whereas, for example, the mainstream feminist movement was concerned with securing a woman's rights to abortion, women of color faced the contrasting position of being targets of sterilization abuse. The mainstream women's movement was curiously silent about this form of abuse in the area of reproductive rights. On a national scale, the early commitment of Black lesbian feminists such as Margaret Sloan, Pat Parker, Audre Lorde, and Barbara Smith was crucial to building the movement in the 1970s. At the time, many heterosexual Black women were reluctant to identify themselves as feminists.[35]

In October 1978, the Combahee River Collective decided to "illuminate the specificity of the feminine" and to connect it to the constitution of "class, race and ethnicity," through sponsoring cultural [read: art, music, dance, film] events.[36] This resulted in Varied Voices of Black Women, a concert tour by Bay Area women-identified composer/pianist Mary Watkins, pianist/singer Gwen Avery, rhythm and blues/jazz vocalist and string bass player Linda Tillery, and poet Pat Parker.[37] The tour demonstrated that White lesbians were not the only ones creating a new women's culture: "Though the concert [tour] was first and foremost a celebration of Black lesbian feminist identity and culture, it was also an attempt to broaden the white feminist community's understanding of feminist and lesbian identity."[38] The Varied Voices of Black Women toured eight cities in the fall of 1978. This also was a watershed event in the history of women-identified music.

A CAPPELLA ENSEMBLES: EAST COAST AND WEST COAST EXAMPLES

The early collaboration of Sweet Honey in the Rock with Olivia Records and the Combahee Collective's sponsorship of the Varied Voices of Black Women tour, both of which took place in the late 1970s, left indelible legacies for Black women in women-identified music. In Process . . . and Linda Tillery and the Cultural Heritage Choir are just two of the groups that, in part, have followed the model of Sweet Honey in the Rock in bringing traditional African American music to the stage. Performances of both ensembles have intersected nodes of the women's music network. Tillery, an original member of the Varied Black Voices tour, routinely praises Bernice Johnson Reagon and Sweet Honey in the Rock for "keeping the flame of African American musical traditions alive." Performances of these a cappella ensembles provide an interesting pathway through which to examine the deployment of Blackness in women-identified music. For Black musicians and consumers, the performance of traditional African American music (a cappella) in women's music contexts is a powerful enactment of Black identity in a gendered frame.

In Process . . . is a seven-member a cappella ensemble in Washington, DC, founded by Bernice Reagon and Sweet Honey in the Rock. The ensemble emerged in 1981 from a vocal workshop Sweet Honey in the Rock held for local women interested in singing and activism. Founded by their need to be "grounded in their home community," the workshop was designed to train another "generation" in the singing of a cappella African American traditional music. Over the years, more than fifty African American women of different political, economic, and social backgrounds have embraced the opportunity to sing, learn, and share a space in the circle of Sweet Honey and In Process . . .[39]

A Sweet Honey workshop participant and early member of In Process . . . shared her introduction to the musical and philosophical sensibilities of the founding ensemble. While selecting songs for their first concert, In Process . . . asked if, in addition to the traditional repertoire of spirituals, hymns, and songs with political and social messages, the group could include songs from the rhythm and blues tradition. Their suggestions inadvertently included songs that Reagon determined contained sexist lyrics. Reagon's discussion of this issue with the group raised their consciousness about gender issues and other social concerns, and In Process . . . became more sensitive in their selection of rhythm and blues standards. They chose and juxtaposed rhythm and blues songs with themes of "good times" ("Dancing in the Street" by Martha & the Vandellas) and love ("In the Still of the Nite" by the Five Satins and "What's Your Name" by the Moments) with politically-oriented songs such as "Chile Your Waters Run Red Through Soweto" and "Abiyoyo"[40] for their first concert under the auspices of the Sweet Honey workshop.[41]

After years of a solo career in women-identified music, rhythm and blues/jazz vocalist and string bassist Linda Tillery established the Bay Area–based ensemble, the Cultural Heritage Choir (CHC) in 1991 (Figure 16.1). At present, the Cultural Heritage Choir is

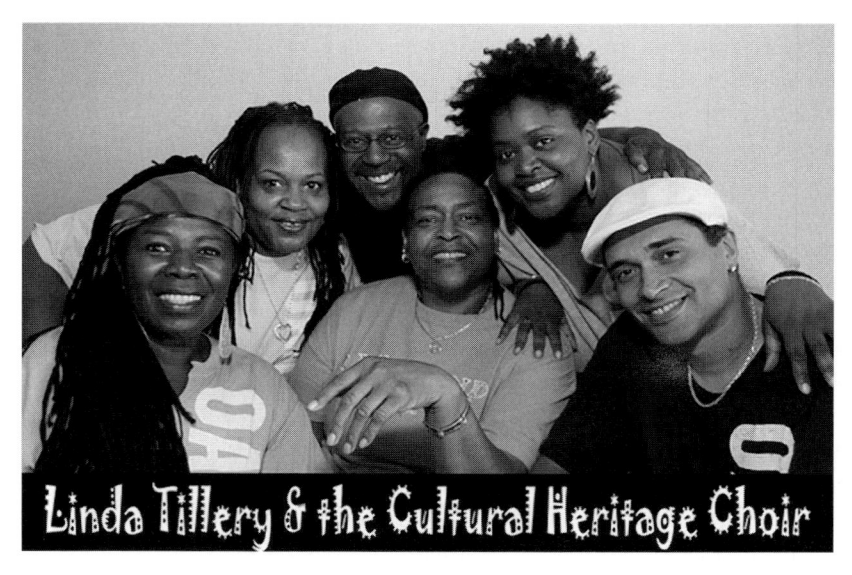

Figure 16.1
Linda Tillery and the Cultural Heritage Choir. Left to right: Elouise Burrell, Ronda Benin, Bryan Dyer, Linda Tillery, Valerie Troutt and Simon Monserrat (conga, percussion).

Photo by Johanna Resta. Courtesy Linda Tillery.

a sextet that includes two men. The ensemble sings primarily a cappella but is sometimes accompanied by harmonica and hand-held percussion instruments, including tambourine, calabash, and pounding stick. The ensemble's arrangements reflect a broad African American tradition that incorporates vocables and in which the voice is used to imitate the instrumental sounds of trombone, trumpet, bass guitar, and trap drum set. Perhaps the most renowned proponent of this practice is singer–composer Bobby McFerrin, with whom several Cultural Heritage Choir members have collaborated. Women's music festival audiences have been delighted by the CHC's vocal approximations of instruments, reminiscent of the style of Sweet Honey in the Rock. The Cultural Heritage Choir performs primarily music of the traditional African American repertoire including work songs, play songs, spirituals, moans, ring shouts, and other genres.

A cappella ensemble members describe their practice of drawing upon traditional African American repertoires as "following in the footsteps" of performers such as folksinger Odetta (1930–2008) and gospel innovator Mahalia Jackson (1912–1972). In bringing religious music to the secular and public stage, ensembles such as In Process . . . , the Cultural Heritage Choir, and Sweet Honey in the Rock have creatively adapted a performance legacy that extends back to the late nineteenth century.

Many African American women musicians interviewed for this study support feminist politics and refer to themselves as "keepers of culture."[42] Black women's a cappella ensembles mark gender concerns in a number of ways, including stage dress, musical style, performance presentation, and thematic content. For Black a cappella singers whose performances intersect nodes of the women's music network, the traditional African American repertoire plays a critical role in the affirmation of their identities as Black women.

THE POLITICS OF AUTHENTICITY: REPERTOIRE AND MUSICAL STYLE

The politics of authenticity take various forms in conversations that take place at women's music festivals. Issues of inclusion and exclusion have arisen as consumers make sense of festival concert rosters that accommodate numerous musical styles. Performances by Black women at festivals encompass a myriad of musical styles (e.g., blues, jazz, country, gospel, spirituals, neo-African drumming, Afro-Celtic). Musicians performing at women-only music festivals range from veteran Judith Casselberry and her band J.U.C.A. (Joy, Understanding, Creativity, Abundance) to groups such as New York's Mz. Fishe and the New Groove, or the South Africa–based The Mahotella Queens.

Diversity in terms of musical style and ethnicity emerges as a critical issue for music festival producers and audience members alike. Festival producers' attempts to diversify programming in terms of musical style and ethnicity means that concert rosters might include some musical acts that embody no obvious performances of lesbian—or, for that matter, women-identified—sensibilities. The backgrounds of The Mahotella Queens, and Mz. Fishe, for example, do not necessarily entail prior involvement in lesbian–feminist politics or a proclamation of lesbian or queer identity through song texts and gesture. Concert promoters have argued that, through performance, musicians such as the Grammy Award–winning Bulgarian Women's Choir (formerly known as the Bulgarian State Radio Women's Chorus), an ensemble specializing in "post-peasant" styles of singing (with traditional text), may transverse or transgress traditional gender boundaries in their home cultures (e.g., ethnic or national) and therefore warrant inclusion in concert rosters of women's music.

Critics and fans observe that women's music festival concert bookings reflect deep racial divisions; commentators submit that this is understandable given that racism permeates social relations among festival attendees. During the period I conducted research, many women of color and like-minded others observed that the musical style of many festival stage acts—that of solo singer accompanied by acoustic guitar—is characterized by the widely circulated (and yet routinely refuted) axiom "wgwg" ("White girl with guitar"). Black singer–percussionist Vicki Randle comments on the history of reception in women's music circles earlier on: "Types of music designated [acceptable] were generally anything soft and quiet: classical, folk music, a cappella vocals. Electric instruments, trap drums, horn sections, jazz, rock, funk, soul, gospel . . . were all considered male-oriented!" As a result, "women who had already broken through the stereotypes by playing electric bass, [electric] guitar, keyboards, horns, trap drums, playing loud dance music and rock, experimental jazz, were initially being told that their music was not affirming to women."[43] As Randle implies, and as I have stated elsewhere, proscriptions such as these contributed to the containment of the genre.[44]

Although women's music activists interviewed suggest that the women's music circuit always included a diverse profile in terms of both race and musical style, for many, the plethora of concert acts were consonant with the soundscape of the 1950s and 1960s folk music revival. For some, this provided evidence that women's music "had become firmly entrenched in what was, for the most part, a European tradition."[45] Ironically, the "wgwg" folk style, derived from post–World War II folk revival groups such as The Weavers, incorporates aesthetic influences of Black performers such as the American blues singer Leadbelly (Huddie Ledbetter). In the cultural politics of women-identified music, the "White" folk style, from which so many consumers sought to distance themselves, actually drew on Black traditions.

The inclusion of Black women performers in studies of women's music festivals necessarily expands the parameters of the genre as defined by earlier scholars, music festival audience members, and listeners.[46] A typology of songs by Black performers reveals a collective repertoire that can be categorized as: (a) songs with lesbian–feminist content; (b) songs concerning oppression–resistance of all types; and (c) songs reflecting Black women's cultural–political heritage (some of these songs, such as neo-African drumming performances, may not have texts).

Some song texts in the collective repertoire such as In Process . . .'s "Patchwork Quilt" or Casselberry-DuPree's "The Last Pioneers" express affiliation with lesbian–gay concerns. At the same time, "Patchwork Quilt," for example, reflects how Black women's involvement with issues such as AIDS transcends one-issue politics. (Songs about the latter reflect concern with the relationship between AIDS and "Africa" and AIDS and the rising number of "boarder babies" [infants who are born drug-dependent] in US urban centers.) "Africanness" is also performed by Black and other musicians at women's music festivals, a phenomenon that admittedly entails issues of cultural appropriation, authenticity, and music appreciation. Attended by predominantly White festigoers, neo-African drumming workshops by Ubaka Hill (Figure 16.2), B. "Wahru" Cleveland, and other artists are popular events in women-only venues. What is striking about the collective repertoire of Black women musicians is the extent to which performers use music to voice

Figure 16.2
Ubaka Hill, artist, percussionist, and master drum teacher.

Courtesy Ubaka Hill.

protest and social conflict. In performances of social criticism, pan-Africanity is evident in both musical style and thematic content; in the years leading up to the release of Nelson Mandela from prison, anti-apartheid songs are the most prevalent among those referencing Africa or the Diaspora.

RECEPTION

At the time of my research, proponents of women-identified music seemed guided in their assessments about the genre's boundaries by a set of symbolically significant features, few of which had to do with standard musical elements (e.g., harmony, melody, rhythm, etc.). Rather, according to festival attendees, extra-musical factors lent coherence to the myriad styles of women-identified music: feminism's concern with women's agency, the significance of women loving women, and the primacy of females in women's lives. My interactions with consumers of women-identified music revealed contested notions of what a woman-identified artist "should sound like" based on her race, cultural heritage, musical style, and acknowledged or rumored sexual identity. Performers, Black and White, often thwart expectations of audience members seeking "women-identifiedness" enacted on stage through mimesis, gesture, or sound. Black consumers, in particular, may likewise be surprised when performances by Black artists fall outside those genres generally thought to comprise the Black music canon.

Music, especially ideas about what constitutes "Black music," has played an integral role in debates about Black identity. Discussions of Black identity have acknowledged the paradox that arises as notions about Blackness, authenticity, and music coincide with and/or fuel essentialized assumptions about Black people. As Ronald Rodano writes:

> While the discourses of authenticity have obviously provided an important defense against a racist and oppressive culture and served in shaping African American collective memory, they have also continued to validate notions of difference that limits the extent of Black self-definition.[47]

During the course of my research, several musicians intimated (sometimes "off the record") that because their musical style falls outside of what is typically regarded as the parameters of "Black music" and because of their women-centered song texts, many Black men and women audience members have regarded them as "not Black enough" on the one hand and as "too lesbian" on the other. Concomitantly, Black performers shared that many White lesbian listeners have regarded them as being "not lesbian enough" and also as "too Black." Against the backdrop of the predominantly White lesbian social field of women's music, the question, "Is this (concert) act women-identified?" emerges frequently in conversation with festival attendees of all backgrounds. Again, the ambiguity of "women-identified" invites diverse and perhaps divergent associations ranging from "lesbian" to "sistah-friend."

These tendencies in critique revolve around the notion of an essential Black and/or lesbian subject. My interviews indicate that for many Black women, the experience of being a musician in the predominantly White lesbian field of women-identified music is one in which audience members may decide that a Black performer embodies no essences felt to be constitutive of either Black or lesbian identity. Interviews with Black women musicians and with music consumers about these same musicians illuminate Black women's experiences as they bridge two different interpretive communities, each of which is comprised of many factions.

To illustrate, I spoke with several audience members during and after a performance by Toshi Reagon (daughter of Sweet Honey's Bernice Reagon), a prominent Black singer–electric guitarist who has performed at numerous women's music festivals. Many audience members appreciated Reagon's socially concerned song texts emphasizing themes of justice and compassion for the homeless and for people with AIDS. Yet, a middle-aged White lesbian couple with whom I spoke reported being "put off" by what they described as Reagon's driving hard rock musical style, which they associated with "maleness." This assessment may seem odd (or at odds) with the many ways festival attendees enact their gender identities, including drawing heavily on male codes in dress, personal carriage, and language. An observer could not be blamed for asking if some consumers did not indeed have a double standard for gender sensibilities evoked through music performance and those evoked through the everyday life of the festival. Some festival attendees, for example, take advantage of the female-only environment to explore more of the full range of gender expression, often to an extent greater than they would in their home communities.

As for whether Reagon's performance was women-identified, some Black audience members maintained that, indeed, her performance fell under the rubric of "women's music." Another interviewee, a White festigoer, opined that Reagon's rendition was not a "Black" performance. My attempt to mention other Black rock guitarists (e.g., Jimi Hendrix) who performed in similar idioms did little to assuage her of that perception, perhaps because of the ambivalence that marked Hendrix's relationship with the Black music community. Another Black festival attendee also mentioned that Reagon's musical style disappointed her expectation for a "Black" performance.

Deidre McCalla, vocalist and acoustic guitar player, suggests that the music she performs, in a "singer/songwriter folk vein," does not typically appeal to a Black audience. As she points out, "The music people are drawn to isn't always connected to their ethnicity."[48] McCalla's attempt to adopt a non-essentialist stance in regard to her music, however, belies the presence of Black musicians historically, who have played in idioms associated with the folk music revival.

Providing a contrasting example, at least one Black composer I interviewed expressed her perception that occasionally the boundaries of inclusion and musical genre are "policed" by music consumers. The composer elaborated that "a lot of White women would not accept jazz from Black women, but would accept it from White composers and players," a phenomenon she found frustrating. The reflections of this composer, who also writes in classical idioms, suggest that the performer presumed to be extending boundaries for her "race" through genre selection accrues more symbolic capital in women-identified spheres.

The exchanges I have recounted illuminate the discursive space created when musicians such as In Process . . . or the Cultural Heritage Choir perform Blackness using identifiable repertoire and performance styles, some of which are rooted in Black church history, versus the discursive space created when musicians such as Toshi Reagon look to other traditions, which also have Black roots, as the source of their inspiration.

CONCLUSION

Predictably, observers of the women's music movement have pondered its future now that its "golden age" (roughly from the early 1970s to the late 1980s) has passed.[49] Observes Arlene Stein:

> The [mainstream pop music] terrain has shifted . . . from lesbian-identified music created in the context of lesbian institutions and communities to music that blandly emulates women's music, playing with signifiers like clothes and hairstyle in order to gain commercial acceptance, but never really identifying itself as lesbian.[50]

Ironically, Stein's sentiments would figure as new information for some of the Black festival attendees I interviewed, some of whom have attended women's music festivals only rather recently. Some, like Kay Young, look forward to the day when "black women in women's music will become more prominent as years go by. . . . Ten years from now, we could have a whole slew of artists in the mainstream."[51]

Regrettably, this is not the case. Singer/songwriter Deidre McCalla's observation speaks to the legacy and hopes of those who have been the most active in this musical sphere: "We've made the world safe for androgyny in the charts, but a few women musicians in the forefront is not what we wanted."[52]

Clearly, the limited consumer base for this music—including that for Black performers—is one of the determinants of its containment. Still, Black women performers and consumers play an important role in this evolving musical realm. Wittingly or unwittingly, the presence of Black women artists challenges the status quo in several ways. First, we are reminded that racial categories were (and are) insufficient in defining or determining musical style. Illuminating also is the tenacity of audience member perceptions that Black women's performances often fall outside the parameters most often associated with women's music festivals. While some Black women seek reinforcement of their collective identity through performance, others seek a space to define themselves as unique. This internal tension has always existed in African American culture. Beyond reclaiming herstories of Black performers of women's music and delineating "how they got over" in this predominantly White lesbian social field, women's music festivals become an even more fruitful area for investigation as lesbian and queer musicians perform their identities in regard to race, sexuality, and the politics of musical style.

ACKNOWLEDGMENTS

I am indebted to the editors for their editorial suggestions and encouragement, which facilitated the revision of this essay.

NOTES

1. Hayes 2010, 1
2. See Penelope and Wolfe 1993, 392–402.
3. See Armstrong 1989, 17.
4. Morris 1999, 3.
5. See Lont 1992, 245.
6. Ibid.
7. Kahn 1995, 5.
8. Faderman 1991, 222.
9. Morris 1999, 156.
10. Ibid., 5.
11. Ibid., 6.
12. Post 1997, 218.
13. Rich 1993.
14. See Kate Brandt's interview with Toni Armstrong in Armstrong 1993.
15. Interview by the author, with Kay Young, Michigan Womyn's Music Festival, 1995.
16. See https://purplesagefem.wordpress.com/2015/03/29/what-it-means-to-be-woman-identified-or-male-identified/ (accessed July 8, 2016); Darty and Potter 1984; Rich 1993.
17. Reagon 1993, 13.
18. See Giddings 1984, 282.
19. Ibid., 293.
20. Reagon 1993, 16.
21. Ibid., 18.

22. Ibid., 32. Sweet Honey members at this time included Bernice Johnson Reagon, Evelyn Maria Harris, Laura Sharp, and Yasmeen Williams.
23. Ibid., 32.
24. Ibid., 33.
25. Ibid., 33, 16.
26. Ibid., 28.
27. E-mail communication from Bernice Johnson Reagon to the author, January 5, 2004.
28. See Lont 1992, 245.
29. Reagon 1993, 34.
30. Evans 1979, 105.
31. Giddings 1984, citing Foner 1980, 489.
32. The collective published *A Black Feminist Statement* in Eisenstein 1979.
33. See Giddings 1984.
34. In Eisenstein 1979, 214.
35. See the introduction to Smith 1983.
36. Ibid.
37. Pat Parker died in 1989; Gwen Avery passed in 2014.
38. Kahn 1995, 7.
39. Reagon 1993, 323.
40. *Abiyoyo* is based on a South African lullaby and folk song popularized by Pete Seeger.
41. Anita Brown in Reagon 1993, 325.
42. Interviews conducted September 1999 through August 2000.
43. Post 1997, 218.
44. See Hayes 1999.
45. Stein 1995, 100.
46. See Petersen 1989; Robertson 1989.
47. Radano 2000, 84.
48. McCalla and Armstrong 1988, 5.
49. See Armstrong 1993; Stein 1993; Post 1997; Morris 1999.
50. Stein 1995, 106.
51. Interview by the author with Kay Young, Michigan Womyn's Music Festival, 1995.
52. Lont 1992, 252.

DISCOGRAPHY

Bulgarian Women's Choir. *Bulgarian Women's Choir: Live, Tour '93*. Globe/JARO 2400, 2005. CD.
Casselberry-DuPree. *Hot Corn in the Fire*. Ladyslipper 204, 2005. CD.
DeMore, Melanie. *Share My Song*. Originally recorded March 1992–June 1992. Redwood RR9203, 1994. CD.
Hill, Ubaka. *Shape Shifters*. Ladyslipper 116, 1995. CD.
———. *Dance the Spiral Dance*. Ladyslipper 118, 1998. CD.
———. *Beyond the Wind*. Splevine 1, 2006. CD.
In Process . . . *In Process . . . In Process . . .* , 2006. CD.
———. *Mission: Love*. In Process . . . , 2006. CD.
Mahotella Queens. *Reign & Shine*. African Cream/African Cream Music, BPP0938, 2007. Digital.
———. *Heart of Africa*. Reflections, 57947, 2012. CD.
McCalla, Deidre. *Everyday Heroes & Heroines*. Olivia Records OL 965, 1993. CD.
———. *With a Little Luck*. Olivia Records 953, 2001. CD.
———. *Playing for Keeps*. Maidenrock Records 3050, 2003. CD.
———. *Don't Doubt It*. Maidenrock Records deidre4, 2005. CD.
Mz. Fishe. *Mz. Fishe and the New Groove*. Mz. Fishe, 2005. CD.
Randle, Vicki. *Sleep City*. Wolf Moon Records, 65410, 2006. CD.
Reagon, Toshi. *The Righteous Ones*. Razor & Tie Entertainment 82839, 1999. CD.
Sweet Honey in the Rock. *Sweet Honey in the Rock*. Originally released 1976. Flying Fish FF 022, 1991. CD.
———. *Live at Carnegie Hall*. Flying Fish/New Rounder FF 70106, 1988. CD.

———. *Sacred Ground*. Earthbeat/Warner Bros. 42580, 1995. CD.
———. *Women Gather*. EarthBeat! 73829, 2003. CD.
———. *Raise Your Voice*. EarthBeat! 76422, 2005. CD.
———. *. . .Twenty-Five . . . .* Rykodisc, 2006. CD.
———. *Experience . . . 101*. Appleseed Records APRCD 1104, 2007. CD.
———. *Go in Grace*. She Rocks 5, 2010. Digital.
———. *Tribute: Live! Jazz at Lincoln Center*. Appleseed Records 1134, 2013. CD.
———. *#LoveInEvolution*. Appleseed Recordings/Red House APRCD 1140, 2015. CD.
Tillery, Linda, and the Cultural Heritage Choir. *Front Porch Music*. Rhino 72881, 1997. CD.
———. *Still We Sing, Still We Rise*. CHC 09, 2010. CD.
The Washington Sisters. *Understated*. Originally released 1987. Shsawa 221, 1997. CD.
———. *Take Two*. Originally released 1991. Ladyslipper SHS222, reissue date unknown. CD.

CHAPTER 17

African American Women and the Dynamics of Gender, Race, and Genre in Rock 'n' Roll

Maureen Mahon

RACE, GENDER, AND GENRE

Although the prevailing tendency is to associate rock music with White practitioners and audiences, Black women have had a continuous and influential presence in the genre since its inception in the 1950s. Attention to their participation challenges some of the fundamental assumptions about rock and African American women's cultural production. An understanding of the race, gender, and power dynamics of the music industry, particularly the race-based genre definitions and the industry's habitual marginalization of women, is necessary to appreciate the treacherous environment in which Black women were working to advance their creative vision. The tendency has been to view Black women in rock as anomalies,[1] but in this article I treat African American women as an inextricable part of rock and demonstrate that the form as we know it would not exist without them.

There are many familiar Black female contributions to rock. In 1956, Elvis Presley had a hit with his cover of Willie Mae "Big Mama" Thornton's "Hound Dog" (1953), borrowing Thornton's forceful vocal style and swagger to craft his rendition of the song. An African American woman named Dorothy La Bostrie wrote the lyrics for Little Richard's hit "Tutti Frutti" (1955). While on a UK tour with the Rolling Stones in the 1960s, Tina Turner taught Mick Jagger how to dance the Pony; he and singer Rod Stewart incorporated Turner's vocal style into their performances. In the years before they were writing their own material, the Beatles performed hits of Black American girl groups such as the Shirelles' "Baby It's You" (1962) and the Marvelettes' "Please Mr. Postman" (1961), infusing their presentation with girl group energy. In 1968, Janis Joplin and her band Big Brother and the Holding Company covered Big Mama Thornton's "Ball and Chain"; Joplin modeled her passionate vocal style and lyrical content on the patterns of Black women singers such as Thornton, Bessie Smith, Sippie Wallace, Billie Holiday, and

Etta James who were forthright about their desires and pains. Joplin acknowledged her debt to Black female musicians, inviting Thornton to play with her on occasional concert dates and helping to pay for a tombstone for Bessie Smith's grave.[2] In 1971, English rockers Led Zeppelin covered Memphis Minnie's "When the Levee Breaks." Memphis Minnie, a rare female instrumentalist working in the blues vernacular, developed a guitar style that, through her presence at the Chess Records studios in the 1950s, influenced Chuck Berry, among others.[3] Similarly, Sister Rosetta Tharpe, a mid-century gospel guitarist, willfully blurred the carefully guarded boundary between the sacred and the secular and approached her instrument with a level of showmanship that was echoed by rock 'n' rollers in the 1950s and 1960s.[4]

Black women were also reappropriating and refashioning, learning from those who had literally and figuratively learned from them. For example, Etta James and Tina Turner incorporated versions of songs written by White rockers into their repertoire. They made these songs their own by reinterpreting them in the rhythm and blues vernacular and stamping them with their personal style. James and Turner also toured the mainstream rock circuit with the Rolling Stones, gaining career-boosting exposure to White audiences. These processes of exchange draw attention to some of the factors that have influenced both Black American women's participation in contemporary popular music and the ways that participation is understood. That James and Turner were "crossing over" by performing rock reveals the rigidity of the racial boundaries that help define American music genres. Rhythm and blues, rock 'n' roll, and rock are distinct but closely intertwined styles. While there is much overlap in terms of musical form, lyrical content, and performance technique, there are also significant differences stemming from the aesthetic choices of the artists who made music and the racially conscious marketing decisions of the people who sold it.

In the 1950s, entrepreneurs who believed that rhythm and blues, the post–World War II sound popular with Black audiences, could potentially appeal to Whites sought ways to help the music "cross over" to the White pop market—especially to teenagers. Those promoting the work of the Black artists who originated rhythm and blues recognized that selling a Black form in the racially segregated United States would require adjustments. Cleveland disc jockey Alan Freed coined the term "rock 'n' roll" to describe the Black rhythm and blues he played on his radio show for a growing White teenage audience. Similarly, record producer Sam Phillips sought a White man with "the Negro sound and the Negro feel."[5] He eventually found Elvis Presley, a young White man who was able to project the energy and rhythmic vitality of rhythm and blues while avoiding the limitations of access and appeal that Black skin almost certainly guaranteed.

Rock 'n' roll advanced through the efforts of both Black and White artists, but in the beginning, the form's leading performers were African American rhythm and blues artists whose music was frequently relabeled "rock 'n' roll." Throughout the 1950s, these artists performed the same repertoire in concert settings that were alternately framed as "rhythm and blues" or "rock 'n' roll" depending on the whims of the promoters. The coexistence of the two labels and the slippage between them has more to do with marketing decisions and racial demographics than musical sound. The energetic performance styles, stylized clothing, playful lyrics, and rhythmic and melodic innovations of these rhythm and blues artists forever changed popular music, and these changes expanded and extended as White artists began to pick up the style. Even as rock 'n' roll began to feature more White artists, the genre remained rooted in African American music traditions; it drew heavily on the musical and vocal inflections, linguistic choices, and body movements of African American performers. Over the years, this Blackness has been recoded and naturalized as White rock 'n' roll attitude—a blend of the rebelliousness, sexuality, and cool that Black Americans often represent. This process enabled Black-identified rock 'n' roll of the 1950s to become White-identified "rock."[6] By the 1960s, White American and British youth had embraced rock 'n' roll and were supporting a network of White bands who drew from Black American blues, rhythm and blues, and rock 'n' roll and mixed these forms with other styles to create the music that by decade's end was known as "rock."

In 1967, a new magazine called *Rolling Stone* announced in an advertisement that "Rock & roll is more than just music, it is the energy of the new culture and youth revolution."[7] This link to the predominantly White youth counterculture of the late 1960s "Whitened" the music and the scene as did accompanying shifts in musical form and presentational aesthetics. The guitar had displaced the saxophone and piano, staples of late 1940s and early 1950s rhythm and blues; this change was set in motion by the innovations of Black rock 'n' roll guitarists like Chuck Berry and Bo Diddley. There was also an increasing acceptance of more rudimentary playing of instruments and an emphasis on what was viewed as authentic self-expression over the vocal and instrumental proficiency that had marked the rhythm and blues milieu. Concept albums replaced single records and social commentary and surrealism were heard alongside love and party lyrics. In rock 'n' roll, audiences and performers alike dressed down, mirroring the increasingly casual fashion trends of the mainstream and replacing rhythm and blues' emphasis on a polished stage show, sharply dressed stars, and impeccably turned-out audiences. Together, these forces distanced rock 'n' roll from its predominantly African American progenitors and early audience, creating a context in which the Black presence and contribution could more easily be forgotten.

Although rock has enabled experimentation with categories of race and sexuality, it is a sharply racialized and gendered terrain. The expression of rebellion against mainstream social constraints has been articulated from White, heterosexual male perspectives. For White men, rock is a platform for defining and performing masculinity, usually in the form of a cool persona that male fans want to be like and female fans want to be with. Prevalent now is the notion that a White man is the proper embodiment of a rock musician and, indeed, those who are not White and male have a difficult time winning acceptance as rock performers. Certainly, White women "in rock" and Black men "in rock" have to participate in race and gender negotiations as they confront rock's White male–dominated scene. For Black women rockers, the challenges increase exponentially. Their gender and race mark them as doubly outside of rock 'n' roll's White male network. Like White women, they are viewed as intruding in male space, and like Black men they are considered to be treading on White territory. As Black women, they have had to fight for recognition and respect as legitimate rock performers. Much of the time, they are overlooked even though they have always been an essential part of the mix.

FOUNDATIONAL FIGURES

When foundational artists like Ruth Brown, LaVern Baker, Etta James (Figure 17.1), and Tina Turner started to perform in the 1950s, they were confined to the segregated rhythm and blues circuit and played to predominantly Black audiences. Their sounds,

Figure 17.1
R&B singer Etta James recording at Fame Studios, circa 1967, in Muscle Shoals, Alabama.
Credit: House of Fame LLC. Photo by House Of Fame LLC/Michael Ochs Archive/Getty Images.

styles, and attitudes shaped rhythm and blues, helped define rock 'n' roll, and continue to reverberate in rock.

Like many of the Black women who have participated in commercial popular music over the years, Ruth Brown began singing in the church, but switched to a secular repertoire. Her voice was compelling enough to win contests, secure performance dates, and attract the interest of Ahmet Ertegun and Herb Abramson, who were launching their independent label Atlantic Records. Once it was time to record Brown, however, her producers were at a loss as to how to best exploit her talent.[8] Eventually, and against Brown's wishes, they focused on a style that took her away from the ballads she preferred to sing and had her record songs that Brown describes as being "different rhythmically from what I was into" and as being "a step ahead of the accepted sound of the day."[9]

This new rhythm, which had been created by African American songwriter and arranger Jesse Stone, and Brown's approach to it, turned out to be the keys to chart success.[10] Starting in October 1950 with "So Long," Brown released a string of songs for Atlantic that climbed *Billboard* magazine's rhythm and blues chart. During the early 1950s, the newly dubbed "Miss Rhythm" enjoyed consistent chart and touring success. She quickly became one of the most influential figures in the developing rhythm and blues genre and one of the principal architects of rock 'n' roll. Her distinctive squeal shaped the sound that a generation of Americans grew up listening to. Little Richard credits Brown with influencing his inflection. Referring to one of his most popular songs, he explains, "This thing you hear me do— 'Lucille-*uh*'—I got that from Ruth Brown. I used to like the way she'd sing 'Mama-*uh*, He Treats Your Daughter Mean.' I put it all together."[11] In 1953, the readers of *DownBeat* magazine voted "Mama" the top rhythm and blues record of the year.

Brown also made an impression on Etta James, another rhythm and blues artist who was part of the growing rock 'n' roll scene. James regarded Brown as

> just too cool. . . . She had all the moves. She wore heavy makeup with painted cat eyes and dark extended eyelashes aimed up to the sky and turned-down lips and Mexican kiss curls plastered on the side of her face.[12]

James also admired Brown's onstage presentation. In James's estimation, Brown "was cute and sassy at the same time" and she knew how to work the stage.[13] Archival footage of Brown singing "Mama" in the mid-1950s shows her alternating between a pout and a playful smile, as she explains to her mother the attraction and frustration she feels toward a man whom she can't satisfy. Playing her tambourine near the side of her head and at the side of her hip with a series of smacks of the hand, she sings the jumping rhythm in a mellow voice with occasional eruptions of her signature squeal.[14] This kind of show-womanship, an inextricable part of the rock 'n' roll package, has its roots in performance practices developed and refined on the rhythm and blues circuit.

In her autobiography, Brown recalls the care she took in choosing her outfits and the importance of arriving on stage in a stunning dress. In the same archival footage, she is wearing one of the elegant gowns for which she was well known, strappy sandals, and has perfectly arranged hair and makeup. The image is black and white, but in her autobiography Brown describes the rainbow of color that was her wardrobe's trademark. On at least one occasion, she dyed her hair red to match her gown. The audience on the rhythm and blues circuit expected that performers would be impeccably attired—the audience itself was well dressed—and one mark of a good show was the artist's sartorial splendor.[15] Both Ruth Brown and Etta James acknowledge their debt to the gay male and transvestite friends who helped them with their makeup, hair, and clothing. These men deployed a level of theatricality and exaggeration that was invaluable to artists seeking to distinguish themselves onstage in a growing field of performers.

Determined to make a forceful statement about her personality, the young Etta James created a singular image. Taking advantage of her light brown complexion and working under the advice of her gay male friends, she presented herself as "an outrageous blonde," cultivating a defiant look with a "sleazy edge."[16] With her impish smile, blonde hair, and dark eyebrows, Etta James created a "bad girl" look. She recalls:

> I wanted to be rare, I wanted to be noticed, I wanted to be glamorous, I wanted to be exotic as a Cotton Club chorus girl, and I wanted to be obvious as the most flamboyant hooker on the street. I just wanted to *be*.[17]

James also had a "bad girl" sound. Born Jamesetta Hawkins, she was renamed Etta James by the well-known Los Angeles bandleader Johnny Otis, whom she met in 1952 when she was fourteen years old. In her first recordings, her subject matter and style of delivery were anything but innocent. "Roll with Me, Henry," a song James wrote as an answer to Hank Ballard and the Midnighters' suggestive 1954 hit "Work with Me, Annie," contains many of the essential ingredients of rock 'n' roll: playful innuendo, sexuality, and outrageousness. James's original title was deemed too racy and the song was released as "The Wallflower" in 1955. Although James has explained that the rolling she refers to in the song meant dancing, throughout her career she has joyfully been "raunchy" in terms of subject matter and bodily movements, highlighting her sexuality and departing from proper mainstream femininity.[18] James has said that she wanted access to a full range of expression and fashioned herself after male singers because she found the dominant female styles of singing too constricting.[19] The sound and image that she projected differed from the other women on the scene in the mid-1950s, and her tough, sexy, and cool persona provided a prototype for the "rock chick," one of the iconic forms of rock 'n' roll femininity.

Working with a rhythm and blues repertoire, LaVern Baker recorded hit records, performed her songs on television and in film, and was a fixture on the blockbuster rock 'n' roll concert circuit that brought the new music to teenage audiences around the United States. Baker started out singing blues and pop in the clubs of Chicago and Detroit under the name Little Miss Sharecropper in the late 1940s. In 1953, she signed to Atlantic Records, becoming a label mate of Ruth Brown's. Like Brown, she was guided to the new, heavy rhythm for which Atlantic was becoming known. Ultimately, she had greater chart success than Brown, recording songs that did well on both the pop and R&B charts. Her hits "Tweedlee Dee" (1954), "Jim Dandy" (1955), and "I Cried a Tear" (1958) broke into the Top 20 pop charts, marking a rare success for an African American rhythm and blues singer during this period. Baker's presence on the pop charts was undercut by the release of covers of songs she had originated, but she offset this displacement through her presence on New York City–based rock 'n' roll concerts organized by Alan Freed, one of her main advocates, and her participation in national rock 'n' roll tours. As one of the headliners on Irvin Feld's "The Biggest Show of Stars" tours that traversed the United States during 1956, 1957, and 1958, Baker was among the artists who first brought live rhythm and blues to rock 'n' roll audiences. She appeared alongside a predominantly Black contingent of artists that included Fats Domino, Bo Diddley, Chuck Berry, the Platters, Big Joe Turner, and Frankie Lymon and the Teenagers as well as White artists such as Bill Haley and His Comets and the Everly Brothers. One of the only women artists in the early rock 'n' roll scene and a Rock 'n' Roll Hall of Fame inductee in 1991, Baker's undeniable presence in the music industry has not translated to a high level of visibility for her in histories of the genre. Perhaps the combination of her elegant appearance (she usually wore evening gowns when she performed), the categorization (and dismissal) of her hits "Tweedlee Dee," "Jim Dandy," and "Bop-Ting-A-Ling" (1955) as "novelty songs," and her race and gender, have made it difficult to see her as a player in the rock 'n' roll field.

In contrast, Tina Turner, who, with Ike Turner, was inducted into the Rock 'n' Roll Hall of Fame in the same year as Baker, has a widely recognized connection to rock and is a hard-to-challenge contender for title of the Queen of Rock. With a career spanning the 1960s, 1970s, 1980s, and 1990s, Turner's longevity is remarkable for any performer in pop music, a medium built on planned obsolescence. Born Anna Mae Bullock and renamed Tina Turner by bandleader Ike Turner even before they married, she began to sing in the gritty, sexy rhythm and blues style for which she has become famous. Her short skirts and high heels accentuated her fabulous legs and helped her create a sexually enticing onstage persona. Wigs—a solution to a catastrophic attempt to go blonde—enabled her and her female backup singers, the Ikettes, to have long, straight, swingable hair that added to the performance electricity. With their strutting, stomping, shimmying dance steps, Turner and the Ikettes put on a show that competed with that of the masterful James Brown. Turner also stood out because of her vocal approach. She has stated that she never had what she calls a "girl's voice," and many commentators have characterized her phrasing and delivery as being similar to that of a man.[20] It is important to note that Turner was following in the tradition of African American women vocalists like Bessie Smith, Sister Rosetta Tharpe, and Big Mama Thornton who used a forceful or "shouting" vocal style that went beyond what were widely perceived as acceptable modes of female expression. Whether she was singing Ike Turner's "Fool in Love" (1960) or Credence Clearwater Revival's "Proud Mary" (1971), playing the Acid Queen in the film of The Who's *Tommy* (1975), or working with producer Phil Spector on "River Deep, Mountain High" (1966), Turner used her relatively low voice to excellent effect and approached her material with an arresting intensity, taking possession of the songs she performed.

Following her 1976 divorce from Ike, Turner launched a solo career; White male rockers and music industry professionals who revered her artistry assisted her on this path.[21] Managed by Roger Davies who encouraged her to emphasize her rock bona fides, Turner appeared with the Rolling Stones and Rod Stewart on their blockbuster tours of the early 1980s. British pop producers Ian Craig Marsh and Martyn Ware, of the new wave band Heaven 17, invited Turner to work with them on a remake of the Temptations' classic "Ball of Confusion." The single's success in Europe led to the album project *Private Dancer*, on which ex-Yardbird Jeff Beck played guitar and to which Mark Knopfler of Dire Straits contributed the title track. Rooted in the electronic pop sound of early 1980s new wave, the album's single "What's Love Got to Do with It?" was an anti-romantic anthem distinguished by Turner's compelling vocals. Always a visual artist, she sold the song in part through a music video that the new and influential music television station MTV put into heavy rotation, introducing her to a new generation of fans. *Private Dancer* took Turner well beyond the rhythm and blues audience that the Ike and Tina Turner Revue had served. She now had the ear of the pop and rock audience, enabling her to sell ten million albums, receive top Grammy awards, mount a record-breaking international tour, and escape the racially segregated rhythm and blues box.

RACIALIZED POLITICAL ECONOMY

The intersection of race and economics, what I have elsewhere called the "racialized political economy" of the US recording industry, played a decisive role in the careers of early rock 'n' rollers and continues to shape the experiences of African American women working in popular music.[22] The financial practices of the industry put recording artists at an economic disadvantage, even when they were earning money for their labels. For example, Ruth Brown contributed significantly to the rise of Atlantic Records. She recorded the young label's first #1 hit and Atlantic is commonly referred to as "The House that Ruth Built." But Brown received comparatively little financial recompense from Atlantic.[23] Like most other rhythm and blues artists, and indeed many White artists, working during this period, Brown was paid a standard flat rate for recording; she was also billed for studio costs and musicians' fees. This system essentially charged performers to make the records that the labels sold and profited from. Rhythm and blues artists in this period made their money through touring, an enterprise that they had to manage and support on their own.[24] Although artists were due royalties once the sale of their records turned a profit, labels often used methods of accounting that shortchanged the artists. Furthermore, some label executives took advantage of working-class Black performers who were often not well educated, did not know the details of the laws of copyright, and did not understand the value of holding on to their publishing rights when they recorded songs they had written. Most of the early R&B women vocalists did not compose their own material and were ineligible for publishing monies.

This widespread situation, which enriched record label executives while leaving the artists uncompensated for their work, was finally addressed in the 1980s when Brown brought a suit against Atlantic Records for unpaid royalties. Chagrined that Ertegun had sold the label for $17 million in the late 1960s, Brown assumed that she was due something, especially because she had received only a handful of royalty checks in the thirty years since she had recorded for Atlantic even though her records continued to sell in the United States and internationally. By adding other Black rhythm and blues artists to the suit, the case revealed the level of exploitation at play during the early years of rock 'n' roll. In addition to spearheading this important legal battle—one she ultimately won—Brown co-founded the Rhythm and Blues Foundation in 1988, an organization dedicated to providing financial support to the musicians who had created rhythm and blues but who had never enjoyed financial compensation commensurate with their contribution to a groundbreaking and influential musical form.[25]

In addition to the industry's economic structure, the racial politics of post–World War II America affected the careers of the early Black rhythm and blues performers. Although this was a period of musical miscegenation and cross-racial listening, with White teenagers being exposed to Black popular music through radio, the prevailing social and political force in the country was segregation. But for a handful of exceptions, Black artists worked in a Black rhythm and blues market that was separate from and, in terms of financial resources and earning potential, unequal to the mainstream White pop music market. General market and later Top 40 radio stations rarely played Black rhythm and blues—although some sponsored a few weekly hours of programming targeted to Black audiences.

Billboard based its pop chart on mainstream radio playlists, while its rhythm and blues chart was based on the records played on the tiny number of stations that served Black audiences. Black rhythm and blues artists struggled to have songs "crossover" to the pop chart. This was a relatively rare occurrence, largely because in order to compete with the onslaught of independently produced Black rhythm and blues, the major labels used contracted White pop singers to record "cover" versions of songs recently released by Black rhythm and blues artists. Performed by White "Suzy Creamcheese" singers, as Etta James disparagingly calls them, these sanitized copies used the same musical arrangements as the originals, but eliminated suggestive lyrics and smoothed the vocals, avoiding the rough timbre associated with R&B vocal style; this muted the audible Blackness and created a version presumed to be more palatable to White audiences. Because the performance of a song is not copyrighted, White artists could copy a Black artist's phrasing and arrangements without owing the Black originator anything. LaVern Baker, whose version of "Tweedlee Dee" was covered by White pop singer Georgia Gibbs, addressed this issue by appealing to her congressman: "Since there is no court to uphold my right," she wrote in 1955,

> . . . maybe my plea for protection will merit some attention from you. After an investigation of the facts you might see some wisdom in introducing a law to make it illegal for one singer to duplicate another's work. It's not that I mind anyone singing a song that I write, or have written for me by someone, but I bitterly resent their arrogance in thefting my music note-for-note.[26]

Cover recordings were promoted and distributed through the far-reaching networks of the major labels, undercutting the versions released by Black artists on comparatively small and resource-limited independent labels. Even covers that added an element of originality, say Elvis Presley's take on Big Mama Thornton's "Hound Dog," followed the dynamic of having a White artist benefit in terms of popularity and earnings by borrowing from Black creativity, and leaving the Black artist uncredited and uncompensated. Furthermore, Black artists did not receive invitations to perform on network television programs, limiting their ability to popularize their music. These forms of racialized marginalization were a sore point for an artist like Ruth Brown who was on the scene a few years before Black performers began to crossover to White audiences. "Throughout my biggest hit-making period," she explains,

> I was forced to stand by as White singers like Georgia Gibbs and Patti Page duplicated my records note for note and were able to plug them on top television shows like *The Ed Sullivan Show*, to which I had no access.[27]

As an early popularizer, Brown paved the way for Little Richard, Chuck Berry, Bo Diddley, and LaVern Baker, who later were able to perform on the mainstream television programs where rock 'n' roll was being promoted. Brown stressed that the primary difference between rock 'n' roll and rhythm and blues had less to do with musical form and more to do with the racial identities of the audience and performer:

> When they called it rock 'n' roll it was only rhythm and blues now being done by white kids and accepted and danced to and being played on the Top 100 and the Top 10 stations. That's all it was. A change in the rhythm pattern, the tempos were upped a little bit, became a little more brassy, a little louder, but it was rhythm and blues. You know. Like Fats Domino said, "I had been singing rock 'n' roll 15 years before they started calling it that." It was rhythm and blues and it still is.[28]

The racialized genres, the segregation of radio stations and music charts, and the practice of covers marginalized African American artists from rock 'n' roll, denying them recognition and compensation for their contributions to the form they had originated.

THE GIRL GROUPS: CARRYING THE TORCH

By the late 1950s, the most prominent male rockers had gone underground: Elvis Presley was in the army, Jerry Lee Lewis was ostracized by the press for marrying his fourteen-year-old cousin, Little Richard had returned to the church, and Chuck Berry had been arrested on charges that he had violated the Mann Act. Between 1957, when the all-female ensemble the Bobettes released "Mr. Love," and 1964, when British bands began to take over the US music charts, "girl groups" were the standard-bearers for rock 'n' roll. The majority of these all-female vocal groups, particularly the ones that made an impact on the charts and the music scene, were Black and their sound was rooted in R&B vocal group style. In fact, it was an African American female group, the Supremes, who posed the only significant challenge to the Beatles, the leaders of the British Invasion that displaced American artists from the top of the pop charts in the mid-1960s. So named because most of their members were teenagers when they started recording, girl groups presented "the first major rock style associated explicitly with women."[29] The roots of girl group music are in the close harmonies of Black gospel vocal quartets and the secular form they influenced, the 1950s doo-wop groups. As fans of Frankie Lymon, the thirteen-year-old lead vocalist of The Teenagers and one of the most popular doo-wop artists of the late 1950s, most girl group members learned to sing rhythm and blues by imitating Lymon's 1956 hit "Why Do Fools Fall in Love?" The Chantels, whose 1958 single "Maybe" is an archetype of girl group music, launched the genre; they were followed by the Shirelles, the Crystals, the Ronettes, Patti LaBelle & the Bluebelles, the Marvelettes, the Supremes, the Chiffons, the Shangri-Las, and many others.

The Shirelles were the first girl group to achieve major pop chart success. Doris Cole, Addie "Micki" Harris, Beverly Lee, and Shirley Owens (who sang lead on most of the group's hit singles), formed their group when they were still high school students; they signed a recording contract with Florence Greenberg in 1958. By December 1960, the quartet from Passaic, New Jersey, had scored a #1 pop hit with "Will You Love Me Tomorrow," the first hit for Greenberg's label Scepter Records. The chart success of a song in which a teenage girl wonders about the repercussions of giving in to her boyfriend's pleas for sex and her own desires, launched a new sound, feel, and attitude in rock 'n' roll. For the first time, the voices and preoccupations of girls and young women were at the center of the music. Once the Shirelles had demonstrated the sales potential of all-female vocal ensembles, recording executives sought them out, creating a critical mass of girl groups on the airwaves. Many of the girl group songs fused the energy and youth focus of rock 'n' roll, rhythm and blues–derived vocal arrangements, and Broadway and Tin Pan Alley–inspired compositions and orchestrations provided by White professional songwriters and arrangers. The resulting music offered a measure of sophistication that differed from the bare bones approach of much 1950s era rock 'n' roll. In fact, this sonic approach eased the crossover of Black artists—significantly, young, relatively unthreatening women—to White audiences. The Shirelles became one of pop music's top acts, following up the success of their first hit, which sold more than

Figure 17.2
The Ronettes, circa 1965.
Photo by Hulton Archive/Getty Images.

nine million records,[30] with a string of successful singles that included "Dedicated to the One I Love" (1961), "Mama Said" (1961), "Baby, It's You" (1962), a Top Ten hit on both the pop and R&B charts, and "Soldier Boy" (1962), a #1 pop hit and their biggest selling record.

While most of the girl groups projected a "good girl" image, the Ronettes (Figure 17.2)—like the White group the Shangri-Las—stood for something a little more daring. Sisters Veronica and Estelle Bennett and their cousin Nedra Talley formed the group when they were New York City high school students in 1960. They began their career singing at sock hops and bar mitzvahs but made a name for themselves as dancers. By applying prodigious amounts of makeup, stuffing their bras, and donning form-fitting dresses, they were able to appear old enough to get into New York's Peppermint Lounge, then one of the city's hottest clubs, even though they were underage.[31]

They were eventually hired to dance in the club, quickly became a celebrated fixture, and were soon on the path that led them to work with the brilliant and eccentric White rock 'n' roll producer, Phil Spector. "Be My Baby" (1963) was the Ronettes' first song with Spector and their most successful release; their other hits, arriving as the girl group era was on the wane, included "Baby I Love You" (1964) and "Walking in the Rain" (1965). Veronica Bennett married Spector in 1968; though they divorced in 1974, she uses Ronnie Spector as her professional name.

Ronnie Spector's voice possessed a unique blend of girlishness and strength. She sang with a compelling vibrato, great emotion, and considerable volume. Hers was an ideal teenage voice, one that somehow conveyed both innocence and sexy confidence. Phil Spector helped secure his status as a central rock 'n' roll innovator by placing that voice against his "wall of sound," the thick and echoey layering of horns, strings, guitars, pianos, percussion, and vocals that stamped the records he made with his musical signature. He perfected this technique through his recordings of African American women singers such as the Ronettes, the Crystals, Darlene Love, and Tina Turner, all of whom had the vocal drama and power to stand out against the loud instrumentation.

The vocal sound and visual style of the Ronettes continued the tough-girl image that Etta James had pioneered. Borrowing from the street culture of the Spanish Harlem neighborhood where they were raised, they teased their long hair, piled on their makeup, and tightened their clothes. In her autobiography, Spector recounts:

> When the audience started responding to our street look, we played along. The songs we sang were already tougher than the stuff the other groups did. While the Shirelles sang about their "Soldier Boy," we were telling the guys, "Turn on Your Love Light." We weren't afraid to be hot. That was our gimmick. When we saw the Shirelles walk onstage with their wide party dresses, we went in the opposite direction and squeezed our bodies into the tightest skirts we could find.[32]

The Ronettes' physical appearance might have added to their appeal. The products of interracial marriages, they left many audience members confused and intrigued by their light complexions and heavy eye makeup—"Are they Spanish . . . or Chinese?" was a common question.[33] Although they were of African descent, they did not look like the brown-skinned members of the other girl groups; they were visibly mixed people performing an audibly mixed form.

In her autobiography, Spector asserts her status as a rock 'n' roller, reiterating the fact that the Ronettes were one of the primary American rock 'n' roll acts of their day. In 1964, the Rolling Stones, then an up-and-coming band, opened for the Ronettes during a British tour; that same year, the Ronettes toured with the Beatles on the English group's first US tour. Spector's self-consciousness about stating her rock 'n' roll credentials may stem from an awareness that as a Black woman, her presence and contribution could easily be erased from a form that, by the 1990s, was widely perceived as White. As critics such as Donna Gaines and Jacqueline Warwick have pointed out, the Ronettes, the Shirelles, and the other girl groups had a more important influence on rock 'n' roll than is usually credited.[34] Their bittersweet harmonies and youthful vocals reverberate in 1970s punk, 1980s and 1990s alternative music, and indie rock of the first decade of the 2000s. Guitar-centered bands who wrote the material they performed became the prototype for rock 'n' roll starting in the mid-1960s. Girl groups, vocal ensembles whose members neither played instruments nor wrote the songs they sang, are often marginalized in accounts of the music's history even though in the early 1960s they were the heart and soul of rock 'n' roll.

THE BLACK BACKUPS

During the late 1960s and early 1970s, African American women had a muted but important presence in rock 'n' roll as backup singers.[35] In her history of women in rock, Gerri Hirshey describes the backup singer as "the Unknown Stalwart of rock and roll" and asserts, "without her, there would be no rock and roll."[36] Never officially members of the band, Black women such as Carolyn and Erma Franklin (Aretha Franklin's sisters), P. P. Arnold, Patti Austin, Madeline Bell, Merry Clayton, Venetta Fields, Gloria Jones, Clydie King, Claudia Lennear, Darlene Love, Minnie Ripperton, Doris Troy, and Dee Dee Warwick, lent their vocal authority to the concert performances and studio recordings of White and Black artists working in rock, rhythm and blues, pop, blues, and folk. A towering example is the Sweet Inspirations, the backup group whose members Cissy Houston, Myrna Smith, Sylvia Shemwell, and Estelle Brown comprised the house backup group for Atlantic Records during the mid-1960s. In addition to singing behind the Drifters, Wilson Pickett, Solomon Burke, Esther Phillips, and Aretha Franklin, they released recordings under their own name ("Sweet Inspiration" [1968] was their biggest hit) and in 1968 became an opening act and backup group for Elvis Presley, who was launching a comeback.

During the 1970s, Merry Clayton was one of the busiest and best-known background singers. A partial list of the artists with whom she has recorded reveals just how pervasive Black women's presence in the genre has been. Clayton is best known for contributing the gripping backup vocal to the Rolling Stones' song "Gimme Shelter" (1969), but she also appears on Carole King's *Tapestry* (1971), five Joe Cocker albums including *With a Little Help from My Friends* (1970) and *I Can Stand a Little Rain* (1974), and recordings by B. B. King, Buffalo Springfield, Leon Russell, Jerry Garcia, Lynyrd Skynyrd, Neil Young, Paul Butterfield Blues Band, Phil Ochs, Rare Earth, and Tina Turner. Clayton sang on the Rolling Stones' albums *Let It Bleed* (1969) and *Exile on Main Street* (1972)—that's her uncredited vocal on "Tumbling Dice"—and she contributed three songs to Mick Jagger's soundtrack for the film *Performance* (1970). She was also the original Acid Queen in the London Symphony Orchestra's 1969 live performance of The Who's rock opera *Tommy*.

Whether the performers were Black or White, the backups helped to deliver "soulful flavor" that derived directly from the gospel vocal style which they had all grown up singing. These women supported the lead vocalist without overshadowing him or her. Professionals, they could be depended on to hit all the notes, even in complicated arrangements; often, they created the vocal arrangements they performed. Many White rockers strategically deployed audible Blackness, sometimes doing their own versions of Black vocals; frequently, though, they achieved or intensified their desired sound through the incorporation of Black female backup singers. In the late 1960s and 1970s, White rock acts such as David Bowie, Joe Cocker, Bob Dylan, Humble Pie, Lynyrd Skynrd, Pink Floyd, the Rolling Stones, Bob Seger, the Small Faces, Steely Dan, Elton John, T-Rex, and Neil Young recorded and performed in concert with Black women vocalists. When contributing to a song, Black women backup singers did their job without calling attention to themselves, but working in the background, they carved an uncontested place for themselves in rock.

OUTRAGEOUS WOMEN: BREAKING OUT OF THE BOX

As the 1960s gave way to a new decade, African American women performers tapped into the zeitgeist of racial, gender, and sexual liberation, added their own spin, and produced notably forward-looking rock 'n' roll performances. The group LaBelle and the solo artist Betty Davis are two exemplars of this spirit. Both were innovators in terms of musical and lyrical content and onstage presentation. Notably, their departures from the strictures of mainstream Black performance made them difficult to categorize and market. This was the case with LaBelle, the trio that had emerged from the 1960s girl group Patti LaBelle & the Bluebelles, a group known for their 1962 hit "I Sold My Heart to the Junkman" and a rhythm and blues–inflected rendition of the standard "Over the Rainbow" (1966). By 1967, Cindy Birdsong had left the Bluebelles to replace Flo Ballard of the Supremes. Patti LaBelle, Sarah Dash, and Nona Hendryx, in consultation with their new manager Vicki Wickham, a former producer of the British music television program *Ready, Steady, Go!*, had decided that in order for the group to survive in the new decade, a serious change was in order.

The Bluebelles of the 1960s fit in the rhythm and blues tradition, singing harmonies and wearing matching outfits, but LaBelle of the 1970s created a new musical and visual profile. After working with White American singer–songwriter Laura Nyro on *Gonna Take a Miracle* (1971), a loving tribute to the girl group and doo-wop era they were leaving behind, they dove into the glam, glitter, and funk of the early 1970s, helping to create the visual image that marks the period. LaBelle exploited the burgeoning glam rock scene in which primarily male performers such as Marc Bolan of T-Rex, David Bowie, and Elton John challenged the standards of heterosexual male identity by wearing makeup and donning exaggerated costumes that featured feathers, lace, tights, high heels. The members of LaBelle were among the first American performers to engage this style (in fact, after working with LaBelle, the designer Larry Le Gaspi went on to design the space-age wardrobes of George Clinton's Parliament-Funkadelic and the rock band Kiss).[37] LaBelle dispensed with wearing identical gowns; instead, each member dressed in one-of-a-kind, way-out pieces. In their skin-tight silver lamé costumes, feathered headdresses, aluminum breastplates, bikini tops, shiny high-heeled boots, and sparkling makeup, LaBelle, Hendryx, and Dash were an outrageous sight to behold. They were also, as music historian Gillian Gaar points out, "virtually the only all-female group that was as flamboyant as the male glam performers."[38]

But LaBelle was about more than style. The group was hailed for its musical capabilities. The vocal talent that had sustained them in the girl group era was still in evidence and, with an outstanding band, they put on spectacular live performances. In the liner notes of *Something Silver*, a 1997 greatest hits collection, critic Vince Aletti describes their stage act:

> Patti's in constant motion, wailing from every corner of the stage, fighting with her costume, mopping her face with a wash cloth, flailing, shimmying, falling to her knees . . . at several of Labelle's most spectacular shows, in fact, Patti descends birdlike from the ceiling, fluttering her arms while the audience roars.[39]

Mixing the emotive stylistics of gospel performance with the exaggerated stage shows of early seventies hard rock acts, LaBelle became a cult favorite among the musical cognoscenti of the mid-1970s.

The very creativity that made them such a compelling live act caused confusion for music industry professionals and radio programmers. Cross-cutting genres of rock, funk, rhythm and blues, gospel, and dance, LaBelle pursued a glam and glitter vision through a mix of original songs, most of which were penned by Nona Hendryx, and covers ranging from an inventive take on Gil Scott-Heron's spoken-word Black-Power litany "The Revolution Will Not Be Televised" (1973) to British band The Who's anthem "Won't Get Fooled Again" (1972). They worked with The Who's producer Kit Lambert on their eponymous album (1971), and with Allen Toussaint, well known for his production of New Orleans–style rhythm and blues and jazz on "Lady Marmalade" (1974), the danceable celebration of a New Orleans "working girl" that was their biggest hit. LaBelle's music was varied, offering messages about love, self-determination, and social concerns wrapped in music one could dance to, feel better to, or make love to. It did not, however, fit into tidy categories. Like the Black rocker Jimi Hendrix, LaBelle challenged race and genre boundaries; as a Black female act, they confronted even more limiting expectations. They were recognized as part of the rock community; *Rolling Stone* devoted coverage to the funky divas in 1974, and they were "the first Black rock group to perform at the New York Metropolitan Opera House."[40] Still, their gender, race, and refreshing brand of Black female independence rendered them nearly incomprehensible to a mainstream unaccustomed to seeing African American women confidently operating outside of the handful of available stereotypes.

Like LaBelle, solo artist Betty Davis created her image through appropriation and manipulation of the symbols of the new era. Davis was inspired by the creative freedom that Jimi Hendrix had represented. In fact, in the late 1960s she introduced Hendrix to her then-husband, Miles Davis, connecting the older jazz great with the burgeoning rock scene and helping him update his sound and image for the new decade. An attractive young woman, she played up her sexiness and also wrote lyrics in which she explained with notable precision what she wanted. Drawing on the blues women's tradition of outspoken lyrics and the forthright sexuality of women such as Etta James and Tina Turner, Betty Davis spoke as a young, liberated Black woman.[41] Her "Anti-Love Song" articulates a counterintuitive message with the narrator praising both her virtues and those of her lover before stating, "I don't want to love you, 'cause I know what you do to me." Her song titles were also provocative: "If I'm in Luck I Might Get Picked Up" and "Game Is My Middle Name." The album cover of her first release, *Betty Davis* (1973), shows her sporting an enormous afro, a midriff-baring blouse, denim hot pants, thigh-high silver platform boots, and a playful smile. Davis toured on the Black music circuit, playing to audiences appreciative of her "nasty" style. For women in particular, this use of sexuality is a double-edged sword. It can be read as a kind of empowering move in which the woman is in control of her body and her desires; at the same time, however, women presenting themselves as sexual agents are often mistaken for sex objects. Furthermore, with sexuality in the foreground, other aspects, importantly the artist's talent, can be easily overshadowed.

Betty Davis's sound combines blues, hard rock, and funk. Her self-titled first album features funk innovators Larry Graham on bass and Greg Ericco on drums (both of Sly and the Family Stone), guitarist Neal Schon, who went on to play with Journey, horn players from Tower of Power, and the Pointer Sisters and future disco star Sylvester as backup singers. Davis dispensed with the gospel-rooted sound typically associated with Black women and used an idiosyncratic vocal style that alternated between an insinuating whisper and a throaty growl. In terms of the acceptance of her music, Davis suffered a problem that has been a commonplace one for Black rock performers: her music was considered "too Black" for White rock radio stations and "too rock" for Black radio, slipping between the cracks of racialized genre and market niches. Not surprisingly, Davis has also slipped through the cracks of most rock and funk histories: the "wrong" race to fit into the rock music story and the "wrong" sound to fit into the Black music story.[42]

OH BONDAGE, UP YOURS: THE BATTLE CONTINUES

The management of image is a constant concern for female performers. Some artists use the strategy of downplaying physical appearance and sexuality. For example, Joan Armatrading, the Black British singer, songwriter, and guitarist who launched her career in the early 1970s, placed the emphasis on her music and lyrics rather than a glittering stage show. Often, she is categorized as a folk musician, the slot in which the majority of women who play guitar are placed.

Armatrading's early recordings foreground her acoustic guitar–centered performances, but she shifted to a pop–rock sound in the early 1980s, recording with a rock band; throughout her career she has enjoyed British pop chart success and developed a committed following in the United States. Arguably, she paved the way for Tracy Chapman, the young singer, songwriter, and guitarist whose debut single, "Fast Car" (1988), was a *Billboard* Top Ten hit; the album *Tracy Chapman* (1988) sold 3.5 million copies and earned Chapman three Grammy Awards including Best New Artist.

The image of stripped-down sincerity projected by Armatrading and Chapman was one mode of expressing a Black female point of view in the rock scene without foregrounding sexuality. Poly Styrene of the 1970s English punk rock band X-Ray Spex took another. Playing against the available female types, she was neither a cool rock chick nor a sexy plaything. Instead, she exploited the emergent punk ethos of androgyny, using it as a platform for a critique of gender stereotypes and excessive consumerism. Born Marianne Elliott in London, the self-named Poly Styrene was not White, but mixed-race (her mother was English, her father was Somali). She wore braces on her teeth, dressed in brightly colored clothing, often of thrift store vintage; she never apologized for not looking like a magazine model or movie star. Instead, she highlighted her individuality. She started the first and most well-known X-Ray Spex single, "Oh Bondage, Up Yours!" (1977), with the innocently uttered phrase, "Some people think little girls should be seen and not heard, but I say . . ."—and next she spoke in a full-bodied shout—"Oh Bondage, up yours!" Backed by the shuffling guitar rhythm and staccato horns that characterized early 1960s Jamaican ska and was popular with British punk rockers, Poly Styrene deconstructed the rigid social rules that bound women to an inferior position. Talking back to the images presented by rock 'n' roll and popular culture more generally, other X-Ray Spex songs critiqued the ways commercial media images of femininity dragged women into a losing cycle of expectations about how one should look and feel. The first prominent front-woman of the punk era in England, Poly Styrene inspired her contemporaries, demonstrated that women could be punk rockers, and influenced the next generation of punk rock women, especially Riot Grrrl bands, the loosely constituted movement of female-led, hard-driving rock bands of the early 1990s.

Whether they opt for high-voltage sexuality or low-key sensuality, audible Blackness or ambiguous musical mixing, Black women rockers have pursued their vision in a largely White, male-dominated arena. Ironically, for all of rock's obvious miscegenation, self-conscious play with gender roles and sexuality, and countercultural spirit, Black women's race and gender difference often impede their ability to secure an equal place in the form. This has not prevented Black women from participating in the genre. Indeed, Black women have forged careers in rock 'n' roll since the beginning of the genre and continue to participate in this wide-ranging musical field. During the 1990s, a new generation of Black women rockers engaged in the ongoing battle to express themselves in terms that made sense to them, even if their sound and style went against dominant expectations for Black women's musical production. Among these performers are Sandra St. Victor of The Family Stand, a band who achieved financial success by writing hits for Paula Abdul and also recorded an eclectic stew of funk and hard rock on the 1991 release *Moon in Scorpio*; Toshi Reagon, a guitarist–singer–songwriter who incorporates elements of rock, folk, funk, blues, and sacred music into beautifully crafted songs captured on recordings such as *The Righteous Ones* (1999) and in riveting live performances; Me'Shell NdegéOcello, a formidable bass player whose debut album *Plantation Lullabies* (1993) reached back to the soul era and who has since explored a wide range of musical sounds and lyrical themes in her uncompromising albums; and Skin, the songwriter and vocalist of the English band Skunk Anansie, who sang provocative material like the song "Intellectualize My Blackness" (1995) and operated in the hard rock tradition following the trail blazed by Joyce Kennedy, the front-woman of 1970s Black funk–metal band Mother's Finest. These artists continue to perform in the 2000s, joined by a new cohort of innovative Black women musicians who include Tamar-Kali, the fierce and soulful punk singer and songwriter, bass player Kamara Thomas of the 70s-inspired hard rock band Earl Greyhound, and the singer and songwriter Santi White, who extended the ska punk of her band Stiffed to include electronica, punk, dub, and hip hop on the 2008 release *Santogold*, a recording that earned critical acclaim and solid sales.

Since the 1950s, Black women in rock 'n' roll have sought to exercise creative self-determination, while making a living in a male-dominated field that devalues women and in a White-dominated field that devalues African Americans. The pioneering artists I have discussed in this article have struggled to break out of the musical boxes that the recording industry assigns them to, advancing their distinctive sounds and styles and leaving an indelible mark on rock music and American culture.

ACKNOWLEDGMENTS

Thanks to Daphne Brooks, Judith Casselberry, Bill Toles, and especially Richard Yarborough for their help with names, sources, and interpretation.

NOTES

1. Jones 1992, 7–8, 10–11, 15, 22.
2. In turn, LaBelle's song "Nightbirds" is a tribute to Joplin; see Gaar 2002, 165. Joplin had a deep respect for Black musicians and contributing to the purchase of a tombstone for one of America's greatest artists was a way for her to publicly and personally acknowledge Bessie Smith's importance both to Joplin and music history. See Echols 1999, 236–237.
3. Garon and Garon 1992, 4.
4. Wald 2007.
5. Guralnick 1994, 501.
6. See Monson 1995.
7. Gaar 2002, 93.
8. Brown and Yule 1996, 60.
9. Ibid., 62–63.
10. For details about Stone's innovation, see Portia Maultsby, "Rhythm and Blues," in *African American Music: An Introduction*, 2nd ed., 244–247.
11. Little Richard quoted in Brown and Yule 1996, 123.
12. James and Ritz 1998, 60.
13. Ibid.
14. *That Rhythm . . . Those Blues*, produced by George T. Nierenberg (Alexandria, VA: The American Experience Series, PBS Video, 1988).
15. Maultsby 1990, 189.
16. James and Ritz 1998, 61.
17. Ibid.
18. Ibid., 49–50.
19. Ibid., 91.
20. Turner quoted in *Celebrate! The Best of Tina Turner*, directed by David Mallet (Chatsworth, CA: Image Entertainment, Inc., 2000).
21. The tumultuous years of physical and mental abuse were popularized in the hit bio-pic *What's Love Got to Do with It?* (Burbank, CA: Touchstone Home Video and Buena Vista Home Video, 1994) and documented in her autobiography (Turner and Loder 1987, 209–215).
22. Mahon 2004.
23. Brown and Yule 1996, 68; Gaar 2002, 7.
24. Stories about the difficulties of touring, especially in the Deep South where there was a core rhythm and blues audience, are a part of every pre–Civil Rights Era Black musician's biography. In addition to the racism and racial segregation that made finding accommodations difficult and that often led to police harassment, these artists also had to fight with club owners for the money they were due. Many, Ruth Brown and Etta James among them, learned to demand their pay before they played lest the club owner "disappear" before the end of the evening with the night's taking.
25. See Brown and Yule 1996 for details of the case and the founding of the Rhythm and Blues Foundation. It is important to note that many of these artists—Little Richard and Big Mama Thornton, for example—have still not received a legal redress in spite of public awareness of and outrage over their mistreatment.
26. Baker quoted in "'Covers vs. Copies'" 1990, 27, 30. Originally published in *Billboard Magazine* (March 1955).
27. Brown and Yule 1996, 76.
28. Ruth Brown quoted in *That Rhythm . . . Those Blues* 1988.
29. Gaar 2002, 31.
30. *Chicago Defender*, December 4, 1962.
31. Spector and Waldron 1990, 27.
32. Ibid., 35.
33. Ibid., 33.
34. Gaines 1997; Warwick 2007.
35. Poet Kate Rushin (1993) used "The Black Back-Ups" as the title for a poem dedicated to her aunts who worked as domestics for White families and the Black women who, in singing behind White rock acts, provided similarly invisible but crucial labor.
36. Hirshey 2001, 53.
37. Gaar 2002, 164.

38. Ibid.
39. Alletti 1997.
40. Gaar 2002, 164.
41. For a discussion of the liberated Black femininity of Betty Davis, see Mahon 2011.
42. See Crazy Horse 2004, a collection of essays that challenges these tendencies and instead marks and analyzes the participation of a broad range of African Americans in the production of rock 'n' roll.

DISCOGRAPHY

Armatrading, Joan. *Love and Affection: Joan Armatrading Classics (1975–1983)*. Originally released as A&M 4936132, 2003. Universal Music TV 9823506, 2004. CD.
Baker, LaVern. *Soul on Fire: The Best of LaVern Baker*. Rhino 7567823112, 1991. CD.
Big Mama Thornton. *Hound Dog: The Peacock Recordings*. MCA MCD 10668, 1992. CD.
Berry, Chuck. *The Great Twenty-Eight*. Originally released as Chess 92500, 1982. Geffen, 2012. CD.
Bo Diddley *Bo Diddley: His Best*. Originally released as Chess MCD 09373, 1997. Chess 1125482, 2001. CD.
Brown, Ruth. *Rockin' in Rhythm: The Best of Ruth Brown*. Originally recorded May 25, 1949–May 7, 1959, Originally released as Rhino Records R2 72450, 1996. Rhino Atlantic, 2005. Digital.
The Chantels. *The Best of The Chantels*. Originally released as Rhino R21S-70954, 1990. Rhino, 2006. Digital.
Chapman, Tracy. *Tracy Chapman*. Originally released as Elektra 7559607742, 1988. Warner Music 8122797965, 2010. CD.
Clayton, Merry. *Merry Clayton*. Originally released as Ode Records 77012, 1971. Repertoire REP 5177, 2010. CD.
Davis, Betty. *Betty Davis*. Originally released as Just Sunshine Records JSS-5, 1973. Ernie B's 154294, 2013. CD.
Diana Ross & The Supremes. *50th Anniversary: The Singles Collections: 1961–1969*. Originally recorded October, 1960. Motown 2778881, 2011. Three CD set.
Ike and Tina Turner. *Best of Ike and Tina Turner*. Capitol Catalog Mkt (C92), 2015. Digital.
James, Etta. *The Essential Etta James*. Legacy/Masterworks 71773, 2010. CD.
———. *25 Greatest Hits*. Marathon Media International Ltd., 2012. Digital.
LaBelle. *Something Silver*. Warner Bros. 46359, 1997. CD.
Little Richard. *Here Is Little Richard*. Concord, 2012. Digital; Concord 7233840, 2012. CD.
The Marvelettes. *Please Mr. Postman*. Originally released as Tamla 228, 1961. Universal Music 0573095, 2012. CD.
NdegéOcello, Me'Shell. *Plantation Lullabies*. Originally released 1993. Sire 9362457542, 1994. CD.
Patti LaBelle and the Bluebells. *Live at The Apollo*. Synergie OMP, 2006. Digital.
Reagon, Toshi. *The Righteous Ones*. Razor & Tie Entertainment 82839, 1999. CD.
The Ronettes. *Be My Baby: The Very Best of the Ronettes*. Originally recorded March 1963. Legacy/Phil Spector Records 88697612862, 2011. CD.
The Shirelles. *The Best of the Shirelles*. Originally released 1992. Ace CDCHD356, 2003. CD.
The Sweet Inspirations. *The Sweet Inspirations*. Originally released as Atlantic SD 8155, 1967. Collectors' Choice Music CCM-700. CD.
Turner, Tina. *Private Dancer 30th Anniversary Edition*. Originally released as Capitol Records ST-12330, 1984. Reissued as Parlophone/Rhino Records RP2 170425, 2015. Two CD set.

CHAPTER 18

"Ain't Nuthin' but a She Thang"
Women in Hip Hop[1]

Cheryl L. Keyes

Hip hop emerged among Black and Latino youth in New York City around the early 1970s. It is defined by its adherents as a youth arts movement comprised of four elements—breakdancing (b-boying/b-girling), graffiti (writing), disc jockeying (DJing), and emceeing (MCing)—and as an expression distinguished by distinct forms of dress, gesture, and language that embody an urban street consciousness. By the late 1970s, hip hop had caught the attention of music entrepreneurs who recognized its commercial potential with the release of the recording "Rapper's Delight" by the Sugarhill Gang (1979). Following the overwhelming success of this recording, hip hop steadily moved from the inner-city streets of New York City into popular mainstream culture. Additionally, the production of hip hop arts via the silver screen, the advertising industry, and underground promotion strategies (e.g., mixtapes) have further contributed to its rise to national prominence.[2] Realizing its viability to a growing youth constituency, entrepreneurs began placing significant value on certain elements of hip hop believed to be more marketable to the average consumer. For example, MCing and DJing were positioned as primary markets of exploitation while breakdancing and graffiti became secondary markets of hip hop. As such, the former two eventually eclipsed in popularity breakdancing and graffiti, thus introducing the music category rap music. Occasionally, critics and aficionados of rap music use the term interchangeably with hip hop, or more specifically, hip hop music.

The existence of hip hop music in the twenty-first century proves its efficacy as a cultural expression embraced by youth around the globe.[3] While it is apparent that hip hop music has flourished exponentially in popular culture and has maintained a competitive edge in the music industry, female representation remains disproportionate to that of male artists of this genre.[4] This status is quite evident when considering the limitation of female MCs heard on radio and the proliferation of highly sexualized and exoticized images of women, who appear in numerous hip hop music videos and who are, for the most part, of African descent. In stark contrast, however, to this one-dimensional stereotyped image and the dwindling number of female MCs, women have been major forces of hip hop in diverse ways, though rarely acknowledged.

This essay provides an overview of women in hip hop music and their prominence as performing artists and as movers and shakers in the boardroom and behind the camera in the shaping of this tradition. Specific attention is given to the conception of a female performative identity and a female sensibility in rap music performance. The following section begins as an overview of women who have pioneered the early development of hip hop.

GODMOTHERS OF HIP HOP: THE PIONEERING YEARS (MID-1970S)

Wreckin' the Mic

During the pre-commercial years of hip hop, artists received token remuneration for their performances. Reputation among peers as the best MC or DJ on the neighborhood block took precedence over making money. MCs, for example, were expected to have a voice resembling that of Black radio personality disc jockeys with an ability to produce superb rhymes, while DJs, on the other hand, needed to be endowed with the biggest, loudest, and highest quality sound system. The typical hip hop "jam" (dance party/gathering) convened in outdoor contexts where

> people used to do jams in the schoolyard or handball court. Someone used to bring their two turntables out and plug it into the lamp post outside and that's how they got their power. People would listen and dance to the music in the streets.[5]

MCs took turns at the microphone as a way to command the crowd. Written history often presents the above outdoor context as male-dominated spaces in which women assumed roles as onlookers rather than creators, innovators, or producers of tradition. But as veteran MC Ms. Melodie noted,

> females were always into rap, had their little crews . . . and were known for rocking parties, schoolyards, whatever it was; and females rocked just as hard as males [but] the male was just first to be put on wax [record].[6]

Among the first all-women hip hop crew known for its deftness on the microphone and dexterity on the "wheels-of-steel" (turntables) was Mercedes Ladies. The multi-member crew from the Bronx formed around the late 1970s. Mercedes Ladies' MC Sheri Sher vividly recalls the early years:

> We used to be out there in the parks . . . along with the rest of the guys, [Grandmaster] Flash, and Theodore and L Brothers. . . . We used to actually watch them perform on the corner and then we decided to start an all-female crew. . . . [We carried] our own equipment [speakers and amps] . . . [and] our own crates of records. . . . It was honor and respect . . . they were like our brothers. . . . We never felt intimidated. . . . We got up there, all psyched up to rock the parties.[7]

Mercedes Ladies delivered their rhymes in a percussive style or "flow," laced with braggadocio; over beats with a repetitive heavy-bass groove, they exploited party themes about having a good time and how they could rock the microphone. Most significantly, they laid the foundation for other all-female crew contemporaries such as the Mellow-D crew with Missy Dee, Lady T, Apple-C, and Easy K; the Choice Girls with Lady T; and the Cheba Girls.[8]

The majority of female hip hop artists during the pioneering years, however, enjoyed tremendous success with male-dominated crews. As part of a male collective, they gained respect, acceptance, and equal footing in the rap music game by demonstrating their abilities at wreckin' the microphone as "hard" (aggressive) as and with a flow indistinguishable from their male cohorts. Such visibility among these early female artists made it possible for other women to enter the rap music stage alongside male artists. Sha-Rock is recognized as the first female MC in the history of hip hop.

Dubbed "Queen of Lady Emcees,"[9] Sha-Rock began her career with the crew Funky Four around 1976. Originating in the Bronx, Funky Four included KK Rockwell, Keith, Rahiem, and Sha-Rock. The crew consisted also of two DJs, Baron and Breakout, known as Sasquatch because of their massive sound system. Eventually, the group's personnel changed when Sha-Rock temporarily left the crew and Rahiem joined Grandmaster Flash and his MCs. They were replaced by two MCs, Lil' Rodney C and Jazzy Jeff (not to be confused with DJ Jazzy Jeff of the Fresh Prince). When Sha-Rock returned to the four member crew circa 1978, the group became known as Funky Four Plus One.

Sha-Rock was not only known for her rhyming capabilities but for her technological innovation with the use of the echo chamber in hip hop. Her proficiency with this device made aspiring emcees like Darryl "D.M.C." McDaniels of Run-D.M.C. take notice:

> I heard this female MC from the group Funky Four Plus One, four dude MCs and she was the Plus One, and her name was Sha-Rock. . . . They had a couple of records out on Sugar Hill and Enjoy. . . . One day I heard something that wasn't Sha-Rock's record [rather] it was a tape of her rhyming over "Seven Minutes of Funk." And she said some crazy dope rhymes that [were] better than eighty-five percent of MCs out today. But this is what was life changing in me. She was rhyming . . . with the echo chamber. . . . I couldn't believe how incredible this girl was with the echo chamber. Then comes along that I get a chance to make a record. I was like "Jay [Jam Master Jay], I got to be like Sha-Rock, I got to have that echo chamber, Sha-Rock is genre changing." . . . Her rhymes were dope. She was doper than the dudes back then. . . . She's not only a legendary pioneer icon female MC, you dudes need to take lessons from Sha-Rock. She changed my life.[10]

Another female MC recognized for wreckin' the microphone was Pebblee-Poo from the Bronx. She once performed with a Harlem-based crew called the Untouchables and eventually joined DJ Kool Herc's crew known as The Herculoids, who hailed from her home borough.[11] Pebblee-Poo's brother, Master Don, soon took notice of her rhymin' skills and invited her to join his group, Master Don and the Def Committee (the first crew to have a Latino MC), replacing female MCs Sondra Dee and Sweet and Sour. More importantly, Pebblee-Poo made history, becoming the first female MC of Kool Herc and the Herculoids around the mid-1970s.[12]

Following in the footsteps of Pebblee-Poo and Sha-Rock yet their junior was Missy Dee, discovered by Grandmaster Flash at the famed Disco Fever hip hop club in the Bronx. She references this encounter as a day she "will never forget."

> I was very young . . . about 15 years old. One day this crew named the People's Choice was there and TJ the DJ was playing some music, "Seven Minutes of Funk" . . . one of my favorite beats to rhyme off. I think Kurtis Blow was in the park. . . . [He] rocked in the Battleground quite often. The People's Choice was the house crew that rocked in the Battleground, and I would get on stage

sometimes. This particular day, I got on and tore that mic up. Grandmaster Flash walked up to me and told me that he wanted me to come up to the Bronx to a club called Disco Fever and rock on the mic. I totally thought I would die. Flash, Grandmaster Flash wanted me to come to the Fever. I ran down the block and upstairs to tell my moms, and can you believe she told me that I couldn't go, that I was too young.[13]

Missy Dee would later perform as an MC with Herc's Herculoids. But because she was considered underage for clubs bookings, she was replaced by Pebblee-Poo. Nonetheless, Missy Dee continued to perform with her crew Mellow-D and recorded "Missy Missy Dee" (c. 1981), a 12-inch single for Universal Record Company (not to be confused with Universal Records). Much to her astonishment, Missy Dee discovered that her debut single eventually became a hip hop classic.

I find it hard to believe that "Missy Missy Dee" is considered to be a classic. There was hardly any real distribution of the song [back in the days]. . . . 12-inches were given away [rather] than sold. When I first saw it being sold online (on ebay) a few years ago [pre-2008], I was totally buggin' out about it.[14]

WOMEN PIONEERS OF EARLY COMMERCIAL HIP HOP (LATE-1970S)

The concept of rocking the parties à la hip hop caught the attention of local nightclub owners throughout the boroughs. The most celebrated clubs during the early years of hip hop were the Dixie Club, Club 371, Disco Fever of the Bronx, Harlem World, The Fun House, Negril, and The Roxy (a former skating rink) of Manhattan. As hip hop moved further into the disco club circuits among Manhattan's mostly White clientele (e.g., the Ritz and Danceteria), one woman was responsible for this shift: Kool Lady Blue. Originally from London, England's Kool Lady Blue was sent to New York City to manage Malcolm McLaren's World's End punk clothing store for one year. But after witnessing the burgeoning hip hop scene in the Bronx, she started promoting hip hop arts at The Roxy and Negril, establishing the former as a nightclub that exclusively showcased hip hop arts. Later she became a promoter-manager for numerous hip hop artists, including Grandmaster Flash and the Rock Steady Crew.

By the late 1970s, independent record producers from the East Coast began to record hip hop acts from nearby boroughs and cities. Hip hop's first record producers were, nonetheless, veterans of rhythm and blues and disco music: Paul Winley (Winley Records), Bobby Robinson (Enjoy Records), and Sylvia and Joe Robinson (Sugar Hill Records).

Paul Winley is best known for producing his daughters on his Harlem-based label, Winley. Co-produced by Winley and his wife Ann, Tanya "Sweet Tee" and Paulette Winley recorded "Rhymin' and Rappin'" (1979), which followed in the style of party-rap rhymes. Sweet Tee succeeded "Rhymin' and Rappin'" as a solo MC on "Vicious Rap" (1980). Although this song was consistent with the party-like themes similar to artists from the pre-commercial years of hip hop, "Vicious Rap" (1980) made a brief social commentary about the government and police repression. Sweet Tee's song joined ranks with other early hip hop songs like "Election '80 Rap" (ALA, 1980) by the Unknown Rapper that "touched on themes of social dislocation and institutional racism [and classism]."[15] Most importantly, "Vicious Rap" set the stage for "The Message" (Sugar Hill Records, 1982) performed by Melle Mel et al. of Grandmaster Flash & the Furious Five, which advanced the concept of the socio-political rap subgenre.

Other pioneering female MCs recorded by Winley included Queen Lisa Lee of the Cosmic Force. She launched her MC career with the Zulu Nation, created by hip hop's DJ-visionary Afrika Bambaataa. Members of the Zulu Nation, addressed as Shaka Kings and Shaka Queens, formed mini-crews that competed artistically via the four elements of hip hop. Although Queen Lisa Lee's associate Queen Kenya was a member of Soul Sonic Force, one of Bambaataa's collectives, she never recorded with them. Lisa Lee, however, recorded with Bambaataa's Cosmic Force. Winley went on to produce Cosmic Force with Queen Lisa Lee on "Zulu Nation Throwdown Part One" (1980). But with Winley's limited understanding of Bambaataa's musical concept, Cosmic Force as well as another of Bambaataa's collectives, Soul Sonic Force, left Winley Records for Tom Silverman's newly established rap music label, Tommy Boy.[16]

A number of enthusiasts and entrepreneurs recognized the talents of women rap artists and began to record them, including Bobby Robinson, a record shop owner in Harlem. His early recording credits were in rhythm and blues, where he had helped launch the careers of The Shirelles, Gladys Knight & the Pips, and jazz vocalist Gloria Lynne. By 1979, he had produced the song "Rappin' and Rockin' the House" by Sha-Rock's rap group, Funky Four Plus One. The accompaniment for "Rappin' and Rockin' the House" was produced by a backup band in lieu of a DJ and incorporated the music from Cheryl Lynn's hit "To Be Real." Among their short lists of recordings, "Rappin and Rockin' the House" was the group's first and only successful recording on Enjoy. Owing to creative differences, Funky Four Plus One left Enjoy to join Sugar Hill Records. On their new label, the group recorded "That's the Joint," deemed a hip hop classic, so much so it landed them a guest-performance spot on NBC's *Saturday Night Live (SNL)* in 1981, hosted by Blondie's Deborah Harry, thus making the group the first hip hop act to appear on *SNL* as well as national network television.

Additionally, Bobby Robinson recorded the single "Funkbox Party" (1983) by the Masterdon Committee (formerly known as Master Don and the Def Committee), which included its lone female MC, Pebblee-Poo. "Funkbox Party" never achieved national success, but it was a local hit for hip hop "heads" (aficionados) in New York City, and popularized such lines as "Everybody say 'Ho,'" "Everybody scream" and "and it make you go 'uh, na na na na.'"[17]

The third early record producers of rap music were R&B–disco singer-turned-record mogul Sylvia (Vanderpool) Robinson and her husband, Joe Robinson (Figure 18.1). They co-founded Sugar Hill Records, named after an exclusive section in Harlem but located in Englewood, New Jersey.

The first time Sylvia Robinson heard rap music was at New York's Harlem World Club. Witnessing how the dance crowd enjoyed watching, she noticed "fellahs rappin'" and concluded "what a hell of a concept; I think that it would be great on record!"[18] The Robinsons recorded a string of 12-inch single hits: "Rapper's Delight" (1979) by the Sugarhill Gang, which became the first rap song to certify gold and platinum; "That's the Joint" (1980) by Funky Four Plus One; "Freedom" (1980), "The Adventures of Grandmaster Flash on the Wheels of Steel" (1981), and "The Message" (1982) by Grandmaster Flash & the Furious Five; "Feel the Heartbeat" (1981) by The Treacherous Three; and "Monster Jam" (1980) with Spoonie Gee. Among the label's first successful female act was the trio The Sequence. Sylvia Robinson discovered them backstage in Columbia, South Carolina, while on a Sugar Hill Records tour and auditioned them on the spot. Consisting

Figure 18.1
Sylvia Robinson, 1983.

Photo by Michael Ochs Archives/Getty Images.

of Cheryl the Pearl, Angie B (a.k.a. Angie Stone), and Blondie, The Sequence's most memorable single was "Funk You Up" (1981).

While the soundtracks for Sugar Hill's acts were mainly produced by the label's house band rather than by a DJ, Sugar Hill Records goes down in history as the first successful independent label to record, produce, and market hip hop music, catapulting it to international recognition. Sylvia Robinson not only co-founded and co-produced acts on Sugar Hill, but she also was the creative force who masterminded the label's trademark sound—live background party-goers' cheers that simulated a party event. Sylvia Robinson also co-wrote lyrics and music with her artists and crafted Sugar Hill's unique production. She had a knack for finding talents for her label, even if it meant buying out or persuading artists from her rivals like Enjoy Records, which once recorded Grandmaster Flash & the Furious Five, Spoonie Gee, and the Treacherous Three, to sign with Sugar Hill. Considered rap music's first female video director, she produced "The Message" as a rap video prior to MTV's programming of rap music. Furthermore, Robinson's keen decision-making acumen in an area dominated by men opened the door for other women to become hip hop entrepreneurs, including Monica Lynch, longtime president of Tommy Boy Records (now Tommy Boy Entertainment), Carmen Ashurst-Watson of Def Jam Records and Rush Communications, and Mona Scott-Young of Monami Entertainment. Because of Sylvia Robinson's pioneering efforts, she earned the moniker the "Mother of Hip Hop."

As Sugar Hill Records became increasingly successful, local independent labels from other areas introduced female MCs. Tec label's artist Lady B of Philadelphia, for example, recorded "To the Beat Y'all" in 1979, making her among the first non–New York City or Tri-borough MC to make a commercial recording. By the 1980s, artists from other genres were experimenting with rap music. Most notably was Blondie's hit single "Rapture" (Chrysalis, 1981) featuring lead singer Deborah Harry. Midway through the song, Harry performed a rap, which references DJ Grandmaster Flash. Blondie's "Rapture" was certified as a gold record within months of its release.

By 1983, the first hip hop film, *Wild Style* by Charles Ahearn, produced by Harry Belafonte, was released. Now considered a cult classic, *Wild Style* is a docudrama that showcases hip hop arts and artists including Fab Five Freddy, Cold Crush Brothers, Busy Bee, Lisa Lee, and graffiti artist Lady Pink, to name a few. Other hip hop films followed suit: *Style Wars* (1983), *Beat Street* (1984), *Breakin'* and *Breakin' 2: Electric Boogaloo* (1984), and *Krush Groove* (1985). *Beat Street*, unlike *Wild Style* and *Style Wars*, featured known actors, Guy Davis and Rae Dawn Chong, who played leading roles alongside actual hip hop artists. The trio called the Us Girls appeared and performed in *Beat Street*. The Us Girls included three pioneering female MCs—Sha-Rock of Funky Four Plus One, Lisa Lee of Cosmic Force, and Debbie Dee of the Mercedes Ladies. Their appearance in *Beat Street* context created visibility for aspiring women of hip hop.

WOMEN AND THE GOLDEN AGE OF HIP HOP

The Answer-Back Rap

Critics identify the mid-1980s through the 1990s as the "Golden Age of Hip Hop."[19] It is characterized by a diverse roster of artists and styles, including party rap, nation conscious rap, gangsta rap, and regional styles (e.g., Miami Bass, chopped and screwed in Houston, crunk of Memphis and Atlanta, and hyphy of the San Francisco bay area). This era also saw hip hop merging with other established genres (e.g., rock, jazz, rhythm and blues, soul, etc.) to create hip hop hybrids. During the golden age, women artists were as influential as their male counterparts in shaping the development of these styles.

The period captures the music's ascent from the underground—streets of the inner city—into the mainstream. It was characterized by the fusion of rap music with rock, introduced by the trio Run-D.M.C. in 1986 with the group's rendition of Aerosmith's "Walk This Way"; the programming of hip hop on music television; the casting of hip hop artists in television commercials and films; the distribution of indie rap music by major labels; and the answer-back rap phenomenon, which served as impetus to a female hip hop commercial concept.

During the golden age of hip hop, individual women continued to stand out as the lone female members in male-dominated collectives, as in the case of Roxanne Shanté of the Juice Crew, which was instrumental to the popularity of the answer-back rap. Shanté, who hails from the Queensbridge Projects of Long Island City, Queens, joined forces with DJ Marley Marl and MC Shan of the Juice Crew at the age of fourteen. The Juice Crew advanced the radio or "answer-back rap" battles that originated with "Mr. Magic's Rap Attack" radio show on New York's WBLS radio and in competition with MC KRS-One and DJ Scott La Rock of Boogie Down Productions (BDP), featured on DJ Red Alert's rap radio program on 98.7 KISS-FM.[20] Shanté's feature on the Crew's radio battle fueled the male/female answer-back raps, popularly remembered as the "Roxanne Battle" raps or "The Roxanne Wars." In the answer-back rap, one rap is posed as a response or "answer" to a previous release.

Ironically, the Roxanne Wars began with Adelaide "Roxanne" Martinez, who immortalized a Roxanne persona, a snobbish female character, in her video stage performance of "Roxanne, Roxanne" (Select, 1984) produced by UTFO and hip hop doo-wop group Full Force.

Capitalizing on the success of "Roxanne, Roxanne," Marley Marl of the Juice Crew provided similar beats from UTFO's Roxanne recording for Roxanne Shanté to rap to. Her Roxanne song, "Roxanne's Revenge" (Pro Arts, 1984) emerged as an explicit retaliatory rant toward UTFO for canceling a scheduled performance produced by members of her crew. Although UTFO eventually countered Shanté (though four years later) with "The Real Roxanne" (Select, 1988) recorded by Elease Jack, the Roxanne songs opened the door for an answer to "Roxanne's Revenge" by MC Sparky Dee.

Sparky Dee, a soon-to-be former member of the hip hop MC crew Playgirls (with Mo-ski and City Slim), launched her solo career when responding to "Roxanne's Revenge" with "Sparky's Turn" (Nia, 1985). Shanté's follow-up to "Sparky's Turn" with "Queen of Rox" gave way to *Round 1* (Spin Records, 1985), an LP that featured the two women. Their battle on wax became verbally aggressive with personalized insult, nonetheless ending with fans crowning Sparky Dee as winner. The Roxanne Wars set the trend for other answer-back raps, in particular, male/female sequels. Examples include: "A Fly Girl" by the Boogie Boys (Capitol, 1985) followed by "A Fly Guy" by Pebblee-Poo (Profile, 1985), and "The Show" by Doug E. Fresh and the Get Fresh Crew (Reality, 1985) followed by "The Show Stoppa (Is Stupid Fresh)" by Salt-N-Pepa (Pop Art Records, 1985).[21]

Subsequent to the answer-back rap trend a legion of female hip hop acts emerged on the rap scene: L'Trimm, a duo affiliated with the Miami bass subgenre, recorded "Cars That Go Boom," (Hot Productions 1988); J.J. Fad, a Los Angeles–based trio, recorded the techno-pop style single "Supersonic" (1988); and Oaktown 3-5-7, a trio from Oakland, affiliated with MC Hammer, recorded "We Like It" and "Yeah, Yeah, Yeah" (Bust It Records, 1989).[22]

Empowering Voices and Shifting Images: Female Rap Identities

During the golden age of hip hop, Black women artists adopted a range of performance personae and their text/lyrics reflected various subject positions. Similar to their female predecessors, some of these women had affiliations with male producers, crews, and mentors. Conversations and interviews with female cultural readers of hip hop—artists, audience members, scholars/critics—revealed that during this period, Black women rappers most frequently projected one of four stage or performance personae: Queen Mother, Fly Girl, Sista with Attitude, and Lesbian.[23] The blurring of categories is to be expected as women rappers negotiate image, social values, political ideologies, and expectations of the music industry.

Queen Mother

The "Queen Mother" prototype encompasses female artists who view themselves as African-centered icons, evoked by their natural, braided, or locked hairstyle, African headdress, and clothing. Hip hop's Queen Mothers rhyme about female empowerment, (inner-city) community issues, and spirituality. They recognize themselves as African, woman, warrior, priestess, Nubian Queen, or simply queen, and, as such, identify with a subgenre of hip hop artists called "nation conscious" hip hop. Although the term "Queen" was initially used in hip hop as a moniker for women who were members of Afrika Bambaataa's Zulu Nation (e.g., Queen Lisa Lee and Queen Kenya), Dana "Queen Latifah" Owens brought the designation to global heights. Latifah, whose translation from Arabic means "feminine, delicate, and kind," explains that her Muslim cousin assigned her the name Latifah when she was eight years old.[24]

Queen Latifah launched her recording career through the release of 12-inch singles on Tommy Boy Records, "Princess of the Posse" and "Wrath of My Madness" (1988), followed by her debut album *All Hail the Queen* (1989). Produced by DJ Mark the 45 King, *All Hail the Queen* firmly established Queen Latifah's regal presence. This album is considered a landmark in hip hop because of its politically-charged Afrocentric pro-woman statement with songs such as "Ladies First," which introduced London-based MC Monie Love. The refrain of "Ladies First" was performed by an ensemble of female MCs—Ms. Melodie, Ice Cream Tee, and Shelly Thunder—singing "Ooo, ladies first . . ."[25] The video version conveys an alternative meaning to hip hop sisterhood, empowerment, and socio-politically charged statements with the superimposition of live footage of South Africa's anti-apartheid riots and photographic stills of central figures in Black political history: Harriet Tubman, Frances Ellen Watkins Harper, Sojourner Truth, Angela Davis, Winnie Mandela, and Rosa Parks.[26] Following Latifah's sophomore album, *Nature of a Sista* (1991), she released a third album on the Motown label, *Black Reign* (1993), which contained the Grammy-winning single "U.N.I.T.Y." that established Latifah as the first female MC to win in the category of "Best Rap Solo Performance."[27]

Queen Latifah opened the door for other Afrocentric female MCs, most notably Lauryn Hill, who became recognized for her subtle yet smooth delivery style and distinct lyrical flow that complemented the Haitian-American rap trio the Fugees (Figure 18.2). The group recorded two albums, *Blunted on Reality* (Ruffhouse/Columbia, 1994) and *The Score* (Ruffhouse/Columbia, 1996). A multi-platinum success, *The Score* produced several singles—"Fu-Gee-La," a cover version of Bob Marley's "No Woman, No Cry," and "Killing Me Softly"—and earned the Fugees two Grammy Awards in the categories of "Best Rap Album" and "Best R&B Performance by a Duo or Group with Vocal" for "Killing Me Softly." Subsequent to "Killing Me Softly," which showcased Hill's vocal prowess, was *The Miseducation of Lauryn Hill* (Ruffhouse/Columbia, 1998), Hill's solo debut album. She won numerous accolades and recognition as the first woman artist to receive ten Grammy nominations and the first female artist to win five Grammys—all at one time. Singles from *Miseducation* ranged from songs about respectability, empowerment, and motherhood, for example, "Doo Wop [That Thing]," Everything Is Everything," and "To Zion," respectively.

Other female MCs who project the Afrocentric Queen Mother image include Sista Soulja, associated with the nation conscious rap group, Public Enemy; Queen Mother Rage and Isis (also known as Lin Que), affiliated with the nation conscious crew, X-Clan; Ms. Melodie, Heather B, and Harmony, female members of Boogie Down Productions; Bahamadia (from Philadelphia), associated with the Gang Starr Foundation collective;

Figure 18.2
Lauryn Hill, 1998.

Photo by Anthony Barboza/Getty Images.

Nonchalant (from Washington, DC); and Lady Mecca (formerly known as Ladybug Mecca) of Digable Planet, to name a few.

Some Queen Mothers of hip hop garner such distinction based on becoming the first female to sign on labels, for example, Nikki D (first female MC to be signed to Def Jam Records) or MC Trouble (first female MC to be signed to Motown), while others, such as Yo-Yo, vacillate between categories.[28] A protégée of Ice Cube, Yo-Yo brought attention to women in hip hop from the West Coast. Advanced by her organization, the Intelligent Black Women's Coalition (IBWC), and through her promotion of Black women's issues and female respectability, as introduced on her debut album, *Make Way for the Motherlode* (EastWest/Atlantic, 1991), Yo-Yo not only represents the Queen Mother category but also that of "fly girl." The latter is embodied in her image—long golden blonde braids, tight-fitting shorts, makeup, and gyrating hips—combined with her singles "You Can't Play with My Yo-Yo" and "Put a Lid on It" that promote female sexual control and responsibility.

Fly Girl

The concept of "flyness" in the hip hop community derives from The Boogie Boys' commercial recording "A Fly Girl" (1985) and its answer rap, "A Fly Guy" (1985), by Pebblee-Poo. In "A Fly Girl," the Boogie Boys described a fly girl as a woman "who wants you to see her name [and] her game"; wears makeup, tight-fitting jeans, leather miniskirts, and abundant gold jewelry; showcases her "voluptuous curves," or full-figure physique; and also speaks her mind. However, the act that canonized the hip hop fly girl look in the golden age of hip hop was Salt-N-Pepa. Originating in Queens, New York, Salt-N-Pepa, composed of Cheryl "Salt" James and Sandra "Pepa" Denton, began their odyssey as female MCs with a modestly successful single, "The Showstopper" (1985), an answer-back to Doug E. Fresh and the Get Fresh Crew's "The Show" (1985). They replaced their DJ, Latoya Hanson, with Deidra "Spinderella" Roper of Brooklyn around the time of the release of their debut album, *Hot, Cool & Vicious* (Next Plateau, 1986). The trio expanded the "Fly Girl" persona to include characterizations of the sexually liberated and independent woman. Although some of their hit singles (e.g., "I'll Take Your Man," 1986; "Push It," 1987; and "Tramp," 1986) were written and produced by their manager–producer Hurby "Luv Bug" Azor—an industry trend where males often penned the lyrics of and produced female MCs—Cheryl "Salt" James began writing and producing for the trio with the single "Expression" (1989), which went platinum. *Blacks' Magic* (1990), the trio's third studio album, also contained "Let's Talk about Sex," initially written by Azor. With growing concern about the AIDS pandemic and its negative impact on the Black community, however, Salt became proactive and rewrote the song's lyrics in 1992 as a public service announcement renamed "Let's Talk about AIDS." The trio's fourth album, *Very Necessary* (1993), achieved multi-platinum status. Contributing to its success are two tracks, "Shoop" and "Whatta Man," backed by En Vogue. In the videos, the trio eyeballs desirable men ranging from corporate types to ruffnecks (a fly guy associated with urban street culture), thus "flippin' the script" (reversing a situation) by referencing men as sexual objects.

Other women who helped to define hip hop's fly girl image are Lisa "Left Eye" Lopes and her trio TLC of Atlanta, Georgia. When TLC entered the scene with the female empowering single "Ain't 2 Proud 2 Beg" from their debut album *Oooooooohhh . . . On the TLC Tip* (LaFace/Artista, 1992), they dressed in baggy, oversized outfits with colored condoms attached. Left Eye, the group's MC, especially stood out, having covered the left lens of her glasses with a condom as well. Although their debut album certified quadruple platinum worldwide, TLC's second album *CrazySexyCool* (LaFace/Arista, 1994) won numerous awards. The single "Waterfalls" advocated TLC's stance against unprotected sex as amplified in the video version. Connecting with increasing public awareness of the AIDS pandemic, "Waterfalls" propelled TLC to mega status, earning two of MTV's most coveted Video Music Awards for "Viewer's Choice" and "Video of the Year" in 1995 and two 1995 Grammy Awards for "Best R&B Album" and "Best R&B Performance by a Duo or Group with Vocal." The Recording Industry Association of America (RIAA) certified *CrazySexyCool* as diamond; the album ultimately sold twenty-three million copies worldwide.

Prior to her untimely death in 2002, Left Eye and her crew TLC recorded a third album, *FanMail* (LaFace/Arista, 1999). Following a five-year hiatus owing to personal and financial challenges, *FanMail* is a testament to their perseverance, maturity, and survival. Of the seventeen tracks of *FanMail*, "No Scrubs," and "Unpretty" landed #1 spots on "Billboard Hot 100" for their messages about undesirable men and issues regarding self-esteem, respectively.

Near the end of the golden age of hip hop enters MC–songwriter–producer Missy "Misdemeanor" Elliott of Portsmouth, Virginia. Elliott's career began with the formation of a neighborhood vocal group, Fayze, with production assistance from her friend Timothy "Timbaland" Mosley. After working behind the scenes songwriting for other artists, Missy Elliott stepped into the forefront as a hip hop fly girl.[29] In so doing, she released her solo debut album *Supa Dupa Fly* (1997) on her own label, Goldmine, distributed by Elektra. Mesmerizing audiences with the album's single "The Rain (Supa Dupa Fly)" and eventually nominated for three MTV awards and two Grammys, Elliott's newfound success with Timbaland prompted salutes to the duo as the "latter-day Ashford and Simpson."[30]

Missy Elliott is unique for her ability to successfully flaunt the latest hip hop fashions on her full-figured frame, together with her finger-wave hairstyle, popularly referred to by her admirers as "Missy waves." In the video of "The Rain (Supa Dupa Fly)," directed by Hype Williams, Elliott confidently dons an overblown blimp-like pantsuit constructed of Black plastic garbage bags. In some scenes, she adds a silver galactic-styled headpiece with sunglasses to her fashion statement. As a full-figured woman, Elliot succeeds in staking her claim to rap music's fly girl category, breaking new ground at that time in an arena that had been off-limits to all but the most slender-proportioned woman.

With her single "She's a Bitch" from her sophomore album *Da Real World* (The Goldmind/Electra, 1999), Elliott appends another image to her fly girl persona. With her face and hairstyle resembling that made popular by singer–actress–model Grace Jones—the *femme fatale* of disco—Elliott's usage of "bitch" makes a lyrical declaration about being an artist–business woman who is a mover and shaker, on- and offstage, in an arena dominated by men. In addressing the status of women rappers in comparison to their male counterparts, Elliot shares much in common with women who fall under the "Sista with Attitude" rubric.

Sista with Attitude

The category "Sista with Attitude" includes hip hop female artists who seem to pride themselves on being direct, or "in yo' face," explicit, and forthcoming, as conveyed in their performances. In general, performers in this category equate "having attitude" with a sense of empowerment. Often, these sistas reclaimed and redefined the term "bitch," viewing it as positive rather than negative by using the title to entertain or provide cathartic release. As Lyndah from BWP (Bytches with Problem) explains, "We use 'Bytches' [to mean] a strong, positive, aggressive woman who goes after what she wants. We take that on today and use it in a positive sense."[31] For other sistas with attitude, "bitch" depicts a callous attitude or stoic demeanor as with Charli Batimore's *Cold as Ice* (Epic, 1999) or Trina's *Da Baddest Bitch* (Slip-N-Slide, 2000).[32]

Roxanne Shanté was among the first to fully exploit the sista with attitude persona to a level that earned her the title "The Millie Jackson of Rap." As previously discussed, Roxanne started her career as a member of the Juice Crew, making an impact with the Roxanne Wars rap. She nurtured her image with follow-up albums, *Bad Sister*

(Cold Chillin, 1989) and *The Bitch Is Back* (Livin' Large/Tommy Boy, 1992). MC Lyte also represents the sista with attitude image. While she does not directly refer to herself as a "bitch" in her lyrics, Lyte was well respected for her no-nonsense attitude and hard-hitting lyrical style intensified via boisterous speech. She flaunts her rhyming skill in a quasi-raspy vocal timbre, which she characterizes as "quick, wicked, and buckwild."[33] She is mostly remembered as the first female MC to project, in a commercial sense, a feminist stance as captured in the singles "I Cram to Understand U (Sam)" and "Paper Thin" from her debut album, *Lyte as a Rock* (First Priority Music, 1988), which reportedly "sold seventy-five thousand copies in a month with virtually no airplay."[34] In these songs, MC Lyte chides Sam, a fictive boyfriend character, for carousing with other women as her statement of female empowerment over a conniving man. What is also noteworthy is how MC Lyte appears on her debut album cover, wearing an athletic suit with sneakers, a unisex look that strategically downplays her gender, forcing listeners to zone-in on her lyrical skills rather than her physical appearance.

While there are numerous female MCs who can be categorized as "Sistas with Attitude," there are those who have notably pushed the boundaries of "attitude." Da Brat, dressed in oversized pants wearing long thick pigtails, for instance was described by critics as "a foul mouth, an admitted tom-boy, [who] cusses like there's no tomorrow [but] has made that 'tude work for her."[35] From Chicago, Da Brat is celebrated as the first female solo rap artist to achieve platinum with her debut album, *Funkdafied* (So So Def/Columbia, 1994). Other women who projected unbridled "attitude" are distinguished as the "first ladies" of their respective male crews: Mia X of Master P's No Limit, Eve of DMX's Ruff Ryders, Gangsta Boo of Three 6 Mafia, and Lady of Rage, the first female act signed to Death Row Records.

The sista with attitude category is augmented with Lil' Kim and Foxy Brown, who conflate flyness and hardcore attitudes with sexually explicit lyrics and seductive dress in their stage performances. Their affiliations with male rappers who employ both hardcore and gangsta-style lyrics—Kim with Notorious B.I.G. and the Junior M.A.F.I.A., and Foxy Brown with Nas's collective, The Firm—undoubtedly bolster their personae to the point where they were perceived by critics as hip hop bad girls, "mack divas," or "Thelma and Louise of rap."[36] Furthermore, Brown, whose name is derived from actress Pam Grier's 1974 screen character, emulates the powerful and desirable yet dangerous woman. While Kim's debut album *Hard Core* (Undeas/Big Beat, 1996) and Brown's *Ill Na Na* (Def Jam, 1997) reached platinum status, with follow-up successes,[37] some female cultural readers feared that the image of Lil' Kim and Foxy Brown would eventually limit the range and possibilities of performance for women. The image of the hyper-sexualized female hip hop artist—partially clad and "'shootin' off the mouth," critics argue, sends mixed messages about feminism and Black women in general. As noted by feminist hip hop commentator Joan Morgan, Black women's power—on- and offstage—is sustained by "those sisters who selectively ration their erotic power."[38] Morgan's candid observation comes near the end of hip hop's golden age when the music industry shifted its preference from a lyrically dexterous female MC to the hyper-sexualized female MC image. The former became a secondary component for securing a record deal as documented in the Black Entertainment Television's documentary, *My Mic Sounds Nice: A Truth about Women and Hip Hop* (2010).

Lesbian

The "queering" of mainstream hip hop was nonexistent during hip hop's golden age. The female MC Queen Pen is credited for disrupting the heteronormative lyrical content employed by other female MCs in the late 1990s. She is considered the first aboveground hip hop artist to openly reference women loving women in her single "Girlfriend," from her debut album *My Melody* (Lil' Man, 1997). Moreover, "Girlfriend" is recognized as a thematic "breakthrough for queer culture" in hip hop.[39] Produced by Teddy Riley, the architect of new jack swing,[40] "Girlfriend" plays on Black lesbian culture as suggested with the inclusion of Me'Shell NdegéOcello, who was openly bisexual, performing on vocals and bass guitar. NdegéOcello's "If That's Your Boyfriend (He Wasn't Last Night)" is sampled throughout "Girlfriend" in which the narrative situates Queen Pen as a suitor in a lesbian relationship. While "Girlfriend" has a hip hop sensibility and a musically resonant funk-driven soundtrack, the hip hop community responded negatively. Queen Pen expressed her dismay: "This song is buggin' everyone out right now. You got Ellen [DeGeneres], you got K. D. Lang. Why shouldn't urban lesbians go to a girl club and hear their own thing?"[41] The song is buggin' everyone out, according to Michael Eric Dyson, because the genre is "notoriously homophobic."[42] Queen Pen's lyrics, in essence, challenge heteronormative presentations and identities in hip hop culture.

Black lesbian culture and identity often have been problematized in hip hop through characterizations that often are either distinctly feminine- or masculine-identified. This dichotomy leaves little room for a fuller representation of the richness of Black lesbian experience. Given that there is no unitary Black lesbian subject position, the inclusion of lesbian as a separate category could prompt confusion. Conversations with female cultural readers seemed to suggest that Queen Pen's persona was also fly in that she wore makeup and stylish clothes. NdegéOcello was noted for her performances of persona more along the continuum of female masculinities.[43] Both Queen Pen and Me'Shell NdegéOcello's images in performance suggest "role-play," though in contrasting ways. Although a music video was not produced for "Girlfriend," Queen Pen exudes a *femme* image in her performances by wearing prominent makeup, fly clothing, and chic hairstyles. Me'Shell NdegéOcello's public persona contrasts that of *femme* as suggested with the wearing of little to no makeup, closely cropped Afro hairstyle, and pants/shirt dress style.[44]

Queen Pen is aware of her significance as an innovator introducing a controversial topic to hip hop, declaring, "Two or three years from now, people will say Queen Pen was the first female to bring the lesbian life to light [in an open way] on wax. It's reality. What's the problem?"[45] Her declaration came into fruition during the post–golden age of hip hop with the August 2014 premiere of the reality show *Sisterhood of Hip Hop* on the Oxygen cable network channel. The show depicts an openly Black and queer female MC, Siya, among a cast of heterosexual female MCs.

Video Models/Video Vixens

As hip hop moved further into mainstream popular culture and its golden age approached an end in the late 1990s, the image of women on album jackets and in videos became highly sexualized. Most notably, as previously stated, the music industry demonstrated a preference for the more revealing dress and hyper-sexualized "bad girl" female MCs rather than the modestly dressed performers with consummate lyrical skills. The sexualized female image in hip hop took root with the controversial album jacket of 2 Live Crew's album, *As Nasty as They Wanna Be* (Luke/Atlantic, 1989), which featured four women, turned backward and posed spreadeagle wearing only bikini thongs, that ushered in the subgenre "booty rap" or "porno rap." As the demand grew for scantily clad female "exotic-type" dancers in the hip hop video market, the strip club and the pornographic film industry became major scouting camps for female extras in rap music videos.[46] Such music videos as 2Pac's adult video version of "How Do You Want It" (Death Row/Interscope, 1996) initiated the casting of porn stars Heather Hunter, Angel Kelly, and Nina Hartley in rap music videos.[47]

Also known as "video models," "video hotties," or "video hos," depending on the explicit contents of a video, men in the music industry describe a video vixen as a woman who is physically attractive or "eye-candy" for/to male viewers. She is perceived as a foxy woman or a fly girl with an attractive face complemented by makeup, long, sculpted nails, well-endowed posterior and breasts, small waistline, and revealing clothing. With gyrating hips and bump and grind movements, she is made to look as though she has stepped out of a fashion magazine. Serving as the ultimate tease and sexual fantasy, the video vixen titillates male desire. Although she is often a woman of color, ideally she is of mixed-race heritage.[48] The proliferation of video vixens in hip hop–oriented magazines signals the reinsertion of a male-centered perspective and ideology in defining the roles and images of women performers in the genre.[49]

There are some women who reject the label "video vixen," preferring instead to be called "video model." One such example is Melyssa Ford, a veteran of the hip hop music video circuit, who gravitated from being a video model to an actress and television personality.[50] Despite the criticism, the proliferation of the video girl in hip hop poses a challenge to female MCs who find that their physical attributes are to be likened to the video vixen as a primary requisite, while wreckin' the microphone takes a backseat.[51]

WOMEN BEHIND THE SCENES IN MUSIC VIDEO INDUSTRY

Beyond the video vixen, women in hip hop have made strides in the music video industry working behind the scenes as directors, a role typically dominated by males. Among hip hop's pioneering female video directors are Millicent Shelton, recognized for her work with Salt-N-Pepa and MC Lyte, and Diane Martel for her works with Gang Starr, LL Cool J, and Onyx. Others include Kia Puriefoy and Nzingha Stewart, who produced videos for 2Pac's group Thug Life, featuring Nate Dogg, and Common, featuring Erykah Badu, respectively.

Other women have advanced in documentary filmmaking, including Rachel Raimist with *Nobody Knows My Name* (1999), which profiles female hip hop artists of Los Angeles's underground scene.[52] Ava DuVernay directed Black Entertainment Television's (BET) first music documentary, *My Mic Sounds Nice: A Truth about Women and Hip Hop* (2010). This work presents poignant perspectives from MC Lyte, Missy Elliott, Eve, Rah Digga, Yo-Yo, and Lady of Rage concerning the pressures and expectations levied upon women by a male-dominated music industry and their growing concerns about a dying breed of female MCs.[53]

Finally, women in hip hop have made significant strides in the trade publication world as well. Among these are Kimberly Osorio, the first female Editor-in-Chief for hip hop premiere magazine, *The Source*; Julia Beverly, founder of *Ozone*, the first nationally successful hip hop–based magazine that profiles hip hop acts from the "Dirty South" (southern hip hop areas of Houston, Miami, and Atlanta); and Jeanette Petri of Belgium, founder of *Anattitude Magazine*, an online international hip hop publication with a penchant for underground hip hop that features women.[54]

One of the important lessons learned in the entertainment industry is the art of reinvention over the course of the artist's life and career cycle. Such is the case with women in hip hop from the golden age, whose influence extends well beyond being MCs, video models, or managers. For example, hip hop manager Mona Scott-Young (formerly Mona Scott), co-founder and former president of Violator Management Entertainment, started her own multi-entertainment conglomerate, Monami Entertainment, LLC.[55] Among her projects are VH1's reality show *Love & Hip Hop*, which inspired similar programs, such as Oxygen channel's *Sisterhood of Hip Hop* (2014). Melyssa Ford, now a veteran video model, landed supporting lead roles in films (i.e. *Love for Sale*, 2008; *Good Hair*, 2009; *Video Girl*, 2011; and the *Think Like a Man* franchise, 2012, 2014) and reality show appearances on Bravo cable network's *Blood, Sweat and Heels* (2014). Lil' Kim was featured as a contestant on *Dancing with the Stars* in 2009, coming in at fifth place. MC Lyte became an actor and philanthropist, as well as the first African American woman to serve as President of the Los Angeles Chapter of the Grammy Organization (2011–2013). She is also author of *Unstoppable—Igniting the Power within to Reach Your Greatest Potential* (2012). Finally, Queen Latifah's star power includes an Oscar nomination, a Grammy nomination, and credits as an author, producer, talk show host, spokesmodel–fashion designer, and perfumer; additionally, she has the distinction of being the only full-figured woman of color ever to become the face of CoverGirl.[56]

HIP HOP WOMEN IN THE INTERNATIONAL SCENE

In 2003, it was clear that women were integral to the legacy of hip hop music and culture. Acknowledging their significance, the National Academy of Recording Arts and Sciences (NARAS) established the category, "Best Female Rap Solo Performance" in 2003. Missy Elliott was the first female MC to win in this category and the last to do so in 2004, when NARAS discontinued the category due to the decline of women MC recording artists.[57] Women who continued to make strides in hip hop in the 2000s included: Lil Mama, Lady Luck, Brianna Perry, Azealia Banks, Diamond, and women of predominantly male collectives, such as Rah Digga of Busta Rhymes' Flipmode Squad and Remy Ma of Fat Joe's Terror Squad. Toni Blackman was recognized as the first hip hop artist selected by the US State Department to serve as a cultural ambassador, while others carved a niche in hip hop for transgender artists like female MCs Katey Red and Big Freedia, to name a few.

Around 2003, hip hop witnessed a diverse roster of female MCs from various global centers, who became household names in a field once dominated by US-based acts. Most notable among these are South African–born sensation Jean Grae, Sri Lankan–British act M.I.A., Trinidadian-born hip hop singer Nicki Minaj, and Australian-born (non-Aborigine) Iggy Azalea.[58] Each of these artists possesses lyrical prowess that contributes to her distinct style of delivery.

Jean Grae, the daughter of South African parents—jazz pianist Abdullah Ibrahim (formerly known as Dollar Brand) and jazz singer Sathima Bea Benjamin—emerged from

New York City's underground scene during the mid-1990s. Followed by her single "Love Song" (Third Earth Music, 2002), Grae's rise to prominence as a solo artist matured when she joined forces with Talib Kweli on his label Blue Sky Black Death to record her solo album, *The Evil Jeanius*, in 2008.

M.I.A. (Missing In Action), a Sri Lankan MC from London, England, combines a chanted MC style with a British accent/dance hall sound over an electronica-driven soundtrack, as heard in her underground hit single, "Galang" (XL/Interscope, 2003). Though better known in international contexts, M.I.A.'s popularity soared in the United States after she received an Academy Award nomination in 2009 for her performance of "O, Saya," co-written by A. R. Rahman, for the Academy Award–winning film *Slumdog Millionaire* (2008). Soon afterwards, she performed alongside noted male MCs Lil' Wayne, T.I., Kanye West, and Jay-Z at the fifty-first Annual Grammy Awards ceremony in 2009. A descendant of Tamil refugee parents from Sri Lanka, M.I.A. confronts political issues such as human genocide in such work as her video "Born Free" (N.E.E.T/Interscope, 2010).[59]

Nicki Minaj surfaced in the hip hop world via the mixtape route. Her lyrical prowess garnered her "Female Artist of the Year" at the Underground Music Awards in 2008. She consequently received offers to record with other labels, becoming "the first artist to sign" with Lil' Wayne's label Young Money.[60] Constructing her persona, she performed under various stage names—Nicki Lewinsky, Roman Zolanski, Nicki Teresa. Often compared to Lil' Kim, Nicki Minaj once stated in *Hip Hop Ruckus*, an online underground publication, "I'm just an all around bad bitch," reinforcing her sista with attitude–bad girl image.[61] Appearing on her platinum-winning debut album *Pink Friday* (2010) were hip hop's luminaries—from Eminem on the track "Roman's Revenge," Drake on "Moment 4 Life," Kanye West on "Blazin'," and Rihanna on "Fly," and a host of artists, Swizz Beatz, will.i.am, and Kane Beatz, just to name a few.[62] Her overall lyrical style combines wit, spunk, and humor, while her sense of fashion embraces multi-colored wigs, sky high platform shoes, flamboyant angular-designed outfits, all of which complement her theatrical stage sensibility. Although her subsequent albums' titles play on her obsession with the color pink, Nicki Minaj has initiated several lyrical disses (insults) with artists Remy Ma, Foxy Brown, and Lil' Kim, thus fueling her sista with attitude façade.[63]

Iggy Azalea began rapping at the age of fourteen in Mullumbimby, New South Wales of Australia. She came to the United States two years later to hone her lyrical skills while living in the "Dirty South." Following her debut album, *Glory* (2012), her sophomore album, *The New Classic* (2013) on Virgin/Def Jam, which featured the single "Fancy" with British singer Charlie XCX, was hailed as her signature classic. With the release of her video single, "Pu$$y," which went viral, Azalea landed a recording contract on T.I.'s label, Grand Hustle, in 2013. Iggy Azalea, similar to Nicki Minaj, exudes a hybridization of rap's fly girl–bad girl with 'tude, though in appearance and stage performance comparable to mega-female pop singers on the scene (e.g., Beyoncé, Lady Gaga, etc.).

As women of hip hop music advance in the contemporary era, they are sometimes criticized for being too "pop," materialistic, hypersexual, and less musically diverse than those from hip hop's golden age.[64] But it is widely understood that female MCs who acquiesce to these formulaic trends are more likely to acquire lucrative record deals. As hip hop continues to reflect youth expressive culture in the global communities, there is promise and fertile ground for continued innovation and change for women in the field.

Such figures as Salome of Iran and Shadia Mansour of Palestinian descent, for example, create lyrics that protest and denounce the sexism and oppression in their native countries, whereas others, like Canadian artist Honey Cocaine of Cambodian descent and German emcee Azize-A of Turkish descent, exploit braggadocio as they address socio-political concerns. As hip hop continues to expand its roster to include female MCs from across the globe, the template from which these artists create and shape their expressive performances are, nonetheless, deeply informed by a set of distinct aesthetic qualities and sensibilities popularized by African American female artists who pioneered in the field during the golden age of hip hop.[65]

CONCLUSION

It is clear that women have been quite integral to the hip hop music scene since its formative years and continue to play a major role in shaping its historical trajectory. Since their appearance on the hip hop scene, women in hip hop have advanced as self-defined multidimensional creative artists. Women continue to move beyond the shadows of their male counterparts in diverse ways. While some have become known for their skills on the microphone and turntables, others have excelled in the areas of directing and producing, thereby often using their artistic craft as a platform to refute, deconstruct, and reconstruct alternative visions of female identity in an arena historically viewed as exclusively male. As a consequence of these innovations, hip hop has become a vehicle by which women are empowered to make choices and create spaces for themselves and other *sistas*, proving that women in hip hop are more than a novelty.

ACKNOWLEDGMENTS

A special thanks to Eileen M. Hayes for her critical insights that facilitated finalizing this essay.

NOTES

1. The first part of the title is taken from the single "Ain't Nuthin' but a She Thing" (1995) by Salt-N-Pepa.
2. A mixtape is a compilation of recordings formulated and produced by a DJ or an independent producer. They are designed to circulate via non-commercial routes and to function as a form of publicity for hip hop artists prior to the official or commercial release of their album. DJs typically play mixtapes at local or neighborhood venues. Such promotional strategies help bolster record sales to two markets: the underground or local hip hop market and to the aboveground or commercial/pop market.
3. See Eryn Brown 2015.
4. Keyes 2002, 186.
5. The Real Roxanne, telephone interview with the author, July 30, 1986, Brooklyn, NY.
6. Pearlman 1988, 25.
7. Refer to the following video interviews: "Meet Hip Hop Pioneer Sherri-Sher of Mercedes Ladies," YouTube, posted April 19, 2009, accessed August 8, 2014, https://youtu.be/xIYlznG8nhE; and "Sherri-Sher of Mercedes Ladies Talks w/ Davey D pt2," YouTube, posted April 20, 2009, accessed August 8, 2014, https://youtu.be/zkkmLNVw2tI. The Mercedes Ladies were managed by a person who went by the name of Trevor, who also managed Grandwizard Theodore and his brothers' MC/DJ collective called the L Brothers.
8. The members of the all-female crews Cheba Girls and Choice Girls are lesser known except for member Lady T, who appeared in other all-female crews, as with Mellow-D crew.

9. DJ Scientist 2008, 43.
10. Darryl "D.M.C." McDaniels comments about Sha-Rock in "DMC of Run-DMC Speaks on Sha-Rock of the Funky 4+1s Influence on His Emceeing," YouTube, posted March 8, 2011, accessed August 7, 2014, https://youtu.be/hyXDNIyQLZk. In the interview, D.M.C. goes on to call Sha-Rock an original [hip hop] icon. See also Sha-Rock's autobiography in Johnson and Brown 2011.
11. DJ Kool Herc (also known as Kool DJ Herc) is considered a major pioneer of hip hop sound production concept. He began DJing parties in the Bronx like others. But unlike contemporary party DJs who would dovetail one recording after the other, Herc tailored his DJ style after the dub music production engineers of Jamaica, his home island country, by mixing musical fragments consisting of bass and percussion interludes, referred to as "breaks" or "break beats." It was the break segment of Herc's mixes that prompted dancers to "break" or breakdance.
12. Refer to "Pebblee Poo: Interview with Troy L. Smith," The Foundation (website), accessed August 7, 2014, http://www.thafoundation.com/peblee.htm.
13. DJ Scientist 2008, 46.
14. Ibid.
15. Chang 2005, 179.
16. Afrika Bambaataa landed a recording deal on Tom Silverman's new rap music label. In 1982, Bambaataa's Soul Sonic Force collective recorded and released "Planet Rock" (1982). Revolutionary for its synthe-mix of electropop samples, vocoder, Roland TR-808 drum machine, and advancing the techno-pop sounds of Kraftwerk and Yellow Magic Orchestra, "Planet Rock" ushered in hip hop's electro funk signature style.
17. The Masterdon Committee's local hit became the basis for Master P's "Make 'Em Say Uhh!" (1997) from the album, *Ghetto D*, which peaked at #16 on the "Billboard Hot 100 Charts."
18. Keyes 2002, 69.
19. See articles Green 2004; Caramanica 2008.
20. The battle began with the "The Bridge" (a diminutive of Queensbridge) by Juice Crew members on WBLS answered by BDP's "South Bronx," responded to by the Juice Crew's "Kill That Noise," and a final verbal round with BDP's "The Bridge Is Over."
21. Others are: "Girls Ain't Nothing but Trouble" (1986) by DJ Jazzy Jeff and the Fresh Prince, followed by "Guys Ain't Nothing but Trouble" (1987) by Ice Cream Tee; "Throw the D" (1986) by 2 Live Crew, followed by "Throw the P" (1986) by MC Anquette; and "Dear Yvette" (1986) by LL Cool J, followed by "E-Vette's Revenge" (1986) by E-Vette Money.
22. The golden age of hip hop also included noted women DJs such as Jazzy Joyce, DJ Pam the Funkstress for The Coup, and DJ Symphony of the Beat Junkies, to name a few. A decade later others made noteworthy accomplishments such as DJ Kuttin Kandi, who became the first female turntablist to make the finals at the American DMC national DJ Championships in 1998. Information on women MCs far outnumbers that about women DJs, and thus is a major lacuna in the historical documentation of hip hop.
23. Keyes 2002, 186–209.
24. Ibid., 190.
25. Although Monie Love's success in the United States was predicated on her appearance alongside Queen Latifah in "Ladies First," other female MCs from England on the scene were: Tarrie B, Cookie Crew, and the Wee Papa Girls. However, their success in the United States was minimal compared to Monie Love, who enjoyed popularity in the United States recording market with her debut album, *Down to Earth* (Mercury, 1990), as well as her affiliation with the Native Tongues Afrocentric/positive collective consisting mainly of Queen Latifah, Tribe Called Quest, De La Soul, and the Jungles Brothers.
26. "Ladies First" was directed by Fab Five Freddy, hip hop pioneer/graffiti artist and hip hop's first veejay for the groundbreaking music television program, *Yo! MTV Raps* in August 1988. For further discussion of this video, see Roberts 1996, 163–184.
27. Latifah closes out the millennium with several projects under her belt, including acting in film and television, and her autobiography, *Ladies First: Revelations of a Strong Woman* (New York: William Morrow, 1999), which became a bestseller. Moreover, Latifah's affiliation with the Afrocentric collective Native Tongues (with Tribe Called Quest, Monie Love, De La Soul, and the Jungle Brothers) cemented her image as a positive force of social consciousness–raising hip hop.
28. MC Trouble's career was short-lived due to an epileptic seizure that induced heart failure. She died at the age of twenty.
29. Some of the artists Missy Elliott penned songs for were SWV, Raven-Symoné, and Aaliyah.
30. Keyes 2002, 198.
31. Quoted in ibid., 200.

32. Albums of these artists are as follows: *It's All Good* (Sick Wid It, 2003) and *Game Related* (Sick Wid It, 1995) by Suga-T; *Good Girl Gone Bad* (No Limit, 1995), *Unlady Like* (No Limit, 1997), and *Mama Drama* (No Limit, 1998) by Mia X; *Let There Be Eve . . . Ruff Ryder's First Lady* (Ruff Ryders, 1999) by Eve; *Necessary Roughness* (Death Row/Interscope, 1997) by Lady of Rage; *Enquiring Minds* (Relativity, 1998) by Gangsta Boo; and *The Bytches* (No Face/Columbia, 1991) by Bytches with Problems (BWP).
33. From the liner notes to *Ain't No Other* (First Priority Music, 1993).
34. Coleman 1988, 29.
35. McGregor 1994, 100.
36. Brown cited in Gonzales 1997, 62.
37. Sophomore releases include *The Notorious K.I.M.* (2000), released on Kim's label, Queen Bee, among others, and *Chyna Doll* (Def Jam, 1999).
38. Morgan 1999, 132.
39. Walters 1998, 60.
40. New jack swing is characterized by rhythm and blues vocals over a hip hop production, popularized during the late 1980s with Riley's group Guy featuring Aaron Hall. Other productions that employ new jack swing include those by Al. B. Sure, Christopher Williams, and New Edition, just to name a few, as well as Riley's signature song and production of Michael Jackson's "Remember the Time" (1992).
41. Queen Pen quoted in Jamison 1998, AR34.
42. Ibid.
43. Walker 1993, 868, 875, 886.
44. For further perspectives on NdegéOcello's music, gender, and sexuality, refer to La France 2002; Wiltz 2005.
45. Queen Pen in Jamison 1998.
46. "The strip club," notes T. Denean Sharpley-Whiting, "is rendered a more complex space. . . . It's a male boardroom atmosphere where deals are brokered, video vixens scouted, invitations to appear on records are extended, and records are broken amid bodies undulating on poles, buttocks shaking furiously, and deep toe-touching bends" (Sharpley-Whiting 2007, 118).
47. 2Pac's video, as well as the pay-per-view X-rated adult program, *Peep Show*, hosted by Luke Campbell of 2 Live Crew in 1996, opened the door for hip hop's connection with the pornography industry in the twenty-first century. Snoop Dogg's *Doggystyle* (2001), produced by Larry Flynt and distributed by Flynt's Hustler enterprise, stars a host of adult film actresses. Following Nelly's (in)famous "Tip Drill" (2005) video, filmmaker Byron Hurt's *Beyond Beats and Rhymes* (2007) goes beyond the scene to expose misogyny and its impact on racial perception in hip hop.
48. In "'I See the Same Ho': Video Vixens, Beauty Culture, and Diasporic Sex Tourism," the opening chapter of her 2007 book, Sharpley-Whiting discusses the desire for the mix-raced woman by video directors/male hip hop artists, and the historical precedence for this age-old perception (Sharpley-Whiting 2007, 23–52).
49. Kimberly Osorio discussed this trend with hip hop magazines on the panel "Media Representations of Women in Hip Hop" (April 9, 2005) at the "Feminism and Hip Hop Conference," sponsored by the Center for the Study of Race, Politics and Culture (conference, University of Chicago, Chicago, IL, April 7–9, 2005).
50. Melyssa Ford discussed the differences between a video model and video "ho" on the panel "Media Representations of Women in Hip Hop" ("Feminism and Hip Hop Conference," 2005). For more information about the conference, see "Center for the Study of Race, Politics and Culture hosts Feminism and Hip Hop conference, April 7–9," University of Chicago News Office, January 21, 2005, accessed August 8, 2014, http://www-news.uchicago.edu/releases/05/050121.hiphop.shtml. For additional perspectives on video vixens, refer to filmmaker Lisa Cunningham's documentary *My Name is Video Vixen*, which features twenty video models interviewed at the Video Vixen Summit in Atlanta, GA, August 2007. Among the interviewees were Tae Heckard, Ashley Ragland, and the Glenn Twins.
51. This issue is further discussed in Ava DuVernay's *My Mic Sounds Nice: A Truth about Women and Hip Hop* (Produced by Black Entertainment Television, 2010).
52. They include Asia One, T-Love, Lisa, and Medusa, dubbed "Queen and High Priestess of the Underground."
53. Academicians also weighed in on the misogyny and objectification of women in hip hop. Important works in this regard include Morgan 1999; Pough 2004; Pough et al. 2007; Sharpley-Whiting 2007; Love 2012. Another work that chronicles the importance of tradition in the making of a female hip hop tradition and its impact on hip hop male artists is Gaunt 2006.

54. At the "Feminism and Hip Hop Conference" (2005), Osorio mentioned the discriminatory treatment by male colleagues at *The Source* magazine, which led her to file a lawsuit with the Equal Employment Opportunity Commission (EEOC). While the court did not find the magazine culpable of harassment or gender discrimination, it did find the magazine guilty of retaliation and defamation against Osorio. She was awarded $7.5 million in damages from *The Source*. In 2012, Osorio returned to *The Source* as Editor-in-Chief.
55. Before branching out from Violator Management, the label was home to noted hip hop artists Missy Elliott, Busta Rhymes, and 50 Cent, and was instrumental for landing commercial spots for their artists. Now, Scott's Monami Entertainment, similar to Russell Simmons's Rush Communications, has a keen interest in film and television projects.
56. Preceding Monami Entertainment, Latifah's Flavor Unit Entertainment, co-founded in 1989 by her lifelong business partner Shakim Compere, became a full-fledged record label in 1993. Latifah then expanded into producing film and television projects, including her HBO film *Bessie*, about blues legend Bessie Smith. Latifah starred as Bessie Smith, and the film earned twelve Emmy nods.
57. The music industry's assumption was that female MCs were on the decline, when, in fact, the industry began to privilege a more contrived pop image as opposed to a more diverse image during hip hop's golden age.
58. Although these MCs are better known in the aboveground circles, there are others in the international hip hop underground community who use MCing as a way to protest political discontent toward their government and the treatment of women by their respective government like Salome of Iran, Shadia Mansour of Palestine, etc.
59. "Born Free" is from M.I.A.'s third studio album, *Maya* (/\/\ /\ Υ /\) (N.E.E.T./Interscope, 2010).
60. Young Money relinquished Nicky Minaj total control of her publishing, creativity, and image.
61. "Nicki Minaj—Beware Sucka MCs," *Hip Hop Ruckus*, August 28, 2008, accessed August 7, 2014, http://hiphopruckus.com/2008/08/on-da-come-up-with-nicki-minaj.html.
62. Because of the signifying or indirect disses (insults), "Roman's Revenge" is a lyrical stab at Lil' Kim.
63. Nicki Minaj even had a lyrical feud with Mariah Carey during Minaj's one-year stint as a judge on *American Idol*.
64. Some of these arguments are captured in Rose 2008 and DuVernay's documentary *My Mic Sounds Nice* (2010).
65. On December 12, 2014, four male hip hop artists from Tunisia and Egypt visited Los Angeles for a conference sponsored by the US Department of State's Creative Arts Exchange (CAE) Program. During the conference, they showcased music videos of Arab rap artists. When I asked them about female MCs of the Arab world, they gave me music video performances of "Hold On" by Tunisian MC Medusa and "We Need to Change" by Palestinian-born Shadia Mansour, dubbed "the First Lady of Arab Rap." I immediately noticed how strikingly similar these women's appearances and performance style were to African American artists labeled the fly girl and sista with attitude.

DISCOGRAPHY

Baltimore, Charli. *Cold as Ice*. Epic/Untertainment Records/Epic 68967, 1999. CD.
Blue Sky Black Death and Jean Grae. *The Evil Jeanius*. Originally released 2008. Instrumentals Babygrande Records 0391, 2009. CD.
Da Brat. *Funkdafied*. Originally released 1994. Chaos Recordings 66164, 2008. CD.
Foxy Brown. *Ill Na Na*. Originally released 1996. Def Jam 5424352, 2000. CD.
Fugees. *Blunted on Reality*. Originally released 1994. Sbme Special Mkts 724289, 2008. CD.
———. *The Score*. Originally released 1996. Col 88697424362, 2009. CD.
Funky Four Plus One. *True School, Vol. 1*. Cold Front Records 3620, 1996. CD.
Grandmaster Flash & the Furious Five. *Adventures of Grandmaster Flash, Melle Mel & the Furious Five: More of the Best*. Originally released 1996. Rhino, 2005. CD.
Grandmaster Flash & the Furious Five (featuring Melle Mel & Duke Bootee). *The Message (Expanded Edition)*. Originally released 1982. Reissued by Castle Music/Sanctuary 2741869, 2010. CD.
Hill, Lauryn. *The Miseducation of Lauryn Hill*. Originally released 1998. Sony Music Distribution 2396, 2009. CD.
Iggy Azalea. *Glory*. Grand Hustle, 2012. Digital.
———. *The New Classic [Deluxe Edition]*. Def Jam 2014. Digital.
J.J. Fad. *Supersonic*. Originally released 1988. Ruthless Records 90959–2, reissue date unknown. CD.

Lil' Kim. *Hard Core*. Originally released 1996. Big Beat/Undeas Recordings 92746, 1998. CD.
MC Lyte. *Lyte as a Rock*. Originally released 1988. Elektra/Rhino, 2002. Digital.
Me'Shell NdegéOcello. *Plantation Lullabies*. Originally released 1993. Includes "If That's Your Boyfriend (He Wasn't Last Night)." Sire 9362457542, 1994. CD.
M.I.A. *Galang*. Originally released 2004. Interscope/XL/XL/Interscope, 2006. Digital.
Missy Elliott. *Supa Dupa Fly*. Originally released 1997. ATG/Atlantic, 2009. Digital.
———. *Da Real World*. Originally released 1999. ATG/Atlantic/Atlantic/Atg, 2009. Digital.
Ms. Melodie. *Diva*. Jive 1210–2-J13, 1989. CD.
Nicky Minaj. *Pink Friday*. Originally released 2010. Universal Distribution, 2011. Digital.
Queen Latifah. *All Hail the Queen*. Originally released 1989. Rhino, 2013. Digital.
———. *Nature of a Sista*. Originally released 1991. Collectors' Choice Music CCM 07262, 2007. CD.
———. *Black Reign*. Originally released 1993. Universal Music 5302722, 1994. CD.
Queen Pen. *My Melody*. Interscope, 1997. Digital.
Roxanne Shanté. *The Bitch Is Back*. Livin' Large Records 3001, 1992. CD.
———. *Bad Sister*. Originally released 1989. Cold Chillin' TEG77514–2, 2010. CD.
Salt-N-Pepa. *Hot, Cool & Vicious*. Originally released 1986. Def Jam /Island/Island/Def Jam, 1992. Digital.
———. *Blacks' Magic*. Def Jam /Island/Island/Def Jam, 1990. Digital.
Sugarhill Gang. *Sugarhill Gang*. Originally released 1980. Rhino, 2012. Digital.
TLC. *Ooooooohhh . . . On the TLC Tip*. Originally released 1992. LaFace 26003, 2009. CD.
———. *CrazySexyCool*. Originally released 1994. BMG 37780, 2006. CD.
The 2 Live Crew. *As Nasty as they Wanna Be*. Originally released 1989. Luke Records 91651–2, reissue date unknown. CD.
Trina. *Da Baddest Bitch*. Originally released 2000. Slip-N-Slide, 2005. Digital.
World Premiere, Vol. 1. Various artists, including Roxanne Shanté and Salt-N-Pepa, among others. Pop Art 8800, 2009. CD.
Yo-Yo. *Make Way for the Motherlode*. EastWest 7567916052, 1991. CD.

PART IV

Musical Agency—African American Music as Resistance

CHAPTER 19

The Antebellum Period
Communal Coherence and Individual Expression

Lawrence W. Levine

It would distort African American music to argue that it has functioned primarily or even largely as a forum for protest. Black Americans have not spent all of their time reacting to the Whites around them, and their songs are filled with comments on all aspects of life. But it would be an even greater distortion to assume that a people occupying the position that African Americans have in American society could create so rich and varied a music with few allusions and responses to their situation. For millions of Black Americans, throughout slavery and long after emancipation, the normal outlets for protest and political expression remained firmly closed. To comprehend their reaction to the system under which they were forced to live, it is necessary to make our definition of resistance less restrictive and more realistic.

Protest has been too easily depicted in exclusively political and institutional terms. By searching too narrowly for signs of political consciousness and revolutionary activity among slaves and freed people, we have missed other manifestations of their group consciousness, sense of pride, and use of their culture to define themselves and comment upon their status. To maintain that Black music and song constituted a form of Black resistance does not mean that it necessarily led to or even called for any tangible and easily identifiable protest, but rather that it served as a mechanism by which American Blacks could be relatively open in a society that rarely accorded them that privilege, could communicate this candor to others whom they would in no other way be able to reach, and could assert their own individuality, aspirations, and sense of being in a repressive society structured to prevent such affirmations. An examination of African American music during slavery and in the decades after emancipation makes this clear.

That antebellum slaves managed to develop their own culture that blended aspects of the White culture around them with many of the African styles, genres, and worldviews they had brought with them was the result of a number of factors. The first of these was that Whites found it easier to justify the enslavement and exploitation of a people whose behavior patterns were sufficiently different to be labeled "primitive" or "childlike." With such important exceptions as the suppression of the drums that had been so central in African music, White masters had an unspoken and perhaps unconscious urge to allow African Americans to stew in their own cultural juices. Slave dancing—which was incorporated into all aspects of slaves' music including the religious "shout"—constitutes an excellent example. With its openly African style of gliding, dragging steps, flexed, fluid bodily position, propulsive rhythm, and concentration upon movement outward from the pelvic region, which many ministers decried as lewd, slave dance was tolerated and even encouraged by a substantial number of masters, as were many of the other distinctive musical practices of the slaves (Figure 19.1).[1]

In addition, as slaves came to understand how few channels of genuine acculturation were open to them and how little the White world offered but the certainty of arbitrary and perpetual bondage, they developed their own cultural universe in which the peer groups and role models remained largely Black. Finally, because they were not inducted into the literate world of their White masters, antebellum slaves, like their African forebears, lived in a world of sound in which the spoken, chanted, sung, or shouted word was the primary form of communication. Slaves, a Northern visitor wrote in 1856, "go singing to their daily labors. The maid sings about the house and the laborer sings in the field."[2] Because the slaves' cultural roots were in an African sacred worldview that never drew modernity's clear line between the religious and the secular, much of what was sung in both house and field were spirituals. They were not sung exclusively in churches but were used as rowing songs, field songs, work songs, and social songs. On the Port Royal Islands, off the coast of South Carolina, Lucy McKim heard the same spiritual, "Poor Rosy," with its final line,

Figure 19.1
"Negro Village on a Southern Plantation," from *Aunt Phillis's Cabin* by Mary H. Eastman, 1852.

"Heab'n shall-a be my home," sung in boats to time the movement of the oars, sung vigorously in the hominy mill to keep the slaves' movements synchronized with the whirling stone, and sung "slowly and mournfully" in the slave quarters at night.[3]

Spirituals also testify to the continuation of a strong sense of community. The overriding antiphonal structure of the spirituals—the call-and-response pattern that Blacks brought with them from Africa and that may have been reinforced in America by the practice of lining out hymns—placed individuals in continual dialogue with each other. The structure of their music presented slaves with an outlet for individual feelings even while it continually drew them back into the communal presence and permitted them the comfort of basking in the warmth of the shared assumptions that permeated slave songs.

The most persistent of those assumptions was rooted in the image of the chosen people. "We are the people of God," slaves sang over and over. "I really do believe I'm a child of God." "I'm born of God, I know I am." Nor is there ever any doubt that "To the promised land I'm bound to go," "I walk de heavenly road," and "I'll hear the trumpet sound/In that morning."[4] For this message of personal worth and confidence to be expressed by Black slaves who were told endlessly that they were members of the lowliest of races offers an insight into the ways slaves could fuse their African worldview and their new religion into barriers against the internalization of the larger society's stereotyped images of them.

The African American worldview forged by slaves allowed them to reach spatially upward to communicate with their gods and temporally backward to touch the lives of their mythic ancestors. The God of whom the slaves sang was neither remote nor abstract but as intimate, personal, and immediate as the gods of Africa had been: "Gwine to argue wid de Father and chatter wid de son, . . . Gwine talk 'bout de bright world dey jes' come from."

Gwine to write to Massa Jesus,
To send some Valiant soldier
To turn back Pharaoh's army, Hallelu![5]

The heroes of the Scriptures—"Sister Mary," "Brudder Jonah," "Brudder Moses," "Brudder Daniel"—were greeted with similar intimacy and immediacy. The slaves not only identified with the acts of their spiritual ancestors, they could recreate them. In 1818, a group of White Quaker students observed slaves doing their counterclockwise ring shout, moving slowly around and around in a circle blowing a tin horn and chanting: "We're traveling to Immanuel's land/Glory! Halle-lu-jah." One of the onlookers gradually realized that he was witnessing "Joshua's chosen men marching around the walls of Jericho, blowing the rams' horns and shouting, until the walls fell."[6]

It is significant that Joshua and Jonah, Daniel and David, Moses and Noah, all of whom fill the lines of the spirituals, were delivered in *this* world, not the next, and delivered in ways that struck the imagination of the slaves. Over and over, their songs dwelt upon the spectacle of the Red Sea opening to allow the Hebrew slaves past before inundating the mighty armies of the Pharaoh. They lingered delightedly upon the image of little David humbling the great Goliath with a stone. They retold in endless variation the stories of the blind and humbled Samson bringing down the mansions of his conquerors, of the ridiculed Noah patiently building the ark that would deliver him from the doom of a mocking world, of the timid Jonah attaining freedom from his confinement through faith. Slaves made it clear that these Old Testament stories had contemporary meaning for them. "O my Lord delivered Daniel," they sang, and responded logically: "O why not deliver me, too?" Slaves rehearsed the triumphs of the Hebrew Children in verse after verse, concluding each with the comforting thought: "And the God dat lived in Moses' [Dan'el's, David's] time is jus' de same today." The "mighty rocky road" that "I must travel," they insisted, is "De rough, rocky road what Moses done travel."[7] Like the heroes they celebrated, the slaves too reached beyond the bonds that confined them. Continually they envisioned the possibility of imminent change: "I look at de worl' an' de worl' look new, . . . I look at my hands an' they look so too. . . . I looked at my feet, my feet was too." "You got a right, I got a right," they sang, "We all got a right to de tree ob life."[8]

These songs manifest clearly the manner in which the sacred world of the slaves was able to combine the precedents of the past, the conditions of the present, and the promise of the future into one connected reality. In no other expressive medium were the slaves permitted to speak so openly of the afflictions of bondage and their longings for freedom. In this sense, there was always an element of protest in the slaves' religious songs. Frederick Douglass asserted that for him and many of his fellow slaves the song, "O Canaan, sweet Canaan,/I am bound for the land of Canaan," symbolized "something more than a hope of reaching heaven. We meant to reach the *North*, and the North was our Canaan," while the lines, "Run to Jesus, shun the danger,/I don't expect to stay much longer here," had a double meaning that first suggested to him the thought of escaping from slavery. Similarly, when Black Civil War troops sang: "We'll soon be free,/When de Lord will call us home," a young drummer boy explained: "Dey tink *de Lord* mean for say *de Yankees*."[9]

Slave songs were filled with innuendo and hidden meaning, and there is no reason to doubt that slaves sometimes used their songs as a means of secret communication. An ex-slave told Lydia Parrish that when slaves "suspicioned" that one of their number was informing, they would sing:

> O Judyas he wuz a 'ceitful man
> He went an' betray a mos' innocen' man.
> Fo' thirty pieces a silver dat it wuz done
> He went in de woods an' 'e self he hung.[10]

Similarly, such spirituals as the commonly heard "Steal away, steal away, steal away to Jesus!" could be used as calls to secret meetings. But it would be a misreading of slave spirituals to think of them as *either* about this world or the next; they were about both simultaneously.[11]

Nowhere is this better demonstrated than during the Civil War itself. It was to be expected that the war would give rise to such new spirituals as the popular "Many Thousand Go," with its jubilant rejection of all the facets of slave life—"No more peck o' corn for me, . . . No more driver's lash for me, . . . No more mistress' call for me." What was as significant was the ease with which slaves' old songs fit their new situation. With so much of their inspiration drawn from the Book of Exodus in the Old Testament and the Book of Revelation in the New, slaves had long sung of the Army of the Lord, of trumpets summoning the faithful, and of vanquishing the hosts of evil. These songs were, as Colonel Thomas Wentworth Higginson put it, "available for camp purposes with very little strain upon their symbolism." "We'll cross de mighty river," his Black troops sang while marching or rowing,

> We'll cross de danger water, . . .
> O Pharaoh's army drownded!
> My army cross over.

But they also found their less overtly militant songs quite as appropriate to warfare. In their most popular marching song they sang: "Jesus call you. Go in de wilderness/To wait upon de Lord." Black Union soldiers found it no more incongruous to accompany their fight for freedom with the sacred songs of their bondage than they had found it inappropriate as slaves to sing their spirituals while picking cotton or shucking corn. Their religious songs, like their religion itself, was of this world as well as the next.[12]

Such uses of sacred music in Black culture never disappeared, and during the Civil Rights Movement of the 1950s and 1960s they were revived. While spirituals may have dominated slave life quantitatively and qualitatively,[13] antebellum Black music contained a striking diversity of songs and dances that were frequently used for purposes quite similar to those of sacred songs. In their tales, Blacks spoke of how they used their music to dupe Whites. In one popular story, a master dropped in on his slave to hear him play the fiddle. The slave, fearful that his master would see the leg of a stolen pig sticking out from under his bed, sang: "Ding-Ding a Dingy—Old Lady put the pig's foot further on the bed." His wife walked to the bed while harmonizing, "Ummmmmmmmm," and jerked the cover down over the pig's foot. "Yessir, that's a new one," the master said, delighting in the improvised song. "Yessir, that's a new one."[14]

Slaves commonly used their songs to speak of the master class with a surprising openness. In 1774, an English visitor, after his first encounter with slave music, wrote in his journal: "In their songs they generally relate the usage they have received from their Masters or Mistresses in a very satirical stile [sic] and manner."[15] On the St. Johns River in Florida during the 1830s, a White passenger on a boat propelled by "a dozen stout negro [sic] rowers" described how the boatmen timed their oars by singing songs "full of rude wit" that satirized everyone on board, Blacks and Whites alike.[16] Harriet Jacobs testified that during the Christmas festivities she and her fellow slaves would ridicule stingy Whites by singing:

> Poor massa, so dey say;
> Down in de heel, so dey say;
> Got no money, so dey say;
> Not one shillin, so dey say;
> God A'mighty bress you, so dey say.[17]

"Once in a while among a mass of nonsense and wild frolic," Frederick Douglass noted, "a sharp hit was given to the meanness of slaveholders":

> We bake de bread,
> Dey gib us de crust;
> We sif de meal,
> Dey gib us de huss;
> We peel de meat,

Dey gib us de skin;
And dat's de way
Dey take us in; . . .[18]

Abram Harris remembered a satirical song sung by himself and his fellow slaves that became part of the minstrel stage and remained part of the Black folk repertory until the mid-twentieth century.

My old Mistis promised me
Dat when she died, she gwine set me free.
But she lived so long en got so po
Dat she lef me diggin wid er garden ho.[19]

In one aspect of their lives after another, slaves used their music and the bodily movement that was an integral element of it to free themselves from the tyranny of their masters' assumptions of superiority. The poet William Cullen Bryant witnessed a series of slave dances on a South Carolina plantation in 1843 that gradually became transformed into a mock military parade, "a sort of burlesque of our militia trainings, in which the words of command . . . were extremely ludicrous."[20] An ex-slave recalled that when she was young in the 1840s,

> Us slaves watched white folks' parties where the guests danced a minuet and then paraded in a grand march, . . . Then we'd do it, too, *but we used to mock 'em*, every step. Sometimes the white folks noticed it, but they seemed to like it; I guess they thought we couldn't dance any better.[21]

Shephard Edmonds described how Tennessee slaves, dressed in "hand-me down finery," would "do a high-kicking, prancing, . . . take-off on the high manners of the white folks in the 'big house,' but their masters who gathered around to watch the fun, missed the point."[22]

These types of musical expression accelerated after the Civil War. As Blacks became increasingly literate and geographically mobile and the culture of the world around them became more accessible, their expressions of resistance tended to be lodged in more purely secular music. If during slavery it was the secular songs that were occasional and the sacred songs that represented the ethos of the Black folk, in freedom this balance gradually began to reverse itself. Many of those antebellum slave and minstrel songs that revolved around grievances against Whites lived on well into freedom. A song that had won "everlasting shouts of applause" for the White minstrel Dan Emmett when he performed it in the 1840s was still being sung by Blacks in Alabama in 1916:

Ol marster was a stingy man
And everybody know'd it;
Kept good likker in his house
And never said here goes it.[23]

Just as slaves had found that they could most safely articulate their longing for freedom by singing of the struggles of the Hebrew Children, so their descendants living in the racially repressive turn-of-the-century South could most safely vent their complaints against Whites and the social system by projecting them into the past and giving them the appearance of nostalgia and not protest. They were able to utilize the commonplaces of the minstrel and folk idioms to criticize, parody, and sharply comment on their society and their situation.

Although such songs lived on, postbellum African American musical resistance took a myriad of contemporary forms. John Jacob Niles, collecting songs among American troops in World War I, found Black troops singing songs markedly different than those they had sung in the Civil War:

> What do the Generals and the Colonels do,
> I'll tell you—I'll tell you,
> Figure out just how the privates ought to do
> The dirty little jobs for Jesus.[24]

Blacks, of course, hardly needed to serve in the armed forces to experience the rigors of hierarchical class and caste discrimination. Black singers commented on everything around them with the same critical, satirical thrust they had exhibited in slavery. Innumerable White bosses found their Black workers using song to make comments, articulate complaints, and issue warnings.

> Captain, O captain, you must be blin'
> You keep hollerin' "hurry" an' I'm darn nigh flyin'.[25]

Charles Peabody, who was supervising the excavation of a mound in Coahoma County, Mississippi, in 1901 and 1902, recorded that his Black workers, deep in the trenches they were digging, used music to convey their feelings to their White employers above:

> One Saturday, a half-holiday, a sing-song came out of the trench,
>
> Mighty long half day, Capta-i-n,

and one evening when my companion and I were playing a game of mumble-the-peg, our final occupation before closing work, our choragus shouted for us to hear,

> I'm so tired I'm almost dead,
> Sittin' up there playing mumblely-peg.[26]

Contrasting industrious Black workers with the indolent Whites above them, which of course turned the popular stereotype on its head, was a common theme in Black song, as were comments concerning the inherent injustice of the situation. Twentieth-century Black turpentine workers in Florida articulated complaints in their version of a song first collected from slaves in 1853:

> Niggers get de turpentine,
> Niggers empty it out,
> White man pockets the money,
> Niggers does without.[27]

Black Texas workers sang in 1895:

> White man goes to college,
> Niggers to the field;
> White man learns to read and write;
> Poor Nigger learns to steal, Honey Babe,
> Poor Nigger learns to steal.[28]

A Black cotton picker on the Sea Islands sang of why she was unable to meet her daily quota of one hundred pounds of cotton: "Black man beat me—White man cheat me/ Won' get my hundud all day."[29] Complaints extended from the workplace to the halls of justice. "If a White man kills a negro, they hardly carry it to court," Blacks in Auburn, Alabama, sang; "If a negro kills a white man, they hang him like a goat." New York Blacks agreed: "Here's a little something that you all should know/They always pinch the nigger and let the white folks go."[30] Georgia workers in the early years of the twentieth century made clear their understanding that the American system was not designed to include them:

*If you work all the week,
An' work all the time,
White man sho' to bring
Nigger out behin'.*[31]

Utilizing a familiar structure and often a familiar tune, and drawing upon a reservoir of hundreds of such familiar lines as, "You don't know my mind," "I'm laughin' to keep from cryin'," "Look down that lonesome road," and "I been down so long, it seems like up to me," Black singers left themselves ample scope to improvise new words that fit their surroundings and their mood. Sam Price, growing up in Waco, Texas, recalled a lynching in the neighboring town of Robinson that elicited a song of protest blending the first two spontaneous lines with the latter two lines from the folk repertory:

*I never have, and I never will
Pick no more cotton in Robinsonville,
Tell me how long will I have to wait,
Can I get you now or must I hesitate?*[32]

Work songs, and Black secular songs in general, were characterized by a realistic depiction of the workers' situation. "You want to say something," a Memphis Black observed, "(and you know how we was situated, so we couldn't say or do a lot of things we wanted to), and so you sing it."[33] In both form and function, the work song was a communal instrument. It allowed workers to blend their physical movements and psychic needs with those of other workers; it provided important outlets for communication, commiseration, and expression; and, as Bruce Jackson has suggested, their songs put "the work into the worker's framework, ... By incorporating the work with their song, ... they make it *theirs* in a way it otherwise is not."[34]

Postbellum Black workers sang not only of themselves and their fellows; they began to sing of symbolic heroes who, unlike the trickster figures of the slaves who triumphed by guile and indirection, confronted contemporary White society openly and directly on its own terms. These modern moral heroes triumphed not by breaking the laws of the larger society—as did the bandit heroes who also assumed a place in the songs of Black workers after the Civil War—but by smashing its expectations and stereotypes and insisting that their lives transcend the traditional roles established for Blacks by the White majority. They were moral figures not only because they never preyed on the Black folk, as Black badmen often did, but because their lives provided more than vehicles for momentary escape: they provided models of action and emulation.

The steel driver John Henry was probably the first, and without question the most popular, hero figure of this type. Songs celebrating his exploits were already widespread in the early 1880s and continued to be sung well into the next century. Fundamental to an understanding of John Henry's significance is the economic plight of Black farmers and workers who faced competition from the growing mechanization represented in "John Henry" by the steam drill. "Dat steam drillers here,/Here a good man to rob," John Henry announces as he determines to engage the machine in a contest to see if with his hammer he could drive steel drills into the rock more quickly and deeply. As he prophesies, his triumph over the steam drill comes at the cost of his life. "A man ain't nothing but a man," he tells his captain, "And before I'll be governed by this old steam drill,/ Lawd, I'll die with the hammer in my hand."

John Henry's longevity in Black song was due to the fact that he became a culture hero: a representative figure whose life and struggle are symbolic of the struggle of worker against machine, individual against society, the lowly against the powerful, Black against White. Black workers saw in the death of John Henry not a defeat but a challenge:

This old hammer
Killed John Henry,
Can't kill me, Lord,
Can't kill me.[35]

The epic song "John Henry" signified an important shift in the Black ethos after emancipation. There was no secular figure equivalent to John Henry in slavery. Postbellum Blacks no longer had to turn exclusively to the Bible to find heroic figures who could openly face the oppressors and triumph. They could now look within their own ranks: John Henry was merely the first of a progression of Black heroes, both mythic and real—Shine, Jack Johnson, Joe Louis—who stood proud, defiant, and fearless in the center of White society and inspired the Black folk to relate their exploits in songs and tales.[36]

Paralleling the rise of a new type of African American secular hero in song was the rise of a new type of African American secular music: the blues. As the new century opened, the images surrounding Black music began to expand. Alongside the work–prayer communal contexts that had dominated nineteenth-century Black music in slavery and freedom, there rose the image of an individual with a guitar giving vent to his or her own emotions without the need of an audience. Individual voices had been prominent in African American music before the rise of the blues. In both sacred music and secular work songs, song leaders were significant but their contributions blended into an antiphonal communal situation with responses from churchgoers or the work gang playing a vital role. Black music in America before the twentieth century did not easily fit into the larger society's performer–audience dichotomy.

In the holler, the cry, the call, and the lullaby, slaves and freed people had the ingredients for a highly personalized music but such music remained occasional, the result of social or spatial isolation. What was necessary for the rise of the blues as a central Black music was not the invention of wholly new musical structures, but rather of new forms of self-conception. The blues was the most completely personalized music African Americans had yet developed. The antiphonal call-and-response form remained, but in blues it was the singer who responded to herself or himself either verbally or on an accompanying instrument. The emergence of the blues, along with the rise of such individual secular heroes as John Henry, represented a major degree of acculturation to the individualized ethos of the larger society—an ethos that was alien to the one African slaves brought to this continent and that remained an important source of difference between Black and White Americans throughout the nineteenth century.

The significance of this change for an understanding of African American music as an instrument of resistance is obvious. From the very beginning, the blues was marked by what Abbe Niles referred to as "the element of pure *self*."[37] Blues songs were solo music not only in musical structure and performance but also in content. The persona of the individual performer entirely dominated the song, which centered upon the singer's own feelings, experiences, fears, dreams, acquaintances, or idiosyncrasies. Blues had its share of the moans and complaints of grieving lovers and poverty-stricken denizens of cities and towns, and it was filled with traditional feelings of protest and anger. But for our purposes, perhaps blues' most important element was the repeated and open sense of pride and self-worth that stood at its very center. "I'm as good as any woman in your town," Bessie Smith insisted after her man left her.

> *Some people call me a hobo, some call me a bum.*
> *Nobody knows my name, nobody knows what I've done.*
> *See that long, lonesome road? Lord, you know it's gotta end.*
> *And I'm a good woman, and I can get plenty men.*[38]

The pain of a broken relationship, for all the complaints it might entail, was commonly mitigated by the singer's sense of self, often expressed in humor. Thus the lyrics "Gwine lay my head right on de railroad track,/'Cause my baby, she won't take me back," are followed by "Gwine lay my head right on de railroad track,/If de train come 'long, I'm gwine to snatch it back."[39] Blues songs were filled with the hardships but also the possibilities of life. Fae Barnes (Maggie Jones) sang of "Going North, child, where I can be free/Where there's no hardship, like in Tennessee," and Cow-Cow Davenport announced: "I'm tired of this Jim Crow, gonna leave this Jim Crow town,/Doggone my Black soul, I'm sweet Chicago bound." "Yes," Charley Patton and scores of other bluesmen and women announced, "I'm worried now but I won't be worried long."[40]

While the personalized, solo elements of the blues indicate a decisive move into twentieth-century American consciousness, the musical style of the blues indicates a holding on to the old roots at the very time when the dispersion of Blacks throughout the country and the rise of the radio and phonograph could have spelled the demise of a distinctive African American musical tradition. Blues, with its emphasis upon improvisation, its retention of important elements of the call-and-response pattern, its polyrhythmic effects, and its use of slides, slurs, vocal leaps, and falsetto in vocal production, was a definite assertion of Black resistance to abandoning the distinctive cultural style that had for so long characterized Black music and society.

The blues allowed women and men greater voice for their individuality than any previous form of African American song but kept them still members of the community, still on familiar ground, still in touch with their peers and their roots. It was a song style created by generations in the flux of change who desired and needed to meet the future without losing the past, who needed to stand alone and yet craved communication with and reassurance from members of the group as they ventured into unfamiliar territories and ways. The blues insisted that the fate of the individual Black woman and man, what happened in their everyday "trivial" affairs, what took place within them—their yearnings, their problems, their frustrations, their dreams—were important, were worth taking note of and sharing in song. Stressing individual expression and communal coherence at one and the same time, the blues was an inward-looking music that insisted upon the significance of Black lives. In these respects it was not only the more obviously angry work songs but the blues as well that were subversive of the American racial order and proved to be an important portent of what was to come in a very few decades.

NOTES

1. Ravenel 1936, 768–769; Latrobe 1951, 49–51, contain descriptions of slave dance by White contemporaries. The WPA Slave Narratives, available at the Library of Congress, are filled with testimony concerning dance by former slaves.
2. "Songs of the Blacks" 1856, 51–52.
3. McKim 1862, 255.
4. These lines were ubiquitous. For these and other examples, see Fenner 1909 (1874), 10–11, 48; Allen, Ware, and Garrison 1951 (1867), 7, 13, 58, 77, 104; Higginson 1962 (1869), 206, 16–17; Marsh 1971 (1880), 136, 67, 78.
5. For these and other examples, see Barton 1899, 19, 30; Allen, Ware, and Garrison 1951 (1867), 2, 7, 15, 97–98; Marsh 1971 (1880), 132.
6. Yoder 1961, 54–55.
7. Hallowell 1901, 30; Fenner 1909 (1874), 21; Barrett 1912, 241; McIlhenny 1933, 248–249; Allen, Ware, and Garrison 1951 (1867), 94; Yetman 1970, 112; Marsh 1971 (1880), 134–135.
8. Seward 1872, 48; Barton 1899, 26; Hallowell 1901, 40; Fenner 1909 (1874), 10, 127; Grissom 1930, 73; Allen, Ware, and Garrison 1951 (1867), 55, 75.
9. Douglass 1962 (1892), 159–160; Higginson 1962 (1869), 217.
10. Parrish 1965 (1942), 247.
11. For the contrary argument that spirituals were primarily secular in their orientation, see Fisher 1963 (1953), 137, passim.
12. For examples of these songs, see *Dwight's Journal of Music* 1862, 149; Barton 1899, 25; Allen, Ware, and Garrison 1951 (1867), 48; Higginson 1962 (1869), 201–202, 11–12.
13. See Levine 1977, Chapter 1.
14. Waugh 1958, 132.
15. *The Journal of Nicholas Creswell* 1925, 18–19.
16. K[innard] 1845, 338.
17. Brent 1973 (1861), 122.
18. Douglass 1962 (1892), 146–147.
19. Interview with Abram Harris, WPA Slave Narratives, Arkansas File, Library of Congress. For the postbellum history of this song, see Levine 1977, 192–193.
20. Bryant 1884, VI: 33.
21. Quoted in Stearns and Stearns 1968, 22.
22. Quoted in Blesh and Janis 1971 (1950), 96.
23. White 1965 (1928), 157.
24. Niles 1927, 50, 60–61, passim; Niles 1932, 69–70.
25. Work 1940, 237. Virtually every collection of Black work songs contains lines like these.
26. Peabody 1903, 150.
27. WPA manuscripts, Florida File, Archive of Folk Culture, Library of Congress. For the original version, see Brown 1969 (1853), 138.
28. Thomas 1926, 165.
29. Parrish 1965 (1942), 247.
30. White 1965 (1928), 382; WPA, "Negroes of New York City," microfilm in the Schomburg Collection of the New York Public Library.
31. Odum 1911, 267.
32. Oliver 1965, 34–35.

33. Lomax 1948, 42.
34. Jackson 1972, xxi–xxii, 25–27.
35. All of the John Henry lyrics quoted here come from the hundreds of variants in Johnson 1929, Chaps. 1–4, 8; Chappell 1933, Chaps. 1–5.
36. See Levine 1977, 420–440.
37. Niles 1926, 292.
38. Bessie Smith, "Young Woman's Blues," *Bessie Smith: Nobody's Blues but Mine* (Columbia Records G3 1093).
39. Handy 1926, 13.
40. Examples can be found in Bessie Smith, "Poor Man's Blues," *Bessie Smith: Empty Bed Blues* (Columbia Records G3 0450); Charley Patton, "Green River Blues," *The Immortal Charley Patton*, no. 1 (Origin Jazz Library recording OJL-1); Oliver 1960, 51; Charters 1963, 67–68; Sackheim 1969, 135.

DISCOGRAPHY

Carawan, Guy. *Been in the Storm So Long*. Originally released 1967. Smithsonian Folkways Recordings SFCD40031, 2004. CD.

John's Island, South Carolina: Its People and Songs. Various artists. Smithsonian Records 3840, 2012. CD.

McIntosh County Shouters. *Slave Shout Songs from the Coast of Georgia*. Smithsonian Records 4344, 2012. CD.

Music Down Home: An Introduction to Negro Folk Music, U.S.A. Various artists. Smithsonian Records 2691, 2012. CD.

Negro Blues and Hollers. Various artists. Originally recorded 1941–1942. Rounder Select/Rounder 1501, 1997. CD.

Ring Games: Line Games and Play Party Songs of Alabama. Various artists. Smithsonian Records 7004, 2012. CD.

Roots of the Blues. Various artists. Originally released 1977. New World Records 80252–2, reissue date unknown. CD.

Smith, Bessie. *Do Your Duty: The Essential Recordings of Bessie Smith*. Includes "St. Louis Blues," "Empty Bed Blues," parts 1 and 2, and others. Recorded February 16, 1923–May 15, 1929. Indigo 2008, 1997. CD.

———. *Sweet Mistreater*. Includes "Poor Man's Blues," "Young Woman's Blues," and "Nobody's Blues But Mine," among others. United States of Distribution 599, 2005. CD.

———. *Bessie Smith: The Complete Columbia Recordings*. Columbia/Sony Legacy 88725403102, 2012. CD.

CHAPTER 20

The Civil Rights Period
Music as an Agent of Social Change

Bernice Johnson Reagon

Beginning with the Montgomery bus boycott in 1955,[1] the equilibrium of American society was racked by waves of social and political protest. African Americans engaging in massive civil disobedience served notice on the nation and the world that they would no longer tolerate the abuses of American racism. The Civil Rights Movement heralded a new era in the African American struggle for equality.

The movement spread throughout the South. Initial organizers were Black college students who set aside their studies to work in segregated rural and urban communities. They received support from local leaders who listened to them, housed, and fed them. Sharecroppers, ministers, hairdressers, restaurant owners, independent business people, students, teachers: these were the first to try to register to vote, apply for a job, or use a public facility previously reserved for Whites.

The response was swift and brutal: economic reprisals, jailings, beatings, and killings. Nonetheless, the movement grew, pulling recruits from all segments of the Black community and Whites who joined the struggle against racism, creating a catalytic force for change in legal, political, and social processes. The essence of the freedom movement lay in the transformation of a people. I grew up in Dougherty County, just outside of Albany, Georgia, in a community steeped in Black southern cultural traditions. From the late 1950s through the mid-1960s, I celebrated and participated in the wedding of our traditional culture with our contemporary struggle for freedom. All of the established academic categories in which I had been educated regarding culture fell apart during this period, revealing culture to be not luxury, not leisure, not entertainment, but the lifeblood of the community. My culture, my traditions, came alive for me as they shaped the context of the Civil Rights Movement.

As a singer and activist in the Albany Movement, I sang and heard the freedom songs, and I saw them pull together sections of the Black community at times when other means of communication were ineffective. It was the first time that I experienced the full power of song as an instrument for the articulation of our community concerns. In Dawson, Georgia, where Blacks made up 75 percent of the population, I sat in a church and felt the chill that ran through a small gathering when the sheriff and his deputies walked in. They stood at the door, making sure everyone knew they were there. Then a song began. And the song made sure that the sheriff and his deputies knew *we* were there. We became visible; our image of ourselves was enlarged when the sounds of the freedom songs filled all the space in that church.

Music has always been integral to the African American struggle for freedom. Its central participants shaped the music culture of the Civil Rights Movement: Black southerners. The freedom songs—though recorded, transcribed, committed to the written page, and read—truly came to life within the context of an older Black oral tradition where song and struggle were inseparable. The power of the songs came from the linking of traditional oral expression with everyday movement experiences.

Most of the singing during movement activities was congregational: songs learned in the singing, unrehearsed. The African American congregational singing tradition has its own set of aesthetics and principles governing the birthing and execution of a song, its own parameters defining the range and use of the vocal instrument, and its own roles for singers within the group.

The songs are initiated by a songleader. Different from a soloist, the songleader raises the song and, if successful, the song is caught by the congregants and raised higher into a full life. The qualities of a good songleader are both musical and organizational. Within communities with strong congregational traditions, all gatherings are usually opened with song and prayer. The songleader is the galvanizer, the person who starts the song and thus begins to pull together a temporary community formed in the process of that specific song rendition. A good songleader must manifest a strength, energy, and enthusiasm that calls each voice into wanting to join in the singing.

The core of freedom song repertoire was formed from the reservoir of traditional songs and older styles of singing. This music base was expanded to include most of the popular secular and sacred music forms and singing techniques of the 1950s and 1960s. From this storehouse, activist songleaders made a new music for a changed time. Lyrics were transformed, traditional melodies were adapted, and procedures associated with old forms were blended with new forms to create freedom songs capable of expressing the force and intent of the movement.

Song as an expression of power and communal unity emerged as early as the 1955 Montgomery, Alabama bus boycott. After Rosa Parks' arrest for refusing to let a White man take her seat on a bus, Black leaders led by the Woman's Political Council called a one-day bus boycott on December 5, 1955.[2] It proved effective, and that night Montgomery's African American community crowded into Holt Street Baptist Church. Martin Luther King Jr., who had been elected leader of the Montgomery Improvement Association, later recalled the singing: "The opening hymn was the old familiar 'Onward Christian Soldiers,' and when that mammoth audience stood to sing, the voices outside swelling the chorus in the church, there was a mighty ring like the glad echo of Heaven itself."[3]

Onward Christian soldiers, marching as to war
With the cross of Jesus, going on before!
Christ, the royal Master, leads against the foe
Forward into battle, see his banner go . . .

This hymn, penned by Sabine Baring-Gould at the end of the Civil War in 1865,[4] was a staple of Sunday school and academic school devotional services. It was often sung without fervor, with the congregation minding text and melody—that is, until it became the contemporary freedom anthem of the Montgomery bus boycott. The text references to the marchers being soldiers and the struggle being a war and a battle with Christ in the lead suited the time and named the situation for many of the participants.

The other hymn that saw a lot of use during that year was Johnson Oatman Jr.'s (1856–1922) "Lift Him Up":

> How to reach the masses, men of every birth
> For an answer Jesus gave the key
> And I, if I be lifted up from the earth,
> Will draw all men unto me.[5]

The White city fathers who ran Montgomery refused to sit in council with African Americans who sought to change the segregated practices by which their communities were run. The lyrics of this hymn were a way of communicating for those who gathered nightly in mass rallies. Here, the text seems to suggest that with Jesus as leader, even the racist city fathers of Montgomery might be drawn to righteousness and to the negotiating table. Also, almost nightly one heard "Leaning on the Everlasting Arms," a hymn that expressed the joy and peace that came from those joined in battle in that community with the assurance that their struggle was in resonance with their commitments to live Christian lives:

> What a fellowship, what a joy divine
> Leaning on the everlasting arms.
> What a blessedness, what a peace is mine
> Leaning on the everlasting arms.
> Leaning on Jesus, Leaning on Jesus
> Safe and secure from all alarm . . .[6]

This hymn by Elisha Albright Hoffman (1839–1929) expresses joy, peace, and safety, and it was a flag bearer for Montgomery participants who risked everything to change things in their community. The year 1955 in Montgomery, Alabama was not a safe time, it was not peaceful, and there was mourning and frustration at a system that refused to enter a dialogue to end injustice for American citizens who happened to be Black. Yet wrapped in the arms of this raised song, the mass meeting created a singing that established a safety zone for the moment. "Leaning" was a very popular freedom hymn, sung "by the book" and in congregational and gospel styles in mass meetings across the South.

While old songs would continue to be given new life throughout the movement, new songs began to appear as the boycott continued and reprisals became more severe. After eighty-nine leaders were arraigned for allegedly organizing a boycott, they walked to the Dexter Avenue Baptist Church. Writing for *The Nation*, Alfred Maund described the scene:

> With the spirit and ingenuity that has characterized the leadership of this historic movement, Reverend Martin Luther King offered a new hymn for the occasion, set to the tune of "Old Time Religion." The stanzas went like this:
>
> > We are moving on to victory . . . (3X) with hope and dignity.
> > We will all stand together . . . (3X) until we all are free.

> Indeed the blending of "Old Time Religion" with a new determination to achieve racial equality is the essence of the boycott.... The meeting that day closed with the singing of "Nobody Knows the Trouble I've Seen." Here were two songs, both a part of Black traditional sacred music repertoire: One, "Old Time Religion," was updated to address an immediate need of the movement; the second, "Nobody Knows the Trouble I've Seen," was sung in its traditional form. On many occasions, the new borrowed from the old in the midst of movement activity. These transformed songs, used in conjunction with older songs, effectively conveyed the message that the Black struggle had a long history.[7]

Montgomery also saw the use of songs and songleaders to mobilize the movement. Mary Ethel Dozier (Jamila Jones), a member of what would become a highly regarded trio of songleaders, was ten years old in 1954 when the Supreme Court decision *Brown v. Board of Education* was issued.

> I was a member of the trio before the movement.... Pretty soon after the first mass meeting in 1955 we started singing for the Montgomery Improvement Association. We were doing songs of the movement, "This Little Light of Mine, I'm Gonna Let It Shine."... We would make up songs. All the songs I remember gave us strength to go on.... It was kind of spontaneous; if somebody started beating us over the head with a billy club we would start singing about the billy club, or either the person's name would come out in a song.[8]

The Montgomery Gospel Trio, made up of Jones, Minnie Hendricks, and Gladys Burnette Carter, later went to the Highlander Folk School in Mt. Eagle, Tennessee, and met Guy Carawan. They appeared at a Carnegie Hall benefit for the Highlander Folk School in 1961. A recording of their music was produced by Carawan and released by Folkways Records.[9] This progression of songs—arising from a rich communal tradition, moving into protest forums, then to supportive concert stages, connecting with the budding folk music revival gathering steam in the Northeast, and culminating in recordings that reached national audiences throughout the 1960s—would occur again and again.

The sit-ins brought young Black college students into the movement in droves. The Greensboro, North Carolina, sit-in at the local Woolworth lunch counter by four freshmen—Ezell Blair Jr., Joseph McNeil, David Richmond, and Franklin McClain—on February 1, 1960, sparked national and international attention and fired the imagination of young people throughout the South to move against segregation practices in their local communities. While sit-ins were staged all over the country, this form of nonviolent resistance was especially successful in southern cities with large Black college populations.

Out of the pressures and needs involved in maintaining group unity while working under conditions of intense hostility and physical threat, student organizers of sit-in campaigns developed their own supportive activist culture—and music was its mainstay. During the early sit-ins, music was not usually a part of the actual street demonstrations. Sit-in leaders wanted to avoid being charged with rowdiness or uncouth behavior. Many demonstrations were carried out in silence, and the media did not miss this aspect. The *Richmond News Leader*, which published an editorial after demonstrations began in that city, made special note of the dignity of the marchers:

> Many a Virginian must have felt a tinge of regret at the state of things as they were reading of Saturday's "sit-downs" by Negro students in Richmond stores. Here were the colored students in coats, white shirts, ties and one of them reading Goethe, and one was taking notes from a biology text. And here, on the sidewalk outside, was a gang of white boys come to heckle; a rag tail rabble, slack-jawed, black-jacketed, grinning to fit to kill, and some of them, God save the mark, were waving the proud and honored flag of the Southern states in the last war fought by gentlemen. Phew! It gives one pause.[10]

Silent marches were the general practice during the early months, and the songs of this period came out of the mass meetings, rallies, and workshop sessions. Still, John Lewis, Nashville, Tennessee, sit-in leader and later chairman of the Student Nonviolent Coordinating Committee (SNCC), explains why, even then, singing sustained marching:

> At the rallies and meetings we sang. One of the earliest songs I remember very well that became very popular was "Amen."
>
> Amen Amen Amen Amen Amen
> Freedom Freedom Freedom Freedom Freedom.
>
> This song represented the coming together, you really felt it—it was like you were part of a crusade, a holy crusade. You felt uplifted and involved in a great battle and a great struggle. We had hundreds and thousands of students from the different colleges and universities around Nashville gathering downtown in a Black Baptist church. That particular song . . . became the heart of the Nashville Movement.[11]

There is a close correlation between the changes that songs underwent during the Nashville struggle—the most highly organized sit-in movement—and those that were heard during the Montgomery bus boycott. "Amen," sung as a traditional Black sacred chant with a one-word lyric, was chanted over and over again. The melodic statement was musically simple and a leader who sang triggered each lilting cycle of "Amen"s:

> *Everybody say*
> *Amen . . .*
> *Let the Church say, . . . Let the Deacons say . . .*

The power of this traditional song came in the singing, singing charged with the richness of Black harmonic techniques and improvisations. In Nashville, it gained a new force by creating collective energy for a direct confrontation with local racist policies. A simple word change from "Amen" to "Freedom" made it a musical statement of the ultimate national goal of the student activists. In Montgomery, the changing of words in the song "Old Time Religion" to "We Are Marching on to Victory," which occurred after the leaders had been arraigned by the local law officials, can be equated with the singing of "Amen" in Nashville after the return to the church from a round of sit-ins. In both cases, the activists were returning to a haven after a confrontation with the system they were seeking to change. Many times it appeared that traditional songs went through text changes when the protesters needed to affirm their commitment to continue in face of seemingly insurmountable odds.

The first freedom songs, such as "Amen," issued from the musical tradition of the Black church. Both Lewis and noted writer Julius Lester, who was at the time a student at Fisk University, identified another important song that was often sung during the rallies. Rallies would start and end with "Lift Every Voice and Sing," which became known as the "Negro National Anthem." This song was composed in 1926 by James Weldon Johnson and set to music by his brother, J. Rosamond Johnson:

> *Lift every voice and sing*
> *Till earth and heaven ring*
> *Ring with the harmonies of liberty;*
> *Let our rejoicing rise*
> *High as the listening skies,*
> *Let it resound loud as the rolling sea.*

Sing a song full of the faith that the dark past has taught us,
Sing a song full of the hope that the present has brought us,
Facing the rising sun of our new day begun
Let us march on till victory is won.[12]

Soon after the Nashville sit-ins began, a quartet was formed that was similar to the local amateur rhythm and blues groups that were formed on most Black campuses and on street corners of Black neighborhoods of that day. The "Nashville Quartet," however, differed from other R&B groups in that their songs were statements of their current political and social struggles. Joseph Carter, Bernard Lafayette, James Bevel, and Samuel Collier were students at the American Baptist Theological Seminary in Nashville. For their freedom songs they used the melodies and arrangement techniques of contemporary R&B hits, which were played on the college jukebox and their favorite radio station. R&B singer Little Willie John's recording of "You'd Better Leave My Kitten Alone" became a freedom song when new lyrics were created:

You better leave segregation alone
Because they love segregation like a hound dog loves a bone . . .
I went down to the dime store to get myself a coke,
The waitress looked at me and said, what's this a joke?
You better leave segregation alone . . .[13]

The R&B tunes of the sit-ins were heavily influenced by the soul music of Ray Charles. Born in Albany, Georgia, Ray Charles reached national prominence in 1954 and throughout the next decade stayed on the record charts. His songs—a rich blend of gospel and blues laced with his earthy, graveled, textured voice—launched a new genre of popular songs that came to be known as soul.

Soon after the breakthrough in Nashville—the citywide integration of lunch counters—James Bevel and Bernard Lafayette took the tune and chorus lyrics of Charles' "Moving On" and produced a song about the approaching demise of the Jim Crow system of segregation:

Segregation's been here from time to time
But we just ain't gonna pay it no mind
It's moving—it's moving on—it's moving on, it's moving on
Moving on Moving on Moving on
Old Jim Crow moving down the track
He's got his bags and he won't be back.[14]

The identification of the new genre as soul is important when one thinks about the fact that neighborhood Black churches hosted the anti-segregation movement. Most marches were prefaced with rallies in churches that began with devotional services that included sacred songs, prayers, and scriptural readings. These devotions served to prepare congregations to more effectively confront the ensuing issues related to the local struggle. When arriving at the protest site, usually a city hall or jail, the marchers held another short rally of song and prayer. If marchers were arrested, the cells rang with singing and prayers. In other words, the church left the buildings and went into the streets and jails, and the popular music called soul, a blend of sacred and secular musics, musically named that evolution in the music and in the seismic shift in the relationship between the church and the street.

The songs poured forth as movement activity increased. The most well-known song of the 1960s, "We Shall Overcome," was not from the hit parade. Although it was recorded, none of these releases made the Top 40 charts, nor did they receive airplay on Top 40 stations. Yet "We Shall Overcome" was known and embraced by people all over the world. As the theme song of the Civil Rights Movement, "We Shall Overcome" was disseminated via live television and radio news clips of demonstrations and mass rallies taking place in communities across the South. All over the world, people heard this song and simultaneously learned of its meaning and function.

"We Shall Overcome" began as a Black church song; it was present in the repertoire of Baptist and Methodist congregations throughout the South. Most congregations sang:

I'll overcome, I'll overcome, I'll overcome, someday
Oh if, in my heart, I do not yield, I'll overcome, someday.

Other verses included "I'll wear a crown . . . ," "I'll be all right . . . ," and "I'll see his face . . ." Around Charleston, South Carolina, Methodist congregations sang their version of the song with a different rhythm, beginning with a moderate tempo, then shifting into a more intense stage using multiple handclaps and foot-stomping rhythms.

I will overcome, I will overcome, I will overcome,
Someday
If in my heart, Oh Lordy I do not yield,
I will overcome, someday . . .

Other verses remain the same, but the songleader might go into a new stanza with the added phrase "I need you Jesus and I will see his face . . ."

In 1901, Charles Albert Tindley, a Methodist minister in Philadelphia, copyrighted a group of songs he had composed as a part of his ministry. Among them was a hymn called "I'll Overcome Someday." The chorus has the same text as the one sung in Baptist and Methodist congregations. There are some views that the congregational song was borrowed from the chorus of Tindley's composition. However, it is also very possible that Tindley took what was already a traditional congregational chorus and created verses to generate his composition. Tindley's work as a songwriter is foundational in that he composed new songs that have become standards in gospel music repertoire.[15] His compositions are considered to be gospel hymns; they use the strophic hymn structure for verses, combining them with choruses based on the spirituals created by slaves. The combination was greatly appreciated by Protestant congregations.

Tindley's most favored songs were typically transmitted orally in African American Christendom and beyond, often without the composer's name. For example, his most popular gospel hymn, "Stand by Me," is often cited as "traditional" without crediting Tindley's authorship. It can be found in the repertoire of most gospel soloists, groups, choirs, and quartets throughout the twentieth century. Most of Tindley's songs that moved into oral tradition retained some of his original text ("Someday," also known as "Beams of Heaven," "Leave It There," "The Storm Is Passing Over," and "Nothing Between," to name a few), although many such arrangements could also vary significantly from the original. Tindley's "I'll Overcome Someday" has never been fully absorbed into oral tradition. Although the chorus has become a standard part of the repertoire among congregations, the verses of this composition are relatively unknown (although they are still occasionally sung in his congregation in Philadelphia). The fact that the verses have not been retained suggests that Tindley's composition was an outgrowth of a preexisting repertoire, rather than the reverse.[16]

The chorus of "I'll Overcome Someday" moved from church worship services to the picket lines in Charleston, South Carolina, as a part of a labor organizing campaign. During the 1940s, the Food, Tobacco, and Agricultural Workers Union organized workers in the American Tobacco Factory. Following a series of fruitless negotiations with company officials, the decision was made to strike. The union always opened their meetings with a song and prayer, and they also sang songs on the picket line. Music was a part of what kept them together, and "We Will Overcome" was the leading song of the picket line. The strike, supported by a national boycott of American Tobacco products, began in October 1945 and lasted through April 1946.

In 1947, after the union won the strike, the work force at the factory was integrated and so was the union. Like many other locals across the South, the Charleston local traveled to the Highlander Folk Center for workshops that focused on their experiences in gaining recognition from the company. The Highlander sessions were always integrated, but to reduce dangers for participants who had to drive through the South to get to the center, Highlander would invite the Black local from one city and the White local from another. The union leaders from Charleston taught "We Will Overcome" to Zilphia Horton, then Highlander's director of music and wife of director and founder Miles Horton; Zilphia liked the song and began to use it in all of her workshops.

Miles Horton, who founded Highlander in 1932, recalled Zilphia hearing the song first when she urged reluctant members of the White local to share some of the songs from their picket lines. They finally sang, "I Will Overcome," citing its use among the Black union members on the picket lines. The Black members who attended Highlander for a workshop were very clear about the community origin of the song and the role it played within their long struggle with the tobacco factory. Union leader Isaiah Bennett talked about the role of music during meetings they attended under the leadership of their sister all-White local:

> The whites would never sing.... We were singing from emotion.... Their meetings were not religious, they just opened the meeting. Sometimes Mrs. Lucille (Simmons), Marie Hodges, S. P. Graham and Joe McKinger would sing, the whites would stand, they had respect, but they didn't sing.[17]

Zilphia Horton taught the song to Pete Seeger when he visited Highlander with Woody Guthrie in 1947. Horton also sent the song in to the *People's Song Bulletin*, a song periodical that featured organizing songs, and it appeared in 1949.[18] Seeger took the song and sang it at Union rallies across the country. Pete Seeger remembered changing "will" to "shall" and adding verses like "the whole wide world around," and "we'll walk hand in hand."[19] By the mid-1950s the song was used in Union gatherings on the East and West Coasts. Zilphia Horton died in 1957 and Guy Carawan, a folksinger and sociologist from California, came to Highlander as music director. He had learned the song from Frank Hamilton in California in 1953. Hamilton had learned it from Merle Hersfeld, who had learned it from Seeger.

During the 1950s, Highlander had shifted its focus and began increasingly to offer its services to southern Black community groups who were working on issues of racial inequities in their communities. Two months before the beginning of the historic Montgomery boycott, Rosa Parks had participated in a workshop at Highlander, later stating that her experience at Highlander was the first time she had been in the company of Whites who treated her as an equal human being.

During the Montgomery boycott, a delegation from the boycott attended a workshop at Highlander. Among this group was a trio of young student singers who sang in the mass meetings and worked in the voter registration drives in Montgomery. Mary Ethel Dozier, of the Montgomery Trio, recounted her first visit to Highlander: "Minnie Hendricks, Gladys Carter and myself. I remember learning 'Michael Rowed the Boat Ashore,' what we were supposed to do was to give songs from our area and learn songs from other participants . . ."[20] The trio returned to Montgomery and one of the songs they sang in voter registration meetings was a new song they had learned from Highlander, "We Shall Overcome." Guy Carawan recounted an occasion in 1959 after Highlander had moved to Knoxville, Tennessee. Highlander was raided by the local police, who put everyone in darkness as they searched the house. Carawan said that someone started to sing, "We Shall Overcome," and then he heard a clear voice sing a new verse that stayed with the song as it moved throughout the movement. Sitting in the dark, this girl began to sing, "We are not afraid, we are not afraid, we are not afraid, today!" That young voice was Mary Ethel Dozier.[21] Then, over Easter weekend, 1960, at a session with sit-in student leaders from Nashville, Guy taught them the song and it began to move out from its Highlander workshop phase, returning to the struggle with the next generation of African Americans who would use it as the theme song of their struggle.

Cordell Hull Reagon, field secretary of the Student Nonviolent Coordinating Committee (SNCC) and founder of the SNCC Freedom Singers (Figure 20.1), describes the

Figure 20.1
The SNCC Freedom Singers, Saratoga Springs, New York, 1963. Left to right: Charles Neblett, Bernice Johnson, Cordell Reagon, Rutha Mae Harris.

Photograph by Joe Alper. Courtesy of the Joe Alper Photo Collection LLC.

The Civil Rights Period   351

first time he felt the song become more than just another freedom song. After the freedom riders had been freed from Parchman Penitentiary, the executive director of the Southern Christian Leadership Conference (SCLC), Ella Josephine Baker, organized a meeting of over two hundred SCLC sit-in student leaders from across the South. The meeting, held on the Shaw College campus in Raleigh, North Carolina, was to give these new activists a chance to decide what their next step would be and whether they might actually become a youth branch of SCLC. The students decided to form their own organization. Reagon said that the first night as they gathered, Guy Carawan led the group in song, but when they began to sing "We Shall Overcome," everybody began to stand, crossing their hands right over left and joining together. Reagon had never heard the song like that before, and from that point it became the theme song of the movement, closing all mass meetings and raised on all the battlefields when needed.[22]

One SNCC field secretary, Reginald Robinson, noted that as movement activities intensified, this anthem became much more than the song, with its union history, that he had learned from the Highlander workshop:

> We put more soul in it, a sort of rocking quality, to stir one's inner feeling. You really have to experience it in action to understand the kind of power it has for us. When you got through singing it, you could walk over a bed of hot coals and you wouldn't feel it.[23]

The theme song went through another transformation in Albany, Georgia, where it was brought more fully into the fold of the rich Black congregational choral tradition with all of its text extrapolations between lines, slurs, and musical punctuations. The opening phrase, "We shall overcome," was answered as if it was a call-and-response with "my Lord," and an extended "Oh—" connected "someday" to "Deep in my heart . . ." All of the ending phrases got multiple-note releases. Then, sung with great compassion and conviction in full-bodied voice and in rich harmony, it became the anthem that would ring throughout the world. Robert Shelton, then music critic for the *New York Times*, described this process:

> "We Shall Overcome" has been called the *Le Marseillaise* of the integration movement. It has passed by word of mouth with great speed despite the fact that no single disk of the song has been issued and no sheet music will be available in the stores next month.[24]

Charles Sherrod, field secretary of the Student Nonviolent Coordinating Committee (SNCC), witnessed how "We Shall Overcome" galvanized the first mass meeting held in Albany, Georgia, at the Mt. Zion Baptist Church (Figure 20.2) in December 1961:

> The church was packed before eight o'clock. People were everywhere, in the aisles, sitting and standing on the choir stands, hanging over the railing of the balcony, sitting in trees outside the window. . . . When the last speaker among the students, Bertha Gober, had finished, there was nothing left to say. Tears filled the eyes of hard grown men who had seen with their own eyes merciless atrocities committed . . . and when we rose to sing "We Shall Overcome," nobody could imagine what kept the church on four corners . . . I threw my head back and sang with my whole body.[25]

Music was a vital part of the culture of the freedom rides organized initially by the Congress of Racial Equality (CORE) and taken up by the sit-in leaders after violence in Alabama led CORE to cancel the rides. This phase of organizing, challenging racial segregation on public interstate transportation, resulted in a ruling by the Interstate Commerce

Figure 20.2
Singing "We Shall Overcome" in the pulpit during a Civil Rights meeting–congregational gathering at Mt. Zion Baptist Church in Albany, Georgia, 1962.

Photo by Ben Cochran. Courtesy The William Anderson Collection.

Commission that outlawed the segregation practice. Like other aspects of the struggle, the battle had its freedom songs.

On May 4, 1961, CORE gathered a group of volunteer riders, Black and White, in Washington, DC, to begin a journey that would take them from the nation's capital to New Orleans, Louisiana. On May 14, Mother's Day, in Anniston, Alabama, the first bus was burned. Later that same day, the second bus was mobbed in Birmingham and the injuries sustained were so severe that CORE decided reluctantly to end the trip. The Nashville and Atlanta sit-in leaders immediately initiated a call for volunteers to take up the ride. On May 20, the reconstructed freedom rides were met with even more extreme violence in Montgomery, Alabama. With the intervention of the Kennedy Justice Department and the imposition of martial law, the bus left Montgomery under escort. According to the riders, when their bus crossed the state line into Mississippi, their protection escort disappeared and songs helped to push back the fear. When they pulled into the bus station at Jackson, Mississippi, they were promptly jailed. But that didn't stop them from singing.[26] Hank Thomas led:

I'm a-taking a ride
On the Greyhound bus line

The Civil Rights Period 353

I'm a-riding the front seat
To Jackson, this time . . .[27]

James Farmer, the executive director of CORE who had rejoined the riders and ended up in Hinds County Jail along with the others, wrote new words to a song he had heard in Chicago during the late 1940s, entitled "Which Side Are You On?" That song had been written during the 1930s Harlan County, Kentucky, coal mine strike by Florence Reese. When the local "goon squad," some of them familiar to Reese, entered her home in search of her husband, Sam Reese, who was a strike leader, she wrote this song which asked "Which side are you on boys, which side are you on?"[28]

In jail, the new lyrics for the verses by Farmer and others explained who the freedom riders were, what had happened as a result of their actions, and their need for "men" instead of "Uncle Toms":

Don't tom for Mister Charlie—Don't listen to his lies
Cause Black folks haven't got a chance unless we organize . . .
Come all you freedom lovers, oh listen while I tell
Oh how the freedom riders came to Jackson to dwell . . .

In every local campaign after this song came forth in the Parchman prison, there were verses added to name and document specific aspects of the community in question. In the 1961–1962 Albany, Georgia, campaign they added this verse about a policeman called "Big Red":

Have you heard about that paddy wagon that Big Red likes to drive?
If you stand up for your rights, he'll take you for a ride . . .

Albany, Georgia, was a powerful singing movement. Mass direct action began with the November 1961 testing of the ICC ruling against segregated facilities serving interstate commerce. The tests were done by members of the local youth chapter of the NAACP who were bailed out of jail after they attempted to purchase tickets at the White-only ticket window of the Trailways bus station. Two students from Albany State College were arrested and refused bail; that led to the first mass demonstration by Albany State College students. This led to the formation of the Albany Movement as an organization of organizations, as well as the first mass meeting. On December 10, SNCC's national office in Atlanta organized an integrated group of riders to travel to Albany by train; they were arrested as soon as they got off the train, along with Bertha Gober and Charles Jones, who were standing in the crowd waiting to greet the riders. Two days later, more than three hundred marchers, mostly students, marched to and around the courthouse in support of the freedom riders who were inside on trial. They were all arrested. Marches followed the next day and the next and after three days over seven hundred people were in jail in Albany. Unable to house these large numbers, Albany rented jail space in surrounding counties. (I was arrested the second day and served time in the Albany City Jail and the Lee County stockade.) The singing in the rallies and the jails provided energy and unity for those who came forward to be a part of a growing struggle.

The music of the Albany Movement attracted national attention. Robert Shelton, folk music critic of the *New York Times*, had journeyed to Albany and written several articles based on music he heard there. One of those pieces captured the power and vitality of the singing in a quote from SNCC Field Secretary Charles Jones:

> There could have been no Albany movement without music. We could not have communicated with the masses of people without music and they could not have communicated with us. . . . But through songs, they expressed years of suppressed hope, suffering, even joy and love. . . .[29]

In Albany, Georgia, during July and August 1962, over one thousand demonstrators were arrested. At the height of tensions, US District Court Judge J. Robert Elliot, a Kennedy-appointed segregationist, issued an injunction ordering Albany Movement leaders to cease further demonstrations. This was a federal order and it created a crisis among the local leadership and Martin Luther King Jr. At the Shiloh mass meeting where Reverend King was scheduled to speak, Reverend Samuel Wells held the crowd as a meeting went on, in the study, where the leaders discussed whether Dr. King should violate a federal order against marching. Finally, Reverend Wells told the waiting crowd that he had not been served an injunction and that he would lead a march down to City Hall. Then a song began, "Ain' Gonna Let No Injunction Turn Me Round," based on the spiritual:

> *Ain' gonna let nobody turn me round,*
> *Turn me round, turn me round,*
> *Ain' gonna let nobody turn me round,*
> *Keep on a-walkin', keep on talkin'*
> *Marching up to Canaan land.*[30]

The song went on for several minutes and each time a new term was inserted signifying an obstacle that would no longer halt the struggle. "Canaan," the goal identified in the last line of the traditional version, was changed to "Freedom" at the Albany meeting:

> *Ain gonna let no injunction, turn me round*
> *. . . Keep on a-walking, keeping on a-talking*
> *Marching up to Freedom land.*

The injunction against demonstrations was later vacated by Federal Judge Elbert Tuttle and the pressure for a forum with the political leadership of Albany continued.

Albany, the county seat of Dougherty County, was the center of a rich congregational choral tradition. For the first time, some of the organizers from SNCC who became a part of the community encountered their first experience with the lined hymn tradition. There were other hymns, Protestant hymns, which were sung with their own melodies and harmony system. The singing of lined hymns differed from the standard hymns melodically, harmonically, metrically, and emotionally. They are called "lined" hymns because the text of the hymn is introduced line by line in a chant-form by the songleader, with the congregation repeating the song text after each line in the appropriate tune and meter.

The lined hymn tradition is practiced in African American and in some White southern Protestant congregations. These hymns within the Black church are sometimes called meter hymns because they are sung in short, common, and long meter. Each meter has a number of tunes that are known within a small geographic region. Any song text that is compatible with a particular meter can be sung to any of that meter's tunes. The tunes are learned and disseminated orally and through performance practice rather than organized rehearsal. Most of the songs that were heard in mass meetings were of the short and common meter category because the long meter tends to be the more complex of the hymn tunes to master.

The metered hymns are slow songs. They create a different force in a congregation because of the way their numerous melodic lines blend to create harmonies. Charles Sherrod, who came to southwest Georgia as a Baptist minister from Virginia, was a singer but had had no prior experience with this traditional repertoire—he described them as creating "a swoon feeling, and reaching deep."[31] Words seem inadequate to describe their power and the ambiance they created within the singing group. The singers actually create and share a common moan that encircles the depth of struggle and pain and rises in peaks of celebration—joy, shouting, never light, always weighted with the burden of the day.

The performance of lined hymns has continued wherever the people who loved and needed them were powerful enough within their congregations to set the worship style in their churches, even as they moved into the twentieth-century gospel era. Thus, one could hear them in mass meetings throughout southwest Georgia, in the urban community of Albany, and in surrounding counties like Terrell, Worth, Mitchell, and Baker.

During the 1960s, when student organizers moved throughout the South, they assumed leadership within the communities into which they moved. This meant that the participants in part shaped the movement culture on the local level. Organizers always brought with them the songs that they had used in other campaigns, and they were usually song styles and repertoire that could be quickly learned in performance.

The transmission of lined hymns was another matter. The song form was non-metrical, highly melismatic, and improvisatory. Learning the form required apprenticeship within a region where the tradition lived. Usually these hymns were heard in gatherings where the songs were a regular part of the worship tradition of that community. One notable exception was Charles Sherrod, an organizer who learned to successfully lead a congregation in a lined hymn even if only a few people present knew the song form.

"A Charge to Keep I Have" was a lined hymn heard more than any other during the movement. This eighteenth-century hymn by Charles Wesley seemed to articulate so much of what the movement activists were trying to express:

A charge to keep I have
A God to glorify
A never dying soul to save
And fit it for the sky

To serve the present age
My calling to fulfill
Oh may it all my power engage
To do my master's will.[32]

In 1963, in a Greenwood, Mississippi, mass meeting, Fannie Lou Hamer lined the common meter hymn, "Must Jesus Bear the Cross Alone," composed in 1852 by George Nelson Allen, as the text for her speech. Hamer, then an SNCC field secretary and one of the most effective organizers of the community struggles in Mississippi, became a national voice and model because of her uncompromising clarity about the purpose of the fight for freedom and because of her brilliance as an orator and songleader. On this night, she lined two verses of this hymn:

> *Must Jesus bear the cross alone*
> *And all the world go free?*
> *No, there's a cross for everyone*
> *And there's a cross for me.*
>
> *The consecrated cross I'll bear*
> *Till death shall set me free*
> *And then go home my crown to wear*
> *For there's a crown for me.*[33]

Hamer saw participation in the movement as a cross. She saw her work in the freedom movement as compatible with her Christian belief. For her, there was no leap for biblical and other sacred texts, like the hymn above, to form the foundation of her activism. Here was an example of a contemporary struggle where the text and worldview learned at the feet of elders presented the strongest ground for sharing meaning. So as they moved to challenge a racist system, local leaders like Mrs. Hamer found that their parents and grandparents had transmitted text that could only be understood in the reality of that challenge.

In the summer of 1963, the night before a Greenwood folk festival, we gathered in a local church for a mass meeting. The meeting opened with the traditional devotional service that began with an upbeat song followed by a lined hymn; this time is was John Newton's "Amazing Grace."

> *Amazing grace, how sweet the sound*
> *That saved a wretch like me*
> *I once was lost, but now I'm found*
> *Was blind, but now I see.*
>
> *Through many dangers, toils and snares,*
> *I have already come;*
> *'Tis grace has brought me safe thus far,*
> *And grace will lead me home.*

As on many other occasions during the freedom struggles that raged throughout the country, as the meeting evolved, in walked the sheriff and some of his deputies. Those gathered responded by giving more fervor to the songs and prayers and testimonies, determined not to give in to fear.

The "Amazing Grace" hymn is one of the most widely known within and outside of the Christian community. The composer John Newton was a captain of a slave ship, engaged in capturing Africans and bringing them across the dreaded middle passage to slavery in the New World. The writing of this hymn was sparked by Newton's newfound commitment to his Christian ideals and his eventual opposition to the slave trade. Joining this eighteenth-century story of redemption is the story of the descendants of these and other African peoples engaged in a struggle for freedom and justice more than two hundred years later, bathing their courage and determination in songs that ring truest when used for major and radical change.

Out of the attention given the singing within the Albany Movement, Pete Seeger, after a trip to Albany, suggested to James Forman, executive director of SNCC, that the organization form a singing group. He talked about the Almanac Singers, a group with which he sang during the 1930s and 1940s, who performed for union rallies. Forman turned to Field Secretary Cordell Reagon, who was the youngest staff member of the student organization. Reagon had been one of the student leaders who, in 1960, led a walk-out at Pearl High into the more college-based Nashville sit-in movement. By the time of his arrival in Albany in 1961, Reagon had gone through the nonviolent workshop training led by Reverend Jim Lawson, been on the student-led revived freedom rides, spent time in the Hinds County Jail and Parchman Penitentiary, participated in demonstrations in Cairo, Illinois, and had traveled and met with activists in Tuskegee, Talladega, and Selma, Alabama. From his experiences he called together some of the strongest singers he had met: Charles Neblett, bass, from Carbondale, Illinois; Dorothy Vales, from Alabama; and Rutha Harris and me, Bernice Johnson, from Albany, Georgia.

In September 1962, at a benefit for SNCC, a Gospel Sing for Freedom at Chicago's McCormick Place featured gospel musicians who performed in support of the movement. The benefit was not financially successful, but it served as one of the first times Cordell Reagon directed a group of SNCC field secretaries who formed a freedom chorus. On November 11 of that same year, Pete Seeger performed a benefit concert for SNCC at Morehouse College's Archer Hall Gymnasium in Atlanta, Georgia. I was then a student at Spelman College and joined in with the group of songleaders Cordell pulled together. Most of the singers were from the Albany Movement: SNCC Field Secretaries Cordell Reagon, Charlie Jones, and Charles Sherrod were joined by Rutha Mae Harris and me. Charles Neblett and Dorothy Vails also formed a part of the singing group. After the concert the group met; Vails returned to school, and Jones and Sherrod went back to organizing in southwest Georgia. The SNCC Freedom Singers' core members remained: Reagon, Neblett, Harris, and me; at times we were joined by Bertha Gober and Charles Neblett's brother, Carver "Chico" Neblett.

Cordell Reagon had met Len Dresler in September; Dresler, a singer and producer, donated a Buick station wagon to the group. The group received a donation of $1,000 from Roberta Yancey. Ella Baker was able to book the first concert for the group, a performance at the joint convention of YWCA and YMCA college chapters held on the University of Illinois–Urbana campus on December 31, 1962. Toshi Seeger agreed to serve as booking agent for the group and, based on the contacts made at that event, began to develop the first tour for the group. Over the next year, we traveled across the country performing freedom songs in concert halls, college campuses, churches, elementary and secondary schools, and homes—accepting any place that was offered for a gathering. The Freedom Singer concerts brought information and the power of the organizing going on throughout the South to audiences and supporters across the nation. In return, we helped to set up support groups for SNCC, raised funds for the SNCC office, and recruited volunteers to come south to join the work of the movement.

This was not the first ensemble that had come together to sing freedom songs; the Montgomery Trio, the Nashville Quartet, and the CORE Freedom Singers were all groups that performed and recorded freedom songs. The SNCC Freedom Singers, however, was the group that was the most organized and that worked within the structure of a movement organization, employed as field secretaries for SNCC who earned a stipend of $10 a week.

There were many others who used performance to support the movement. Harry Belafonte was unrelenting in not only giving direct support but also in organizing support and using his network of artists to get them involved directly in fiscally sustaining the organizations that were carrying on the day-to-day work. Mahalia Jackson, the gospel singer who performed the first gospel solo concert at Carnegie Hall, was a fierce supporter of the movement. She organized a benefit concert for SCLC and could be called upon to join Dr. King in his speaking engagements whenever her schedule allowed. Roebuck Staples of the Staple Singers called Dr. King and also offered to join him in his efforts to support the freedom campaign. Staples wrote "Why Am I Treated So Bad" as a part of his witness to the need for the struggle. In February 1963, there was a benefit concert at Carnegie Hall for SNCC, featuring jazz artists Thelonious Monk, Charlie Mingus, the SNCC Freedom Singers, and Tony Bennett. Later that year, a Carnegie Hall concert featured the Freedom Singers with Mahalia Jackson in a joint benefit for SCLC and SNCC. A review of a benefit concert at Carnegie Hall featuring Mahalia Jackson stated that:

> Even if the quartet was not dealing in matters so urgent as the topical freedom songs of the integration movement, it would be outstanding for its singing. The unaccompanied voices, the rhythmic drive and the sense of conviction put the Freedom Singers in the top level of American folk groups. . . . The Freedom singers are the ablest performing group to come out of what is perhaps the most spontaneous and widespread singing movement in the world today.[34]

The Freedom Singers stimulated an increase in unaccompanied singing among folk artists who sometimes seemed to be vocal extensions of their guitars and banjos. The Freedom Singers were invited to the Newport Folk Festival in 1963, the closest thing the folksong revival had to a "National Convention." Almost every top performer or performing group there included an unaccompanied selection and/or a freedom song in their set.

Topical songwriters, a vital part of the folksong revival, increasingly incorporated issues raised by the Civil Rights struggle into their new work. Singer–songwriters like Pete Seeger, Bob Dylan, Phil Ochs, and Len Chandler reflected specific aspects of movement activity as well as events and ideas that in a more symbolic way addressed the nature of the crisis gripping the nation. Bob Dylan's "Oxford Town," written in the fall of 1962 when James Meredith's entrance into the University of Mississippi resulted in riot and a call-up of the National Guard, is illustrative:

> *He went down to Oxford Town*
> *Guns and clubs followed him down*
> *All because his face was brown*
> *Better get away from Oxford Town.*[35]

Pete Seeger and Lee Hays' "Hammer Song" became popular within folk revival circles and within the southern-based movement. This song's lyrics talked about using a hammer and a song to sing out justice, freedom, and love all over the world.

Seeger shared his stages with the Freedom Singers at Orchestra Hall in Chicago and at their first concert in the Bay Area. Toshi Seeger booked the group at the Ashgrove folk club in Los Angeles, where they were at the time of the March on Washington. Harry Belafonte intervened and got the Freedom Singers on a chartered plane, full of supporters from the film industry, from Los Angeles to Washington in time for the March. As a result, the March on Washington featured songs performed by Joan Baez; Peter, Paul, and Mary; Bob Dylan; a special choir organized by Eva Jessye; Marian Anderson; Mahalia Jackson; and the SNCC Freedom Singers.

Others who offered support from the music industry were the Smothers Brothers, who assisted in the production of two recordings of SNCC Freedom Singers by their label, Mercury Records. Guy Carawan organized several conferences that brought together freedom songleaders with traditional singers such as the Georgia Sea Island Singers, Dock Reed from Texas, and the Moving Star Hall Singers. They were often joined by topical songwriters like Len Chandler, Ralph Rinzler (who worked as program director of the Newport Folk Festival), Alan Lomax, and Josh Dunson, who worked for *Sing Out Magazine*. All of the Newport Festivals from 1963 to 1965 featured a delegation of singers from the Southern movement pulled together by Cordell Reagon. In 1965, Fannie Lou Hamer was featured at the festival.

Fannie Lou Hamer was a powerful leader shaped by her life in Mississippi and her urge to have a chance to do something to change the lives of Black people. Hamer credits Reverend James Bevel, then an SNCC field secretary, for making her believe that the time and opportunity had come. After attending a voter registration meeting and hearing him talk about the importance of voting, she volunteered to try to register. As a result of her actions, she and her family were put off the farm where she had worked weighing cotton for almost twenty years. In the months and years that followed, Hamer was jailed, beaten, and shot at, but she never wavered in her sense of purpose as a woman, as a Black person, as a Mississippian, and as an American. Hamer was a powerfully riveting speaker who based her presentations on biblical and sacred scripture and always started with a song, usually "This Little Light of Mine."

Hamer's story is an excellent example of the relationships among living, fighting for freedom, speaking, and singing as a way of evidencing your reality. For her, once she came into the movement and it came into her, there were no distinctions between any of these ways of being. Organizing, talking, singing, and being a human being were all seamless, very unlike the Western tendency toward compartmentalization. But it would be wrong to give the notion that Hamer was alone and had no company. The movement was full of witnesses who gave all they had and more in every way, without holding back. Because one way of participating was songleading, Hamer and her singing colleagues presented a different definition of art and music for contemporary times.

Although Hamer traveled as much as she could, she was always grounded in Mississippi. In contrast, the SNCC Freedom Singers followed the hybrid model of professional musician and movement activist. We were on the road full-time, only returning home for organizational meetings and short periods in the field. After Los Angeles and the March on Washington, the Freedom Singers returned to Atlanta and a second group was formed. Harris began to do work for SCLC and I, now married to Cordell, began to prepare for our family.

The second group of Freedom Singers featured Charles Neblett and Matthew and Marshall Jones as the core members, and at various times they were joined by Emory Harris, Betty Mae Fikes, Cordell Reagon, Willie Peacock, Carver "Chico" Neblett, and Bill Perlman (guitar). The Freedom Voices, a third group organized by Cordell Reagon with Bill Harris and Willie Peacock, performed for a short time until Reagon rejoined the second group of Freedom Singers. This group continued to perform freedom songs from the South but expanded their repertoire with new songs composed by Matthew Jones and arrangements with strong jazz influences.

Every Black community had its songleaders, and some of them joined the movement with their time and their voices. The staff of the Civil Rights organizations had great singers, and SNCC was richly endowed: Charles Sherrod, Cordell Hull Reagon, Willie Peacock, Sam Block, Hollis Watkins, Bob Zellner, Fannie Lou Hamer, James Bevel, and Bernard Lafayette. SCLC had able songleaders in Dorothy Cotton, Jimmy Collier, Reverend Frederick Douglas Kirkpatrick, Reverend Andrew Young, Reverend Wyatt T. Walker, and Reverend Fred Shuttlesworth. Joining Reverend Shuttlesworth in Birmingham was the dynamic Carlton Reese, with Cleo Kennedy and Mamie Smith.

Birmingham, Alabama, had long been a strong center of gospel music, so when demonstrations exploded in the summer of 1963, it was to the songs of Carlton Reese, founder and director of the Alabama Christian Movement Choir, that the leaders and community turned for inspiration. One of Reese's most powerful songs was his reworking of "Ninety-Nine and a Half Won't Do." The lyrics of this song proclaimed a commitment to completing a task and an awareness that nothing less than total involvement in the struggle was required. Reese kept the standard gospel text intact except for the insertion of the word "freedom":

Oh Lord, I'm running
Lord, I'm running trying to make a hundred
Running for Freedom
Lord, I'm running trying to make a hundred
Ninety-nine
Ninety-nine
And a half
And a half
Won't do
No it won't do!

This song was charged by Reese's powerful lead vocals and the thundering response by the choir, all of it driven by his accompaniment on the Hammond organ with Leslie speakers.

Birmingham represented a new level in street demonstrations. The use of children in its D-Day March on April 30, 1963, was severely criticized in the press. The response by the authorities was unequaled in its brutality and violence. One of the most dynamic songs from Birmingham grew out of the use of dogs and fire hoses against peaceful demonstrators by Sheriff "Bull" Connor, who instantly became the visible symbol of the unleashed wrath of White segregationists. This song, together with stark images of the event captured by television crews and photojournalists, stirred the nation's conscience and infused the movement with new determination:

Ain' scared of your dogs
'Cause I want my Freedom
I want my Freedom now . . .[36]

There were original songs that came from activists responding to powerful events taking place around them. One of the earliest came as a pivotal musical statement that eulogized the death of Reverend Herbert Lee, an early supporter of the 1961 voter registration drive, who was murdered in McComb, Mississippi. Bertha Gober, the student arrested with Blanton Hall in Albany, Georgia, in 1961, was a beautiful singer. Suspended from Albany State College for her activities, she returned to Atlanta and, learning about the death of Reverend Lee, wrote "We'll Never Turn Back." This song became important throughout the expanding activist communities, but especially so in Mississippi because the danger of working in voter registration for Blacks was so great. Its message was that despite the fact that the presence of Civil Rights organizers increased danger for local people—whose support of the movement automatically made them targets for physical abuse—there was no turning back:

> *We've been 'buked and we been scorned*
> *We've been talked about sure you're born*
> *But we'll never turn back*
> *No we'll never turn back*
> *Until we've all been freed*
> *And we have equality*
> *We have hung our heads and cried*
> *Cried for those like Lee who died*
> *Died for you and died for me*
> *Died for the cause of equality . . .*[37]

SNCC Field Secretary Matthew Jones, a leading force in the second group of Freedom Singers, was probably the most prolific creator of songs documenting the movement. Jones was in solitary confinement at the Danville County Farm in Danville, Virginia, when a young Black soldier named Private First Class Buford Holt was put into the same cell. Holt had been arrested while demonstrating in his hometown with his uniform on. Jones captured the glaring contradiction in his brilliant composition, "Demonstrating GI." The song, written on jail cell toilet paper, tells the story of a soldier who could fight for freedom overseas but could be thrown in jail for fighting for freedom for his people at home. When Medgar Evers, the state director of the NAACP for Mississippi, was murdered by Byron de la Beckwith during the summer of 1963, Matthew Jones began work on a freedom song that became the "Ballad for Medgar Evers." Jones was prompted to complete the song after personally meeting Merlie Evers and her children and being greatly impacted by the killing of the four girls attending Sunday School in Birmingham, Alabama.[38] "Ballad for Medgar Evers" became an important tribute to Evers in the Freedom Singers repertoire.

On June 21, 1964, when three Civil Rights organizers who had gone out to investigate a church bombing near Philadelphia, Mississippi, were reported missing,[39] another song memorializing the cost of freedom began to be heard on the Oxford, Ohio, campus where volunteers were being trained to spend the summer in statewide organizing in Mississippi:

> *They say that freedom is a constant struggle (3X)*
> *Oh Lord, we've struggled so long,*
> *We must be free, we must be free . . .*[40]

Other lines included ". . . freedom is a constant dying . . ." and ". . . freedom is a constant mourning. . . ."

The Selma campaign was so bloody that when the 1965 march from Selma to Montgomery began, the marchers were surrounded by United States Army troops for protection. Jimmie Lee Jackson and Reverend James Reeb had been murdered and marchers had been stormed on Pettus Bridge. Songs supplied a steady spiritual nourishment throughout activities of that march; the verses that people fashioned expressed their intentions and reasons for being there. This song was created with new lyrics by James Orange, an organizer for SCLC, from a recording called "Kidnapper" by Ruby and the Jewels:

I don't want no mess
I don't want no jive
I want my freedom
In sixty-five
Oh Wallace, you never can jail us all
Oh Wallace, segregation's bound to fall . . .[41]

The song documents the arrival in Selma of hundreds of volunteers to participate in the historic march from Selma to Montgomery. After the march, Viola Liuzzo, a Detroit mother of four who volunteered to drive people home from the march, was killed. Topical songwriter Len Chandler passed the scene as he drove back to Atlanta, and by the time he reached my house he had written this song:

There's murder on the roads of Alabama (2X)
If you're black or if you're white
If you're trying to do what's right
You're a target in the night in Alabama.

Oh, we know who is to blame (2X)
She caught two bullets in the brain
Before we learned to say her name
And George Wallace is the shame of Alabama . . .[42]

The High Priestess of Soul, Nina Simone, who, with other recording artists like Odetta and Miriam Makeba, gave voice and support to the struggle for freedom, expressed her outrage in the 1963 composition she called, "Mississippi Goddam":

Alabama's got me so upset
Tennessee makes me lose my rest
And everybody knows about Mississippi
Goddam!! . . .[43]

When SCLC moved to Chicago, Jimmy Collier, a singer and organizer, wrote songs that mirrored the urban discontent that led to riots and rebellions in Watts, Newark, and Detroit:

Middle of the summer,
Bitten by flies and fleas
Sitting in a crowded apartment
about a hundred and 10 degrees
I went outside
It was the middle of the night
All I had was a match in my hands
And I wanted to fight

The Civil Rights Period   363

So I said Burn Baby Burn
Nowhere to be, no one to see
Nowhere to turn
Burn Baby Burn . . .[44]

The music of the Top 40 charts began to resonate with the crisis created by more than a decade of intense activism. One of the strongest voices was the Impressions out of Chicago, singing the songs of Curtis Mayfield:

People get ready, there's a train a-coming
You don't need no ticket, you just get on board,
All you need is faith to hear the diesel humming
You don't need no ticket, you just thank the Lord . . .[45]

Some radio stations refused to play Mayfield's anthem, "Keep on Pushing!"[46]

Along with increasing unrest and strain that occurred when movement activities moved out of the South to urban centers, nonviolence (although challenged) continued to be the bedrock of the movement's strategy and song. Frederick Douglas Kirkpatrick, a founder of the Louisiana Deacons for Defense, was converted to nonviolence and became a staff organizer for SCLC. He was one of the major organizers who led a contingent of marchers and campers to the SCLC-sponsored Poor People's March on Washington, DC, in 1968. This tent city on the federal mall had been called for by Martin Luther King Jr. before his assassination on April 4, 1968, in Memphis, Tennessee. Kirkpatrick, a powerful singer, songwriter, and organizer, sang a blues song he had written called "The Cities Are Burning"; it captured the rebellions and burnings that followed King's death. He also created one of the most important songs that summer for the Poor People's March, signaling changes in activism that questioned not only racism but also the violence of poverty in a land as rich as the United States:

Everybody's got a right to live
Everybody's got a right to live
And before this campaign fail
We'll all go down in jail
Everybody's got a right to live.

We are down in Washington, feeling mighty bad
Thinking about an income, that we've never had
Everybody's got a right . . .[47]

You could not organize Black people without singing, and the singing of the Civil Rights Movement was powerful and inseparable from the organizing and formation of strategies; so, too, were the prayers and the testimonies, sermons, and speeches. Here was a twentieth-century example of music as an integral part of Black life, charged by a community in intense struggle for transformation. The sound of the collective voice was an aural witness as thousands who offered their bodies and often risked their lives moved within the sound of their singing. The Civil Rights Movement was a "borning" struggle, breaking new ground and laying the foundation for ever-widening segments of the society to call for fundamental rights and human dignity. And as African Americans raised their voices in a fight for freedom, they were joined by all who were willing to offer their lives to challenge racism. And they came singing . . .

ACKNOWLEDGMENTS

This essay is based on the accompanying booklet for *Voices of the Civil Rights Movement: African American Freedom Songs, 1955–1965*, Smithsonian Folkways Recording (originally released, 1980; new CD box release, 1998). Material is also drawn from my article. "The Lined Hymn as a Song of Freedom," *Black Music Research Bulletin* 12, no. 1 (1990): 4–7.

NOTES

1. Most studies begin Civil Rights Movement history with the 1954 Supreme Court decision, *Brown v. The Board of Education*, which struck down segregated school systems as unconstitutional, and the murder of Emmett Till in Mississippi. However, there was a bus boycott in Baton Rouge, Louisiana, in 1954, and in 1951 Harry T. Moore and his wife, leaders of the NAACP in the state of Florida, were killed because of their organizing. In spite of trials following the crimes, no one has been convicted of the murders of Moore and Till.
2. Robinson 1987, 45.
3. King 1958, 50.
4. The American Baptist Publication Society 1920 (1881), Hymn #421.
5. *The New National Baptist Hymnal* 1977, 411.
6. McClain, Cleveland, and Nix 1981, 53.
7. Maund 1956, 168.
8. Mary Ethel Dozier (now Jamila Jones), interview conducted by Jesse Johnson Jr., November 1974.
9. Guy Carawan, producer, *We Shall Overcome: Songs of the Freedom Riders and the Sit-Ins* (Washington, DC: Folkways FH5591, 1961).
10. "Editorial" 1960, 5.
11. John Lewis, interview conducted by Bernice Johnson Reagon, Atlanta, Georgia, November 1974.
12. James Weldon Johnson and his brother J. Rosamond Johnson wrote this hymn for a performance in celebration of Abraham Lincoln's birthday by the students of Stanton Grammar School, the school Johnson had attended and been principal. Within the next decade this song became known as the "Negro National Anthem" (Bond and Kathryn 2000; also see Nelson 2003, available at http://www.anb.org).
13. Carawan and Carawan 1963, 26.
14. Ibid., 42.
15. In the process of completing this article, I received a reference to the singing of "We Will Overcome" as "that old Union song," from a 1910 record of an Alabama Union meeting. If this proves to be an accurate accounting, it would shift the date by a few decades for the use of the song as an organizing song and the change of "I" to "We" in the text.
16. See Reagon 1992b.
17. Isaiah Bennett, personal interview, Charleston, SC, October 5, 1974.
18. Miles Horton, interview conducted by the author, New Market, Tennessee, August 20, 1973.
19. Peter Seeger, interview conducted by the author, Beacon, New York, August 1974. Cited in Reagon 1975.
20. Mary Ethel Dozier, interview conducted by Jesse Johnson Jr., Atlanta, Georgia, November 1970. Cited in Reagon 1975.
21. Carawan as quoted by Lowens 1965, 2–8.
22. Cordell Hull Reagon, interview conducted by the author, New York City, August 8, 1973.
23. Quoted from Sherman 1963, 67.
24. Shelton 1963b, 22.
25. Zinn 1964, 128–129.
26. For a more detailed account of the freedom rides and the role of songs, see Farmer 1985.
27. Farmer 1985, 5.
28. Carawan and Carawan 1963, 45.
29. Shelton 1961–1962, 4–7.
30. For the song, see Carawan and Carawan 1963, 62. Also see the account in Branch 1988, 524–561.
31. Charles Sherrod, speaking at the Voices of the Civil Rights Movement Conference, Smithsonian Institution National Museum of American History, January 30–February 3, 1980. Available from the audio and video collection at the SI-NMAH Archive Center.

32. United Methodist Hymnal #413. *The United Methodist Hymnal*. Nashville: The United Methodist Publishing House, 1989.
33. Moses Moon Collection, Smithsonian Institution Museum of American History Archive Center, Washington, DC.
34. Shelton 1963a, 15.
35. "Oxford Town" was originally released on *Freewheelin' Bob Dylan* (Columbia Records 8786, 1963). Lyrics: "Oxford Town," by Bob Dylan. Copyright © 1963 by Warner Bros. Inc. Copyright renewed 1991 by Special Rider Music. All rights reserved. International copyright secured. Reprinted by permission.
36. "Ain't Scared of Nobody" on *Voices of the Civil Rights Movement: Black American Freedom Songs 1960–1966.*
37. "We'll Never Turn Back," by Bertha Gober. Copyright © 1963 (Renewed) Unichappell Music Inc. (BMI). All rights reserved. Used by Permission. Warner Bros. Publications US Inc., Miami, FL 33014.
38. Matthew Jones, written correspondence, August 2004.
39. Michael Schwerner was a CORE organizer and Andrew Goodman was a summer volunteer, both Jews from New York; James Cheney was Black from Meridian, Mississippi. The search for the missing workers included more than four hundred servicemen and fifty FBI agents before their bodies were found on August 4 in a shallow grave.
40. "Freedom Is a Constant Struggle" on *Freedom Is a Constant Struggle: Songs of the Mississippi Civil Rights Movement*. Also visit: http://www.crmvet.org/crmpics/albums/ms_movt.pdf.
41. James Orange in Carawan and Carawan 1963, 264.
42. Len Chandler in Carawan and Carawan 1963, 268. Lyrics reprinted by permission of Len Chandler.
43. "Mississippi, Goddam," by Nina Simone. Copyright © 1964 (Renewed) WB Music Corp. (ASCAP). All rights reserved. Used by Permission. Warner Bros. Publications US Inc., Miami, FL 33014.
44. Jimmy Collier in Carawan and Carawan 1963, 284. Lyrics: "Burn, Baby, Burn," by Jimmy Collier, © Copyright 1966 by Sanga Music, Inc. All rights reserved. Used by permission.
45. "People Get Ready," by Curtis Mayfield, Copyright © 1964 (Renewed) Warner–Tamerlane Publishing Corp. (BMI) and Mijac Music (BMI). All rights reserved. Used by Permission. Warner Bros. Publications US Inc., Miami, FL 33014.
46. Carawan and Carawan 1963, 288.
47. "Everybody's Got A Right To Live," by Frederick Douglass Kirkpatrick, © Copyright 1968 (renewed) by Sanga Music, Inc. All rights reserved. Used by permission.

DISCOGRAPHY

The Best of Broadside, 1962–1988. Various artists. Originally recorded 1962–1970. Smithsonian Folkways Recording 40130, 2000. CD.

Dylan, Bob. *Freewheelin' Bob Dylan*. Originally released 1963. Mobile Fidelity Sound Lab 2081, 2012. Super Audio Hybrid CD.

Freedom Is a Constant Struggle: Songs of the Mississippi Civil Rights Movement. Various artists. Folk Era Records FE1419, 1994. CD.

Jackson, Mahalia. *How I Got Over*. Includes "I've Been 'Buked and I've Been Scorned," "Move On Up a Little Higher," and others. Columbia C34073. 1976. LP.

———. *Mahalia Jackson 21 Greatest Hits*. Kenwood Records 20510, 1979. LP.

———. *Mahalia Jackson: I Sing Because I'm Happy*. Compiled by Jules Schwerin. Folkways 31101 and 31102, 1979. Reissue, Smithsonian/Folkways Special Projects, SFSP900002, 1992.

Let Freedom Sing! Music of the Civil Rights Movement. Various artists. Time/Life Music 80051, 2009. CD.

Mayfield, Curtis. *Curtis Live!* Originally released 1971. Warner Music 909245, 2010. CD.

———. *People Get Ready: The Curtis Mayfield Story*. Includes "Keep On Pushing" and "People Get Ready," among others. Rhino/Warner Bros. 72262, 1996. CD Box Set.

The Montgomery Gospel Trio, The Nashville Quartet, and Guy Carawan. *We Shall Overcome: Songs of the Freedom Riders and the Sit-ins*. Originally released 1961. Smithsonian Folkways Recordings 5591, 2004. CD.

Moving Star Hall Singers. *Been in the Storm So Long: Spirituals & Shouts*. Smithsonian Records 3842, 2012. CD.

Seeger, Pete. *If I Had a Hammer: Songs of Hope and Struggle*. Smithsonian Folkways Recordings SFWCD 40096, 1998. CD.

Seeger, Pete with The Freedom Voices, and Len Chandler. *WNEW's Story of Selma*. Originally released 1965. Smithsonian Records 5595, 2012. CD.
Sing for Freedom: Civil Rights Movement Songs. Various artists. Smithsonian Folkways Recordings 40032, 1992. CD.
Staple Singers. *The Best of the Staple Singers*. Stax 125, 1998. CD.
Sweet Honey in the Rock and James Horner. *Freedom Song*. Original Television Soundtrack. Sony Classical 89147, 2000. CD.
Voices of the Civil Rights Movement: Black American Freedom Songs, 1960–1966. Various artists. Smithsonian Folkways Recording 40084, 1997. CD.

CHAPTER 21

The Post-Civil Rights Period
The Politics of Musical Creativity

Mark Anthony Neal

The quality and breadth of Black protest art during the late 1960s and early 1970s is perhaps unprecedented in any other historical moment. Underlying many of these vibrant expressions of political and cultural resistance were efforts to maintain the "communities of resistance" that produced the Civil Rights and Black Power Movements. By "communities of resistance," I am referring to the loose networks of civil rights activists, anti–Vietnam War protesters, Black Power proponents, Black feminists, and "God-fearing" everyday folk, who sought to challenge the prevailing logic of racism, sexism, and "war mongering" in the United States. As such, the post-Civil Rights era, or what Nelson George first referred to as the "Post-Soul" era of Black culture,[1] created new opportunities for Black musical expression but also produced new challenges, as Black popular music became commodified, seemingly with an intensity that matched the erosion of public and social space within Black communities. With the slow demise of these spaces, which were integral to the development of the "communities of resistance," Black popular music, particularly songs that contained distinct political commentary, was increasingly impacted by the ebb and flow of the recording industry. More often than not, music executives were less concerned with artistic integrity or meaningful political commentary than were Black artists and activists. The post-soul era also represented a period where the very definition of "resistance" for the Black community expanded beyond the issue of racial discrimination. Thus, the burgeoning feminist and gay rights movements also had implications within the Black community as fundamental understandings of Black identity were broadened beyond race to acknowledge the roles of gender, sexuality, and class in shaping the concept of African American identity. In this context, many Black artists embraced modes of resistance that pushed the boundaries of Blackness beyond race.

"FIGHT THE POWER": POST-SOUL RESISTANCE

When the political rhetoric of Malcolm X and the Nation of Islam began to circulate throughout the mainstream, it represented a breach with historical forces such as the notorious "Black codes," which readily circumscribed various modes of Black public expression. While Malcolm X was demonized and vilified in the mainstream for his outspoken opinions regarding White supremacy and American race relations, the relative "freedom" he had to speak was an inspiration to African Americans as they strove to address the realities of race relations in the late 1950s and 1960s. Although various forms of Black expression continued to be repressed, figures like Malcolm X, Angela Davis, Robert F. Williams (via his *Radio Free Dixie* program, broadcast from Havana, Cuba), and others created an atmosphere where Blacks were more willing to openly express themselves publicly, whether through political rhetoric or displays of cultural pride such as wearing dashikis, Afro hairdos, or exhibiting the Black Power fist. One could not imagine the "Black Power fist" protest of American sprinters John Carlos, Tommie Smith, and Lee Evans at the 1968 Olympics in Mexico City, for example, without these earlier models.

It is in this context that Black musical and cultural forms also began to blatantly address Black social and political conditions, both in terms of lyrics and production styles. For example, the studio production styles of Norman Whitfield and James Brown, with regards to their use of electric guitars and bass as witnessed on songs like "Ball of Confusion" (The Temptations, 1970) and "Give It Up or Turnit a Loose" (James Brown, 1969), respectively, reflected the urgency with which Blacks demanded equality in the streets. Musicians as varied as Sly and the Family Stone ("Thank You Falettinme Be Mice Elf Agin," 1970); John Lee Hooker ("[I Don't Wanna Go to] Vietnam," 1969); Aretha Franklin ("Respect," 1967); Roberta Flack, Eddie Harris, and Les McCann ("Compared to What," 1972); Julian "Cannonball" Adderley ("The Price You Gotta Pay to Be Free," 1972); Gil Scott-Heron ("The Revolution Will Not Be Televised," 1970); Nikki Giovanni ("Great Pax Whitey," 1971); The Last Poets ("Niggers Are Scared of Revolution," 1970); and Nina Simone ("Mississippi Goddam," 1962) addressed issues such as police brutality, the Vietnam War, Black pride, and Black rage in their music. It is important to note that most of these artists lodged their "musical protest" while recording for decidedly mainstream (i.e., White-controlled) record labels including Epic, Atlantic, and RCA. Even the Motown label, which generally eschewed politically-charged lyrics in their music, allowed releases by the Temptations ("Ball of Confusion," 1970) and Marvin Gaye ("What's Going On?," 1971) to address the social and political conditions of the day. Motown also produced the Black Forum label, which distributed the speeches of Martin Luther King Jr. and Stokely Carmichael.

Ironically, some of the most powerful of these musical critiques were circulated at a time when the Civil Rights and Black Power Movements were literally under siege and being undermined by covert efforts on the part of the United States government to destabilize and destroy the Black protest movement. The period of 1968–1972, particularly after the election of Richard M. Nixon as president, is arguably one of the most repressive in twentieth-century American history. The impact of this era of repression on Black political and social struggle has been widely documented, as leaders were murdered and incarcerated, organizations like the Black Panther Party and the Student Nonviolent

Coordinating Committee (SNCC) were largely eradicated, and the influence of other groups like the Nation of Islam and Southern Christian Leadership Conference (SCLC) began to wane in the 1970s. Moderate organizations like the National Association for the Advancement of Colored People (NAACP), the Urban League, and Operation Push/The Rainbow Coalition were increasingly the frontline players in advocating for the maintenance of Civil Rights–era gains and increased sensitivity towards the concerns of the Black community in public policy.[2]

Operation Push, in an earlier incarnation known as "Operation Breadbasket," was a Chicago-based grassroots organization founded in 1971 by Reverend Jesse Jackson.[3] At the time, Jackson was known as the "Country Preacher," a title that was immortalized when the Cannonball Adderley Quintet recorded a track called "Country Preacher" (1969), which was written by band member Joe Zawinul in tribute to Jackson's activism. The song was the title track of a live disc by the quintet recorded at Operation Breadbasket's offices in Chicago. Adderley and his band often lent their talents to Jackson's organization in an effort to raise funds for, and the profile of, the organization. It was one of the great examples of how Black musicians and activists worked in direct concert with each other in the context of Black political struggle. This example is notable because, increasingly, Black musical protests were produced outside of the context of sustained social movements on the scale of the Civil Rights Movement.

Beginning in the early 1980s, political narratives in Black popular music were even more informed by various social malaises that reverberated in many Black communities. Recordings such as Paul Laurence's "Strung Out" (1985), Grandmaster Melle Mel's "King of the Streets" (1984), Oran "Juice" Jones' "Pipe Dreams" (1990), and Isaac Hayes' "Hey Love" (1986), for example, all discussed the significance of crack cocaine addiction in the Black community. In other examples, artists recorded songs in support of a Martin Luther King Jr. holiday (Stevie Wonder's "Happy Birthday," 1980) and Jesse Jackson's run for the presidency (Melle Mel's "Run, Jesse, Run," 1984). In some cases, political narratives in Black popular music took on an international flavor, addressing the continued incarceration of Nelson Mandela, South African apartheid, and, in the most celebrated example, in support of famine relief in Ethiopia and the Sudan. The song "We Are the World" (1985), written by Michael Jackson and produced by Quincy Jones, helped bring attention to famine in Africa via the USA for Africa organization.

The commercial success of "We Are the World" highlighted one of the more troubling aspects of "protest" music in the post-Civil Rights era. Increasingly, such music was reduced to musical "styles" that could be intensely consumed and appropriated by the mainstream until different styles of music emerged. More broadly, political events and icons themselves were reduced to commodities to be exchanged in the markets of popular opinion and popular taste. The wide availability of Black protest expression in the mainstream (even The Last Poets charted in the Top 40 in 1969) mirrored the increasing mass mediation of the Black protest movement, facilitating the conditions under which modes of political expression and resistance could be conflated with modes of consumption. Thus, even in the late 1960s, real acts of political resistance were at times reduced to elements of style and fashion, as Afro-wigs, "Free Huey" T-shirts, "red, black and green" Afro-picks, James Brown recordings ("Say It Loud," 1969), and cinematic depictions of "cartooned" Black folks "overtaking the Man" became the limits of Black political expression for some. By the 1980s and 1990s, seminal protest events such as Woodstock were

"MTVed" for "Generation X," the Martin Luther King Jr. holiday was used to peddle pseudo-diversity in the name of selling cotton sheets and hamburgers via the use of King's image and ideas, and a militant international figure like Che Guevara was caricatured as a Chihuahua by a fast food restaurant.

The intense popularity of hip hop music and culture is instructive in this regard. Although many of the early recordings and performances of hip hop in the late 1970s and early 1980s firmly embraced an ethos of "party and bullshit," distinct strains of hip hop began to emerge that spoke lucidly about Black societal conditions. Grandmaster Flash & the Furious Five's "The Message" (1982) is generally recognized as the first significant "political" hip hop recording, as the track distilled the crisis of ghetto life with lines such as "It's like a jungle sometimes." Even hip hop's first major crossover act, Run-D.M.C., featured social commentary on some of their early recordings, notably "It's Like That" (1983) and "Hard Times" (1984). Increasingly, hip hop's oppositional stance against the mainstream (more cultural and social than legitimately political) was integrated into it, thus making it ripe to become one of the core texts of an emerging Generation X that was being socialized via music videos, animated cartoons funded by toy manufacturers, and cable television.

In 1988, MTV comfortably debuted the hip hop program *Yo! MTV Raps*, only a few years after Rick James and others criticized the network for the lack of Black artists on their video playlists. Hip hop stars themselves, such as Queen Latifah, LL Cool J, and Will Smith, appeared in innocuous, and at times foolish, television sitcoms (and later Hollywood films) without even the taint of oppositional realities that marked the genre's emergence. In addition, by the end of the 1980s, although there was a full-blown Black Nationalist/Afrocentric movement emanating out of hip hop culture in the music of Public Enemy, KRS-One and Boogie Down Productions, the X-Clan, Poor Righteous Teachers, Brand Nubian, Paris, and others, this style was replaced, seemingly overnight, by the nihilistic sounds of "gangsta rap" largely parlayed in the music of West Coast–based acts such as the late Eazy-E, N.W.A. (Niggaz with Attitude), DJ Quick, and Compton's Most Wanted. Although the music of some of these acts contained political elements—N.W.A.'s critiques of racial profiling and police brutality, for example—many of these acts became media stars to young Whites, at the expense of some of the more politically conscious rap acts. In the absence of a sustained social and political movement, so-called conscious hip hop had become little more than an "old-school" style of hip hop.

SOUL OUT THE BOX: REDEFINING BLACK RESISTANCE

In the aftermath of the political struggles of the late 1960s, resistance within the context of the Black community began to more accurately reflect diverse interests within the "community." At stake were efforts to redefine Black identity not only in the context of race, but also gender, sexuality, class, and spirituality. In other cases, there were efforts to redefine what exactly "Black music" was, as some artists such as Mother's Finest, Fishbone, Living Colour, Bad Brains, Lenny Kravitz, and The Family Stand began to embrace musical styles that were not usually thought of as being "Black," although the lyrics of these artists continued to address issues concerning the Black community.[4] Thus issues such as those specific to the experiences of Black women (including their ability to define their own sexuality), Black male sexuality, and class divisions within the Black community took on a certain prominence in Black musical resistance, particularly after the emergence of hip hop.

Perhaps no one group of artists captured the new terrain of Black musical resistance in the early 1970s better than the trio LaBelle. Founded in 1962, in their earliest incarnation the group was a quartet known as the Ordettes and later the Bluebelles, as the group's lead singer Patsy Holte was renamed Patti LaBelle. The group was a favorite on the "chitlin' circuit," the loose network of Black clubs, restaurants, taverns, and dance halls that catered to largely segregated Black audiences, and they achieved several "turntable" hits with tracks like "Over the Rainbow" (1965) and "You'll Never Walk Alone" (1964). Under the new management of Vicki Wickham (who also guided the career of Dusty Springfield) the group, now reduced to three members, was simply renamed LaBelle. According to Patti LaBelle, Wickham envisioned the new version of the group as "three black women singing about racism, sexism and eroticism."[5] Wickham's comments were a firm reference to the tradition of girl groups like the Supremes and others who donned the pretty uniforms of pleasure and sophistication for audiences at places like the Copacabana, but rarely addressed issues of racism, sexuality, and political disenfranchisement in their music, which more often than not was written and produced by men.

In this regard, LaBelle and their records from the early 1970s are useful in framing the contours of resistance in the post-Civil Rights era. Arguably, this was the first generation of Black women to wield such creative control over their art since figures like Bessie Smith and Ma Rainey emerged in the 1920s. Artists like Roberta Flack, Valerie Simpson (who recorded two brilliant though obscure discs for Motown in the early 1970s), Janis Ian, Betty Davis, and, of course, LaBelle all took advantage of these new artistic opportunities. Increasingly, the LaBelle sound became more distinct with the maturation of Nona Hendryx's songwriting skills. Songs like "Sunday's News" (1972), "If I Can't Have You" (1972), and "Can I Speak to You Before You Go to Hollywood?" (1973) were all deeply personal tracks, which the trio fluidly embellished across a range of emotions including rage, defiance, joy, and pleasure.

On the Patti LaBelle and Nona Hendryx–penned "Shades of Difference" from *LaBelle* (1971), the trio sings the song's hook, "Hey yeah, we don't care if you fade away/We gonna save the world today," as though they were pre–*Powerpuff Girls* superhero feminists seriously aiming to "save the world."[6] On "I Believe That I've Finally Made It Home" (1972, written by Hendryx) the group addresses how distinct spheres of feminist thought are often thought to be out of sync with reality. Countering a doctor's notion that it was "too late, and out of date" for their "emancipation," the trio sings, "I believe that I've finally made it home/I believe that with me there's a'nothing wrong/I believe . . . that I'm alright and this whole political world has gone insane."

On their first two recordings, *LaBelle* (1971) and *Moon Shadow* (1972), LaBelle also took liberties with songs written and performed by established acts such as the Rolling Stones ("Wild Horses"), Cat Stevens ("Moonshadow"), The Who ("Won't Get Fooled Again"), and Laura Nyro ("Time and Love"), with whom the trio would collaborate on a collection of doo-wop and Motown classics (*Gonna Take a Miracle*, 1971). Because many of these "covers" were originally written by and for male artists, LaBelle often used their own vocal arrangements, allowing them a "voice" in narratives in which Black women had been largely marginalized. The best example of this was LaBelle's combined cover of

Thunderclap Newman's "Something in the Air" and Gil Scott-Heron's "The Revolution Will Not Be Televised," which appeared on their third disc, *Pressure Cookin'* (1973).

LaBelle's most popular recording, "Lady Marmalade," appeared on their fourth disc, *Nightbirds* (1974). "Lady Marmalade" was a tribute to one of few public spaces where women were allowed some sense of autonomous expression. Produced by Allen Toussaint, who scored a year earlier with the Pointer Sisters' "Yes, We Can, Can," and written by Kenny Noland and Bob Crewe, "Lady Marmalade" became the trio's only million-seller. The classic chorus lyric, "Voulez-vous coucher avec moi ce soir?" ("Do you want to sleep with me tonight?"), is one of the most memorable lines in all of 1970s pop music. In the hands of LaBelle, the song became an anthem of sexual assertion and empowerment, rather than a camp story about prostitution.

During the decade of the 1970s, popular books by Erica Jong and others were published that celebrated human sexuality in ways not possible during earlier generations. The film industry's Production Code Administration, which had sanctioned puritanical representations of sex acts and sexuality on screen, were challenged by a litany of films including *Carnal Knowledge* (1971) and *Bob & Carol & Ted & Alice* (1969). The allowance of more liberal and even vulgar presentations of sexuality in popular culture during the 1970s had an obvious impact within Black popular culture. In the past, full explorations (and celebrations) of Black sexuality were constrained, not only by the general conservatism of American society, but also by calculated attempts by various forces to fabricate and deny various aspects of Black sexuality. Very often, Black folks engaged in self-censorship, to counter widespread myths that Black women were insatiable (thus deserving of some forms of sexual violence, particularly in the South) or that Black men possessed "unnaturally" large sex organs and appetites for White women (thus deserving of forms of violent control in order to protect White women). LaBelle's "Lady Marmalade" was evidence that even Black women could now engage in the sexual freedoms of the time, although race continued to temper how such freedoms would be interpreted in a society that still traded heavily in the same tropes of Black sexuality that had circulated in previous generations.

In previous generations, Black performers deftly negotiated issues of sexuality by engaging in forms of play or double entendre, a well-known literary and rhetorical strategy that Blacks have utilized for hundreds of years, that escaped the scrutiny of censors and affirmed healthy Black sexualities.[7] Songs such as Bull Moose Jackson's "Big Ten Inch Record" (1952, later covered by Aerosmith) or Dinah Washington's "Long John Blues" (1948) were popular examples of these strategies.[8] The decidedly restrained sexualities of Sam Cooke, Jackie Wilson, Johnny Mathis, Harry Belafonte, and Nat "King" Cole—who were all legitimate sex symbols—represent yet another strategy that was employed by artists. The constraints of the presentation of Black sexuality were most dramatically challenged by Melvin Van Peebles' film *Sweet Sweetback's Baadasssss Song* (1971), which chronicled the life of a sex worker on the run for killing a police officer. "Sweetback" was the most sexual Black character to appear in popular culture at the time of the film's release, and Van Peebles consciously conflated that sexuality with issues of Black political struggle. In many ways, "Sweetback" was seen as fornicating in the name of Black political struggle. "Sweetback" struck a chord among Black audiences because his image liberated the counterimage of the docile Black male, which had been embraced by Black men, in part to protect themselves from racial violence.

Accordingly, Black male musical artists picked up on this energy as Black male sexuality was blatantly celebrated in the music of Major Harris and Marvin Gaye, who traveled from the protest politics of his *What's Going On* (1971) to the bedroom politics of *Let's Get It On* (1973) in two short years. Harris' "Love Won't Let Me Wait" (1975) and Gaye's "Since I Had You" (1975), for example, both featured the feigned sounds of female orgasms in the background, suggesting that both artists were accomplished at pleasuring women, both musically and sexually. Disco diva Donna Summer offered an alternative. Performing her own orgasmic sounds on the song "Love to Love You Baby" (1975), she in effect placed her own sexual pleasure at the center of the narrative instead of being objectified in the narratives of her male counterparts. Whereas Black male musical artists were relatively free to pursue hypersexual and hypermasculine themes in their music—think of the longevity of blues artist Marvin Sease, who has had a relatively successful commercial career recording songs in the vein of his best known track "Candy Licker" (1986)—the decision of Black women artists to aggressively pursue hypersexual themes in their music has often reinforced centuries-old notions of Black women as hypersexual "creatures" who thus "deserved" to be demeaned.

As the commercial stakes for Black music artists increased in the post-Civil Rights era, many Black women performers were forced to appeal to base sexual desires among their audiences, often at the expense of the music that they produced. Examples include artists as varied as Aretha Franklin, who made the transition from the "Queen Mother of Soul" image that appeared on her discs *Amazing Grace* (1972) and *Young, Gifted, and Black* (1972) to a more sexualized image on the discs *Let Me in Your Life* (1974) and *With Everything I Feel in Me* (1974) (the cover art on the latter disc showed Franklin's cleavage); Toni Braxton; Adina Howard ("Freak Like Me," 1994); and hip hop artists Lil' Kim and Foxy Brown. As Black women performers were continuously reduced to sexual images, particularly after music video channels became indispensable to the promotion of pop artists, it became increasingly difficult for those Black women who didn't fit the requisite "'lite' and bright" criteria, such as Jill Scott, Angie Stone, Kelly Price, and Sandra St. Victor, to get a fair hearing (and viewing) in the marketplace.

Despite the new freedoms associated with Black sexuality in popular music, much of what was produced was largely presented in heterosexist contexts. Although all artists were constrained by the homophobia of the recording industry and among pop music audiences, there were White artists whose homosexuality or bisexuality—Elton John, Dusty Springfield, and Freddie Mercury of Queen, for example—were fairly well known and to some extent accepted. An artist like David Bowie, for instance, blatantly took advantage commercially of the perceived ambiguous nature of his sexuality, in a way that few Black artists had been able to, save Little Richard. The point here is that there have been few Black artists who have been able to be openly gay or bisexual within the context of Black popular music.

The popularity of Patti LaBelle after the breakup of LaBelle in 1977 is also instructive in examining themes of homosexuality or rather fluid sexualities in Black popular music. For much of her career, dating back to the early days of Patti LaBelle & the Bluebelles, LaBelle's version of "Over the Rainbow" (1965) has been her signature tune. The song is, of course, historically linked to Judy Garland, who first performed the song in the film *The Wizard of Oz* (1939). Although Garland's difficulties with alcohol, prescription drugs, and fame in general have been widely documented, less so has been her significance to gay and lesbian community, where Garland became a template for some post–World War II White male homosexuals.[9] LaBelle's performance of Garland's signature tune links LaBelle to Garland and, not surprisingly, LaBelle has become a template for Black male homosexuals who embrace a more feminine model of homosexuality.

Although South Shore Commission's "Free Man" (1975) has been acknowledged as an anthem of Black male homosexuality in the 1970s, disco artist Sylvester became one of the first openly gay Black men to emerge in Black popular music. With recordings like "You Make Me Feel (Mighty Real)" (1978) and "Dance (Disco Heat)" (1978), Sylvester was one of the most popular disco artists in the late 1970s. Sylvester acknowledged the influence of Patti LaBelle on his live recording *Living Proof* (1979), where he performed a version of the LaBelle-penned "You Are My Friend." Sylvester remained the most well-known homosexual or bisexual Black musician until the emergence of Me'Shell NdegéOcello (Figure 21.1). NdegéOcello's debut release *Plantation Lullabies* (1983)

Figure 21.1
Me'Shell NdegéOcello at Lifebeat party at NV, New York City, April 6, 1996.

Photograph by Tina Paul, reproduced with permission.

melded old-school funk with hip hop across a vibrant and imaginative urban (musical) landscape. NdegéOcello's name, which means "Free Like a Bird" in Swahili, was the perfect metaphor for the fluidity of themes and styles that pervaded her music. Openly bisexual, NdegéOcello challenges both homophobia within the Black community and the provincialism of gays and lesbians regarding bisexuality on tracks such as "Barryfarms" (*Cookie: The Anthropological Mixtape*, 2002) and "Leviticus Faggot" (*Peace Beyond Passion*, 1996). The latter track is also notable because Black Entertainment Television (BET), for a long time the primary venue for the distribution of Black music videos, refused to air the song, which was deemed "too controversial."[10] But NdegéOcello's political palate has extended well beyond the politics of Black sexuality to engage issues ranging from Black dysfunction ("Jabril," 2002), icon worship ("Dead Nigga Blvd," 2002), and crass commercialism ("GOD.FEAR.MONEY," 2002). In this regard, NdegéOcello has bridged the sexual politics that make her voice so significant within Black popular music with the more traditional protest politics of the Black community.

It has largely been in the context of hip hop that many of the "old-school" narratives of political resistance have been maintained. Even NdegéOcello acknowledges this, as the title of her disc *Cookie: The Anthropological Mixtape* (2002) is a direct reference to the underground "mixtape culture" where hip hop vocalists and DJs earn their "street credibility." The political narratives of groups such as Public Enemy, Paris, Ice Cube, and other "conscious" hip hop artists have diverged little from the narratives of Malcolm X, H. Rap Brown, Kwame Toure (Stokely Carmichael), and other well-known Black Nationalists. More than anything, "political" hip hop has helped valorize Black Nationalist icons for the post-Civil Rights generation. Generally speaking, though, hip hop music, even that which was not "conscious," has been useful in highlighting the more pronounced class divisions within the Black community over the last three decades.

In the best instances, hip hop has countered the hegemony of liberal bourgeois spokespersons in the Black community by never shrinking from "speaking truth to power" and providing a beat reporter's view of life in the inner city. Thus tracks like "The Message" (Grandmaster Flash & the Furious Five, 1982), KRS-One's "Love Is Gonna Get Cha" (1990), or N.W.A.'s "Straight Outta Compton" (1989) spoke of the illicit realities of inner-city life, providing a context for the gang violence, drug dealing, and petty criminality that were deeply imbricated in the mainstream's perceptions of Black urban life. In another example, Public Enemy's "911 Is a Joke" (1990) comically addressed the state of emergency services in poor Black and Latino communities, where folks often wait for great lengths of time before a response. With the song, Public Enemy suggests that the response time is much quicker in predominately White communities.

More broadly, hip hop music and culture was perceived within the Black community as the antithesis of Black middle- and working-class sensibilities, in part mirroring the nationalist–integrationist split that defined the political struggles of the 1960s and early 1970s. Musically, this was expressed by the lethargic pace with which Black-owned radio stations integrated hip hop music onto their playlists. Crucial to this rift, which is also generational, are fundamental ways in which the Civil Rights and post-Civil Rights generations held differing opinions about the use of certain modes of address in the public and commercial spheres, whether it be the use of profanity and "vulgar" descriptions of

Black female sexuality or critiques of Civil Rights icons (the controversy over comments made about Rosa Parks and Martin Luther King Jr. in the film *Barbershop* [2002] is an example).[11] Ironically, the Black-owned radio stations which "banned" rap music on their airwaves had little compunction about accepting ads from malt liquor companies, whose products could also be traced to "dysfunctional" attitudes among the so-called hip hop generation. Public Enemy and The Family Stand explicitly addressed problems that some younger artists had with "Black radio" on tracks such as "Don't Believe the Hype" (1988) and "Plantation Radio" (1992), respectively.

Although class divisions have been an obvious part of the Black experience in America, dating back to the classic "field nigger vs. house nigger" narrative, these divisions were rarely played out publicly in such a way that the larger society could detect a significant lack of social and political cohesiveness within segregated Black communities. In this regard, the façade of "unity" within the Black public proper helped serve the political interests of the Black community by positing the community as being of "one voice." The animosities between followers of Malcolm X (El Hajj Malik El-Shabazz) and Martin Luther King Jr. reflected the class fissures within the Black community just as the differences in organizing styles and political ideologies between the two men were also a reflection of their different class origins. Concerns about class divisions within "Black America" became much more pronounced with the growth of the Black middle class in the post-Civil Rights era. Anxieties within the emerging Black middle class can be identified in some of the pop culture artifacts of the 1970s, including films like *Let's Do It Again* (1975) and *A Piece of the Action* (1978) and the musical productions of Kenneth Gamble and Leon Huff of Philadelphia International Records. The Harold Melvin and the Blue Notes' recording "Be for Real" (1972), written and produced by Gamble and Huff, offers an example of some of these anxieties as lead vocalist Teddy Pendergrass narrates the struggles of trying to remain connected to the "old community" after he and his wife have "come up in the world" and achieved a level of financial stability not shared by many of their friends.

Hip hop has consistently addressed these issues in mantras like "keepin' real" that are meant to frame issues of authenticity for an emerging generation of pop culture crossovers like Sean "P. Diddy" Combs, Russell Simmons, Shaquille O'Neal, Allen Iverson, and Ice Cube, and crossover "wannabes" who dream of living the lifestyle of those icons. The concept of "ghetto fabulous," which celebrates certain notions of a normative "ghetto" experience, is another marker of distinct class allegiances within the post-Civil Rights generation. "Ghetto fabulous" can be defined as a stylish embrace of certain aspects of a poor, ghetto experience, thus illustrating how members of these communities creatively find ways to not only survive, but even thrive amidst distasteful circumstances. One example of "ghetto fabulousness" is Jaheim's 2002 track "Fabulous," which provides humorous commentary on folks who use "pre-paid cellies [cell phones] for local calls" (because their local service was turned off because of unpaid bills) and "name their kids them funny names" (providing their kids with a distinct individuality).

On the one hand, "ghetto fabulousness" has allowed ghetto denizens, who don't have the material resources of their icons, the ability to relish their lifestyles (as they are celebrated in music videos and movies). On the other hand, the icons themselves get to authenticate themselves via ghetto culture, despite their upper-middle-class status as entertainers and artists. Of course, any attempt to define Black middle class and its sensibilities is further complicated by issues of skin caste and educational attainment, although various sentiments about these attributes, especially skin color, are rarely publicly addressed by Blacks in terms of the issues of earned income or wealth. The point here is that hip hop artists with access to wealth may consciously embrace a "ghettocentric" aesthetic to validate themselves among their less affluent fans.

The music video for Florida-based rap artist Trick Daddy's song "I'm a Thug" (2001) is a comical exploration of the differing opinions about what constitutes middle-class identity within the Black community. In the video, the parents of Trick Daddy's upper-middle-class girlfriend despise him for his style of dress and the music that he makes (so-called gangsta rap), which, not so ironically, their young son listens to. In a pivotal scene in the video, Trick Daddy accompanies his girlfriend and her parents to an upscale "five-star" restaurant. Not feeling the need to validate himself among the Black bourgeois, Trick Daddy "orders in" a bucket of fried chicken. The point of the video is that distinct differences in class sensibilities exist between the traditional Black middle class and "ghetto fabulous" rap artists, even though they may possess comparable wealth. Hip hop has heightened these distinctions because hip hop culture has created a distinct population of upper-middle-class performers and industry executives (at least in terms of income and wealth), who did not emerge from within the context of traditional middle-class professionals and whose educational attainment and socialization differ.[12]

But Trick Daddy's consumption habits are also instructive in the twenty-first century, because video depictions of material consumption have been interpreted by many within the hip hop generation as acts of resistance in and of themselves. Thus, the acquisitions of material goods and the development of boutique labels within the recording industry have taken on a perceived political component that, in many regards, undermines traditional forms of political engagement. The "performance" of resistance, often as an "aesthetic of consumption," has become an integral feature of contemporary hip hop music.

CONCLUSION

In the post-Civil Rights era, Black musical performers experienced greater freedom with regard to their ability to address the various political dynamics of Black life and culture. Unlike previous generations of artists, particularly those recording at the height of the Civil Rights Movement, the post-Civil Rights generation often recorded tomes of resistance outside of the context of sustained political movements. Lacking specific political foci, particularly in the context of intensified commodification of Black popular expression, many "political" performances were rendered as little more than stylistic choices among certain artists. In the future, Black musical performers interested in recording politically progressive music will have to struggle to maintain strong ties to progressive social movements and create ways to garner commercial support of their projects outside of the context of the mainstream recording industry and its various organs, particularly music video networks that at this time have little interest in music that doesn't turn huge profits.

NOTES

1. For a discussion of the "Post-Soul" era, see Nelson George 1992.
2. For details about these organizations, see Garrow 2001; Marable 2001; Churchill and Vander Wall 2002.
3. "Operation Breadbasket" was first established in 1962 as an economic arm of SCLC.
4. See Mahon 2000.
5. LaBelle and Randolph 1996, 154.
6. The *Powerpuff Girls* is an animated series that is broadcast on the Cartoon Network. Part of the show's appeal across age groups is that it posits the three members of the group, Buttercup, Blossom, and Bubbles, as the first self-defined female superheroes. The group's mantra is that they "save the world before bedtime."
7. For a thoughtful discussion of the political significance of forms of play or what Scott calls the "hidden transcripts" of political relationships, see Scott 1990.
8. See Neal 2001.
9. For more information, see Gross 2000; Davis 2001.
10. Jones 2001, 93.
11. For detailed studies of generational shifts within Black communities, particularly within the realm of culture, see Boyd 2002; Neal 2002.
12. See Boyd 2002.

DISCOGRAPHY

Brand Nubian. *In God We Trust*. Elektra 7559613812, 1993. CD.
Brown. James. *Live at the Apollo (1962)*. Originally recorded October 24, 1962. Polydor B 171502, 2004. CD.
———. *Live at the Apollo, Vol. II*. Originally released 1968. Universal/Polydor 90572, 2007. CD.
———. *Star Time*. Originally released 1991. Polydor/Strategic Marketing 007063885, 2009. Digital.
Davis, Betty. *Betty Davis*. Originally released 1973. Ernie B's 154294, 2013. CD.
Dr. Dre. *The Chronic [Re-Lit and From the Vault]*. Originally released 1992. WIDEawake Entertainment Group/Death Row 21012, 2009. CD & DVD.
Franklin, Aretha. *Live at Fillmore West*. Originally recorded February 5, 1971 and February 7, 1971. Rhino 127956, 2007. CD.
———. *Aretha Franklin: 30 Greatest Hits*. Originally released 1985. Atlantic 81668 ACD, 2011. CD.
Grandmaster Flash & the Furious Five (featuring Melle Mel & Duke Bootee). *The Message (Expanded Edition)*. Originally released 1982. Reissued by Castle Music/Sanctuary 2741869, 2010. CD.
Hendryx, Nona. *Nona Hendryx*. Originally released 1977. Superbird TBIRD 0036, 2010. CD.
KRS-One and the Temple of Hiphop. *Spiritual Minded*. Koch KOCCD 8376, 2002. CD.
LaBelle. *Moon Shadow*. Originally released 1972. Wounded Bird WOU 2618, 2000. CD.
———. *Pressure Cookin'*. Originally released 1973. Soul Music SMCR 5123, 2014. CD.
———. *Something Silver*. Warner Bros. 46359, 1997. CD.
The Last Poets. *The Last Poets*. Rev-Ola Records CRREV 90, 2008. CD.
NdegéOcello, Me'Shell. *Plantation Lullabies*. Originally released 1993. Sire 9362457542, 1994. CD.
N.W.A. *Straight Outta Compton*. Originally released 1988. Reissued by Priority B 002309502, 2015. CD.
Paris. *Sleeping with the Enemy [2009 Deluxe Edition]*. Originally released 1992. Reissued by Guerrilla Funk 19, 2009. CD.
Patti LaBelle and the Bluebelles. *Golden "Philly" Classics*. Collectables 5090, 1993. CD.
Public Enemy. *It Takes a Nation of Millions to Hold Us Back [Deluxe Edition]*. Originally released 1988. Reissued by Def Jam 3773708, 2014. CD and DVD.
———. *Fear of a Black Planet [Deluxe Edition]*. Originally released 1990. Reissued by Def Jam/Virgin EMI 4704574, 2014. CD.
Queen Latifah. *Black Reign*. Originally released 1993. Universal Music 5302722, 1994. CD.
Run-D.M.C. *Run-D.M.C. [Deluxe Edition]*. Originally released 1984. Reissued by Arista 88697507172, 2009. CD.
Scott, Jill. *Who Is Jill Scott? Words and Sounds, Vol. 1*. Originally released 2000, Sony Music Distribution 8187, 2007. CD.

Simone, Nina. *Nina Simone in Concert*. Recorded March 21, 1964–April 6, 1964. JDC Records 12100, 2010. CD.

Sly & The Family Stone. *There's a Riot Goin' On*. Originally released 1971. Get On Down GET 9009, 2013. CD.

———. *The Essential Sly & the Family Stone*. Recorded 1967–1975. Originally released 2002. Epic/Legacy 5100182, 2009. CD.

Stone, Angie. *Black Diamond*. Arista 19092, 1999. CD.

Wonder, Stevie. *Talking Book*. Originally released 1972. Reissued by Universal Distribution 91470, 2009. CD.

———. *Innervisions*. Originally released 1973. Reissued by Universal Distribution 91471, 2009. CD.

Wu Tang Clan. *Enter the Wu-Tang (36 Chambers)*. Originally released 1993. Reissued by BMG 21203672, 2000. CD.

Bibliography

Adams, Dolly. *Oral History Digest*. New Orleans: Hogan Jazz Archive, Tulane University, April 18, 1962.
African Methodist Episcopal Church. *The African Methodist Episcopal Church Bicentennial Hymnal*. Nashville, TN: African Methodist Episcopal Church, 1984.
Agawu, Kofi. "Does Music Theory Need Musicology?" *Current Musicology* 53 (1993): 89–98.
———. "Analyzing Music under the New Musicological Regime." *Journal of Musicology* 15, (1997): 297–307.
Ake, David. *Jazz Cultures*. Berkeley: University of California Press, 2002.
———, Charles Hiroshi Garrett, and Daniel Goldmark, eds. *Jazz/Not Jazz: The Music and Its Boundaries*. Berkeley: University of California Press, 2012.
Albertson, Chris. *Bessie Smith: Empress of the Blues*. New York: Walter Kane and Son, 1975.
Albiez, Sean. "Post-Soul Futurama: African American Cultural Politics and Early Detroit Techno." *European Journal of American Culture* 24, no. 2 (2005): 131–52. doi: 10.1386/ejac.24.2.131/1
Allen, Candace. *Valaida: A Novel*. London: Virago Press, 2005.
Allen, William Francis, Charles Pickard Ware, and Lucy McKim Garrison, eds. *Slave Songs of the United States*. 1867. Reprint, New York: Peter Smith, 1951. E-text available at www.docsouth.unc.edu/church/allen/allen.html.
Alletti, Vince. *Liner Notes to Something Silver*. New York: Warner Brothers, 1997.
Altschuler, Glenn C. *All Shook Up: How Rock 'n' Roll Changed America*. New York: Oxford University Press, 2003.
The American Baptist Publication Society. *Baptist Hymnal*. 1881. New ed., Valley Forge, PA: Judson Press, 1920.
"America's Most Amazing Family: The Famous Gordys of Detroit." *Color*, June 1949, 4–8.
"ANC Mothers Inaugural Banquet." *Los Angeles Sentinel*, May 1, 1986, A1.
Anderson, Allan. "The Azusa Street Revival and the Emergence of Pentecostal Missions in the Early Twentieth Century." *Transformation* 23, no. 2 (2006): 107–18.
Anderson, Chris. "The Long Tail." *Wired*, October 2004. Available from http://www.wired.com/wired/archive/12.10/tail.html.
Anderson, Iain. "Jazz Outside the Marketplace: Free Improvisation and Non-Profit Sponsorship of the Arts, 1965–1980." *American Music* 20, no. 2 (2002): 131–67.
Anderson, Victor. "The Black Church and the Curious Body of the Black Homosexual." In *Loving the Body: Religious Studies and the Erotic*, edited by Anthony Pinn and Dwight Hopkins, 297–312. New York: Palgrave, 2004.
"Ann Cooper Plays with Bibbs' Band." *Chicago Defender*, February 17, 1940, 20.
"Ann Cooper to 'Darlings of Rhythm' Band." *Chicago Defender*, August 19, 1944, 6.
"Anti-Apartheid Telethon on Drawing Board." *Los Angeles Sentinel*, April 17, 1986, A1.

Anzaldúa, Gloria, ed. *Making Face, Making Soul/Haciendo Caras: Creative and Critical Perspectives by Women of Color.* 1st ed. San Francisco: Aunt Lute Foundation Books, 1990.

Arbus, Doon. "James Brown Is Out of Sight," *The New York Herald Tribune*, March 20, 1966. Reprint in *The James Brown Reader: 50 Years of Writing about the Godfather of Soul*, edited by Nelson George and Alan Leeds, 18–34. New York: A Plum Book/Penguin Press, 2008.

Armstrong, Louis. *Swing That Music.* 1936. Reprint, New York: Da Capo, 1993.

Armstrong, Toni, Jr. "An Endangered Species: Women's Music By, For, and About Women." *HOT WIRE: The Journal of Women's Music and Culture* 5, no. 3 (September 1989): 17–19.

———. "Midwife to the Culture: Hot Wire." In *Happy Endings: Lesbian Writers Talk About Their Lives and Work*, edited by Kate Brandt, 161–70. Tallahassee, FL: The Naiad Press, Inc., 1993.

Associated Press. "Tye Tribbett Discusses the Infidelity in his Marriage." *Eurweb*, October 21, 2010. Available from http://www.eurweb.com/2010/10/tye-tribbett-discusses-the-infidelity-in-his-marriage/.

Attali, Jacques. *Noise: The Political Economy of Music.* Translated by Brian Massumi. Minneapolis: University of Minnesota Press, 1985. Originally published in *Bruits: Essai sur l'Économie Poliltique de la Musique* (Paris: Presses Universitaires de France, 1977).

Austerlitz, Paul. *Jazz Consciousness: Music, Race, and Humanity.* Middletown, CT: Wesleyan University Press, 2005.

Bailey, Marlon. *Butch Queens Up in Pumps: Gender, Performance, and Ballroom Culture in Detroit.* Ann Arbor: The University of Michigan Press, 2013.

Bakkum, Nathan C. "Point of Departure: Recording and the Jazz Event." *Jazz Perspectives* 8, no. 1 (2014): 73–91.

Banfield, William. *Musical Landscapes in Color: Conversations with Black American Composers.* Lanham, MD: Scarecrow Press, 2003.

Baraka, Amiri (LeRoi Jones). *Blues People: Negro Music in White America.* New York: William Morrow, 1963. Reprint, New York: William Morrow, 1966.

———. *Blues People: Negro Music in White America.* New York: Morrow, 1963. Reprint, New York: HarperCollins, 1999.

Barker, Danny. *Buddy Bolden and the Last Days of Storyville.* New York: Cassell, 1998.

Barlow, William. *"Looking Up At Down": The Emergence of Blues Culture.* Philadelphia: Temple University Press, 1989.

———. *Voice Over: The Making of Black Radio.* Philadelphia: Temple University Press, 1999.

Barrett, Harris. "Negro Folk Songs." *Southern Workman* 41, (1912): 238–45.

Barton, William E. *Old Plantation Hymns: A Collection of Hitherto Unpublished Melodies of the Slaves and the Freedmen.* Boston: Lamson, Wolffe, 1899.

Barzel, Tamar. "Subsidy, Advocacy, Theory: Experimental Music in the Academy, in New York City, and Beyond." In *People Get Ready: The Future of Jazz Is Now!*, edited by Ajay Heble and Rob Wallace, 153–65. Durham, NC: Duke University Press, 2013.

Basie, Count (as told to Albert Murray). *Good Morning Blues: The Autobiography of Count Basie.* London: Paladin, 1987.

Bastin, Bruce. *Red River Blues: The Blues Tradition in the Southeast.* 1986. Reprint, Urbana: University of Illinois Press, 1995.

Bauer, William R. "Billie Holiday and Betty Carter: Emotion and Style in the Jazz Vocal Line." *Annual Review of Jazz Studies* 6, (1993): 99–152.

———. "Scat Singing: A Timbral and Phonemic Analysis." *Current Musicology* 71–73, (2001–02): 303–23.

Bayles, Martha, Ran Blake, Scott Deveaux, Michael Dorf, Jon Faddis, Lorraine Gordon, Robin D. G. Kelley, Joe Lovano, Jason Moran, Joshua Redman, Roswell Rudd, Terry Teachout, and Steve Wilson. "Watching 'Jazz' for Its High Notes and Low." *The New York Times*, January 7, 2001, 33, 40. Available from http://www.nytimes.com/2001/01/07/arts/music-watching-jazz-for-its-high-notes-and-low.html?pagewanted=all&pagewanted=print.

Bebey, Francis. *African Music: A People's Art.* Translated by Josephine Bennett. Brooklyn, NY: Lawrence Hill & Co., 1975. Originally published in *Musique De L'Afrique* (n.p.: Horizons de France, 1969).

Becker, Judith. "Is Western Art Music Superior?" *Musical Quarterly* 72, no. 3 (1986): 341–59.

Beerbohm, Constance. "The 'Cake-Walk' and How to Dance It: A Chat with the Prima Donna of 'In Dahomey'." *The Tatler*, no. 105 (July 1, 1903).

Bego, Mark. *Aretha Franklin: The Queen of Soul.* Exp. ed., New York: Da Capo Press, 2001. First published 1989 by St. Martin's Press.

Beltz, Carl. *The Story of Rock.* 2nd ed. New York: Oxford University Press, 1972.

Berkman, Franya J. "Appropriating Universality: The Coltranes and Sixties Spirituality." *American Studies* 48, no. 1 (Spring 2007): 41–62.

———. *Monument Eternal: The Music of Alice Coltrane*. Middletown, CT: Wesleyan University Press, 2010.

Berliner, Paul F. *Thinking in Jazz: The Infinite Art of Improvisation*. Chicago: University of Chicago Press, 1994.

Bertrand, Michael T. *Race, Rock, and Elvis*. Urbana: University of Illinois Press, 2005.

Betts, Graham. *Motown Encyclopedia*. AC Publishing, 2014.

Bianco, David. *Heat Wave: The Motown Fact Book*. Ann Arbor, MI: Pierian Press, 1988.

"Billboard Adopts 'R&B' as New Name for 2 Charts." *Billboard*, October 27, 1990, 6, 35.

Bird, Brian. *Skiffle*. London: Robert Hale, 1958.

Bjorn, Lars. *Before Motown: A History of Jazz in Detroit, 1920–1960*. Ann Arbor: University of Michigan Press, 2001.

Blair, Leonardo. "Pastor E. Dewey Smith Says Criticism of Church Hypocrisy on Treatment of Gays in Viral Video Taken Out of Context." *Christian Post*. July 27, 2015. Available from http://www.christianpost.com/news/pastor-e-dewey-smith-says-criticism-of-church-hypocrisy-on-treatment-of-gays-in-viral-video-taken-out-of-context-141975/.

Blesh, Rudi, and Harriet Janis. *They All Played Ragtime: The True Story of an American Music*. 1950. 4th ed., New York: Oak Publications, 1971.

Block, Rory. *Rory Block Official Life Story*. Online resource [cited April 22, 2003]. Available from http://www.roryblock.com/Pages/LifeStory.htm.

Bockris, Victor. *Keith Richards*. New York: Poseidon, 1992.

Bond, Julian, and Sondra Kathryn, eds. *Lift Every Voice and Sing: A Celebration of the Negro National Anthem: 100 Years, 100 Voices*. New York: Random House, 2000.

Bonilla-Silva, Eduardo. *Racism without Racists: Color-Blind Racism and the Persistence of Racial Inequality in the United States*. Lanham, MD: Rowan and Littlefield, 2010.

———. "The Invisible Weight of Whiteness: The Racial Grammar of Everyday Life in Contemporary America." *Ethnic and Racial Studies* 35, no. 2 (2012): 173–94.

Borzillo, Carrie. "Franklin, Family Cross Lines: Gospo-Centric Act Multichart Success." *Billboard*, February 25, 1995, 22–3.

Bosman, William. *A New and Accurate Description of the Coast of Guinea, Divided into the Gold, the Slave, and the Ivory Coasts*. London: Printed for J. Knapton, 1721.

"Bostic Urges Gospel Folk to Be Militant." *Billboard*, August 30, 1975, 1, 12.

Bowdich, Edward. *Mission from Cape Coast Castle to Ashanti*. London: John Murray, 1819.

Bowman, Robert M. J. *Soulsville, U.S.A.: The Story of Stax Records*. New York: Schirmer Books, 1997.

Boyd, Stacy C. *Black Men Worshipping: Intersecting Anxieties of Race, Gender, and Christian Embodiment*. New York: Palgrave Macmillan, 2011.

Boyd, Todd. *The New H.N.I.C.: The Death of Civil Rights and the Reign of Hip-Hop*. New York: New York University Press, 2002.

Boyer, Horace. "Kenneth Morris: Composer and Dean of Black Gospel Music Publishers." In *We'll Understand It Better By and By: Pioneering African American Gospel Composers*, edited by Bernice Johnson Reagon, 309–27. Washington, DC: Smithsonian Institution Press, 1992a.

———. "Lucie E. Campbell: Composer for the National Baptist Convention." In *We'll Understand It Better By and By: Pioneering African American Gospel Composers*, edited by Bernice Johnson Reagon, 81–108. Washington, DC: Smithsonian Institution Press, 1992b.

———. "Roberta Martin: Innovator of Modern Gospel Music." In *We'll Understand It Better By and By: Pioneering African American Gospel Composers*, edited by Bernice Johnson Reagon, 275–86. Washington, DC: Smithsonian Institution Press, 1992c.

Brackett, John. "Subsidizing the Experimental Muse: Rereading Ribot." In *People Get Ready: The Future of Jazz Is Now!*, edited by Ajay Heble and Rob Wallace, 166–74. Durham, NC: Duke University Press, 2013.

Branch, Taylor. *Parting the Waters: America in the King Years, 1954–63*. New York: Simon and Schuster, 1988.

Brent, Linda, [Harriet Brent Jacobs]. *Incidents in the Life of a Slave Girl*. 1861. Reprint, New York: Harcourt Brace Jovanovich, 1973.

Brewster, William H. "Rememberings." In *We'll Understand It Better By and By: Pioneering African American Gospel Composers*, edited by Bernice Johnson Reagon, 185–210. Washington, DC: Smithsonian Institution Press, 1992.

Bricker, Rebecca. "Take One." *People*, April 4, 1983. Available from http://www.people.com/people/article/020084656,00.html.

Brooks, Daphne A. *Bodies in Dissent: Spectacular Performances of Race and Freedom, 1850–1910*. Durham and London: Duke University Press, 2006.

Brooks, Tim. *Lost Sounds: Blacks and the Birth of the Recording Industry, 1890–1919*. Chicago: University of Illinois Press, 2004.

Broven, John. *Rhythm and Blues in New Orleans*. 1974. Reprint, Gretna, LA: Pelican Publishing, 1995.

Brown, Ernest D. "Something from Nothing and More from Something: The Making and Playing of Musical Instruments in African American Culture." *Selected Reports in Ethnomusicology* 8, (1990): 275–91.

———. "African American Instrument Construction and Music Making." In *African American Music: An Introduction*, 2nd ed., edited by Mellonee V. Burnim and Portia K. Maultsby, 23–33. New York: Routledge, 2015.

Brown, Eryn. "Pop Music's Most Important Revolution? That Would Be Hip-Hop, Science Reveals." *Los Angeles Times*, May 6, 2015. Accessed June 23, 2015. Available from http://www.latimes.com/science/sciencenow/la-sci-sn-pop-music-trends-20150505-story.html.

Brown, James, and Bruce Tucker. *James Brown: The Godfather of Soul*. New York: Collier Macmillan, 1986.

Brown, Jayna Jennifer. "Dat Var Negressen Walaida Snow." In "Recall and Response: Black Women Performers and the Mapping of Memory," edited by Jayna Jennifer Brown and Tavia Nyong'o, special issue, *Women and Performance: A Journal of Feminist Theory* 16, no. 1 (March 2006): 51–70.

———. *Babylon Girls: Black Women Performers and the Shaping of the Modern*. Durham and London: Duke University Press, 2008a.

———. "From the Point of View of the Pavement: A Geopolitics of Black Dance." In *Big Ears: Listening for Gender in Jazz Studies*, edited by Nichole T. Rustin and Sherrie Tucker, 157–79. Durham: Duke University Press, 2008b.

Brown, Lee B. "Review of *Representing Jazz* and *Jazz among the Discourses*, edited by Krin Gabbard." *Journal of Aesthetics and Art Criticism* 55, no. 3 (1997): 325–29.

———. "Jazz: America's Classical Music?" *Philosophy and Literature* 26, no. 1 (2002): 157–72.

Brown, Rae Linda. "William Grant Still, Florence Price, and William Dawson: Echoes of the Harlem Renaissance." In *Black Music in the Harlem Renaissance: A Collection of Essays*, edited by Samuel A. Floyd, Jr., 71–86. Westport, CT: Greenwood Press, 1990.

Brown, Ruth, and Andrew Yule. *Miss Rhythm: The Autobiography of Ruth Brown, Rhythm and Blues Legend*. New York: Donald Fine Books, 1996.

Brown, Warren. "Sorrow, Pomp, Anger Mark Mahalia's Rites," *Jet*, February 17, 1972, 17–34.

Brown, William Wells. *Clotel, or, the President's Daughter*. 1853. Reprint, New York: Citadel Press, 1969.

Bryant, Clora, Buddy Collette, William Green, Steve Isoardi, and Marl Young, eds. *Central Avenue Sounds: Jazz in Los Angeles*. Berkeley and Los Angeles: University of California Press, 1998.

Bryant, William Cullen. "A Tour in the Old South." In *Prose of William Cullen Bryant*, vol. 2, edited by Parke Godwin, 23–50. New York: D. Appleton and Company, 1884.

Buckner, Reginald T., and Steven Weiland, eds. *Jazz in Mind: Essays on the History and Meanings of Jazz*. Detroit: Wayne State University Press, 1991.

Burnett, Robert. *The Global Jukebox: The International Music Industry*. New York: Routledge, 1996.

Burnim, Mellonee V. "The Black Gospel Tradition: A Complex of Ideology, Aesthetic, and Behavior." In *More Than Dancing: Essays on Afro-American Music and Musicians*, edited by Irene V. Jackson, 147–67. Westport, CT: Greenwood, 1985.

———. "The Performance of Black Gospel Music as Transformation." In *Concilium: International Review of Theology, Vol. 2*, edited by Mary Collins, David Powers, and Mellonee Burnim, 52–61. Edinburgh: T&T Clark Ltd., 1989.

———. "The Gospel Music Industry." In *African American Music: An Introduction*, edited by Mellonee V. Burnim and Portia K. Maultsby, 416–29. New York: Routledge, 2006.

———, and Portia K. Maultsby. "From Backwoods to City Streets: The Afro-American Musical Journey." In *Expressively Black: The Cultural Basis of Ethnic Identity*, edited by Geneva Gay and Willie L. Baber, 109–36. New York: Praeger, 1987.

Caesar, Shirley. *The Lady, the Melody, and the Word: An Autobiography*. Nashville: Thomas Nelson, 1998.

Cantor, Louis. *Wheelin' on Beale: How WDIA-Memphis Became the Nation's First All-Black Radio Station and Created the Sound That Changed America*. New York: Pharos Books, 1992.

Cantwell, Robert. *When We Were Good: The Folk Revival*. Cambridge, MA: Harvard University Press, 1996.

Caramanica, Jon. "The Mining of Hip-Hop's Golden Age." *The New York Times*, September 12, 2008. Available from http://www.nytimes.com/2008/09/14/arts/music/14cara.html?pagewanted=all&_r=2.

Carawan, Guy. *A Personal Story through Sight and Sound*. Online resource [cited November 14, 2002]. Available from http://photo.ucr.edu/projects/carawan/.

———, and Candie Carawan, comps. *We Shall Overcome! Songs of the Southern Freedom Movement*. New York: Oak Publications, 1963.

Carby, Hazel. "'It Jus' Be's Dat Way Sometime': The Sexual Politics of Women's Blues." *Radical America* 20, no. 4 (1986): 9–24.

Carlos Santana Biography. Santana: *The Official Carlos Santana Web Site*, 2014. Accessed August 12, 2016. Available from www.santana.com.

Carlos Santana: Influences. Warner Brothers Publications. DVD. 2004.

Carmichael, Hoagland "Hoagy." *Washboard Blues*. Sheet music and lyrics. In Indiana University Digital Library Program, Hoagy Carmichael Collection. Online resource [cited March 23, 2003]. Available from http://www.dlib.indiana.edu/collections/hoagy/index.html.

Carner, Gary. "Introduction." *Black American Literature Forum* 25, no. 3 (1991): 441–48.

Carpenter, Delores, ed. *African American Heritage Hymnal*. Chicago: GIA, 2001.

Carr, Ian. *Miles Davis: A Critical Biography*. London: Quartet Books, 1982.

Carson, Annette. *Jeff Beck: Crazy Fingers*. San Francisco: Backbeat Books, 2001.

Carson, David. *Rockin' Down the Dial*. Troy, MI: Momentum, 2000.

Cavin, Susan. "Missing Women: On the Voodoo Trail to Jazz." *Journal of Jazz Studies* 3, no. 1 (Fall 1975): 4–27.

Chamberlain, Charles. "The Goodson Sisters: Women Pianists and the Function of Gender in the Jazz Age." *The Jazz Archivist: A Newsletter of the William Ransom Hogan Jazz Archive* 15, (2001): 1–9.

Chambers, Jack. *Milestones 2: The Music and Times of Miles Davis since 1960*. New York: Quill, 1989.

Chang, Jeff. *Can't Stop, Won't Stop: A History of the Hip-Hop Generation*. New York: St. Martin's Press, 2005.

Chappell, Louis W. *John Henry: A Folk-Lore Study*. Jena: Frommann, 1933.

Charters, Samuel B. *The Country Blues*. New York: Rinehart and Company, Inc., 1959.

———. *Poetry of the Blues*. New York: Oak Publications, 1963.

———. Liner notes. *The Prestige/Folklore Years, Volume 2: The New City Blues*. Fantasy, Inc. PRCD-9902-2, 1994.

Cheers, Ahmad. "Hate, Homophobia, and Heteropatriarchy at the Hampton Minister's Conference." *Huffpost Black Voices* (blog): *The Huffington Post*. Last modified June 9, 2015. Available from http://www.huffingtonpost.com/ahmad-cheers-hampton-ministers-conference-delman-coates_b_7538016.html.

Chilton, Karen. *Hazel Scott: The Pioneering Journey of a Jazz Pianist from Café Society to Hollywood to HUAC*. Ann Arbor: University of Michigan Press, 2008.

Chinen, Nate. "As Open as the Genre It Celebrates." *New York Times*, January 26, 2013, Sec. C: 1–2.

Cho, Sumi. "Post-Racialism." *Iowa Law Review* 94, (2009): 1591–649.

Christgau, Robert. *Any Old Way You Choose It: Rock and Other Pop Music 1967–1973*. Baltimore: Penguin Books, 1973.

Chura, Hillary. "Cornelius Still On Track." *Advertising Age*, March 7, 2005. Accessed September 1, 2015. Available from http://adage.com/article/special-report-syndication/cornelius-track/102286.

Churchill, Ward, and Jim Vander Wall. *Agents of Repression: The FBI's Secret Wars against the Black Panther Party and the American Indian*. 2nd ed., Boston: Turnaround, 2002.

Cintron, Esperanza Malave. "The History of the Bell Broadcasting Company: Black Owned and Operated Radio in Detroit, 1954–1981." M.A. thesis, Wayne State University, 1982.

Cohen, Richard. "San Francisco Blues Festival." *Living Blues*, no. 7 (Winter 1971–72): 46–7.

Cohen, Ronald D., ed. *"Wasn't That a Time!": Firsthand Accounts of the Folk Music Revival*. Metuchen, NJ: The Scarecrow Press, 1995.

Cohn, Nik. *Rock from the Beginning*. New York: Stein and Day, 1969.

———. *Awopbopaloobop Alopbamboom: The Golden Age of Rock*. 1970. Reprint, New York: Grove Press, 2001.

Coleman, Bill. "Female Rappers Give Males Run for the Money." *Billboard*, May 21, 1988, 1, 29.

Coleman, Rick. *Blue Monday: Fats Domino and the Lost Dawn of Rock 'n' Roll*. New York: Da Capo Press, 2006.

Collins, Lisa. "Making a Difference: Vicki Mack Lataillade." *Score* (July/August 1994): 27.

Collins, Patricia H. *Black Feminist Thought: Knowledge, Consciousness, and the Politics of Empowerment*. Boston: Unwin Hyman, 1990.

Cook, Olivia Charlot. *Oral History Interview*. New Orleans: Hogan Jazz Archive, Tulane University, August 30, 1999.
Coolman, Todd F. "The Miles Davis Quintet of the Mid-1960s: Synthesis of Improvisational and Compositional Elements." PhD diss., New York: New York University, 1997.
"'Covers vs. Copies' Sparking New Hubbub in Rhythm & Blues Field." In *First Pressings: The History of Rhythm and Blues*. Vol. 5 of *First Pressings: Rock History as Chronicled in Billboard Magazine*, compiled and edited by Galen Gart. Milford, NH: Big Nickel Publications, 1990. Originally published in *Billboard Magazine*, March 1955, 27, 30.
Crazy Horse, Kandia, ed. *Rip It Up: The Black Experience in Rock 'n' Roll*. New York: Palgrave Macmillan, 2004.
Crenshaw, Kimberlé, Garry Peller, Kendall Thomas, and Neil Gotanda, eds., *Critical Race Theory: The Key Writings That Formed the Movement*. New York: The New Press, 1995.
Cresswell, Nicholas (Samuel Thornley). *The Journal of Nicholas Cresswell, 1774–1777*. London: J. Cape, 1925.
Cruz, Jon. *Culture on the Margins: The Black Spiritual and the Rise of American Cultural Interpretation*. Princeton, NJ: Princeton University Press, 1999.
Cuff, Daniel F. "Warner Names Head of Elektra Record Unit." *The New York Times*, January 12, 1983, D2.
Cummings, Tony. *The Sound of Philadelphia*. London: Methuen, 1975.
Cuney-Hare, Maude. *Negro Musicians and Their Music*. 1936. Reprint, New York: Da Capo Press, 1974.
Currie, James. "Music after All." *Journal of the American Musicological Society* 62, no. 1 (2009): 145–203.
Cusic, Don. *The Sound of Light: A History of Gospel Music*. Bowling Green, OH: Bowling Green State University Popular Press, 1990.
Cusset, François. *French Theory: How Foucault, Derrida, Deleuze and Co. Transformed the Intellectual Life of the United States*. Translated by Jeff Fort. Minneapolis: University of Minnesota Press, 2008. Originally published in *French Theory: Foucault, Derrida, Deleuze et Cie et les Mutations de la vie intellectuelle aux Etats-Unis* (Paris: Découverte, 2003).
Dahl, Linda. *Stormy Weather: The Music and Lives of a Century of Jazz Women*. New York: Limelight Editions, 1989.
———. *Morning Glory: A Biography of Mary Lou Williams*. Berkeley, Los Angeles: University of California Press, 1999.
Dallas, Karl. Liner Notes. *Troubadours of British Folk, Volume 1*. Rhino Records R2 72160, 1995.
Daniels, Douglas Henry. "Oral History, Masks, and Protocol in the Jazz Community." *Oral History Review* 15, no. 1 (1987): 143–64.
———. *Lester Leaps In: The Life and Times of Lester "Pres" Young*. Boston: Beacon Press, 2002.
Danielsen, Anne. *Presence and Pleasure: The Funk Groove of James Brown and Parliament*. Middletown, CT: Wesleyan University Press, 2006.
Dannen, Frederic. *Hit Men: Power Brokers and Fast Money inside the Music Business*. New York: Vintage, 1991.
Darden, Bob. "Contemporary Christian Music," *Billboard*, April 30, 1994, 35, 47.
Dargan, William Thomas, and Kathy White Bullock. "Willie Mae Ford Smith of St. Louis: A Shaping Influence Upon Black Gospel Singing Style." *Black Music Research Journal* 9, no. 2 (1989): 249–70.
Darty, Trudy, and Sandee Potter, eds. *Women-Identified Women*. Palo Alto, CA: Mayfield Publishing Company, 1984.
Davis, Angela Y. *Blues Legacies and Black Feminism: Gertrude "Ma" Rainey, Bessie Smith, and Billie Holiday*. New York: Pantheon, 1998.
Davis, Clive. *Clive: Inside the Record Business*. New York: Ballantine, 1976.
Davis, Reid. "What Woz: Lost Objects, Repeat Viewings, and the Sissy Warrior." *Film Quarterly* 55, no. 2 (2001): 2–13.
De Jong, Nanette. "Women of the Association for the Advancement of Creative Musicians: Four Narratives." In *Black Women and Music: More Than the Blues*, edited by Eileen M. Hayes and Linda F. Williams, 134–52. Urbana: University of Illinois Press, 2007.
DeNora, Tia. *After Adorno: Rethinking Music Sociology*. Cambridge: Cambridge University Press, 2003.
Deutsche, Rosalyn, and Cara Gendel Ryan. "The Fine Art of Gentrification." *October* 31, (Winter 1984): 91–111.
DeVeaux, Scott. "Constructing the Jazz Tradition: Jazz Historiography." *Black American Literature Forum* 25, no. 3 (1991): 525–60.
———. *The Birth of Bebop: A Social and Musical History*. Berkeley: University of California Press, 1997.
"Dick Griffey Concerts." *Los Angeles Sentinel*, July 21, 1983, B8.
Dixon, Robert M.W., and John Godrich. *Recording the Blues*. New York: Stein and Day, 1970.
Dixon, Willie, and Don Snowden. *I Am the Blues: The Willie Dixon Story*. New York: Da Capo, 1989.

DjeDje, Jacqueline Cogdell, and Eddie Meadows, eds. *California Soul: Music of African Americans in the West*. Los Angeles: University of California Press, 1998.
DJ Scientist. "Missy Dee." *Anattitude Magazine*, September, 2008, 42–6. Available from http://issuu.com/anattitudemagazine/docs/anattitudemagazine_issue03.
Dolins, Barry, and "Little" Milton Campbell. "Interview with 'Little' Milton Campbell." In *Speakin' of the Blues Series*. Chicago: Chicago Blues Archives, Chicago Public Library, 1996. Oral history interview.
"Don Cornelius Is Guest on WBEE's 'Minority Forum'." *Chicago Defender (Daily Edition)*, October 17, 1974, 15.
Dorsey, Thomas A. "Gospel Music." In *Reflections on Afro-American Music*, edited by Dominique-René de Lerma, 189–95. Kent, OH: Kent State University Press, 1973.
Douglass, Frederick. *Life and Times of Frederick Douglass*. 1892. Reprint, New York: Collier Books, 1962.
Driggs, Frank. *Women in Jazz: A Survey*. New York: Stash Records, 1977.
Du Bois, W.E.B. *The Souls of Black Folk: Essays and Sketches*. 1903. Reprint, Greenwich, CT: Fawcett, 1961.
Dyson, Michael E. *Race Rules: Navigating the Color Line*. Reading, MA: Addison-Wesley Publishing Company, Inc., 1996.
———. *Holler If You Hear Me: Searching for Tupac Shakur*. New York: Basic Civitas Books, 2001.
Echols, Alice. *Scars of Sweet Paradise: The Life and Times of Janis Joplin*. New York: Metropolitan Books, 1999.
"Editorial." *The Richmond News Leader*, February 22, 1960, 5.
Edwards, David "Honeyboy." *The World Don't Owe Me Nothing: The Life and Times of Delta Bluesman Honeyboy Edwards*, edited by Janis Martinson and Michael Robert Frank. Chicago: Chicago Review Press, 1997.
"The Edwin Hawkins Singers, 'Oh Happy Day'." *Sepia* 19, no. 8 (August 1969): 66–8.
Eisen, Jonathan, ed. *The Age of Rock: Sounds of the American Cultural Revolution*. New York: Vintage Books, 1969.
Eisenstein, Zillah R., ed. *Capitalist Patriarchy and the Case for Social Feminism*. New York: Monthly Review Press, 1979.
Eliot, Marc. *Rockonomics: The Money Behind the Music*. New York: Franklin Watts, 1989.
Ellison, Ralph. *Shadow and Act*. New York: Vintage, 1964. Reprint, New York: Quality Paperback, 1994.
———. *Going to the Territory*. New York: Random House, 1986.
Ennis, Philip H. *The Seventh Stream: The Emergence of Rock 'n' Roll in American Popular Music*. London: Wesleyan University Press, 1992.
Epstein, Dena J. *Sinful Tunes and Spirituals: Black Folk Music to the Civil War*. 1977. Reprint with additional preface, Urbana: University of Illinois Press, 2003.
Equiano, Olaudah. *The Interesting Narrative of the Life of Olaudah Equiano, or Gustavas Vassa, the African: Written by Himself*. London: Printed by W. Durrell, 1791.
Erlwine, Michael, Vladimir Bogadanov, Chris Woodstra, and Cub Koda. *All Music Guide to the Blues: The Expert's Guide to the Best Blues Recordings*. San Francisco: Miller Freeman Books, 1996.
Evans, David. *Big Road Blues: Tradition and Creativity in the Folk Blues*. Berkeley: University of California Press, 1982.
Evans, Sara. *Personal Politics: The Roots of Women's Liberation in the Civil Rights Movement and the New Left*. New York: Vintage, 1979.
Faderman, Lillian. *Odd Girls and Twilight Lovers*. New York: Penguin, 1991.
Farmer, James. *Lay Bare the Heart*. New York: Arbor House, 1985.
Feather, Leonard. *The Jazz Years: Earwitness to an Era*. New York: Da Capo Press, 1987.
Feeney, Jim. "Chicago Blues Club Guide." Unpublished manuscript. 1997.
Feld, Steven. "Aesthetics as Iconicity of Style, or 'Lift-Up-Over-Sounding': Getting into the Kaluli Groove." *Yearbook for Traditional Music* 20, (1988): 74–113.
Fenner, Thomas P. *Religious Songs of the Negro as Sung on the Plantations*. 1874. Revised ed., Hampton, VA: The Institute Press, 1909.
Fernandez, Raul. *The Perfect Combination/La Combinacion Perfecta: Latin Jazz*. San Francisco: Chronicle Books, 2002.
Filene, Benjamin. *Romancing the Folk*. Chapel Hill: University of North Carolina Press, 2000.
Fischlin, Daniel, and Ajay Heble, eds. *The Other Side of Nowhere: Jazz, Improvisation, and Communities in Dialogue*. Middletown, CT: Wesleyan University Press, 2004.
Fisher, Miles Mark. *Negro Slave Songs in the United States*. 1953. 2nd ed., New York: Citadel Press, 1963.
Floyd, Samuel A. "Ring Shout! Literary Studies, Historical Studies and Black Music Inquiry." *Black Music Research Journal* 11, no. 2 (1991): 265–87.

———. *The Power of Black Music: Interpreting Its History from Africa to the United States.* New York: Oxford University Press, 1995.

Foner, Philip S. *Women and the American Labor Movement: From World War I to the Present.* New York: Free Press, 1980.

Fong-Torres, Ben. "'Oh Happy Day': A Pop Godsend." *Rolling Stone*, May 17, 1969, 12.

Forlenza, Jeff. "Rudy Van Gelder: Jazz's Master Engineer." *Mix*, October 1993, 54–8, 62–4, 254.

Franklin, Aretha, and David Ritz. *Aretha: From These Roots.* New York: Crown, 1999.

Franklin, Kirk, with Jim Nelson Black. *Church Boy: My Music and My Life.* Nashville: Word Publishing, 1998.

Gaar, Gillian G. *She's a Rebel: The History of Women in Rock & Roll.* 2nd ed., New York: Seal Press, 2002.

Gabbard, Krin, ed. *Jazz among the Discourses.* Durham, NC: Duke University Press, 1995a.

———, ed. *Representing Jazz.* Durham, NC: Duke University Press, 1995b.

Gaines, Donna. "Girl Groups: A Ballad of Codependency." In *Trouble Girls: The Rolling Stone Book of Women in Rock*, edited by Barbara O'Dair, 103–15. New York: Random House, 1997.

Garland, Phyl. *The Sound of Soul.* Chicago: Henry Regnery, 1969.

Garofalo, Reebee. "Black Popular Music: Crossing Over or Going Under?" In *Rock and Popular Music*, edited by Tony Bennett, Simon Furth, Lawrence Grossberg, John Shepherd, and Graeme Turner, 231–48. New York: Routledge, 1993.

———. "Culture versus Commerce: The Marketing of Black Popular Music." In *The Black Public Sphere*, edited by The Black Public Sphere Collective, 279–92. Chicago: University of Chicago Press, 1995.

———. *Rockin' Out: Popular Music in the U.S.A.* 5th ed. Englewood Cliffs, NJ: Prentice Hall, 2011.

———, and Steve Waksman. *Rockin' Out: Popular Music in the U.S.A.* 6th ed., Boston: Pearson, 2014.

Garon, Paul. *White Blues.* Online resource, 1995 [cited 2000]. Available from http://www.bluesworld.com/whiteblues.html.

———, and Beth Garon. *Woman with Guitar: Memphis Minnie's Blues.* New York: Da Capo Press, 1992.

Garrow, David. *The FBI and Martin Luther King, Jr.: From "Solo" to Memphis.* New and Enlarged ed., New Haven, CT: Yale University Press, 2001.

Gates, Henry Lewis, Jr. *The Signifying Monkey: A Theory of Afro-American Literary Criticism.* New York: Oxford University Press, 1988.

Gaunt, Kyra D. *The Games Black Girls Play: Learning the Ropes from Double-Dutch to Hip-Hop.* New York: New York University Press, 2006.

Gehman, Mary, and Nancy Ries. *A History of Women and New Orleans.* New Orleans: Margaret Media, 1988.

Gellert, Lawrence. *Negro Songs of Protest.* New York: Carl Fischer, Inc., 1936.

"Gender Composition by Religious Group" (2014). Pew Research Center: Religion and Public Life. Accessed September 9, 2015. Available from http://www.pewforum.org/religious-landscape-study/gender-composition.

Gendron, Bernard. "'Moldy Figs' and Modernists: Jazz at War (1942–1946)." In *Jazz among the Discourses*, edited by Krin Gabbard, 31–56. Durham, NC: Duke University Press, 1995.

Gennari, John. "Jazz Criticism: Its Development and Ideologies." *Black American Literature Forum* 25 (1991): 449–523.

———. *Blowin' Hot and Cool: Jazz and Its Critics.* Chicago: University of Chicago Press, 2006.

George, Emmett. "Cameo's Secret Omen." *Sepia*, January 1, 1980, 30–4.

George, Luvenia. "Lucie Eddie Campbell Williams: Her Nurturing and Expansion of Gospel Music in the National Baptist Convention, U.S.A., Inc." In *We'll Understand It Better By and By: Pioneering African American Gospel Composers*, edited by Bernice Johnson Reagon, 109–19. Washington, DC: Smithsonian Institution Press, 1992.

George, Nelson. *The Death of Rhythm and Blues.* New York: Pantheon Books, 1988.

———. *Buppies, B-Boys, Baps, and Bohos: Notes on Post-Soul Black Culture.* New York: Harper Collins Publishers, 1992.

George-Warren, Holly, and Patricia Romanowski, eds. *Rolling Stone Encyclopedia of Rock 'n' Roll*, 3rd ed., revised and updated for the 21st century. New York: A Rolling Stone Press Book, 2001.

Giddings, Paula. *When and Where I Enter: The Impact of Black Women on Race and Sex in America.* New York: Bantam Books, 1984.

Gilbert, Jeremy, and Ewan Pearson. *Discographies: Dance, Music, Culture, and the Politics of Sound.* New York: Routledge, 1999.

Gillett, Charlie. *The Sound of the City: The Rise of Rock and Roll.* New York: Outerbridge and Dienstfrey, 1970.

———. *Making Tracks: Atlantic Records and the Growth of a Multi-Billion-Dollar Industry.* New York: E. P. Dutton, 1974.

———. *The Sound of the City: The Rise of Rock and Roll.* 1970. Rev. and Exp. ed., New York: Pantheon Books, 1984.
Gilroy, Paul. "Sounds Authentic." *Black Music Research Journal* 11, no. 2 (1991): 111–36.
Goehr, Lydia. *The Imaginary Museum of Musical Works: An Essay in the Philosophy of Music.* Oxford: Clarendon Press, 1992.
Goldman, Albert. "Does He Teach Us the Meaning of 'Black is Beautiful'?" In *The James Brown Reader: 50 Years of Writing about the Godfather of Soul*, edited by Nelson George and Alan Leeds, 39–43. New York: A Plum Book/Penguin Press, 2008. Originally published in *The New York Times*, June 9, 1968.
Gonzales, Michael. "Mack Divas." *The Source*, February, 1997, 62–7.
Goodrich, Andrew L. "Jazz in Historically Black Colleges." *Jazz Education Journal* 34, no. 3 (2001): 54–8.
Gordon, Robert. *Can't Be Satisfied: The Life and Times of Muddy Waters.* Boston: Little, Brown and Company, 2002.
Gordy, Berry. *To Be Loved: The Music, the Magic, the Memories of Motown.* New York: Warner Books, 1994.
Goreau, Lauraine. *Just Mahalia, Baby.* Waco, TX: Word Books, 1975.
"The Gospel According To . . ." *Freeing the Spirit* 1, no. 2 (Spring 1972): 7–9.
Gottschild, Brenda Dixon. *Digging the Africanist Presence in American Performance: Dance and Other Contexts.* Westport, CT: Praeger, 1998.
Gourse, Leslie. *Madame Jazz: Contemporary Women Instrumentalists.* New York and Oxford: Oxford University Press, 1995.
Graff, Gary. "Renewing Motown: Buyer Wants Gordy, Tops Back." *Detroit Free Press*, August 4, 1993.
———. "Motown's Move Was Bad for Music." *Detroit Free Press*, November 5, 1994.
Grant, Jacquelyn. *White Women's Christ and Black Women's Jesus.* Atlanta, GA: Scholars Press, 1989.
Graustark, Barbara. "Disco Takes Over." *Newsweek*, April 2, 1979, 56–64.
Green, Tony. "Remembering the Golden Age of Hip-Hop." Today.com. August 2, 2004. Accessed August 1, 2015. Available from http://www.today.com/id/5430999#.VubF8vkrLIV.
Greenway, John. *American Songs of Protest.* New York: S. Barnes and Company, Inc., 1960.
Griffin, Farah Jasmine. *If You Can't Be Free, Be a Mystery: In Search of Billie Holiday.* New York: The Free Press, 2001.
———. "When Malindy Sings: A Meditation on Black Women's Vocality." In *Uptown Conversation: The New Jazz Studies*, edited by Robert G. O'Meally, Brent Hayes Edwards, and Farah Jasmine Griffin, 102–25. New York: Columbia University Press, 2004.
Griffin, Horace. *Their Own Receive Them Not: African American Lesbians and Gays in Black Churches.* Cleveland, OH: Pilgrim Press, 2006.
Grissom, Mary Ellen. *The Negro Sings a New Heaven.* Chapel Hill: University of North Carolina Press, 1930.
Groom, Bob. *The Blues Revival.* In the Blues Paperback Series, edited by Paul Oliver. London: Studio Vista, Ltd., 1971.
Gross, Michael Joseph. "The Queen Is Dead." *The Atlantic Monthly*, August, 2000, 62–70.
Guillory, John. *Cultural Capital: The Problem of Literary Canon Formation.* Chicago: University of Chicago Press, 1993.
Guillory, Monique, and Richard C. Green. *Soul: Black Power, Politics, and Pleasure.* New York: New York University Press, 1998.
Guralnick, Peter. *Feel Like Going Home: Portraits in Blues and Rock 'n' Roll.* New York: E.P. Dutton, 1971.
———. *Last Train to Memphis: The Rise of Elvis Presley.* Boston: Little, Brown, 1994.
———. *Sweet Soul Music: Rhythm and Blues and the Southern Dream of Freedom.* 1986. Reprint, New York: Harper and Row, 1999.
Guy, Buddy, Jim O'Neal, and Tim Zorn. "Living Blues Interview: Buddy Guy." *Living Blues* 1, (1970): 3–9.
"Guys & Dolls Host Jim Brown Night." *Los Angeles Sentinel*, December 31, 1964, B4.
Hairston, Monica. "The Wrong Place for the Right People? Café Society, Jazz, and Gender, 1938–1947." PhD diss., New York: New York University, 2009.
Hajdu, David. *Positively 4th Street: The Lives and Times of Joan Baez, Bob Dylan, Mimi Baez Fariña, and Richard Fariña.* New York: North Point Press, 2001.
Hall, Stuart. "Race, Articulation and Societies Structured in Dominance." In *Sociological Theories: Race and Colonialism*, 305–45. Paris: UNESCO, 1980.
———. "What Is This 'Black' in Black Popular Culture?" In *Representing Blackness: Issues in Film and Video*, edited by Valerie Smith, 123–33. New Brunswick, NJ: Rutgers University Press, 1997.
———. and Paul du Gay, eds. *Questions of Cultural Identity.* Thousand Oaks, CA: Sage, 1996.
Hallowell, Emily. *Calhoun Plantation Songs.* Boston: C.W. Thompson, 1901.

Halperin, David. "Homosexuality's Closet." *Michigan Quarterly Review* 41, no. 1 (2002): 21–55.

Hammond, John Henry, and Irving Townsend. *John Hammond on Record: An Autobiography*. New York: Penguin, 1981. First published 1977 by Ridge Press.

Handy, D. Antoinette. *Black Women in American Bands and Orchestras*. 2nd ed., Metuchen, NJ: Scarecrow Press, 1998.

Handy, William C., ed. *Blues: An Anthology*. New York: A. & C. Boni, 1926.

———. *Father of the Blues: An Autobiography*, edited by Arna Bontemps. 1941. Reprint, New York: Collier Books, 1970.

Haralambos, Michael. *Right On: From Blues to Soul in Black America*. 1974. Reprint, Ormskirk, UK: Causeway Press, 1994.

Harper, Phillip Brian. *Are We Not Men?: Masculine Anxiety and the Problem of African-American Identity*. New York, NY: Oxford University Press, 1996.

Harris, Michael W. *The Rise of Gospel Blues: The Music of Thomas Andrew Dorsey in the Urban Church*. New York: Oxford University Press, 1992.

Harrison, Christina M. "Sunday Best: The Mediation of the Sacred and Secular in a Gospel Competition." MA thesis, Bloomington: Indiana University, 2012.

Harrison, Daphne Duval. *Black Pearls: Blues Queens of the 1920s*. New Brunswick, NJ: Rutgers University Press, 1988.

Hartman, Laura M. "Consuming Christ: The Role of Jesus in Christian Food Ethics." *Journal of the Society of Christian Ethics* 30, no. 1 (2010): 45–62.

Haskins, James, and Kathleen Benson. *Nat King Cole: A Personal and Professional Biography of a Man as Unforgettable as His Music*. New York: Stein and Day, 1984.

Hayes, Eileen M. "Black Women Performers of Women-Identified Music: They Cut Off My Voice, I Grew Two Voices." PhD diss., Seattle: University of Washington, 1999.

———. "To Bebop or To Be Pop: Sarah Vaughan and the Politics of Cross Over." PhD diss., Philadelphia: University of Pennsylvania, 2004.

———, and Linda Williams, eds. *Black Women and Music: More Than the Blues*. Urbana: University of Illinois Press, 2007.

Hayes, Eileen M. *Songs in Black and Lavender: Race, Sexual Politics, and Women's Music*. Urbana: University of Illinois Press, 2010.

Hays, Timothy Odell. "The Music Department in Higher Education: History, Connections, and Conflicts, 1865–1998." PhD diss., Chicago: Loyola University of Chicago, 1999.

Hazzard-Gordon, Katrina. *Jookin': The Rise of Social Dance Formations in African American Culture*. Philadelphia: Temple University Press, 1990.

Heble, Ajay. *Landing on the Wrong Note: Jazz, Dissonance, and Critical Practice*. New York: Routledge, 2000.

———, and Gillian Sidall. "Nice Work If You Can Get It: Women in Jazz." In *Landing on the Wrong Note: Jazz, Dissonance, and Critical Practice*, 141–66. New York: Routledge, 2000.

———, and Rob Wallace, eds. *People Get Ready: The Future of Jazz Is Now!* Durham, NC: Duke University Press, 2013.

Heffley, Mike. *Northern Sun, Southern Moon: Europe's Reinvention of Jazz*. New Haven, CT: Yale University Press, 2005.

Hernandez, Deborah Pacini. *Oye Como Va! Hybridity and Identity in Latino Popular Music*. Philadelphia: Temple University Press, 2010.

Henderson, Alex. "Active Indies." *Billboard*, December 24, 1988, R6, R16, R20.

Hersch, Charles B. *Subversive Sounds: Race and the Birth of Jazz in New Orleans*. Chicago: University of Chicago Press, 2009.

Higginson, Thomas Wentworth. *Army Life in a Black Regiment*. 1869. Reprint, Boston: Beacon Press, 1962.

———. "Negro Spirituals." First published in *Atlanta Monthly*, 19 (June 1867), 685–94. Reprinted in Bruce Jackson, *The Negro and His Folklore in Nineteenth-Century Periodicals*, 82–102. Published for the American Folklore Society. Austin: University of Texas Press, 1967.

Hinson, Glenn. *Fire in My Bones: Transcendence and the Holy Spirit in African American Gospel*. Philadelphia: University of Pennsylvania Press, 2000.

Hirshey, Gerri. *Nowhere to Run: The Story of Soul Music*. New York: Times Books, 1984.

———. *We Gotta Get out of This Place: The True, Tough Story of Women in Rock*. New York: Atlantic Monthly Press, 2001.

Hoffman, Lawrence, comp. and annotator. *Mean Old World: The Blues from 1940 to 1994*. Washington, DC: Smithsonian Institution Press, 1996.

hooks, bell. *Talking Back: Thinking Feminist, Thinking Black.* Toronto: Between the Lines, 1988.
———. *Yearning: Race, Gender, and Cultural Politics.* Boston: South End Press, 1990.
———. *Black Looks: Race and Representation.* Boston: South End Press, 1992.
———. *Outlaw Culture: Resisting Representations.* New York: Routledge, 1994.
"How Da T.R.U.T.H. Overcame the Love Triangle that Rocked the Gospel Industry: Path MEGAzine Interview." YouTube. Posted February 5, 2011. Accessed January 28, 2016. Available from https://www.youtube.com/watch?v=qE4b9D4553g.
Hubbard, Karen, and Terry Monaghan. "Negotiating Compromise on a Burnished Wood Floor: Social Dancing at the Savoy." In *Ballroom, Boogie, Shimmy Sham, Shake: A Social and Popular Dance Reader*, edited by Julie Malnig, 72–92. Urbana and Chicago: University of Illinois Press, 2009.
Hull, Gloria T., Patricia Bell Scott, and Barbara Smith, eds. *All the Women Are White, All the Blacks Are Men, But Some of Us Are Brave: Black Women's Studies.* Old Westbury, NY: Feminist Press, 1982.
Hunt, Danica Stein. "Women Who Play Jazz: A Study of the Experience of Three Los Angeles Musicians." PhD diss., Los Angeles: University of California, Los Angeles, 1994.
Hunt, Darnell, and Ana Christina Ramón, eds. *Black Los Angeles: American Dreams and Racial Realities.* New York: New York University Press, 2010.
Hunt, Dennis. "Griffey: Kingpin of Soul Promoters." *Los Angeles Times*, August 9, 1973, C24.
Hunter, Tera W. "'Sexual Pantomimes,' the Blues Aesthetic, and Black Women in the New South." In *Music and the Racial Imagination*, edited by Ronald Radano and Philip V. Bohlman, 145–64. Chicago: The University of Chicago Press, 2000.
Hurston, Zora Neale. "Spirituals and Neo-Spirituals." 1935. Reprint in *Voices from the Harlem Renaissance*, edited by Nathan Huggins, 344–7. New York: Oxford University Press, 1976.
———. "Card Game." 1935. Reprint in *Mules and Men*, 152–9. Bloomington: Indiana University Press, 1978.
———. *The Sanctified Church.* Berkeley: Turtle Island Foundation, 1981.
"Interview Transcript: Midnight Star (Reggie Calloway)." Karen Shearer Collection. Collector's No. SE 84-15. Archives of African American Music and Culture, Indiana University. April 2, 1984. 6 typed leaves.
"Interview Transcript: Midnight Star (Reggie Calloway)." Karen Shearer Collection. Collector's No. 2735A. Archives of African American Music and Culture, Indiana University. December 12, 1984. 22 typed leaves.
"Interview Transcript: Zapp (Roger Troutman)." Karen Shearer Collection. Collector's No. 1357. Archives of African American Music and Culture, Indiana University. August 1982. 26 typed leaves.
Isoardi, Steven L. *The Dark Tree: Jazz and the Community Arts in Los Angeles.* Berkeley: University of California Press, 2006.
"It's 'I Care about Detroit' Sunday." *Detroit Free Press*, August 8, 1969.
Jackson, Blair. "Joe Lovano and Gunther Schuller: A Classic Pairing." *Mix*, June, 1995a, 163, 171–3.
———. "Leon Parker: A Different Drummer." *Mix*, June, 1995b, 162, 169–71.
Jackson, Bruce. *Wake up Dead Man: Afro-American Worksongs from Texas Prisons.* Cambridge, MA: Harvard University Press, 1972.
Jackson, John A. *Big Beat: Alan Freed and the Early Years of Rock 'n' Roll.* New York: Schirmer Books, 1991.
Jackson, Mahalia, and Evan McLeod Wylie. *Movin' on Up.* New York: Hawthorn, 1966.
Jackson, Travis. "Jazz Performance as Ritual: The Blues Aesthetic and the African Diaspora." In *The African Diaspora: A Musical Perspective*, edited by Ingrid Monson, 23–82. New York: Garland, 2000.
———. "Interpreting Jazz." In *African American Music: An Introduction*, edited by Mellonee V. Burnim and Portia K. Maultsby, 167–83. New York: Routledge, 2006.
———. *Blowin' the Blues Away: Performance and Meaning on the New York Jazz Scene.* Berkeley: University of California Press, 2012.
Jacques, Geoffrey, Sherrie Tucker, Scott DeVeaux, Krin Gabbard, and Bernard Gendron. "A Roundtable on Ken Burns's *Jazz*." *Journal of Popular Music Studies* 13, no. 2 (2001): 207–25.
James, Etta, and David Ritz. *Rage to Survive: The Etta James Story.* New York: Villard Books, 1998.
James, Joy. *Transcending the Talented Tenth: Black Leaders and American Intellectuals.* New York: Routledge, 1997.
Jamison, Laura. "A Fiesty Female Rapper Breaks a Hip-Hop Taboo." *New York Times*, January 18, 1998, AR34. Available from http://www.nytimes.com/1998/01/18/arts/pop-jazz-a-feisty-female-rapper-breaks-a-hip-hop-taboo.html.
Jefferson, Thomas. *Notes on the State of Virginia.* 1781. Reprint, Chapel Hill: Institute of Early American History and Culture, University of North Carolina Press, 1954.

"Jimmy Jam and Terry Lewis Have Become Synonymous With Recording Excellence." Waxpoetics.com. Accessed November 22, 2015. Available from http://waxpoetics.com/features/articles/jimmy-jam-interview.

Joe, Radcliffe A. *This Business of Disco*. New York: Billboard Books, 1980.

Johnson, Guy. *John Henry: Tracking Down a Negro Legend*. Chapel Hill: University of North Carolina Press, 1929.

Johnson, James Weldon, and J. Rosamond Johnson. *The Books of American Negro Spirituals, Including the Book of American Negro Spirituals and the Second Book of Negro Spirituals*. 1925, 1926. Reprint, New York: Da Capo, 1989.

Johnson, Maria. "Black Women Electric Guitarists and Authenticity in the Blues." In *Black Women and Music: More Than the Blues*, edited by Eileen Hayes and Linda Williams, 51–71. Urbana: University of Illinois Press, 2007.

Johnson, Sharon "Sha-Rock," and Iesha Brown. *Luminary Icon: The Story of the Beginning and End of Hip Hop's First Female MC*. [n.p.]: Pearlie Gates Publishing, 2011.

Jones, Alisha. "We Are a Peculiar People: Meaning, Masculinity, and Competence in Gendered Gospel Performance." PhD diss., Chicago: University of Chicago, ProQuest, 2015.

Jones, Anderson. "Invisible Lover: Does BET Censor Gay Images from Music Videos?" *Advocate*, January 16, 2001, 93–4.

Jones, Lisa. "This Is Faith: Tribal Grunge Takes Manhattan." *Village Voice Rock & Roll Quarterly* (Winter 1992): 7–8, 10–11, 15, 22.

———. "Kirk Franklin: New Gospel Sensation," *Ebony*, October 1995, 64–7, 144.

Joyce, Mike. "Etta James and the Roots Band." *The Washington Post*, June 26, 2002.

Kahn, Karen. *Front Line Feminism, 1975–1995: Essays from Sojourners First 20 Years*. San Francisco: Aunt Lute Books, 1995.

Kartomi, Margaret. "The Processes and Results of Musical Culture Contact: A Discussion of Terminology and Concepts." *Ethnomusicology* 35, no. 2 (1981): 227–49.

Katz, Larry. "Can The New Motown Recapture the Old Magic," CNN.com, March 26, 1998, http://www.cnn.com/SHOWBIZ/9803/26/motown.anniversary.lat/.

Keil, Charles. *Urban Blues*. Chicago: University of Chicago Press, 1966.

———, and Steven Feld. *Music Grooves: Essays and Dialogues*. 2nd ed., Tucson, Arizona: Fenestra, 2005. First published 1994 by University of Chicago Press.

Kelley, Robin D.G. "In a Mist: Thoughts on Ken Burns's *Jazz*." *Institute for Studies in American Music Newsletter* 30, no. 2 (Spring 2001): 8–10, 15.

———. "The Jazz Wife: Muse and Manager." *The New York Times*, July 21, 2002, 24.

———. *Africa Speaks, America Answers: Modern Jazz in Revolutionary Times*. Cambridge, MA: Harvard University Press, 2012.

Kennedy, Al. *Chord Changes on the Chalkboard: How Public School Teachers Shaped Jazz and the Music of New Orleans*. Lanham, MD: Scarecrow Press, 2002.

Kennedy, Rick and Randy McNutt. *Little Labels—Big Sound*. Bloomington: Indiana University Press, 1999.

Kernfeld, Barry Dean. *The New Grove Dictionary of Jazz*. 3 vols. 2nd ed., New York: Grove's Dictionaries Inc., 2002.

Kernodle, Tammy L. *Soul on Soul: The Life and Music of Mary Lou Williams*. Boston: Northeastern University Press, 2004.

———. "Freedom is a Constant Struggle: Alice Coltrane and the Redefining of the Jazz Avant-Garde." In *John Coltrane and Black America's Quest for Freedom: Spirituality and the Music*, edited by Leonard L. Brown, 73–98. Oxford: Oxford University Press, 2010.

Keyes, Cheryl. *Rap Music and Street Consciousness*. Urbana: University of Illinois Press, 2002.

King, Martin Luther, Jr. *Stride Toward Freedom*. New York: Harper and Row, 1958.

K[innard] Jr., J. "Who Are Our National Poets?" *Knickerbocker Magazine* 26, (1845): 331–41.

Kitts, Jeff, and Harold Steinblatt, eds. *Guitar World Presents Stevie Ray Vaughan: In His Own Words*. Milwaukee: Hal Leonard Corporation, 1997.

Kmen, Henry. *Music in New Orleans: The Formative Years, 1791–1841*. Baton Rouge: Louisiana State University Press, 1966.

Koenig, Karl, ed. "Women Pianists in Early New Orleans Jazz." In *The Jazz Lectures*. Running Springs, CA: Basin Street Press, 1996.

Kubik, Gerhard. *Africa and the Blues*. Jackson: University of Mississippi Press, 1999.

LaBelle, Patti, and Laura B. Randolph. *Don't Block the Blessings: Revelations of a Lifetime*. New York: Riverhead Books, 1996.

La France, Mélisse. "Textural Subversions: The Narrative Sabotage of Race, Gender, and Desire in the Music of Me Shell Ndegeocello." In *Disruptive Divas: Feminism, Identity and Popular Music*, edited by Lori Burns and Mélisse La France, 133–47. New York: Routledge, 2002.

Latrobe, Benjamin Boneval. *Impressions Respecting New Orleans: Diary & Sketches, 1818–1820*, edited by S. Wilson, Jr. New York: Columbia University Press, 1951.

Leeds, Jeff. "Warner Restructuring Black Music Unit." *Los Angeles Times*, November 14, 2001. Accessed September 1, 2015. Available from http://articles.latimes.com/2001/nov/14/business/fi-3879.

Lees, Gene. *Cats of Any Color: Jazz, Black and White*. New York: Oxford University Press, 1994.

———. *You Can't Steal a Gift: Dizzy, Clark, Milt, and Nat*. New Haven, CT: Yale University Press, 2001.

Levine, Lawrence W. *Black Culture and Black Consciousness: Afro-American Folk Thought from Slavery to Freedom*. New York: Oxford University Press, 1977.

Lewis, George E. *A Power Stronger than Itself: The AACM and American Experimental Music*. Chicago: University of Chicago Press, 2008.

Leyshon, Andrew, David Matless, and George Revill, eds. *The Place of Music*. New York: Guilford Press, 1998.

Lieb, Sandra R. *Mother of the Blues: A Study of Ma Rainey*. Amherst: University of Massachusetts Press, 1981.

Lincoln, C. Eric, and Lawrence H. Mamiya. *The Black Church in the African-American Experience*. Durham, NC: Duke University Press, 1990.

Lomax, Alan. "I Got the Blues." *Common Ground* 8, (1948): 38–52.

———, and John Avery Lomax. *Negro Folk Songs as Sung by Leadbelly*. New York: Macmillan, 1936.

Long, Alecia P. *The Great Southern Babylon: Sex, Race, and Respectability in New Orleans, 1865–1920*. Baton Rouge: Louisiana State University Press, 2004.

Lont, Cynthia. "Women's Music: No Longer a Small Private Party." In *Rockin' the Boat: Mass Music and Mass Movements*, edited by Reebee Garofalo, 240–5. Boston: South End Press, 1992.

Looker, Benjamin. *Point from Which Creation Begins: The Black Artists' Group of St. Louis*. St. Louis: Missouri Historical Society Press, 2004.

Lott, Eric. *Love and Theft: Blackface Minstrelsy and the American Working Class*. 1993. Reprint, New York: Oxford University Press, 1995.

Lotz, Rainer. *Black People: Entertainers of African Descent in Europe and Germany*. Bonn, Germany: Bigit Lotz, 1997.

Love, Bettina L. *Hip Hop's Li'l Sistas Speak: Negotiating Hip Hop Identities and Politics in the New South*. New York: Peter Lang, 2012.

Lowens, Irvin. "We Shall Overcome: Origins of Rights Songs." *The Sunday Washington Star*, (July 1965): 2–8.

Lydon, Michael. *Rock Folk: Portraits from the Rock 'n' Roll Pantheon*. New York: Dial Press, 1971.

———. *Ray Charles: Man and Music*. Rev. ed., New York: Routledge, 2004.

MacDonald, J. Fred. *Don't Touch That Dial! Radio Programming in American Life, 1920–1960*. Chicago: Nelson-Hall, 1979.

MacDonald, Raymond, Graeme Wilson, and Dorothy Miell. "Improvisation as a Creative Process within Contemporary Music." In *Musical Imaginations: Multidisciplinary Perspectives on Creativity, Performance and Perception*, edited by David Hargreaves, Dorothy Miell, and Raymond MacDonald, 242–56. Oxford: Oxford University Press, 2012.

Macías, Anthony. "Rock con Raza, Raza con Jazz: Latinos/as and Post–World War II Popular American Music." In *Musical Migrations: Transnationalism and Cultural Hybridity in Latin/o America*, Volume 1, ed. Frances R. Aparicio and Cándida F. Jáquez with María Elena Cepeda, 183–97. New York: Palgrave Macmilan, 2003.

———. *Mexican American Mojo: Popular Music, Dance, and Urban Culture in Los Angeles, 1935–1968*. Durham, NC: Duke University Press, 2008.

Mahon, Maureen. "Black Like This: Race, Generation, and Rock in the Post–Civil Rights Era." *American Ethnologist* 27, no. 2 (2000): 283–311.

———. *Right to Rock: The Black Rock Coalition and the Cultural Politics of Race*. Durham, NC: Duke University Press, 2004.

———. "They Say She's Different: Race, Gender, and Genre and the Liberated Black Femininity of Betty Davis." *Journal of Popular Music Studies* 23, no. 2 (June 2011): 146–65.

Malnig, Julie, ed. *Ballroom, Boogie, Shimmy Sham, Shake: A Social and Popular Dance Reader*. Urbana: University of Illinois Press, 2009.

Malone, Bill. *Country Music USA*. Austin: University of Texas Press, 1968.

———. *Southern Music, American Music*. Lexington: The University Press of Kentucky, 1979.

Malone, Jacqui. *Steppin' on the Blues: The Visible Rhythms of African American Dance*. Urbana and Chicago: University of Illinois Press, 1996.

Manetta, Manuel. *Oral History Digest*, March 28, 1957. New Orleans: Hogan Jazz Archive, Tulane University, 1957. Four reels.

Marable, Manning. *Race Reform and Rebellion: The Second Reconstruction in Black America, 1945–2000*. 3rd ed., Jackson: University Press of Mississippi, 2001.

Marcus, Greil. *Mystery Train: Images of America in Rock 'n' Roll Music*. 6th ed., New York: Plume, 2015. First published 1975.

Marsh, J.B.T. *The Story of the Jubilee Singers: With Their Songs*. London: Hodder and Stoughton, 1880. Reprint, Boston: Houghton Mifflin, 1971.

Martin, Sallie, and Kenneth Morris. *The New Angelic Gospelodium, Songbook Number 1*. Chicago: Martin and Morris, Inc., 1970.

Massey, Howard. *Behind the Glass, Volume II: Top Record Producers Tell How They Craft the Hits*. San Francisco: Backbeat Books, 2009.

Maultsby, Portia K. "Africanisms in African-American Music." In *Africanisms in American Culture*, edited by Joseph E. Holloway, 185–210. Bloomington: Indiana University Press, 1990.

———. "The Impact of Gospel Music on the Secular Music Industry." In *We'll Understand It Better By and By: African American Pioneering Gospel Composers*, edited by Bernice Johnson Reagon, 19–33. Washington, DC: Smithsonian Institution Press, 1992.

———. "Music." In *Encyclopedia of African-American Culture and History*, edited by J. Salzman, D.L. Smith and Cornel West, 818–907. New York: Macmillan Library Reference, 1996.

———. "The Translated African Cultural and Musical Past." In *African American Music: An Introduction*, 2nd ed., edited by Mellonee V. Burnim and Portia K. Maultsby, 3–22. New York: Routledge, 2015.

———, and Mellonee V. Burnim with contributions from Susan Oehler. "Intellectual History." In *African American Music: An Introduction*, edited by Mellonee V. Burnim and Portia K. Maultsby, 7–32. New York: Routledge, 2006.

Matthews, Bob. "Black Executives in the Record Business." *Los Angeles Sentinel*, December 29, 1977, 7, 15, 31.

Maund, Alfred. "Around the USA: 'We Will All Stand Together'." *The Nation*, March 3, 1956, 168.

Maxwell, William J. "Black Arts Survivals in the New New Jazz Studies." *American Literary History* 23, no. 4 (2011): 873–84.

Mays, Benjamin, and Joseph Nicholson. *The Negro's Church*. New York: Institute of Social and Religious Research, 1933.

McCalla, Deidre, and Toni Armstrong. "Deidre McCalla: Interviewed by Toni L. Armstrong." *HOT WIRE: Journal of Women's Music and Culture* 4, no. 3 (July 1988): 2–5.

McCollum, Brian. "Andre Harrell Is Ready to Lead Motown Records Back to Glory and Back to Its Roots," *Detroit Free Press*, March 24, 1996.

McClain, William B., J. Jefferson Cleveland, and Verolga Nix. *Songs of Zion*. Nashville, TN: Abingdon Press, 1981.

McGee, Kristin Ann. "The Gendered Jazz Aesthetics of *That Man of Mine*: The International Sweethearts of Rhythm and Independent Black Sound Film." In *Big Ears: Listening for Gender in Jazz Studies*, edited by Nichole T. Rustin and Sherrie Tucker, 393–422. Durham, NC: Duke University Press, 2008.

———. *Some Liked It Hot: Jazz Women in Film and Television, 1928–1959*. Middletown, CT: Wesleyan University Press, 2009.

McGhee, Cece. "Tye Tribbett on His Infidelity: 103.9 Praise Philadelphia Interview." YouTube. Posted October 11, 2010. Accessed on January 28, 2016. Available from https://www.youtube.com/watch?v=qf06nIn8zB8.

McGregor, Tracii. "Sittin' on Top of the World." *The Source*, October 1994, 98–104.

McIlhenny, E.A. *Befo' De War Spirituals*. Boston: Christopher Pub. House, 1933.

McKim, Lucy. "Songs of the Port Royal 'Contrabands'." *Dwight's Journal of Music* 22, no. 6 (1862): 254–5.

McLeese, Don. "Anatomy of an Anti-Disco Riot." *In These Times*, August 29–September 4, 1979, 23.

McPartland, Marion. *All in Good Time*. New: Oxford University Press, 1987.

Meadows, Eddie S. *Blues, Funk, Rhythm and Blues, Soul, Hip Hop, and Rap: A Research and Information Guide*. New York: Routledge, 2010.

Metcalf, Ralph, and Theresa Needham. "Interview with Theresa Needham." In *Speakin' of the Blues Series*. Chicago: Chicago Blues Archives, Chicago Public Library, 1989. Oral history interview.

Miller, Karl Hagstrom. *Segregating Sound: Inventing Folk and Pop Music in the Age of Jim Crow*. Durham, NC: Duke University Press, 2010.

Miller, Mark. *Such Melodious Racket: The Lost History of Jazz in Canada, 1914–1949*. 1st ed. Toronto: Mercury Press, 1997.

———. *High Hat Trumpet and Rhythm: The Life and Music of Valaida Snow*. Toronto: Mercury Press, 2007.

Miller, Norma, and Evette Jensen. *Swingin' at the Savoy: The Memoir of a Jazz Dancer*. Philadelphia: Temple University Press, 1996.

Mitchell, Gail. "Black Execs Downsized," *Billboard*, July 30, 2005, 24–5.

Monaghan, Peter. "The Riffs of Jazz Inspire Social and Political Studies of Black Music." *Chronicle of Higher Education*, May 1, 1998, A16–A17.

Monson, Ingrid. "The Problem with White Hipness: Race, Gender, and Cultural Conceptions in Jazz Historical Discourse." *Journal of the American Musicological Society* 48, no. 3 (1995): 396–422.

———. *Saying Something: Jazz Improvisation and Interaction*. Chicago: University of Chicago Press, 1996.

———. "Review of *Representing Jazz* and *Jazz Among the Discourses*, edited by Krin Gabbard," *American Music* 15, no. 1 (1997): 110–13.

———. "Oh Freedom: George Russell, John Coltrane, and Modal Jazz." In *In the Course of Performance: Studies in the World of Musical Improvisation*, edited by Bruno Nettl and Melinda Russell, 149–68. Chicago: University of Chicago Press, 1998.

———. "Riffs, Repetition, and Theories of Globalization." *Ethnomusicology* 43 (1999): 31–65.

———. *Freedom Sounds: Jazz, Civil Rights, and Africa, 1950–1967*. New York: Oxford University Press, 2007.

———. "Fitting the Part." In *Big Ears: Listening for Gender in Jazz Studies*, edited by Nichole T. Rustin and Sherrie Tucker, 267–87. Durham, NC: Duke University Press, 2008.

Moraga, Cherríe, and Gloria Anzaldúa, eds. *This Bridge Called My Back: Writings by Radical Women of Color*. 2nd ed. New York: Kitchen Table, Women of Color Press, 1983.

Morath, Max. *100 Ragtime Classics*. Denver: Donn Printing, 1963.

———. "May Aufderheide and the Ragtime Women." In *Ragtime: Its History, Composers, and Music*, edited by John Edward Hasse, 154–65. London: Macmillan, 1985.

Morgan, Joan. *When Chickenheads Come Home to Roost: My Life as a Hip-Hop Feminist*. New York: Simon and Schuster, 1999.

Morris, Bonnie J. *Eden Built by Eves: The Culture of Women's Music Festivals*. New York: Alyson Books, 1999.

Morrison. Keith. "To Hell and Back." *NBC News*. Last modified August 13, 2006. Available from http://www.nbcnews.com/id/14337492/#.VoibZTaYfdk.

Morrow, Latrea. "'Forward in Faith' BET's Celebration of Gospel Highest Ratings in 14 years." *Examiner.com*. Last modified April 8, 2014. Accessed January 28, 2016. Available from http://www.examiner.com/article/forward-faith-bet-s-celebration-of-gospel-highest-ratings-14-years.

Morton, David C., and Charles K. Wolfe. *Deford Bailey*. Knoxville: The University of Tennessee Press, 1991.

"Motown Moves to Los Angeles." *Bay State Banner*, June 29, 1972, 10.

Mulhern, Francis. "The Politics of Cultural Studies." *Monthly Review: An Independent Socialist Magazine* 47, no. 3 (1995): 31–40.

Muller, Carol Ann, and Sathima Bea Benjamin. *Musical Echoes: South African Women Thinking in Jazz*. Durham, NC: Duke University Press, 2011.

Murphy, Dan. "Jazz Studies in American Schools and Colleges: A Brief History." *Jazz Educators Journal* 26, no. 3 (March 1994): 34–8.

"Music Abroad." *Dwight's Journal of Music* 21, no. 19 (August 1862): 149–50.

Myers, Brenda T. "An Afternoon with Dick Griffey: His Philosophy and Thoughts on Business, with Reflections." *African American Review* 29, no. 2 (1995): 341–6.

Nash, Alanna. *The Colonel: The Extraordinary Story of Colonel Tom Parker and Elvis Presley*. Chicago: Chicago Review Press, 2004. First published in 2003.

National Association of Schools of Music. *Handbook 2013–14*. Reston, VA: National Association of Schools of Music, 2013.

National Baptist Publishing Board. *The New National Baptist Hymnal*. Nashville, TN: National Baptist Publishing Board, 1977.

Neal, Mark Anthony. "Another Man Is Beating My Time: Gender and Sexuality in Rhythm and Blues." In *American Popular Music*, edited by Jeffrey Melnick and Rachel Rubin, 127–40. Amherst: University of Massachusetts Press, 2001.

———. *Soul Babies: Black Popular Culture and the Post-Soul Aesthetic*. New York: Routledge, 2002.

Negro Population in the United States, 1790–1915. Department of Commerce, Bureau of Census: Government Printing Office, 1918.

Nelson, Cary, comp. *American National Biography Online.* In American Council of Learned Societies and Oxford University Press. Online resource [cited 2003]. Available from http://www.anb.org.

Nettl, Bruno, and Melinda Russell, eds. *In the Course of Performance: Studies in the World of Musical Improvisation.* Chicago: University of Chicago Press, 1998.

Nicholson, Stuart. *Is Jazz Dead? (Or Has It Moved to a New Address).* New York: Routledge, 2005.

Niles, Abbe. "Blue Notes." *New Republic* 45, (1926): 292.

Niles, John J. *Singing Soldiers.* New York: Crown Publishers, 1927.

———. "White Pioneers and Black." *Musical Quarterly* 18, (1932): 69–70.

Nketia, J.H. Kwabena. "The Study of African and Afro-American Music." *Black Perspective in Music* 1, no. 1 (1973): 7–15.

———. "African Roots of Music in the Americas: An African View." In *Report of the 12th Congress*, edited by Daniel Heartz and Bonnie C. Wade, 82–8. Berkeley: American Musicological Society, 1981.

Obrecht, Jas, ed. *Rollin' and Tumblin': The Postwar Blues Guitarists.* San Francisco: Miller Freeman Books, 2000.

O'Connell, Monica Hairston, ed. Special issue, *Black Music Research Journal* 34, no. 1 (Spring 2014).

Odum, Howard. "Folk-Song and Folk-Poetry as Found in the Secular Songs of the Southern Negroes." *Journal of American Folklore* 24, no. 93–94 (1911): 255–94, 351–96.

Oehler, Susan E. "Aesthetics and Meaning in Professional Blues Performance: An Ethnographic Examination of an African-American Music in Intercultural Context." PhD diss., Bloomington: Indiana University, 2001.

Ogren, Kathy J. *The Jazz Revolution: Twenties America and the Meaning of Jazz.* New York: Oxford University Press, 1989.

———. "Review of *Representing Jazz* and *Jazz among the Discourses*," edited by Krin Gabbard, *Journal of American History* 83, no. 1 (1996): 261–3.

Oja, Carol. "'New Music' and the 'New Negro': The Background of William Grant Still's *Afro-American Symphony*." *Black Music Research Journal* 12, no. 2 (1992): 145–69.

———. "New Music Notes." *Institute for Studies in American Music Newsletter* 31, no. 2 (2002): 6, 14.

Oliver, Paul. *Blues Fell This Morning: Meaning in the Blues.* London: Cassell, 1960.

———. *Conversation with the Blues.* New York: Horizon Press, 1965.

———. "Overseas Blues: Europeans and the Blues." In *Sounds of the South*, edited by Daniel W. Patterson, 57–72. Chapel Hill: Southern Folklife Collection, University of North Carolina, 1991.

O'Meally, Robert. *Lady Day: The Many Faces of Billie Holiday.* New York: Arcade Publishing, 1991.

———, ed. *The Jazz Cadence of American Culture.* New York: Columbia University Press, 1998.

———, Brent Hayes Edwards, and Farah Jasmine Griffin, eds. *Uptown Conversation: The New Jazz Studies.* New York: Columbia University Press, 2004.

Omi, Michael, and Howard Winant. *Racial Formation in the United States: From the 1960s to the 1990s.* 2nd ed., London: Routledge, 1994.

———. *Racial Formation in the United States: From the 1960s to the 1990s.* 3rd ed., New York: Routledge, 2015.

O'Neal, Amy. "Koko Taylor." *Living Blues*, no. 40 (1978): 46–7 (Reprint). Originally published in *Living Blues*, no. 7 (Winter 1971–72): 11–13.

O'Neal, Jim. "Sara Martin." *Living Blues*, no. 52 (Spring 1982): 23.

———. "I Once Was Lost, but Now I'm Found: The Blues Revival of the 1960s." In *Nothing but the Blues: The Music and the Musicians*, edited by Lawrence Cohn, 347–87. New York: Abbeville, 1993.

———, and Amy Van Singel, eds. *The Voice of the Blues: Classic Interviews from Living Blues Magazine.* New York: Routledge, 2002.

Otis, Johnny. *Upside Your Head! Rhythm and Blues on Central Avenue.* Hanover, NH: University Press of New England, 1993.

Palmer, Richard. "Review of *Representing Jazz* and *Jazz among the Discourses*," edited by Krin Gabbard, *Journal of American Studies* 30, no. 2, Part 2 (1996): 289–90.

Palmer, Robert. "The Pop Life." *New York Times*, August 4, 1978, Sec. C: 24.

———, and Eric Clapton. "Eric Clapton (Interview by Robert Palmer, 1985)." In *The Rolling Stone Interviews: The 1980s*, edited by Sid Holt, 169–79. New York: St. Martin's Press and Rolling Stone Press, 1989.

Parchoma, Gale. "The Contested Ontology of Affordances: Implications for Researching Technological Affordances for Collaborative Knowledge Production." *Computers in Human Behavior* 37, no. 9 (2014): 360–8.

Pareles, Jon. "Jazz Suite with a Park View." *New York Times*, May 23, 2000, Sec. E: 1, 3.

Parker, Willie. *Oral History Transcript*, November 7, 1958. New Orleans: Hogan Jazz Archive, Tulane University, 1958.
Parrish, Lydia. *Slave Songs of the Georgia Sea Islands*. 1942. Reprint, Hatboro, PA: Folklore Associates, 1965.
Peabody, Charles. "Notes on Negro Music." *Journal of American Folklore* 16, (1903): 148–52.
Pearlman, Jill. "Girls Rappin' Round the Table." *The Paper* (Summer 1988): 25–7.
Pearson, Carlton. *The Gospel of Inclusion: Reaching Beyond Religious Fundamentalism to the True Love of God and Self*. New York: Atria Books, 2009.
Pecknold, Diane, ed. *Hidden in the Mix: The African American Presence in Country Music*. Durham, NC: Duke University Press, 2013.
Pekar, Harvey. "Miles Davis: 1964–69 Recordings." In *A Miles Davis Reader*, edited by Bill Kirchner, 164–83. Washington, DC: Smithsonian Institution Press, 1997.
Pellegrinelli, Lara. "The Song Is Who? Locating Singers on the Jazz Scene." PhD diss., Cambridge: Harvard University, 2005.
———. "Separated at 'Birth': Singing and the History of Jazz." In *Big Ears: Listening for Gender in Jazz Studies*, edited by Nichole T. Rustin and Sherrie Tucker, 31–47. Durham, NC: Duke University Press, 2008.
Penelope, Julia, and Susan Wolfe, eds. *Lesbian Culture: An Anthology*. Freedom, CA: The Crossing Press, 1993.
Perchard, Tom. "Writing Jazz Biography: Race, Research and Narrative Representation." *Popular Music History* 2, no. 2 (2007): 119–45.
Peretti, Burton W. *The Creation of Jazz: Music, Race and Culture in Urban America*. Urbana: University of Illinois Press, 1992.
Person-Lynn, Kwaku. "Insider Perspectives on the American Afrikan Popular Music Industry." In *California Soul: Music of African Americans in the West*, edited by Jacqueline DjeDje and Eddie Meadows, 179–212. Los Angeles: University of California Press, 1998.
Petersen, Karen. "An Investigation of Women-Identified Music in the United States." In *Women and Music in Cross-Cultural Perspective*, edited by Ellen Koskoff, 203–12. Urbana: University of Illinois Press, 1989.
Philips, John Edward. "The African Heritage of White America." In *Africanisms in American Culture*, edited by Joseph Holloway, 225–39. Bloomington: Indiana University Press, 1990.
Phinney, Kevin. *Souled America: How Black Music Transformed White Culture*. New York: Billboard Books/Watson-Guptill Publications, 2005.
Placksin, Sally. *Jazzwomen: 1900 to the Present, Their Words, Lives, and Music*. London: Pluto Press, 1985. Originally published in *American Women in Jazz, 1900 to the Present: Their Words, Lives, and Music* (New York: Wideview Books, 1982).
PoKempner, Marc, and Wolfgang Schorlau. *Down at Theresa's . . . Chicago Blues: The Photographs of Marc PoKempner*. London: Prestel, 2000.
Ponce de Leon, Charles L. *Fortunate Son: The Life of Elvis Presley*. New York: Hill and Wang, 2006.
Pond, Steven F. *Head Hunters: The Making of Jazz's First Platinum Album*. Ann Arbor: University of Michigan Press, 2005.
Porter, Eric. *What Is This Thing Called Jazz? African American Musicians as Artists, Critics, and Activists*. Berkeley: University of California Press, 2002.
———. "Rethinking Jazz through the 1970s." *Jazz Perspectives* 4, no. 1 (2010): 1–5.
Porter, Lewis. "Guidelines for Jazz Research." *Bulletin of the Council for Research in Music Education*, no. 95 (1987): 3–12.
Posner, Gerald. *Motown: Music, Money, Sex, and Power*. New York: Random House, 2002.
Post, Laura. *Backstage Pass: Interviews with Women in Music*. Norwich, VT: New Victoria Publishers, 1997.
Pough, Gwendolyn D. *Check It While I Wreck It: Black Womanhood, Hip-Hop Culture, and the Public Sphere*. Boston: Northeastern University Press, 2004.
———, Elaine Richardson, Aisha Durham, and Rachel Raimist, eds. *Home Girl Makes Some Noise: Hip-Hop Feminist Anthology*. Mira Loma, CA: Parker Publishing, LLC, 2007.
Price, Emmett G., Tammy L. Kernodle, and Horace Maxille, eds. *Encyclopedia of African American Music*. Santa Barbara, CA: Greenwood Press, 2010.
Prouty, Kenneth E. "The History of Jazz Education: A Critical Reassessment." *Journal of Historical Research in Music Education* 26, no. 2 (2005): 79–100.
———. "The 'Finite' Art of Improvisation: Pedagogy and Power in Jazz Education." *Critical Studies in Improvisation/Études Critiques en Improvisation* 4, no. 1 (2008): n.p.
Radano, Ronald M. *New Musical Figurations: Anthony Braxton's Cultural Critique*. Chicago: University of Chicago Press, 1993.
———. *Lying Up a Nation: Race and Black Music*. Chicago: University of Chicago Press, 2003.

———, and Philip V. Bohlman. *Music and the Racial Imagination*. Chicago: University of Chicago Press, 2000.
Ramsey, Guthrie P., Jr. "Review of *Representing Jazz* and *Jazz among the Discourses*, edited by Krin Gabbard." *African-American Review* 31, no. 2 (1997): 348–50.
———. *Race Music: Black Cultures from Bebop to Hip-Hop*. Berkeley: University of California Press, 2003.
———. "The Pot Liquor Principle: Developing a Black Music Criticism in American Music Studies." *American Music* 22, no. 2 (Summer 2004): 284–95.
———. "Secrets, Lies, and Transcriptions: Revisions on Race, Black Music and Culture." In *Western Music and Race*, edited by Julie Brown, 24–36. New York: Cambridge University Press, 2007.
Rasula, Jed. "The Media of Memory: The Seductive Menace of Records in Jazz History." In *Jazz among the Discourses*, edited by Krin Gabbard, 134–62. Durham, NC: Duke University Press, 1995.
Ravenel, Henry William. "Recollections of Southern Plantation Life." *Yale Review* 25 (1936): 768–9.
Reagon, Bernice Johnson. "Songs of the Civil Rights Movement, 1955–1965: A Study in Culture History." PhD diss., Washington, DC: Howard University, 1975.
———. "Kenneth Morris: I'll be a Servant for the Lord." In *We'll Understand It Better By and By: Pioneering African American Gospel Composers*, edited by Bernice Johnson Reagon, 329–41. Washington, DC: Smithsonian Institution Press, 1992a.
———. "Searching for Tindley." In *We'll Understand It Better By and By: Pioneering African American Gospel Composers*, edited by Bernice Johnson Reagon, 37–52. Washington, DC: Smithsonian Institution Press, 1992b.
———. *We Who Believe in Freedom: Sweet Honey in the Rock . . . Still on the Journey*. New York: Anchor Books, 1993.
Reed, Ishmael. *Mumbo Jumbo*. New York: Scribner, 1996. Originally published in Garden City, NJ: Doubleday, 1972.
Reed, Rochelle. "James Brown: Flamboyant Showman of Soul." *Soul Illustrated* (Summer 1968): 41–8.
Reeves, Martha. *Dancing in the Street: Confessions of a Motown Diva*. New York: Hyperion, 1994.
Resner, Hillel. "Orrin Keepnews: Past Master." *Mix* (January 1996): 92–8.
Reuss, Richard A. "American Folklore and Left-Wing Politics, 1927–1957." PhD diss., Bloomington: Indiana University, 1971.
Reyes Schramm, Adelaide. "Exploration in Urban Ethnomusicology: Hard Lessons from the Spectacularly Ordinary." *Yearbook for Traditional Music* 14 (1982): 1–14.
Reynolds, Rhonda. "Must Black Firms Stay in Black Hands?" *Black Enterprise* 26, no. 1 (August 1995): 191–2, 194, 198.
Ribot, Marc. "Days of Bread and Roses." In *People Get Ready: The Future of Jazz Is Now!*, edited by Ajay Heble and Rob Wallace, 141–52. Durham, NC: Duke University Press, 2013.
Rich, Adrienne. "Compulsory Heterosexuality and Lesbian Existence." 1980. Reprinted in *The Lesbian and Gay Studies Reader*, edited by Henry Abelove, Michèle Aina Barale, David M. Halperin, 227–54. New York: Routledge, 1993.
Roberts, Robin. *Ladies First: Women in Music Videos*. Jackson: University Press of Mississippi, 1996.
Robertson, Carol E. "Power and Gender in the Musical Experiences of Women." In *Women and Music in Cross-Cultural Perspective*, edited by Ellen Koskoff, 225–44. Urbana: University of Illinois Press, 1989.
Robinson, Jo Ann Gibson. *The Montgomery Bus Boycott and the Women Who Started It: The Memoir of Jo Ann Gibson Robinson*. Knoxville: University of Tennessee Press, 1987.
Robinson, Paul, "Race, Space, and the Evolution of Black Los Angeles." In *Black Los Angeles: American Dreams and Racial Realities*, edited by Darnell Hunt and Ana Christina Ramón, 21–59. New York: New York University Press, 2010.
Robinson, Smokey. *Smokey: Inside My Life*. London: Headline, 1989.
Rockwell, John. "Presley Gave Rock Its Style." *The New York Times*, August 17, 1977, 1, D18.
Rose, Al, and Edmond Souchon. *New Orleans Jazz: A Family Album*. 1967. 3rd ed., Rev. and Enlarged. Baton Rouge: Louisiana State University Press, 1984.
Rose, Cynthia. *Living in America: The Soul Saga of James Brown*. London: Serpent's Tail, 1990.
Rose, Tricia. *Black Noise: Rap Music and Black Culture in Contemporary America*. Hanover, NH: Wesleyan University Press/University Press of New England, 1994.
———. *The Hip Hop Wars: What We Talk About When We Talk About Hip Hop—and Why It Matters*. New York: Basic Civitas, 2008.
Rowe, Billy. "Big Music Beef at Home Why Fund African Gestapo." *New York Amsterdam News*, July 28, 1984, 18.

Rudolph, Eric. "Jacky Terrasson: Capturing Jazz Piano with a 'Cello'." *Mix*, June, 1996, 190, 194–6.
Rushin, Kate. *The Black Back-Ups*. Ithaca, NY: Firebrand Books, 1993.
Rustin, Nichole T. "Mary Lou Williams Plays Like a Man! Gender, Genius, and Difference in Black Music Discourse." *The South Atlantic Quarterly* 104, no. 3 (Summer 2005): 445–62.
Rustin, Nichole T., and Sherrie Tucker, eds. *Big Ears: Listening for Gender in Jazz Studies*. Durham, NC: Duke University Press, 2008a.
———. "Introduction." In *Big Ears: Listening for Gender in Jazz Studies*, edited by Nichole T. Rustin and Sherrie Tucker, 1–32. Durham, NC: Duke University Press, 2008b.
Rye, Howard. "What the Papers Said: The Harlem Play-Girls and Dixie Rhythm Girls (and Dixie Sweethearts)." *Storyville* (2007): 173–87.
Sackheim, Eric. *The Blues Line: A Collection of Blues Lyrics*. New York: Grossman Publishers, 1969.
Sanders, Charles. "Aretha." *Ebony* 27, no. 2 (December 1971): 124–34.
Sandke, Randall. *Where the Dark and the Light Folks Meet: Race and the Mythology, Politics, and Business of Jazz*. Lanham, MD: Scarecrow Press, 2010.
———. "Unforgiveable Whiteness." *Journal of Jazz Studies* 7, no. 1 (2011): 104–20.
Sanjek, David. "One Size Does Not Fit All: The Precarious Position of the African American Entrepreneur in Post-World War II American Popular Music." *American Music* 15, no. 4 (1997): 535–62.
Sanjek, Russell. *American Popular Music and Its Business: The First Four Hundred Years*: Vol. 3, *From 1900 to 1984*. New York: Oxford University Press, 1988.
Sanneh, Kalefa. "Revelations: A Gospel Singer Comes Out." *The New Yorker*, February 8, 2010. Available from http://www.newyorker.com/magazine/2010/02/08/revelations-3.
Sarath, Ed, Patricia Shehan Campbell, David Myers, Juan Chattah, Lee Higgins, Victoria Lindsay Levine, . . . and Timothy Rice. *Transforming Music Study from Its Foundations: A Manifesto for Progressive Change in the Undergraduate Preparation of Music Majors*. Missoula, MT: College Music Society, 2014.
Schipper, Henry. "Dick Clark." *Rolling Stone*, April 19, 1990, 67–70, 126.
Schloss, Joseph G., Larry Starr, and Christopher Waterman. *Rock: Music, Culture, and Business*. New York: Oxford University Press, 2012.
Schwerin, Jules. *Got to Tell It: Mahalia Jackson, Queen of Gospel*. New York: Oxford University Press, 1992.
Scott, James. *Domination and the Arts of Resistance*. New Haven, CT: Yale University Press, 1990.
Sculatti, Gene. "Pop Music: 'Home Runs, No Bunts'—Solar Power on the Rise." *Los Angeles Times*, December 6, 1981, K76.
Segrave, Kerry. *Jukeboxes: An American Social History*. Jefferson, NC: MacFarland Books, 2002.
Seward, Theodore F., comp. *Jubilee Songs as Sung by the Fisk Jubilee Singers of Fisk University*. New York: Biglow and Main, 1872.
Sharpley-Whiting, T. Denean. *Pimps Up Ho's Down: Hip Hop's Hold on Young Black Women*. New York: New York University Press, 2007.
Shaw, Arnold. *The World of Soul: Black America's Contribution to the Pop Music Scene*. New York: Cowles Book Company, 1970.
———. *Honkers and Shouters: The Golden Years of Rhythm and Blues*. New York: Macmillan Collier Books, 1978.
———. *Black Popular Music in America: From the Spirituals, Minstrels, & Ragtime to Soul, Disco, & Hip Hop*. New York: Schirmer, 1986.
Shelton, Robert. "Singing for Freedom: Music of the Integration Movement." *Sing Out Magazine*, December–January 1961–62, 4–7.
———. "Negro Songs Here Aid Rights Drive." *The New York Times*, July 23, 1963a, 15.
———. "Rights Song Has Own History of Integration." *The New York Times*, July 23, 1963b, 22.
Sherman, Robert. "Sing a Song of Freedom." *Saturday Review*, September 28, 1963, 65–7, 81.
"Shirelles Come Up with Another Hit in 'Lover'." *Chicago Defender (Daily Edition)*, December 4, 1962, 17.
Sidran, Ben. *Talking Jazz: An Oral History*. Exp. ed., New York: Da Capo, 1995. Originally published in San Francisco: Pomegranate Artbooks, 1992.
Slutsky, Allan "Dr. Licks." *Standing in the Shadows of Motown: The Life and Music of Legendary Bassist James Jamerson*. Wynnewood, PA: Dr. Licks Publishing, 1989.
Smith, Aaron. "Technology Trends Among People of Color." *Pew Internet & American Life Project*. September 17, 2010. Accessed September 1, 2015. Available from http://www.pewinternet.org/Commentary/2010/September/Technology-Trends-Among-People-of-Color.aspx#.

Smith, Barbara, ed. *Home Girls: A Black Feminist Anthology*. New York: Kitchen Table: Women of Color Press, 1983.

Smith, Suzanne E. *Dancing in the Street: Motown and the Cultural Politics of Detroit*. Cambridge, MA: Harvard University Press, 1999.

Snorton, C. Riley. *Nobody is Supposed to Know: Black Sexuality on the Down Low*. Minneapolis: University of Minnesota Press, 2014.

Snyder, Jean. "A Great and Noble School of Music: Dvořák, Harry Burleigh, and the African American Spiritual." In *Dvořák in America*, edited by John C. Tibbetts, 1234–248. Portland, OR: Amadeus Press, 1993.

"Solar Chief Keynotes Ebonics Awards." *Los Angeles Sentinel*, June 19, 1986, A3.

"Solar Launches National Dance Contest." *Los Angeles Sentinel*, November 16, 1978, B1A.

Solis, Gabriel. *Monk's Music: Thelonious Monk and Jazz History in the Making*. Berkeley: University of California Press, 2008.

———, and Bruno Nettl, eds. *Musical Improvisation: Art, Education, and Society*. Urbana: University of Illinois Press, 2009.

"Songs of the Blacks." *Dwight's Journal of Music* 10, no. 7 (November 15 1856): 51–2.

"The Soul of Ray Charles." *Ebony*, September 1960, 99–107.

"'Soul Train' Back for 2nd Season TV Series." *Chicago Daily Defender (Daily Edition)*, September 20, 1972, 12.

"Soul Train Hit with Teens." *Chicago Daily Defender (Daily Edition)*, September 21, 1970, 13.

Southern, Eileen. *The Music of Black Americans: A History*. 1971. 3rd ed., New York: W.W. Norton, 1997.

———, and Josephine Wright. *African American Traditions in Song, Sermon, Tale, and Dance, 1600s–1920: An Annotated Bibliography of Literature, Collections, and Artworks*. New York: Greenwood Press, 1990.

Spector, Ronnie, and Vince Waldron. *Be My Baby: How I Survived Mascara, Mini Skirts, and Madness, or My Life as a Fabulous Ronette*. New York: Harmony, 1990.

Spooner, Tom, and Lee Rainie. "African-Americans and the Internet." *Pew Internet & American Life Project*. October 22, 2000. Accessed September 1, 2015. Available from http://www.pewinternet.org/~/media//Files/Reports/2000/PIP_African_Americans_Report.pdf.pdf.

Stanford, Karin L. *Beyond the Boundaries: Reverend Jesse Jackson in International Affairs*. Albany: State University of New York Press, 1997.

Starr, Larry, and Christopher Waterman. *American Popular Music: From Minstrelsy to Mp3*. 3rd ed., New York: Oxford Press, 2010.

Stearns, Marshall, and Jean Stearns. *Jazz Dance: The Story of American Vernacular Dance*. New York: Macmillan, 1968.

Stein, Arlene, ed. *Sisters, Sexperts, Queers: Beyond the Lesbian Nation*. New York: Penguin Books, 1995.

Stelter, Brian. "After Decades, a New Owner for 'Soul Train'." *New York Times*, June 17, 2008. Accessed September 1, 2015. Available from http://query.nytimes.com/gst/fullpage.html?res=9E0CE3DE1E3BF934A25755C0A96E9C8B.

"Student Music Guide: Where to Study Jazz 2015." *DownBeat*, October, 2014, 73–176.

Suhor, Charles. *Jazz in New Orleans: The Postwar Years through 1970*. Lanham, MD: Scarecrow Press, 2001.

Sunderland, Patricia. "Cultural Meanings and Identity: Women of the African American Art World of Jazz." PhD diss., Burlington: University of Vermont, 1992.

Swartz, Nellie. *A New Day for the Colored Woman Worker: A Study of Colored Women in Industry in New York City*. New York: Consumer League, March 1919. Pamphlet.

Sykes, Charles. "Profiles of Record Labels: Motown." In *African American Music: An Introduction*, edited by Mellonee V. Burnim and Portia K. Maultsby, 431–52. New York: Routledge, 2006.

———. "The Black Forum Label: Motown Joins the Revolution." *Association for Recorded Sound Collections* 46 (2015): 1–41.

Synan, Vinson. "Pentecostal Roots." In *The Century of the Holy Spirit: 100 Years of Pentecostal and Charismatic Renewal*, edited by Vinson Synan, 14–37. Nashville, TN: Thomas Nelson, Inc., 2001.

Szwed, John F. *So What: The Life of Miles Davis*. New York: Simon and Schuster, 2002.

Tagg, Philip. "Open Letter: 'Black Music', 'Afro-American Music' and 'European Music'." *Popular Music* 8, (October 1989): 285–98.

Talbot, Michael, ed. *The Musical Work: Reality or Invention?* Liverpool: Liverpool University Press, 2000.

Tapscott, Horace. *Songs of the Unsung: The Musical and Social Journey of Horace Tapscott*, edited by Steven L. Isoardi. Durham, NC: Duke University Press, 2001.

Tate, Greg. *Everything But the Burden: What White People Are Taking from Black Culture*. New York: Broadway Book, 2003a.

———. *Midnight Lightning: Jimi Hendrix and the Black Experience*. Chicago: Lawrence Hill Books. 2003b.

Taylor, Arthur. *Notes and Tones: Musician-to-Musician Interviews*. 1977. Exp. ed., New York: Da Capo, 1993.

Taylor, Jeffrey. "With Lovie and Lil: Rediscovering Two Chicago Pianists of the 1920s." In *Big Ears: Listening for Gender in Jazz Studies*, edited by Nichole T. Rustin and Sherrie Tucker, 48–63. Durham, NC: Duke University Press, 2008.

Tenzer, Michael. "Integrating Music: Personal and Global Transformations." In *Analytical and Cross-Cultural Studies in World Music*, edited by Michael Tenzer and John Roeder, 357–87. New York: Oxford University Press, 2011.

"They Blew Horns." *New York Amsterdam News*, January 29, 1938, 19.

Thomas, Gates. "South Texas Negro Work-Songs: Collected and Uncollected." In *Rainbow in the Morning*, edited by J. Frank Dobie, 154–80. Publications of the Texas Folklore Society 5. Hatboro, PA: Texas Folklore Society, 1926.

Thomas, Richard. *Life for Us Is What We Make It*. Bloomington: Indiana University Press, 1992.

Thurston, Chuck, "Motown Moving to California." *Detroit Free Press*, June 15, 1972.

Tipaldi, Art. *Children of the Blues: 49 Musicians Shaping a New Blues Tradition*. San Francisco: Back Beat Books, 2002.

Titon, Jeff Todd. "Reconstructing the Blues: Reflections on the 1960s Blues Revival." In *Transforming Tradition*, edited by Neil V. Rosenberg, 220–40. Urbana: University of Illinois Press, 1993.

———. *Early Downhome Blues: A Musical and Cultural Analysis*. 1977. 2nd ed., Chapel Hill: The University of North Carolina Press, 1994.

Tolleson, Robin. "Recording Cassandra Wilson's 'New Moon Daughter'." *Mix*, July, 1996, 186, 190–8.

———. "Recording James Carter's 'Layin' in the Cut'." *Mix*, June, 2001, 177, 190–2.

Tomlinson, Gary. "The Web of Culture: A Context for Musicology." *19th Century Music* 7, (1984): 350–62.

"Top Contemporary Christian Chart," *Billboard*, September 16, 1995, 40.

"Top Gospel Albums," *Billboard, One Hundredth Anniversary Issue, 1894–1994*, November 1, 1994, 246.

Touré. *Never Drank The Kool-Aid*. New York: Picador, 2006.

Toynbee, Jason, Catherine Tackley, and Mark Doffman, eds. *Black British Jazz: Routes, Ownership and Performance*. Farnham, Surrey: Ashgate, 2014.

Toynbee, Jason, and Linda Wilks. "Audiences, Cosmopolitanism, and Inequality in Black British Jazz." *Black Music Research Journal* 33, no. 1 (2013): 27–48.

Tucker, Mark. "Musicology and the New Jazz Studies." (Review of *Representing Jazz* and *Jazz among the Discourses*," edited by Krin Gabbard), *Journal of the American Musicological Society* 51, no. 1 (1998): 131–48.

Tucker, Sherrie. *Swing Shift: "All-Girl" Bands of the 1940s*. Durham, NC: Duke University Press, 2000.

———. "Women." In *New Grove Dictionary of Jazz*, edited by Barry Kernfeld, 249–55. New York: Macmillan, 2001.

———. "Big Ears: Listening for Gender in Jazz Studies." *Current Musicology*, no. 71–73 (2001–2002): 375–408.

———. "Beyond the Brass Ceiling: Dolly Jones Trumpets Modernity in Oscar Micheaux's *Swing!*" *Jazz Perspectives* 3, no. 1 (April 2009): 3–34.

———. "Deconstructing the Jazz Tradition: The 'Subjectless Subject' of New Jazz Studies." In *Jazz/Not Jazz: The Music and Its Boundaries*, edited by David Ake, Charles Hiroshi Garrett, and Daniel Goldmark, 264–84. Berkeley: University of California Press, 2012.

Turner, Tina, and Kurt Loder. *I, Tina*. New York: Avon Books, 1987.

"Tutu's U.S. Visit Stirs New Anti-Apartheid Awareness." *Los Angeles Sentinel*, January 30, 1986, A16.

"Two Cities Pay Tribute to Mahalia Jackson," *Ebony*, April 1972, 62–72.

University of Illinois Campus Folksong Club, coll. "Robert Johnson, 23 February, Urbana, Illinois." Indiana University Archives of Traditional Music 65–044-F, EC 541–44, 1963.

Unterbrink, Mary. *Jazz Women at the Keyboard*. Jefferson, NC: McFarland, 1983.

Volk, Terese M. "The History and Development of Multicultural Music Education as Evidenced in the Music Educators Journal, 1967–1992." *Journal of Research in Music Education* 41, no. 2 (1993): 137–55.

Wald, Elijah. *Josh White, Society Blues*. Amherst: University of Massachusetts Press, 2000.

Wald, Gayle. *Shout, Sister Shout! The Untold Story of Rock-and-Roll Trailblazer Sister Rosetta Tharpe*. Boston: Beacon Press, 2007.

Walker, Rev. Charles. "Lucie E. Campbell Williams: A Cultural Biography." In *We'll Understand It Better By and By: Pioneering African American Gospel Composers*, edited by Bernice Johnson Reagon, 121–40. Washington, DC: Smithsonian Institution Press, 1992.

Walker, Juliet. *The History of Black Business in America: Capitalism, Race, Entrepreneurship*. New York: Macmillan, 1998.

Walker, Lisa M. "How to Recognize a Lesbian: The Cultural Politics of Looking Like What You Are." *Signs: Journal of Women in Culture and Society* 18, no 4 (1993): 886–9.

Walser, Robert. "'Out of Notes': Signification, Interpretation, and the Problem of Miles Davis." In *Jazz among the Discourses*, edited by Krin Gabbard, 165–88. Durham, NC: Duke University Press, 1995.

———, ed. *Keeping Time: Readings in Jazz History*. New York: Oxford University Press, 1999.

Walters, Barry. "Review of Queen Pen, My Melody." *Advocate*, March 17, 1998, 59–60.

Warwick, Jacqueline. *Girl Groups, Girl Culture: Popular Music and Identity in the 1960s*. New York: Routledge, 2007.

Waters, Keith. *The Studio Recordings of the Miles Davis Quintet, 1965–68*. New York: Oxford University Press, 2011.

Waugh, Butler H. "Negro Tales of John Kendry from Indianapolis." *Midwest Folklore* 8, no. 3 (1958): 125–41.

Welch, Chris. *Cream*. San Francisco: Miller Freeman Books, 2000.

Wellman, David T. *Portraits of White Racism*. 2nd ed. Cambridge: Cambridge University Press, 1993. Originally published in 1977.

Werner, Craig. *A Change Is Gonna Come: Music, Race, and the Soul of America*. New York: Plume, 1999.

———. *Higher Ground: Stevie Wonder, Aretha Franklin, Curtis Mayfield, and the Rise and Fall of American Soul*. New York: Crown Publishers, 2004.

Wesley, Fred, Jr. *Hit Me, Fred: Recollections of a Sideman*. Durham, NC: Duke University Press, 2002.

West, Cornel. "Race and Modernity." In *The Cornel West Reader*, 55–86. New York: Basic Civitas Books, 1999.

"The Whispers Say: And the Beat Goes On." *Los Angeles Sentinel*, April 24, 1980, B.

Whitburn, Joel. *Top R&B Singles, 1942–1988*. Menomonee Falls, WI: Record Research, 1988.

———. *Top Pop Singles, 1955–1990*. Menomonee Falls, WI: Record Research, 1990.

———. *Top R&B/Hip-Hop Singles 1942–2004*. Menomonee Falls, WI: Record Research, Inc. 2004.

White, Bob W. "The Promise of World Music: Strategies for Non-Essentialist Listening." In *Music and Globalization: Critical Encounters*, edited by Bob W. White, 189–218. Bloomington: Indiana University Press, 2012.

White, Charles. *The Life and Times of Little Richard: The Quasar of Rock and Roll*. New York: Harmony Books, 1984.

White, Cliff. "After 21 Years, Still Refusing To Lose . . ." In *The James Brown Reader: 50 Years of Writing about the Godfather of Soul*, edited by Nelson George and Alan Leeds, 124–41. New York: Plume/Penguin Group, 2008. Originally published in *Black Music*, April 1, 1977.

White, Newman Ivey. *American Negro Folk-Songs*. 1928. Reprint, Hatboro, PA: Folklore Associates, 1965.

Whyton, Tony. *Jazz Icons: Heroes, Myths and the Jazz Tradition*. Cambridge: Cambridge University Press, 2010.

Wiggins, Daphne C. *Righteous Content: Black Women's Perspectives of Church and Faith*. New York: New York University Press, 2005.

Wilcock, Donald E., and Buddy Guy. *Damn Right I've Got the Blues: Buddy Guy and the Blues Roots of Rock-and-Roll*. San Francisco: Woodford Press, 1993.

Williams, Edward Wyckoff. "The Black Gay-Straight Alliance." *The Root*, October 5, 2012. Available from http://www.theroot.com/articles/culture/2012/10/the_rev_delman_coates_on_gay_marriage_the_black_gaystraight_alliance.html.

Williams, Linda Faye. "The Impact of African American Music on Jazz in Zimbabwe: An Exploration in Radical Empiricism." PhD diss., Bloomington: Indiana University, 1995.

———. "Black Women, Jazz, and Feminism." In *Black Women and Music: More than the Blues*, edited by Eileen M. Hayes and Linda F. Williams, 119–33. Urbana: University of Illinois Press, 2007.

Williams, Otis. *Temptations*. New York: Putnam, 1998.

Williams, Paul. *Outlaw Blues: A Book of Rock Music*. New York: E.P Dutton and Co., Inc., 1969.

Wilmer, Valerie. *As Serious as Your Life: The Story of the New Jazz*. 1977. 1st U.S. ed., Westport, CT: Lawrence Hill & Company, 1980.

Wilson, Mary. *Dreamgirl: My Life as a Supreme*. New York: St. Martin's Press, 1986.

Wilson, Olly. "The Significance of the Relationship between Afro-American Music and West Africa." *Black Perspective in Music* 2, no. 1 (1974): 3–22.

———. "Black Music as an Art Form." *Black Music Research Journal* 3, (Winter 1983): 1–22.

———. "The Association of Movement and Music as a Manifestation of a Black Conceptual Approach to Music-Making." 1977. Reprint in *More Than Dancing: Essays on Afro-American Music and Musicians*, edited by Irene Jackson, 10–23. Westport, CT: Greenwood Press, Inc., 1985.

——— "The Heterogeneous Sound Ideal in African-American Music." 1981. Reprint, In *New Perspectives on Music: Essays in Honor of Eileen Southern*, edited by Josephine Wright and Samuel A. Floyd Jr., 327–38. Detroit, MI: Harmonie Park Press, 1992.

Wiltz, Teresa. "Meshell Ndegeocello Breaks Step with Pop." *The Washington Post*, June 19, 2005, N01. Available from http://www.washingtonpost.com/wp-dyn/content/article/2005/06/17/AR2005061700715.html.

Windsor, W. Luke, and Christophe de Bézenac. "Music and Affordances." *Musicae Scientiae* 16, no. 1 (2012): 102–20.

Wolff, Daniel, S.R. Crain, Clifton White, and G. David Tenenbaum. *You Send Me: The Life and Times of Sam Cooke*. New York: Quill, 1995.

Wolkin, Jan Mark, and Bill Keenom. *Michael Bloomfield: If You Love These Blues*. San Francisco: Miller Freeman Books, 2000.

Work, John W., Jr., *Folk Songs of the American Negro*. 1915. Reprint, New York: Negro Universities Press, 1969.

Work, John W., III., ed. *American Negro Songs and Spirituals: A Comprehensive Collection of 230 Folk Songs, Religious and Secular*. New York: Bonanza Books, 1940.

Wright, Josephine, and Samuel A. Floyd Jr., eds. *New Perspectives on Music: Essays in Honor of Eileen Southern*. Detroit, MI: Harmonie Park Press, 1992.

Yetman, Norman, ed. *Life Under the "Peculiar Institution": Selections from the Slave Narrative Collection*. New York: Rinehart and Winston, 1970.

Yoder, Don. *Pennsylvania Spirituals*. Lancaster: Pennsylvania Folklife Society, 1961.

Yoshida, George. *Reminiscing in Swingtime: Japanese Americans in American Popular Music, 1925–1960*. San Francisco: National Japanese American Historical Society, 1997.

Zarlenga, Brian. "The Recession Compounds the Crisis in Recorded Music Sales." *Music Business Journal*, January 27, 2009. Available from http://www.thembj.org/2009/01/the-recession-compounds-the-crisis-in-recorded-music-sales/.

Zimmerman, Phil, coll. "New York, Rochester. University of Rochester. First Annual Rochester Folk Festival, 11–12 February." Indiana University Archives of Traditional Music 66–225-F, 1966.

Zinn, Howard. *SNCC: The New Abolitionists*. Boston: Beacon Press, 1964.

Zorn, John, ed. *Arcana: Musicians on Music*. New York: Granary Books, 2000.

Editors and Contributors

EDITORS

MELLONEE V. BURNIM is Professor of Ethnomusicology in the Department of Folklore and Ethnomusicology, Adjunct Professor of African American and African Diaspora Studies, and Director of the Archives of African American Music and Culture at Indiana University. She is a Distinguished Alumnus of the University of North Texas and was selected as the first Distinguished Faculty Fellow in Ethnomusicology and Ritual Studies at the Yale Institute for Sacred Music in 2004. As a performer-scholar, Burnim has done fieldwork and led workshops on African American religious music across the United States, as well as in Cuba, Liberia, and Malawi. Co-editor of *African American Music: An Introduction*, second edition, her writings on African American religious music and theoretical issues in ethnomusicology appear in various edited volumes and journals, including *Ethnomusicology*, *The Western Journal of Black Studies*, and *The Music Educator's Journal*, among others.

PORTIA K. MAULTSBY is Laura Boulton Professor Emerita of Ethnomusicology in the Department of Folklore and Ethnomusicology, and Research Associate in the Archives of African American Music and Culture at Indiana University. In the spring of 1998, she was the Belle van Zuylen Professor of African American Music in the Department of Musicology at Utrecht University, the Netherlands. Maultsby is co-editor of *African American Music: An Introduction*, second edition, and her writings on African American religious and popular music appear in various journal and edited volumes, including *Ethnomusicology*, *The Black Perspective in Music*, *Journal of Popular Culture*, *The Western Journal of Black Studies*, *Bulgarian Musicology*, *The Harvard Guide to African-American History* (Harvard Press, 2001), and *Ashgate Research Companion to Popular Musicology* (Ashgate, 2009). In addition to her scholarly work, she is a keyboard player and the founding director of the IU Soul Revue, a touring ensemble specializing in the performance of African American popular music. Her current project examines issues of transnationalism, focusing on Euro-Dutch choirs in the Netherlands specializing in Black gospel music as a case study.

CONTRIBUTORS

ROB BOWMAN has been writing professionally about rhythm and blues, rock, country, jazz, and gospel for over forty years. Nominated for five Grammy Awards, in 1996 Bowman won the Grammy in the "Best Album Notes" category for a 47,000-word monograph he penned to accompany a ten-CD box set that he also co-produced, *The Complete Stax/Volt Soul Singles Volume 3: 1972–1975* (Fantasy Records). He is also the author of *Soulsville U.S.A.: The Story of Stax Records* (Schirmer Books), winner of the 1998 ASCAP-Deems Taylor and ARSC Awards for Excellence in Music Research. In 2013 *Soulsville U.S.A.* was inducted into the Blues Hall of Fame. On top of his popular press and liner note work, Bowman played a seminal role in the founding and creation of The Stax Museum of American Soul Music (opened in Memphis in 2003), wrote the four-part television documentary series *The Industry*, has co-produced numerous music documentaries, and has helped pioneer the study and teaching of popular music in the world of academia. A tenured professor at York University in Toronto, Bowman regularly lectures on popular music around the world.

SCOT BROWN is Associate Professor of History and African American studies at the University of California at Los Angeles. He is the author of *Fighting for Us* (2003), a study of cultural nationalism and the Black Power movement during the 1960s and '70s, and numerous articles on social movements, music, and popular culture. Brown is the editor of the collection *Discourse on Africana Studies: James Turner and Paradigms of Knowledge* (2016), and he is completing a book on the soul and funk music scene in Dayton, Ohio. Also a musician, he produced and co-wrote Kalamu ya Salaam's CD *Catfish and Yellow Grits*, scheduled to be released in 2016. Brown has served as historian and music commentator for numerous television and film documentaries, on cable networks including PBS, TV One, Centric/BET, and VH1.

TYRON COOPER is Assistant Professor in the Department of African American and African Diaspora Studies, Indiana University–Bloomington (IU), and director of the IU Soul Revue—an ensemble course that examines and performs Black popular music post–World War II to the present. Cooper holds a BA in music education from Bethune-Cookman University along with an MA in Jazz Studies and PhD in Ethnomusicology, both from IU. As a singer, guitarist, arranger, and music director, Cooper has performed and recorded with national artists in various genres such as Angela Brown, Marietta Simpson, The Soulful Symphony, Donnie McClurkin, Kim Burrell, Kathy Taylor, Bishop Leonard Scott, Jason Nelson, Max Roach, Bo Diddley, and A Taste of Honey, to name a few. Finally, Cooper is a two-time Emmy Award winner for his role as talent and composer for PBS documentaries, *Strange Fruit: The Salt Project* and *Bobby 'Slick' Leonard: Heart of a Hoosier*.

REEBEE GAROFALO is Professor Emeritus at University of Massachusetts–Boston, where he taught for thirty-three years. His most recent book (co-authored with Steve Waksman) is *Rockin' Out: Popular Music in the USA*. He has written numerous articles on popular music for popular as well as scholarly publications and has lectured internationally on a broad range of subjects relating to the operations of the music industry. Garofalo is a member of the executive committee and past chairperson of the International Association for the Study of Popular Music-US, and an editor for several popular music journals, including the *Journal of Popular Music Studies*. At the local level, Garofalo serves on the organizing committee for the annual HONK! Festival of Activist Street Bands. He enjoys drumming and singing with the Blue Suede Boppers, a fifties rock 'n' roll band, and the Second Line Social Aid and Pleasure Society Brass Band, an activist New Orleans–style brass band.

DAPHNE DUVAL HARRISON, Professor Emeritus, University of Maryland Baltimore County, was Chair of the African American Studies Department and later the founding director of the university's Center for the Humanities. She is the author of *Black Pearls: Blues Queens of the 1920s* (Rutgers University Press, 1988) and numerous articles, as well as presentations on African American and African musical traditions and performance, particularly as they pertain to women.

EILEEN M. HAYES is Professor and Chair of the Department of Music at Towson University. She holds the Bachelor of Music from Temple University, the Master of Arts in Folklore from Indiana University, and the PhD in Music from the University of Washington. An ethnomusicologist, her research interests include African American music, feminist theories, queer studies in music and the social sciences, and race in American popular culture. Hayes pursues these interests in *Songs in Black and Lavender: Race, Sexual Politics, and Women's Music* (University of Illinois Press, 2010), a study that tracks the emergence of Black feminist consciousness in women's music. The latter network emerged from a subculture of lesbian feminism in the early 1970s. She has presented papers at numerous conferences including the Society for Ethnomusicology, the College Music Society, Feminist Theory and Music, the Society for American Music, meetings of the German Musicological Society, and the Center for Black Music Research. She is the co-editor with Linda Williams of *Black Women and Music: More Than the Blues* (University of Illinois Press, 2007), nominated for the 2008 Letitia Woods Brown Memorial Book Prize sponsored by the Association of Black Women Historians (ABWH). Hayes is a Ford Foundation Postdoctoral, Danforth, and DAAD Fellow. Her research into the interactions of race, gender, and sexuality in regard to African American music cultures is complemented by her personal and professional advocacy on behalf of women, people of color, and other underrepresented constituencies in departments and schools of music.

JOHN A. JACKSON is the author of *A House on Fire: The Rise and Fall of Philadelphia Soul* (Oxford University Press, 2004), *American Bandstand: Dick Clark and the Making of a Rock and Roll Empire* (Oxford University Press, 1997), and *Big Beat Heat: Alan Freed and the Early Years of Rock and Roll* (Schirmer Books, 1991). He has lectured extensively on the early years of rock music and has twice won the Ralph J. Gleason Award and the Association for Recorded Sound Collections Award for Best Research in the field of Rock, Rhythm and Blues, and Soul.

TRAVIS A. JACKSON is Associate Professor of Music and the Humanities at the University of Chicago. He is the author of *Blowin' the Blues Away: Performance and Meaning on the New York Jazz Scene* (2012). His other writings include essays on jazz history and historiography, intersections between jazz and poetry, Duke Ellington's "travel suites" and world music, the politics of punk, and popular music and recording technology. He is currently conducting research for a monograph on post-punk music, graphic design, discourses of branding, and attitudes regarding race and empire in the United Kingdom between 1977 and 1984.

ALISHA LOLA JONES is Assistant Professor in the Department of Folklore and Ethnomusicology, affiliated faculty in the Department of Gender Studies, and research associate for the Archives of African American Music and Culture at Indiana University. Jones is a graduate of University of Chicago (PhD), Oberlin Conservatory (BM), Yale Divinity School (MDiv), and Yale Institute of Sacred Music (ISM). She has received academic acclaim and support for her research with fellowships from Andrew W. Mellon; the University of Chicago's Center for the Study of Race, Politics, and Culture (CSRPC) and the Center for the Study of Gender and Sexuality (CSGS) joint residency; Martin Marty Center for the Advanced Study of Religion; and the Franke Institute for the Humanities, among others. As a performer-scholar, Jones has done fieldwork and led workshops on religious music and masculinity in the United States, Brazil, Germany, England, and Spain. Her writings on African American religious music and gender in ethnomusicology appear in edited volumes such as *The Oxford Handbook on Voice Studies* and *There Is a Mystery: Esotericism, Gnosticism, and Mysticism in African American Religious Experience*.

CHERYL L. KEYES is Professor of Ethnomusicology at the University of California at Los Angeles (UCLA). Her areas of specialty include African American music, gender, and popular music studies. She is the author of *Rap Music and Street Consciousness* (University of Illinois Press, 2004), which received a CHOICE award for outstanding academic book title, and a recipient of an NAACP Image Award for "Outstanding World Music Album" for her album, *Let Me Take You There* (2008).

LAWRENCE W. LEVINE (1933–2006), past president of the Organization of American Historians and a former MacArthur Prize Fellow, was Professor of History and Cultural Studies at George Mason University, and Margaret Byrne Professor of History Emeritus at the University of California, Berkeley. His publications include *Defender of the Faith: William Jennings Bryan, The Last Decade* (Oxford University Press, 1977); *Highbrow/Lowbrow: The Emergence of Cultural Hierarchy in America* (Harvard University Press, 1988); *The Unpredictable Past: Explorations in American Cultural History* (Oxford University Press, 1993); *The Opening of the American Mind: Canons, Culture, and History* (Beacon Press, 1996); and, with Cornelia R. Levine, *The People and the President: America's Conversations with FDR* (Beacon Press, 2002). At his death he was writing a study of American culture during the Great Depression.

MAUREEN MAHON, a cultural anthropologist, is Associate Professor in the Department of Music at New York University. She is the author of *Right to Rock: The Black Rock Coalition and the Cultural Politics of Race* (Duke University Press, 2004), and articles on music and African American cultural studies that have appeared in *American Ethnologist*, *Journal of Popular Music Studies*, *Women and Music: A Journal of Gender and Culture*, *Journal of the American Musicological Society*, *Ethnomusicology*, EbonyJet.com, and the Rock and Roll Hall of Fame and Museum website. She received a 2013–14 National Endowment for the Humanities Fellowship for her research on the contribution of African American women such as Big Mama Thornton, the Shirelles, Tina Turner, LaBelle, and Betty Davis to popular music. Her book on the subject, *Beyond Brown Sugar: Voices of African American Women in Rock and Roll, 1953–1984*, is under contract with Duke University Press.

MARK ANTHONY NEAL is the author of several books including *What the Music Said: Black Popular Music and Black Public Culture* (Routledge, 1998), *Soul Babies: Black Popular Culture and the Post-Soul Aesthetic* (Routledge, 2002), and *Looking for Leroy: Illegible Black Masculinities* (2013). The tenth anniversary edition of his *New Black Man: Rethinking Black Masculinity* (Routledge) was published in 2015. Neal is also the co-editor (with Murray Forman) of *That's the Joint!: The Hip-Hop Studies Reader* (Routledge), now in its second edition. Neal's essays have been anthologized in more than a half dozen books, including the 2004 edition of the acclaimed series *Da Capo Best Music Writing*, edited by Mickey Hart. Neal is Professor of African and African American Studies and the founding director of the Center for Arts, Digital Culture, and Entrepreneurship (CADCE) at Duke University.

SUSAN OEHLER HERRICK is an independent educational consultant based in Phoenix, Arizona, who holds advanced degrees in ethnomusicology (PhD Indiana University) and education (MEd Vanderbilt University.) Herrick primarily serves clients who seek to integrate music into humanities instruction and support teacher professional development. Experience includes managing educational programs for non-profits, such as the Rock and Roll Hall of Fame and Museum (2004–2008), and teaching across the K–16 spectrum. Publications center on the blues, pedagogy, and applied ethnomusicology—most recently appearing in *The Oxford Handbook of Applied Ethnomusicology* (2015), a special issue of the *Journal of Popular Music Studies* (2009), and reviews in the *Journal of American Folklore* (2011), *Ethnomusicology* (2010), and *Journal of Folklore Research* (2009).

BERNICE JOHNSON REAGON is a historian, composer, singer, music producer, author, and cultural activist. She has received major recognition for her pioneering work as a scholar, teacher, and artist in the history and evolution of African American culture, including the MacArthur Fellowship (1989), the Heinz Award for the Arts and Humanities (Heinz Family Foundation, 2003), the Leeway National Award for Women in the Arts (2000), and the 1995 Presidential Medal for contribution to public understanding of the Humanities. She is Curator Emeritus at Smithsonian Institution National Museum of American History, Professor of History Emeritus at American University, and former performer with Sweet Honey in the Rock, the internationally renowned a cappella ensemble she founded in 1973.

CHARLES E. SYKES is Executive Director of Indiana University's African American Arts Institute, Adjunct Professor in IU's Department of Folklore and Ethnomusicology and Department of African American and African Diaspora Studies, and Research Associate with the Archives of African American Music and Culture. His research focuses on African American popular music, with emphasis on Motown. He has served on a consultant panel for the Motown Historical Museum, is co-contributor of text for the study guide and souvenir program for *Motown the Musical*, and developed the first noted course on the history of Motown, which he teaches at Indiana University. Author of "Motown" in the first edition of *African American Music: An Introduction*, he also contributed an article on Motown's Black Forum label in the Spring 2015 issue of the *Association for Recorded Sound Collections Journal*.

SHERRIE TUCKER, Professor of American Studies at University of Kansas, is the author of *Dance Floor Democracy: The Social Geography of Memory at the Hollywood Canteen* (Duke, 2014), *Swing Shift: "All-Girl" Bands of the 1940s* (Duke, 2000) and co-editor, with Nichole T. Rustin, of *Big Ears: Listening for Gender in Jazz Studies* (Duke, 2008). She is a member of Improvisation, Community, and Social Practice (ICASP), International Institutes for Critical Improvisation Studies (IISCI), the Melba Liston Research Collective, the Adaptive Use Musical Instrument (AUMI) research team led by Pauline Oliveros, and the AUMI-KU InterArts, one of six member institutions of the AUMI Research Consortium. She was the Louis Armstrong Visiting Professor at the Center for Jazz Studies at Columbia University in 2004–2005. She is co-editor, with Randal M. Jelks, of *American Studies* and a series editor, with Deborah Wong and Jeremy Wallach, for Music/Culture at Wesleyan University Press.

OLLY WILSON is the recipient of numerous awards for his creative work as a composer, including awards from the Guggenheim, Koussevitzky, Rockefeller, Fromm, and Lila Wallace foundations; the National Endowment for the Arts; and the Chamber Music Society of Lincoln Center. His works have been commissioned and/or performed by the Boston, Chicago, New York, and Moscow philharmonics; the Cleveland and San Francisco symphonies; and many other orchestras in the United States and abroad. In 1995 he was elected to the American Academy of Arts and Letters. He has published scholarly articles on African and African American music and conducted numerous concerts of contemporary music. After teaching at Florida A&M University and the Oberlin Conservatory, in 1970 he joined the faculty of the University of California, Berkeley. He is currently Professor of Music Emeritus.

Index

Page numbers in italics refer to illustrations; page numbers in bold refer to tables

Adams, Dolly 263–5
Adorno, Theodor 32, 45n44
Africa: African music "living sound" 50; "African traits" 52; pan-Africanism 176–7; "Queen Mother" rap identity 310, 313–14, 324n16, 324n25, 325n27; social importance of music 68–9
Alexander, James 143–4
Alexenburg, Ron 155, 159
All about Jazz (website) 38
Allen, Johnny 123, 142, 145
Anderson, Marian 71, 204, 360
Apostolic church 181–3, 185, 195n5, 211, 228
Archie Bell & the Drells 153–4, 162
Armstrong, Lil Hardin 244
Armstrong, Louis 9, 66, 95, 244
art music: "double consciousness" identity and 68–9; Mahalia Jackson career and 208–10; orchestral 72; ragtime influence from 69–70; spirituals influence from 70–1; vernacular influence in 67–8, 72–4
Atkins, Cholly 116–17, 119
Austin, Lovie 243–4, 265
Axton, Estelle 135–7, 140

Baker, David 72
Baker, LaVern 289–90, 292–3, 295
Bakhtin, Mikhail 37
Ball, Marcia 3–5
band music 69
Baptist Church: blues and 248, 250; Civil Rights Movement and 344–5, 347–9, 352–3; Dick Griffey affiliation 166; Elvis affiliation 57; Franklin family affiliation 79, 235n42; gendered leadership in 221–2, 224–5, 232–3; Great Migration and 238–9; Indianapolis gospel music and 191; Lucie Campbell affiliation 202–5; Mahalia Jackson affiliation 208
Baraka, Amiri 40, **113**, 119, 133n38
Baring-Gould, Sabine 344–5
Bar-Kays 137, 140, 143–4
Basie, William Allen "Count" 59, 95, 115
Bebey, Francis 50
Bell, Al 140–8
Bell, Thom 99, 152, 154, 157–8
Benjamin, Walter 37
Benson, George 101
Berry, Chuck 13, 55, 288, 289, 296
Beyoncé 105, 106
Black Entertainment Television (BET) 102, 194, 195n4, 229–30, 318, 320, 376
Black Nationalism 112, 274–5, 371, 376
Black-owned labels: advantages of 177–8; Black entrepreneurship and 110–15; Civil Rights Movement and 97–8; female-owned GospoCentric 82; independent rap labels 103–5; industry consolidation and 165; race record market and 93–6; Stax integrated management and 148–9; *see also* Motown Records; Philadelphia International Records; recording industry; SOLAR; Tyscot Records
Blackwell, Otis 58
Bland, Bobby "Blue" 20, 24, 25
Bley, Paul 42

410

Block, Rory 18
Bloomfield, Mike 14, 20–1
blues: blues compositions 246; blues festivals 15–16; blues revival 16–25; country blues 94; early recordings of 91–3, *92*; female vocal styles 243–4; "jump blues" 249; Mahalia Jackson influence from 207; origins 3, 339–41; "race" records 10, 93–4, *93*; racial identity and 22–3, 25–5, 256, 258–60; racial segregation era and 6–7. radio broadcasts 7, 11, 248–9; "shouting" vocal style 19, 243–5, 253, 293; southern Black "chitlin' circuit" 25, 372; urban blues 12; White blues scenes 20–5; White popular music influence from 7; women in blues 93, 202, 238–43
body: Black pride display and 369–70; blues performing persona and 244; monitoring of Black entertainers 8; performance attire of R&B women 291, 293, 300–1; physical motion in music making 68; *see also* dance
boogie-woogie 58, 62n11, 64n72, 116, 151–2, 246, 249
Booker, T. and the MGs 135, 137–40, 142–3, 149
Boyd, Stacy C. 217
Boyer, Horace 204
brass bands 258, 263
Broonzy, Big Bill (William Lee Conley) 13, 15, 94, 245–6
Brown, Foxy 318
Brown, James 48–51, 52–3, 98, 100, 369–70
Brown, Ruth 13, 249, 289–92, 294–5
Bryant, Charles Anthony 221–7
Burleigh, Harry 69–70, 91
Burnim, Mellonee 50, 180, 187
Butler, Melvin L. 218

Caesar, Shirley 83–4
Campbell, "Little" Milton 11, 20, 25, 145
Campbell, Lucie 202–6, *203*
Carawan, Guy 346, 350–2, 360
Carey, Mariah 102, 104
Carmichael, Stokley **113**, 119, 369, 376
Carr, Ian 34
Carson, David 121
Charles, Ray 57, 63n69, 97, 348
Chicago: blues on radio 7; Great Migration and 238–9, 241; New Orleans jazz in 265–6; Southside blues clubs 14, 20–2, 25, 245; as Stax sales market 141; White blues scene 20–2, 25
Cho, Sumi 60
churches: Apostolic 181–3, 185, 195n5, 211, 228; COGIC 80, 85, 185, 228, 231–2, 248; Methodist *192*, 204, 239, 349; Pentecostal/Sanctified 181–2, 184–5, 187, 195n5, 219, 227–32, 239, 248; *see also* Baptist Church

Civil Rights Movement: "Amazing Grace" and 357; Bernice Reagon role in 274, 276; Berry Gordy contributions 114–15, 120–3, 132n8, 133n37; Black entrepreneurs in Detroit and 111–12; blues experience and 6; as community of resistance 368; Detroit riots and recovery 114–15; Dick Griffey economic empowerment agenda 167, 176–8; *Ed Sullivan Show* and 120; effect on entertainment business 11–12; folk music revival and 350–2, 357, 359–60; freedom songs 343–64, *351*; grassroots organizations 369–70; Mahalia Jackson role 207; music industry and 97–8; silent marches 346–7; spirituals importance for 335; Stax support for 98, 135, 147; "We Shall Overcome" 16, 349–53, *353*; *see also* resistance
Clapton, Eric 16, 19, 25, 60
class: African American music tastes 103; ghetto fabulousness 377–8; gospel music class status 208–9; "lady" designation and 264–5; R&B as working-class music 95
Clayton, Merry 299
Coates, Delman 232–3
COGIC (Church of God in Christ) 80, 85, 185, 228, 231–2, 248
Cohen, Richard 252
Cole, Nat "King" 95, 119, 209, 373
Collage 166, 175
Connor, Charles 58, 64n79
Cooke, Sam 79, 87, 97, 98
Cooper, Anna Julia 256
Cornelius, Don 100, 167–9, *168*
Cox, Ida 93, 243, 246–7
Cropper, Steve 136–9, 143
crossovers: Berry Gordy crossover strategy 111, 121–3, *122*; Black covers of White rock 288; Columbia interest in 155–7; cross-racial duets 102–3; DJs' role in 97; gospel crossovers 79–88; *Hot Buttered Soul* significance 143–4, 155; James Brown style and 51; Mahalia Jackson recordings and 210; payola scandals and 160–1; Philadelphia International Records approach 153; pop culture crossovers 377; *see also* transculturation
Cruz, Jon 53
Cusic, Don 85–6

Da Brat 318
Dahl, Linda 257–9, 262
Dailey, Patrick 222
dance: breakdancing 306, 324n22; disco 51, 100–1, 159, 162, 170; James Brown performances/recordings and 49; monitoring of Black entertainers 8; Motown stage routines 110; role in jazz history 259; slave dancing 332, *332*, 336; SOLAR dance contests 170; *Soul Train* dance

Index **411**

promotion 167–9; syncopated dance music 91–2; *see also* body
Daniels, Douglas Henry 41
Danielsen, Anne 53
Dannen, Frederic 160–1
Davis, Angela 259, 314, 369
Davis, Betty 300–2
Davis, Miles 32–4, *33*, 39–40, 43n20, 115
Davis, Sammy, Jr. **113**
Deele, The 165, 172–3, 175–6
Detroit 111–15, *117*, *118*, 124, 129–30, 131
digital music 105, 106–7, 189
disco 51, 100–1, 159, 162, 170; *see also* funk
Dixon, Bill 42
DJing: Black-appeal radio and 12–13; crossovers and 122; Detroit DJs 116–17; disco DJs 101; early hip hop DJs 306–9, 324n11, 324n22; independent radio DJs 96; rock DJs 54, 96–7; transcultural appeal and 11
DJ Kool Herc 308, 324n11
Domino, Fats 55, 58, 64n79, 95, 96
doo-wop vocal tradition 118, 125, 296
Dorsey, Thomas 79, 81, 85, 204, 243, 248
Dranes, Arizona 201, 248
Dr. Dre 107, 177
Driggs, Frank 262
DuBois, W. E. B. 67, 223
Dyson, Michael Eric 224

economy: Black entrepreneurs in Detroit 111–12; Black music economy emergence 53–4, 172; Black sexuality in music and 374; commodification of Black popular music 368; corporate sponsorship in television 209, 261; Dick Griffey economic empowerment agenda 167, 176–8; digital music consumer habits 189; industry dismantling of Black music divisions 104–5; 1980s artist managers 102; post-1965 Black broadcast leadership 98–9; recording industry racialized political economy 294–6; soul music "Harvard Report" 99; *Soul Train* as financial cooperation model 167–9, *168*; superstar economic growth model 104–5; Tyscot faith-based business model 182–3, 188–90, 192–5; *see also* Black-owned labels
Edwin Hawkins Singers 80–2, *80*, 86–7
Eliot, Marc 58, 64n70
Ellington, Edward Kennedy "Duke" 66, 70, 91, 95, 115
Elliott, Missy 317, 320–1
Ellison, Ralph 6, 66–7, 74
entertainment industry: Black show business 66; chitlin' circuit 25, 372; Civil Rights Movement and 11–12, 97–8; corporate sponsors for Black shows 209; crossovers 85–6, 111, 121–3, *122*; Dick Griffey economic empowerment agenda 167, 176–8; early Black women entertainers 239–41; marketing categories in 24; MTV racial exclusion 101–2, 162; racial exclusion in 7, 101–2, 162, 260–1; racial integration in 5; racialized genre and market niches 301; superstar economic growth model 104–5; treatment of rap in 103; *see also* film and video; publishing; radio; recording industry; television
Evans, David 18
Evans, Sara 276

festival: blues festivals 15–16; folk festivals 10, 15–16, 23, 359; jazz festivals 15–16, 262; "women's music" festivals 270–3, 279–83
film and video: Black-directed films 104; blaxploitation films 145–7, 155; disco films 101; early rock films 55; Elvis films 57; gospel music films 79; hip hop films 103, 312; hip hop video models/vixens 319–20, 325nn46–48; James Brown live performances 49; orchestrated blues in 249; *Say Amen, Somebody* 211; *Shaft* soundtrack significance 145–7, *146*; Stax promotional videos 147–8; *Sweet Sweetback's Baadasssss Song* 147, 155, 373; Tyscot film productions 189–90, 196n38; women as video producers 320–1; *see also* television
Fink, Sue 270
Finkelstein, Sidney 259
Fisk Jubilee Singers 201, 241, 259
folk music revival: blues revival in America 16–25; Civil Rights Movement and 350–2, 357, 359–60; cultural pluralism ideal in 18; declining blues market and 14–15; folk as industry genre 302; folk festivals 10, 15–16, 23, 359; Highlander Folk School 346, 350–2; industry field recordings 94; performance practice in 19–20, 24–5; transcultural working of 9–10; White blues scenes 20–5; *see also* vernacular music
Four Tops 110, **113**, 121, 126–30, 166
Franklin, Aretha 53, 79, 81, 98, 100, 103, 143, 166, 369, 374
Franklin, Kirk 81–7, 180, 192–3, 230
Freed, Alan 54, 97, 288, 292
Freedom Singers 274, 351, *351*, 358–61
funk 25, 51, 62n30, 100–2, 159, 172; *see also* disco

Gaar, Gillian 300
Gabbard, Krin 34–7, 44n27
Gabler, Milt 55
Gaines, Donna 298
Gamble, Kenny 99, 151–63, 168–9
Garofalo, Reebee 53–4, 85–6
Gaye, Marvin 110, **113**, 114, 119, 126–30, 144, 166, 369, 374
gender: Fly Girl female identity 316–19, 320, 322; gendered instrumentation 260, 264;

hetero-patriarchy in churches 217–34, 235n42; masculine identity in gospel music 216–27; masculine identity in preaching 218–27; rock as gendered music 289; Sista with Attitude rap identity 317–18; *see also* LGBT issues; sexuality; women
George, Luvenia 204
George, Nelson 51, 95, 102, 368
Giddings, Paula 274
Gillespie, Dizzy 39, 45n45, 266
Gillett, Charlie 57
Gladys Knight & the Pips **113**, 166
Goldman, Albert 50
Gordy, Berry 82, 98, 110–34, *113*, *118*; *see also* Motown Records
gospel music: Black gospel promotional strategies 86–7; choir director charisma 225, 227; choir director gender performance 216–27; Civil Rights Movement and 358; Contemporary Christian genre and 86; crossovers 85–8; Detroit gospel music 117–18; Edwin Hawkins Singers 80–2, *80*, 86–7; girl groups influence from 296; gospel go-go 219, 234n12; instrumentalists 225–6; Kirk Franklin success 81–7; Lucie Campbell role in 202–6, *203*; Mahalia Jackson role 83, 87, 201, 204, 206–11, *206*; masculine identity in 216–27; musical border crossings to 79–80; "Oh Happy Day" success 80–1, 83–5; racially stratified market 86–8; radio broadcasts 248; Tyscot faith-based business model 180, 182–3, 188–90, 192–5; Willie Mae Ford Smith role in 211–13; women as prominent singers 201–14
GospoCentric Records 82–3, 192, 196n41
Gottschild, Brenda Dixon 256–7
Grae, Jean 321–2
Graustark, Barbara 100
Great Migration 12, 238–9
Griffey, Dick 166–78, *168*; *see also* SOLAR
Griffin, Farah Jasmine 258–9
Guralnick, Peter 48, 56, 62n11
Guy, Buddy 15, 16, 23, 25, 48, 60, 252–3

Haddon, Deitrick 189–90, 196n32, 228–31
Halperin, David 221–2
Hamer, Fannie Lou 356–7, 360
Handy, D. Antoinette 257–8, 262
Hardin, Lillian 243–4, 260, 264–5
Harold Melvin and the Blue Notes 157–8, *157*, 160
Harper, Philip Brian 217
Harrison, Christina 194
Hawkins, Edwin 80–3, *80*, 86–7
Hayes, Isaac 138–40, 143–7, *146*, 154, 370
Hill, Lauryn 314–15, *315*
hip hop 103–4, 177–8, 306–27, 371, 376–7; *see also* DJing; MCing; rap
Hirshey, Gerri 299

Holiday, Billie 115–16, 249, 259
hooks, bell 213
Howland, John 37
Huff, Leon 99, 151–63, 168–9
Hughes, Langston **113**, 119
hymns: Civil Rights Movement and 344–5, 349, 355–7; as gospel sources 84–5; "Lift Every Voice and Sing" 347–8, 365n12; lined hymns 225, 333, 355–7; Sweet Honey use of 278

instrumentalists: blues accompaniment 244–5; guitar emergence as rock centerpiece 289; jazz women instrumentalists 256–7, 260, 263–7
intellectual property: Atlantic royalties lawsuit 294; "Oh Happy Day" arrangement 84–7; racial exclusion in copyrights 91; White covers of blues and R&B 16, 47, 295; *see also* publishing

Jackson, Mahalia 83, 87, 201, 204, 206–11, *206*, 279, 359–60
Jackson, Michael 100, 102–4, 129–30, 370
Jackson 5 (The Jacksons) **113**, 129–30, 166
James, Etta 250, 288, 289–92, *290*, 298
jazz: corporate and capital support for 30; Detroit jazz 115–16; early recordings of 91; free jazz 30, 31; *Hot Buttered Soul* significance 143–4; improvisation 38, 42n8, 44–5n40; jazz festivals 15–16, 262; jazz fusion 31; jazz studies 30–41, 44n27, 44n39, 44nn31–33, 45n51, 59; performing and recording revenue 38–9; as racial resistance 259, 261; sidemen as important in 32–4, 43n20; White appropriation of 95; women as instrumentalists 256–7, 260; women in jazz 44n33, 262–7
Jefferson, Blind Lemon 94, 243
Jefferson, Thomas 68
Johnson, Francis 69–70
Johnson, James Weldon 91, 201, 239, 347
Johnson, J. Rosamond 91, 239, 347–8
Johnson, Robert 17, 94
Jones, Bobby 181, 187, 195n4
Jones, Booker T. 137–8, 140–2
Joplin, Janis 16, 19, 251–2, 287–8
Joplin, Scott 69–70, 90, 239
Jr. Walker & the All Stars **113**, 114, 127–8
jukeboxes 94

Kartomi, Margaret 143
Kelley, Robin D. G. 37, 260
King, Martin Luther Jr. 112, **113**, 119, 344, 355, 369
King, Riley "B. B." 3, 5, 13–14, 18, 19, 23, 299
King Records 48–51, 95, 251
Klymaxx 165, 166, 172–4, *174*
Koenig, Karl 263
Krehbiel, Henry E. 70

Index **413**

LaBelle 300–1, 372–3
LaBelle, Patti 103, 163, 296, 300, 372, 374–5
Lakeside 165, 172–3
Lamb, Bill 105
LaSalle, Denise 20, 24, *24*, 25, 252
Lataillade, Vicki Mack 82–4, 86–7, 192–3
Leadbelly (Huddie Ledbetter) 10, 15, 94
Left Eye (Lisa Lopes) 316–17
Levine, Lawrence 238
Lewis, George E. 37, 39, 42
Lewis, Jerry Lee 13, 56, 296
Lewis, John 347
Leyshon, Andrew 143
LGBT issues: gay rights movement 368; gospel choirs and 216–34, 234n1; homosexuality in rap music 374–5; lesbianism as blues theme 247–8; lesbian rap identity 319; "women's music" and 270–83; *see also* gender; sexuality
Lil' Kim 318
Lincoln, C. Eric 218
Liston, Melba 257–8, 260, 266–7
Little Richard (Richard Penniman) 13, 55–8, 63n69, 64n79, 287, 291, 296
LL Cool J 100, 103, 320, 371
Lomax, Alan 10, 15, 23, 94, 360
Lomax, John 94
Lont, Cynthia 271
Los Angeles: as advocacy locale 176; Guys & Dolls club 166; Lakeside residency in 172; Motown relocation to 111, 129; New Orleans jazz in 265; *Soul Train* relocation to 167; WattsStax event 147
Lucas, Carrie 165–6, 168, 170–1, 173

Macero, Teo 43n20
Malcolm X 112, 132n8, 369, 376–7
Malone, Bill C. 8, 56
Mamiya, Lawrence H. 218
Martha & the Vandellas 110, **113**, 121, 125, 128
Martin, Roberta 83, 204
Martin, Sallie 86, 201, 248, 249
Martin, Sarah 93, 243
Marvelettes 110, 121, 125, 127–8, 287, 296
Matless, David 143
Maultsby, Portia K. 83
Maund, Alfred 345–6
Maxwell, William J. 36
Mayfield, Curtis 98, 144, 364
Mays, Benjamin 223
McCalla, Deidre 272, 283–4
McClurkin, Donnie 229, 231
McCoy, Van 159
McFerrin, Bobby 279
MCing 306–23, 324n22, 326nn57–58
McKenzie, Ed "Jack the Bellboy" 116–18
McKim, Lucy 332–3
McNeill, Tony 219–20, 222, 224–5, 227
McPartland, Marian 41

medicine shows 242–3
Memphis Minnie 243, 245–7, 288
Methodist Church *192*, 204, 239, 349
MFSB 153, 158
M.I.A. 322
Michigan Womyn's Music Festival 270–3
Midnight Star 165, 172–4
Minaj, Nicki 322
minstrelsy: Black show business and 66; "coon" songs recordings 91, 241; White "Negro dialect" songs 91; White popular music influence from 7; women entertainers 239–41
Missy Dee 308–9
mixtapes 306, 322, 323n2
Monson, Ingrid 35–7, 44n27
Moore, Arnold Dwight "Gatemouth" 79
Moore, Wild Bill 54, 63n62
Morgan, Joan 318
Morris, Bonnie 271–2
Morris, Kenneth 84–6
Moss, James 228
Motown Records: assembly-line process 110–11, 115, 123–4; Berry Gordy crossover strategy 121–3, *122*, 132n16; Civil Rights Movement and 97, 114–15, 120–3, 132n8, 133n37, 369; decline of 165–6; Detroit association with 111–15, *117*, *118*, 124, 129–30, 131; founding 82, 98, 111–15; influence on SOLAR 170; "Motown Sound" *113*, 124–31, 131n2, 132n5
Musselwhite, Charlie 13–14, 18, 20, 22

Nathan, Syd 48–51
NdegéOcello, Me'Shell 303, 319, 375–6, *375*
new jack swing 186, 319, 325n40
New Orleans 207–8, 241, 258, 260, 263–6
Newsome, Sam 42
New York City: blues on radio 7; hip hop emergence 306–12, 324n11; James Brown Apollo Theater recording 48–50; music and gentrification 38–9; rap emergence and *52*
Nicholson, Joseph Williams 223
Niles, Abbe 340
Niles, John Jacob 337
Nketia, J. H. Kwabena 50, 53

Odetta 10, 279, 363
Ogren, Kathy 35
O'Jays 157–8, 160–3
Oliver, Paul 15, 22–3
Oliver, Robin 191, 193–4
O'Meally, Robert G. 37, 259
Omi, Michael 60
Osorio, Kimberly 320–1, 326n54
Otis, Johnny 62n11, 250–1, 292

Pace, Harry 93, 241
Palmer, Richard 35–6

Palmer, Robert 45n45
Parks, Rosa 314, 344, 350–1, 377
Parrish, Lydia 334
Patton, Charley 17, 94
Paul, Billy 157–8
Peabody, Charles 337
Pearson, Carlton 232–3
Peer, Ralph 93
Pegglee-Poo 308
Pekar, Harvey 33–4
Pentecostal/Sanctified Church 181–2, 184–5, 187, 195n5, 219, 227–32, 239, 248
performance: audience role in Black performance 48–51; blues performing persona 244; blues revival transcultural performance 17–20, 24–5; concert promotion 167; "*disengaged engagement*" aesthetic performance 53; female rap identities 313–17; gender performance in choral music 216–34; glam performance 300–1; hip hop jams 307; lined hymns 355–7; racial performance of women vocalists 256, 258–60; R&B transcultural performance 48
Philadelphia International Records: assembly-line process 153–4; Civil Rights initiatives 158–9, 161–2; Columbia deal 154–6; decline of 157–62, 166; founding 151; soft soul and 99; *Soul Train* collaboration 168, 171; "Sound of Philadelphia" style 151–3, 157–9, 163, 169
Phillips, Esther 249, 251, 299
Pickett, Wilson 143, 153
Placksin, Sally 257–8, 262
Polydor Records 50–1
Poly Styrene 302–3
popular music: blues influence on 7; commodification of Black popular music 368; Detroit era "Motown Sound" 124–31; James Brown and 51; 1980s African American artists in 102; racial erasure and 47, 54–5, 57–60; Tin Pan Alley 12, 90, 95, 97, 241
Powell, Maxine 119, 121, 176
preaching 19, 49, 218, 223–8, 235n42
Presley, Elvis: Black music influence in 13–16; "Hound Dog" cover 60, 63n69, 251, 287, 295; military service 57, 296; pop repertoire of 64n70; racial erasure attributed to 57–8, 60, 64n81, 288; R&B hits of 121; rock 'n' roll emergence and 56–7; television appearances 63n69
Prince 102, 175–6
Public Enemy 103–4, 314, 371, 376–7
publishing (of music): ASCAP-BMI dispute 95; folk music publication 10; gospel music 86; Lieber and Stoller songwriting 98; Pace & Handy 241; published arrangements of spirituals 53–4, 69, 70; racial segregation in 90–1, 241; ragtime and art music 69–70, 90–1; Tin Pan Alley 12, 90, 95, 97, 241; *see also* intellectual property
punk 298, 302–3

Queen Latifah 104, 313–14, 321, 324n25, 325n27, 326n56, 371
Queen Pen 319

race: authenticity and 23, 139, 279–82; "*blackness as practice*" 52–3; Creole-of-color racial identity 263–4; cultural orientations to music and 8; "double consciousness" racial identity 67–8; historical erasure of jazz women 256–7, 266–7, 267n6; musical agency and 39; racial agency in jazz 32, 39–41, 45n51; racial erasure in R&B covers 47, 54–5, 57–61, 295; racial identity in blues 22–3, 25–6; social racism 5–6; White expectations in blues performance 19; women-identified music and 273, 281–4
racism: Bell as Stax owner and 148; Creoles-of-color racial status 263–4; devaluation of Blackness in blues 25–6; "*disengaged engagement*" aesthetic performance and 53; disruption of interracial blues experiences 13–14; gentrification 39; Great Migration as escape from 238–9; Jim Crow era protest music 5; monitoring of Black entertainers 8; touring and 202, 260, 304n24
Radano, Ronald 53
radio: album-oriented FM radio 99; Berry Gordy exposure to 115; Black-appeal radio 12–14; blues music broadcasts 7, 11, 248; Detroit Black radio programming 116–17; disco and 100–1; exclusion of Black artists 94–5; independent radio 96; Mahalia Jackson radio show 207, 209; Motown crossover recordings 121; "Oh Happy Day" success and 86; payola scandals 97, 159–61; Petrillo bans 250; prevalence of White imitators (of Black music) on 9; public accessibility of Black music 53–4; rap on Black-owned radio 377; rock 'n' roll emergence and 54; Urban Contemporary genre 101; *see also* entertainment industry
ragtime 69–70, 90–1
Rainey, Ma 9, 238, 241–6, 248
Ramsey, Guthrie P. Jr. 35, 52
Randle, Vicki 272–3, 280
rap: answer-back rap 312–13, 324n20; on Black-owned radio 377; "double consciousness" identity and 68; on MTV 102; as R&B successor 51, *52*; *see also* hip hop
Rawls, Lou 151, 161–3
Ray, Johnnie 64n70, 121
Reagon, Bernice Johnson 274–9, 282–3
Reagon, Cordell Hull 351, 358, 360–1
Reagon, Toshi 282–3, 303
recording industry: assembly-line processes 110–11, 115, 123–4, 153–4; Black music divisions 99, 155, 165; dismantling of Black music divisions 104–5; early African American recordings 91; folk revival labels 16–17; hip hop producers 309–10; industry consolidation

Index 415

154, 165; jukeboxes 94; live concert recordings 48–51; mixtapes 306, 322, 323n2; multi-track recording 125–6; payola scandals 97, 159–61; Petrillo bans 250; post-WWII R&B labels 95–6; protest music and 369–70; public accessibility of Black music 53–4; "race" records 10, 93–4, *93*; racialized political economy of 294–6; recordings as transcultural devices 9; Spector "wall of sound" technique 298; Stax live recording process 139–40; vocoder and talk box technology 173; *see also* Black-owned labels; entertainment industry; GospoCentric Records; King Records; Motown Records; Philadelphia International Records; SOLAR; Stax Records; Tyscot Records
Redding, Otis 135, 138, 140, 149
Redman, Joshua 42
Reed, Ishmael 40
Reed, Jimmy 13, 14, 274
Reese, Carlton 361
Reeves, Martha 124, 127–8
resistance: African American protest music 331, 337–9; Afrocentric hip hop 371, 376–7; Black feminist organizations 276–7; Black Power movement 98, 167, 261, 368–9; blues as resistance 5–7, 18, 202; communities of resistance 368; cultural feminism 271; female rap identities and 313–15; freedom songs 343–64, *351*; genres of resistance 237–8; gospel music as resistance 210; heroic figures and 339; jazz as resistance 259, 261; Kenny Gamble social initiatives 158–9, 161–2; pan-Africanism 176–7; Post-Soul resistance 368–72; silence as 346–7; "We Are the World" and 103, 370; *see also* Civil Rights Movement
Revill, George 143
rhythm and blues: Berry Gordy exposure to 115; *Billboard* coverage of 98; blues artists and 20; choo-choo beat 57–8, 64n79; freedom songs and 348; independent radio DJs and 96, 121; new jack swing 186, 319, 325n40; post-WWII R&B labels 95–6; racial erasure in White covers 13, 16, 47, 54–5, 57–61, 64n81, 295; racialized political economy of 294–6; rap as successor to 51, *52*; recording industry and 13, 24; rock 'n' roll emergence and 54, 288–9; sexual innuendo in 292; soul music as successor to 98; White youth subculture and 15; women artists 289–93; working-class popularity of 95
Ribot, Marc 38–9
Rich, Adrienne 273
Richie, Lionel 102, 103
Riley, Teddy 319, 325n40
Robeson, Paul 11, 71
Robinson, Bobby 309–10
Robinson, Smokey 48–51, 110, 112, 114–15, 123, 125–30

Robinson, Sylvia and Joe 309–11, *311*
rockabilly 13
"Rock Island Line" (Leadbelly, Lonnie Donegan) 15
rock 'n' roll: African American women in 287–8, 292–3, 302–3; Alan Freed role in 54, 288; backup singers 53, 154, 256, 293, 299–300; blues relationship with 5, 11, 16; blues rock 25; British rock blues influence 15–16; counterculture and 289; Elvis emergence and 56–7; girl groups 97, 118, 125, 296–9, 300, 372; historiography 55–6, 59; racial erasure and 47, 54–5, 57–60, 288–9; White covers of blues 13, 16, 47, 64n81; White youth subculture and 15
Rockwell, John 56
Rodano, Rolando 282
Rolling Stones 15–16, 148, 287–8, 293, 298–9, 372
Ronettes 296–8, *297*
Rose, Tricia 58
Ross, Diana 102–3, 110, **113**, 119, 120, 126–30
Run-D.M.C. 103, 308, 312, 371
Rustin, Nichole T. 34

Salt-N-Pepa 149, 316, 320
Salvatore, Nick 235n42
Sam and Dave 135, 139, 143, 149
Sandke, Randall 45n51
Scott, Bryant 186–90
Scott, Christine 192, *192*
Scott, Leonard 180–95, *192*
Scott, Melanie 190–1
Scott, Sydney 184, 191–2
Scott-Heron, Gil 301, 369, 373
Seeger, Pete 11, 350, 357–9
sexuality: androgyny as sexual performance 302–3; Black sexual expression 373–4; blues sexual innuendo 247–50, 252; Fly Girl rap identity 316–19, 320, 322; hip hop video models/vixens 319–20, 325nn46–48; masculine identity in choral music 216–27; masculine identity in preaching 218–37; minstrelsy presentation of 7; New Orleans sex industry 265; R&B sexual innuendo 250, 292; sexualized imagery in hip hop 306–7; *see also* gender; LGBT issues
Shalamar 165, 168, 170–1, 173, 179n20
Shanté, Roxanne 312, 317–18
Sha-Rock 308, 310, 312
Shaw, Arnold 56
Shelton, Robert 352, 354–5
Sheri Sher 307
Sherrod, Charles 352, 356
Shirelles 98, 287, 296–7
Shorter, Wayne 32–4, 43n20
Sidran, Ben 39–41, 45n47
Simon, George T. 59
Simon and Garfunkle 53
skiffle 15

slavery 68–9, 259, 331–2, 333–6
Sly and the Family Stone 99–100, 301–2, 369
Smith, Bessie 9, 74, *92*, 93, 207, 241–7, 250, 258–9, 287–8, 293, 326n56, 340, 372
Smith, E. Dewey 225
Smith, Mabel Louise "Big Maybelle" 251
Smith, Mamie 91–3, 241–2, *242*, 244, 258, 361
Smith, Suzanne 112, 122
Smith, Trixie 93, *93*, 243
Smith, Will 104, 149, 171, 371
Smith, Willie Mae Ford 83, 202, 211–13
Smokey Robinson and the Miracles 110, **113**, 114–15, 121
Snoop Dogg 149, 177
Snorton, C. Riley 217–18
Snow, Valaida 257, 262, 265–6
Snyder, Jean 70–1
SOLAR (Sound of Los Angeles Records) 165, 168–78
Soul Messengers 181
soul music: "blue-eyed soul" music 98; blues artists and 20; as blues successor 12; Detroit era "Motown Sound" 124–31; "Harvard Report" on 99–100; *Hot Buttered Soul* significance 143–4, 155; live concert recordings 48–51; psychedelic soul 128–9; as R&B successor 98; soft soul music 99; soul blues 24–5; *Soul Train* 100
Southern, Eileen 69
Sparky Dee 313
Spector, Phil 98, 298
spirituals: antebellum spirituals 333–6; Civil Rights Movement and 335; Fisk Jubilee Quartet 241; published arrangements of 53–4, 69, 70; seeds of resistance in 237; solo art song spirituals 70–1; women as prominent singers 201
Spivey, Victoria 93, 243–4, 246
Staple Singers 143, 145
Stax Records: acquisition by Al Bell 139–43, *141*; acquisition by Gulf and Western 99; bankruptcy 148–9, 166; Civil Rights Movement and 98, 135, 147; founding 135; *Hot Buttered Soul* significance 143–4, 155; live recording process 139–40; *Shaft* blaxploitation soundtrack 145–7, *146*; "Stax Sound" 136, 138–9, 142–4
Stein, Arlene 283–4
Stewart, Jim 135, 139–41, *141*, 148
Strachwitz, Chris 16–17
Strong, Barrett **113**, 125, 128–9, 155
Sugarhill Gang 306, 310
Sugar Hill Records 103, 166, 308, 310–11
Supremes 110–11, **113**, 119, 120, 121, 125–30, 296, 372
Sweet Honey in the Rock 272, 274–9, 282–3
swing 12, 19, 59, 62n11, 94, 115
Sylvers, Leon III 169–73, *169*, 175, 179n20
Sylvester 302, 375
Szwed, John F. 43n20

Tagg, Philip *52*
Taylor, Arthur 39, 45nn44–45
Taylor, Johnnie 20, 24, 142, 145
Taylor, Koko 252–3, *253*
television: Alan Freed on 55; *American Bandstand* 98, 100, 155; Aretha Franklin on 86; Black culture emergence in 155; Black Entertainment Television 102, 194, 195n4, 229–30, 318, 320, 376; early television racial exclusion 260–1; *Ed Sullivan Show* 102, 119; effect on radio audience 96; Elvis exposure on 57, 63n69; hip hop programming 371; Mahalia Jackson appearances 207, 209–10; MTV racial exclusion 101–2, 162; *Soul Train* 100, 155, 167–9, *168*; *see also* entertainment industry; film and video
Temptations 110, **113**, 116–18, *117*, 121, 123, 126–30, 166, 369
Terry, Sonny 13, 15, 17
Tharpe, Rosetta 246, 249, 288
Thomas, Richard 111
Thomas, Rufus 13, 136–7, 144, 148
Thornton, Willie Mae "Big Mama" 60, 63n69, 251–2, 287, 295
Tillery, Linda 277–8
Titon, Jeff Todd 17, 248
Tonéx (Anthony C. Williams II; B. Slade) 230–2
transculturation: blues on radio and 7; blues revival performance and 17–19; Cold War effect on 11; cultural impulse for 143; folk music revival and 9–10; formal musical training and 9; 1980s cross-racial duets 102–3; R&B record sales 13; radio as transcultural medium 11, 13–14, 248–9; recordings as transcultural medium 9; segregated repertoire in blues performance 8; Stax Records founding 136–8; traditional music interchanges 8–9; transcultural performance 48; White disruption of musical integration 13; *see also* crossovers; White imitators
Tribbett, Tye 228–31
Tucker, Mark 35–8, 41, 44n33
Tucker, Sherrie 34, 36
Turner, Tina 102, 287–8, 293, 299
Tyscot Records 180–8, 191–2
Tyson, Craig 181–4

Van Peebles, Melvin 373
vaudeville 5, 91, 242–3, 245
vernacular music: African American vernacular style 67–8; African musical practices 68–9; antebellum music and dance 331–6; art music influence from 67–8, 72–4; drum and fife music 14; freedom songs derived from 343–7, 355; genres of resistance 237–8; Stax live recording process and 139–40; transcultural influences in 8; vernacular blues traditions 9–10, 14; vocal precursors to jazz 259; work songs 337–9; *see also* folk music revival

Index **417**

Wald, Elijah 37
Walker, Albertina 87
Walker, Anthony "Tony" 227
Walker, Clarence 204
Wallace, Sippie 93, 243, 246, 252, 254, 287
Waller, Fats 95, 244
Ward, Clara 201, 203–4
Warwick, Jacqueline 298
Washington, Dinah 249–51, 373
Waters, Muddy 14–15, 18, 20
Wells, Junior 20, *21*, 252–4
Wells, Mary 110, 121, 125–7, 130
Werner, Craig 40–1
West, Cornell 122
Westbrooks, Logan 155, 165, *168*
Wexler, Jerry 140, 250
Whispers 165, 168–71, 173, 175
White, Cliff 49
White imitators: "blue-eyed soul" music 98; counterculture and 289; in disco 101; Elvis covers 57–8, 251, 288; prevalence on radio 9; racial erasure in jazz 95; racial erasure in R&B covers 13, 16, 47, 54–5, 57–61, 64n81, 295; racial erasure in rock 47, 54–5, 57–60, 288–9; *see also* crossovers; Presley, Elvis; transculturation
Whitfield, Norman 125, 128–9, 155, 369
Wiggins, Daphne C. 223
Wiggins, Raynetta 180
Williams, Joe Lee "Big Joe" 17, 20, 22
Wilson, Olly 50, 52, 72–4, *73*, 263
Wilson, Steve 42
Winant, Howard 60
Winley, Paul 309–10
women: all-woman bands 260–2, *261*; Black feminist organizations 276–7; exceptionalist narratives of 260; female rap identities 313–14; gospel music women 201–14; historical erasure in jazz history 256–7, 266–7, 267n6; Klymaxx all-women band 174–5; as ministers 223, 232; post-Soul sexual expression and 374; racial performance of women vocalists 256, 258–60; rock girl groups 97, 118, 125, 296–300, 372; Willie Mae Ford Smith role in 211–13; women-identified music 270–3, 279–84; women in blues 93, 202, 238–43; women in gospel music 83; women in hip hop 307–23; women in jazz 44n33, 262–7; women in R&B 289–93; women in rock 287–8, 292–3; *see also* gender
Wonder, Stevie 101, 102, 110, **113**, 121, 125, 128–31, 144
Woodson, Josiah 226